Pseudodoxia Epidemica

Or
Enquiries Into
Very Many Received Tenents and
Commonly Presumed Truths,
Which When Examined Prove but

VULGAR AND COMMON ERRORS.

(Volumes I and II)

by
Sir Thomas Browne

Edited by
Simon Wilkins, F.L.S.

© 2007 Benediction Classics, Oxford

Volume I

CONTENTS TO VOL. I.

PSEUDODOXIA EPIDEMICA, Books I. to IV.
    Editor's Preface lxxi

    (The Author) to the Reader 1

        THE FIRST BOOK; *containing the general part.*

Chap. 1. Of the first cause of common errors; the common infirmity of human nature 7
Chap. 2. A further illustration of the same 12
Chap. 3. Of the second cause of common errors; the erroneous disposition of the people 16
Chap. 4. Of the more immediate causes of common errors, both in the wiser and common sort; and first, of misapprehension and fallacy, or false deduction 26
Chap. 5. Of other more immediate causes of error: viz. credulity and supinity 33
Chap. 6. Of another more immediate cause of error: viz. obstinate adherence unto antiquity 39
Chap. 7. Of another of the more immediate causes of error: viz. adherence unto authority 51
Chap. 8. Of authors who have most promoted popular conceit . 59
Chap. 9. Of others indirectly effecting the same 72
Chap. 10. Of the last and great promoter of false opinions, the endeavours of Satan 75
Chap. 11. A further illustration of the same 86

THE SECOND BOOK; *beginning the particular part. Of popular and received tenets concerning mineral and vegetable bodies.*

Chap. 1. That crystal is nothing else but ice strongly congealed . 94
Chap. 2. Concerning the loadstone; of things particularly spoken thereof, evidently or probably true . . . 112

CONTENTS.

PAGE

Chap. 3. Concerning the loadstone; a rejection of sundry common opinions and relations thereof; natural, medical, historical, magical 133

Chap. 4. Of bodies electrical 157

Chap. 5. Compendiously of sundry other common tenets concerning minerals and terreous bodies, which, examined, prove either false or dubious. That a diamond is softened or broken by the blood of a goat; that glass is poison, and that it is malleable; of the cordial quality of gold; that a pot full of ashes will contain as much water as it would without them; of white powder that kills without report; that coral is soft under water, but hardeneth in the air; that porcelain lies under the earth an hundred years in preparation; that a carbuncle gives a light in the dark; of the eagle stone; of fairy stones; with some others 166

Chap. 6. Of sundry tenets concerning vegetables or plants, which, examined, prove either false or dubious. Of mandrakes; that cinnamon, ginger, cloves, mace, are but the parts or fruits of the same tree; that miseltoe is bred upon trees, from seeds which birds let fall thereon; of the rose of Jericho, that flowereth every year upon Christmas Eve; of Glastonbury thorn; that Sferra Cavallo hath a power to break or loosen iron; that bays preserve from the mischief of lightning and thunder; that bitter almonds are preservatives against ebriety 192

Chap. 7. Of some insects and the properties of several plants. Of the death-watch; the presages drawn from oak-apple insects; whether all plants have seeds; whether the sap of trees runs to the ground in winter; of the effects of camphor; with many others 210

THE THIRD BOOK; *the particular part continued. Of popular and received tenets concerning animals.*

Chap. 1. That an elephant hath no joints, &c. 220
Chap. 2. That the horse hath no gall 232
Chap. 3. That a pigeon hath no gall 235
Chap. 4. That a beaver, to escape the hunter, bites off his testicles or stones 240
Chap. 5. That a badger hath the legs of one side shorter than of the other 245
Chap. 6. That a bear brings forth her cubs informous or unshaped 247
Chap. 7. Of the basilisk 250
Chap. 8. That a wolf first seeing a man begets a dumbness in him 261
Chap. 9. Of the long life of the deer 262
Chap. 10. That a kingfisher, hanged by the bill, showeth where the wind lay 270
Chap. 11. Of griffins 273

CONTENTS.

	PAGE
Chap. 12. Of the phœnix	276
Chap. 13. Of frogs, toads, and toad-stone	284
Chap. 14. That a salamander lives in the fire	291
Chap. 15. Of the amphisbæna	294
Chap. 16. That young vipers force their way through the bowels of their dam	297
Chap. 17. That hares are both male and female	305
Chap. 18. That moles are blind	312
Chap. 19. That lampreys have many eyes	316
Chap. 20. That snails have no eyes	318
Chap. 21. That the chameleon lives only upon air	321
Chap. 22. That the ostrich digesteth iron	334
Chap. 23. Of the unicorn's horn	337
Chap. 24. That all animals of the land are in their kind in the sea	344
Chap. 25. Concerning the common course of our diet, in making choice of some animals and abstaining from eating others	346
Chap. 26. Of the spermaceti whale	353
Chap. 27. Compendiously, of the musical note of swans before their death; that the flesh of peacocks corrupteth not: that they are ashamed of their legs: that storks will only live in republicks and free states; of the noise of a bittern by putting the bill in a reed; that whelps are blind nine days; of the antipathy between a toad and a spider, a lion and a cock; that an earwig hath no wings; of worms; that flies make that humming noise by their mouths or wings; of the tainct or small red spider; of the glow-worm; of the providence of pismires in biting off the ends of corn	357
Chap. 28. That the chicken is made out of the yolk of the egg; that snakes sting; of the tarantula; the lamb of Tartary; the swiftness of tigers; with sundry queries	373

THE FOURTH BOOK; *the particular part continued. Of many popular and received tenets concerning man.*

Chap. 1. That only man hath an erect figure	379
Chap. 2. That the heart is on the left side	383
Chap. 3. That pleurisies are only on the left side	385
Chap. 4. Of the ring finger	386
Chap. 5. Of the right and left hand	391
Chap. 6. On swimming and floating	402
Chap. 7. That men weigh heavier dead than alive, and before meat than after	405
Chap. 8. That there are several passages for meat and drink	408
Chap. 9. On saluting upon sneezing	410
Chap. 10. That Jews stink	413
Chap. 11. Of pigmies	421
Chap. 12. Of the great climacterical year, that is, sixty-three	425
Chap. 13. Of the canicular or dog-days	446

EDITOR'S PREFACE

TO PSEUDODOXIA EPIDEMICA.

If the conception and plan of the present work is not to be ascribed to the mental activity of its author *alone*,—if we are not to regard it *solely* as the result of his own native and irrepressible thirst for knowledge, and of that unrelenting spirit of investigation which led him to scrutinize every position before he admitted it; if, in short, we are to allow, that Sir Thomas Browne might have been, in some degree, impelled to this undertaking by the suggestions of another, may we not with great probability attribute the impulse to the opinions expressed by Lord Bacon as to the *Use of Doubts*, and the advantages which might result from drawing up a *Calendar of Doubts, Falsehoods*, and *Popular Errors?* In support of this conjecture, I will insert some of those opinions (from Mr. Basil Montagu's Lectures on Bacon, with which I have been favoured by that gentleman, at the request of my kind friend Mr. Amyot), with Mr. Montagu's remarks.

"'The recording and proposing of doubts hath in it a two-fold use. One, that it munites and fortifies philosophy against error, when that which is not altogether so clear and evident is not defined and avouched (lest error should beget error), but a judgment upon it is suspended and not definitive.'—It will be seen in a future lecture, that Lord Bacon enumerates a tendency to hasty assent among the idols of the understanding by which we are diverted from the truth. In this place, he contents himself with incidentally noticing, that a record of doubts has a tendency to prevent the influence of this idol.—'The other, that the entry of doubts, and recording of them, are so many sponges which continually draw and suck unto them an increase and improvement of knowledge; whereby it comes to pass that those things which, without the suggestion of doubts, had been slightly and without observation, passed over, are, by occasion of such dubitations, more seriously and attentively considered.'—Lord

Bacon, in various parts of his works, admonishes us of our duty to keep our minds open to improvement, and not to admit as truths what may be either false, or only a proper subject for doubts. He warns us in his doctrine of the idols of the understanding, that, from our love of truth, we are anxious to possess it, and too ready to imagine ourselves enriched by the possession of counterfeit, instead of real coin. He says—'The mind of man doth wonderfully endeavour and extremely covet, that it may not be pensile; but that it may light upon something fixed and immoveable, on which, as on a firmament, it may support itself in its swift motions and disquisitions. Aristotle endeavours to prove that, in all motions of bodies, there is some point quiescent, and very elegantly expounds the fable of Atlas, who stood fixed, and bare up the heavens from falling, to be meant of the poles of the world, whereupon the conversion is accomplished. In like manner, men do earnestly seek to have some Atlas, or axis of their cogitations within themselves, which may, in some measure, moderate the fluctuations and wheelings of the understanding, fearing it may be the falling of their heaven. An impatience of doubt, and an unadvised haste of assertion, without due and mature supension of the judgment, is an error in the conduct of the understanding. For the two ways of contemplation are not unlike the two ways of action, commonly spoken of by the ancients; of which the one was a plain and smooth way in the beginning, but in the end impassable;—the other rough and troublesome in the entrance, but after a while fair and even. So it is in contemplations:—if a man will begin in certainties, he shall end in doubts; but if he be content to begin with doubts, and have patience a while, he shall end in certainties. * * * Wherefore I report as deficient a *calendar of dubitations*, or problems in nature, and approve the undertaking of such a work as a profitable pains; so care be had that, as knowledge daily grows up (which certainly will come to pass if men hearken unto us), such doubts as be clearly discussed, and brought to resolution, be rased out of the catalogue of problems. It would be a very profitable course to adjoin to the calendar of doubts and non-liquets, *a calendar of falsehoods, and of popular errors*, now passing unargued in natural history and opinions, that sciences be no longer distempered and debased by them.'

"Since Lord Bacon's time, there have been publications on vulgar errors, or erroneous opinions received as truths by the community. The first was published in the year 1646, by Sir Thomas Browne. It is entitled, *Pseudodoxia Epidemica, or Enquiries into very many received Tenets, and commonly received Truths, by Sir Thomas Browne, Knt. M.D.* (From his preface it will be found, that before Lord Bacon's time, as I conceive, but certainly before the time of Sir Thomas Browne, there were other works upon this subject.) Of this work, Mr. Jeremy Bentham, in his work on Fallacies, says, 'Vulgar Errors is a denomination which, from a work on this subject by a physician of name in the 17th century, has obtained a certain degree of celebrity. Not the moral (of which the political is a department), but the physical was the field of the errors, which it was the object of Sir Thomas Browne to hunt out and bring to view; but of this restriction, no intimation is given by the words of which the title of his work is composed.' It is rather interesting to see that antipathy to improvement in the time of Sir Thomas Browne was, as it is, and to a certain extent ever will be, so rife, that he thought it expedient to guard against such prejudices by an amulet to charm priests, physicians, and philosophers."—*Mr. Montagu's MS.*[h]

By whatever inducements, however, we may suppose Browne to have been stimulated to the production of the *Pseudodoxia Epidemica*, few will hesitate to admit that he was peculiarly qualified for the task. It was in his very nature to inquire (as I have remarked), and he was not content to receive any thing, without scrutiny,—except in matters of faith. The exception may be given in his own words. "In philosophy, where truth seems double-faced, there is no man more paradoxical than myself; but in divinity, I love to keep the road: and, though not in an implicit, yet an humble faith, follow the great wheel of the church, by which I move, not reserving any proper poles, or motion from the epicycle of my own brain."[i] Again:—"where the scripture is silent, the church is my text; where that speaks, 'tis but my comment; where both are silent,"[k] &c. If we add to these passages the following avowal,—"I am, I confess, naturally inclined to that which misguided zeal terms superstition,"[l] —we are furnished with the true key to explain his belief in witchcraft, and Satanic influence, as well his partiality for the Ptolemaic system of the universe. He regarded these all as being to a certain extent, subjects of revelation; and therefore[m] to be received implicitly. But every thing not so supported, fell under the process of his excruciation. His very curious and extensive reading,—his daily and ardent pursuit of every branch of natural history,—the labour he was constantly willing (as Dr. Johnson observes)[n] to pay for truth, in patient and reiterated experiments

[h] "See his preface, in which he says, 'we cannot expect the frown of theology herein, &c. &c.' to the end of the paragraph."
[i] *Rel. Med.*   [k] *Rel. Med.*   [l] *Rel. Med.*
[m] See this ground stated by his annotator Dean Wren, who with still greater vehemence advocated Browne's astronomical belief.
[n] In his *Life of Browne*, vol. i.

upon even the most trifling or absurd questions,—together with the ready access, which his great celebrity and extended acquaintance procured him, to the collections and observations of the literary and scientific men of his day; all these supplied him with copious materials for the exercise of his inquisitive propensities. Every doubt was brought to the test of experiment and examination. His *Common-place Books* exhibit abundant evidence that he trusted nothing to memory, but noted down, at the moment they struck him, the experiments and inquiries he deemed necessary to be made, together with results as they arose. That this process of accumulation began early in life, is evident from the date of his first edition; while subsequent alterations, and the constant accessions of new matter,[p] (some even now first printed) may serve to convince us, that throughout life he continued, as the constantly increasing "diversion" of his business or acquaintance allowed him opportunity, to enrich his treasury of doubts and speculations.

Let us now proceed to enumerate the editions and translations which have appeared.

The First Edition is in pot folio, with the following title-page.[p] *Pseudodoxia Epidemica: or, Enquiries into very many received Tenets, and commonly presumed Truths. By Thomas Browne, Dr. of Physick. Jul. Scaliy. Ex libris colligere quæ prodiderunt autho. es, longe est periculosissimum ; rerum ipsarum cognitio vera e rebus ipsis est. London, Printed by T. H. for Edward Dod, and are to be sold in Ivie Lane.* 1646. On the leaf opposite the title is *Downame's Imprimatur.*[q]

The Second Edition is the handsomest, as to typography, which has hitherto appeared. It is in foolscap folio. The title is, *Pseudodoxia,* &c. (as before); *Second Edition, corrected and much enlarged by the author, Together with some Marginal Observations, and a Table alphabeticall at the end. London, Printed by A. Miller, for Edw. Dod and Nath. Ekins, at the Gunne in Ivie Lane.* 1650.

The Third Edition, with some additions, appeared in folio, in

---

[p] These alterations and additions are pointed out in the notes to the present edition. They occur chiefly in the 2nd and 3rd editions, and in the 6th, the last which the author revised. The 4th and 5th editions differ little from the 3rd.

[q] *Downame's Imprimatur.*] "March the 14th, 1645. I have perused these learned Animadversions upon the Common Tenets and Opinions of Men in former and in these present times, entitled *Pseudodoxia Epidemica*; and finding them much transcending vulgar conceipt, and adorned with great variety of matter, and multiplicity of reading, I approve them as very worthy to be printed and published.

"JOHN DOWNAME."

1658. It is printed on the model of the second, but is very inferior.

The Fourth Edition was printed in the same year, in 4to. with the Hydriotaphia and Garden of Cyrus—two Discourses which had just appeared in 8vo. The title is *Pseudodoxia, &c. The Fourth Edition, with Marginal Observations, and a Table Alphabetical. Whereunto are now added two Discourses:—the one of Urn Burial, or Sepulchrall Urns, lately found in Norfolk: the other, of the Garden of Cyrus, or Network Plantations of the Antients. Both newly written by the same Author. Ex libris, &c. London, Printed for Edward Dod, and are to be sould by Andrew Crook, at the Green Dragon in Paul's Church-yard.* 1658. No sooner had Dod brought out this edition, so enriched, than Ekins, his former partner, printed, in double column, not only the Tracts appended by Dod, but also Religio Medici:—and thus, in 1659, produced, as altogether new, his unsold copies of the 3rd edition, with these enrichments, preceded by this title-page:—*Religio Medici: whereunto is added a Discourse of the Sepulchrall Urns, lately found in Norfolk. Together with the Garden of Cyrus; or the Quincunciall Lozenge, or Network Plantations of the Ancients, Artificially, Naturally, Mistically Considered. With sundry Observations. By Thomas Brown, Doctour of Physick, Printed for the good of the Commonwealth;* —the whole set forth with a new title-page to the volume, calling it *The Last Edition*, with the date 1659.

The Fifth Edition, in 4to. by the Assigns of Dod, in 1669, is nearly a reprint of his Fourth, and contains the two Discourses. It is remarkable for having a portrait (the first, I believe, which appeared) of the author; but so different from all others I have seen, that it is not easy to suppose them to have had a common original. Mr. Ottley, of the British Museum, has had the kindness to give me his opinion as to the engraver, that it may probably have been executed by John Dunstall.

The Sixth Edition, published by Ekins, under the author's especial superintendence, and with his final revision and improvements,[1] and the last which appeared during his life-time, came out in 1672, in 4to. with this title:—*Pseudodoxia, &c. The Sixth and last Edition, corrected and enlarged by the Author, with many Explanations, Additions, and Alterations throughout. Together with many more Marginal Observations, and a Table Alphabetical at the end. London, Printed by J. R. for Nath. Ekins.* 1672. A portrait by Van Hove

---

[1] As declared in the Postscript. Of this edition there were *large papers*.

accompanied it; which, in all probability, had a common original with all the subsequent portraits:—viz. that of Van der Banc, published with the *Miscellany Tracts*, in 1683—that of White, with the *Works*, in 1686—that of Van der Gucht, with the *Posthumous Works*, in 1712—that of Trotter, in *Malcolm's Lives of Topographers*—together with a Dutch 4to. print, which probably accompanied a Dutch translation of the Works.

In 1686, Abp. Tenison published the folio volume, which contained the Seventh Edition of Pseudodoxia, Religio Medici, Hydriotaphia, and the Quincunx, together with the Miscellany Tracts, which he had himself first edited in 1683 (but of which many copies have a reprint title with the date 1684), with this title, in red and black ink.

I know of but three translations of Pseudodoxia: two of which are those of Grundal and Knorr, in 1668 and 1680; the third is a French translation, in 2 vol. 12mo. of the seventh edition.[u] I cannot say by whom it was made, unless by Peter Briot, the translator of Ricault's Ottoman Empire, and several other works into French.

Watt mentions an edition of the Works of Browne in Latin, in 1682; but I have never seen it, nor any other mention of it. Peti, a mathematician, who wrote on comets, is mentioned as having translated some part into Latin; and Isaac Gruter[x] corresponded with Sir Thomas, respecting a translation which he was preparing; but which I believe never appeared.

In 1652 our old enemy, Alexander Ross, again took up arms, and made an attack at the same time on our author, and on Lord Bacon, Dr. Harvey, and others, in his *Arcana Microcosmi*.[y]

---

[u] With this title:—*Essai sur les Erreurs Populaires, ou Examen de plusieurs Opinions reçues comme vrayes, qui sont fausses ou douteuses. Traduit de l'Anglois de Thom. Brown, Chevalier et Docteur en Medecine. Nouvelle edition revue et corrigée. Ex libris, &c. Jul. Scalig. A Paris, chez Briasson, Rue Saint Jacques, à la Science et à l'Ange Gardien.* MDCCXXXVIII. *Avec Approbation et privilège du Roy.* My copy of this work has also reprint titles, with the date 1753.

[x] Gruter published several of Lord Bacon's pieces in Latin; and Abp. Tenison in his *Baconiana* (Lond. 1679, sm. 8vo.) has given, at p. 221, several Latin letters on the subject, from Isaac Gruter to Dr. Rawley.

[y] *Arcana Microcosmi: or, The hid Secrets of Man's Body discovered; in an Anatomical Duel between Aristotle and Galen concerning the Parts thereof: as also by a discovery of the Strange and marvellous Diseases, Symptomes, and Accidents of Man's Body. With a Refutation of Doctor Brown's Vulgar Errors, the Lord Bacon's Natural History, and Doctor*

To assail at once three such men, must be admitted as a proof that Alexander was not wanting in spirit; and to say the truth, there is much amusement to be found in the volume.[a] He adheres to antiquity, "through thick and thin," as John Gilpin hath it; but in his very blunders and wrongheadedness, he often shows a quaintness and humour which not a little atones for them.

The next, and I believe the only other attack which appeared in print, was the *Still Gale* of John Robinson,[b] a pompous and somewhat coxcombical personage, who calls himself "his fellow

Harvy's Book de Generatione, Comenius, and Others; whereto is annexed a Letter from Doctor Pr. to the Author, and his Answer thereto, touching Doctor Harvy's Book de Generatione. By A. R. London.

[a] Dr. Kippis remarks, that "the *Arcana* is far from being so mean a piece as many have represented it. There is in it a great deal of vanity, and more spleen; but withal there wants not truth, learning, and some sense."

[b] He published in 1649 a work entitled *Miscellaneous Propositions and Quæres, by J. R. Dr. in Physick in Norwich*—with this motto: *Fabricanda Fabri Fimus*, enclosed in a wreath. *London, Printed for R. Royston, at the Angel in Ivie Lane.* That they are truly *Miscellaneous*, will be sufficiently proved by their enumeration:—1. of a Church. 2. of Ministers. 3. of Sacraments. 4. of Adam. 5. of Marriage. 6. of Sympathy. 7. of an Egge. 8. of Swimming or Floating. 9. of Remedies. 10. of Telesmes. From this work it appears, that he was an Independent, in his opinions on church government, and the ministerial office. He held marriage to be a civil, not a religious institution. He seems to have been a person of some acuteness, and his belief in Satanic agency, resembled that of his fellow citizen Sir Thomas, as appears by his last chapter on "Telesmes," whose effect in removing Epidemical diseases, "if any," he would ascribe "unto the Prince of the Air." This work he translated into Latin and published with two additional pieces, under the following title:— *Endoxa seu Questionum quarundam Miscellanearum examen probabile, ut et Lapis ad Altare, sive Exploratio Locorum paucorum difficiliorum S. Scripturæ, una cum Pseudodoxiæ Epidemicæ Ventilatione tranquilla, per Johannem Robinsonum, M.D.* (here occurs a rude wood-cut of 3 faces, with this motto:) *Sunt variæ quamvis facies mentesque alienæ, Unus fit cordis nexus amore boni. Londini, &c.* 1656. Two years afterwards the work made its appearance, with slight alterations, in English, under this title:—*Endoxa, or some probable Inquiries into Truth, both Divine and Humane: together with a Stone to the Altar, or short Disquisitions on a few difficult places of Scripture; as also a Calm Ventilation of Pseudodoxia Epidemica, by John Robinson, Doctor of Physick, Translated and Augmented by the Author.* (*Four faces in a heart.*)

Though divers heads; faces averse you see;
Yet, for truth's sake, they all in heart agree.

London, *Printed by J. Streater, for Francis Tylor.* 1658.

citizen and collegian." There was little in this *gale* to ruffle a far more excitable antagonist than Sir Thomas; and it seems to have died away unnoticed.

The present Edition is printed from the folio of 1686, and all the important variations of that edition, from preceding ones, are pointed out in notes. The fifth book contains some pages of new matter, from the MSS. in the British Museum.

In speaking of the notes which accompany it, I must first mention those marked *Wr*. They were written by Dr. Christopher Wren, Dean of Windsor, and father of the architect of St. Paul's, on the margins of a copy of the first edition. This copy, preserved in the Bodleian Library at Oxford, caught the attention of my very kind friend Dr. Bliss, who enabled me to obtain a transcript of the entire notes. I hope that in printing nearly the whole of these notes, I shall be allowed to have really enhanced both the interest and the value of this edition, by adding the very curious commentary of a learned and distinguished contemporary. In extent of reading, as well as in acuteness, the commentator was probably far inferior to Browne; but he went beyond him, though at the same time strongly resembling him, in a certain superstitious tinge of feeling, and in love of the marvellous; he was inclined to believe in astrology; and was a regarder of dreams; of which a very curious instance is recorded in the *Parentalia*, as having been written by him on the margin of *Aubrey's Miscellanies*, cap. v. p. 52.[c] He, moreover, admired Sir Thomas for being (like himself) a stout adherent to the falling fortunes of the Ptolemaic system of astronomy.

Browne has enumerated in his preface several works similar and anterior to his own.[d] Several others may here be

[c] "Sir C. W. being at his father's home, *anno* 1651, at Knoyle, Wilts, dreamt that he saw a fight in a great market-place, which he knew not, where some were flying, and others pursuing; and among those that fled, he saw a kinsman of his, who went into Scotland to the king's army. They heard in the country that the king was come into England, but whereabout he was they could not tell. The next night his kinsman came to his father's at Knoyle, and was the first that brought the news of the fight at Worcester, fought Sep. 3.

"When Sir C. W. was at Paris, about 1665, he was taken ill and feverish, made but little water, and had a pain in his reins: he sent for a physician, who advised him to let blood, thinking he had a pleurisy; but bleeding much disagreeing with his constitution, he would defer it a day longer; that night he dreamt that he was in a place where palm-trees grew (suppose Egypt), and that a woman in a romantick habit reached him dates. The next day he sent for dates, which cured him of the pain in his reins."

[d] Respecting Primrose, *De Vulgi Erroribus*, I may add that his first

mentioned; though many have very probably escaped my notice.

Espagne John d'. *Erreurs Populaires en Points Généraux qui concernent l'intelligence de la Religion.* To this work there is no date, nor do I find it in the British Museum, which contains several other of his works. He was a French Protestant divine of the 17th century.

ΠΕΡΙΑΜΜΑ ’ΕΠΙΔΗ'ΜΙΟΝ: or, *Vulgar Errors in practice censured. Also the Art of Oratory*, composed for the benefit of young students, cap. 8vo. Lond. *Royston*, 1659, pp. 112. The *Vulgar Errours in practice censured* are, 1. That of reproaching red-haired men. 2. That of censuring some professions. 3. That of reproaching the feminine sex. 4. The neglect of many writers to defend the deity of Christ. 5. The vanity of epitaphs. 6. The running from one extreme in religion to another. 7. The common practice of railing against an adversary.

Ralph Battell. *Vulgar Errors in Divinity Removed*, Lond. 8vo. 1683, containing, with title, &c. pp. 152. These relate to, 1. Reprobation. 2. Kingly government. 3. God's house and service in it. 4. Man's will. 5. Man's redemption. 6. Praying by the Spirit.

Two works on popular superstitions, viz. *Traité des Superstitions*, by M. Thiers, published in 1679, and *L'Histoire Critique des pratiques superstitieuses qui ont séduit les peuples, et embarrassé les Savans*, by Pierre Le Brun, published in 2 vols. at Rouan, in 1702 and 1732,—were published together in 1733 in one vol. fol. with plates. One of these gives several figures of mandrakes.

Fovargue Stephen. *A New Catalogue of Vulgar Errors*, 8vo. pp. 202, Camb. 1767. A work of slight pretension, and of slender merit; introduced by a preface somewhat flippant and in bad taste. Two of his errors had been already noticed by Sir Thomas Browne, and many of the rest are by no means generally received opinions.

Vulgar Errors, Lond. Debrett [8vo. 1784.] A political pamphlet against Mr. Pitt, at the time of the coalition between Lord North and Mr. Fox. The "Errors" enumerated are six:—
1. That the union between Lord North and Mr. Fox was interested, and without any public spirit to support it. 2. That Mr. Fox's India bill was a violation of charters. 3. That it was a confiscation of property. 4. That, in the issue of this contest, the people will take part against the House of Commons. 5. That the king must succeed in the struggle by dissolving

edition was in Latin, Amst. 1639:—it was that which Wittie translated: subsequent editions appeared, and in 1668 one very much enlarged at Rotterdam; it was this which De Rostagny translated.

parliament. 6. That the opposition to the present ministers has been carried on with violence. These six positions the author terms "Vulgar Errors," and professes to disprove.

A notice of some Vulgar Errors, as to points of law, will be found in *Barrington on the Statutes*, 4to. 1775, p. 474.

S. W.

London, June 17, 1835.

In the Sloanian MSS. in the British Museum, No. 1839, there is a very neatly-written MS. extending to 85 pages, 4to., of *Observations on Ps. Ep.* which is proved to have proceeded from the pen of Sir Hamon L'Estrange.

The knight commences by thus expressing his admiration of his author:—"Boterus, magnifying the latitude of the pope's power, sayes that he hath *una jurisditione che no conosce oriente*, 'a command that knows no east,' and another dedicates a booke to the king of Spaine, thus, 'To the great king, to whom the sun never sets.' I cannot but prædicate the vast expanse of the Dr.'s learning, reading, and knowledge, from the cedar to the hyssope." He then begins his observations by pointing out, in Browne's chapter on magnetism and the compass, several remarks which had not been made by previous writers;—Borough, Norman, or Gilbert. He goes on successively to notice Browne's remarks on electricity, flies in amber, white powder, and the rose of Jericho. After noticing, in connection with this last topic, several marvellous stories of omens, apparitions, and miracles, (among which this one, told to the writer by the old Countess of Arundel, respecting her father, Lord Dacre of the North, that he had a pasture on the scite of an old abbey, and that his sheep never failed, if within that scite, to produce twins:)—he thus proceeds. "And I see no barr against mee to think that in the dayes of darkness and ignorance of popery, some cloysterers might truck with the devil (att a deare rate) for an ape's trick (as witches do) for the shewing, effecting, and continuance of such pranks and toyes, whereby to acquire a stupendous reputation of working miracles (of which they were not a little ambitious,) to drawe affection, respect, and honour, to their religion and profession, and to celebrate the place with a mark and character of extraordinary sanctity for the future," p. 6. After touching upon *Deer casting their horns*, he mentions, on the subject of *Griffins*, having seen in Sir Rob. Cotton's library *a griffin's claw*, p. 7. Discussing the story of the *ostrich* swallowing iron, he mentions having seen one eat pellets of chewed paper as large as a walnut. He gives also, as a parallel, the following story:—"About 1638, as I walked London streets, I sawe the picture of a strange fowle hang out upon a . . . .[e] and my selfe, with one or two more then in company, went in to see it. It was kept in a chamber, and was a great

---

[e] A burnt hole occurs here in MS.

fowle, somewhat bigger than the largest turkey-cock, and so legged and footed, but shorter and thicker, and of a more erect shape, coulourd before like the breast of yong cock fesan, and on the back of dunn or deare coulour. The keeper called it a Dodo, and in the ende of a chimney in the chamber there lay an heap of large pebble stones, whereof hee gave it many in our sight, some as bigg as nutmegs, and the keeper told us shee eate them, conducing unto digestion ; and though I remember not how far the keeper was questioned herein, yet I am confident that afterwards he cast them all agayne." He goes on to mention other instances of birds swallowing stones, &c. for the same purpose—which he concludes to be the most probable solution of the alleged fact that the ostrich (or estridge, as he calls it,) swallowing iron, pp. 8—12. Then follows a lengthened notice of the five kinds of one-horned animals noticed by Browne ;—the *Indian ox* and *ass*, the *oryx*, *rhinoceros*, and *monoceros*. His opinion is that three "might exist ; some one or more of several sorts of monsters in nature, through some errour or vitiosity in generation or conception, which might bear one horne ; and such a creature once seen might multiply fast enough in report, and (*ex traduce*) naturalists readily follow one another, as wild geese flye." He concludes the unicorn of Job to be the *rhinoceros*, after many pages of careful and argumentative examination of his "shape and strength, and the seate, position, and portage of his horne," pp. 13—26. At p. 27, we find the notice (adverted to in his letter to Browne) of the *whale*, beginning thus : "In June, 1626, a whale was cast up upon my shoare or sea liberty, sometyme parcel of the possessions of the abbey of Ramsey, &c." Notices of the *dolphin*, the *toad and spider, seal, dottrel, basilisk, swallows in mud*, &c. occupy from p. 28 to p. 46 :—from the last of which I must extract the following very lively incident—" About 16 or 20 years since, upon a hot, bright, and cleare daye, (a little before noone,) hapning in the midst of March, as I leaned over my garden wall, and looking steadfastly into my mote, (which is on that syde very cleare, leane, and hungry water,) I espied sundry small creatures (of a dark or dusky coulour, longwise shaped, and of forme of beetle or scarabee) to rise out of the mud from the bottom of the mote to the topp of the water, and some of them to settle themselves speedily downe againe into the mud, others to rayse themselves above the water five or six inches, others a foote, others more, and some some yards, with a slanting or sloaping mount, and a like descent and falling downe hastened to the bottome ;[1] and being much pleased with this speculation, I hastily rann unto mine house, and called out mine eldest sonne, (then a man growne and of yeares,) both to participate and bee a witnesse of this discovery ; wee observed againe as before, and att last (among sundry essayes of many of these creatures, we perceived

---

[1] I must suspect that the Knight was deceived, probably by reflection, as to "these creatures" (which must be supposed the larvæ of *libellulæ*, or dragon flies,) having mounted out of the water before they acquired their wings—or having returned into the water after they had once taken their leave of it.

one of them to rise from the bottom to the top of the water, and found itselfe so full sunned and perfected as it raysed it selfe above the water, and after two or three turnes and circinations in the ayre, it mounted cleane out of sight," p. 40. He proceeds to remark on the *passenger falcon*, (p. 42, 43,) *toads found in oaks, shell stones*, (Pholas,) p. 44, *St. Hierome*, p. 46, and last, but not least, *Pope Joan*, whose existence he believes, and devotes the remaining forty pages of his paper to a most learned and ingenious examination of the arguments for and against the story—and still further to a discussion of the sense in which those Apocalyptic passages are to be understood—in which the whore of Babylon is foretold and denounced, concluded by a courteous expression of personal respect to many who are of that faith, pp. 47—85.

TO THE READER.

Would truth dispense, we could be content, with Plato, that knowledge were but remembrance; that intellectual acquisition were but reminiscential evocation, and new impressions but the colourishing of old stamps which stood pale in the soul before.[1] For (what is worse) knowledge is made by oblivion, and, to purchase a clear and warrantable body of truth, we must forget and part with much we know; —our tender enquiries taking up learning at large, and, together with true and assured notions, receiving many, wherein our reviewing judgments do find no satisfaction. And, therefore, in this encyclopædie and round of knowledge, like the great and exemplary wheels of heaven, we must observe two circles; that, while we are daily carried about and whirled on by the swing and rapt of the one, we may maintain a natural and proper course in the slow and sober wheel of the other. And this we shall more readily perform, if we timely survey our knowledge; impartially singling out those encroachments which junior compliance and popular credulity hath admitted. Whereof at present we have endeavoured a long and serious adviso; proposing not only a large and copious list, but from experience and reason attempting their decisions.

And first we crave exceeding pardon in the audacity of the attempt; humbly acknowledging a work of such concernment unto truth, and difficulty in itself, did well deserve the conjunction of many heads. And surely more advantageous had it been unto truth, to have fallen into the endeavours of

---

[1] *the colourishing, &c.*] "The pictures drawn in our minds are laid in fading colours; and if not sometimes refreshed, vanish and disappear."—*Locke.*

some co-operating advancers, that might have performed it to the life, and added authority thereto; which the privacy of our condition, and unequal abilities cannot expect. Whereby notwithstanding we have not been diverted; nor have our solitary attempts been so discouraged, as to despair the favourable look of learning upon our single and unsupported endeavours.

Nor have we let fall our pen upon discouragement of contradiction, unbelief, and difficulty of dissuasion from radicated beliefs, and points of high prescription; although we are very sensible how hardly teaching years do learn, what roots old age contracteth unto errors, and how such as are but acorns in our younger brows grow oaks in our elder heads, and become inflexible unto the powerfullest arm of reason. Although we have also beheld, what cold requitals others have found in their several redemptions of truth; and how their ingenuous enquiries have been dismissed with censure, and obloquy of singularities.[2]

Some consideration we hope from the course of our profession, which though it leadeth us into many truths that pass undiscerned by others, yet doth it disturb their communications, and much interrupt the office of our pens in their well-intended transmissions. And therefore surely in this work attempts will exceed performances; it being composed by snatches of time, as medical vacations, and the fruitless importunity of uroscopy* would permit us.[3] And therefore also, perhaps it hath not found that regular and constant style, those infallible experiments, and those assured determinations, which the subject sometime requireth, and might be expected from others, whose quiet doors and unmolested hours afford no such distractions. Although whoever shall indifferently perpend the exceeding difficulty, which either the obscurity of the subject or unavoidable paradoxology must often put upon the attemptor, he will easily discern a work of this nature is not to be performed upon one legg; and should smell of oyle, if duly and deservedly handled.

* Inspection of urines.

[2] *Although we have also beheld, &c.*] Nota justam Doctoris querimoniam.—*Wr.*

[3] *fruitless importunity, &c.*] See book i. chap. 3.

Our first intentions, considering the common interest of truth, resolved to propose it unto the Latin republick and equal judges of Europe, but, owing in the first place this service unto our country, and therein especially unto its ingenuous gentry, we have declared ourselves in a language best conceived. Although I confess the quality of the subject will sometime carry us into expressions beyond mere English apprehensions.[4] And, indeed, if elegancy still proceedeth, and English pens maintain that stream we have of late observed to flow from many, we shall, within few years, be fain to learn Latin to understand English, and a work will prove of equal facility in either.[5] Nor have we addressed our pen or style unto the people, (whom books do not redress, and [who] are this way incapable of reduction,) but unto the knowing and leading part of learning. As well understanding (at least probably hoping) except they be watered from higher regions, and fructifying meteors of knowledge, these weeds must lose their alimental sap, and wither of themselves. Whose conserving influence could our endeavours prevent, we should trust the rest unto the scythe of time, and hopeful dominion of truth.

We hope it will not be unconsidered, that we find no open tract, or constant manuduction in this labyrinth, but are ofttimes fain to wander in the America and untravelled parts of truth.[6] For though, not many years past, Dr. Primrose hath made a learned discourse of Vulgar Errors in Physick,[7] yet have we discussed but two or three thereof.

[4] *expressions beyond, &c.*] That our naturall English consistes for the moste parte of monosyllables, as appeares by the names of all creatures in our tounge and all our actions, and in all the parts of our bodye, except such things as wee have borrowed from other nations. Scarce one word of ten, in our common talke, is of more than one syllable. In this very shorte note which conteynes sixty words, there bee not above eleven (and those of Latin derivation) which are not (all of them) monosyllables.—*Wr.*

[5] *we shall within, &c.*] To which desirable end, it must be confessed, Browne has, in this work, used his best endeavours.—*Crossley, in London Mag.* vol. iv. p. 436.

[6] *America, &c.*] Little more than 150 years had elapsed since the discovery of America, of which many parts were still *untravelled* and unknown.—*Br.*

[7] *Dr. Primrose hath made, &c.*] The work here alluded to is the *De Vulgi Erroribus in Medicinâ*, of which there is a translation into French,

Scipio Mercurii hath also left an excellent tract in Italian, concerning Popular Errors; but, confining himself only unto those in physick, he hath little conduced unto the generality of our doctrine.[8] Laurentius Joubertus,[9] by the same title, led our expectation into thoughts of great relief; whereby notwithstanding, we reaped no advantage, it answering scarce at all the promise of the inscription. Nor perhaps (if it were yet extant), should we find any further assistance from that ancient piece of Andreas,*[1] pretending the same title. And, therefore, we are often constrained to stand alone against the strength of opinion, and to meet the Goliah and giant of authority, with contemptible pebbles and feeble arguments, drawn from the scrip and slender stock of ourselves. Nor have we, indeed, scarce named any author whose name we do not honour; and if detraction could invite us, discretion surely would contain us from any derogatory intention, where highest pens and friendliest eloquence must fail in commendation.

And therefore also we cannot but hope the equitable con-

* περὶ τῶν ψευδῶς πεπιστευμένων, Athenæi, lib. 7.

by Rostagny, and another into English, by Dr. Wittie; the latter was published in 8vo. in 1651. Dr. James Primrose, the author, who wrote several other medical treatises, likewise in Latin, was the son of Gilbert Primrose, or Primerose, D.D., a Scotch divine, minister of the French church in London, and chaplain to James I. He practised at Paris for some time and afterwards settled in Yorkshire.—*Br.*

[8] *Scipio Mercurii, &c.*] Not mentioned in the *first edition.*
"*Degli errori popolari d' Italia,*" 1603, by Girolamo Mercurii, who had assumed the name of Scipio, when travelling through Europe as a physician, after having thrown aside the religious habit of the Dominicans. This work is a verbose but amusing performance, containing much curious information relative to the opinions and customs of the period at which it was published, and usefully correcting many errors, though it inculcates others of equal magnitude.—*Br.*

[9] *Laurentius Joubertus, &c.*] The *Erreurs populaires touchant la Médecine,* of Laurent Joubert, first published at Bourdeaux, in 1579, is the most distinguished of all the works of that celebrated medical professor. It obtained immediate popularity, being reprinted ten times in six months. The levity of its style, and the nature of some of the subjects discussed in it, appear to have contributed in a great degree to its popularity.—*Br.*

[1] *Andreas.*] Nothing appears to be known of this work of Andreas, who was himself a physician, besides this reference to it by Athenæus. Concerning the author, see *Fabricius' Elenchus Medicorum Veterum, Biblioth. Græc.* vol. xiii. p. 57.—*Br.*

siderations, and candour of reasonable minds. We cannot expect the frown of theology herein; nor can they which behold the present state of things,[2] and controversy of points so long received in divinity, condemn our sober enquiries in the doubtful appertinences of arts, and receptaries of philosophy. Surely philologers and critical discoursers, who look beyond the shell and obvious exteriours of things, will not be angry with our narrower explorations. And we cannot doubt, our brothers in physick (whose knowledge in naturals will lead them into a nearer apprehension of many things delivered) will friendly accept, if not countenance, our endeavours. Nor can we conceive it may be unwelcome unto those honoured worthies who endeavour the advancement of learning; as being likely to find a clearer progression, when so many rubs are levelled, and many untruths taken off, which passing as principles with common beliefs, disturb the tranquillity of axioms which otherwise might be raised. And wise men cannot but know, that arts and learning want this expurgation; and if the course of truth be permitted unto itself, like that of time and uncorrected computations,[3] it cannot escape many errors, which duration still enlargeth.

Lastly, we are not magisterial in opinions, nor have we dictator-like[4] obtruded our conceptions; but, in the humility of inquiries or disquisitions, have only proposed them unto more ocular discerners. And therefore opinions are free; and open it is for any to think or declare the contrary. And we shall so far encourage contradiction, as to promise no disturbance, or re-oppose any pen, that shall fallaciously or captiously[5] refute us; that shall only lay hold of our lapses, single out digressions, corollaries, or ornamental conceptions, to evidence his own in as indifferent truths. And shall only take notice of such, whose experimental and judicious knowledge shall solemnly look upon it; not only to destroy of ours

---

[2] *present state, &c.*] Written in 1645.

[3] *time, &c.*] Dean Wren, in a long note on this passage, proposes methods of correcting the calendar: but as the correction has long ago been made, the interest of the note appears to me scarcely to equal its length; I have therefore omitted it.

[4] *dictator-like, &c.*] Ut Julius Cæsar Scaliger in literis dictaturam arripuit.—*Wr.*

[5] *fallaciously.*] Elenchically, in *first edition.*

but to establish of his own; not to traduce or extenuate, but to explain and dilucidate, to add and ampliate, according to the laudable custom of the ancients in their sober promotions of learning. Unto whom notwithstanding, we shall not contentiously rejoin, or only to justify our own, but to applaud or confirm his maturer assertions; and shall confer what is in us unto his name and honour: ready to be swallowed in any worthy enlarger;—as having acquired our end, if any way, or under any name, we may obtain a work, so much desired, and yet desiderated,[6] of truth.

THOMAS BROWNE.

THE POSTSCRIPT.[7]

READERS,

To inform you of the advantages of the present impression, and disabuse your expectations of any future enlargements;—these are to advertise you, that this edition comes forth with very many explanations, additions, and alterations throughout, besides that of one entire chapter; and now this work is compleat and perfect, expect no further additions.

[6] *desired and yet desiderated, &c.*] The first edition reads, " desired, *at least* desiderated." Dean Wren in the margin asks, "What's the difference?" By collectors, everything which they do not possess is classed among *desiderata*, whether *desirable* for its rarity or not: Browne evidently meant to say, that his work was *at least* among the *desiderata* of literature, if not *desired* or *desirable*.

[7] POSTSCRIPT.] To the sixth edition: the last published in the author's life.

PSEUDODOXIA EPIDEMICA.

THE FIRST BOOK.

CONTAINING THE GENERAL PART.

CHAPTER I.

Of the first Cause of Common Errors; the common infirmity of Human Nature.

THE first and father cause of common error is the common infirmity of human nature; of whose deceptible condition, although, perhaps, there should not need any other eviction than the frequent errors we shall ourselves commit, even in the express declarement hereof, yet shall we illustrate the same from more infallible constitutions, and persons presumed as far from us in condition as time, that is, our first and ingenerated forefathers. From whom, as we derive our being, and the several wounds of constitution, so may we in some manner excuse our infirmities in the depravity of those parts, whose traductions were pure in them, and their originals but once removed from God. Who, notwithstanding, (if posterity may take leave to judge of the fact, as they are assured to suffer in the punishment,) were grossly deceived in their perfection, and so weakly deluded in the clarity of their understanding, that it hath left no small obscurity in ours, how error should gain upon them.

For first, they were deceived by Satan; and that not in an invisible insinuation, but an open and discoverable apparition, that is, in the form of a serpent; whereby, although there were many occasions of suspicion, and such as could not easily escape a weaker circumspection, yet did the unwary apprehension of Eve take no advantage thereof. It hath therefore seemed strange unto some, she should be deluded by a serpent, or subject her reason to a beast, which God had subjected unto hers. It hath empuzzled the enquiries of others to apprehend, and enforced them unto strange conceptions, to make out, how without fear or doubt she could discourse with such a creature, or hear a serpent speak, without suspicion of imposture.[1] The wits of others have been so bold as to accuse her simplicity, in receiving his temptation so coldly; and, when such specious effects of the fruit were promised as to make them like gods, not to desire, at least not to wonder, he pursued not that benefit himself. And had it been their own case, would perhaps have replyed, if the taste of this fruit maketh the eaters like gods why remainest thou a beast? If it maketh us but *like* gods, we are so already. If thereby our eyes shall be opened hereafter, they are at present quick enough to discover thy deceit; and we desire them no opener to behold our own shame. If to know good and evil be our advantage, although we have free will unto both, we desire to perform but one. We know 'tis good to obey the commandment of God, but evil if we transgress it.

They were deceived by one another, and in the greatest disadvantage of delusion, that is, the stronger by the weaker: for Eve presented the fruit, and Adam received it from her. Thus the serpent was cunning enough to begin the deceit in the weaker: and the weaker of strength sufficient to consummate the fraud in the stronger. Art and fallacy was used unto her; a naked offer proved sufficient to him; so his superstruction was his ruin, and the fertility of his sleep an issue of death unto him. And although the condition of sex, and posteriority of creation, might somewhat extenuate the error of the woman, yet was it very strange and inexcusable in the man: especially, if, as some affirm, he was the wisest of all men since; or if, as others have conceived, he was not ignorant of the fall of the angels, and had thereby example and punishment to deter him.

They were deceived from themselves, and their own apprehensions; for Eve either mistook or traduced the commandment of God. " Of every tree of the garden thou mayest

---

[1] *how without fear, &c.*] See *Religio Medici*, p. 15, note 9.

freely eat, but of the tree of knowledge of good and evil thou shalt not eat: for in the day thou eatest thereof, thou shalt surely dye." Now Eve upon the question of the serpent, returned the precept in different terms: "You shall not eat of it, neither shall you touch it, lest perhaps you dye." In which delivery there were no less than two mistakes, or rather additional mendacities: for the commandment forbad not the touch of the fruit; and positively said, ye shall surely dye, but she extenuating replied, *ne forte moriamini*, lest perhaps ye dye. For so in the vulgar translation it runneth, and so it is expressed in the Thargum or paraphrase of Jonathan. And therefore although it be said, and that very truly, that the Devil was a lyer from the beginning, yet was the woman herein the first express beginner, and falsified twice, before the reply of Satan. And therefore also, to speak strictly, the sin of the fruit was not the first offence. They first transgressed the rule of their own reason, and after, the commandment of God.[2]

They were deceived through the conduct of their senses, and by temptations from the object itself; whereby although their intellectuals had not failed in the theory[3] of truth, yet did the inservient and brutal faculties controll the suggestion of reason: pleasure and profit already overswaying the instructions of honesty, and sensuality perturbing the reasonable commands of virtue. For so it is delivered in the text; that when the woman saw "that the tree was good for food," and "that it was pleasant unto the eye," and "a tree to be desired to make one wise, she took of the fruit thereof and did eat." Now hereby it appeareth, that Eve, before the fall, was by the same and beaten way of allurements inveigled, whereby her posterity hath been deluded ever since; that is, those three delivered by St. John, "the lust of the flesh, the lust of the eye, and the pride of life:" where indeed they seemed as weakly to fail, as their debilitated posterity, ever after. Whereof, notwithstanding, some in their imperfection have resisted more powerful temptations, and in many moralities condemned the facility of their seductions.

[2] *and after, the commandment of God.*] As indeed none can transgress his commandment without first transgressing reason.—*Capel Loft.*
[3] *theory.*] Theorys, in Greeke signifies, search into the nature of things.—*Wr.*

Again, they might, for ought we know, be still deceived in the unbelief of their mortality, even after they had eat of the fruit. For, Eve observing no immediate execution of the curse, she delivered the fruit unto Adam; who after the taste thereof, perceiving himself still to live, might yet remain in doubt, whether he had incurred death; which perhaps he did not indubitably believe, until he was after convicted in the visible example of Abel. For he that would not believe the menace of God at first, it may be doubted whether, before an ocular example, he believed the curse at last. And therefore they are not without all reason, who have disputed the fact of Cain; that is, although he purposed to do mischief, whether he intended to kill his brother; or designed that, whereof he had not beheld an example in his own kind. There might be somewhat in it, that he would not have done, or desired undone, when he brake forth as desperately, as before he had done uncivilly, my iniquity is greater than can be forgiven me.[4]

Some niceties I confess there are which extenuate, but many more that aggravate this delusion; which exceeding the bounds of this discourse, and perhaps our satisfaction, we shall at present pass over. And therefore whether the sin of our first parents were the greatest of any since; whether the transgression of Eve seducing did not exceed that of Adam seduced; or whether the resistibility of his reason did not equivalence the facility of her seduction, we shall refer it to the schoolman. Whether there was not in Eve as great injustice in deceiving her husband, as imprudence in being deceived herself, especially, if fore-tasting the fruit, her eyes were opened before his, and she knew the effect of it, before he tasted of it, we leave it unto the moralist. Whether the whole relation be not allegorical, that is, whether the temptation of the man by the woman be not the seduction of the rational and higher parts by the inferior

---

[4] "*My iniquity,*" &c.] The authorized version gives the passage thus; "my *punishment* is greater than I can *bear.*" Sir Thomas prefers the marginal reading, which he contrasts with the surly question of Cain, in the 9th verse;—"Am I my brother's keeper?"—Drs. Clarke and Robertson give the same meaning to the words of the sentence, but the former makes it interrogative:—"Is my *sin* too great to be *forgiven?*"

and feminine faculties; or whether the tree in the midst of the garden, were not that part in the centre of the body, in which was afterward the appointment of circumcision in males, we leave it unto the thalmudist.[5] Whether there were any policy in the devil to tempt them before the conjunction, or whether the issue, before tentation, might in justice have suffered with those after, we leave it unto the lawyer. Whether Adam foreknew the advent of Christ, or the reparation of his error by his Saviour; how the execution of the curse should have been ordered, if, after Eve had eaten, Adam had yet refused; whether, if they had tasted the tree of life, before that of good and evil, they had yet suffered the curse of mortality; or whether the efficacy of the one had not overpowered the penalty of the other, we leave it unto God. For he alone can truly determine these, and all things else; who, as he hath proposed the world unto our disputation, so hath he reserved many things unto his own resolution; whose determination we cannot hope from flesh, but must with reverence suspend unto that great day, whose justice shall either condemn our curiosities, or resolve our disquisitions.

Lastly, man was not only deceivable in his integrity, but the angels of light in all their clarity.[6] He that said, he would be like the highest, did err, if in some way he conceived not himself so already: but in attempting so high an effect from himself, he misunderstood the nature of God, and held a false apprehension of his own; whereby vainly attempting not only insolencies, but impossibilities, he deceived himself as low as hell. In brief, there is nothing infallible but God, who cannot possibly err. For things are really true, as they correspond unto His conception;[7] and

---

[5] *whether the tree, &c.*] See the *Count de Gabalis*, p. 54, Lond. 1714. This is the theory of Hadrian Beverland's celebrated work, *De Peccato originali*, 1679, 8vo. It may be observed by the way, as a fact not generally known, that many curious papers and MSS. of this singular writer, throwing great light on that period of his life which he passed in England, may be found in the British Museum.—*J. C.*

[6] *Man was not only deceivable, &c.*] More correctly, "not only was man deceivable in his integrity, but the angels of light in all their clarity."

[7] *For things are really true as they correspond, &c.*] But not arbitrarily.—They conform to his conception, because they are true; and he

have so much verity, as they hold of conformity unto that intellect, in whose idea they had their first determinations. And, therefore, being the rule, He cannot be irregular; nor, being truth itself, conceivably admit the impossible society of error.

CHAPTER II.

A further Illustration of the same.

BEING thus deluded before the fall, it is no wonder if their conceptions were deceitful, and could scarce speak without an error after. For, what is very remarkable (and no man that I know hath yet observed) in the relations of Scripture before the flood, there is but one speech delivered by man, wherein there is not an erroneous conception;[8] and, strictly examined, most heinously injurious unto truth. The pen of Moses is brief in the account before the flood, and the speeches recorded are but six. The first is that of Adam, when, upon the expostulation of God, he replied, " I heard thy voice in the garden, and, because I was naked, I hid myself." In which reply there was included a very gross mistake, and, if with pertinacity maintained, a high and capital error. For, thinking by this retirement to obscure himself from God, he infringed the omnisciency and essential ubiquity of his Maker: who, as he created all things, so is he beyond and in them all; not only in power, as under his subjection, or in his presence, as being in his cognition; but in his very essence, as being the soul of their causalities, and the essential cause of their existencies. Certainly, his posterity at this distance, and after so perpetuated an impairment, cannot but condemn the poverty of his conception, that thought to obscure himself from his Creator in the shade of the garden, who had beheld him before in the darkness of his chaos, and the great obscurity of nothing; that thought to fly from God, which could not fly himself;

seeth all things as they are; and maketh their physical constitution to be what it is: and knoweth the moral relations thereunto belonging according to eternal rectitude, which is his nature.—*Capel Loft.*

[8] *There is but one speech, &c.*] Adverting probably to the speech of Lamech at the birth of Noah.

or imagined that one tree should conceal his nakedness from God's eye, as another had revealed it unto his own. Those tormented spirits that wish the mountains to cover them, have fallen upon desires of minor absurdity, and chosen ways of less improbable concealment. Though this be also as ridiculous unto reason, as fruitless unto their desires; for he that laid the foundations of the earth cannot be excluded the secrecy of the mountains; nor can there anything escape the perspicacity of those eyes which were before light, and in whose optics there is no opacity. This is the consolation of all good men, unto whom his ubiquity affordeth continual comfort and security: and this is the infliction of hell, unto whom it affordeth despair and remediless calamity. For those restless spirits that fly the face of the Almighty, being deprived the fruition of his eye, would also avoid the extent of his hand; which, being impossible, their sufferings are desperate, and their afflictions without evasion; until they can get out of Trismegistus his circle, that is, to extend their wings above the universe, and pitch beyond ubiquity.

The second is that speech of Adam unto God, "The woman whom thou gavest me to be with me, she gave me of the tree, and I did eat." This indeed was an unsatisfactory reply, and therein was involved a very impious error, as implying God the author of sin, and accusing his maker of his transgression. As if he had said, "If thou hadst not given me a woman, I had not been deceived; thou promisedst to make her a help, but she hath proved destruction unto me: had I remained alone, I had not sinned; but thou gavest me a consort, and so I became seduced." This was a bold and open accusation of God, making the fountain of good the contriver of evil; and the forbidder of the crime, an abettor of the fact prohibited. Surely his mercy was great, that did not revenge the impeachment of his justice; and his goodness to be admired, that it refuted not his argument in the punishment of his excusation,[9] and only pursued the first transgression, without a penalty of this the second.

The third was that of Eve, "The serpent beguiled me, and I did eat." In which reply there was not only a very feeble

---

[9] *his goodness to be admired, &c.*] Meaning that God's goodness withheld him from proving himself *just*, by punishing Adam for his implied charge of *injustice*.

excuse, but an erroneous translating her own offence upon another; extenuating her sin from that which was an aggravation, that is, to excuse the fact at all, much more upon the suggestion of a beast, which was before, in the strictest terms, prohibited by her God. For although we now do hope the mercies of God will consider our degenerated *integrities* unto some minoration of our offences; yet, had not the sincerity of our first parents so colourable expectations, unto whom the commandment was but single, and their *integrities* best able to resist the motions of its transgression. And therefore so heinous conceptions have risen hereof, that some have seemed more angry therewith than God himself: being so exasperated with the offence, as to call in question their salvation, and to dispute the eternal punishment of their maker.[1] Assuredly with better reason may posterity accuse them, than they the serpent, or one another; and the displeasure of the Pelagians must needs be irreconcilable, who, peremptorily maintaining they can fulfil the whole law, will insatisfactorily[2] condemn the nonobservation of one.

The fourth was that speech of Cain, upon the demand of God, "Where is thy brother?" and he said, "I know not." In which negation, beside the open impudence, there was implyed a notable error; for, returning a lie unto his maker, and presuming in this manner to put off the searcher of hearts, he denied the omnisciency of God, whereunto there is nothing concealable. The answer of Satan, in the case of Job, had more of truth, wisdom, and reverence than this: "Whence comest thou, Satan?" and he said, "From compassing the earth." For, though an enemy of God, and hater of all truth, his wisdom will hardly permit him to falsifie with the Almighty. For, well understanding the omniscience of his nature, he is not so ready to deceive himself as to falsifie unto him, whose cognition is no way deludable. And, therefore, when in the tentation of Christ he played upon the fallacy, and thought to deceive the author of truth, the method of this proceeding arose from

---

[1] *to dispute the eternal punishment of their maker.*] To dispute his justice in inflicting for the offence of our first parents, eternal punishment on their posterity.

[2] *insatisfactorily.*] i. e. urappeasably.—*Wr.*

the uncertainty of his divinity; whereof had he remained assured, he had continued silent, nor would his discretion attempt so unsucceedable a temptation. And so again at the last day, when our offences shall be drawn into accompt, the subtilty of that inquisitor shall not present unto God a bundle of calumnies or confutable accusations, but will discreetly offer up unto his omnisciency a true and undenyable list of our transgressions.[3]

The fifth is another reply of Cain, upon the denouncement of his curse: "My iniquity is greater than can be forgiven;" for so it is expressed in some translations. The assertion was not only desperate, but the conceit erroneous, overthrowing that glorious attribute of God, his mercy, and conceiving the sin of murder unpardonable. Which, how great soever, is not above the repentance of man, but far below the mercies of God, and was (as some conceive) expiated in that punishment he suffered temporally for it. There are but two examples of this error[4] in Holy Scripture, and they both for murder, and both as it were of the same person, for Christ was mystically slain in Abel, and, therefore, Cain had some influence on his death, as well as Judas; but the sin had a different effect on Cain from that it had on Judas; and most that since have fallen into it. For they, like Judas, desire death, and not unfrequently pursue it. Cain, on the contrary, grew afraid thereof, and obtained a securement from it. Assuredly, if his despair continued, there was punishment enough in life, and justice sufficient in the mercy of his protection. For the life of the desperate equalls the anxieties of death; who in uncessant inquietudes, but act the life of the damned, and anticipate the desolations of hell. 'Tis indeed a sin in man, but a punishment only in devils; who offend not God, but afflict themselves, in the appointed despair of his mercies. And, as to be without

---

[3] *And so again at the last day, &c.*] Here is an evident allusion to that singular passage in which Satan is spoken of as the *accuser* of the *brethren*, which accused them before God day and night. But surely it would be incorrect to conclude from thence, that he will stand up at the judgment day as the accuser of *all men*. On the contrary, we are expressly told that men will then be judged, "according to those things which were written in the books."

[4] *this error.*] Namely, despair of God's mercy.

hope is the affliction of the damned, so is it the happiness of the blessed; who having all their expectations present, are not distracted with futurities. So is it also their felicity to have no faith; for enjoying the beatifical vision, there is nothing unto them inevident: and in the fruition of the object of faith, they have received the full evacuation of it.

The last speech was that of Lamech, "I have slain a man to my wound, and a young man to my hurt: If Cain be avenged seven fold, truly Lamech seventy and seven fold." Now herein there seems to be a very erroneous illation: from the indulgence of God unto Cain concluding an immunity unto himself; that is, a regular protection from a single example, and an exemption from punishment in a fact that naturally deserved it. The error of this offender was contrary to that of Cain, whom the Rabbins conceive that Lamech at this time killed. He despaired of God's mercy in the same fact, where this presumed of it; he by a decollation of all hope annihilated his mercy, this by an immoderancy thereof destroyed his justice. Though the sin were less, the error was as great: for, as it is untrue that his mercy will not forgive offenders, or his benignity co-operate to their conversions, so is it also of no less falsity to affirm His justice will not exact account of sinners, or punish such as continue in their transgressions.

Thus may we perceive how weakly our fathers did err before the flood; how continually, and upon common discourse, they fell upon errors after; it is therefore no wonder we have been erroneous ever since. And being now at greatest distance from the beginning of error, are almost lost in its dissemination, whose ways are boundless, and confess no circumscription.

CHAPTER III.

Of the second Cause of Common Errors; the erroneous Disposition of the People.

HAVING thus declared the fallible nature of man, even from his first production, we have beheld the general cause of error. But as for popular errors, they are more nearly founded upon an erroneous inclination of the people; as being the most deceptable part of mankind, and ready with open arms to receive the encroachments of error. Which condition of theirs, although deducible from many grounds, yet shall we evidence it but from a few, and such as most nearly and undeniably declare their natures.

How unequal discerners of truth they are, and openly exposed unto error, will first appear from their unqualified intellectuals, unable to umpire the difficulty of its dissentious. For error, to speak largely, is a false judgment of things, or an assent unto falsity. Now, whether the object whereunto they deliver up their assent be true or false, they are incompetent judges.

For the assured truth of things is derived from the prinples of knowledge, and causes which determine their verities. Whereof their uncultivated understandings scarce holding any theory, they are but bad discerners of verity, and in the numerous track of error, but casually do hit the point and unity of truth.

Their understanding is so feeble in the discernment of falsities, and averting the errors of reason, that it submitteth to the fallacies of sense, and is unable to rectifie the error of its sensations. Thus the greater part of mankind, having but one eye of sense and reason, conceive the earth far bigger than the sun, the fixed stars lesser than the moon, their figures plain, and their spaces from the earth equidistant. For thus their sense informeth them, and herein their reason cannot rectifie them; and, therefore, hopelessly continuing in mistakes, they live and die in their absurdities; passing their dayes in perverted apprehensions and conceptions of the world, derogatory unto God and the wisdom of the creation.

Again, being so illiterate in the point of intellect, and their sense so incorrected, they are further indisposed ever to attain unto truth; as commonly proceeding in those wayes, which have most reference unto sense, and wherein there lyeth most notable and popular delusion.

For being unable to wield the intellectual arms of reason, they are fain to betake themselves unto wasters,[5] and the

---

[5] *wasters.*] A kind of cudgel.

blunter weapons of truth: affecting the gross and sensible ways of doctrine, and such as will not consist with strict and subtile reason. Thus unto them a piece of rhetorick is a sufficient argument of logick; an epilogue* of Æsop, beyond syllogisms in barbara,[6] parables than propositions, and proverbs more powerful than demonstrations. And therefore are they led rather by example than precept; receiving persuasions from visible inducements, before intellectual instructions. And, therefore also they judge of human actions by the event; for, being uncapable of operable circumstances,[7] or rightly to judge the prudentiality of affairs, they only gaze upon the visible success, and, therefore, condemn or cry up the whole progression. And so, from this ground, in the lecture of Holy Scripture, their apprehensions are commonly confined unto the literal sense of the text, from whence have ensued the gross and duller sort of heresies. For not attaining the deuteroscopy,[8] and second intention of the words, they are fain to omit the super-consequences, coherences, figures, or tropologies: and are not sometimes persuaded by fire[9] beyond their literalities. And,

* Fable.

[6] *syllogisms in barbara.*] *Barbara*, among logicians, the first mode of the first figure of syllogism. A syllogism in *barbara*, is one whereof all the propositions are universal and affirmative; the middle term being the subject of the first proposition, and attribute in the second.
Example:—
  bar—Every wicked man is miserable:
  ba —All tyrants are wicked men:
  ra —Therefore all tyrants are miserable.—*Enc. Brit.*

[7] *uncapable of operable circumstances.*] "Not capable of judging what is to be done under any given circumstances." This passage is Dr. Johnson's solitary authority for the word *operable*, which he observes is *not in use*.

[8] *deuteroscopy.*] i. e. the inward and spiritual meaning, which is sometimes
Allegorical, and by a continual metaphor or allusion, or similitude or parable, proposes the greatest depths of divinitye:
Tropological, tending to the reformation of the manners and life of a Christian: as by the forbidding of swine's flesh, expressing God's detestation of all filthiness in the flesh and the spirit:—
Anagogicall; inducing us by the vilitye, unstabilitye, and vexatious fruition of earthly things to the love of that future blisse, wherein shall wee noe defect, noe change, noe dislike for ever.—*Wr.*

[9] ***by fire.***] He seems to refer to *the stake.* But, surely, martyrdom

therefore also, things invisible but unto intellectual discernments, to humour the grossness of their comprehensions, have been degraded from their proper forms, and God himself dishonoured into manual expressions.[1] And so likewise being unprovided, or unsufficient for higher speculations, they will always betake themselves unto sensible representations, and can hardly be restrained the dulness of idolatry. A sin or folly not only derogatory unto God but men; overthrowing their reason, as well as his divinity. In brief, a reciprocation, or rather an inversion of the creation, making God one way, as he made us another; that is, after our image,[2] as he made us after his own.

Moreover, their understanding, thus weak in itself, and perverted by sensible delusions, is yet farther impaired by the dominion of their appetite; that is, the irrational and brutal part of the soul, which, lording it over the sovereign faculty, interrupts the actions of that noble part, and choaks those tender sparks, which Adam hath left them of reason. And, therefore, they do not only swarm with errors, but vices depending thereon. Thus they commonly affect[3] no man any further than he deserts his reason, or complies with their aberrances. Hence they embrace not virtue for itself, but its reward; and the argument from pleasure or utility is far more powerful than that from virtuous honesty: which Mahomet and his contrivers well understood, when he set out the felicity of his heaven, by the contentments of flesh and the delight of sense, slightly passing over the accomplishment of the soul, and the beatitude of that part which earth and visibilities too weakly affect. But the wisdom of our Saviour, and the simplicity of his truth proceeded another

---

has, in a vast majority of instances, been undergone in defence of truth, rather than from ignorant adherence to *vulgar error*.

[1] *God himself dishonoured into manual expressions.*] On the ancient heresy of the *Anthropomorphites*, who ascribed to the Almighty a bodily shape, see *Augustin contra Epist. Manichæi*, c. 23;—*Epiphanius*, tom i. lib. iii. *Hæres.* 70; *Theodoret.* lib. iv. c. 10. In 1654, this extraordinary error was advocated by Mr. J. Biddle, in his " *Briefe Scripture Catechisme,*" which produced a reply in the following year from the celebrated Dr. Owen, his *Vindiciæ Evangelicæ,* or *The Mystery of the Gospel Vindicated.*

[2] *image.*] i. e. *imagination.*—*Wr.*

[3] *affect.*] In the sense of "being pleased with."

way; defying the popular provisions of happiness from sensible expectations; placing his felicity in things removed from sense, and [in] the intellectual enjoyment of God. And, therefore, the doctrine of the one was never afraid of universities, or endeavoured the banishment of learning, like the other. And though Galen doth sometimes nibble at Moses, and, beside the apostate Christian,* some heathens have questioned his philosophical part, or treaty[4] of the creation, yet is there surely no reasonable pagan that will not admire the rational and well-grounded precepts of Christ; whose life, as it was comformable unto his doctrine, so was that unto the highest rules of reason, and must therefore flourish in the advancement of learning, and the perfection of parts best able to comprehend it.

Again, their individual imperfections being great, they are, moreover, enlarged by their aggregation; and being erroneous in their single numbers, once huddled together, they will be error itself. For being a confusion of knaves and fools, and a farraginous concurrence of all conditions, tempers, sexes, and ages, it is but natural if their determinations be monstrous, and many ways inconsistent with truth. And, therefore, wise men have always applauded their own judgment, in the contradiction of that of the people; and their soberest adversaries have ever afforded them the style of fools and madmen; and, to speak impartially, their actions have made good these epithets. Had Orestes been judge, he would not have acquitted that Lystrian rabble of madness,† who,—upon a visible miracle falling into so high a conceit of Paul and Barnabas, that they termed the one Jupiter, the other Mercurius, that they brought oxen and garlands, and were hardly restrained from sacrificing unto them,—did, notwithstanding, suddenly after fall upon Paul, and, having stoned him, drew him for dead out of the city. It might have hazarded the sides of Democritus, had he been present at that tumult of Demetrius; when the people flocking together in great numbers, some crying one thing and some another, and the assembly was confused, and the most part knew not wherefore they were come together, notwithstand-

---

* Julian.   † Non sani esse hominis, non sanus juret Orestes.

[4] *treaty.*] In the sense of *treatise;* but the word is obsolete.—*Wr.*

ing, all with one voice, for the space of two hours cried out, "Great is Diana of the Ephesians." It had overcome the patience of Job, as it did the meekness of Moses, and would surely have mastered any but the longanimity and lasting sufferance of God, had they beheld the mutiny in the wilderness; when, after ten great miracles in Egypt, and some in the same place, they melted down their stolen[5] ear-rings into a calf, and monstrously cried out, "These are thy gods, O Israel, that brought thee out of the land of Egypt." It much accuseth the impatience of Peter, who could not endure the staves of the multitude, and is the greatest example of lenity in our Saviour, when he desired of God forgiveness unto those, who having one day brought him into the city in triumph, did presently after act all dishonour upon him, and nothing could be heard but *crucifige* in their courts. Certainly, he that considereth these things in God's peculiar people, will easily discern how little of truth there is in the ways of the multitude; and though sometimes they are flattered with that aphorism, will hardly believe "The voice of the people to be the voice of God."

Lastly, being thus divided from truth in themselves, they are yet farther removed by advenient deception. For true it is (and I hope I shall not offend their vulgarities if I say) they are daily mocked into error by subtiler devisors, and have been expressly deluded by all professions and ages. Thus the priests of elder time have put upon them many incredible conceits, not only deluding their apprehensions with ariolation, soothsaying,[6] and such oblique idolatries, but winning their credulities unto the literal and downright adorement of cats, lizards, and beetles.[7] And thus also in

---

[5] *stolen.*] Neither *stolen* nor *borrowed*, but *freely given* to the solicitations of the Israelites, to whom "The Lord had given favour in the sight of the Egyptians." The LXX and Vulgate, with the Syriac, Chaldee, Samaritan, Coptic, and Persian all agree in this interpretation of Exod. iii. 22, and xii. 35, 36. The idea of dishonesty so universally attached to this transaction, in consequence of our unfortunate version of the passage, is a *vulgar error*, which cannot be too generally corrected.

[6] *ariolation, soothsaying.*] Synonymous terms.

[7] *adorement of cats, lizards, and beetles.*] This, no doubt, is an allusion to the ancient Egyptians, by whom all these animals were worshipped, but whether as *incarnations* or as mere *symbols* of certain

some Christian churches (wherein is presumed an irreprovable truth) if all be true that is suspected, or half what is related, there have not wanted many strange deceptions, and some thereof are still confessed by the name of pious frauds.[8]

divinities, it seems difficult to determine. It would, indeed, appear probable, that the animals which were at first worshipped in Egypt, as representative symbols only of the deities to whom they were respectively sacred, were in the progress of idolatry adored as manifestations upon earth of those divinities themselves. The CAT, many embalmed bodies of which animal have been found in the Egyptian sepulchres, appears to have been sacred either to Isis or to her half-sister Nephthys. In mentioning the worship of LIZARDS, the author doubtless alludes to that of the crocodile, the affinity of which to the lizard was observed and recorded by the Greek writers, who, when travelling in Egypt, bestowed on that animal called *temsah* by the natives, the name of Κροκοδειλος, previously applied to a lizard, common in Greece. Strabo, relating his own observations, states, that "in the city of Arsinoë, which was formerly called Crocodilopolis, (in Upper Egypt, now called Medinet-el-Fay-yúm,) the crocodile is worshipped, and a sacred crocodile is kept in a pond, who is perfectly tame, and familiar with the priests. He is called Suchus ; they feed him with corn, and meat, and wine, which are continually brought him by strangers." One of the Egyptian divinities, apparently that to whom the crocodile was consecrated, was pictured as having a crocodile's head ; and is denoted, in the hieroglyphic inscriptions, by a representation of that animal with the tail turned under it. The BEETLE was regarded by the Egyptians as the symbol of a particular personification of Phthah, the father of the gods ; that insect is used in hieroglyphics for the name of this deity, whose head in the pictural representations of him, either bears a beetle, or is itself in the form of a beetle ; and in other instances the beetle, in hieroglyphics, has clearly a reference to generation or reproduction, which is a sense attributed to this symbol by all antiquity, and from which Dr. Young, in hieroglyphical researches, inferred its relation to Phthah ; an inference since confirmed by the inquiries of Champollion. The Egyptians embalmed and preserved all the animals they adored ; and in the Royal Egyptian Museum at Berlin are some mummies of the sacred beetle. In these instances of the worship of animals, however, it may be questioned whether the priests who conducted it were not themselves the subjects of delusion, in a degree equal to, or perhaps greater than, that of their followers. Possibly, therefore, they were not *wholly* deserving of the censure cast upon them by our author.—*Br.*

[8] *And thus also, &c.*] It would be easy to justify the charge which is only insinuated in this sentence, by a host of examples of the monkish trickery of pretended miracles and relicks. But the task would be endless ; and surely it is becoming daily less necessary to contradict what is daily less believed. It happened to the editor, some years since, to visit the cathedral of Aachen (*Gallicè, Aix-la-Chapelle*) where,

Thus Theudas,[9] an impostor, was able to lead away four thousand into the wilderness; and the delusions of Mahomet almost the fourth part of mankind. Thus all heresies, how gross soever, have found a welcome with the people. For thus many of the Jews were wrought into the belief that Herod was the Messias:[1] and David George, of Leyden,[2] and Arden, were not without a party amongst the people, who maintained the same opinion of themselves almost in our days.

Physicians (many at least that make profession thereof) besides divers less discoverable ways of fraud, have made them believe there is the book of fate, or the power of Aaron's breast-plate,[3] in urines. And, therefore, hereunto

among a profusion of relicks, was exhibited a *fragment* of one of the nails used in the crucifixion: and we were gravely assured by the priest in attendance, that *the other part* of that nail was in the cathedral of Nostre Dame, at Paris. There, accordingly, we made a point of inquiring for it, but in vain; our guide averred that there was no such bit of nail among the relicks of the place, nor ever had been!

[9] *Theudas.*] Theudas or Theodas was a Jewish impostor and magician, in the first century of the Christian church, who so well deluded the people as to collect together above four hundred (not *thousand*) men, whom he persuaded to quit the town; assuring them that he could dry up the waters of the Jordan by speaking a single word. His followers, however, were exterminated, and Theudas himself was killed, and his head brought to Jerusalem. *Acts* v.; *Eusebius*, lib. ii. cap. x.; *Dict. de Moréri, edit. par Drouet, sub nom.—Br.*

[1] *many of the Jews, &c.*] "Tacco de Judaismi hereticis . . . . quod Herodiani Herodem regem suscepere pro Christo." *Hieoronymus, adv. Luciferianos*, cap. 8—*J. K.*

[2] *David George, of Leyden.*] Or, as some say, of Ghent, was a glazier or a painter on glass, who began to preach, about the year 1525, that he was the true Messiah, the third David, and (like the well-known enthusiast of our own times, Richard Brothers) *the nephew of God*, not according to the flesh, but according to the spirit. He appears to have been an enthusiast of the worst order, uniting with this profession of being the Messiah, the teaching of many sentiments inimical alike to Christianity and to morals. However, he gained followers, and sustained the delusion even to his last hour. He died at Basle in 1556, having declared to his disciples, a short time previous to his death, that he should rise again on the third day after his decease. In order to expose the delusion, and confound the believers in his mad professions, the Senate of Basle had his body disinterred on the third day, and caused it to be burnt, together with his writings. *Dict. de Moréri. edit. par Drouet, sub nom.* and other authorities.—*Br.*

[3] *power of Aaron's breastplate.*] Josephus and others maintain that

they have recourse, as unto the oracle of life, the great determinator of virginity, conception, fertility, and the inscrutable infirmities of the whole body. For, as though there were a seminality in urine,[4] or that, like the seed, it carried with it the idea of every part, they foolishly conceive, we visibly behold therein the anatomy of every particle, and can thereby indigitate their diseases: and, running into any demands, expect from us a sudden resolution in things, whereon the Devil of Delphos[5] would demur: and we know hath taken respite of some days to answer easier questions.

Saltimbancoes,[6] quacksalvers,[7] and charlatans, deceive them in lower degrees. Were Æsop alive, the Piazza and Pont-Neuf* could not but speak their fallacies.[8] Meanwhile there are too many whose cries cannot conceal their mischiefs: for their impostures are full of cruelty, and worse than any other; deluding not only unto pecuniary defraudations, but the irreparable deceit of death.

Astrologers, which pretend to be of Cabala with the stars[9] (such I mean as abuse that worthy enquiry) have not been wanting in their deceptions: who, having won their belief unto principles, whereof they make great doubt themselves, have made them believe, that arbitrary events below, have necessary causes above. Whereupon their credulities assent unto any prognosticks, and daily swallow the predictions of men; which, considering the independency of their causes,

* Places in Venice and Paris, where mountebanks play their pranks.

the precious stones of Aaron's breastplate were the *Urim* and *Thummim*, and that they discovered the will of God by their extraordinary lustre, thereby predicting the issue of events to those who consulted them.

[4] *For as though there were a seminality in urine.*] See *Primrose's Vulgar Errors*, translated by *Wittie*, p. 64.—J. Cr.

[5] *the Devil of Delphos.*] Meaning the oracle of Apollo, at Delphos.

[6] *Saltimbancoes.*] Mountebanks: *saltare in banco*.

[7] *quacksalvers.*] Originally those who made, sold, or applied ointments or oils; *salve-quacks*. Applied to travelling quacks or *charlatans*.

[8] *Were Æsop alive, the Piazza and Pont Neuf, &c.*] Alluding probably to Æsop's fable of the "Astrologer and Traveller," and meaning to intimate that the *Piazza* and *Pont Neuf* would have suggested to the fabulist abundant materials for fresh apologues.

[9] *of Cabala with the stars.*] "Possessed of the key to their secrets." *Cabbala*, a Hebrew word signifying *tradition;* applied originally to the secret science of the rabbinical doctors, and thence used to designate any secret science.

and contingency in their events, are only in the prescience of God.

Fortune-tellers, jugglers, geomancers,[1] and the like incantatory impostors, though commonly men of inferior rank, and from whom, without illumination, they can expect no more than from themselves, do daily and professedly delude them. Unto whom (what is deplorable in men and Christians) too many applying themselves, betwixt jest and earnest, betray the cause of truth, and insensibly make up the legionary body of error.

Statists and politicians, unto whom *ragione di stato* is the first considerable,[2] as though it were their business to deceive the people, as a maxim do hold, that truth is to be concealed from them; unto whom although they reveal the visible design, yet do they commonly conceal the capital intention. And therefore have they[3] ever been the instruments of great designs, yet seldom understood the true intention of any; accomplishing the drifts of wiser heads, as inanimate and ignorant agents the general design of the world, who, though in some latitude of sense, and in a natural cognition [they] perform their proper actions, yet do they unknowingly concur unto higher ends, and blindly advance the great intention of nature. Now how far they may be kept in ignorance, a great example there is in the people of Rome, who never knew the true and proper name of their own city. For, beside that common appellation received by the citizens, it had a proper and secret name concealed from them; *cujus alterum nomen*[4] *dicere secretis ceremoniarum nefas habetur*, saith Pliny. Lest the name thereof being discovered unto their enemies, their *penates* and patronal god might be called forth by charms and incantations. For, according unto the tradition of magicians, the tutelary spirits will not remove at common appellations, but at the proper names of things whereunto they are protectors.

[1] *geomancers.*] A geomancer is a caster of figures : a cheat, who pretends to foretell futurity by other means than the astrologer.—*Johnson.*

[2] *unto whom* ragione di stato, *&c.*] To whom *reasons of state* are of the first consideration.

[3] *have they.*] The vulgar have.—*Wr.*

[4] *secret name concealed from them, &c.*—This name was *Valentias*, for revealing which Soranus was put to deathe.—*Wr.*

Thus, having been deceived by themselves, and continually deluded by others, they must needs be stuffed with errors, and even overrun with these inferior falsities. Whereunto whosoever shall resign their reasons, either from the root of deceit in themselves, or inability to resist such trivial deceptions[5] from others, although their condition and fortunes may place them many spheres above the multitude, yet are they still within the line of vulgarity, and democratical enemies of truth.

CHAPTER IV.

Of the more immediate causes of Common Errors, both in the wiser an common sort; and first, of Misapprehension and Fallacy, or false Deduction.

THE first is a mistake, or a misconception of things, either in their first apprehension, or secondary relations. So Eve mistook the commandment, either from the immediate injunction of God, or from the secondary narration of her husband. So might the disciples mistake our Saviour, in his answer unto Peter concerning the death of John, as is delivered John xxi. "Peter seeing John, saith unto Jesus, Lord, and what shall this man do? Jesus saith, If I will that he tarry till I come, what is that unto thee? Then went this saying abroad among the brethren, that that disciple should not die." Thus began the conceit and opinion of the Centaurs; that is, in the mistake of the first beholders, as is declared by Servius.[6] When some young

---

[5] *deceptions.*] The first five editions read *ingannations*.

[6] *In the mistake, &c.*] A mistake similar to that which is recorded by Herrera, the Spanish historian of America, to have been committed by the people of New Spain, when they first beheld the Spanish cavalry. They imagined the horse and his rider to be some monstrous animal of a terrible form, and supposing that their food was the same as that of men, brought flesh and bread to nourish them. No representation, however, of horsemen occurs, which might indicate that the artist regarded the horse and his rider as one animal, among the various specimens of Mexican *picture-writing*, which have been published by Purchas, Thevenot, Robertson, Humboldt, and others.—*Br.*

Ross says, "there is no doubt then but Centaurs, as well as other monsters, are produced, partly by the influence of the stars, and partly by other causes," &c.

Thessalians on horseback were beheld afar off, while their horses watered, that is, while their heads were depressed, they were conceived by the first spectators to be but one animal; and answerable hereunto have their pictures been drawn ever since.

And, as simple mistakes commonly beget fallacies, so men rest not in false apprehensions, without absurd and inconsequent deductions; from fallacious foundations, and misapprehended mediums, erecting conclusions no way inferrible from their premises. Now the fallacies whereby men deceive others, and are deceived themselves, the ancients have divided into verbal and real. Of the verbal, and such as conclude from mistakes of the word, although there be no less than six, yet are there but two thereof worthy our notation, and unto which the rest may be referred; that is, the fallacy of equivocation and amphibology, which conclude from the ambiguity of some one word, or the ambiguous syntaxis of many put together. From this fallacy arose that calamitous error of the Jews, misapprehending the prophecies of their Messias, and expounding them always unto literal and temporal expectations. By this way many errors crept in, and perverted the doctrine of Pythagoras, whilst men received his precepts in a different sense from his intention; converting metaphors into proprieties,[7] and receiving as literal expressions obscure and involved truths. Thus when he enjoined his disciples an abstinence from beans, many conceived they were with severity debarred the use of that pulse, which, notwithstanding, could not be his meaning; for as Aristoxenus, who wrote his life, averreth, he delighted much in that kind of food himself. But herein, as Plutarch observeth, he had no other intention than to dissuade men from magistracy, or undertaking the publick offices of state: for by beans was the magistrate elected in some parts of Greece; and after his days, we read, in Thucydides, of the Council of the Bean in Athens. The same word also in Greek doth signify a testicle, and hath been thought by some, an injunction only of continency, as Aulus Gellius

---

[7] *converting metaphors into* proprieties.] "Taking an expression or representation which only by *simile* applies to a subject, as if it had properly (or *of propriety*) belonged to it." *Proprieties* here implies *literalities*.

hath expounded, and as Empedocles may also be interpreted,* that is, *testiculis miseri dextras subducite.* And [this] might be the original intention of Pythagoras, as having a notable hint hereof in beans,[8] from the natural signature of the venereal organs of both sexes. Again, his injunction is, not to harbour swallows in our houses; whose advice notwithstanding we do not contemn, who daily admit and cherish them. For herein a caution is only implied, not to entertain ungrateful and thankless persons, which like the swallow, are no way commodious unto us, but having made use of our habitations, and served their own turns, forsake us. So he commands to deface the print of a cauldron in the ashes, after it hath boiled; which strictly to observe, were condemnable superstition. But hereby he covertly adviseth us not to persevere in anger, but after our choler hath boiled, to retain no impression thereof. In the like sense are to be received, when he adviseth his disciples to give the right hand but to few, to put no viands in a chamber-pot, not to pass over a balance, not to take up fire with a sword, or piss against the sun. Which ænigmatical deliveries comprehend useful verities, but being mistaken by literal expositors at the first, they have been misunderstood by most since, and may be occasion of error to verbal capacities for ever.

This fallacy is the first delusion Satan put upon Eve, and his whole tentation might be the same continued.[9] So when he said, "Ye shall not die," that was, in his equivocation, "ye shall not incur a present death," or a destruction immediately ensuing your transgression; "Your eyes shall be opened," that is, not to the enlargement of your knowledge, but discovery of your shame and proper confusion; "Ye shall know good and evil," that is, ye shall have knowledge of good by its privation, but cognizance of evil by sense and

* πᾶν δείλοι κυαμῶν ἀπὸ χεῖρας ἔχεσθε.

[8] *as having, &c.*] See a curious paper on the ancient superstitions concerning beans and peas, in the *Working Bee*, iii. p. 11.—*J.*

[9] *the same continued.*] The early editions read, "the same *elench* continued." Dean Wren remarks that *elench* is wrongly used here; meaning rather the detection of a sophistry than the sophistry itself. The author seems himself to have seen the error, and omitted the word.

visible experience. And the same fallacy or way of deceit, so well succeeding in Paradise, he continued in his oracles through all the world. Which had not men more warily understood, they might have performed many acts inconsistent with his intention. Brutus might have made haste with Tarquine to have kissed his own mother.[1] The Athenians might have built them wooden walls,[2] or doubled the altar at Delphos.[3]

The circle of this fallacy is very large; and herein may be comprised all ironical mistakes, for intended expressions receiving inverted significations; all deductions from metaphors, parables, allegories, unto real and rigid interpretations. Whereby have risen, not only popular errors in philosophy, but vulgar and senseless heresies in divinity, as will be evident unto any that shall examine their foundations, as they stand related by Epiphanius,[4] Austin, or Prateolus.[5]

Other ways there are of deceit; which consist not in false apprehension of words, that is, verbal expressions, or sentential significations, but fraudulent deductions, or inconsequent illations, from a false conception of things. Of these extra-

---

[1] *Brutus might have made haste, &c.*] Alluding to his interpretation of the Delphian reply to the Tarquinii: " Young men, whichever of you shall first kiss your mother, he shall possess the sovereign power at Rome." Brutus, who was present, fell to the ground, as if accidentally, and touched with his lips his mother, *earth*.

[2] *The Athenians, &c.*] When the oracle advised them, on the approach of Xerxes, to take refuge within their *wooden walls*, which, by the advice of Themistocles, they understood to mean *their fleet*.

[3] *or doubled the altar at Delphos.*] This refers to the demand of the *Delian oracle*, "to double his cubical altar," which gave occasion to a long series of geometrical inventions. See *Gillies' Anc. Greece*, part 2, vol. ii. p. 130, and the authorities he refers to.

[4] *Epiphanius, &c.*] Epiphanius, *contra octoginta Hæreses Panarium*; Augustinus, *De Hæresibus*.

[5] *Gabriel Prateolus.*] Vernacularly *du Preau*, was a voluminous French ecclesiastical writer of the 16th century. He was distinguished by the ardour of his zeal for the Roman catholic church, in opposition to those whom she has been pleased to stigmatize by the name of heretics. This spirit is manifested in all his works, but that to which Browne refers is doubtless the following: "De vitis, lectis, et dogmatibus, omnium hæreticorum, qui ab orbe condito, ad nostra usque tempora, et veterum et recentium monumentis proditi sunt, elenchus alphabeticus," &c.—*Br.*

dictionary[6] and real fallacies, Aristotle and logicians make in number six, but we observe that men are most commonly deceived by four thereof: those are, *petitio principii; a dicto secundum quid ad dictum simpliciter; a non causa pro causa;* and, *fallacia consequentis.*

The first is, *petitio principii*. Which fallacy is committed when a question is made a medium, or we assume a medium as granted, whereof we remain as unsatisfied as of the question. Briefly, where that is assumed as a principle to prove another thing, which is not conceded as true itself.[7] By this fallacy was Eve deceived, when she took for granted, the false assertion of the Devil: " Ye shall not surely die; for God doth know, that in the day ye shall eat thereof, your eyes shall be opened, and you shall be as gods." Which was but a bare affirmation of Satan, without any proof or probable inducement, contrary unto the command of God, and former belief of herself. And this was the logick of the Jews when they accused our Saviour unto Pilate; who demanding a reasonable impeachment, or the allegation of some crime worthy of condemnation, they only replied, "If he had not been worthy of death, we would not have brought him before thee." Wherein there was neither accusation of the person nor satisfaction of the judge, who well understood a bare accusation was no presumption of guilt, and the clamours of the people no accusation at all. The same fallacy is sometimes used in the dispute between Job and his friends, they often taking that for granted which afterwards he disproveth.

The second is, *A dicto secundum quid ad dictum simpliciter,* when from that which is but true in a qualified sense, an inconditional and absolute verity is inferred; transferring the special consideration of things unto their general acceptions, or concluding from their strict acception unto that without all limitation. This fallacy men commit when they argue from a particular to a general; as when we conclude the vices or qualities of a few, upon a whole nation, or from a

---

[6] *extradictionary.*] Johnson, citing the present passage, explains the word, " not relating to words but realities."

[7] *where that is assumed as a principle, &c.*] More clearly, "where that which is not conceded as true itself, is assumed as a principle to prove another thing."

part unto the whole. Thus the Devil argued with our Saviour; and by this he would persuade him he might be secure if he cast himself from the pinnacle: "For," said he, "it is written, He shall give his angels charge concerning thee, and in their hands they shall bear thee up, lest at any time thou dash thy foot against a stone." But this illation was fallacious, leaving out part of the text, (Psalm 91,) "He shall keep thee in all thy ways;" that is, in the ways of righteousness, and not of rash attempts: so he urged a part for the whole, and inferred more in the conclusion than was contained in the premises. By the same fallacy we proceed, when we conclude from the sign unto the thing signified. By this encroachment idolatry first crept in, men converting the symbolical use of idols into their proper worship, and receiving the representation of things as the substance and thing itself.[8] So the statue of Belus, at first erected in his memory, was in aftertimes adored as a divinity. And so also in the sacrament of the Eucharist, the bread and wine which were but the signals or visible signs, were made the things signified, and worshipped as the body of Christ. And hereby generally men are deceived, that take things spoken in some latitude without any at all. Hereby the Jews were deceived concerning the commandment of the Sabbath, accusing our Saviour for healing the sick, and his disciples for plucking the ears of corn upon that day. And, by this deplorable mistake, they were deceived unto destruction, upon the assault of Pompey the Great, made upon that day;[9] by whose superstitious observation they could not defend themselves, or perform any labour whatever.

The third is, *A non causa pro causa*, when that is pretended for a cause which is not, or not in that sense which is inferred. Upon this consequence the law of Mahomet

---

[8] *By this encroachment, &c.*] The conversion of the "symbolical use" of such "idols" as consisted of natural objects or their representations "into their proper worship," is beautifully though concisely explained in Kirby and Spence's *Introduction to Entomology*, vol. iv. p. 401-403.—*Br.*

[9] *And by this deplorable mistake, &c.*] The reader will find the particulars of this event recorded by Josephus, in his *Antiquities of the Jews*, book xiv. chap. 4, to which some pertinent illustrations from other parts of the Jewish history have been added by Whiston.—*Br.*

forbids the use of wine;[1] and his successors abolished universities. By this, also, many Christians have condemned literature, misunderstanding the counsel of Saint Paul, who adviseth no further than to beware of philosophy.[2] On this foundation were built the conclusions of soothsayers in their augurial and tripudiary divinations, collecting presages from voice or food of birds, and conjoining events unto causes of no connection. Hereupon also are grounded the gross mistakes in the cure of many diseases, not only from the last medicine and sympathetical receipts, but amulets, charms, and all incantatory applications; deriving effects not only from inconcurring causes, but things devoid of all efficiency whatever.

The fourth is, the fallacy of the consequent; which, if strictly taken, may be a fallacious illation in reference unto antecedency, or consequency; as, to conclude, from the position of the antecedent, to the position of the consequent, or from the remotion of the consequent, to the remotion of the antecedent. This is usually committed when in connexed propositions the terms adhere contingently. This is frequent in oratory illations; and thus the Pharisees, because he canversed with publicans and sinners, accused the holiness of Christ. But, if this fallacy be largely taken, it is committed in any vicious illation, offending the rules of good consequence; and so it may be very large, and comprehend all false illations against the settled laws of logick. But the most usual inconsequencies are from particulars, from nega-

[1] *Upon this consequence, &c.*] Meaning probably that Mahomet forbad the *use* of wine, when his motive was to prevent its *abuse* only; but his experience had taught him that the only means of effecting this would be to prohibit it altogether.

[2] *Philosophy.*] The apostle bids beware of vaine philosophie: where the worde (vaine) is a sufficient commentarye to a Christian, that by forbidding that which is indeed vaine, he advanceth true philosophye: such as is that of the hexameron, or six dayes creation: whereon many of the ancient Christians have left admirable treatises, setting forth in those workes the incomprehensible wisdom, and majesty and omnipotency of the Creator, and his unpromerited inexhausted goodness unto us, for whom he ordained the use of them all: that by our acknowledgment, the abundant grace might redound to his glorye; as itt hath don in all ages by that divine philosophical treatise of Moses philosophie, mentioned in the 20th page, line 6, in the passage beginning "And though Galen," &c.—*Wr.*

tives, and from affirmative conclusions in the second figure, wherein, indeed, offences are most frequent, and their discoveries not difficult.

CHAPTER V.

Of other more immediate Causes of Error ;—viz. Credulity and Supinity.

A THIRD cause of common errors[3] is, the credulity of men, that is, an easy assent to what is obtruded, or a believing, at first ear, what is delivered by others. This is a weakness in the understanding, without examination assenting unto things which, from their natures and causes, do carry no persuasion; whereby men often swallow falsities for truths, dubiosities for certainties, feasibilities for possibilities, and things impossible as possibilities themselves. Which, though a weakness of the intellect, and most discoverable in vulgar heads, yet hath it sometime fallen upon wiser brains, and great advancers of truth. Thus many wise Athenians so far forgot their philosophy, and the nature of human production, that they descended unto belief that the original of their nation was from the earth, and had no other beginning, than from the seminality and womb of their great mother. Thus it is not without wonder how those learned Arabicks so tamely delivered up their belief unto the absurdities of the Alcoran. How the noble Geber, Avicenna, and Almanzor should rest satisfied in the nature and causes of earthquakes, delivered from the doctrine of their prophet; that is, from the motion of a great bull, upon whose horns all the earth is poised.[4]

[3] *A third cause of common errors.*] The first cause being *mistake*, or *misapprehension*; the second *fallacious*, or *false inferences*.

[4] *How the noble Geber, &c.*] Sale's Koran having been in vain examined for some justification of this passage, I requested my learned friend, Mr. W. H. Black, to refer to the works of Geber, Almanzor, and Avicenna, in the library of the British Museum. He did so, without success, as appears from the following extracts from his obliging reply:—

"I have diligently perused (but in vain) the *Rhasis of Almanzor*, (1497, folio), and *Taraqua's Alphabetical Arrangement or Common Place Book of Avicenna* (Burdigal, 4to. 1520), and two editions of Geber, the latter being, as I think, the same book as you mean. . . . . .

"This little duodecimo volume contains several curious tracts not named in the title, all which I have also perused, and the only notice

How their faiths could decline so low as to concede their generations in heaven to be made by the smell of a citron, or that the felicity of their paradise should consist in a jubilee of conjunction, that is, a coition of one act prolonged unto fifty years.[5] Thus is it almost beyond wonder, how the belief of reasonable creatures should ever submit unto idolatry; and the credulity of those men scarce credible (without presumption of a second fall) who could believe a Deity in the work of their own hands. For although in that ancient and diffused adoration of idols unto the priests and subtiler heads, the worship, perhaps, might be symbolical, and as those images some way related unto their deities; yet was the idolatry direct and downright in the people; whose credulity is illimitable, who may be made believe that anything is God; and may be made believe there is no God at all.

And, as credulity is the cause of error, so incredulity oftentimes of not enjoying truth: and that not only an obstinate incredulity, whereby we will not acknowledge assent unto what is reasonably inferred, but any academical reservation in matters of easy truth, or rather sceptical infidelity against the evidence of reason and sense. For these are conceptions

of *earthquakes* I can any where find, is in "*Avicennæ Mineralia,*" p. 248, in the beginning of the 2nd chapter. "De Causa Montium."

"Montes quoque quandoque fiunt ex causa essentiali, quandoque ex causa accidentali. Ex essentiali causa, ut ex *vehementi motu terræ* elevatur terra et fit mons."

[5] *How their faiths, &c.*] It will be sufficient merely to remark, that the ridiculous conceits respecting "generations in heaven" and the "felicity of Paradise," here attributed to Mohammed, are not to be found in the Korân, or in any genuine commentary upon it. They have much the air of Rabbinical fancies, foisted upon the Mohammedans by their inventors. At the same time, the real dogmas of the prophet of Mecca upon both points, afford, perhaps, as good an illustration of the credulity of the Arabian philosophers as those erroneously ascribed to him in the text. For "according to the saying of the prophet," if any of the faithful in Paradise be desirous of issue, it shall be *conceived* by their Houri wives, *born*, and *grown up, within the space of an hour*. And the other extraordinary notion alluded to by Browne (for doubtless he was not the originator of it), may have been derived from the declaration of Mohammed, that in order to qualify the blessed for the full enjoyment of the pleasures and delights of Paradise, which they would otherwise sink under, "God will give to every one the abilities of an hundred men." Vide *Sale's Korân, Prelim. Disc.* sect. iv.—*Br.*

befalling wise men, as absurd as the apprehensions of fools, and the credulity of the people, which promiscuously swallow any thing. For this is not only derogatory unto the wisdom of God, who hath proposed the world unto our knowledge, and thereby the notion of himself, but also detractory unto the intellect and sense of man, expressedly disposed for that inquisition. And therefore, *hoc tantum scio, quod nihil scio*, is not to be received in an absolute sense, but is comparatively expressed unto the number of things whereof our knowledge is ignorant. Nor will it acquit the insatisfaction of those who quarrel with all things, or dispute of matters concerning whose verities we have conviction from reason, or decision from the inerrable and requisite conditions of sense. And, therefore, if any affirm the earth doth move, and will not believe with us, it standeth still;[6] because he

---

[6] *it standeth still.*] [In] the booke of God, from Moses unto Christ, there are no lesse than eighty and odd expresse places, affirming in plaine and overt termes the naturall and perpetuall motion of the sun and the moon ; and that the stop or stay of that motion was one of the greatest miracles that ever the whole world beheld: others the rising and setting of them: others, their diurnal course and vigorous activitye upon this lowest world : others, their circulation on this world or earth not only daylye, but annually, by a declination from the midline on both sides, North and South : others (as expressly) the impossibility of any (other) motion in the earth, than that terrible and pœnal motion of his shaking itt, that made it: others that it cannot be moved totally in his place, nor removed universal out of his place. Soe that were itt nothing else than the veneration and firme beliefe of that Word of His, which the penmen thereof spake not of themselves, but by inspiration of the Holy Ghost. they that profess Christianitye should not dare, much lesse adventure to call the letter thereof in question concerning things soe plainly, frequently, constantly, delivered ; should tremble at that curse which is denounced against those that adde any thing unto itt, or diminish any tittle of itt : should feare to raise such a hellish suspition in vulgar mindes, as the Romish church, by undervalewing the majesty and authority thereof, hath done : should bee affrighted to follow that audacious and pernicious suggestion, which Satan used, and thereby undid us all in our first parents ; that God had a double meaning in his commands, in effect condemning God of amphibologye. And all this boldness and overweaning having no other ground, but a seeming argument of some phænomena forsooth ; which notwithstanding, we know the learned Tycho ὁ Ἀστρονομάρχων, who lived (fifty-two) years since Copernicus, hath by admirable and matchlesse instruments, and many yeares exact observations proved to bee noe better than a dreame.—*Wr.*

hath probable[7] reasons for it, and I no infallible sense, nor reason against it,[8] I will not quarrel with his assertion. But if, like Zeno, he shall walk about, and yet deny there is any motion in nature, surely that man was constituted for Anticyra[9] and were a fit companion for those who, having a

[7] *probable.*] Seeminge.—*Wr.*
[8] *reason against it.*]—Other than God's perpetual dictate.—*Wr.*
[9] *Anticyra.*] Two cities of the same name, the one in Phocis, the other in Thessaly, famous for producing hellebore, which was esteemed among the ancients the great remedy for madness.

Hence the proverb mentioned by Horace, *Naviget Anticyram*, which was applied to a person deemed insane ; and hence also the allusion in the text.

A remarkable illustration of Browne's remarks on obstinate and irrational scepticism is afforded by the history of *meteorites*, or of the bodies cast down upon the earth by meteors in the atmosphere. The fall of metallic and stony bodies from the atmosphere, is recorded by writers of every age of classical antiquity, many of whom narrated instances of it that had occured in their own times, or even within their own knowledge. Evidence of the same kind is abundantly to be found throughout the middle and dark ages ; and after the reformation, the fall of meteorites was witnessed and described by several natural philosophers of approved eminence and undoubted credit, during the sixteenth and seventeenth century, with the same attendant phænomena as had been described by the historians and writers of all the epochs we have mentioned. In the eighteenth century similar events took place, and were attested by irrefragable moral evidence. But the opinion, that nothing was to be believed which could not directly be accounted for, was now very prevalent. The accounts of the fall of meteoric stones were consequently rejected as impossible, and incompatible with the laws of nature ; and specimens of stones and iron that had been seen to fall by hundreds of people, were preserved in cabinets of natural history, as ordinary minerals, "which the credulous and superstitious regarded as having fallen from the clouds." Towards the latter end of the eighteenth century, the attention of several candid men of science was attracted to the subject by some remarkable cases which then occurred : but so powerful was the inclination to negative the question, that accounts of the fall of three similar stones, in as many districts of country, attested in the most convincing manner, could not obtain credence in the minds of a committee of the French Academy of Sciences, one of whom was the celebrated Lavoisier. At length, however, all the powers of inductive research were exerted upon the subject, which was subjected, in 1801, by the late Mr. Edward Howard, F.R.S., to a train of exact research : stones stated to have fallen from meteors in various parts of the world were collected and examined, and shown to bear a decided resemblance to each other, whilst they were altogether dissimilar from every known mineral. In England, this evidence gradually vanquished incredulity, but many foreign *savans*

conceit they are dead, cannot be convicted into the society of the living.

The fourth is a supinity, or neglect of enquiry, even of matters whereof we doubt; rather believing than going to see, or doubting with ease and gratis than believing with difficulty or purchase. Whereby, either from a temperamental inactivity, we are unready to put in execution the suggestions or dictates of reason: or by a content and acquiescence in every species of truth, we embrace the shadow thereof, or so much as may palliate its just and substantial acquirements. Had our forefathers sat down in these resolutions, or had their curiosities been sedentary, who pursued the knowledge of things through all the corners of nature, the face of truth had been obscure unto us, whose lustre in some part their industries have revealed.

Certainly the sweat of their labours was not salt unto them, and they took delight in the dust of their endeavours. For, questionless, in knowledge there is no slender difficulty; and truth, which wise men say doth lie in a well, is not recoverable by exantlation.[1] It were some extenuation of the curse, if *in sudore vultûs tui* were confinable unto corporal exercitations, and there still remained a Paradise, or unthorny place of knowledge. But now, our understandings being eclipsed, as well as our tempers infirmed, we must betake ourselves to ways of reparation, and depend upon the illumination of our endeavours. For thus we may, in some measure, repair our primary ruins, and build ourselves men again. And though the attempts of some have been precipitous, and their enquiries so audacious as to come within command of the flaming swords, and lost themselves in attempts above humanity; yet have the enquiries of most defected by the way, and tired within the sober circumference of knowledge.

And this is the reason why some have transcribed anything; and although they cannot but doubt thereof, yet

---

refused to believe it, and the bulk of the French philosophers were yet undecided what to think, when the fall of some thousands of stones at L'Aigle, in Normandy, the testimonies to which were scrutinized with judicial circumspection and jealousy, compelled the most determined scepticism to an unwilling assent.—*Br.*

[1] *by exantlation.*] By *being drawn out.* See *Christian Morals*, p. ii. § 5.

neither make experiment by sense, nor enquiry by reason, but live in doubts of things, whose satisfaction is in their own power; which is, indeed, the inexcusable part of our ignorance, and may, perhaps, fill up the charge of the last day.[2] For, not obeying the dictates of reason, and neglecting the crys of truth, we fail, not only in the trust of our undertakings, but in the intention of man itself. Which, although more venial in ordinary constitutions, and such as are not framed beyond the capacity of beaten notions; yet will it inexcusably condemn some men, who, having received excellent endowments, have yet sat down by the way, and frustrated the intention of their abilities. For certainly, as some men have sinned in the principles of humanity, and must answer for not being men; so others offend if they be not more. *Magis extra vitia, quàm cum virtutibus*, would commend those: these are not excusable without an excellency. For, great constitutions, and such as are constellated unto knowledge, do nothing till they out-do all; they come short of themselves, if they go not beyond others; and must not sit down under the degree of worthies. God expects no lustre from the minor stars; but if the sun should not illuminate all, it were a sin in nature. *Ultimus bonorum*, will not excuse every man, nor is it sufficient for all to hold the common level. Men's names should not only distinguish them. A man should be something, that all men are not, and individual in somewhat beside his proper name.[3] Thus, while it exceeds not the bounds of reason and modesty, we cannot condemn singularity. *Nos numerus sumus*, is the motto of the multitude, and for that reason are they fools. For things, as they recede from unity, the more they approach to imperfection and deformity; for they hold their perfection in their simplicities, and as they nearest approach unto God.

Now, as there are many great wits to be condemned, who have neglected the increment of arts, and the sedulous pursuit of knowledge; so are there not a few very much to be pitied, whose industry being not attended with natural parts, they have sweat to little purpose, and rolled the stone in vain. Which chiefly proceedeth from natural incapacity,

---

[2] *may, perhaps, fill up the charge, &c.*] Audi et time!—*Wr.*
[3] *A man should be, &c.*] A right and able man should.--*Wr.*

and genial indisposition, at least, to those particulars whereunto they apply their endeavours. And this is one reason why, though universities be full of men, they are oftentimes empty of learning; why, as there are some men do much without learning,[4] so others but little with it, and few that attain to any measure of it. For many heads, that undertake it, were never squared, nor timber'd for it. There are not only particular men, but whole nations indisposed[5] for learning; whereunto is required, not only education, but a pregnant Minerva, and teeming constitution. For the wisdom of God hath divided the genius of men according to the different affairs of the world, and varied their inclinations according to the variety of actions to be performed therein. Which they who consider not, rudely rushing upon professions and ways of life unequal to their natures, dishonour not only themselves and their functions, but pervert the harmony of the whole world. For, if the world went on as God hath ordained it, and were every one employed in points concordant to their natures, professions, arts, and commonwealths, would rise up of themselves, nor needed we a lanthorn to find a man in Athens.

CHAPTER VI.

Of another more immediate Cause of Error; viz. obstinate Adherence unto Antiquity.

But the mortallest enemy unto knowledge, and that which hath done the greatest execution upon truth, hath been a peremptory adhesion unto authority; and more especially, the establishing of our belief upon the dictates of antiquity. For (as every capacity may observe) most men, of ages present, so superstitiously do look upon ages past, that the authorities of the one exceed the reasons of the other. Whose persons indeed being far removed from our times, their works, which seldom with us pass uncontrolled,

---

[4] *why, as there are some men, &c.*] These observations are well amplified by the author in his *Christian Morals*, p. ii. § 4.—*J. Cr.*

[5] *whole nations, &c.*] Surely so sweeping an assertion as this would fall under the author's own censure, in Religio Medici, p. 93.

either by contemporaries, or immediate successors, are now become out of the distance of envies; and, the farther removed from present times, are conceived to approach the nearer unto truth itself. Now hereby methinks we manifestly delude ourselves, and widely walk out of the track of truth.

For, first, men hereby impose a thraldom on their times, which the ingenuity of no age should endure, or indeed the presumption of any did ever yet enjoin. Thus Hippocrates about two thousand years ago, conceived it no injustice, either to examine or refute the doctrines of his predecessors; Galen the like, and Aristotle the most of any. Yet did not any of these conceive themselves infallible, or set down their dictates as verities irrefragable: but when they either deliver their own inventions, or reject other men's opinions, they proceed with judgment and ingenuity; establishing their assertions, not only with great solidity, but submitting them also unto the correction of future discovery.

Secondly, Men that adore times past consider not that those times were once present, that is, as our own are at this instant; and we ourselves unto those to come, as they unto us at present; as we rely on them, even so will those on us, and magnify us hereafter, who at present condemn ourselves. Which very absurdity is daily committed amongst us, even in the esteem and censure of our own times. And, to speak impartially, old men, from whom we should expect the greatest example of wisdom, do most exceed in this point of folly; commending the days of their youth, which they scarce remember, at least well understood not, extolling those times their younger years have heard their fathers condemn, and condemning those times the grey heads of their posterity shall commend. And thus is it the humour of many heads to extol the days of their forefathers, and declaim against the wickedness of times present. Which notwithstanding they cannot handsomely do, without the borrowed help and satires of times past; condemning the vices of their own times, by the expressions of vices in times which they commend, which cannot but argue the community of vice in both. Horace, therefore, Juvenal, and Persius, were no prophets, although their lines did seem to indigitate and point at our times. There is a certain list of vices[6] committed in all ages, and declaimed against by all authors, which will last as long as human nature; which digested into common places, may serve for any theme, and never be out of date until doomsday.

Thirdly, The testimonies of antiquity, and such as pass oraculously amongst us, were not, if we consider them, always so exact as to examine the doctrine they delivered. For some, and those the acutest of them, have left unto us many things of falsity; controllable not only by critical and collective reason, but common and country observation.

Hereof there want not many examples in Aristotle, through all his book of animals; we shall instance only in three of his problems, and all contained under one section. The first enquireth, why a man doth cough, but not an ox or cow; whereas notwithstanding the contrary is often observed by husbandmen, and stands confirmed by those who have expressly treated *De re rustica*, and have also delivered divers remedies for it. Why juments, as horses, oxen, and asses, have no eructation or belching; whereas indeed the contrary is often observed, and also delivered by Columella. And thirdly, why man alone hath grey hairs; whereas it cannot escape the eyes, and ordinary observation of all men, that horses, dogs, and foxes, wax grey with age in our countrys;[7] and in the colder regions, many other animals without it. And though favourable constructions may somewhat extenu-

[6] *There is a certain list of vices.*] "Qualia sunt quæ semper velantur sed semper retinentur," saith old Livius.—*Wr.*

[7] *Why man alone hath grey hairs, &c.*] The author's previous reference to the problems of Aristotle, of which this is one, is so ambiguous, that it might induce a reader, unacquainted with the works of the Stagirite, to suppose that the problems formed part of the "Book of Animals," which is not the case. From a passage in the latter work, however, apparently unknown to our author, it is to be inferred that Aristotle was aware of the fact, that other animals become grey by age, and that he is speaking not in an absolute but in a comparative sense, when he asks the above question in the problems. For in the *History of Animals*, lib. iii. cap. xi., speaking of animals in general, he observes that "the colour of the hair changes in old age, in men becoming white, undergoing the same change in other animals, but not very manifestly, except in the horse," which latter is one of the instances cited in the paragraph before us, in contradiction of Aristotle. The other subjects, coughing and eructation, are not noticed in the *History of Animals*. —*Br.*

ate the rigour of these concessions[8] yet will scarce any palliate that in the fourth of his meteors, that salt is easiest dissolvable in cold water;[9] nor that of Dioscorides, that quicksilver is best preserved in vessels of tin and lead.

Other authors write often dubiously, even in matters wherein is expected a strict and definitive truth, extenuating their affirmations with *aiunt, ferunt, fortasse;*[1] as Dioscorides, Galen, Aristotle, and many more. Others by hearsay, taking upon trust most they have delivered; whose volumes are mere collections, drawn from the mouths or leaves of other authors, as may be observed in Pliny, Ælian, Athenæus, and many more. Not a few transcriptively, subscribing their names unto other men's endeavours, and merely transcribing almost all they have written. The Arabs transcribing the Greeks, the Greeks and Latins each other.

And though favourable constructions, &c.] Added in second edition.

[9] *That salt is easiest dissolvable in cold water.*] Upon examining the entire chapter (vi.) of the Meteors here cited, I found that our author had altogether mistaken the meaning of the passage relating to the solubility of salts. Aristotle does not use the term "cold moisture" (for this is the sense of the original, not *cold water*, as Browne has rendered it) in contradiction to *hot moisture*, he does not intend to say, as our author infers, that nitre and salts are more readily soluble in cold water than in hot; but he uses the phrase "cold moisture" as the opposite to "dry heat." Not far from the beginning of the chapter, he had previously defined water to be "a cold moisture;" and in the passage in question he says that salts and nitre (the νίτρον of the Greeks, which was not our nitre, or saltpetre, but the *natron* of North Africa, one of the *carbonates of soda* of modern chemistry) are soluble in moisture, using that term to denote humid substances in general, yet not in all moisture, "but in that which is cold." He adds, immediately, which proves this view of the subject to be the true one, "hence they are liquefied by water, and by aqueous fluids in general; (ὕδατος εἴη :) but they are not liquefied by oil;" evidently regarding the latter fluid as not being "a cold moisture." It may be remarked also, as an indication of the degree of acquaintance with such subjects possessed by our author, and by the generality of physical inquirers in his time, that he would, to a considerable extent, be himself in error, even had the assertion of Aristotle really been as he represents it; for common salt and several others are actually "easiest dissolvable in cold water."—*Br.*

[1] *aiunt, ferunt, fortasse.*] These three terms, and such like, argue so much modesty in those magazines of all human [learning?] as might well free them from a censure.—*Wr.*

Thus hath Justine[2] borrowed all from Trogus Pompeius, and Julius Solinus in a manner transcribed Pliny. Thus have Lucian and Apuleius served Lucius Pratensis; men both living in the same time, and both transcribing the same author, in those famous books, entituled Lucius by the one, and Aureus Asinus by the other. In the same measure hath Simocrates, in his tract De Nilo, dealt with Diodorus Siculus, as may be observed in that work annexed unto Herodotus, and translated by Jungermannus. Thus Eratosthenes wholly translated Timotheus de Insulis, not reserving the very preface. The same doth Strabo report of Eudorus, and Arstion, in a treatise entituled De Milo. Clemens Alexandrinus hath observed many examples hereof among the Greeks; and Pliny speaketh very plainly in his preface, that conferring his authors, and comparing their works together, he generally found those that went before *verbatim* transcribed by those that followed after, and their originals never so much as mentioned. To omit how much the wittiest[*] piece of Ovid is beholden unto Parthenius Chius; even the magnified Virgil hath borrowed almost all his works; his Eclogues from Theocritus, his Georgicks from Hesiod and Aratus, his Æneids from Homer, the second book whereof containing the exploit of Sinon and the Trojan Horse (as Macrobius observeth) he hath *verbatim* derived from Pisander. Our own profession is not excusable herein. Thus Oribasius, Ætiuus, and Ægineta, have in a manner transcribed Galen. But Marcellus Empericus, who hath left a famous work De Medicamentis, hath word for word transcribed all Scribonius Largus De Compositione Medicamentorum, and not left out his very peroration. Thus may we perceive the ancients were but men, even like ourselves. The practice of transcription in our days was no monster in theirs. Plagiary had not its nativity with printing, but began in times when thefts were difficult, and the paucity of books scarce wanted that invention.

Nor did they only make large use of other authors, but often without mention of their names. Aristotle, who seems to have borrowed many things from Hippocrates, in the most favourable construction, makes mention but once of him,[†] and that by the bye, and without reference unto his present

---

[*] His Metamorphoses.   [†] In his Politicks.

[2] *Justine.*] He cannot be properly said to borrow who professes only an epitome.—*Wr.*

doctrine. Virgil, so much beholding unto Homer,[3] hath not his name in all his works; and Pliny, who seems to borrow many authors out of Dioscorides, hath taken no notice of him. I wish men were not still content to plume themselves with others' feathers. Fear of discovery, not single ingenuity,[4] affords quotations rather than transcriptions; wherein, notwithstanding, the plagiarism of many makes little consideration,[5] whereof though great authors may complain, small ones cannot but take notice.[6]

Fourthly, while we so eagerly adhere unto antiquity, and the accounts of elder times, we are to consider the fabulous condition thereof. And that we shall not deny, if we call to mind the mendacity of Greece, from whom wee have received most relations; and that a considerable part of ancient times was by the Greeks themselves termed μύθικον, that is, made up, or stuffed out with fables.[7] And surely the

---

[3] *beholding unto Homer.*] "Very corruptly written," says Johnson, "for *beholden, held in obligation*, from the Dutch *gehouden.*" But Sir Thomas probably uses the word in the sense of "*looking* unto Homer," as to an authority or a source of information.

[4] *single ingenuity.*] "Simple ingenuousness."

[5] *the plagiarism, &c.*] That is, "plagiarism against many authors, who are little known, often escapes detection."

[6] *Nor did they, &c.*] Added in sixth edition.

[7] *By the Greeks themselves termed μύθικον, that is, made up, or stuffed out with fables.*] Our author seems here to misinterpret to a certain extent the term μύθικον, as applied to the earlier ages of Grecian history; and as his view of this point enters into the consideration of many other subjects discussed in the Pseudodoxia, it may be useful to the reader to offer in this place a few remarks upon what appears to be the true meaning of that term, as employed by the ancients themselves. The remains of Grecian, Egyptian, and Indian antiquity which have come down to us, and the modern investigation of the *mythi* of the ancients in general, abundantly evince that it was the custom with mankind, at periods of very remote antiquity, to couch whatever instructions or intellectual contemplations they wished to be conveyed to posterity, under the form of a *historical relation*, but intermingled with circumstances so extraordinary, as showed it was not designed to be literally apprehended. In process of time, however, the meaning of the symbols thus used was forgotten; and then the narratives composed by their aid, being accompanied in their descent to posterity by a feeling of respect which prevented their total rejection, began to be understood according to their literal meaning only, and mankind were lost in amazement at the marvellous things, which they supposed their ancestors to have witnessed. Thus the vulgar, in the latter ages of Greece

fabulous inclination of those days was greater than any since; which swarmed so with fables, and from such slender grounds took hints for fictions, poisoning the world ever after: wherein how far they succeeded may be exemplified

and Rome, looked back with admiration at the times when their heroes went to school to the Centaurs, and when sacred statues or holy shields fell from heaven for the protection of favoured cities. And further: the people of the earliest ages of the world appear to have been of a turn of mind so devoted to exalted sentiments and sublime contemplations, that they seem never to have thought of committing to writing accounts of common or historical occurrences: for which reason, as the researches of our own and the preceding age have amply proved, no authentic history of political or civil events, of any very great antiquity, exists, with the exception of the inspired books given through Moses.—Hence, and now we arrive at the true meaning of the term μυθικον—the well known remark of Varro: that the space of time before the flood was αδηλον—the period of utter obscurity; that the age from the flood to the first Olympiad was μυθικον—the period of *mythi* or of *mystery*,—not the part of history made up of fables, in the common sense of the term, as our author supposes: and that it was only with the first Olympiad that commenced the period ιστορικον —that of literal or true history.—With this general view of the subject, (for which I must acknowledge myself indebted, substantially, to Lect. vi. of Noble's *Plenary Inspiration of the Scriptures*,) the results of the profound researches of M. Julius Klaproth into the history and philological antiquities of Asia, especially with respect to the comparative state and nature of history among the Hindûs and the Chinese, entirely concur. The sense here attributed to μυθικον may also in particular be confirmed from the results at which M. Klaproth has arrived; as used by Varro, it must of course have been suggested by the consideration, principally, of Greek and early Roman history; but M. Klaproth, from the consideration, principally, of the ancient history of Asia, divides the history of ancient nations into *mythology*, doubtful history, and authentic history; the first of which he states to be "*truth in part*, enveloped in an impenetrable darkness of fable and *allegory*," and generally consisting (as M. Klaproth, perhaps somewhat too comprehensively, infers), "of subsequently calculated astronomical periods, metamorphosed into dynasties and heroes."

If the views submitted in this note be borne in mind, and much might be added in further confirmation of their truth, from the most recent and satisfactory investigations of the *mythi*, by the most soberminded inquirers and critics, of all countries, and all schools of ancient literature, the reader will often be enabled to arrive at a more satisfactory solution of the marvellous relations of classical antiquity, than those adopted by our author. To what extent we may receive the explanations of them he has given from *Palæphatus* and others, may in some degree be inferred from the circumstances mentioned in our note upon the "fable of *Charon*," p. 47.—*Br.*

from Palæphatus,* in his book of Fabulous Narrations. That fable of Orpheus, who by the melody of his musick made woods and trees to follow him, was raised upon a slender foundation; for there were a crew of mad women retired unto a mountain, from whence, being pacified by his musick, they descended with boughs in their hands; which, unto the fabulosity of those times, proved a sufficient ground to celebrate unto all posterity the magick of Orpheus's harp, and its power to attract the senseless trees about it.[8] That Medea, the famous sorceress, could renew youth, and make old men young again, was nothing else, but that from the knowledge of simples, she had a receipt to make white hair black, and reduce old heads into the tincture of youth again. The fable of Geryon and Cerberus with three heads was this: Geryon was of the city Tricarinia,[9] that is, of three heads, and Cerberus of the same place, was one of his dogs, which, running into a cave upon pursuit of his master's

---

* An ancient author who writ Περὶ ἀπίστων, *sive de incredibilibus*, whereof some part is yet extant.

[8] *Orpheus' Harp, &c.*] Dr. Delany, in his life of David, produces some ingenious arguments to prove that Orpheus was in reality the same person with David.—*J.*

We are tempted to insert (rather for *ornament* than illustration) a *jeu d'esprit* of the late ..... Lisle: See *Aiken's Vocal Poetry*, 8vo. 1810, p. 228:—

> When Orpheus went down to the regions below,
>   Which men are forbidden to see,
> He tuned up his lyre, as old histories show,
>   To set his Eurydice free.
>
> All hell was astonish'd, a person so wise
>   Should rashly endanger his life,
> And venture so far—but how vast their surprise,
>   When they found that he came for his wife!
>
> To find out a punishment due for his fault,
>   Old Pluto long puzzled his brain;
> But hell had not torments sufficient he thought,
>   —So he gave him his wife back again.
>
> But pity succeeding soon vanquish'd his heart,
>   And, pleas'd with his playing so well,
> He took her again, in reward of his art;—
>   Such power had music in hell!

[9] *Tricarinia.*—Read *Trinacria.*—*Wr.*

oxen, Hercules perforce drew him out of that place; from whence the conceits of those days affirmed no less than that Hercules descended into hell, and brought up Cerberus into the habitation of the living. Upon the like grounds was raised the figment of Briareus, who, dwelling in a city called Hecatonchiria, the fancies of those times assigned him an hundred hands. 'Twas ground enough to fancy wings unto Dædalus, in that he stole out of a window from Minos, and sailed away with his son Icarus; who, steering his course wisely, escaped, but his son carrying too high a sail was drowned. That Niobe, weeping over her children, was turned into a stone, was nothing else but that during her life she erected over their sepulchres a marble tomb of her own. When Acteon had undone himself with dogs, and the prodigal attendants of hunting, they made a solemn story how he was devoured by his hounds. And upon the like grounds was raised the anthropophagie* of Diomedes his horses. Upon a slender foundation was built the fable of the Minotaure; for one Taurus, a servant of Minos, gat his mistress, Pasiphae, with child, from whence the infant was named Minotaurus. Now this unto the fabulosity of those times, was thought sufficient to accuse Pasiphae of beastiality, or admitting conjunction with a bull; and in succeeding ages gave a hint of depravity unto Domitian to act the fable into a reality. In like manner, as Diodorus plainly delivereth, the famous fable of Charon had its nativity; who, being no other but the common ferry-man of Egypt that wafted over the dead bodies from Memphis, was made by the Greeks to be the ferry-man of hell, and solemn stories raised after of him.[1]

* Eating of man's flesh.

[1] *In like manner, as Diodorus plainly delivereth, the famous fable of Charon had its nativity, &c.*] Two circumstances, for the knowledge of which we are indebted to the modern researches into the literature and antiquities of Egypt (for which the late Dr. Thomas Young opened the way, by his discovery of the method of deciphering the *Hieroglyphics*), concur to prove, not only that Diodorus has faithfully reported the information he received from the Egyptian priests, but also that he was truly informed by them respecting their rites and ceremonies. Both of these occur in the very passages (*Diod. Sic. Bib. Hist.* Wess. § 92, 96) in which is delivered the statement alluded to in the text, relative to the fable of *Charon.* One of them is a remarkable numerical coincidence, pointed out and commented upon by Dr. Young. (*Art.* EGYPT,

OBSTINATE ADHERENCE [BOOK I.

Lastly, we shall not need to enlarge, if that be true which grounded the generation of Castor and Helena out of an

Supp. Ency. (*Brit.* p. 52) between the statement of Diodorus, and the delineations as well as enumerations, of the Egyptian papyri. The other, the importance of which Dr. Young appears not to have observed, although it has become apparent through his researches alone, relates to the name *Charon.* Dr. Young, in his translation of one of the passages in question (*Account of Recent Discoveries in Egypt. Antiq.* p. 104), has, from his knowledge of the Egyptian language, interpolated " the Silent." as the literal meaning of this appellation. Now, that Charon should be an Egyptian word, and that such should be its signification, are circumstances in themselves further strongly corroborative of the truth of the relation of Diodorus; for, with respect to the latter, it was the office of the "ferry-man of *Egypt*, that wafted over the dead bodies from *Memphis*," to wait with his boat, in the presence of the judges, until judgment had been passed upon the deceased, which, as Charon had no part to take in the ceremony, until judgment had been pronounced, he would of course do in solemn silence.

But that the Greeks actually derived their *mythus*, of Charon and his office, from the mere funeral ceremonies of the Egyptians, as represented to Diodorus by the priests, is a notion which rests, it will be perceived, upon their testimony alone; and that it is untrue various considerations concur to evince. From our present knowledge of the Egyptian mythology, it appears that the ceremonies through which every mummy had to pass, before it was allowed sepulture, formed a kind of mythic drama, intended to represent the successive stages of the judgment, through which the soul of the deceased had to pass, prior to its final allotment to happiness or misery. But the object of all the allegations of the Egyptian priests to Diodorus, being, as is manifest, the aggrandizement of their own country, while they truly related their ceremonies to him, they appear sedulously to have concealed the dogmas, or *mythi*, of which those ceremonies were representative. Hence their statement, that the Greek *mythus* of Charon had been derived from their mere funeral ceremony; while the fact doubtless was, as the entire tenour of mythological literature shows, either that the Greek *mythi* in general (and that of *Charon* as one of them) were derived originally, not from the mere ceremonies, as the priests would have had us believe, but from the *mythi* themselves, of the Egyptians; or that both nations had derived their *mythi* from an anterior common source. *Charon* was in all probability originally the name of the mythic boatman, and subsequently applied also to his mortal representative, so that the proof of the veracity of Diodorus, derived from it, will remain equally valid under the view of the subject now taken. The recent investigations of the *mythi* of the Greeks by Heyne, and other scholars equally competent to the inquiry, have shown that the origins assigned to them by Palæphatus and others, which Browne usually adopts, are for the most part untenable; and even some of those related, from the Egyptian priests, by Diodorus, notwithstanding the authenticity we have found to belong to his relations,

egg, because they were born and brought up in an upper room, according unto the word ὦον, which with the Lacedæmonians had also that signification.

Fifthly, We applaud many things delivered by the ancients, which are in themselves ordinary, and come short of our conceptions. Thus we usually extol, and our orations cannot escape the sayings of the wise men of Greece. *Nosce teipsum*, of Thales; *Nosce tempus*, of Pittacus; *Nihil nimis*, of Cleobulus; which, notwithstanding, to speak indifferently, are but vulgar precepts in morality, carrying with them nothing above the line, or beyond the extemporary sententiosity of common conceits with us. Thus we magnifie the apothegms or reputed replies of wisdom, whereof many are to be seen in Laertius, more in Lycosthenes, not a few in the second book of Macrobius, in the Salts of Cicero, Augustus, and the comical wits of those times: in most whereof there is not much to admire, and are, methinks, exceeded, not only in the replies of wise men, but the passages of society, and urbanities of our times. And thus we extol their adages or proverbs; and Erasmus hath taken great pains to make collections of them, whereof, notwithstanding, the greater part will, I believe, unto indifferent judges, be esteemed no extraordinaries; and may be paralleled, if not exceeded, by those of more unlearned nations, and many of our own.

Sixthly, We urge authorities in points that need not, and introduce the testimony of ancient writers, to confirm things evidently believed, and whereto no reasonable hearer but would assent without them; such as are *nemo mortalium omnibus horis sapit. Virtute nil præstantius, nil pulchrius. Omnia vincit amor. Præclarum quiddam veritas.* All which, although known and vulgar, are frequently urged by many men; and though trivial verities in our mouths, yet noted from Plato, Ovid, and Cicero, they become reputed

---

appear, as Dr. Young has observed. (*Account, &c.* p. 111) to rest upon "analogies all too slight to be admitted as anything like evidence." The application to these doubtful points, however, so far as the relations of Diodorus are concerned, of the fact already noticed, that the Egyptian ceremonies alluded to were *mythic dramas*, would certainly contribute greatly to their elucidation.—*Br.*

The passage which forms the subject of Mr. Brayley's preceding note was first added in the second edition.

elegancies. For many hundred to instance in one we meet with while we are writing. Antonius Guevara, that elegant Spaniard, in his book entituled, The Dial of Princes, beginneth his epistle thus: "Apollonius Thyanæus, disputing with the scholars of Hiarchas, said, that among all the affections of nature, nothing was more natural than the desire all have to preserve life." Which, being a confessed truth, and a verity acknowledged by all, it was a superfluous affectation to derive its authority from Apollonius, or seek a confirmation thereof as far as India, and the learned scholars of Hiarchas.[2] Which, whether it be not all one as to strengthen common dignities and principles, known by themselves, with the authority of mathematicians; or [to] think a man should believe, 'the whole is greater than its parts,' rather upon the authority of Euclide, than if it were propounded alone, I leave unto the second and wiser cogitations of all men. 'Tis sure a practice that savours much of pedantry; a reserve of puerility we have not shaken off from school; where, being seasoned with minor sentences, by a neglect of higher enquiries, they prescribe upon our riper ears, and are never worn out, but with our memories.

Lastly, While we so devoutly adhere unto antiquity in some things, we do not consider we have deserted them in several others. For they, indeed, have not only been imperfect in the conceit of some things, but either ignorant or erroneous in many more. They understood not the motion of the eighth sphere from west to east, and so conceived the longitude of the stars invariable. They conceived the Torrid Zone unhabitable, and so made frustrate the goodliest part of the earth. But we now know 'tis very well empeopled,[3] and the habitation thereof esteemed so happy, that some have made it the proper seat of Paradise; and been so far from judging it unhabitable, that they have made it the first

---

[2] *Antonius Guevara, &c.*] This practice is well ridiculed by Sterne:—"Tis either Plato, or Plutarch, or Seneca, or Xenophon, or Epictetus, or Theophrastus, or Lucian, or some one perhaps of later date,—either Cardan, or Buddæus, or Petrarch, or Stella, or possibly it may be some divine or father of the Church, St. Austin, or St. Cyprian, or Bernard, who affirms that it is an irresistible and natural passion to weep for the loss of our friends or children, &c., &c."—*J. Cr.*

[3] *But we now know 'tis very well empeopled.*] See *Sir T. P. Blount's Essays,* p. 137.—*J. Cr.*

habitation of all. Many of the ancients denied the Antipodes, and some unto the penalty of contrary affirmations;[4] but the experience of our enlarged navigations can now assert them beyond all dubitation. Having thus totally relinquished them in some things, it may not be presumptuous to examine them in others; but surely most unreasonable to adhere to them in all, as though they were infallible, or could not err in any.

CHAPTER VII.

Of another of the more immediate Causes of Error;—viz. Adherence unto Authority.

NOR is only a resolved prostration unto antiquity a powerful enemy unto knowledge, but any confident adherence unto authority, or resignation of our judgments upon the testimony of any age or author whatsoever.

For, first, to speak generally, an argument from authority, to wiser examinations, is but a weaker kind of proof; it being but a topical probation, and as we term it, an inartificial argument, depending upon a naked asseveration, wherein neither declaring the causes, affections, or adjuncts, of what we believe, it carrieth not with it the reasonable inducements of knowledge. And therefore *contra negantem principia, ipse dixit,* or *oportet discentem credere*,[5] although pos-

[4] *and some, &c.*] Alluding to Virgilius; See *Rel. Med.* p. 39, note 2.

[5] *contra negantem, &c.*] These three rules althoughe they bee founded on the grounds of universall reason, yet they have theire limits and boundaryes, by which they must be circumscribed. The first reachinge only such perverse spirits, as denye those universall principles of reason and nature, wherein the wisest and soberest judgments of all times have held an unanimous and full consent, and whereon the perpetuall and uncontrouled experience of all mankinde hath agreed. As that the snow is white; and that fire does burne. The former whereof, althoughe some have made not only dispute, but deniall, yet they purchast nothing but scorne and the censure as of brainsick men.

The second is noe where of universall authoritye, save in the booke of God: all other dictates of men, how specious soever, being noe farther authenticall to enforce beleefe, then as the reasons are, whereon they are built: but the only reason in God's booke is, because wee know, Hee, whose worditt is, is truth ittselfe, and can neither lye, nor deceave, nor bee deceaved: and therefore hath the whole and sole

tulates very accommodable unto junior indoctrinations, yet are their authorities but temporary, and not to be embraced beyond the minority of our intellectuals. For our advanced beliefs are not to be built upon dictates, but having received the probable inducements of truth, we become emancipated from testimonial engagements, and are to erect upon the surer base of reason.

Secondly, unto reasonable perpensions[6] it hath no place in some sciences, small in others, and suffereth many restrictions even where it is most admitted. It is of no validity in the mathematics, especially the mother part thereof, arithmetic and geometry. For these sciences, concluding from dignities and principles known by themselves, receive not satisfaction from probable reasons, much less from bare and peremptory asseverations. And, therefore, if all Athens should decree, that in every triangle, two sides, whichsoever be taken, are greater than the side remaining, or that, in rectangle triangles, the square which is made of the side that subtendeth the right angle, is equal to the squares which are made of the sides containing the right angle; although there be a certain truth therein, geometricians, notwithstanding, would not receive satisfaction without demonstration thereof. 'Tis true, by the vulgarity of philosophers there are many points believed without probation; nor if a man affirm from Ptolemy, that the sun is bigger than the earth, shall he probably meet with any contradiction; whereunto notwithstanding astronomers will not assent without some convincing argument or demonstrative proof thereof. And therefore certainly of all men a philosopher should be no swearer: for an oath which is the end of controversies in law, cannot determine any here; nor are the deepest sacraments or desperate imprecations of any force to persuade, where reason only, and necessary mediums must induce.

In natural philosophy, and which is more generally pur-

empire of authoritye, to which all humane reason must submitte without dispute or hæsitancye.

The last rule concerns none but those who yeeld up themselves to the instructions and information of others, from whom they must perforce take up upon truste the principles of that arte, which they desire to gaine, till they come to attain unto itt.—*Wr.*

[6] *perpensions.*] Considerations.

sued amongst us, it carrieth but slender consideration; for that also proceeding from settled principles, therein is expected a satisfaction from scientifical progressions, and such as beget a sure rational belief. For if authority might have made out the assertions of philosophy, we might have held, that snow was black, that the sea was but the sweat of the earth, and many of the like absurdities.[7] Then was Aristotle injurious to fall upon Melissus, to reject the assertions of Anaxagoras, Anaximander, and Empedocles;[8] then were we also ungrateful unto himself: from whom our junior endeavours embracing many things on his authority, our mature and secondary enquiries are forced to quit those receptions, and to adhere unto the nearer accounts of reason. And although it be not unusual, even in philosophical tractates, to make enumeration of authors, yet are there reasons usually introduced, and to ingenious readers do carry the stroke in the persuasion. And surely if we account it reasonable among ourselves, and not injurious unto rational authors, no farther to abett their opinions, than as they are supported by solid reasons, certainly with more excusable reservation may we shrink at their bare testimonies, whose argument is but precarious, and subsists upon the charity of our assentments.

In morality, rhetorick, law, and history, there is I confess a frequent and allowable use of testimony; and yet herein I perceive it is not unlimitable, but admitteth many restrictions. Thus, in law both civil and divine, that is only esteemed a legal testimony, which receives comprobation from the mouths of at least two witnesses; and that not only for prevention of calumny, but assurance against mistake. Whereas notwithstanding, the solid reason of one man is as sufficient as the clamour of a whole nation, and with imprejudicate apprehensions, begets as firm a belief as the authority or aggregated testimony of many hundreds. For reason being the very root of our natures, and the principles thereof common unto all, what is against the laws of true reason, or the unerring understanding of any one, if rightly apprehended,

---

[7] *that snow was black, &c.*] Attributed to Anaxagoras, a Clazomenian philosopher, who flourished above 400 years B.C.

[8] *Then was Aristotle, &c.*] See Aristotle's discussion of the opinions of these philosophers, in his *Physicks*, lib. i. c. 2, 3, 4.

must be disclaimed by all nations, and rejected even by mankind.

Again, a testimony is of small validity, if deduced from men out of their own professions. So, if Lactantius affirm the figure of the earth is plain,[9] or Austin deny there are Antipodes,[1] though venerable fathers of the church, and ever to be honoured, yet will not their authorities prove sufficient to ground a belief thereon. Whereas, notwithstanding the solid reason,[2] or confirmed experience of any man, is very approvable, in what profession soever. So Raymund Sebund, a physician of Tholouze, besides his learned dialogues *De natura humana*, hath written a natural theology; demonstrating therein the attributes of God, and attempting the like in most points of religion. So Hugo Grotius, a civilian, did write an excellent tract in Dutch, of the Verity of the Christian Religion.[3] Wherein most rationally delivering themselves, their works will be embraced by most that understand them, and their reasons enforce belief, even from prejudicate readers. Neither, indeed, have the authorities of men been ever so awful, but that by some they have been rejected, even in their own professions. Thus Aristotle, affirming the birth of the infant, or time of its gestation, extendeth some times unto the eleventh month, but

---

[9] *if Lactantius affirm, &c.*] See *Lactantius De Falsa Sapientia*, l. iii. c. 23.

[1] *or Austin deny, &c.*] "Quod vero et Antipodas esse fabulantur, ... nulla ratione credendum est."—*S. Aug. De Civitate Dei*, l. xvi. c. 9.

[2] *the solid reason.*] This is a golden rule, worthye to be written in marble and golde. For as among those that have the persons of men in adoration, and (for something they admire in them) swallow all that they say as gospel, truth is manye times silentlye smothered, and sometimes violently and furiously not only opposed but oppressed; soe among sober men, and such as entertaine and embrace truth, wherever they find her, shee sodenly advances them to such a hight of honor and reputation, that they become the leaders of learninge and knowledge to after ages, and that deservedly.—*Wr.*

[3] *did write an excellent tract, &c.*] In the first edition, "did write an excellent tract, in Dutch, of the Verity of Christian Religion, and hath since contracted the same into six books in Latin." "Grotius, while a prisoner in the castle of Louvain, wrote, in the Dutch language, 'A Treatise on the Truth of the Christian Religion.' He afterwards *enlarged* it, and translated it, so enlarged, into Latin."—*Butler's Life of Grotius*, p. 148.

Hippocrates averring that it exceedeth not the tenth;[4] Adrian, the emperor, in a solemn process, determined for Aristotle, but Justinian many years after took in with Hippocrates, and reversed the decree of the other. Thus have councils not only condemned private men, but the decrees and acts of one another. So Galen, after all his veneration of Hippocrates, in some things hath fallen from him; Avicen in many from Galen; and others succeeding from him. And although the singularity of Paracelsus be intolerable, who sparing only Hippocrates, hath reviled not only the authors, but almost all the learning that went before him;[5] yet it is not much less injurious unto knowledge, obstinately and inconvincibly to side with

[4] *Thus Aristotle, &c.*] Although Aristotle (in his *Hist. Animal.* vii. cap. 4,) gives instances in which the period of human gestation extends to the eleventh month, he evidently considers them as extreme cases, and agrees with Hippocrates in regarding the tenth as very generally the extreme limit. See his *De Generat. Animal.* l. iv. c. 4. In this opinion they are borne out by the general consent of modern authority both physical and judicial. The doubt indeed is whether even that limit is not too wide. From the *Medical Jurisprudence* of Dr. Paris and Fonblanque, where the subject will be found most elaborately treated—it appears that although there exists a very general opinion among lawyers and medical men, that the period may be protracted to ten calendar months, it is a point scarcely admitting of proof: and many high authorities reject the opinion as untenable. "Each side is supported by a considerable list of partisans, and we perceive that upon this occasion the two celebrated medico-jurisconsults of France are opposed to each other; *Mahon* having associated his name with those of *Bohn, Hebensteit, Astruc, Mauriceau, De La Motte, Rœderer,* and *Baudelocque,* who reject the belief in *retarded delivery* as impossible, and contrary to the immutable law of nature; while the name of *Foderé* ranges with those who support the contrary opinion, as *Teichmeyer, Heister, Albert, Vallentini, Bartholin, Haller, Antoine Petit, Lictaud, Vicq d'Azyr,* and *Capuran,* also *Dr. Hamilton,* who may boast of the support of *Hippocrates, Aristotle,* and *Pliny.*" (*Medical Jurisprudence,* vol. i. p. 247.)—By the law of Scotland, as stated by Paris and Fonblanque, a child born *ten* months after the death of the father is considered as legitimate; and the civil code of France decrees three hundred days, or *ten* months, to be the most distant period at which the legitimacy of a birth shall be allowed.—*Br.*

[5] *although the singularity of* Paracelsus *be intolerable, &c.*] "Paracelsus began his professional career by burning publicly, in his class-room, and in the presence of his pupils, the works of Galen and Avicenna, assuring his hearers that the strings of his shoes possessed more knowledge than those two celebrated physicians. All the universities

any one. Which humour⁶ unhappily possessing many, they have by prejudice withdrawn themselves into parties, and contemning the sovereignty of truth, seditiously abetted the private divisions of error.

Moreover, a testimony in points historical, and where it is of unavoidable use, is of no illation⁷ in the negative; nor is it of consequence,⁸ that Herodotus writing nothing of Rome, there was therefore no such city in his time, or because Dioscorides hath made no mention of unicorn's horn, there is therefore no such thing in nature. Indeed, intending an accurate enumeration of medical materials, the omission

---

united had not, he assured them, as much knowledge as was contained in his own beard, and the hairs upon his head were better informed than all the writers that ever existed put together." This statement is derived from Dr. Thomson's *History of Chemistry* (forming part of the National Library,) vol. i. p. 145, where also, in the following page, is given an extract from the preface to a tract by Paracelsus, entitled *Paragranum*, the arrogance of which amply vindicates the justice of the preceding representation. It may be doubted, however, whether this extreme arrogance and contempt was really felt by Paracelsus, or whether it was merely assumed for the sake of singularity and effect. In a letter written by him to Christopher Clauser, a physician of Zurich, he admits the claims, not only of Hippocrates, but also of Avicenna, Galen, and Marsilius, to be considered the greatest physicians of their respective countries, assuming, however, that he was himself, beyond dispute, the greatest physician among the Germans. The contempt and arrogance with which, however, Paracelsus, in public, certainly treated almost every preceding practitioner and teacher of medical science, were probably required in order to overcome the slavish and superstitious deference to ancient authority which had so long prevailed. As Dr. Thomson has observed (*Hist. of Chem.* vol. i. p. 146,) he "shook the medical throne of Galen and Avicenna to its very foundation; he roused the latent energies of the human mind, which had for so long a period lain torpid; he freed medical men from those trammels, and put an end to that despotism which had existed for five centuries."—*Br.*

⁶ *Which humour, &c.*] This humour is itt which hath engaged the whole world into factions, not only amongst Christians, but even Jews, Turks, and Infidels. And being once planted is hardly ever rooted out. For that they who have once swallowed an error (act of ignorance, inadvertence, or the tye of observance and relation to some on whom they depend) are ever loath to acknowledge, but more to renounce itt, though in pointe of conscience they be often convinced of itt; least, being thought to have faultered in one thing, they may come to question, and bring into suspicion, whatever they shall allow for the future.—*Wr.*

⁷ *is of no illation.*] "Affords no inference."

⁸ *nor is it of consequence.*] "Nor does it follow as a consequence."

hereof affords some probability it was not used by the ancients, but will not conclude the non-existence thereof. For so may we annihilate many simples unknown to his enquiries, as senna, rhubarb, bezoa, ambergris, and divers others. Whereas indeed the reason of man hath not such restraint; concluding not only affirmatively, but negatively; not only affirming there is no magnitude beyond the last heavens, but also denying there is any vacuity within them. Although it be confessed, the affirmative hath the prerogative illation, and barbara[9] engrosseth the powerful demonstration.

Lastly, the strange relations made by authors may sufficiently discourage our adherence unto authority, and which, if we believe, we must be apt to swallow any thing. Thus Basil[1] will tell us, the serpent went erect like man, and that that beast could speak before the fall. Tostatus would make us believe that Nilus encreaseth every new moon. Leonardo Fioravanti, an Italian physician, beside many other secrets, assumeth unto himself the discovery of one concerning pellitory of the wall; that is, that it never groweth in the sight of the North star,—("*dove si possa vedere la stella Tramontana;*") wherein how wide he is from truth is easily discoverable unto every one, who hath but astronomy enough to know that star. Franciscus Sanctius, in a laudable comment upon Alciat's emblems, affirmeth, and that from experience, a nightingale hath no tongue; ("*avem Philomelam lingua carere pro certo affirmare possum, nisi me oculi fallunt;*") which if any man for a while shall believe upon his experience, he may at his leisure refute it by his own. What fool almost would believe, at least, what wise man would rely upon, that antidote delivered by Pierius in his hieroglyphicks against the sting of a scorpion,—that is to sit upon an ass

---

[9] *barbara.*] The affirmative proposition: see note [6], p. 18.

[1] *Thus Basil.*] See Book v. chap. iv. And this is the only reason that holds the church of Rome in an obstinate maintenance of some ridiculous, some scandalous, some pernicious, some blasphemous doctrines: For feare that by the acknowledgement of them they shall loose their credit and authoritye. And that the acknowledgement enforcing their renunciation and desertion of them, they shall withall loose the merit, profit, and gaine, which they reape from the numerous proselytes: whose consciences they have fettered and chained unto them, by these powerfull overawinge chaines, and (as they call them) pious fraudes.—*Wr.*

with one's face towards his tail, for so the pain leaveth the man, and passeth into the beast. It were, methinks, but an uncomfortable receipt for a quartane ague (and yet as good perhaps as many others used) to have recourse unto the receipt of Sammonicus; that is, to lay the fourth book of Homer's Iliad under one's head, according to the precept of that physician and poet, *Mæoniæ Iliados quartum suppone trementi.* There are surely few that have belief to swallow, or hope enough to experiment the *collyrium** of Albertus, which promiseth a strange effect, and such as thieves would count inestimable, that is, to make one see in the dark; yet thus much, according unto his receipt, will the right eye of an hedgehog boiled in oil, and preserved in a brazen vessel, effect. As strange it is, and unto vicious inclinations were worth a night's lodging with Lais,† what is delivered in Kiranides; that the left stone of a weasel, wrapt up in the skin of a she-mule, is able to secure incontinency from conception.

These, with swarms of others, have men delivered in their writings, whose verities are only supported by their authorities; but being neither consonant unto reason, nor correspondent unto experiment, their affirmations are unto us no axioms. We esteem thereof as things unsaid, and account them but in the list of nothing. I wish herein the chymists had been more sparing; who, over-magnifying their preparations, inveigle the curiosity of many, and delude the security of most. For if experiments would answer their encomiums, the stone and quartane agues were not opprobrious unto physicians;[2] we might contemn that first and most uncomfortable aphorism of Hippocrates,‡ for surely that art were soon attained, that hath so general remedies, and life could not be short, were there such to prolong it.

* An eye medicine. † Ten thousand drachms.
‡ Ars longa, vita brevis.

[2] *opprobrious unto physicians.*] By being very difficult to cure.

CHAPTER VIII.

Of Authors who have most promoted Popular Conceit.

Now, forasmuch as we have discoursed of authority, and there is scarce any tradition or popular error but stands also delivered by some good author, we shall endeavour a short discovery of such as for the major part have given authority hereto; who, though excellent and useful authors, yet either being transcriptive, or following common relations, their accounts are not to be swallowed at large, or entertained without all circumspection. In whom *ipse dixit*, although it be no powerful argument in any, is yet less authentic than in many other, because they deliver not their own experiences, but others' affirmations, and write from others, as we ourselves from them.

1. The first in order, as also in time, shall be Herodotus, of Halicarnassus,[3] an excellent and very elegant historian;

---

[3] *Herodotus of Halicarnassus.*] It will be useful to place in apposition with our author's statement, respecting the writings of this historian, the opinion of their authenticity and character, so far as they relate to the history of Egypt, formed by one of the most sagacious investigators of ancient history of the present age. Since the early history of Egypt claims a much higher antiquity than that of almost any other nation, and is consequently involved in obscurity more impenetrable, if the relations of any ancient writer *respecting it* are found to be substantially correct, we may conclude, *a fortiori*, that his account of *other nations* also deserves our confidence.

"The only original authorities," observes Dr. Young, "on which we can depend for the early history of Egypt, are those of *Herodotus*, Manetho, Eratosthenes, Diodorus Siculus, and Strabo; all of whom had been more or less in the country. *Herodotus* lived soon after the conquest of Egypt by Cambyses, when the names of the later monarchs could not easily have been forgotten. The earlier part of his history is of a much more apocryphal nature: he does not, however, continue the series of the kings further back than Sesostris and Moeris: so that almost all his names are sufficiently recent to be considered as completely within the province of legitimate history." * * * * "The stories of Herodotus, though told with an elegant simplicity, and with every appearance of good faith, are by no means free from a frequent mixture of fable; and, with respect to his Egyptian etymologies, he is almost universally mistaken; but his account of the ceremonies observed in the preparation of the mummies has many marks of authenticity, and he is perfectly correct in asserting, that the most splendid of the

whose books of history were so well received in his own days, that, at their rehearsal in the Olympick games, they obtained the names of the nine muses; and continued in such

coffins are formed in imitation of the figures of Osiris; a circumstance which he could not easily have conjectured without direct and accurate information." *Supp. Ency. Brit. art.* EGYPT, p. 47, 52.

Of the above testimony to the fidelity of Herodotus, the writer of the present note is enabled to give a strong confirmation in one particular. Dr. Young, arguing from general grounds, observes, as above, that the account of the preparation of the mummies given by that historian " has many marks of authenticity." But the minute examination to which a very perfect mummy was subjected by Dr. Granville, a few years since, appeared to justify strong doubts of the correctness of the statements of Herodotus respecting the Egyptian processes of embalming; the mummy in question having been prepared by a very different method. However, another mummy, in as perfect a condition as the former, has recently been described by Mr. Osburn, Secretary to the Philosophical and Literary Society of Leeds, which, as he has shown, must have been prepared, in every particular, by the process described by Herodotus and Diodorus Siculus as the most perfect mode of embalming practised by the Egyptians. The opinion antecedently expressed by Dr. Young, before any perfect mummies had been examined, is therefore fully confirmed, and the authority of Herodotus supported, on a subject of Egyptian history, on which, of almost all others, it must have been most difficult to acquire precise and correct knowledge. The weight which this train of circumstances imparts to the character of Herodotus, as a faithful historian, will readily be appreciated by the student of ancient history. *Phil. Trans.* 1825; *Phil. Mag. and Annals, N. S.* vol. v. p. 57, 1829. Some very remarkable and important points, in which even the *minute* accuracy of Herodotus has been established, are conected with his account (lib. i. s. 74) of the eclipse stated to have been predicted by Thales, and which, owing to a very singular coincidence, put an end to a furious war that raged between Cyaxases King of Media, and Alyattes King of Lydia. The investigations by which his accuracy on these points has been determined cannot be detailed in this place, but a full account of them will be found in " *Brayley's Utility of the Knowledge of Nature considered; with reference to the Introduction of Instruction in the Physical Sciences into the General Education of Youth.*" London, 1831, 8vo.

As the extreme accuracy which we have thus seen the statements of Herodotus to possess, with relation to subjects on which it must have been difficult to obtain correct information, and with respect also to others requiring very nice observation, unquestionably guarantee his general fidelity, we have entered into these remarks, for the purpose of showing that he is much more worthy of the title of *Historiarum parens*, than of that of *Mendaciorum pater*. With the exceptions arising from the facts we have detailed, and viewed agreeably to the general bearing of those facts, the character of Herodotus given by our author may be regarded as substantially corect.—*Br.*

esteem unto descending ages that Cicero termed him *historiarum parens*; and Dionysius, his countryman, in an epistle to Pompey, after an express comparison, affords him the better of *Thucydides*. All which notwithstanding, he hath received from some the style of *mendaciorum pater*. His authority was much infringed by Plutarch, who, being offended with him, as Polybius had been with Philarchus, for speaking too coldly of his countrymen, hath left a particular tract, *De malignitate Herodoti*. But in this latter century Camerarius and Stephanus have stepped in, and, by their witty apologies, effectually endeavoured to frustrate the arguments of Plutarch or any other. Now, in this author, as may be observed in our ensuing discourse, and is better discernable in the perusal of himself, there are many things fabulously delivered, and not to be accepted as truths; whereby, nevertheless, if any man be deceived, the author is not so culpable as the believer. For he, indeed, imitating the father poet, whose life he hath also written, and as Thucydides observeth, as well intending the delight as benefit of his reader, hath besprinkled his work with many fabulosities; whereby if any man be led into error he mistaketh the intention of the author (who plainly confesseth he writeth many things by hearsay) and forgetteth a very considerable caution of his; that is, *Ego quæ fando cognovi, exponere narratione mea debeo omnia: credere autem esse vera omnia, non debeo.*

2. In the second place is Ctesias the Cnidian,[4] physician

---

[4] *Ctesias the Cnidian.*] The sum of our author's remarks on the authority of Ctesias is probably very near the truth; but in this instance again the researches of modern science have in a great degree rescued from obloquy the statements of ancient history. The descriptions given by Ctesias of many animals, which, as he alleges, are found in Persia and India, and his relations concerning the uses to which many objects of nature are applied by the inhabitants of those countries, are now known either to be actually true, or at least to be founded in truth. In other cases it has been shown that he has correctly described certain objects as represented in paintings or sculptures, but has erroneously attributed an actual existence to what were merely the offspring of the imagination of the artists or of the priests who instructed them. The historical relations of Ctesias, like those of Manetho and others, which have until recently been deemed altogether apocryphal, have received confirmation in many points, from the researches into the early history of Asia and Egypt, which our own age has witnessed; and it is impossible to say how many which yet appear untrue, may

unto Artaxerxes, king of Persia. His books are often recited by ancient writers, and, by the industry of Stephanus and Rhodomanus, there are extant some fragments thereof in our days. He wrote the history of Persia, and many narrations of India. In the first, as having a fair opportunity to know the truth, and as Diodorus affirmeth, the perusal of Persian records, his testimony is acceptable.[5] In his Indian relations, wherein are contained strange and incredible accounts, he is surely to be read with suspension. These were they which weakened his authority with former ages; for, as we may observe, he is seldom mentioned without a derogatory parenthesis in any author. Aristotle, besides the frequent undervaluing of his authority in his books of animals, gives him the lie no less than twice con-

be attributable to the errors of transcribers. As an instance of his marvellous and incredible relations which have proved to be positively true, we will cite an anticipation of modern discovery contained in his fragments relating to India, which was pointed out a few years since, by the late Rev. J. J. Conybeare, successively professor of Anglo-Saxon and of poetry in the University of Oxford. Ctesias relates (*Ex Ctes. Ind. Hist. Excerpt. in app. Herodot. Wesseling. sub initio*, p. 1827,) that a certain variety of iron is found in India, which, when fixed into the ground, has the power of averting storms and lightnings. See *Annals of Philosophy, Sec. Ser.* vol. iv. p. 439. This evidently describes an anticipation of the use of conductors for lightning. Prior, however, to the discovery of the nature of lightning, and to the invention, founded upon that discovery, of metallic conductors for conveying the electric fluid, of which lightning is a manifestation, silently and innocuously to the earth, about the middle of the last century, every reader would suppose that Ctesias, in the passage before us, was relating, not a philosophical truth, but an unfounded absurdity; and would regard it as one of the "strange and incredible accounts," which, according to our author, are contained "in his *Indian* relations."

Bearing all these circumstances in mind, the reader, by comparing our author's remarks on Ctesias with the following notes, (marked *Br.*,) will have the means of forming a correct opinion respecting the merits of that writer.—*Br.*

[5] *perusal of Persian records, &c.*] In his account of the origin of the Assyrian empire, however, which he professes to have derived from the regal archives of the Medes, he differs considerably from Herodotus, who must be regarded, in this case, as by far the most authentic historian; and he also attributes to the conquests of Ninus and Semiramis an extent towards the west, which is absolutely incompatible with the Jewish and Egyptian history of the same periods. (See Cuvier, *Discours sur les Revolutions de la Surface du Globe*, 4to. Paris, 1826, p. 101.)—*Br.*

cerning the seed of elephants. Strabo, in his eleventh book, hath left a harder censure of him:[6] *Equidem facilius Hesiodo et Homero aliquis fidem adhibuerit, itemque tragicis poetis, quam Ctesiæ, Herodoto, Hellanico et eorum similibus.* But Lucian hath spoken more plainly than any: *Scripsit Ctesias de Indorum regione, deque iis quæ apud illos sunt, ea quæ nec ipse vidit, neque ex ullius sermone audivit.* Yet were his relations taken up by some succeeding writers, and many thereof revived by our countryman, Sir John Mandevil, knight and doctor in physick; who, after thirty years' peregrination, died at Liege, and was there honourably interred.[7] He left a book of his travels, which hath been honoured with the translation of many languages, and now continued above three hundred years; herein he often attesteth the fabulous relations of Ctesias, and seems to con-

---

[6] *Strabo, in his eleventh book, &c.*] Cuvier has remarked (*Discours, ubi sup.* p. 102) that Strabo was apparently led to this censure from the want of accordance between the various accounts of the antiquity of the Assyrian empire given by Ctesias and other ancient writers. But his ranking Ctesias with Herodotus, whose veracity has been established in modern times, in a manner so irrefragable, is in fact a testimony of considerable weight to the fidelity of the former. In reference to this particular subject Cuvier also alludes to the manifest errors of transcribers, in the fragments of Ctesias which are extant. Upon the whole, therefore, this writer ought not in any degree to suffer in our estimation on account of Strabo's censure.—*Br.*

[7] *Sir John Mandeville, &c.*] Though spoken of by Sale (in his Preliminary Discourse, p. 177, *note*), by Parkhurst (Heb. Lex. p. 259, third edition), and by Chalmers, as entitled to more credit than has been usually assigned him, Mandeville's work is pronounced by Dr. Hugh Murray, to be "a pure and entire fabrication." Chalmers remarks, "that Sir John honestly acknowledges that his book was made partly of hearsay, and partly of his own knowledge; and that he prefaces his most improbable relations with some such words as these, *thei seyne*, or *men seyn, but I have not sene it:*"—and concludes that "there does not appear to be any very good reason *why Sir John should not be believed in anything that he relates on his own observation.*" He further observes that some of his improbabilities have been since verified; e. g. his hens that bore wool, &c. &c. Murray, on the other hand, asserts that Mandeville, not content with transplanting the fictions of Oderic, and other writers into his narrative, declares himself to have actually *seen* what they had only heard of. He is quite of opinion that Sir John compiled the greater and the most valuable part of his travels from Oderic, Carpini, Rubruquis, &c. and *that what he has added of his own, consists, quite exclusively, of monstrous lies.*

firm the refuted accounts of antiquity. All which may still be received in some acceptions of morality, and to a pregnant invention may afford commendable mythology; but in a natural and proper exposition, it containeth impossibilities, and things inconsistent with truth.[8]

3. There is a book, *De mirandis auditionibus*, ascribed unto Aristotle; another, *De mirabilibus narrationibus*, written long after by Antigonus; another also of the same title by Plegon Trallianus, translated by Xilander, and with the annotations of Meursius, all whereof make good the promise of their titles, and may be read with caution. Which if any man shall likewise observe in the lecture of Philostratus concerning the life of Apollonius, and even in some passages of the sober and learned Plutarchus, or not only in ancient writers, but shall carry a wary eye on Paulus Venetus, Jovius, Olaus Magnus, Nierembergius, and many others, I think his circumspection is laudable, and he may thereby decline occasion of error.

4. Dioscorides Anazarbeus, he wrote many books in physick, but six thereof, *De Materia Medica*, have found the greatest esteem. He is an author of good antiquity and better use, preferred by Galen before Cratevas, Pamphilus, and all that attempted the like description before him; yet all he delivereth therein is not to be conceived oraculous. For beside that (following the wars under Anthony,) the course of his life would not permit a punctual *examen* in all, there are many things concerning the nature of simples traditionally delivered, and to which I believe he gave no assent himself. It had been an excellent receipt, and in his time when saddles were scarce in fashion,[9] of very great use, if

---

[8] *All which may still be received, &c.*] The truth and sagacity of this remark, taken in application to Ctesias himself, is beautifully illustrated by the following circumstances noticed by Cuvier, (*ubi sup.* p. 40):— When treating of the mythological (or rather *mythical*) animals of the Persians, he observes, "Ctesias, who has described these animals as actually existing, has been regarded by many authors as an inventor of fables, while, in fact, he has merely attributed reality to emblematical figures;" and he shows, in the sequel, that the imaginary beings in question (such as the griffin, &c.) are represented in the sculptures of Persepolis, from which, or from similar works of art, it is manifest that Ctesias described them.—*Br.*

[9] *when saddles were scarce in fashion.*] They were not invented till

that were true which he delivers, that *vitex*¹ or *agnus castus* held only in the hand, preserveth the rider from galling. It were a strange effect, and whores would forsake the experiment of *savine*, if that were a truth which he delivereth of brake or female fearn, that only treading over it, it causes a sudden abortion.* It were to be wished true, and women would idolize him, could that be made out which he recordeth of phyllon, mercury, and other vegetables, that the juice of the male plant drunk, or the leaves but applied unto the genitals, determines their conceptions unto males. In these relations although he be more sparing, his predecessors were very numerous, and Galen hereof most sharply accuseth Pamphilus. Many of the like nature we meet sometimes in Oribasius, Ætius, Trallianus, Serapion, Evax, and Marcellus, whereof some containing no colour of verity, we may at first sight reject them; others which seem to carry some face of truth, we may reduce unto experiment. And herein we shall rather perform good offices unto truth, than any disservice unto their relators, who have well deserved of succeeding ages; from whom having received the conceptions of former times, we have the readier hint of their conformity with ours, and may accordingly explore and sift their verities.

5. Plinius Secundus,² of Verona; a man of great elo-

* A like opinion there is now of elder.—*Note first added in Second Edition.*

long after, probably about the fourth century: though some kinds of horse cloths composed of various materials more or less costly were used at a much earlier period. See *Beckman's History of Inventions and Discoveries*, vol. ii. 247.

¹ *that vitex.*] Yet that is true which hee sayes, that *persicaria* bruised, and layd under ye saddle, cures a galled horse in the jornye.—*Wr.*

² *Plinius Secundus.*] It will be interesting to compare, with our author's estimate of the authority of Pliny, the following view of the merits of a considerable portion of the contents of his Natural History, taken by a modern man of science, profoundly versed in the history of the science whose progress he details, and to which the portion of Pliny in question principally relates. "The only exception to this general neglect and contempt for all the arts and trades, is Pliny the Elder, whose object, in his Natural History, was to collect into one focus every thing that was known at the period when he lived. His work displays prodigious reading, and a vast fund of erudition. It is to him that we are chiefly indebted for the knowledge of the chemical arts that were prac-

quence, and industry indefatigable, as may appear by his writings, especially those now extant, and which are never like to perish, but even with learning itself; that is his *Natural History*. He was the greatest collector or rhapsodist[3] of all the Latins, and as Suetonius de Viris Illustribus observeth, he collected this piece out of two thousand Latin and Greek authors. Now what is very strange, there is scarce a popular error passant in our days, which is not either directly expressed, or deductively contained in this work; which being in the hands of most men, hath proved a powerful occasion of their propagation. Wherein, notwithstanding, the credulity of the reader is more condemnable than the curiosity of the author; for commonly he nameth the authors from whom he received those accounts, and writes but as he reads, as in his preface to Vespasian he acknowledgeth.

6. Claudius Ælianus, who flourished not long after, in the reign of Trajan, unto whom he dedicated his Tacticks; an elegant and miscellaneous author. He hath left two books which are in the hands of every one, his History of Animals, and his Varia Historia. Wherein are contained many things suspicious, not a few false, some impossible; he is much beholding[4] unto Ctesias, and in many uncertainties writes more confidently than Pliny.

7. Julius Solinus, who lived also about his time. He left a work entitled Polyhistor, containing great variety of matter, and is with most in good request at this day. But to speak freely what cannot be concealed, it is but Pliny varied, or a transcription of his Natural History; nor is it without all wonder it hath continued so long, but is now likely, and

tised by the ancients. But the low estimation in which these arts were held appears evident, from the wonderful want of information which Pliny so frequently displays, and the erroneous statements which he has recorded respecting these processes. Still a great deal may be drawn from the information which has been collected and transmitted to us by this indefatigable natural historian." (*Thomson's History of Chemistry*, vol. i. p. 50.)—*Br.*

[3] *rhapsodist.*] One who writes without any regular dependance of one part upon another.—*Johnson.* I am, however, much more inclined to think that Sir Thomas meant by *rhapsodist*, one who packs together (from ῥάπτω, *consarcino*,) materials collected from various sources.

[4] *beholding.*] See note, chap. vi. p. 44.

deserves indeed to live for ever, not only for the elegancy of the text, but the excellency of the comment, lately performed by Salmasius, under the name of Plinian Exercitations.

8. Athenæus,[5] a delectable author, and very various, and justly styled by Casaubon, Græcorum Plinius. There is extant of his, a famous piece, under the name of Deipnosophista, or Cœna Sapientium, containing the discourse of many learned men, at a feast provided by Laurentius. It is a laborious collection out of many authors, and some whereof are mentioned no where else. It containeth strange and singular relations, not without some spice or sprinkling of all learning. The author was probably a better grammarian than philosopher, dealing but hardly with Aristotle and Plato, and betrayeth himself much in his chapter *De Curiositate Aristotelis*. In brief, he is an author of excellent use, and may with discretion be read unto great advantage; and hath therefore well deserved the comments of Casaubon and Dalecampins. But being miscellaneous in many things, he is to be received with suspicion;[6] for such as amass all relations must erre in some, and may without offence be unbelieved in many.

9. We will not omit the works of Nicander, a poet of good antiquity; that is, his Theriaca, and Alexipharmaca, translated and commented by Gorræus: for therein are contained several traditions, and popular conceits of venomous beasts; which only deducted, the work is to be embraced, as containing the first description of poisons and their antidotes, whereof Dioscorides, Pliny, and Galen, have made especial use in elder times; and Ardoynus Grevinus, and others, in times more near our own. We might perhaps let pass Oppianus, that famous Cilician poet. There are extant of his in Greek, four books of Cynegeticks or Venation, five of Halieuticks or Piscation, commented and published by Ritterhusius; wherein, describing beasts of

---

[5] *Athenæus.*] A very favourite author with Sir Thomas. See his *Remarks on Athenæus*.

[6] *he is to be received with suspicion.*] We need have noe great suspition of him, going under the garde of these learned men; who will not suffer you to bee led by him, into any knowne or suspected error.—*Wr.*

venery, and fishes, he hath indeed but sparingly inserted the vulgar conceptions thereof. So that abating the annual mutation of sexes in the hyæna, the single sex in the rhinoceros, the antipathy between two drums, of a lamb and a wolf's skin, the informity of cubs, the venation of Centaures, the copulation of the murena and the viper, with some few others, he may be read with great delight and profit. It is not without some wonder his elegant lines are so neglected. Surely, hereby we reject one of the best epic poets,* and much condemn the judgment of Antoninus, whose apprehensions so honoured his poems that, as some report, for every verse he assigned him a stater of gold.

10. More warily are we to receive the relations of Philes, who, in Greek iambicks, delivered the proprieties of animals; for herein he hath amassed the vulgar accounts recorded by the ancients, and hath therein especially followed Ælian. And likewise Johannes Tzetzes,[7] a grammarian, who, besides a comment upon Hesiod and Homer, hath left us *Chiliads de Varia Historia;* wherein delivering the accounts of Ctesias, Herodotus, and most of the ancients, he is to be embraced with caution, and as a transcriptive relator.[8]

11. We cannot, without partiality, omit all caution even of holy writers, and such whose names are venerable unto all posterity. Not to meddle at all with miraculous authors, or any legendary relators, we are not without circumspection to receive some books even of authentic and renowned fathers. So are we to read the leaves of Basil and Ambrose, in their books entituled *Hexameron,*[9] or The Description of the Creation; wherein, delivering particular accounts of all the creatures, they have left us relations suitable to those of Ælian, Pliny, and other natural writers, whose authorities

---

* That write hexameters, or long verses.

[7] *Johannes Tzetzes.*] Tzetzes ventisossimus.—*Wr.*

[8] *a transcriptive relator.*] N.B. justissimam censuram.—*Wr.*

[9] *Hexameron.*] St. Basil and St. Ambrose in their hexameron: instead whereof wee have Du Bartas, an elegant and modest writer: justly honoured by (two) excellent poets, his translatores: Hieronymus Vida of Cremona, a second Virgil, who turned him into Latin verse, most smoothlye; and our Sylvester, a second Spencer, who hath soe finely fitted him with an English garbe, that itt seemes to become him as handsomelie, as his owne native French.—*Wr.*

herein they followed, and from whom, most probably, they desumed their narrations. And the like hath been committed by Epiphanius in his Physiology; that is, a book he hath left concerning the nature of animals. With no less caution must we look on Isidore, bishop of Seville; who, having left in twenty books an accurate work *De Originibus*, hath to the etymology of words superadded their received natures; wherein, most generally, he consents with common opinions and authors which have delivered them.

12. Albertus, bishop of Ratisbone, for his great learning and latitude of knowledge, surnamed Magnus. Besides divinity, he hath written many tracts in philosophy; what we are chiefly to receive with caution, are his Natural Tractates, more especially those of minerals, vegetables, and animals, which are indeed chiefly collections out of Aristotle, Ælian, and Pliny, and respectively contain many of our popular errors. A man who hath much advanced these opinions by the authority of his name, and delivered most conceits, with strict enquiry into few. In the same classes may well be placed Vincentius Belluacensis,[1] or rather he from whom he collected his *Speculum Naturale*, that is, Gulielmus de Conchis, and also Hortus Sanitatis, and Bartholomeus Glanvil, sirnamed Anglicus, who writ *De proprietatibus Rerum*. Hither also may be referred Kiranides, which is a collection out of Harpocration, the Greek, and sundry Arabic writers; delivering not only the natural but magical propriety of things; a work as full of vanity as variety, con-

---

[1] *Vincentius Belluacensis.*] The following statement of the merits of Vincent of Beauvais is given by the late Rev. J. J. Conybeare, in his account of the *Symbola Aureæ Mensæ Duodecim Nationum* of Michael Maier, published in the *Annals of Philosophy, Sec. Ser.* vol. vi. p. 428: —"Vincent of Beauvais, . . . certainly one of the most laborious and generally informed writers of the middle ages. His *Speculum Naturale* is the largest and most interesting Encyclopædia which I know of the philosophy and natural history of that period. It seems to have been laid under contribution pretty largely, if not altogether copied, in a work better known to our own black letter students, '*Bartholomæus de proprietatibus rerum*' (alluded to by our author in the same paragraph.) I have now before me what a bibliographer would term a venerable and perfect copy of Vincent's S. N. (Cologne, 1494.) The sixth and seventh books contain much alchemical matter, chiefly extracted from Avicenna and a work termed **Alchemiste**."—*Br.*

taining many relations, whose invention is as difficult as their beliefs, and their experiments sometime as hard as either.

13. We had almost forgot Jeronymus Cardanus,[2] that famous physician of Milan, a great enquirer of truth, but too greedy a receiver of it. He hath left many excellent discourses, medical, natural, and astrological; the most suspicious are those two he wrote by admonition in a dream, that is, *De Subtilitate* and *Varietate Rerum*. Assuredly this learned man hath taken many things upon trust, and although he examined some, hath let slip many others. He is of singular use unto a prudent reader; but unto him that only desireth *hoties*,[3] or to replenish his head with varieties, like many others before related, either in the original or confirmation, he may become no small occasion of error.

14. Lastly, authors are also suspicious, not greedily to be swallowed, who pretend to write of secrets, to deliver antipathies, sympathies, and the occult abstrusities of things; in the list whereof may be accounted, Alex. Pedimontanus, Antonius Mizaldus, Trinum Magicum, and many others. Not omitting that famous philosopher of Naples, Baptista Porta; in whose works, although there be contained many excellent things, and verified upon his own experience, yet are there many also receptary,[4] and such as will not endure the test. Who, although he hath delivered many strange relations in his Phytognomonica,[5] and his Villa, yet hath he more remarkably expressed himself in his Natural Magick,[6]

---

[2] *Cardanus.*] There is a most copious and interesting account of Cardan, and review of his works (ascribed to James Crossley, Esq., of Manchester), in *the Retrospective Review*, vol. i. p. 94—112.

[3] *hoties.*] i. e. the quiddities of things, for τὸ ὅτι, in Greek, signifies the quiddity, that is, the essential or formal cause of every thing in nature.—*Wr.*

[4] *receptary.*] "Generally or popularly admitted." Dr. Johnson quotes the present passage, but spells the word *receptory*.

[5] *Phytognomonica.*] "I would recommend the treatise of Baptista Porta, on Physiognomy, as an excellent commentary on that of Aristotle." Thos. Taylor's Introduction to his translation of Aristotle's *History of Animals* and *Treatise on Physiognomy*, p. xx.—*Br.*

[6] *Natural Magick.*] "That strange mixture of learning and absurdity:" J. J. Conybeare, *Ann. Phil. Sec. Ser.* vol. iv. p. 436. A judgment quite in accordance with our author's on the merits of the works of Baptista Porta in general.—*Br.*

and the miraculous effects of nature. Which containing various and delectable subjects, with all promising wondrous and easy effects, they are entertained by readers at all hands; whereof the major part sit down in his authority, and thereby omit not only the certainty of truth, but the pleasure of its experiment.

Thus have we made a brief enumeration of these learned men; not willing any to decline their works (without which it is not easy to attain any measure of general knowledge), but to apply themselves with caution thereunto. And seeing the lapses of these worthy pens, to cast a wary eye on those diminutive and pamphlet treatises[7] daily published amongst us. Pieces maintaining rather typography than verity, authors presumably writing by common places, wherein for many years promiscuously amassing all that makes for their subject, they break forth at last in trite and fruitless rhapsodies,[8] doing thereby not only open injury unto learning, but committing a secret treachery upon truth. For their relations falling upon credulous readers, they meet with prepared beliefs; whose supinities[9] had rather assent unto all, than adventure the trial of any.

Thus, I say, must these authors be read, and thus must we be read[1] ourselves; for discoursing of matters dubious, and many controvertible truths, we cannot without arrogancy entreat a credulity, or implore any further assent, than the probability of our reasons and verity of experiments induce.

[7] *And seeing the lapses of these worthy pens, to cast a wary eye on those diminutive and pamphlet treatises.*] A most useful and prudent caution.—*Wr.*

[8] *rhapsodies.*] Things thrown together without mutual relation: mere collections.

[9] *whose supinities.*] Whose indolence.

[1] *and thus must we be read.*] This is such a modest profession, as makes me wonder that any man should undertake to quarrel with him, as one of late hath professedly done.—*Wr.*

The Dean refers of course to Alexander Ross's *Arcana Microcosmi,* and Robinson's *Endoxa.*

CHAPTER IX.

Of others indirectly effecting the same.

THERE are, besides these authors and such as have positively promoted errors, divers other which are in some way accessory; whose verities, although they do not directly assert, yet do they obliquely concur unto their beliefs.[2] In which account are many holy writers, preachers, moralists, rhetoricians, orators, and poets; for they depending upon invention, deduce their mediums from all things whatsoever; and playing much upon the simile, or illustrative argumentation, to induce their enthymemes unto the people,[3] they take up popular conceits, and from traditions unjustifiable, or really false, illustrate matters of undeniable truth. Wherein, although their intention be sincere, and that course not much condemnable, yet doth it notoriously strengthen common errors, and authorise opinions injurious unto truth.

Thus have some divines drawn into argument the fable of the phœnix, made use of that of the salamander, pelican, basilisk, and divers relations of Pliny, deducing from thence most worthy morals, and even upon our Saviour. Now, although this be not prejudicial unto wiser judgments, who are but weakly moved with such arguments, yet is it ofttimes occasion of error unto vulgar heads, who expect in the fable as equal a truth as in the moral, and conceive that infallible philosophy, which is in any sense delivered by divinity. But wiser discerners do well understand that every art hath its own circle; that the effects of things are best examined by sciences wherein are delivered their causes: that strict and definitive expressions are always required in philosophy, but a loose and popular delivery will serve oftentimes in

---

[2] *unto their beliefs.*] Unto the belief *of errors.*

[3] *to induce their enthymemes, &c.*] An *enthymem* is an imperfect syllogism, where either the *major* or the *minor* is omitted, as being easily supplied by the understanding. The term, however, seems used here in no such precise signification. The author merely means to say, that, to obtain readier assent to the *maxims* or *propositions* delivered, preachers, moralists, &c., have garnished them with popular though erroneous conceits.

divinity.[4] As may be observed even in Holy Scripture, which often omitteth the exact account of things, describing them rather to our apprehensions, than leaving doubts in vulgar minds upon their unknown and philosophical descriptions. Thus it termeth the sun and the moon, the two great lights of heaven. Now if any shall from hence conclude the moon is second in magnitude unto the sun, he must excuse my belief: and it cannot be strange if[5] herein I rather adhere unto the demonstration of Ptolemy, than the popular description of Moses. Thus it said (2 Chron. iv. 2,) "That Solomon made a molten sea of ten cubits from brim to brim round in compass, and five cubits the height thereof, and a line of thirty cubits did compass it round about." Now in this description the circumference is made just treble unto the diameter: that is, as 10 to 30, or 7 to 21. But Archimedes demonstrates [in his Cyclometria] that the proportion of the diameter unto the circumference is as 7 unto almost 22, which will occasion a sensible difference, that is almost a cubit. Now, if herein I adhere unto Archimedes, who speaketh exactly, rather than the sacred text, which speaketh largely, I hope I shall not offend divinity; I am sure I shall have reason and experience of every circle to support me.

Thus moral writers, rhetoricians, and orators, make use of several relations, which will not consist with verity. Aristotle in his ethics takes up the conceit of the beaver, and the divulsion of his testicles. The tradition of the bear, the viper, and divers others are frequent amongst orators. All which, although unto the illiterate and undiscerning hearers [it] may seem a confirmation of their realities, yet this is no reasonable establishment unto others, who will not depend hereon, otherwise than on common apologues; which

[4] *a loose and popular delivery, &c.*] The author's illustration and application of this position in the remainder of the paragraph, might have well served as a reply to the tirade of Dean Wren against the Copernican system of astronomy, in his note at page 35, and has been used by some of the most eminent of our modern geologists, in attempting to show that certain opinions, which they have deduced from geological phenomena, are only apparently and not really at variance with the Mosaic account of creation.

[5] *and it cannot be strange if.*] *Ed.* 1646 reads, "and I think it cannot be taken for heresy, if."

being of impossible falsities, do notwithstanding include wholesome moralities, and such as expiate the trespass of their absurdities.

The hieroglyphical doctrine of the Egyptians (which in their four hundred years' cohabitation some conjecture they learned from the Hebrews) hath much advanced many popular conceits. For, using an alphabet of things, and not of words, through the image and pictures thereof they endeavoured to speak their hidden conceits in the letters and language of nature. In pursuit whereof, although in many things they exceeded not their true and real apprehensions, yet in some other they, either framing the story or taking up the tradition conducible unto their intentions, obliquely confirmed many falsities; which, as authentic and conceded truths, did after pass unto the Greeks, from them unto other nations, and are still retained by symbolical writers, emblematists, heralds, and others. Whereof some are strictly maintained for truths, as naturally making good their artificial representations; others, symbolically intended, are literally received, and swallowed in the first sense, without all gust of the second. Whereby we pervert the profound and mysterious knowledge of Egypt; containing the arcana of Greek antiquities, the key of many obscurities and ancient learning extant. Famous herein in former ages were Heraiseus, Cheremon, and Epius: especially Orus Apollo Niliaeus, who lived in the reign of Theodosius, and in Egyptian language left two books of hieroglyphics, translated into Greek by Philippus, and a large collection of all made after by Pierius. But no man is likely to profound the ocean of that doctrine, beyond that eminent example of industrious learning, Kircherus.

Painters, who are the visible representers of things, and such as by the learned sense of the eye endeavour to inform the understanding, are not inculpable herein, who, either describing naturals as they are or actions as they have been, have oftentimes erred in their delineations. Which, being the books that all can read, are fruitful advancers of these conceptions, especially in common and popular apprehensions, who being unable for further enquiry, must rest in the draught and letter of their descriptions.

Lastly, poets and poetical writers have in this point

exceeded others, trimly advancing the Egyptian notions[6] of harpies, phœnix, griffins, and many more. Now, however to make use of fictions, apologues, and fables be not unwarrantable, and the intent of these inventions might point at laudable ends, yet do they afford our junior capacities a frequent occasion of error, settling impressions in our tender memories which our advanced judgments generally neglect to expunge. This way the vain and idle fictions of the Gentiles did first insinuate into the heads of Christians, and thus are they continued even unto our days. Our first and literary apprehensions being commonly instructed in authors which handle nothing else, wherewith our memories being stuffed, our inventions become pedantic, and cannot avoid their allusions; driving at these as at the highest elegancies, which are but the frigidities of wit, and become not the genius of manly ingenuities. It were, therefore, no loss like that of Galen's library,[7] if these had found the same fate; and would in some way requite the neglect of solid authors, if they were less pursued. For, were a pregnant wit educated in ignorance hereof, receiving only impressions from realities, upon such solid foundations, it must surely raise more substantial superstructions, and fall upon very many excellent strains, which have been justled off by their intrusions.

CHAPTER X.

Of the last and great promoter of false opinions, the endeavours of Satan.

BUT, beside the infirmities of human nature, the seed of error within ourselves, and the several ways of delusion from each other, there is an invisible agent, the secret promoter without us, whose activity is undiscerned, and plays in the dark upon us: and that is the first contriver of error, and professed opposer of truth, the devil. For though, permitted

---

[6] *trimly advancing the Egyptian notions.*] "Leaving unto us the notions:"—*Ed.* 1646.

[7] *It were therefore no loss, &c.*] i. e. "had all such fabulous works been burnt, the loss would not have been comparable to that of Galen's library." He wrote 300 works, the greater part of which were burnt in the Temple of Peace, at Rome.

unto his proper principles, Adam, perhaps, would have sinned without the suggestion of Satan, and from the transgressive infirmities of himself might have erred alone, as well as the angels before him; and although were there no devil at all, yet there is now in our natures a confessed sufficiency unto corruption, and the frailty of our own economy were able to betray us out of truth; yet wants there not another agent, who taking advantage hereof proceedeth to obscure the diviner part, and efface all tract[8] of its traduction. To attempt a particular of all his wiles, is too bold an arithmetic for man: what most considerably concerneth his popular and practised ways of delusion, he first deceiveth mankind in five main points concerning God and himself.

And first, his endeavours have ever been, and they cease not yet, to instil a belief in the mind of man, there is no God at all. And this he principally endeavours to establish in a direct and literal apprehension; that is, that there is no such reality existent, that the necessity of his entity dependeth upon ours, and is but a political chimera; that the natural truth of God is an artificial erection of man, and the Creator himself but a subtile invention of the creature. Where he succeeds not thus high, he labours to introduce a secondary and deductive atheism; that although men concede there is a God, yet should they deny his providence. And therefore assertions have flown about, that he intendeth only the care of the species or common natures, but letteth loose the guard of individuals, and single existencies therein; that he looks not below the moon, but hath designed the regiment of sublunary affairs unto inferior deputations. To promote which apprehensions, or empuzzle their due conceptions, he casteth in the notions of fate, destiny, fortune, chance, and necessity; terms commonly misconceived by vulgar heads, and their propriety sometime perverted by the wisest. Whereby extinguishing in minds the compensation of virtue and vice, the hope and fear of heaven and hell, they comply in their actions unto the drift of his delusions, and live like creatures below the capacity of either.

Now hereby he not only undermineth the base of religion, and destroyeth the principle preambulous unto all belief, but

---

[8] *tract.*] In the sense of *track*. So used also by Shakspeare.

puts upon us the remotest error from truth. For atheism is the greatest falsity, and to affirm there is no God, the highest lie in nature. And therefore strictly taken, some men will say his labour is in vain; for many there are, who cannot conceive there was ever any absolute atheist, or such as could determine there was no God, without all check from himself, or contradiction from his other opinions. And therefore those few so called by elder times, might be the best of Pagans; suffering that name rather in relation to the gods of the Gentiles, than the true Creator of all. A conceit that cannot befall his greatest enemy, or him that would induce the same in us; who hath a sensible apprehension hereof, for he believeth with trembling. To speak yet more strictly and comformably unto some opinions, no creature can wish thus much; nor can the will which hath a power to run into velleities,[9] and wishes of impossibilities, have any *utinam* of this. For to desire there were no God, were plainly to unwish their own being, which must needs be annihilated in the subtraction of that essence which substantially supporteth them, and restrains them from regression into nothing. And if, as some contend, no creature can desire his own annihilation, that nothing is not appetible, and not to be at all, is worse than to be in the miserablest condition of something; the devil himself could not embrace that motion, nor would the enemy of God be freed by such a redemption.

But coldly thriving in this design, as being repulsed by the principles of humanity, and the dictates of that production which cannot deny its original, he fetcheth a wider circle: and when he cannot make men conceive there is no God at all, he endeavours to make them believe there is not one, but many: wherein he hath been so successful with common heads, that he hath led their belief through all the works of nature.

Now in this latter attempt, the subtilty of his circumvention hath indirectly obtained the former. For although to opinion there be many gods may seem an excess in religion, and such as cannot at all consist with atheism, yet doth it deductively and upon inference include the same; for unity is the inseparable and essential attribute of deity, and if there be more than one God, it is no atheism to say there is no God at all.

[9] *velleities.*] Velleity is the school term used to signify the lowest degree of desire.

And herein though Socrates only suffered, yet were Plato and Aristotle guilty of the same truth; who demonstratively understanding the simplicity of perfection, and the indivisible condition of the first causator, it was not in the power of earth, or areopagy* of hell to work them from it. For, holding an apodictical† knowledge and assured science of its verity, to persuade their apprehensions unto a plurality of gods in the world, were to make Euclid believe there were more than one centre in a circle, or one right angle in a triangle: which were indeed a fruitless attempt, and inferreth absurdities beyond the evasion of hell. For though mechanic and vulgar heads ascend not unto such comprehensions, who live not commonly unto half the advantage of their principles, yet did they not escape the eye of wiser Minervas, and such as made good the genealogy of Jupiter's brains; who, although they had divers styles for God, yet under many appellations acknowledged one divinity; rather conceiving thereby, the evidence or acts of his power in several ways and places, than a multiplication of essence, or real distraction of unity in any one.

Again, to render our errors more monstrous, (and what unto miracle sets forth the patience of God,) he hath endeavoured to make the world believe, that he was God himself; and failing of his first attempt to be but like the highest in heaven, he hath obtained with men to be the same on earth. And hath accordingly assumed the annexes of divinity, and the prerogatives of the Creator, drawing into practice the operation of miracles, and the prescience of things to come. Thus hath he in a specious way wrought cures upon the sick, played over the wondrous acts of prophets, and counterfeited many miracles of Christ and his apostles. Thus hath he openly contended with God, and to this effect his insolency was not ashamed to play a solemn prize with Moses; wherein, although his performance were very specious, and beyond the common apprehension of any power below a deity, yet was it not such as could make good his omnipotency. For he was wholly confounded in the conversion of dust into lice. An act philosophy can scarce deny to be above the power of nature, nor upon a requisite predisposition beyond the efficacy of the sun. Wherein

---

* Areopagus, the severe court of Athens.   † Demonstrative.

CHAP. X.] THE GREAT PROMOTER OF FALSE OPINIONS. 79

notwithstanding, the head of the old serpent was confessedly too weak for Moses's hand, and the arm of his magicians too short for the finger of God.[1]

[1] *to play a solemn prize with Moses, &c.*] The following curious parallel to this passage, is contained in a fragment of a discourse on Acts vii. 22, which forms part of the "Remains" of the unfortunate H. Kirke White. The writer is inquiring into the nature of the "wisdom of the Egyptians," mentioned in his text; and after some remarks on the scientific knowledge of that people, he proceeds thus: "The great objects of attention were the occult sciences. It was the magicians who swayed the people with a power almost imperial. It was the magicians who spread their fame over all the civilized world, and attached a reverential awe to the name of an Egyptian. The mysteries of these arts the magi preserved with the most scrupulous care, they were imparted to none but their immediate descendants, they were not entrusted to writing, but were locked up in the breasts of their jealous possessors. There is reason to believe, that a portion of judicial astrology was mixed with their magic, but they seem to have relied more on the incantation of spirits for the accomplishment of their purposes. Who does not read the accounts contained in the book of Exodus, of the wonders they performed in emulation of Moses, with surprise and astonishment? This prompt re-duplication of the miracles wrought by the power of God, is such, as we cannot readily conceive to have been effected by art, or simulated by deception, and there remains no other possible mode of accounting for their power, than by presuming that they did really maintain that intercourse with fallen spirits to which they pretend. I am aware that sneers of vain philosophy will be directed against such a supposition, but the course of all history, sacred and profane, countenances the idea; and after the body of evidence afforded by the ancient writers on this point, to express unqualified and unhesitating disbelief, can only argue an utter ignorance of the grounds on which we can alone judge in this mysterious subject. Let any one, however, read with attention the history of the ancient world, and he will see strong reason for believing that a very great part of mankind was given up to the government of unclean spirits. He will find that their gods were rather devils, worse than the very worst of their followers; that their religious institutions were a compound of imposture, avarice, and the most abominable wickedness; yet he will find their oracles often true in their predictions, and maintaining for a long series of years the reputation of being inspired. It was thus in Egypt at the time of the Exodus; the spirits of darkness held uncontrolled dominion over the people through the medium of the magicians, and had arrived at such a pitch of audacity, as almost to fly in the face of Almighty God himself, and measure their powers with his. But we see in the Scripture how they were defeated. They could not follow the arm of the Lord in his wonders. They could not even save their unhappy votaries from his plagues, for "*the magicians could not stand before Moses, because of the boils, for the boil was with the magicians.*" That they knew the evil character of the spirits they served,

Thus hath he also made men believe that he can raise the dead, that he hath the key of life and death, and a prerogative above that principle which makes no regression from privations.² The stoics, that opinioned the souls of wise men dwelt about the moon, and those of fools wandered about the earth, advantaged the conceit of this effect;³ wherein the Epicureans, who held that death was nothing, nor nothing after death, must contradict their principles to be deceived. Nor could the Pythagorean or such as maintained the transmigration of souls give easy admittance hereto; for, holding that separated souls successively supplied other bodies, they could hardly allow the raising of souls from other worlds, which at the same time, they conceived conjoined unto bodies in this. More inconsistent with these opinions is the error of Christians, who holding the dead do rest in the Lord, do yet believe they are the lure of the devil; that he who is in bonds himself commandeth the fetters of the dead, and dwelling in the bottomless lake, the blessed from Abraham's bosom; that can believe the real resurrection of Samuel; or that there is any thing but delusion in the practice of * necromancy and popular raising of ghosts.

He hath moreover endeavoured the opinion of deity, by the delusion of dreams, and the discovery of things to come in sleep, above the prescience of our waked senses. In this expectation he persuaded the credulity of elder times to take up their lodging before his temple, in skins of their own sacrifices, till his reservedness had contrived answers, whose

* Divination by the dead.

and were aware of their subordination to the true Jehovah, is manifest from the confession extorted by the wonders wrought by Moses, when, unable to equal him in his miracles, they exclaimed to Pharoah, "*This is the finger of God.*" *Remains of Henry Kirke White,* vol. iii. p. 183—185. Edit. 1822.—*Br.*

² *that principle which makes no regression from privations.*] That *law* or principle, by which life once lost is irrecoverable. "The artist, who shall first recall to life a human being in a case of natural death, by the same resuscitative process which is applied to cases of violent death, becomes the founder of a new era, and of a new name in the annals of humanity, of medicine, and of science." *Whiter on the Disorder of Death,* pref. p. ix.

³ *advantaged the conceit of this effect.*] Meaning that this opinion of the stoics somewhat facilitated the opinion that Satan can raise the dead, &c.

accomplishments were in his power, or not beyond his presagement. Which way although it had pleased Almighty God sometimes to reveal himself, yet was the proceeding very different. For the revelations of heaven are conveyed by new impressions, and the immediate illumination of the soul; whereas the deceiving spirit, by concitation of humours, produceth his conceited phantasm, or by compounding the species already residing, doth make up words which mentally speak his intentions.

But above all other he most advanced his deity in the solemn practice of oracles, wherein in several parts of the world he publicly professed his divinity; but how short they flew of that spirit whose omniscience they would resemble, their weakness sufficiently declared. What juggling there was therein, the orator* plainly confessed, who being good at the same game himself, could say that Pythia Philippised. Who can but laugh at the carriage of Ammon unto Alexander, who addressing unto him as a God, was made to believe he was a God himself? How openly did he betray his indivinity unto Crœsus, who being ruined by his amphibology, and expostulating with him for so ungrateful a deceit, received no higher answer than the excuse of his impotency upon the contradiction of fate, and the settled law of powers beyond his power to control! What more than sublunary directions, or such as might proceed from the oracle of human reason, was in his advice unto the Spartans in the time of a great plague; when for the cessation thereof, he wished them to have recourse unto a fawn, that is, in open terms, unto one Nebrus,† a good physician of those days? From no diviner a spirit came his reply unto Caracalla, who requiring a remedy for his gout, received no other counsel than to refrain cold drink; which was but a dietetical caution, and such as without a journey unto Æsculapius, culinary prescription and kitchen aphorisms might have afforded at home. Nor surely if any truth there were therein, of more than natural activity was his counsel unto Democritus, when for the falling sickness he commended the maggot in a goat's head. For many things secret are true; sympathies and antipathies are safely authentic unto us, who ignorant of their causes may yet

* Demosthenes.   † Nebros, in Greek, a fawn.

acknowledge their effects. Beside, being a natural magician he may perform many acts in ways above our knowledge, though not transcending our natural power, when our knowledge shall direct it. Part hereof hath been discovered by himself, and some by human indagation, which though magnified as fresh inventions unto us, are stale unto his cognition. I hardly believe he hath from elder times unknown the verticity of the loadstone; surely his perspicacity discerned it to respect the north, when ours beheld it indeterminately. Many secrets there are in nature of difficult discovery unto man, of easy knowledge unto Satan. Whereof some his vain glory cannot conceal, others his envy will not discover.

Again, such is the mystery of his delusion, that although he labour to make us believe that he is God, and supremest nature whatsoever, yet would he also persuade our beliefs that he is less than angels or men, and his condition not only subjected unto rational powers, but the action of things which have no efficacy on ourselves. Thus hath he inveigled no small part of the world into a credulity of artificial magic; that there is an art, which without compact commandeth the powers of hell; whence some have delivered the polity of spirits, and left an account even to their provincial dominions, that they stand in awe of charms, spells, and conjurations, that he is afraid of letters and characters, of notes and dashes, which, set together, do signifie nothing, not only in the dictionary of man, but the subtiler vocabulary of Satan. That there is any power in bitumen, pitch or brimstone, to purifie the air from his uncleanness, that any virtue there is in hypericon[4] to make good the name of *Fuga Dæmonis** any such magic as is ascribed unto the root *baaras* by Jose-

---

* St. John's wort, so called by magicians.

[4] *hypericon.*] This subject is thus alluded to by Stukely, in his *Palæographia Sacra,* p. 16 : "*Hypericon,* called ' fuga demonum,' reckoned among sacred magical plants, on account of the Druids using them." The plant is the *Hypericum perforatum* of botanists, and will be found described and depicted in Sowerby's *English Botany,* tab. 295. It was probably employed in the Druidical rites, on account of its aromatic qualities, and of the flowers yielding a red essential oil ; all plants having powerful effects upon the senses or upon the animal economy, being supposed, in former times, to possess mystical virtues, either in the way of propitiating good spirits or deities, or in that of charming away evil ones.—*Br.*

phus, or *cynospastus* by Ælianus, it is not easy to believe, nor is it naturally made out what is delivered of Tobias, that by the fume of a fish's liver he put to flight Asmodeus. That they are afraid of the pentangle of Solomon,*[5] though so set forth with the body of man, as to touch and point out the five places wherein our Saviour was wounded, I know not how to assent. If, perhaps, he hath fled from holy water, if he cares not to hear the sound of Tetragrammaton, † if his eye delight not in the sign of the cross, and that sometimes he will seem to be charmed with words of holy scripture, and to fly from the letter and dead verbality, who must only start at the life and animated interiors thereof:— it may be feared they are but Parthian flights, ambuscado retreats, and elusory tergiversations; whereby to confirm our credulities, he will comply with the opinion of such powers, which in themselves have no activities. Whereof, having once begot in our minds an assured dependence, he makes us rely on powers which he but precariously obeys, and to desert those true and only charms which hell cannot withstand.

Lastly, to lead us farther into darkness, and quite to lose us in this maze of error, he would make men believe there is no such creature as himself, and that he is not only subject unto inferior creatures, but in the rank of nothing,—insinuating into men's minds there is no devil at all; and contriveth, accordingly, many ways to conceal or indubitate[6] his existence. Wherein, beside that he annihilates the blessed angels and spirits in the rank of his creation, he begets a security of himself, and a careless eye unto the last remunerations. And, therefore, hereto he inveigleth, not only Sad-

---

* Three triangles intersected and made of five lines.
† Implying Jehovah, which in Hebrew consisteth of four letters.

[5] *pentangle of Solomon.*] After the unexpected discovery of the treasury in Misticot's grave, by Sir Arthur Wardour and his friends, in "The Antiquary," the writer introduces into Oldbuck's attack upon the German adept, Dousterswivel, on the latter pretending that the discovery had been effected by means of his magical arts, the following allusion to the pentangle:—"You have used neither charm, lamen, sigil, talisman, spell, crystal, *pentacle*, magic mirror, nor geomantic figure." *The Antiquary*, edit. with author's notes, vol. ii. p. 32.—*Br.*
[6] *indubitate.*] To bring into doubt; for in English the adjective signifies doubtless.—*Wr.*

ducees and such as retain unto the church of God, but is also content that Epicurus, Democritus, or any heathen should hold the same. And to this effect he maketh men believe that apparitions, and such as confirm his existence, are either deceptions of sight, or melancholy depravements of fancy. Thus when he had not only appeared but spake unto Brutus; Cassius, the Epicurean, was ready at hand to persuade him it was but a mistake in his weary imagination, and that indeed there were no such realities in nature. Thus he endeavours to propagate the unbelief of witches, whose concessions infers his coexistency; by this means also he advanceth the opinion of total death, and staggereth the immortality of the soul; for, such as deny there are spirits subsistent without bodies, will with more difficulty affirm the separated existence of their own.[7]

Now, to induce and bring about these falsities, he hath laboured to destroy the evidence of truth, that is, the revealed verity and written word of God. To which intent he hath obtained with some to repudiate the books of Moses,

[7] *Lastly, &c.*] Most certainly the Devil would have work enough on his hands, if he were concerned in all the mischief, real and imaginary, which has been attributed to him by many great men, and, among others, by our author. As an admirer of Browne, I cannot but regret most deeply the share which his views of Satanic influence led him to take in the trial of Amy Duny and Rose Cullendon, who were condemned and executed as witches, in 1664, at Bury, before one of the greatest and best men of his time, Sir Matthew Hale.—But, on the other hand, although we attribute to popular superstition the belief in *modern* witchcraft, and although it be conceded to the research and ingenuity of recent very eminent physiologists, that many of the best attested cases of apparitions were spectral illusions, attributable to physical causes,—we must not hence be supposed to doubt the existence and active agency of the Devil;—nor to question the *scriptural* relation of witches, and spiritual appearances. I am by no means inclined to admit that apparitions "confirm the existence of the Devil;" but I feel no greater difficulty in believing that such spiritual manifestations *may* still be occasionally permitted to take place, than in admitting that spiritual existence is not subject to the same laws as those which govern material existence. The spirit, at death, leaves the body *permanently* no more to resume its tenement on earth; why then should not a *transient* separation during life take place, and the spirit—bound by no laws of time and space—pay its monitory visit to some distant friend? See *Hibbert's Philosophy of Apparitions; Alderson's Essay on Apparitions; Ross,* p. 72, § 6.

others those of the prophets, and some both; to deny the gospel and authentic histories of Christ; to reject that of John, and to receive that of Judas; to disallow all, and erect another of Thomas.[8] And when neither their corruption by Valentinus and Arrius, their mutilation by Marcion, Manes, and Ebion, could satisfy his design, he attempted the ruin and total destruction thereof; as he sedulously endeavoured, by the power and subtilty of Julian, Maximinus, and Dioclesian.

But the longevity of that piece, which hath so long escaped the common fate, and the providence of that spirit which ever waketh over it, may at last discourage such attempts, and if not make doubtful its mortality, at least, indubitably declare this is a stone too big for Satan's mouth, and a bit indeed oblivion cannot swallow.

And thus how strangely he possesseth us with errors may clearly be observed, deluding us into contradictory and inconsistent falsities; whilst he would make us believe,—That there is no God—that there are many—that he himself is God—that he is less than angels or men—that he is nothing at all.

Nor hath he only by these wiles depraved the conception of the Creator, but with such riddles hath also entangled the nature of our Redeemer.[9] Some denying his humanity, and that he was one of the angels, as Ebion; that the Father and Son were but one person, as Sabellius. That his body was phantastical, as Manes, Basilides, Priscillian, Jovinianus; that he only passed through Mary, as Eutyches and Valentinus. Some denying his divinity; that he was begotten of human principles, and the seminal son of Joseph, as Carpocras, Symmachus, Photinus: that he was Seth, the son of

---

[8] *to receive that of Judas, &c.*] In *Fabricii Codex Apocryphus* and in Jones's *Method of settling the Canonical authority of the New Testament*, accounts are to be found of these Apocryphal gospels. There were two under the name of *Judas;* one of Judas Iscariot, and the other of Judas Thaddeus, but they are not now extant. Of the gospel of Thomas, some fragments yet remain, under the name of "the gospel of our Saviour's infancy."

[9] *nature of our Redeemer.*] The doctrines of the Heresiarchs enumerated in this paragraph, are, upon the whole, accurately stated by our author: detailed views of most of them will be found in Mosheim's *Ecclesiastical History.—Br.*

Adam, as the Sethians; that he was less than angels, as Cerinthus; that he was inferior unto Melchisedec, as Theodotus; that he was not God, but God dwelt in him, as Nicolaus; and some embroiling them both. So did they which converted the trinity into a quaternity, and affirmed two persons in Christ, as Paulus Samosatenus; that held he was a man without a soul, and that the word performed that office in him, as Apollinaris; that he was both Son and Father, as Montanus; that Jesus suffered, but Christ remained impatible, as Cherinthus. Thus he endeavours to entangle truth; and, when he cannot possibly destroy its substance, he cunningly confounds its apprehensions—that from the inconsistent and contrary determinations thereof, consectary impieties[1] and hopeful conclusions may arise, there's no such thing at all.

CHAPTER XI.

A further Illustration of the same.

Now, although these ways of delusion most Christians have escaped, yet are there many other whereunto we are daily betrayed; and these we meet with in obvious occurrents of the world,[2] wherein he induceth us to ascribe effects unto causes of no cognation;[3] and, distorting the order and theory of causes perpendicular to their effects, he draws them aside unto things whereto they run parallel, and in their proper motions would never meet together.

Thus doth he sometime delude us in the conceits of stars and meteors, beside their allowable actions ascribing effects thereunto of independent causations. Thus hath he also made the ignorant sort believe that natural effects immediately and commonly proceed from supernatural powers: and these he usually derives from Heaven, and his own principality the air, and meteors therein; which, being of themselves the effects of natural and created causes, and such as, upon a due conjunction of actives and passives, without a

---

[1] *consectary impieties.*] "Consequent impieties."
[2] *occurrents of the world.*] "Occurrences of the world."
[3] *of no cognation.*] "Of no *relation*."

miracle, must arise unto what they appear, are always looked on by ignorant spectators as supernatural spectacles, and made the causes or signs of most succeeding contingencies. To behold a rainbow in the night, is no prodigy unto a philosopher. Than eclipses of sun or moon, nothing is more natural: yet with what superstition they have been beheld since the tragedy of Nicias and his army,[4] many examples declare.

True it is, and we will not deny it, that although, these being natural productions from second and settled causes, we need not alway look upon them as the immediate hand of God, or of his ministering spirits: yet do they sometimes admit a respect therein; and even in their naturals, the indifferency of their existences, contemporised unto our actions, admits a farther consideration.

That two or three suns or moons appear in any man's life or reign, it is not worth the wonder. But that the same should fall out at a remarkable time, or point of some decisive action; that the contingency of its appearance should be confirmed unto that time; that those two should make but one line in the book of fate, and stand together in the great ephemerides of God; beside the philosophical assignment of the cause, it may admit a Christian apprehension in the signality.

But, above all he deceiveth us, when we ascribe the effects of things unto evident and seeming casualties, which arise from the secret and undiscerned action of himself. Thus hath he deluded many nations in his augurial and extispicious[5] inventions, from casual and uncontrived contingencies divining events succeeding. Which Tuscan superstition seizing upon Rome, hath since possessed all Europe. When Augustus found two galls in his sacrifice, the credulity of the city concluded a hope of peace with Anthony, and the conjunction of persons in choler with each other. Because Brutus and Cassius met a blackmoor, and Pompey had on a dark or sad-coloured garment at Pharsalia; these were pre-

[4] *Nicias and his army.*] He lost his army before Syracuse, by delaying to embark it, at the favourable moment, on account of an eclipse of the moon which suddenly came on. *Plutarch in Vit.*

[5] *extispicious.*] "Relating to the inspection of entrails in order to prognostication."

sages of their overthrow.⁶ Which notwithstanding are scarce rhetorical sequels; concluding metaphors from realities, and from conceptions metaphorical inferring realities again.

Now these divinations concerning events, being in his power to force, contrive, prevent, or further, they must generally fall out conformably unto his predictions. When Gracchus was slain, the same day the chickens refused to come out of the coop; and Claudius Pulcher underwent the like success, when he condemned the tripudiary augurations; they died, not because the pullets would not feed, but, because the devil foresaw⁷ their death, he contrived that abstinence in them. So was there no natural dependence of the event upon the sign, but an artificial contrivance of the sign unto the event. An unexpected way of delusion, and whereby he more easily led away the incircumspection of their belief. Which fallacy he might excellently have acted before the death of Saul; for that being within his power to foretell, was not beyond his ability to foreshow, and might have contrived signs thereof through all the creatures, which, visibly confirmed by the event, had proved authentic unto those times, and advanced the art ever after.

He deludeth us also by philters, ligatures, charms, ungrounded amulets, characters, and many superstitious ways in the cure of common diseases; seconding herein the expectation of men with events of his own contriving, which while some, unwilling to fall directly upon magick, impute unto the power of imagination, or the efficacy of hidden causes, he obtains a bloody advantage; for thereby he begets not only a false opinion, but such as leadeth the open way to destruction. In maladies admitting natural reliefs, making men rely on remedies, neither of real operation in themselves, nor more than seeming efficacy in his concurrence. Which whensoever he pleaseth to withdraw, they stand naked unto the mischief of their diseases, and revenge the contempt of the medicines of the earth which God hath created for them. And therefore, when neither miracle is

⁵ *Because Brutus and Cassius met a blackmoor.*] The Ethiopian, who met the standard-bearer opening the gate of the camp, and was cut in pieces by the soldiers, as affording an ill omen.

⁷ *the Devil foresaw, &c.*] "Because he foresaw the death of Gracchus and Claudius Pulcher, he contrived that abstinence in the birds."

expected, nor connection of cause unto effect from natural grounds concluded, however it be sometime successful, it cannot be safe to rely on such practices, and desert the known and authentic provisions of God. In which rank of remedies, if nothing in our knowledge or their proper power be able to relieve us, we must with patience submit unto that restraint, and expect the will of the restrainer.

Now in these effects although he seem ofttimes to imitate, yet doth he concur unto their productions in a different way from that spirit which sometimes, in natural means, produceth effects above nature. For whether he worketh by causes which have relation or none unto the effect, he maketh it out by secret and undiscerned ways of nature. So, when Caius the blind, in the reign of Antoninus, was commanded to pass from the right side of the altar unto the left, to lay five fingers of one hand thereon, and five of the other upon his eyes; although the cure succeeded, and all the people wondered, there was not any thing in the action which did produce it, nor any thing in his power that could enable it thereunto. So for the same infirmity, when Aper was counselled by him to make a collyrium or ocular medicine with the blood of a white cock and honey, and apply it to his eyes for three days; when Julian for his spitting of blood, was cured by honey and pine nuts taken from his altar; when Lucius for the pain in his side, applied thereto the ashes from his altar with wine; although the remedies were somewhat rational, and not without a natural virtue unto such intentions, yet need we not believe that by their proper faculties they produced these effects.

But the effects of powers divine flow from another operation; who, either proceeding by visible means or not unto visible effects, is able to conjoin them by his co-operation. And therefore those sensible ways which seem of indifferent natures, are not idle ceremonies, but may be causes by his command, and arise unto productions beyond their regular activities. If Naaman the Syrian had washed in Jordan without the command of the prophet, I believe he had been cleansed by them no more than by the waters of Damascus. I doubt, if any beside Elisha had cast in salt, the waters of Jericho had not been made wholesome. I know that a decoction of wild gourd or *colocynthis* (though somewhat qualified) will not from every hand be dulcified unto aliment by an addition of flour or meal. There was some natural virtue in the plaster of figs applied unto Hezechiah; we find that gall is very mundificative, and was a proper medicine to clear the eyes of Tobit; which carrying in themselves some action of their own, they were additionally promoted by that power, which can extend their natures unto the production of effects beyond their created efficiencies. And thus may he operate also from causes of no power unto their visible effects; for he that hath determined their actions unto certain effects, hath not so emptied his own, but that he can make them effectual unto any other.

Again, although his delusions run highest in points of practice, whose errors draw on offensive or penal enormities, yet doth he also deal in points of speculation, and things whose knowledge terminates in themselves. Whose cognition although it seems indifferent, and therefore its aberration directly to condemn no man, yet doth he hereby preparatively dispose us unto errors, and deductively deject us into destructive conclusions.

That the sun, moon, and stars, are living creatures, endued with soul and life, seems an innocent error, and an harmless digression from truth; yet hereby he confirmed their idolatry, and made it more plausibly embraced. For, wisely mistrusting that reasonable spirits would never firmly be lost in the adorement of things inanimate, and in the lowest form of nature, he begat an opinion that they were living creatures, and could not decay for ever.

That spirits are corporeal, seems at first view a conceit derogative unto himself, and such as he should rather labour to overthrow; yet hereby he establisheth the doctrine of lustrations, amulets, and charms, as we have declared before.

That there are two principles of all things, one good and another evil; from the one proceeding virtue, love, light, and unity: from the other, division, discord, darkness, and deformity, was the speculation of Pythagoras, Empedocles, and many ancient philosophers, and was no more than Oromasdes and Arimanius of Zoroaster.[6] Yet hereby he obtained the advantage of adoration, and as the terrible

---

[6] *Oromasdes and Arimanius of Zoroaster.*] These were the two deities of Zoroaster, the founder of the Magi in Persia.—*Wr.*

principle became more dreadful than his Maker, and therefore not willing to let it fall, he furthered the conceit in succeeding ages, and raised the faction of Manes to maintain it.

That the feminine sex have no generative emission, affording no seminal principles of conception, was Aristotle's opinion of old, maintained still by some, and will be countenanced by him[9] for ever. For hereby he disparageth the fruit of the Virgin, frustrateth the fundamental prophecy, nor can the seed of the woman then break the head of the serpent.

Nor doth he only sport in speculative errors, which are of consequent impieties, but the unquietness of his malice haunts after simple lapses, and such whose falsities do only condemn our understandings. Thus if Xenophanes will say there is another world in the moon;[1] if Heraclitus, with his adherents, will hold the sun is no bigger than it appeareth; if Anaxagoras affirm that snow is black; if any other opinion there are no Antipodes, or that stars do fall, he shall not want herein the applause or advocacy of Satan. For maligning the tranquillity of truth, he delighteth to trouble its streams; and, being a professed enemy unto God (who is truth itself) he promoteth any error as derogatory to his nature, and revengeth himself in every deformity from truth. If, therefore, at any time he speak or practise truth, it is upon design, and a subtle inversion of the precept of God, to do good that evil may come of it. And therefore, sometime we meet with wholesome doctrines from hell; *Nosce teipsum*, the motto of Delphos, was a good precept in morality; that a just man is beloved of the gods, an uncontrollable verity. 'Twas a good deed, though not well done,

---

[9] *by him.*] That is, by the devil.
[1] *if* Xenophanes *will say there is another world in the moon.*] Xenophanes was a pantheistical philosopher, born at Colophon, B. C. 556, who founded the Eleatic sect in Sicily, and died in Magna Græcia at the age of a century, having occupied the Pythagorean chair of philosophy for nearly seventy years. His doctrines, both philosophical and astronomical, if they have been rightly represented, were wild and incongruous; but perhaps it may be inferred, from the reasonableness of his tenet that *the moon was an inhabited world*, that, as suspected by Brucker and others, they have been misrepresented. This is of course the notion alluded to by our author. See *Bruckeri Hist. Crit. Philosophiæ*, tom. i. p. 1143, 1148, 1155.—*Br*

which he wrought by Vespasian, when by the touch of his foot he restored a lame man, and by the stroke of his hand another that was blind, but the intention hereof drived at his own advantage; for hereby he not only confirmed the opinion of his power with the people, but his integrity with princes, in whose power he knew it lay to overthrow his oracles, and silence the practice of his delusions.

But of such a diffused nature, and so large is the empire of truth, that it hath place within the walls of hell, and the devils themselves are daily forced to practise it; not only as being true themselves, in a metaphysical verity, that is, as having their essence comformable unto the intellect of their maker, but making use of moral and logical verities, that is, whether in the conformity of words unto things, or things unto their own conceptions, they practise truth in common among themselves. For, although without speech they intuitively conceive each other, yet do their apprehensions proceed through realities; and they conceive each other by species, which carry the true and proper notions of things conceived. And so also in moral verities, although they deceive us, they lie not unto each other, as well understanding that all community is continued by truth, and that of hell cannot consist without it.

To come yet nearer the point, and draw into a sharper angle: they do not only speak and practise truth, but may be said well-wishers hereunto, and, in some sense, do really desire its enlargement. For many things which in themselves are false, they do desire were true. He cannot but wish he were as he professeth, that he had the knowledge of future events; were it in his power, the Jews should be in the right, and the Messias yet to come. Could his desires effect it, the opinion of Aristotle should be true, the world should have no end,[2] but be as immortal as himself. For thereby he might evade the accomplishment of those afflictions he now but gradually endureth; for comparatively unto those flames, he is but in *balneo*, then begins his *ignis rotæ*,[3]

---

[2] *the world should have no end.*] Aristotle unquestionably held this doctrine, as appears from the entire argument of his treatise *On the Heavens.—Br.*

[3] *he is but yet in* balneo, *then begins his* ignis rotæ.] These terms are derived from the technical language of the old chemists. *In balneo* refers

and terrible fire, which will determine its disputed subtilty, and even hazard his immortality.

But to speak strictly he is in these wishes no promoter of verity, but, if considered, some ways injurious unto truth; for (besides that if things were true, which now are false, it were but an exchange of their natures, and things must then be false, which now are true) the settled and determined order of the world would be perverted, and that course of things disturbed which seemed best unto the immutable contriver. For whilst they murmur against the present disposure of things, regulating determined realities unto their private optations, they rest not in their established natures, but unwishing their unalterable verities, do tacitly desire in them a difformity from the primitive rule, and the idea of that mind that formed all things best. And thus he offendeth truth even in his first attempt; for, not content with his created nature, and thinking it too low to be the highest creature of God, he offended the ordainer, not only in the attempt, but in the wish and simple volition thereof.

---

to the gentle or comparatively low heat obtained by immersing the vessel containing the substance to be heated in a *bath* of heated water, oil, sand, or other convenient medium; whence the *water bath* and *sand bath*, or sand heat of modern chemistry. The *ignis rotæ* was a naked fire disposed in a circle round a crucible, in which ignition or calcination, operations requiring an intense heat were to be performed. Thus understood, the meaning of our author's application of these terms is obvious.—*Br.*

THE SECOND BOOK,

BEGINNING THE PARTICULAR PART.

OF POPULAR AND RECEIVED TENETS CONCERNING MINERAL AND VEGETABLE BODIES.

CHAPTER I.

That Crystal is nothing else but Ice strongly congealed.

HEREOF the common opinion hath been, and still remaineth amongst us, that crystal is nothing else but ice or snow concreted, and, by duration of time, congealed beyond liquation. Of which assertion, if prescription of time, and numerosity of assertors were a sufficient demonstration, we might sit down herein, as an unquestionable truth, nor should there need ulterior disquisition; for few opinions there are which have found so many friends, or been so popularly received, through all professions and ages. Pliny is positive in this opinion; *Crystallus fit gelu vehementius concreto:*[1] the same is followed by Seneca, elegantly described by Claudian, not denied by Scaliger, some way affirmed by Albertus, Brassavolus, and directly by many others.[2] The venerable fathers of the church have also assented hereto; as Basil, in his *Hexameron,* Isidore, in his *Etymologies,* and not only Austin, a Latine father, but Gregory the Great, and Jerom upon occasion of that term expressed in the first of Ezekiel.

[1] *Crystallus fit gelu, &c.*] This opinion is given by Pliny, *Hist. Nat.* lib. xxxvii. cap. 2.—*Br.*
[2] *by many others.*] Thucydides clearly uses the word κρύσταλλος in the sense of *ice;* See *Hist.* iii. 23.—4to. vol. 1, p. 438.

All which notwithstanding, upon a strict enquiry, we find the matter controvertible, and with much more reason denied, than is as yet affirmed. For though many have passed it over with easy affirmatives, yet there are also many authors that deny it, and the exactest mineralogists have rejected it. Diodorus, in his eleventh book, denieth it (if crystal be there taken in its proper acception, as Rhodiginus hath used it, and not for a diamond, as Salmasius hath expounded it), for in that place he affirmeth, *crystallum esse lapidem ex aqua pura concretum, non tamen frigore sed divini caloris vi.* Solinus, who transcribed Pliny, and, therefore, in almost all subscribed unto him, hath in this point dissented from him. *Putant quidam glaciem coire, et in crystallum corporari, sed frustra.* Matthiolus, in his comment upon Dioscorides, hath with confidence rejected it.[3] The same hath been performed by Agricola, *De natura fossilium*, by Cardan, Boëtius de Boot, Cæsius Bernardus, Sennertus, and many more.

Now, besides authority against it, there may be many reasons, deduced from their several differences, which seem to overthrow it. And first a difference is probable in their concretion. For, if crystal be a stone (as in the number thereof it is confessedly received),[4] it is not immediately concreted by the efficacy of cold, but rather by a mineral spirit and lapidifical principles of its own; and, therefore, while it lay *in solutis principiis*, and remained in a fluid body, it was a subject very unapt for proper conglaciation; for mineral spirits do generally resist, and scarce submit thereto. So we observe that many waters and springs will never freeze,[5] and many parts in rivers and lakes, where

---

[3] *with confidence rejected it.*] "With confidence, and not without reason, rejected it."—*Ed.* 1646.

[4] *as in the number thereof it is, &c.*] i. e. in the number whereof it is, &c.

Ross, with his usual wrong-headedness, argues stoutly for the ancient opinion. "The cold of some waters," he observes, "metamorphose sticks, leaves, and trees, pieces of leather, nutshells, and such like stuff into stones; why then may not cold convert ice into a higher degree of hardness, and prepare it for reception of a new form, which gives it the essence and name of crystal?"—*Arcana*, p. 189.

[5] *many waters and springs will never freeze.*] Our author is mistaken in ascribing this phenomenon to the mineral contents of the water ex-

there are mineral eruptions, will still persist without congelation: as we also observe in aqua fortis, or any mineral solution, either of vitriol, alum, saltpetre, ammoniac, or tartar, which, although to some degree exhaled, and placed in cold conservatories, will crystallize and shoot into white and glacious bodies: yet is not this a congelation primarily effected by cold, but an intrinsical induration from themselves; and a retreat into their proper solidities, which were absorbed by the liquor, and lost in a full imbibition thereof before. And so, also, when wood and many other bodies do petrify, either by the sea, other waters, or earths abounding in such spirits, we do not usually ascribe their induration to cold, but rather unto salinous spirits, concretive juices, and causes circumjacent, which do assimilate all bodies not indisposed for their impressions.

But ice is only water congealed by the frigidity of the air, whereby it acquireth no new form, but rather a consistence or determination of its diffluency, and amitteth not its essence, but condition of fluidity. Neither doth there any thing properly conglaciate but water, or watery humidity; for the determination of quicksilver is properly fixation, that

hibiting it: no springs are so strongly impregnated with mineral substances as to have their freezing points affected by it in any considerable degree. The true cause of the phenomenon is, in the case of springs and lakes, their depth, and in that of rivers, their depth in conjunction with the rapidity with which they flow. For, owing to the mobility of the particles of water, and to the circumstance that, like all other bodies, it becomes heavier, in consequence of its contraction in bulk, in proportion as its temperature is reduced (with a particular exception, which it is unnecessary now to mention), when the surface or upper portion of the water gives out its heat to the atmosphere, on account of the temperature of that medium becoming inferior to its own, the portion of water so cooled down, becoming heavier than the subjacent portion, sinks towards the bottom, and an uncooled portion takes its place, which, in its turn, is cooled, and rendered heavier by the same process. Until, therefore, the whole of the water has been reduced to the freezing point by the continuance of this operation, no ice can form upon it; for, until then, the temperature of that portion which is in contact with the atmosphere will be above the freezing point. In the case of deep wells and lakes, this occupies so long a time, that, in temperate climates, the cold season has passed away, and the temperature of the atmosphere has ceased to be inferior to that of the upper portion of the water, before the whole has been reduced to the freezing point.—*Br.*

of milk coagulation, and that of oil and unctious bodies only incrassation. And, therefore, Aristotle makes a trial of the fertility of human seed, from the experiment of congelation; for that, saith he, which is not watery and improlifical will not conglaciate: which, perhaps, must not be taken strictly, but in the germ and spirited particles; for eggs, I observe, will freeze in the albugineous part[6] thereof. And upon this ground Paracelsus, in his *Archidoxis*, extracteth the magistery of wine; after four months' digestion in horse-dung, exposing it unto the extremity of cold, whereby the aqueous parts will freeze, but the spirit retire, and be found uncongealed in the centre.

But whether this congelation be simply made by cold, or also by co-operation of any nitrous coagulum,[7] or spirit of salt, the principle of concretion, whereby we observe that ice may be made with salt and snow by the fire-side, as is also observable from ice made by saltpetre and water, duly mixed and strongly agitated, at any time of the year, were a very considerable enquiry. For thereby we might clear the generation of snow, hail, and hoary frosts, the piercing quali-

[6] *eggs, I observe, &c.*] That point in the *Chalaza*, the spark of vivification, I wish it might freeze: it would rid my trees from caterpillars, which can continue their noxious species, by their hybernating eggs.— *Robinson's Endoxa*.

[7] *or also by co-operation of any nitrous coagulum.*] The doubt here expressed, whether the congelation of water is simply owing to cold, or whether the operation of cold may not be aided by saltpetre, or some analogous principle, is a remnant of the notions entertained of that salt by the alchemists, and the older operators in true chemistry who immediately succeeded them, of both whose ideas on such subjects our author retained a few, though (considering the state of science in his time) but very few indeed, and those of minor importance only. The arguments which he adduces in favour of this doubt are as fallacious as the supposition itself, which it involves, "That ice may be made with salt and snow by the fire-side," arises, not from any peculiar congealing virtue in the salt, but merely from the circumstance that the affinity it has for water produces a rapid liquefaction of the snow, which, robbing the surrounding bodies of their heat, in order itself to assume the liquid form (their *sensible* heat thus becoming *latent* in the resulting water) produces the cold. The case is similar with respect to the "ice made by saltpetre and water;" for here, the water subjected to experiment is reduced to the solid form by the abstraction of its sensible heat, consequent upon the liquefaction of the salt, in the solution of which it becomes latent.—*Br*.

ties of some winds, the coldness of caverns, and some cells. We might more sensibly conceive how saltpetre fixeth the flying spirits of minerals in chemical preparations, and how by this congealing quality it becomes an useful medicine in fevers.[8]

Again, the difference of their concretion is collectible from their dissolution, which being many ways performable in ice, is few ways effected[9] in crystal. Now the causes of liquation are contrary to those of concretion; and, as the atoms and indivisible parcels are united, so are they in an opposite way disjoined. That which is concreted by exsiccation or expression of humidity,[1] will be resolved by humectation, as earth, dirt, and clay; that which is coagulated by a fiery siccity, will suffer colliquation from an aqueous humidity, as salt and sugar, which are easily dissoluble in water, but not without difficulty in oil and well rectified spirits of wine. That which is concreted by cold, will dissolve by a moist heat, if it consist of watery parts, as gums arabic, tragacanth, ammoniac, and others, in an airy heat or oil, as all resinous bodies, turpentine, pitch, and frankincense; in both, as gummy resinous bodies, mastic, camphor, and storax; in neither, as neutrals, and bodies anomalous hereto, as bdellium, myrrh, and others. Some by a violent dry heat, as metals; which although corrodible by waters, yet will they not suffer a liquation[2] from the powerfullest heat communicable unto that element. Some will dissolve by this heat,

---

[8] *But whether, &c.*] This paragraph was added in *Second Edition*.

[9] *is few ways effected.*] "Is not in the same manner effected."—*Ed.* 1646.

[1] *that which is concreted by exsiccation, &c.*] The statements here made by our author respecting the causes of liquation and concretion, &c., are evidently derived from Aristotle. *Met.* lib. iv. cap. 6. See also the notes to *Pseudodoxia*, book i. chap. vi. p. 42.—*Br*

[2] *yet will they not suffer a liquation.*] Modern chemistry shows our author to be in error in his opinion, that heat of a peculiar nature is required for the fusion of metals. The only reason why the generality of metals cannot be melted by hot water is, that they require a higher temperature for their liquefaction than can be given to that fluid under ordinary circumstances. But there is an alloy of bismuth, lead, and tin, which melts at a temperature inferior to that of boiling water, (commonly called on that account *fusible metal*), and which accordingly melts when immersed in that fluid. Under pressure, as when heated in Papin's digester for instance, water can be raised to a much higher

although their ingredients be earthy, as glass,[3] whose materials are fine sand, and the ashes of kali or fern; and so will salt run with fire, although it be concreted by heat. And this way may be effected a liquation in crystal, but not without some difficulty, that is, calcination or reducing it by art into a subtle powder, by which way and a vitreous commixture, glasses are sometime made hereof, and it becomes the chiefest ground for artificial and factitious gems. But the same way of solution is common also unto many stones; and not only beryls and cornelians, but flints and pebbles are subject unto fusion, and will run like glass in fire.

But ice will dissolve in any way of heat, for it will dissolve with fire, it will colliquate in water, or warm oil, nor doth it only submit unto an actual heat, but not endure the potential calidity of many waters. For it will presently dissolve in cold aqua fortis, spirit of vitriol, salt or tartar, nor will it long continue its fixation in spirits of wine, as may be observed in ice injected therein.

Again, the concretion of ice will not endure a dry attrition[4] without liquation; for if it be rubbed long with a cloth, it melteth. But crystal will calefy unto electricity,[5]

temperature than that at which it boils under the common pressure of the atmosphere; and thus can be made to melt lead, which is quite infusible in common boiling water.—*Br.*

[3] *glass.*] In the *Manchester Memoirs*, vol. 2. p. 95, there are some interesting "Remarks on the Knowledge of the Ancients respecting Glass," by Dr. Falconer.

[4] *the concretion of ice will not endure a dry attrition, &c.*] A similar exertion of ingenuity to that which has discovered a knowledge of the true chemical mixture of the atmosphere in certain mythological tales of the Egyptian priests, and of that of the constituents of water in some of the speculations of Lucretius, might, with far less aberration from the truth, affirm that in this sentence of our author is virtually an anticipation of Sir H. Davy's experiment, in which ice was melted by the mere friction of two pieces of it together. For as a cloth would be a very bad conductor of heat, the experiment of our author might, with care, be so made as to cause the fusion of the ice by the heat generated by the friction alone, independent of that which might (without care) be conducted from the hand of the experimenter through the cloth, and of that also which would be derived from the cloth itself, if not previously reduced to the freezing temperature. It is plain, also, from the author's use of the word "calefy" in the next period, that he believed the ice to be melted by the heat generated by the friction, and not by the friction alone, mechanically considered.—*Br.*

[5] *But crystal will calefy unto electricity.*] It is an accurate observa-

that is, a power to attract straws or light bodies, and convert the needle freely placed :—which is a declarement of very different parts, wherein we shall not enlarge, as having discoursed concerning such bodies in the chapter of electrics.

They are differenced by supernatation or floating upon water;[6] for crystal will sink in water, as carrying in its own bulk a greater ponderosity than the space in any water it doth occupy, and will therefore only swim in molten metal and quicksilver. But ice will swim in water[7] of what thinness soever; and, though it sink in oil, will float in spirits of wine or aqua vitæ. And therefore it may swim in water, not only as being water itself, and in its proper place, but perhaps as weighing somewhat less[8] than the water it possesseth. And therefore, as it will not sink unto the bottom, so neither will it float above, like lighter bodies, but, being near in weight, lie superficially or almost horizontally

---

tion that rock-crystal becomes electric by friction; but our author is mistaken in attributing the excitation of electricity to the heat produced by the friction. In this case, and in all others of electricity so excited, the agency of the friction appears to be merely mechanical. —*Br.*

[6] *They are differenced, &c.*] They; i. e. ice and crystal. Here again we have Ross's ingenious reply; it's no wonder to see a stone sink and ice swim; for crystal when it was ice, swimmed, being now a stone sinks; as being a body more compact, hard, solid, and ponderous; so a stick will swim, but when it is converted to a stone, it sinks. The argument therefore is good thus; crystal sinks, ice swims; therefore crystal *is* not ice; but it will not follow, therefore, crystal *was* not ice." —*Arcana,* p. 189.

[7] *But ice will swim in water.*] The whole of this paragraph is excellent, in assertion as well as in argument, giving a very accurate view of the facts described. It is quite true that the ice weighs "somewhat less than the water it possesseth," specifically; that is, a bulk of ice equal to that of the water in its liquid form would weigh less than the water; and that this is the reason why it swims upon water. It is also true that ordinary ice is less compact, less continuous in its solidity than other crystalline bodies, and that it is full of spunes and bubbles, and "which abate its gravity." The last statement, that the freezing of water is at the same time condensation and rarefaction, is also correct: that its solid state must imply a kind of condensation, some sort of molecular approximation, is clear; and yet it expands in freezing, and thus unquestionably undergoes rarefaction.—*Br.*

[8] *somewhat less.*] "No more."—*Ed.* 1646. The specific gravity of ice is to that of water, as 8 to 9. Its greater lightness was discovered by Galileo.

unto it. And therefore also, an ice or congelation of salt or sugar, although it descend not unto the bottom, yet will it abate, and decline below the surface in thin water, but very sensibly in spirits of wine. For ice, although it seemeth as transparent and compact as crystal, yet is it short in either;[9] for its atoms are not concreted into continuity, which doth diminish its translucency; it is also full of spumes and bubbles, which may abate its gravity. And therefore, waters frozen in pans and open glasses, after their dissolution, do commonly leave a froth and spume upon them, which are caused by the airy parts diffused in the congelable mixture, which, uniting themselves, and finding no passage at the surface, do elevate the mass, and make the liquor take up a greater place than before: as may be observed in glasses filled with water, which, being frozen will seem to swell above the brim. So that if, in this condensation, any one affirmeth there is also some rarefaction, experience may assert it.[1]

They are distinguished, in substance of parts, and the accidents thereof:[2] that is, in colour and figure: for ice is a similary body, and homogeneous concretion, whose material is properly water, and but accidentally exceeding the simplicity of that element. But the body of crystal is mixed, its ingredients many, and sensibly containeth those principles into which mixed bodies are reduced. For beside the spirit and mercurial principle,[3] it containeth a sulphur or inflam-

[9] *yet is it short in either.*] "Yet is it inferior to crystal, both in transparency and compactness."

[1] *which are, &c.*] From l. 11 to the end of the paragraph was added in 2*nd Edit.*

[2] *They are distinguished, &c.*] Ross again meets the author on the hypothesis, that no present difference between ice and crystal can prove that the one may never have been the other. "Crystal is not so much distinguished either in substance or accidents from ice, as a chick is from an egg, and yet the chick was an egg."—*Arcana*, 190.

[3] *For besides the spirit and mercurial principle, &c.*] Our author's notions of the chemical nature of rock-crystal are those of the alchemists, and are wholly unfounded. There is neither spirit, mercury, nor sulphur, in rock-crystal; at least, nothing to which those appellations can properly be applied: it is *silica*, or the earth of flints, in a pure crystallized form, itself composed of equal weights of *silicon* (a single combustible substance), and oxygen. It may be suspected, with some plausibility, however, that the notion of the alchemists, that

mable part, and that in no small quantity; for, besides its electric attraction, which is made by a sulphureous effluvium, it will strike fire upon percussion, like many other stones, and, upon collision with steel, actively send forth its sparks. not much inferiorly unto a flint. Now such bodies as strike fire,[4] as have sulphureous or ignitable parts within

such bodies as rock-crystal and the precious stones contained sulphur, might have arisen from their having, in some of their multifarious operations, actually separated its combustible base ; they always attributing combustibility to the presence of sulphur. Although they were altogether ignorant of the true nature of the processes which they employed, and of the effects which they witnessed, it cannot be doubted, that in their operations many of the simple as well as compound bodies, which modern chemists have described, would occasionally be evolved, though, in most instances, they would be caused again to enter into combination immediately, or be confounded with other well-known bodies, and, in either case, they would of course escape detection and record.—*Br.*

[4] *Now such bodies strike fire, as have, &c.*] The scientific reader might at first infer, from the perusal of this passage, that, as the *Pseudodoxia* was first published in 1646, our author had anticipated the celebrated Hooke in his experimental investigation of the nature of the sparks produced by the collision of flint and steel. A comparison, however, of the passage as it stands in the edition of 1672 (the last revised by the author), with the corresponding one in all the previous editions, and a reference to a further allusion to the subject in book iii. will show that Browne's statements on the subject were corrected and matured subsequently to the promulgation of Hooke's results, and that all his definite knowledge respecting it was borrowed from the latter, as, indeed, he has fairly, though indirectly, acknowledged. As the present annotator at first made the above inference himself, and (the subject being of some importance in the history of science) was induced to examine the seeming anticipation somewhat minutely, it may be as well to introduce here the entire examination ; this, while it proves that Browne's knowledge on the point was derived from Hooke, as just stated, will evince also the diligence with which he investigated, and the candour with which he adopted the discoveries of his contemporaries.

It will first be proper to cite the statement of Dr. Hooke.—He informs us in his *Micrographia* (published in 1665), p. 44—46, that, about eight years before, he came, from experiment, to the following conclusions : that a spark struck from a flint and steel was nothing else but a small piece of the steel or flint, but most commonly of the steel. which, by the violence of the stroke, is at the same time severed and heated red-hot, and that sometimes to such a degree, as to make it melt into a small globule of steel, and sometimes further to vitrify it ; phenomena which he ascribes to the existence in iron or steel of a very combustible sulphureous body " which the air very readily preys upon,

them, and those strike best which abound most in them. For these scintillations are not the accension of the air, upon the collision of two hard bodies, but rather the inflammable effluencies or vitrified sparks discharged from the bodies collided. For diamonds, marbles, heliotropes, and agaths, though hard bodies, will not readily strike fire with a

as soon as the body is a little violently heated." That such is truly the nature of such sparks he proves by experiment and by microscopical observation; and if we regard his supposition of the combustible sulphureous body in steel as merely another mode of describing the combustible nature of the metal, his explanation is perfectly correct, and in accordance with the results of modern chemical discovery: the oxygen in the air "preys upon" the metal, when heated by the percussion which separates it from the mass, converts it into an oxide, which the heat is also often sufficiently intense to vitrify.

In book iii. chap. xxi. of the *Pseudodoxia*, editions 1672 and 1686, we find the following recurrence to the collision of flint and steel, introduced in the discussion of another subject. "As first, how fire is stricken out of flints? That is, not by kindling the air from the collision of two hard bodies; for then diamonds should do the like better than flints; but rather from sulphureous, inflamed, and even *vitrified effluviums* and *particles*, as hath been observed of late."—(1672, p. 176; 1686, p. 124). Upon comparing these two passages from the editions of 1672 and 1686 with the corresponding passages in earlier editions, we find the following differences with respect to the point now before us. Book ii. chap. i.: the words, "or vitrified sparks," do not occur in the earlier editions. Book iii. chap. xxi.: instead of the words, "but rather from sulphureous, &c.," as above, to the end of the extract, in the editions of 1672 and 1686, we have in the earlier editions only these: "but rather from the sulphur and inflammable effluviums contained in them."

It is clear, therefore, that the *Micrographia* of Hooke having appeared in the interval between the publication of the first and that of the sixth edition of the *Pseudodoxia*, our author had perused the work of his great contemporary, and interwoven the results of his experimental investigation of the phenomena of the collision of steel with hard bodies with his own previous hypothetical explanation of them—adding, in the first notice of the subject, to the expression, "inflammable effluencies," that of "or vitrified sparks," and also introducing the words, "vitrified" and "particles," into the second.

Browne is in error, however, with respect to diamonds, heliotropes, and agates; all which, if their shape be adapted to the purpose, will readily strike fire with steel, and also with each other. If by "marble" he means, as is most probable, the more beautiful rocks and mineral substances employed in building and ornamental architecture in general, he is further in error; for most of these will also strike fire; but few of the substances, however, to which the term marble is now usually applied, possess that property.—*Br*.

steel, much less with one another. Nor a flint so readily with a steel if they both be very wet, for then the sparks are sometimes quenched in the eruption.

It containeth also a salt,[5] and that in some plenty, which may occasion its fragility, as is also observable in coral. This is separable by the art of chemistry, unto the operations whereof, as calcination, reverberation, sublimation, distillation, it is liable, with other concretions. And in the preparation of crystal Paracelsus[*] hath made a rule for that of gems. Briefly, it consisteth of parts so far from an icy dissolution, that powerful menstruums are made for its emollition, whereby it may receive the tincture of minerals, and so resemble gems (as Boetius hath declared in the distillation of urine, spirits of wine, and turpentine); and is not only triturable, and reducible into powder by contrition, but will subsist in a violent fire, and endure a vitrification. Whereby are testified its earthy and fixed parts: for vitrification is the last work of fire,[6] and a fusion of the salt and earth, which are the fixed elements of the composition, wherein the fusible salt draws the earth and infusible part into one *continuum;* and, therefore, ashes will not run from whence the salt is drawn, as bone ashes prepared for the test of metals. Common fusion in metals is also made by a violent heat, acting upon the volatile and fixed, the dry and humid parts of those bodies; which, notwithstanding, are so united that, upon attenuation from heat, the humid parts will not fly away, but draw the fixed ones into fluor with them. Ordinary liquation, in wax and oily bodies, is made by a gentler heat, where the oil and salt, the fixed and fluid principles, will not easily separate. All which, whether by vitrification,

* Paracelsus *de præparationibus.*

[5] *It containeth also a salt.*] It is scarcely requisite to observe that this statement is not correct, and must have originated in some mistake in conducting chemical experiments on rock-crystal.—*Br.*

[6] *for vitrification, &c.*] Instead of the remainder of this paragraph (altered in the 2nd edition) *Ed.* 1646 reads thus:—" For vitrification is the last work of fire, and when that arriveth, humidity is exhaled, for powdered glass emits no fume or exhalation, although it be laid upon red-hot iron. And, therefore, when some commend the powder of burnt glass against the stone, they fall not under my comprehension, who cannot conceive how a body should be farther burnt which hath already passed the extreamest test of fire."

fusion, or liquation, being forced into fluent consistencies, do naturally regress into their former solidities. Whereas, the melting of ice is a simple resolution, or return from solid to fluid parts, wherein it naturally resteth.

As for colour, although crystal, in its pellucid body, seems to have none at all, yet in its reduction into powder, it hath a vail and shadow of blue; and in its coarser pieces is of a sadder hue than the powder of Venice glass;[7] and this complexion it will maintain, although it long endure the fire. Which, notwithstanding, needs not move us unto wonder; for vitrified and pellucid bodies are of a clearer complexion in their continuities than in their powders and atomical divisions. So *stibium*, or glass of antimony, appears somewhat red in glass, but in its powder yellow; so painted glass of a sanguine red will not ascend in powder above a murrey.[8]

As for the figure of crystal (which is very strange, and forced Pliny to despair of resolution), it is for the most part hexagonal, or six-cornered; being built upon a confused matter, from whence, as it were from a root, angular figures arise, even as in the amethyst and basaltes. Which regular figuration hath made some opinion, it hath not its determination from circumscription, or as conforming unto contiguities, but rather from a seminal root, and formative principle of its own,[9] even as we observe in several other concre-

---

[7] *Venice glass.*] A glass made at Venice, of a pebble called *cuogolo*, resembling white marble, found in the bed of the Tesino.

[8] *murrey.*] Dark, purplish, red: used in this sense by Bacon and Boyle.

[9] *formative principle of its own.*] With respect to rock-crystal, and also gallstones and other substances, as he observes, this is perfectly true: their crystalline forms are not impressed upon them by the surrounding bodies, but are the result of "a formative principle,"—the peculiar molecular attraction which is inherent in each substance. But all the bodies he subsequently mentions in this paragraph, as far as the *cornu ammonis* inclusive, although their forms also have undoubtedly arisen from formative principles of their own, do not owe their forms to crystalline attraction, but to *organization;* for they are all either parts of animals in a fossil state, or natural casts from them; which Browne, with the error common to his age, evidently supposes to be strictly mineral bodies, and not derived from animals; although, as is very remarkable, he actually, in his note to this passage, compares one of these fossils with a recent marine body belonging to the same natural group, the *echinidæ*.—See ch. v. of this book, sec. 10. In this

tions. So the stones, which are sometimes found in the gall of a man, are most triangular and pyramidal, although the figure of that part seems not to co-operate thereto. So the *asteria*, or *lapis stellaris* hath on it the figure of a star; so *lapis Judaicus* hath circular lines in length all down its body, and equidistant, as though they had been turned by art. So that we call a fairy-stone,* and is often found in gravel pits amongst us, being of an hemispherical figure, hath five double lines arising from the centre of its basis, which, if no accretion distract them, do commonly concur, and meet in the pole thereof. The figures are regular in many other stones, as in *belemnites, lapis anguinus, cornu ammonis*, and many more; as by those which have not the experience hereof, may be observed in their figures expressed by mineralogists. But ice receiveth its figure according unto the surface wherein it concreteth, or the circumambiency which conformeth it. So it is plain upon the surface of water, but round in hail, which is also a glaciation, and figured in its guttulous descent from the air, and so growing greater[1] or lesser according unto the accretion or pluvious aggelation about the mother and fundamental atoms thereof; which seems to be some feathery particles of snow, although snow itself be sexangular, or at least of a starry and many-pointed figure.

They are also differenced in the places of their generation; for, though crystal be found in cold countries, and where ice remaineth long, and the air exceedeth in cold, yet is it also found in regions where ice is seldom seen, or soon dissolved:

---

* Which seemeth to be *echinites decima Aldrovandi; Musæi Metallici*, lib. 4. Rather *echinometrites*, as best resembling the *echinometra* found commonly on our sea shore.

point, however, our author's distinction of crystal from ice is fallacious; for although the latter (as well as the former also occasionally) receives its figure from that of the bodies upon or among which it is formed; it, too, has a formative principle of its own, and occasionally crystallizes; its *structure* being always crystalline, even when its external form, as in general, is amorphous.—*Br.*

[1] *and so, &c.*] Thus altered in the 2nd edition. *Ed.* 1646 reads— "And, therefore, Aristotle, in his Meteors, concludeth that hail which is not round is congealed nearer the earth, for that which falleth from on high is, by the length of its journey, corraded, and descendeth, therefore, in a lesser magnitude, but in a greater rotundity unto us."

as Pliny and Agricola relate of Cyprus, Caramania, and an island in the Red Sea. It hath been also found in the veins of minerals, sometimes agglutinated unto lead,[2] sometimes in rocks, opacous stones, and the marble face of Octavius, duke of Parma.* It hath also constant veins: as, besides others, that of mount Salvino, about the territory of Bergamo, from whence, if part be taken, in no long tract of time, out of the same place, as from its mineral matrix, others are observed to arise. Which made the learned Cerautus to conclude, *videant hi an sit glacies, an verò corpus fossile.* It is also found sometimes in common earth. But as for ice, it will not readily concrete but in the approachment of the air, as we have made trial in glasses of water, covered an inch with oil, which will not easily freeze in the hardest frosts of our climate. For water commonly concreteth first in its surface, and so conglaciates downward; and so will it do, although it be exposed in the coldest metal of lead, which well accordeth with that expression of Job, " the waters are hid as with a stone, and the face of the deep is frozen." † But whether water which hath been boiled or heated doth sooner receive this congelation, as commonly is delivered, we rest in the experiment of Cabeus,[3] who hath rejected the same in his excellent discourse of meteors.

They have contrary qualities elemental, and uses medicinal; for ice is cold and moist, of the quality of water; but crystal is cold and dry, according to the condition of earth. The use of ice is condemned by most physicians, that of crystal commended by many. For, although Dioscorides and Galen have left no mention thereof, yet hath Matthiolus, Agricola, and many, commended it in dysenteries and fluxes; all, for the increase of milk, most chemists, for the stone, and some, as Brassavolus and Boëtius, as an antidote against poison. Which occult and specifical operations are not expectable from ice; for, being but water congealed, it can never make

* Wherein the sculptor found a piece of pure crystal.   † Chap. 38.

[2] *sometimes agglutinated, &c.*] This, and the two following sentences were added in the 3rd edition.

[3] *Cabeus.*] Nicol. Cabeus, *In libros Meteorologicorum Aristotelis Commentaria et Quæstiones,* 4 tom. fol. Romæ, 1646. This passage was added in *Ed.* 1650.

good such qualities, nor will it reasonably admit of secret proprieties, which are the affections of forms and compositions at distance from their elements.

Having thus declared what crystal is not, it may afford some satisfaction to manifest what it is. To deliver, therefore, what, with the judgment of approved authors and best reason consisteth.—It is a mineral body, in the difference of stones,[4] and reduced by some unto that subdivision which comprehendeth gems; transparent, and resembling glass or ice, made of a lentous percolation[5] of earth, drawn from the most pure and limpid juice thereof, owing unto the coldness of the earth some concurrence or coadjuvancy, but not immediate determination and efficiency, which are wrought by the hand of its concretive spirit, the seeds of petrification and *Gorgon* of itself. As sensible philosophers[6] conceive of the generation of diamonds, iris,[7] beryls; not making them of frozen icicles, or from mere aqueous and glaciable substances, condensing them by frosts into solidities, vainly to be expected even from polary congelations, but from thin and finest earths, so well contempered and resolved, that transparency is not hindered, and containing lapidifical spirits, able to make good their solidities against the opposition and activity of outward contraries; and so leave a sensible difference between the bonds of glaciation, which, in the mountains of ice about the northern seas, are easily dissolved by ordinary heat of the sun, and between the finer ligatures of petrification whereby not only the harder concretions of diamonds and saphires, but the softer veins of crystal remain indis-

[4] *In the difference of stones.*] That is, "in the class or *division* of stones."

[5] *a lentous percolation.*] Dr. Johnson explains the word *lentous* (for which he cites no other authority than Browne) as meaning *viscous* and *tenacious*; but it is evidently used here to express "a *gradual* filtration or straining."

[6] *as sensible philosophers.*] Instead of the remainder of this paragraph (so altered in 3rd edition), *Ed.* 1646 has the following passage:—"as we may conceive in stones and gems; as diamonds, beryls, saphires and the like, whose generation we cannot with satisfaction confine unto the remote activity of the sun, or the common operation of coldness in the earth, but may more safely refer it unto a lapidificall siccity and congelitive principle, which determines prepared materials unto special concretions."

[7] *iris.*] Perhaps he refers to opal, or irisated quartz.

solvable in scorching territories, and the negro land of Congo.

And, therefore, I fear⁸ we commonly consider subterraneities not in contemplations sufficiently respective unto the creation. For, though Moses have left no mention of minerals, nor made any other description than suits unto the apparent and visible creation, yet is there, unquestionably, a very large class of creatures in the earth, far above the condition of elementarity. And, although not in a distinct and indisputable way of vivency, or answering in all points the properties or affections of plants, yet in inferior and descending constitutions they do, like these, contain specifical distinctions, and are determined by seminalities, that is, created and defined seeds committed unto the earth from the beginning. Wherein, although they attain not the indubitable requisites of animation, yet have they a near affinity thereto. And, though we want a proper name and expressive appellation, yet are they not to be closed up in the general name of concretions, or lightly passed over, as only elementary and subterraneous mixtions.

The principal and most gemmary affection is its tralucency:⁹ as for irradiancy or sparkling, which is found in many gems, it is not discoverable in this, for it cometh short of their compactness and durity; and, therefore, requireth not the emery, as the saphire, granite, and topaz, but will receive impression from steel, in a manner like the turquoise. As for its diaphanity or perspicuity, it enjoyeth that most eminently; and the reason thereof is its continuity, as having its earthy and salinous parts so exactly resolved, that its body is left imporous, and not discreted by atomical terminations. For that continuity of parts is the cause of perspicuity,¹ is made perspicuous by two ways of

⁸ *And, therefore, I fear.*] This paragraph gives an excellent and very accurate view of the nature of the beings composing the mineral kingdom,—if by "seeds" we understand *formative principles.—Br.*

⁹ *tralucency.*] For "translucency." Johnson gives *tralucent,* citing Davies and B. Jonson—but not *tralucency.*

¹ *continuity of parts is the cause of perspicuity.*] The explanation of the cause of transparency in this paragraph is quite accurate, so far as it goes; but to make it satisfactory, it must be added, that continuity of parts is necessary to transparency, because, in that case, the refrac-

experiment. That is, either in effecting transparency in those bodies which were not so before, or at least far short of the additional degree: so snow becomes transparent upon liquation; so horns and bodies resolvable into continued parts or jelly; the like is observable in oiled paper, wherein, the interstitial divisions being continuated by the accession of oil, it becometh more transparent, and admits the visible rays with less umbrosity. Or else the same is effected by rendering those bodies opacous which were before pellucid and perspicuous: so glass, which was before diaphanous, being by powder reduced into multiplicity of superficies, becomes an opacous body, and will not transmit the light: so it is in crystal powdered, and so it is also before, for if it be made hot in a crucible, and presently projected upon water, it will grow dim, and abate its diaphanity: for the water, entering the body, begets a division of parts, and a termination of atoms united before unto continuity.[2]

The ground of this opinion[3] might be, first, the conclusions of some men from experience; for as much as crystal is found sometimes in rocks, and in some places not much unlike the stirious or stillicidious dependencies of ice.[4] Which,

---

tive effect upon the rays of light is uniform throughout the body, so that the rays (however those which do not fall upon the surface in a direction perpendicular to it may be diverted from their original course,) come unbroken to the eye; whereas, when the continuity is broken, as in the case of powdered glass, the interstices of which are filled with air, which has a different refractive power from the particles of glass, the rays are again and again broken, and turned from their course, so that they cannot reach the eye *through* the substance, so as to present images of the bodies on the other side.—*Br.*

[2] *for if it be made hot, &c.*] This statement also is generally true, but the cause of the opacity produced is not the entering of the water into the crystal, but its being filled with cracks arising from the sudden cooling, and these, whether filled with water or with air, having a different refractive power from the crystal itself, an effect takes place corresponding to that explained above.

It may be observed, upon the whole, that there is much excellent reasoning and much real science in this chapter, but mingled, of course, with occasional fallacies, and with some now antiquated prejudices. —*Br.*

[3] *The ground of this opinion.*] Namely, "that crystal is ice congealed beyond liquation."

[4] *the stirious or stillicidious, &c.*] *Stirious,* like icicles: *stillicidious,* falling in drops.

notwithstanding, may happen, either in places which have been forsaken or left bare by the earth, or may be petrifications, or mineral indurations, like other gems, proceeding from percolations of the earth disposed unto such concretions.

The second and most common ground is from the name *crystallus*, whereby in Greek both ice and crystal are expressed; which many not duly considering, have, from their community of name, conceived a community of nature, and what was ascribed unto the one, not unfitly appliable unto the other. But this is a fallacy of equivocation, from a society in name inferring an identity in nature. By this fallacy was he deceived that drank *aqua fortis* for strong water:[5] by this are they deluded who conceive *spermaceti*, which is found about the head, to be the spawn of the whale; or take *sanguis draconis*, which is the gum of a tree, to be the blood of a dragon. By the same logic we may infer the crystalline humour of the eye, or rather the crystalline heaven above, to be of the substance of crystal here below; or that God sendeth down crystal, because it is delivered in the vulgate translation, Ps. 47: *mittit crystallum suum sicut buccellas*. Which translation, although it literally express the septuagint, yet is there no more meant thereby than what our translation in plain English expresseth, that is, "he casteth forth his ice like morsels;" or what Tremellius and Junius as clearly deliver, *dejicit gelu suum sicut frusta, coram frigore ejus quis consistet?* which proper and Latin expressions, had they been observed in ancient translations, elder expositors had not been misguided by the synonymy: nor had they afforded occasion unto Austin, the Gloss,[6] Lyranus, and many others, to have taken up the common conceit, and spoken of this text conformably unto the opinion rejected.

[5] aqua fortis, &c.] An Englishman gave occasion to this error; who, translating that tract (of the French Ld. ****) of Salt and Fire, renders it so, out of a gross pernicious ignorance, which I wisht might be corrected.—*Wr.*

[6] *the Gloss.*] Referring probably to the annotations of Walafridus Strabo, who flourished in the ninth century. They were called *glossa ordinaria*, and for many years were received as the only authorized interpretation of the Bible. The best edition of the Gloss of Strabo, as well of the *Postilla*, or expositions of Nicolas de Lyra, or Lyranus, was published in folio, at Antwerp, in 1684.

CHAPTER II.

Concerning the Loadstone: of things particularly spoken thereof, evidently or probably true.

AND first, we conceive the earth to be a magnetical body.[7] A magnetical body, we term, not only that which hath a power attractive, but that which, seated in a convenient medium, naturally disposeth itself to one invariable and fixed

---

[7] *And first, we conceive the earth, &c.*] The chapter which begins with this opinion, though containing many errors, is yet characterized by the sagacity and acuteness so often displayed by the author in treating of a complex and difficult subject of science, and also by those philosophic views in which he occasionally anticipated the most profound results attained in the modern investigations of the powers of nature. The remark now immediately before us partakes, in all respects, of the character of the chapter itself. That the earth is "a magnetical body," in the senses in which we apply that term to the magnet itself, and to the metals, iron, nickel, and some others, is a notion for which there is no foundation whatever; nor have we any reason for supposing that the "polary position" of the earth, or the direction of its axis in space, is produced by magnetism. And further, there is a deep error in philosophy in the fundamental notion of the author, that a magnetical body, as he defines it, naturally "disposeth itself" to one invariable and fixed situation; the fact being, as all the phenomena of magnetism conspire to evince, that magnetized bodies which apparently possess that property are in reality *disposed to it*, by the influence of a subtle agent permeating them, and the action of which is in some unknown manner connected with an arrangement in space, having a particular relation to the figure and position, and probably to some of the material constituents also of the earth. Supposing it to be true (which at present, however, we have no reason to suppose) that if the whole earth could be violently removed, it would "return unto its polary position again," that effect would not result from an inherent virtue in the planet itself, but from its being so constituted as to receive and obey the action of the vortical or other motions of the subtle ethereal fluid, in which (from the recent investigations of Encke and others) we now know it to be placed, and by which also we know it to be pervaded: this would cause it to return to its position, much in the same way as a ball held by strings in a particular position returns to that position after displacement, by their action upon it; or, which is a closer representation of the circumstances, as a magnetic needle, after disturbance, returns to its original direction, to the magnetic north and south, by the force of terrestrial magnetism acting upon it.—*Br.*

situation. And such a magnetical virtue we conceive to be in the globe of the earth, whereby, as unto its natural points and proper terms, it disposeth itself unto the poles; being so framed, constituted, and ordered unto these points, that those parts which are now at the poles, would not naturally abide unto the equator, nor Greenland remain in the place of Magellanica. And if the whole earth were violently removed, yet would it not forego its primitive points, nor pitch in the east or west, but return unto its polary position again. For, though by compactness or gravity it may acquire the lowest place, and become the centre of the universe,⁸ yet, that it makes good that point, not varying at all by the accession of bodies upon, or secession thereof from its surface, perturbing the equilibration of either hemisphere (whereby the altitude of the stars might vary), or that it strictly maintains the north and southern points, that neither upon the motions of the heavens, air, and winds without, large eruptions and divisions of parts within its polary parts, should never incline or veer unto the equator (whereby the latitude of places should also vary), it cannot so well be salved from gravity, as a magnetical verticity. This is, probably, that foundation the wisdom of the Creator hath laid unto the earth; in this sense we may more nearly apprehend, and sensibly make out the expressions of holy scripture, as, *Firmavit orbem terræ qui non commovebitur*, "he hath made the round world so sure, that it cannot be moved;"* as when it is said by Job, *extendit aquilonem super vacuo, &c.*, "he stretcheth forth the north upon the empty place, and hangeth the earth upon nothing."† And this is the most probable answer unto that great question, "Whereupon are the foundations of the earth fastened, or who laid the corner-stone thereof?" Had they been acquainted with this principle, Anaxagoras, Socrates, and Democritus, had better made out the ground of this stability; Xenophanes had not been fain to say, the earth

* Psalm xciii.   † Job xxxviii.

⁸ *and become the centre of the universe.*] It must be borne in mind that the author was not a convert to the Copernican system of astronomy. His opposite opinions on this science will be observed to pervade all his reasonings, and to tinge all his feelings.

hath no bottom; and Thales Milesius, to make it swim in water.[9]

Nor is the vigour of this great body included only in itself, or circumferenced by its surface, but diffused at indeterminate distances through the air, water, and all bodies circumjacent; exciting and impregnating magnetical bodies within its surface or without it, and performing, in a secret and invisible way, what we evidently behold effected by the loadstone. For these effluxions penetrate all bodies, and like the species of visible objects are ever ready in the medium, and lay hold on all bodies proportionate or capable of their action; those bodies likewise, being of a congenerous nature, do readily receive the impressions of their motor; and, if not fettered by their gravity, conform themselves to situations wherein they best unite unto their animator. And this will sufficiently appear from the observations that are to follow, which can no better way be made out, than by this we speak of, the magnetical vigour of the earth.[1] Now, whether these effluviums do fly by striated atoms and winding particles, as Renatus des Cartes conceiveth, or glide by streams attracted from either pole and hemisphere of the earth unto the equator, as Sir Kenelm Digby excellently declareth, it takes not away[2] this virtue of the earth; but more distinctly sets down the gests and progress thereof, and are conceits of emi-

---

[9] *water.*] The first edition continues thus:—"Now whether the earth stand still, or moveth circularly, we may concede this magnetical stability: for although it move, in that conversion the poles and centre may still remain the same, as is conceived in the magnetical bodies of heaven, especially Jupiter and the sun; which, according to Galileus, Kepler, and Fabricius, are observed to have dinetical motions and certain revolutions about their proper centres; and though the one in about the space of ten days, the other in less than one, accomplish this revolution, yet do they observe a constant habitude unto their poles, and firme themselves thereon in their gyration."

[1] *the magnetical vigour of the earth.*] Having stated, in the preceding note, in what sense we are not to regard the earth as a magnet, we may now admit that in the sense of a body permeated by the magnetic fluid (whatever that may be) the earth may be regarded as a great complex magnet, or rather as a collection of substances, many of which, under certain circumstances, are susceptible of the magnetic influence, and display accordingly magnetic phenomena.—*Br.*

[2] *it takes not away.*] Read, "they take not away, &c." viz. "Neither of these opinions takes away, &c."—*Wr.*

nent use to salve magnetical phenomena. And, as in astronomy, those hypotheses (though never so strange) are best esteemed which best do salve appearances, so surely in philosophy those principles (though seeming monstrous) may with advantage be embraced, which best confirm experiment, and afford the readiest reason of observation. And truly the doctrine of effluxions,[3] their penetrating natures, their invisible paths, and insuspected effects, are very considerable; for, besides this magnetical one of the earth, several effusions there may be from divers other bodies, which invisibly act their parts at any time, and, perhaps, through any medium; a part of philosophy but yet in discovery, and will, I fear, prove the last leaf to be turned over in the book of nature.

First, therefore, it is true, and confirmable by every experiment, that steel and good iron never excited by the loadstone, discover in themselves a verticity;[4] that is, a directive or polary faculty, whereby, conveniently placed, they do septentrionate* at one extreme, and australise† at another. This is manifestable in long and thin plates of steel perforated in the middle and equilibrated; or by an easier way in long wires equiponderate with untwisted silk

* Point to the north. † Point to the south.

[3] *And truly the doctrine of effluxions.*] The remarks in the passage commencing with these words may be considered to have been made good by the discoveries of the present century, if we regard the notion of "effluxions" to result from an obscure perception of the existence and functions of those ethereal fluids, to the motions of which the united results of modern science lead us to attribute the phenomena of heat, light, electricity, magnetism, &c. It is requisite, however, to observe, that what Browne, as well as some of his predecessors and contemporaries, appears to have supposed to consist of subtle *emanations* from grosser bodies, must be regarded contrariwise, agreeably to the most profound researches of our time, as the principles from which all ordinary ponderable matter derives its activity—from which it takes all its force and energy.—*Br.*

[4] *steel and good iron, &c.*] This, in the sense in which the author intends us to understand it, is an error; unmagnetized iron or steel has no directive power; the experiments apparently alluded to must have been performed with steel plates, wires, and needles, which had, in reality, become magnetic, although they might not have been actually "excited by the loadstone." As an observation that the magnetic virtue is possessed by bodies which have not been so excited, it is quite worthy of Browne.—*Br.*

and soft wax; for, in this manner pendulous, they will conform themselves meridionally, directing one extreme unto the north, another to the south. The same is also manifested in steel wires thrust through little spheres or globes of cork and floated on the water, or in naked needles gently let fall thereon; for, so disposed, they will not rest until they have found out the meridian, and as near as they can, lie parallel unto the axis of the earth; sometimes the eye, sometimes the point, northward in divers needles, but the same point always in most; conforming themselves unto the whole earth, in the same manner as they do unto every loadstone. For, if a needle untouched be hanged above a loadstone, it will convert into a parallel position thereto; for in this situation it can best receive its verticity, and be excited proportionably at both extremes. Now this direction proceeds, not primitively from themselves, but is derivative and contracted from the magnetical effluxions of the earth, which they have winded in their hammering and formation, or else, by long continuance in one position, as we shall declare hereafter.

It is likewise true what is delivered of irons heated in the fire, that they contract a verticity in their refrigeration;[5]

[5] *They contract a verticity, &c.*] The statements here made, to the end of the period, are probably true, provided the cooling takes place in a direction corresponding, or nearly corresponding, to that of the dip; but the extent to which they are true, so far as modern experiments afford us the means of verifying them, may be best seen, perhaps, by comparing them with the following observations made by Mr. Barlow, and published in the *Encyclopædia Metropolitana*, Treatise on Magnetism, § v. 38, 39:—For certain purposes of research, which it is unnecessary here to state, Mr. Barlow heated in a furnace a bar of soft iron and a bar of cast-iron, nearly of equal dimensions, placing them in an inclined position, in the direction of the dip of the needle, and ascertaining their attractive effect upon the horizontal or common magnetic needle previously to the application of heat. As soon as the bars arrived at a high blood-red heat, they began to exercise an increased power of attraction upon the needle, and in a minute or two this attained its maximum, which was far greater than the attractive power of the bars when cold; the deviation produced by one of them being in the latter case 24° 20′, but in the former, 78° 30′. In the course of these experiments the following facts were observed, which bear directly upon the passage of our author now before us:—" It should be observed here, that the great attraction produced by the heat did not subside with it, provided the bar remained in its place undis-

for, heated red-hot and cooled in the meridian from north to south, they presently contract a polary power, and being poised in air or water, convert that part unto the north which respected that point in its refrigeration; so that if they had no sensible verticity before, it may be acquired by this way, or if they had any, it might be exchanged by contrary position in the cooling. For by the fire they amit not only many drossy and scorious parts, but whatsoever they had received either from the earth or loadstone; and so being naked and despoiled of all verticity, the magnetical atoms invade their bodies with more effect and agility.[6]

turbed; for after some days it was found that the power of the bar continued just the same as at the time of making the experiment when it had not been displaced; but then the bar upon trial was always found to possess a certain degree of fixed magnetism, its other extremity producing an opposite effect upon the needle; but if the bar was inverted, while it retained any visible colour from the heat, both ends produced exactly the same deflection: as to the magnetic effect to which we have alluded above, it was lost, or at least a great part of it, after leaving the bar for some time horizontal, or, after its being thrown about with other pieces of iron."—*Br.*

[6] *For by the fire they amit, &c. . . . . whatsoever they had received either from the earth or loadstone; and so, &c.*] This statement is true in itself, but unless viewed in connexion with other facts it may produce an erroneous impression upon the mind. Mr. Barlow's experiments have also elucidated this subject; his results on which will be appropriately introduced by an historical notice of it, derived from the Treatise on Magnetism cited in the preceding note, from which the comparative amount and nature of our author's knowledge respecting it may be inferred, by contrasting it with his own remarks. "The effect of temperature, in changing and destroying the magnetic power of iron bodies had been long imperfectly known, but it had never been satisfactorily established prior to Mr. Barlow's experiments. It is, for example, stated in Newton's *Optics*, that red-hot iron has no magnetic property, while Father Kircher asserts, that the magnet will attract red-hot iron as well as cold; Mr. Cavallo again found, that although iron at a red heat had a greater power over the magnet than when cold, yet at the white heat it had less; but he was not aware that it was entirely lost at a white heat."—(*Encyc. Metrop.* Magnetism, § vi. 41.) The last-mentioned fact, viz. that the magnetic action of iron is destroyed by a white heat, was ascertained by Mr. Barlow in the experiments already noticed, and he observed, on the same occasion, an extraordinary phænomenon, the consideration of which will explain some of the apparently contradictory facts which are related by our author in this chapter. It is, that "after the iron loses its entire power of attraction at the white heat, it acquires, as that colour subsides into the bright red and red, an attractive power, the reverse of what it had

Neither is it only true what Gilbertus first observed, that irons refrigerated north and south acquire a directive faculty, but, if they be cooled upright and perpendicularly,[7] they will also obtain the same: that part which is cooled towards the north, on this side of the equator, converting itself unto the north, and attracting the south point of the needle; the other and highest extreme respecting the south, and attracting the northern, according unto the laws magnetical: for (what must be observed) contrary poles or faces attract each other, as the north the south; and the like decline each other, as the north the north. Now on this side[8] of the equator, that extreme which is next the earth is animated unto the north, and the contrary unto the south, so that in coition it applies itself quite oppositely, the coition or attraction being contrary to the verticity or direction. Contrary, if we speak according unto common use, yet alike, if we conceive the virtue of the north pole to diffuse itself, and open at the south, and the south at the north again.

This polarity from refrigeration, upon extremity, and in defect of a loadstone, might serve to invigorate and touch a needle any where; and this, allowing variation, is also the readiest way at any season to discover the north or south; and surely far more certain than what is affirmed of the

been when cold; so that if the bar and needle are so situated that the north end [of the needle] is attracted when the iron is cold, the south end will be attracted during the above interval," that is, while it is passing through the high temperatures indicated by the shades of colour just mentioned; after which the usual attractive power again takes place in the increased degree stated in the preceding note.—*Br.*

[7] *but if they be cooled upright, &c.*] This statement is quite accurate; and, in fact, a nearly perpendicular position is more favourable to the reception of magnetism by the iron than the horizontal. The effect depends upon the suitable position of the iron for receiving and retaining a portion of the magnetism of the earth, and the position in which the greatest effect is exerted by the earth's magnetism is when the iron is placed in the position of the *dipping needle*; that is, inclined to the magnetic north at an angle (in these latitudes, and at the *present* time) of about 69¾ degrees with the horizon. The subject is resumed, and with equal correctness, towards the end of the next paragraph, which has evidently been written from experiment. Both are replete with just representations of the facts.—*Br.*

[8] *Now on this side, &c.*] Itt is certainly knowne that beyond the line the needle keeps his posture to the north, as truly as att the first setting out of England.—*Wr.*

grains and circles in trees, or the figure in the root of fern. For if we erect a red-hot wire until it cool, then hang it up with wax and untwisted silk, where the lower end and that which cooled next the earth doth rest, that is the northern point; and this we affirm will still be true, whether it be cooled in the air or extinguished in water, oil of vitriol, *aqua fortis*, or quicksilver. And this is also evidenced in culinary utensils, and irons that often feel the force of fire, as tongs, fire-shovels, prongs, and andirons; all of which acquire a magnetical and polary condition, and, being suspended, convert their lower extremes unto the north; with the same attracting the southern point of the needle. For easier experiment, if we place a needle touched at the foot of tongs or andirons, it will obvert or turn aside its lily or north point, and conform its *cuspis* or south extreme unto the andiron. The like verticity, though more obscurely, is also contracted by bricks and tiles,[9] as we have made trial in some taken out of the backs of chimneys. Now, to contract this direction, there needs not a total ignition, nor is it necessary the irons should be red-hot all over. For if a wire be heated only at one end, according as that end is cooled upward or downward, it respectively acquires a verticity, as we have declared in wires totally candent. Nor is it absolutely requisite they should be cooled perpendicularly, or strictly lie in the meridian; for, whether they be refrigerated inclinatorily or somewhat equinoxially, that is, towards the eastern or western points, though in a lesser degree, they discover some verticity.

Nor is this only true in irons, but in the loadstone itself.

---

[9] *The like verticity, &c.*] The cause of this is doubtless the magnetism acquired by the particles of oxide of iron disseminated throughout the clay of which bricks and tiles are made, and which, of course, remain distributed in the same sensibly uniform manner in the bricks and tiles themselves. Each particle itself acquiring, by being placed in a position not greatly deviating from that of the dipping needle, magnetical polarity of the same kind as the rest, the result is a general polarity of all, which, freely permeating the earthy matter, appears to be possessed by the brick or tile itself. Assuming the author's experiment to be correct (and this there is no reason to doubt), such must be the explanation of the facts. The subject will be resumed under another form, when commenting upon the passage "*Of rocks magnetical*," in the following chapter.—*Br.*

For if a loadstone be made red-hot, it loseth the magnetical vigour it had before in itself, and acquires another from the earth in its refrigeration; for that part which cooleth toward the earth will acquire the respect of the north, and attract the southern point or *cuspis* of the needle. The experiment hereof we made in a loadstone of a parallelogram or long square figure; wherein only inverting the extremes, as it came out of the fire, we altered the poles or faces thereof at pleasure.

It is also true what is delivered of the direction and coition of irons, that they contract a verticity by long and continued position; that is, not only being placed from north to south, and lying in the meridian, but respecting the zenith and perpendicular unto the centre of the earth; as is manifest in bars of windows, casements, hinges, and the like. For if we present the needle unto their lower extremes, it wheels about and turns its southern point unto them. The same condition in long time do bricks contract which are placed in walls, and, therefore, it may be a fallible way to find out the meridian by placing the needle on a wall; for some bricks therein, by a long and continued position, are often magnetically enabled to distract the polarity of the needle. And, therefore, those irons which are said to have been converted into loadstones, whether they were real conversions or only attractive augmentations, might be much promoted by this position: as the iron cross of an hundred weight upon the church of St. John, in Ariminum, or that loadstoned iron of Cæsar Moderatus, set down by Aldrovandus.*[1]

Lastly, irons do manifest a verticity, not only upon refrigeration and constant situation, but (what is wonderful, and advanceth the magnetical hypothesis) they evidence the same by mere position, according as they are inverted, and their extremes disposed respectively unto the earth. For if an iron or steel, not firmly excited, be held perpendicularly or inclinatorily unto the needle, the lower end thereof will attract the *cuspis* or southern point; but if the same extreme be inverted and held under the needle, it will then

---

* *De Mineralibus.*

· **And, therefore, those irons, &c.**] Added in the 2nd edition.

attract the lilly or northern point ; for by inversion it changeth its direction acquired before, and receiveth a new and southern polarity from the earth, as being the upper extreme.[2] Now, if an iron be touched before, it varieth not in this manner; for then it admits not this magnetical impression, as being already informed by the loadstone, and polarily determined by its preaction.

And from these grounds may we best determine why the northern pole of the loadstone attracted a greater weight than the southern on this side the equator; why the stone is best preserved in a natural and polary situation ; and why, as Gilbertus observeth, it respecteth that pole, out of the earth, which it regarded in its mineral bed and subterraneous position.

It is likewise true and wonderful, what is delivered of the inclination or declination of the loadstone;[3] that is, the de-

---

[2] *For if an iron or steel, &c.*] The magnetism of the earth appears to emanate from it in curves, originating far within the earth, or perhaps at its centre, their planes being magnetic meridians, but which, for small distances, are sensibly straight lines. The angles which they form with the horizon, or, what is practically the same, with the earth's surface, is the angle of the dip of the needle for each latitude respectively, being, as already stated, about $69\frac{3}{4}$ degrees for the British Islands at the present time. The dipping needle, therefore, is nothing but a magnetized body freely obeying the tendency imparted to it by these curves, and, in fact, exhibiting their direction at each particular spot. Now, if a bar of soft iron, or other body susceptible of magnetism, but perfectly free from it, be held in the direction of the dipping needle it acquires polarity, for the time, the lower end becoming a south pole, attracting the north end of a compass needle ; and the upper a north pole, attracting the south end of the needle. If the bar be inverted, but its direction still preserved, the end which was before the north pole will become the south pole, and *vice versâ*. If, however, it has already received permanent magnetism, these effects do not take place ; agreeably to our author's statement.—*Br.*

[3] *inclination or declination of the loadstone.*] The phænomena described in this and the succeeding paragraph, are those of the *dip* of the magnetic needle, now usually observed by means of a needle placed in a circle divided into degrees, &c., in order to show the amount of the dip, or the angle formed with the horizon by the needle when allowed freely to obey the influence of terrestrial magnetism. The reader will be enabled to form correct ideas on this subject from the present brief remarks, if taken in conjunction with the three preceding notes, and also with the next, by the same annotator, in which the history of the dipping needle is continued.—*Br.*

scent of the needle below the plane of the horizon. For long needles, which stood before upon their axis parallel unto the horizon, being vigorously excited, incline and bend downward, depressing the north extreme below the horizon; that is, the north on this, the south on the other side of the equator; and at the very line or middle circle stand without deflexion. And this is evidenced, not only from observations of the needle in several parts of the earth, but sundry experiments in any part thereof, as in a long steel wire, equilibrated or evenly balanced in the air; for excited by a vigorous loadstone it will somewhat depress its animated extreme, and intersect the horizontal circumference. It is also manifest in a needle pierced through a globe of cork so cut away and pared by degrees, that it will swim under water, yet sink not unto the bottom, which may be well effected; for if the cork be a thought too light to sink under the surface, the body of the water may be attenuated with spirits of wine; if too heavy, it may be incrassated with salt; and if by chance too much be added, it may again be thinned by a proportionable addition of fresh water. If, then, the needle be taken out, actively touched, and put in again, it will depress and bow down its northern head toward the bottom, and advance its southern extremity towards the brim. This way, invented by Gilbertus, may seem of difficulty; the same, with less labour, may be observed in a needled sphere of cork equally contiguous unto the surface of the water; for if the needle be not exactly equiponderant, that end which is a thought too light, if touched, becometh even; that needle, also, which will but just swim under water, if forcibly touched, will sink deeper, and sometimes unto the bottom. If, likewise, that inclinatory virtue be destroyed by a touch from the contrary pole, that end which before was elevated will then decline; and this might perhaps be observed in some scales exactly balanced, and in such needles which, for their bulk, can hardly be supported by the water. For, if they be powerfully excited, and equally let fall, they commonly sink down and break the water at that extreme whereat they were septentrionally excited; and by this way it is conceived there may be some fraud in the weighing of precious commodities, and such as carry a value in quarter-grains, by placing a powerful loadstone above or below, according as we intend to depress or elevate one extreme.

Now if these magnetical emissions be only qualities, and the gravity of bodies incline them only unto the earth, surely that which alone moveth other bodies to descent, carrieth not the stroke in this, but rather the magnetical alliciency of the earth; unto which with alacrity it applieth itself, and in the very same way unto the whole earth, as it doth unto a single loadstone. For if an untouched needle be at a distance suspended over a loadstone, it will not hang parallel, but decline at the north extreme, and at that part will first salute its director. Again, what is also wonderful, this inclination is not invariable; for just under the line the needle lieth parallel with the horizon,[4] but sailing north or south it

---

[4] *just under the line, &c.*] This statement, in the terms in which it is made, is incorrect; for it is found by experiment, that while under the line or equator of the earth, in some places, the dip is still considerable, in some places south of the equator it continues to be north, and conversely in some places north of the equator it is south. But if we substitute *magnetic equator* for "the line" or true equator, and the *magnetic poles* for the poles of the earth, it becomes accurate. According to Mr. Barlow (*Phil. Trans.* 1831. p. 105), the results obtained by Sir E. Parry, and by the late Captain Foster, for the situation of the magnetic poles, give a *magnetic equator*, which cuts the true equator in about 14° east, and 166° west longitude.

The following principles of the geometrical construction of what is called the *magnetic sphere* will enable the reader accurately to estimate the degree of truth which exists in our author's remarks on terrestrial magnetism: they are derived from Mr. Barlow's "Treatise" already referred to, § xxii. 193. "The two centres which give direction to magnetised needles at the earth's surface, are situated in two points indefinitely near to each other in the centre of the terrestrial sphere. If we conceive the indefinitely short lines which unite these centres to be produced both ways to the surface, the diameter thus formed is called the *terrestrial magnetic axis*. The circle cutting this at right angles is the *terrestrial magnetic equator*; and the extremities of this axis, or diameter, are the poles of this equator, or the *terrestrial magnetic poles*.

"If the magnetic poles coincided with the poles of the earth, the magnetic equator would, in like manner, fall upon the terrestrial equator; and the magnetic and geographic meridians would also coincide, and the needle, in all places, would point duly north and south: moreover, a needle upon the equator would, in that case, be equally distant, and under equal influence from both poles, or rather from both centres, and would, therefore, have no dip or inclination.

"We know, however, that the needle does not everywhere point duly

beginneth to incline, and increaseth according as it approacheth unto either pole and would at last endeavour to erect itself.[5] And this is no more than what it doth upon the north and south, and that the circle on the globe, in which the needle has no inclination, is not coincident with the terrestrial equator."—*Br.*

[5] *would at last endeavour to erect itself.*] The phænomena thus predicted by the author from his (theoretically) correct reasoning, is actually found to occur.

Mr. Barlow gives a table containing the computed situation of the magnetic north pole of the earth, derived from twenty-three sets of observations on the dip, in different places, the results of those observations themselves being also given. From this it appears that Captain Parry found the dip, at Melville Island (N. Lat. 74° 47′, W. Long. 110° 48′), to be 88° 43′, deviating only 1° 17′ from the vertical position or 90°. Sir John Franklin observed a still closer approximation; finding the dip, in North America (N. Lat. 68° 18′, W. Long. 109° 25′) to be 89° 31′, or within less than half a degree of 90°. But the positions of the north magnetic pole computed from these observations differ; Capt. Parry's indicating it to be situated in N. Lat. 73° 12′, W. Long. 102° 46′, and Capt. Franklin's in N. Lat. 68° 50′, and W. Long. 107° 33′; while Mr. Barlow has more recently computed (*Phil. Trans.* 1831, p. 105) from the mean results of the observations of Capt. Parry and the late Capt. Foster, that the position of the magnetic axis is in N. and S. Lat. 72° and corresponding to W. Long. 76°. But further observations have been made in the last voyage of Capt. Ross, an account of which, by Commander J. C. Ross, was read before the Royal Society on the 19th December last, of which the following is an abstract, as given in the *Proceedings of the Royal Society*. "The author remarks that the discordances in former observations, made with a view to determine the position of the magnetic pole, have arisen partly from the irregularity of distribution in the earth of the substances which exert magnetic power, and partly from the great distances from the magnetic poles, at which these observations have been made. The latter cause of uncertainty has been now, in a great measure, removed, by the numerous and accurate observations made during the late arctic expeditions. The object of the present paper is to put on record those which were made in the last voyage of Capt. Ross, in which a spot was reached corresponding to the true north magnetic pole on the surface of the earth. The nature of the instruments, and the difficulties encountered in their practical employment, under the circumstances of the expedition, are fully stated. Having arrived, on the 1st of June, at N. Lat. 70° 5′ 17″, and W. Long. 96° 45′ 48″, the horizontal magnetic needle exhibited no determinate directive tendency, and the dipping needle was within a minute of the vertical position, a quantity which may be supposed to come within the limits of the errors of observation; hence the author concludes that this spot may be considered as the true magnetic pole, or as a very near approximation to it, as far, at least, as could be ascertained with the limited means of determination of which he was then in possession." The following extract from Mr. Barlow's treatise,

loadstone, and that more plainly upon the terrella or spherical magnet cosmographically set out with circles of the globe. For at the equator thereof, the needle will stand rectangularly; but approaching northward toward the tropic it will regard the stone obliquely, and when it attaineth the pole, directly; and if its bulk be no impediment, erect itself and stand perpendicularly thereon. And therefore, upon strict observation of this inclination in several latitudes and due records preserved, instruments are made, whereby, without the help of sun or star, the latitude of the place may be discovered. And yet it appears the observations of men have not as yet been so just and equal as is desirable, for, of those tables of declination which I have perused, there are not any two that punctually agree; though some have been thought exactly calculated, especially that which Ridley received from Mr. Briggs, in our time geometry professor in Oxford.

It is also probable, what is delivered concerning the variation of the compass, that is, the cause and ground thereof;

already referred to, will explain the apparent anomalies just described, and thus complete that general view of the subject which will enable the reader fully to appreciate our author's views and statements respecting it.

"On these results it may be observed that, although in determinations relative to the dip and variation of the needle, we cannot expect the utmost accuracy, yet it is very obvious from the preceding table, that the aberrations in the latitude and longitude of the magnetic pole are much greater than can be attributed to errors of observation. It will be seen that the place assigned to it differs in longitude as much as 57° between one set of observations and another, and as much as 14° in latitude. It will also be observed, that the more we approach the north and west, the more westerly we find the place of the pole; and the more easterly the place of observation, the greater is its latitude. In short, it is evident, from the few examples we have taken, that every place has its particular polarizing axis, which, probably in all cases, falls within the arctic circle; but that this is the narrowest limit we are able to assign; that is, the local attraction or particular influence which the compass in every place is under, besides that of the general directive power of the globe, is such, as to displace the needle so much from its natural direction, *as to give a different pole to almost every different set of observations*; so that instead of the magnetism of the earth possessing that degree of uniformity which appertains to a perfectly formed iron ball, it may rather be said to resemble that species of action which we might expect to find in an irregularly formed mass of iron, approximating in its general character to that of a globe, but not perfectly such."—*Br.*

for the manner, as being confirmed by observation, we shall not at all dispute. The variation of the compass is an arch of the horizon intercepted between the true and magnetical meridian; or more plainly, a deflexion and siding east and west from the true meridian. The true meridian is a major circle passing through the poles of the world, and the zenith or vertex of any place, exactly dividing the east from the west. Now on this line the needle exactly lieth not, but diverts and varieth its point, that is the north point on this side the equator, the south on the other; sometimes unto the east, sometimes towards the west, and in some few places varieth not at all. First, therefore, it is observed that, betwixt the shores of Ireland, France, Spain, Guinea, and the Azores, the north point varieth towards the east, and that in some variety; at London it varieth eleven degrees, at Antwerp nine, at Rome but five: at some part of the Azores it deflecteth not, but lieth in the true meridian: on the other side of the Azores, and this side of the equator, the north point of the needle wheeleth to the west; so that in the latitude of thirty-six, near the shore, the variation is about eleven degrees; but on the other side the equator, it is quite otherwise; for about Capo Frio in Brazil, the south point varieth twelve degrees unto the west, and about the mouth of the Straits of Magellan five or six; but, elongating from the coast of Brazil toward the shore of Africa, it varieth eastward, and arriving at Capo de las Agullas, it resteth in the meridian, and looketh neither way.

Now the cause of this variation was thought by Gilbertus to be the inequality of the earth, variously disposed, and differently intermixed with the sea: withal the different disposure of its magnetical vigor in the eminences and stronger parts thereof. For the needle naturally endeavours to conform unto the meridian; but, being distracted, driveth that way where the greater and powerfuller part of the earth is placed. Which may be illustrated from what hath been delivered before, and may be conceived by any, that understands the generalities of geography. For whereas on this side the meridian, or the isles of Azores, where the first meridian is placed, the needle varieth eastward; it may be occasioned by that vast tract of earth, that is, of Europe, Asia, and Africa, seated towards the east, and disposing the needle that way. For arriving at some part of the Azores, or islands of Saint Michael, which have a middle situation between these continents, and that vast and almost answerable tract of America, it seemeth equally distracted by both; and diverting unto neither, doth parallel and place itself upon the true meridian. But, sailing farther, it veers its lily to the west, and regardeth that quarter wherein the land is nearer or greater, and in the same latitude, as it approacheth the shore, augmenteth its variation. And therefore as some observe, if Columbus, or whoever first discovered America, had apprehended the cause of this variation, having passed more than half the way, he might have been confirmed in the discovery, and assuredly foretold there lay a vast and mighty continent toward the west. The reason I confess and inference is good, but the instance perhaps not so. For Columbus knew not the variation of the compass, whereof Sebastian Cabot first took notice, who after made discovery of the northern part of that continent. And it happened, indeed, that part of America was first discovered, which was on this side farthest distant, that is, Jamaica, Cuba, and the isles in the bay of Mexico. And from this variation do some new discoverers deduce a probability in the attempts of the northern passage toward the Indies.

Now, because, where the greater continents are joined, the action and effluence is also greater, therefore those needles do suffer the greatest variation which are in countries which most do feel that action. And therefore, hath Rome far less variation than London, for on the west side of Rome are seated the great continents of France, Spain, Germany, which take off the exuberance, and in some way balance the vigor of the eastern parts. But unto England there is almost no earth west, but the whole extent of Europe and Asia lieth eastward: and therefore at London it varieth eleven degrees, that is, almost one rhumb. Thus, also, by reason of the great continent of Brazil, Peru, and Chili, the needle deflecteth toward the land twelve degrees; but at the Straits of Magellan, where the land is narrowed, and the sea on the other side, it varieth but five or six. And so likewise, because the Cape de las Agullas hath sea on both sides near it, and other land remote, and, as it were, equidistant from it, therefore at that point the needle conforms unto the true meridian, and is not distracted by the vicinity of adjacencies. This is the general and great cause of variation. But, if in certain creeks and vallies the needle prove irregular, and vary beyond expectation, it may be imputed unto some vigorous part of the earth, or magnetical eminence not far distant. And this was the invention of D. Gilbert,[6] not many years past, a physician in London. And therefore, although some assume the invention of its direction, and other have had the glory of the card, yet in the experiments, grounds, and causes thereof, England produced the father philosopher, and discovered more in it, than Columbus or Americus did ever by it.

Unto this, in great part true, the reason of Kircherus may be added: that this variation proceedeth, not only from terrestrious eminences and magnetical veins of the earth, laterally respecting the needle, but the different coagmentation of the earth disposed unto the poles, lying under the sea and waters, which affect the needle with great or lesser variation, according to the vigour or imbecility of these subterraneous lines, or the entire or broken compagination of the magnetical fabric under it. As is observable from several loadstones placed at the bottom of any water; for a loadstone or needle upon the surface will variously conform itself, according to the vigour or faintness of the loadstones under it.

Thus also a reason may be alleged for the variation of the variation, and why, according to observation, the variation of the needle hath after some years been found to vary in some places. For this may proceed from mutations of the earth, by subterraneous fires, fumes, mineral spirits, or otherwise; which altering the constitution of the magnetical parts, in process of time, doth vary the variation over the place.[7]

[6] *Gilbert, &c.*] Herschel (in his Preliminary Discourse) says, "Our countryman, Dr. Gilbert, of Colchester, in 1500, published a treatise on magnetism, full of valuable facts and experiments, ingeniously reasoned on; and he likewise extended his enquiries to a variety of other subjects, in particular to electricity."

The title of this work, which is now very scarce, is *Gulielmi Gilberti Colcestrensis, Medici Londinensis, De Magnete, Magneticisque corporibus, et de magno magnete tellure; physiologia nova, plurimis et argumentis et experimentis demonstrata*: fol. pp. 240, Londini, 1506.

[7] *Unto this, &c.*] These two paragraphs were added in the 2nd edition

It is also probable, what is conceived of its antiquity, that the knowledge of its polary power and direction unto the north was unknown unto the ancients, and (though Levinus Lemnius, and Cælius Calcagninus, are of another belief), is justly placed with new inventions by Pancirollus. For their Achilles and strongest argument is an expression in Plautus, a very ancient author and contemporary unto Ennius. *Hic ventus jam secundus est, cape modo versoriam.* Now this *versorium* they construe to be the compass, which, notwithstanding, according unto Pineda, who hath discussed the point, Turnebus,[8] Cabeus, and divers others, is better interpreted the rope that helps to turn the ship, or, as we say, doth make it tack about; the compass declaring rather the ship is turned, than conferring unto its conversion. As for the long expeditions and sundry voyages of elder times which might confirm the antiquity of this invention, it is not improbable[9] they were performed by the help of stars; and so might the Phœnician navigators, and also Ulysses, sail about the Mediterranean, by the flight of birds, or keeping near the shore; and so might Hanno coast about Africa, or, by the help of oars, as is expressed in the voyage of Jonah. And, whereas, it is contended that this verticity was not unknown unto Solomon, in whom is presumed an universality of knowledge, it will as forcibly follow, he knew the art of typography, powder, and guns, or had the philosopher's stone, yet sent unto Ophir for gold. It is not to be denied, that, besides his political wisdom, his knowledge in philosophy was very large; and perhaps from his works therein, the ancient philosophers, especially Aristotle, who had the assistance of Alexander's acquirements, collected great observables. Yet, if he knew the use of the compass, his ships were surely very slow, that made a three years' voyage from Eziongeber in the Red Sea unto Ophir, which is supposed to be Taprobana or Malacca in the Indies, not many months' sail;[1] and since, in the same or lesser time, Drake and Cavendish performed their voyage about the earth.

[8] *Turnebus.*] Otherwise *Turnbull*, whose father was a Scotchman. —*Jef.*

[9] *improbable.*] Ross reads *probable*, and so indulges in a long discourse to refute the position.

[1] *a three years' voyage, &c.*] That the voyage from Eziongeber to

And, as the knowledge of its verticity is not so old as some conceive, so is it more ancient than most believe, nor had its discovery with guns, printing, or as many think, some years before the discovery of America; for it was not unknown unto Petrus Peregrinus, a Frenchman, who, two hundred years since,[2] left a tract of the magnet, and a per-

Ophir occupied three years is by no means to be inferred from the expressions used by the sacred historian: see 1 Kings x. 22; 2 Chron. ix. 21.

If, in his identification of the ancient *Taprobane* with Malacca, Sir Thomas may be supposed to have included the adjacent islands of Sumatra, Borneos, and Java, which is extremely probable, his opinion is supported by the high authority of Sir T. Stamford Raffles; though other modern geographers have considered it to be Ceylon.

The true situation of *Ophir*, however, has been the subject of very many conflicting hypotheses. One of the most recent, and perhaps most probable, is that of Mr. C. T. Beke, who supposes it to have been situated at the northern extremity of the Persian gulph. See his *Origines Biblicæ*, vol. i. p. 114.

[2] *two hundred years since.*] The knowledge of the directive power or polarity of the magnet, is now known to be of a date considerably earlier than this. Sir John F. W. Herschel, in his *Preliminary Discourse on the Study of Natural Philosophy*, p. 326, thus concisely states the present amount of our information on the subject: "It does not appear that the ancients had any knowledge of this property of the magnet, though its attraction of iron was well known to them. The first mention of it in modern times cannot be traced earlier than 1180, though it was probably known to the Chinese before that time. "The following passage from the late Professor Sir John Leslie's Dissertation on the Progress of Mathematical and Physical Science, prefixed to the seventh edition of the Encyclopædia Britannica, gives a more circumstantial view of the history of the compass, which is further interesting, when contrasted with the previous passage of the text, as showing that the notions respecting the antiquity of the knowledge of magnetic polarity, which are therein contemned by Browne, have been revived and supported by high modern authority. "The magnetic compass, with the art of distillation, which was never practised by the ancient Greeks or Romans, seems to have been discovered in Upper Asia, and thence communicated by their Tartarian conquerors, to the Chinese. From them again, the knowledge of the invention spread gradually over the East. The Crusaders, during the occupation of their bloody conquests in those regions, had leisure to admire the arts acquired by their more civilized rivals. Having their curiosity thus awakened, they appear, about the latter part of the twelfth century, to have imported into Europe the *compass*, along with the substance which, mistaking it for *natron*, they called *saltpetre*, and of which they had learned the deflagrating property. That invaluable instrument was at first very rudely formed, consisting merely of a piece of the native mineral fixed to a broad cork, and set to float

petual motion to be made thereby, preserved by Gasserus. Paulus Venetus, and, about five hundred years past, Albertus Magnus, make mention hereof, and quote for it a book of Aristotle, *De Lapide;* which book, although we find in the catalogue of Laertius, yet, with Cabeus, we may rather judge it to be the work of some Arabic writer, not many years before the days of Albertus.

Lastly, it is likewise true, what some have delivered of *crocus Martis,* that is, steel corroded with vinegar, sulphur, or otherwise, and after reverberated by fire. For the loadstone will not at all attract it, nor will it adhere, but lie therein like sand.[3] This is to be undertood of *crocus Martis* well reverberated, and into a violet colour; for common *chalybs præparatus,* or corroded and powdered steel, the loadstone attracts, like ordinary filings of iron, and many times most of that which passeth for *crocus Martis.* So that this way may serve as a test of its preparation, after which, it becometh a very good medicine in fluxes. The like may be affirmed of flakes of iron that are rusty and begin to tend unto earth; for their cognation then expireth, and the loadstone will not regard them.

---

in a dish of water. An artist, of the opulent town of Amalphi, the great emporium of the East, and seated on the shore of Calabria, in the direct route of the Crusaders, improved the construction, and marked the north point by a *fleur-de-lis,* the armorial bearing of the kingdom of Naples. From its directive property, it was now called, in English, the *loadstone,* or *leadingstone.—Br.*

[3] *but lie therein like sand.*] Some explanatory remarks are requisite in this place. The *crocus martis* described by the author, is the *peroxide* of iron of modern chemists, that is, iron combined with the greatest proportion of oxygen with which it is capable of uniting, in which state of combination the metal ceases to obey the magnetic influence. But the "common *chalybs præparatus,*" which he afterwards mentions, consists merely of steel, in which the metal retains, in great measure, its metallic form, but is mixed and disguised with variable proportions of its oxides, and chiefly of the *black oxide,* and this, containing less oxygen than the peroxide, is like the unoxidated metal attracted by the magnet; which explains why this preparation is attracted by "the loadstone," . . . . "like ordinary filings of iron." While the "flakes of iron that are rusty," &c. adverted to at the conclusion of the paragraph, are only in the state of black oxide, they also obey the magnet; but when they have acquired their full dose of oxygen, and thus become peroxide, "their cognation then expireth, and the loadstone will not regard them."—*Br.*

And therefore, this may serve as a trial of good steel,⁴ the loadstone taking up a greater mass of that which is most pure. It may also decide the conversion of wood into iron, as is pretended, from some waters; and the common conversion of iron into copper, by the mediation of blue copperas; for the loadstone will not attract it. Although it may be questioned, whether, in this operation, the iron or copperas be transmuted,⁵ as may be doubted from the cognation of copperas with copper, and the quantity of iron remaining after the conversion. And the same may be useful

⁴ *as a trial of good steel.*] This statement is no further true than that the magnet, if caused to act upon filings of iron or steel in which the metal fully retained its metallic form, free from oxidation, and also upon similar filings which had become partially oxidated, would attract a greater quantity of the former than of the latter. As a trial of the purity or goodness of iron or steel in the mass, the proposed test is quite nugatory.—*Br.*

⁵ *whether in this operation the iron or copperas be transmuted.*] This alleged conversion of iron into copper is an experiment of the alchymists and of the old chemists their successors ; the true nature of which has been explained by modern chemists, and appears, from the passage before us, to have been suspected also by Browne. The metallic salt, here termed "blue copperas" (or blue vitriol, as it is also called), is properly a *hydrated persulphate of copper*,—a combination of the peroxide of that metal with the sulphuric acid and with water. But iron, having a stronger chemical attraction for oxygen than copper has, when immersed in a solution of this salt, attracts and unites with the oxygen of a part of the peroxide of copper, thus separating an equivalent quantity of the copper itself, which being precipitated, in its pure metallic state, upon the iron, imparts to it externally the appearance of copper, just as gilding would impart that of gold. It was formerly imagined, however (and the experiment was cited as demonstrating the transmutability of metals into one another), that part of the iron was actually converted into copper. But our author, knowing the "cognation of [blue] copperas with copper," and considering "the quantity of iron remaining after the conversion," justly questions whether the iron or the "copperas" "be transmuted." It is evident from this, that he entertained as correct a notion upon the subject as it was possible to arrive at in the existing state of chemical knowledge ; for, although in reality a particle of iron becomes dissolved in the solution for every particle of copper which is precipitated from it, yet, in the manner in which the experiment is commonly made, and as it was always made formerly, the iron is not sensibly diminished in substance, and continues unaltered in form, so that the obvious essential change takes place with the metallic salt only. The last sentence of the first period alluding to this subject would be more readily intelligible, were it read "for the loadstone will not attract the *copperas.*"—*Br.*

to some discovery concerning vitriol or copperas of *Mars*,⁶ by some called salt of steel, made by the spirits of vitriol or sulphur. For the corroded powder of steel will, after ablution, be actively attracted by the loadstone, and also remaineth in little diminished quantity; and therefore, whether those shooting salts partake but little of steel, and be not rather the vitriolous spirits fixed into salt by the effluvium or odour of steel, is not without good question.⁷

CHAPTER III.

Concerning the Loadstone; a rejection of sundry common opinions and relations thereof; natural, medical, historical, magical.

And first, not only a simple heterodox, but a very hard paradox, it will seem, and of great absurdity unto obstinate ears, if we say, attraction is unjustly appropriated unto the loadstone, and that perhaps we speak not properly, when we say vulgarly and appropriately, the loadstone draweth iron; and yet herein we should not want experiment and great authority. The words of Renatus des Cartes, in his *Principles of Philosophy*, are very plain. *Præterea magnes trahit ferrum, sive potiùs magnes et ferrum ad invicem acce-*

⁶ *some discovery concerning vitriol or copperas of Mars.*] The salt here alluded to, commonly termed *green vitriol*, is the *hydrated protosulphate of iron*,—a combination of the protoxide of iron with the sulphuric acid and with water, bearing nearly the same relation to metallic iron which *blue vitriol* bears to metallic copper. The manner in which Browne adverts to these substances, evinces that he entertained approximately correct ideas respecting the nature of the several salts termed *copperas*. But when he supposes that "those shooting salts" (meaning thereby the hydrated protosulphate of iron), "partake but little" of the metal from which they are formed, he is entirely mistaken. He appears to have been led into this error by the application of his own proposed magnetic test: finding that the "corroded powder of steel," the nature of which is explained in our preceding note, was readily attracted by the magnet, but that the "copperas of Mars" was not, he seems to have inferred that that salt could not be materially related to the metal from which it is formed; not knowing that those substances which obey the magnet in their metallic state, and in some instances in their oxidated form also, cease to be amenable to its influence when united with acids into *salts.*—*Br.*

⁷ *And therefore, &c.*] Added in 2nd edition.

dunt, neque enim ulla ibi tractio est. The same is solemnly determined by Cabeus. *Nec magnes trahit propriè ferrum, nec ferrum ad se magnetem provocat; sed ambo pari conatu ad inricem confluunt.* Concordant hereto is the assertion of Dr. Ridley, physician to the emperor of Russia, in his tract *Of Magnetical Bodies*, defining magnetical attraction to be a natural incitation and disposition conforming unto contiguity, an union of one magnetical body with another, and no violent haling of the weak unto the stronger. And this is also the doctrine of Gilbertus, by whom this motion is termed coition, and that not made by any faculty attractive of one, but a *syndrome* and concourse of each,[1] a coition always of their vigours, and also of their bodies, if bulk or impediment prevent not. And therefore, those contrary actions, which flow from opposite poles or faces, are not so properly expulsion and attraction, as *sequela* and *fuga*, a mutual flight and following. Consonant whereto are also the determinations of Helmontius, Kircherus, and Licetus.[2]

The same is also confirmed by experiment; for if a piece of iron be fastened in the side of a bowl or basin of water, a loadstone, swimming freely in a boat of cork, will presently make unto it. So if a steel or knife untouched be offered toward the needle that is touched, the needle nimbly moveth toward it, and conformeth unto a union with the steel that moveth not. Again, if a loadstone be finely filed, the atoms or dust thereof will adhere unto iron that was never touched, even as the powder of iron doth also unto the loadstone. And, lastly, if in two skiffs of cork, a loadstone and steel be placed within the orb of their activities, the one doth not move, the other standing still, but both hoist sail and steer unto each other. So that if the loadstone attract, the steel hath also its attraction; for in this action the alliciency is reciprocal, which jointly felt, they mutually approach and run into each other's arms.

[1] *concourse of each.*] Ross, on the ground that "no end can be assigned why the loadstone should move towards the iron," denies that they move towards each other; thinking it more reasonable to suppose that iron *and other metals* move towards the loadstone as to their matrix. —*Arcana,* p. 141.

[2] *Consonant, &c.*] Added in the 2nd edition.

And therefore, surely, more moderate expressions become this action, than what the ancients have used; which some have delivered in the most violent terms of their language; so Austin calls it, *mirabilem ferri raptorem*: Hippocrates, λίθος ὅ τι τὸν σίδηρον ἁρπάζει, *lapis qui ferrum rapit*. Galen, disputing against Epicurus, useth the term ἕλκειν, but this also is too violent; among the ancients, Aristotle spake most warily, λίθος ὅστις τὸν σίδηρον κινεῖ, *lapis qui ferrum movet*: and in some tolerable exception do run the expressions of Aquinas, Scaliger, and Cusanus.

Many relations are made, and great expectations are raised from the *magnes carneus*, or a loadstone that hath a faculty to attract not only iron, but flesh; but this, upon enquiry, and as Cabeus hath also observed, is nothing else but a weak and inanimate kind of loadstone, veined here and there with a few magnetical and ferreous lines, but chiefly consisting of a bolary and clammy substance, whereby it adheres like *hæmatites* or *terra Lemnia*, unto the lips. And this is that stone which is to be understood, when physicians join it with *ætites*, or the eagle-stone, and promise therein a virtue against abortion.

There is sometimes a mistake concerning the variation of the compass, and therein one point is taken for another. For beyond the equator some men account its variation by the diversion of the northern point; whereas beyond that circle, the southern point[3] is sovereign, and the north submits his pre-eminency. For in the southern coast, either of America or Africa, the southern point deflects and varieth toward the land, as being disposed and spirited that way by the meridional and proper hemisphere. And, therefore, on that side of the earth, the varying point is best accounted by the south. And therefore, also, the writings of some, and maps of others, are to be enquired, that make the needle decline unto the east twelve degrees at Capo Frio, and six at the straits of Magellan; accounting hereby one point for

---

[3] *beyond that circle, &c.*] The author was here much mistaken: the southern pointe having noe soveranty at all—noe not in the southern clymats, as our navigators unanimously affirme.—*Wr.*

The dean's contradiction must be flatly thrown back upon him. The fact is found to bear out our author's assertion, which is correct both as to substance and literality.

another, and preferring the north in the liberties and province of the south.[4]

But certainly false it is, what is commonly affirmed and believed, that garlick doth hinder the attraction of the loadstone;[5] which is, notwithstanding, delivered by grave and worthy writers, by Pliny, Solinus, Ptolemy, Plutarch, Albertus, Matthiolus, Rueus, Langius, and many more. An effect as strange as that of Homer's *Moly*, and the garlick that Mercury bestowed upon Ulysses. But that it is evidently false, many experiments declare. For an iron wire heated red hot and quenched in the juice of garlick, doth, notwithstanding, contract a verticity from the earth, and attracteth the southern point of the needle. If, also, the tooth of a loadstone be covered or stuck in garlick, it will, notwithstanding, attract; and needles, excited and fixed in garlick, until they begin to rust, do yet retain their attractive and polary respects.

Of the same stamp is that which is obtruded upon us by authors ancient and modern, that an adamant or diamond prevents or suspends the attraction of the loadstone; as is in open terms delivered by Pliny: *Adamas dissidet cum magnete lapide, ut juxtà positus ferrum non patiatur abstrahi, aut si admotus magnes apprehenderit, rapiat atque auferit.* For if a diamond be placed between a needle and a loadstone, there will, nevertheless, ensue a coition even over the body of the diamond. And an easy matter it is to touch or excite a needle through a diamond, by placing it at the tooth of a loadstone: and, therefore, the relation is false; or our estimation of these gems untrue,[6] nor are they diamonds which carry that name amongst us.

[4] *and preferring, &c.*] Itt is certaine that the needle holds the same posture to the northe, and moves to iron on the south side the line, in the self-same manner as itt did being toucht in England, and that the south pointe of the needle does [there] fly from iron as itt does here.—*Wr.*

[5] *garlick doth hinder, &c.*] Nothing can afford a more perfect example of implicit adherence to antiquity, than the following passage from Ross:—"I cannot think the ancient sages would write so confidently of that which they had no experience of, being a thing so obvious and easy to try; therefore I suppose they had a *stronger kind of garlick than is with us!*"—*Arcana*, p. 192.

[6] *and therefore the relation, &c.*] The paragraph containing this result, the preceding, and the two following ones, all furnish examples

It is not suddenly to be received what Paracelsus* affirmeth, that if a loadstone be anointed with mercurial oil, or only put into quicksilver, it amitteth its attraction for ever. For we have found that loadstones and touched needles, which have laid long time in quicksilver, have not amitted their attraction. And we also find that red hot needles or wires, extinguished in quicksilver, do yet acquire a verticity according to the laws of position in extinction. Of greater repugnancy unto reason is that which he delivers concerning its graduation, that heated in the fire and often extinguished in oil of Mars or iron, it acquires an ability to extract or draw forth a nail fastened in a wall; for, as we have declared before, the vigour of the loadstone is destroyed by fire; nor will it be re-impregnated by any other magnet than the earth.[7]

Nor is it to be made out, what seemeth very plausible, and formerly hath deceived us, that a loadstone will not attract an iron or steel red hot.[8] The falsity hereof, discovered first by Kircherus, we can confirm by iterated experiment; very sensibly in armed loadstones, and obscurely in any other.

True it is, that, besides fire, some other ways there are of its destruction; as age, rust, and, what is least dreamt on, an unnatural or contrary situation. For, being impolarily adjoined unto a more vigorous loadstone, it will in a short time exchange its poles; or, being kept in undue position, that is, not lying on the meridian, or else with its poles inverted, it receives in longer time impair in activity, exchange of faces; and is more powerfully preserved by position than

---

* *De generatione rerum.*

of Browne's rigorous experimental scrutiny of the statements made by authors; in the present instance, as in all others adverted to in these paragraphs, "the relation is false," the discrepancy not arising from any error relative to the diamond, although several substances are probably confounded together under that appellation, by Pliny.— *Br.*

[7] *nor will it be re-impregnated, &c.*] This is untrue, if understood of an artificial magnet, which may readily be re-magnetized by the usual means, after being deprived of its magnetism by heat; but the statement is probably true, if understood of the natural loadstone, or magnetic iron ore.—*Br.*

[8] *Nor is it, &c.*] Added in the 2nd edition.

by the dust of steel. But the sudden and surest way is fire; that is, fire not only actual but potential; the one surely and suddenly, the other slowly and imperfectly; the one changing, the other destroying the figure. For if distilled vinegar or *aqua fortis* be poured upon the powder of loadstone, the subsiding powder dried, retains some magnetical virtue, and will be attracted by the loadstone; but if the *menstruum* or dissolvent be evaporated to a consistence, and afterward doth shoot into icicles or crystals, the loadstone hath no power upon them; and if in a full dissolution of steel, a separation of parts be made by preciptitation or exhalation, the exsiccated powder hath lost its wings, and ascends not unto the loadstone. And though a loadstone fired doth presently amit its proper virtue, and according to the position in cooling contracts a new verticity from the earth, yet if the same be laid awhile in *aqua fortis*, or other corrosive water, and taken out before a considerable corrosion, it still reserves its attraction, and will convert the needle according to former polarity. And that, duly preserved from violent corrosion, or the natural disease of rust, it may long conserve its virtue,—beside the magnetical virtue of the earth which hath lasted since the creation, a great example we have from the observation of our learned friend, Mr. Graves,* in an Egyptian idol cut out of loadstone, and found among the mummies, which still retains its attraction, though probably taken out of the mine about two thousand years ago.[9]

It is improbable, what Pliny affirmeth concerning the object of its attraction, that it attracts not only ferreous bodies, but also *liquorem vitri*; for in the body of glass there is no ferreous or magnetical nature which might occasion attraction. For, of the glass we use, the purest is made of the finest sand and the ashes of chaly or glasswort; and the coarser or green sort, of the ashes of brake or other plants. True it is, that in the making of glass, it hath been an ancient practice to cast in pieces of magnet, or, perhaps, manganese, conceiving it carried away all ferreous and earthy parts from the pure and running portion of glass, which the loadstone would not

---

* In his learned *Pyramidography*.

[9] *And that, &c.*] Added in the 2nd edition.

respect; and, therefore, if that attraction were not rather electrical than magnetical, it was a wondrous effect what Helmont delivered concerning a glass wherein the magistery of loadstone was prepared, which after retained an attractive quality.[1]

But, whether the magnet attracteth more than common iron, may be tried in other bodies. It seems to attract the *smyris* or emery in powder.[2] It draweth the shining or glassy powder brought from the Indies,[3] and usually employed in writing dust. There is also in smith's cinders, by some adhesion of iron,[4] whereby they appear as it were glazed,

---

[1] *True it is, &c.*] Instead of the rest of this paragraph (thus altered in 2nd edit.) edit. 1646 read thus:—" Beside vitrification is the last or utmost fusion of a body vitrifiable, and is performed by a strong and violent heat, which keeps the melted glass red hot. Now certain it is, and we have showed it before, that the loadstone will not attract even steel itself that is candent, much less the incongenerous body of glass being fired. For fire destroys the loadstone; and therefore it declines in its own defence, and seeks no union with it."

[2] *seems to attract, &c.*] Emery itself, in its natural state a massive and granular variety of corundum, the mineral of which the saphire and the ruby are also varieties, is not attracted by the magnet; but it is almost always mingled with a considerable proportion of particles of magnetic iron ore (or loadstone) which of course are subject to attraction. By the use of a magnet, indeed, nearly the whole of this may be separated, leaving the emery nearly pure, especially if the mass has previously been reduced into a fine powder. It was by this means that the late accomplished chemical analyst, Mr. Smithson Tennant, separated the magnetic iron ore from the emery, his examination of which first evinced the true nature of that substance as a variety of corundum. See *Phil. Trans.* 1802, p. 399.

The foregoing explanation has been given on the supposition that our author alludes to the mineral properly designated *emery*; but that term has also been applied, in commerce and in the arts, to various other substances, and among them to some of the ores of iron; Browne, therefore, may perhaps allude in reality to some of the latter; but in either case the fact is explained in conformity with the obvious and known properties of the magnet, and without leaving room for any suspicion that other bodies, not properly magnetic, are attractable by it under ordinary circumstances.—*Br.*

[3] *shining or glassy powder, &c.*] This powder consists almost entirely of minute crystals or grains of magnetic iron ore, so that, as in the case of the attractable particles in emery, we have here merely the loadstone or the magnet attracting particles of loadstone itself.—*Br.*

[4] *There is also in smith's cinders, &c.*] The scales which are detached from the surface of iron while undergoing the operations of the smith, consist of the black oxide of that metal, which agrees in its chemical

sometimes to be found a magnetical operation; for some thereof applied have power to move the needle. But, whether the ashes of vegetables, which grow over iron mines, contract a magnetical quality, as containing some mineral particles, which by sublimation ascend unto their roots, and are attracted together with their nourishment, according, as some affirm from the like observations upon the mines of silver, quicksilver, and gold, we must refer unto further experiment.[5]

It is also improbable and something singular, what some conceive, and Eusebius Nierembergius, a learned jesuit of Spain, delivers, that the body of man is magnetical, and, being placed in a boat, the vessel will never rest until the head respecteth the north.[6] If this be true, the bodies of Christians do lie unnaturally in their graves. King Cheops in his tomb, and the Jews in their beds, have fallen upon the natural position; who reverentially declining the situation of their temple, nor willing to lie as that stood, do place their beds from north to south, and delight to sleep meridionally. This opinion confirmed, would much advance the microcosmical conceit and commend the geography of Paracelsus, who, according to the cardinal points of the world, divideth the body of man; and, therefore, working upon human ordure, and by long preparation rendering it odoriferous, he terms it *zibeta occidentalis*, western civet; making the face the east, but the posteriors the America or western part of his microcosm. The verity hereof[7] might easily be tried in Wales, where there are portable boats, and made of leather, which would convert upon the impulsion of any ver-

---

nature with the magnetic iron ore or native loadstone, being composed, like that mineral, of the protoxide and the peroxide of iron united. These scales are of course magnetic, and may be, indeed, what the author alludes to; but should he in reality refer merely to the cinders of the small coal used in the forge, their magnetism may readily be accounted for on the supposition that the scales of black oxide, with which they are so frequently brought into contact, must often become intimately mingled with them by the partial fusion of both.—*Br.*

[5] *But whether the ashes, &c.*] Added in 2nd edition.

[6] *the vessel, &c.*] How easye it is to sifte out this, and save the dispute.—*Wr.*

[7] *The verity hereof.*] "The verity, or rather falsity hereof."—*Edit.* 1646.

ticity; and seem to be the same whereof, in his description of Britain, Cæsar hath left some mention.[8]

Another kind of verticity is that which *Angelus doce mihi jus*,* alias, Michael Sundevogis, in a tract *De Sulphure*, discovereth in vegetables, from sticks let fall or depressed under water; which, equally framed and permitted unto themselves, will ascend at the upper end, or that which was vertical in their vegetation; wherein, notwithstanding, as yet, we have not found satisfaction: although, perhaps, too greedy of magnalities, we are apt to make but favourable experiments concerning welcome truths, and such desired verities.

It is also wondrous strange, what Lælius Bisciola reporteth, that if unto ten ounces of loadstone one of iron be added, it increaseth not unto eleven, but weighs ten ounces still. A relation inexcusable in a work of leisureable hours;† the examination being as ready as the relation, and the falsity tried as easily as delivered. Nor is it to be omitted, what is taken up by Cæsius Bernardus, a late mineralogist, and originally confirmed by Porta, that needles

---

* Anagrammatically.   † *Horæ Subsecivæ*.

[8] *in Wales, where, &c.*] "The fishermen on the Teivi, and some of the other rivers of Wales, use a boat of a singular construction, called in Welsh *corwg*, and anglicized *coracle*, which is probably coeval with the earliest population of the island. (See *Cæsar, Bell. Civ.* lib. i. c. 54.) The form of this vessel is nearly oval, flattened at one end like the keel of a common boat: its length is usually from five to six feet, and its breadth about four feet. The frame is formed of split rods, which are plaited like basket-work: these are afterwards covered on the outside with a raw hide, or more commonly with strong coarse flannel, which is rendered water tight by a thick coating of pitch and tar. A narrow board is fastened across the middle: when on the water, this forms the fisherman's seat, whence, with his paddle, he directs his bark at pleasure. They are not adapted to carry more than one person conveniently. When proceeding to their work, or returning, the men fasten these vessels on their backs by means of a leather strap attached to the seat, which they pass round their bodies. Their appearance, when thus equipped, has been aptly compared to that of a large tortoise walking on its hind legs. Their usual weight may be about forty or fifty pounds; but according to an old Welsh adage (*Llwyth gur ei gorwg*), it was thought necessary that they should form as heavy a load as the individual could carry, before they would bear him on the water."—*Rees's Beauties of South Wales*, p. 391.

touched with a diamond contract a verticity, even as they do with a loadstone, which will not consist with experiment. And, therefore, as Gilbertus observeth, he might be deceived in touching such needles with diamonds, which had a verticity before, as we have declared most needles to have; and so, had he touched them with gold or silver, he might have concluded a magnetical virtue therein.

In the same form may we place Fracastorius his attraction of silver, Philostratus his *Pantarbes*, Apollodorus and Beda their relation of the loadstone that attracted only in the night. But most inexcusable is Franciscus Rueus, a man of our own profession; who, in his discourse of gems mentioned in the Apocalypse, undertakes a chapter of the loadstone. Wherein substantially and upon experiment he scarce delivereth anything; making long enumeration of its traditional qualities, whereof he seemeth to believe many, and some, above convicted by experience, he is fain to salve as impostures of the devil. But Boëtius de Boot, physician unto Rodolphus the second, hath recompensed this defect; and in his tract, *De Lapidibus et Gemmis*, speaks very materially hereof, and his discourse is consonant unto experience and reason.

As for relations historical, though many there be of less account, yet two alone deserve consideration; the first concerneth magnetical rocks and attractive mountains in several parts of the earth. The other, the tomb of Mahomet, and bodies suspended in the air. Of rocks magnetical there are likewise two relations; for some are delivered to be in the Indies, and some in the extremity of the north, and about the very pole. The northern account is commonly ascribed unto Olaus Magnus, archbishop of Upsale, who, out of his predecessor, Joannes Saxo, and others, compiled a history of some northern nations; but this assertion we have not discovered in that work of his, which commonly passeth amongst us; and should believe his geography herein no more than that in the first line of his book; when he affirmeth that Biarmia (which is not seventy degrees in latitude) hath the pole for its zenith, and equinoctial for the horizon.

Now, upon this foundation, how uncertain soever, men have erected mighty illations, ascribing thereto the cause of the need e's direction, and conceiving the effluxions from these mountains and rocks invite the lily toward the north. Which conceit, though countenanced by learned men, is not made out either by experience or reason; for no man hath yet attained or given a sensible account of the pole by some degrees. It is also observed the needle doth very much vary as it approacheth the pole; whereas, were there such direction from the rocks, upon a nearer approachment it would more directly respect them. Besides, were there such magnetical rocks under the pole, yet being so far removed, they would produce no such effect. For they that sail by the isle of Ilua, now called Elba, in the Tuscan sea, which abounds in the veins of loadstone, observe no variation or inclination of the needle; much less may they expect a direction from rocks at the end of the earth. And, lastly, men that ascribe thus much unto rocks of the north, must presume or discover the like magneticals at the south; for in the southern seas, and far beyond the equator, variations are large, and declinations as constant as in the northern ocean.

The other relation, of loadstone mines and rocks[9] in the

---

[9] *loadstone mines and rocks.*] The author's facts and reasoning, in the preceding paragraphs, relative to the absurd notion that the direction of the magnetic needle is caused by the attraction of magnetical rocks, situated at or near the north pole of the earth, are equally correct; as also is the evidence of the navigators upon which he decides, in the paragraph now before us, that no rocks exist having the power of drawing the iron nails out of the ships which sail past them. But when he infers, as the marginal note intimates, that therefore " (probably), there be no magnetical rocks," he is himself in error, for there are many such, which have a very powerful effect upon the compass needle, in producing a local deviation from its ordinary north and south direction. The known existence of these, in connection with other circumstances, has probably led to the fabrication of some of the stories just alluded to, respecting rocks and islands of loadstone destroying ships approaching them, by drawing out their bolts and other iron fastenings, or by their attractive force exerted upon the iron, drawing the ships themselves out of their course, and at length detaining them on shore. It may be remarked, by the way, that supposing magnetic rocks to possess sufficient power, and to be capable of exerting it to such distances as these stories imply, the latter would be the effect that would really happen; the former, under any supposition, would be impossible; for, not to mention the manner in which the fastenings of ships must neces-

shore of India, is delivered of old by Pliny; wherein, saith he, they are so placed both in abundance and vigour, that sarily be interlaced with each other, and with the timbers, the adhesion of wood to iron nails, screws, and bolts, is so powerful, that the *vis inertiæ* and weight of the vessel would yield to it, and the vessel itself, by the aggregate magnetic attraction upon all the separate masses of iron which it contained, would be drawn towards, and finally affixed to the rock.

In some of these stories, however, this, which is the only possible effect of such a power of attraction as they suppose, is actually related, as will appear from the subjoined extracts from Hole's "Remarks on the Arabian Nights' Entertainments," an elegant and ingenious commentary on those marvellous narratives, in which many of the incidents, which occur in them, are illustrated in a very satisfactory and interesting manner.

"The account of vessels being wrecked by the attractive power of a magnetic rock, appears to have been a long-established opinion in the eastern world. In the history of the Third Calendar (in the Arabian Nights), we meet with a mountain of adamant, possessing the same properties: and Aboulfoneris, the Sinbad of the Persian Tales, is wrecked by means of a magnetic rock; for that must be intended by a mountain which resembled polished steel, and which, by virtue of a talisman, rendered every vessel that approached it stationary and immoveable." After making these observations, Mr. Hole cites our author's quotation from Serapion, and then proceeds as follows: "It is not probable that Mandeville ever saw Serapion, yet he gives the same account: 'In an isle clept Crues, ben schippes withouten nayles of iren, or bonds, for the rockes of the adamandes; for they ben alle fulle there aboute in that see, that it is marveyle to spaken of. And gif a schipp passed by the marches, and hadde either iren bandes or iren nayles, anon he sholde ben perishet. For the adamande of this kinde draws the iren to him; and so wolde it draw to him the schipp, because of the iren; that he sholde never departen fro it, ne never go thens.'" It is proper to state, that these extracts are taken from a review of Mr. Hole's book, in the European Magazine for December, 1798, vol. xxxiv. pp. 395, 396.

In order fully to illustrate our author's allusions to magnetic rocks, we must now proceed to give a concise account of some of the most remarkable of those rocks which are at present known, and of their properties, with a reference also to some of his previous observations on magnetic bodies. It will be appropriate to commence this with a notice of the rocks of Magnesia, in Asia Minor, a locality of the loadstone well known to the ancients, and from which that substance is said to have derived the name of *magnes*, or "magnet," now extended to bodies artificially magnetised, and in fact often applied to them emphatically, in contradistinction from the natural magnet, loadstone, or magnetic iron ore. A particular account of these rocks of Magnesia, by Dr. Yates, was submitted, not long since, to the Philosophical Society of Cambridge:

it proves an adventure of hazard to pass those coasts in a ship with iron nails. Serapion, the Moor, an author of

the important facts, as given in the substance of Dr. Yates' paper, published in the Athenæum, for January 4th, 1834, are as follows:

"The ancient town of Magnesia, in Asia Minor (the supposed origin of the term "magnet"), stands at the base of mount Sipylus.... The rocky heights of mount Sipylus are remarkable for their extraordinary influence over the mariner's compass....... We ascended the castle hill, a part of the Sipylus range. Having proceeded about a quarter of an hour, a little to the westward of the castle, we took the first observation, in order to determine the bearing of a sugar-loaf mountain, which was beyond the river Hermus (probably a part of the range of mount Temnus). We found it to be two degrees westward of north. As yet, the compass indicated no change. Ascending in the same direction, we took very numerous observations, keeping always as a fixed point, the sugar-loaf mountain. At length the compass was found to vary 12 degrees *easterly*, and the variation continued to increase gradually in the same course, until it amounted to 56 degrees *easterly*. A short time before we approached the summit, the needle began to recede, and was suddenly attracted to the south-west. It was evident there must be some powerful cause for the change, and, in proportion as we advanced, the degree of variation *diminished*, from which we inferred that the great source of attraction was *now* behind us; we, therefore, retraced our steps, and immediately there was a corresponding change in the compass. We forthwith set ourselves to explore the district: the variation went on steadily increasing, until we approached a mass of dark rock, which had a most astonishing influence over the instrument, which was no sooner placed upon it, than it became considerably agitated, and trembled as if drawn from its course *downwards*, by a powerful magnetic source *beneath the surface*: on placing the needle on the ground, either at our feet, or a few yards off, the effect produced was the same; it did not point to the rock, but fairly dipped: it *trembled*, and was *drawn down* as before, and only returned to its former variation, as we retired from the spot; from which we concluded that the phænomenon did not depend on the mass in question, but on something *below the surface*: besides, we carried home portions of the rock, but did not find that they exhibited any magnetic power.

"On quitting this remarkable spot, the needle ceased to tremble, and gradually returned to its previous degree of variation. Our ascent had been westerly; we went nearly to the summit of the mountain, where nothing particular was noticed, and afterwards we descended by a path to the eastward of the castle..... The compasses sustained no injury: we had taken two with us, in order to compare the results—one of them was smaller than the other, and, of course, more sensibly affected. The rocks of the whole district contained a great deal of iron in various states of oxydation."

"The mountainous parts about Magnesia," says Chishull (Travels in Turkey, 1747), "were anciently famous for the production of the load-

good esteem and reasonable antiquity, confirmeth the same, whose expression in the word *magnes* is this:— "The mine of this stone is in the sea-coast of India, whereto when ships approach, there is no iron in them which flies not like a bird unto those mountains; and, therefore, their ships are fastened not with iron but wood, for otherwise they would be torn to pieces." But this assertion, how positive soever, is contradicted * by all navigators that pass that way, which are now many, and of our own nation; and might

* (Probably) there be no magnetical rocks.

stone, though, indeed, it is disparaged by Pliny, and accounted less attractive than that of other places. However, this probably was the city, from whence, as Lucretius says, that stone took the name of magnet: as from the whole country of Lydia, the touchstone likewise was called *lapis Lydius*. This hint gave us the curiosity to carry a sea compass up the castle hill, where we had the satisfaction to see it point to different stones, and quickly after entirely to lose its whole virtue: two effects which are natural to the magnetic needle when injured by the nearness of other bodies impregnated with the same quality."

Macfarlane tells us (Constantinople in 1828), that his pocket compass proved the accuracy of Chishull's statement of the magnetic qualities of these mountains. "In several places in my ascent," says he, "I found the needle affected, seeing it tremble and vary from the pole; but, on the summit of the castle hill, to the west, on producing it, it pointed due east, in the direction of a dark mass of rock, which, on examination, offered nothing to distinguish it from the general appearance of the Sipylus; and, rather lower down, behind the castle, in the deep hollow which separates the castle hill from the Sipylus, on placing it on a flat stone, the needle wavered, and stood in succession at nearly every point of the compass, and this suddenly, and as if by jerks, being any thing now rather than an emblem of constancy." The same author also mentions, that the day before his visit to the castle hill, [in] a chasm of mount Sipylus, to the east of Magnesia, near the road which leads to Sardes, he also detected the variations of his pocket compass; but the needle was not affected to such a degree, as on the hill of the Acropolis.

Certain trap rocks in Nova Scotia, recently described by Messrs. Jackson and Alger, in a memoir on the mineralogy and geology of that country, published in the Memoirs of the American Academy of Arts and Sciences, No. VIII. vol. i. p. 223, are magnetic; surveyors who have to run lines in different parts of Digby peninsula, which is occupied by them, find their compasses very sensibly influenced.

Further particulars relating to the action of magnetic rocks upon the compass, will be found in several papers by Dr. Macculloch, published in the Transactions of the Geological Society, especially in a paper on the Geology of Glen Tilt. *Trans. Geol. Soc.* vol. iii. p. 324—332.—*Br.*

surely have been controlled by Nearchus, the admiral of Alexander, who not knowing the compass, was fain to coast that shore.

For the relation concerning Mahomet, it is generally believed his tomb, at Medina Talnabi, in Arabia, without any visible supporters, hangeth in the air between two loadstones artificially contrived both above and below; which conceit is fabulous and evidently false, from the testimony of ocular testators, who affirm his tomb is made of stone, and lieth upon the ground; as (besides others) the learned Vossius observeth, from Gabriel Sionita and Joannes Hefronita, two Maronites, in their relations hereof. Of such intentions and attempt by Mahometans we read in some relators, and that might be the occasion of the fable, which by tradition of time and distance of place [was] enlarged into the story of being accomplished. And this hath been promoted by attempts of the like nature; for we read in Pliny, that one Dinocrates began to arch the temple of Arsinoe in Alexandria, with loadstone, that so her statue might be suspended in the air to the amazement of the beholders. And, to lead on our credulity herein, confirmation may be drawn from history and writers of good authority. So is it reported by Ruffinus, that in the temple of Serapis there was an iron chariot suspended by loadstones in the air, which stones removed, the chariot fell and dashed into pieces. The like doth Beda report of Bellerophon's horse, which, framed of iron, and placed between two loadstones, with wings expanded, hung pendulous in the air.

The verity of these stories we shall not further dispute; their possibility we may in some way determine: if we conceive (what no man will deny) that bodies suspended in the air have this suspension from one or many loadstones placed both above and below it, or else by one or many placed only above it; likewise the body to be suspended in respect of the loadstone above, is either placed first at a pendulous distance in the medium, or else attracted unto that site by the vigour of the loadstone. And so we first affirm, that possible it is a body may be suspended between two loadstones; that is, it being so equally attracted unto both, that it determineth itself unto neither. But surely this position will be of no duration; for if the air be agitated, or the body waved either way, it amits the equilibration, and disposeth itself unto the nearest attractor. Again, it is not impossible (though hardly feasible) by a single loadstone to suspend an iron in the air, the iron being artificially placed, and at a distance guided toward the stone, until it find the neutral point, wherein its gravity just equals the magnetical quality, the one exactly extolling as much as the other depresseth. And lastly, impossible it is, that if an iron rest upon the ground, and a loadstone be placed over it, it should ever so arise as to hang in the way or medium; for that vigour, which at a distance is able to overcome the resistance of its gravity, and to lift it up from the earth, will, as it approacheth nearer, be still more able to attract it; never remaining in the middle that could not abide in the extreme. Now, the way of Baptista Porta, that by a thread fasteneth a needle to a table, and then so guides and orders the same, that by the attraction of the loadstone, it abideth in the air, infringeth not this reason; for this is a violent retention, and, if the thread be loosened, the needle ascends and adheres unto the attractor.

The third consideration concerneth medical relations; wherein, whatever effects are delivered, they are either derived from its mineral and ferreous condition, or else magnetical operation. Unto the ferreous and mineral quality pertaineth, what Dioscorides, an ancient writer and soldier under Anthony and Cleopatra, affirmeth, that half a dram of loadstone given with honey and water, proves a purgative medicine and evacuateth gross humours; but this is a quality of great incertainty; for, omitting the vehicle of water and honey, which is of a laxative power itself, the powder of some loadstones in this dose doth rather constipate and bind, than purge and loosen the belly; and if sometimes it cause any laxity, it is probably in the same way with iron and steel unprepared, which will disturb some bodies, and work by purge and vomit. And therefore, whereas it is delivered in a book ascribed unto Galen, that it is a good medicine in dropsies, and evacuates the waters of persons so affected;— it may, I confess, by siccity and astriction, afford a confirmation unto parts relaxed, and such as be hydropically disposed; and by these qualities it may be useful in *hernia*, or ruptures, and for these it is commended by Ætius,

Ægineta, and Oribasius, who only affirm that it contains the virtue of *hæmatites*, and being burnt was sometimes vended for it. Wherein notwithstanding there is an higher virtue; and in the same prepared, or in rich veins thereof though crude, we have observed the effects of chalybeate medicines; and the benefits of iron and steel in strong obstructions. And therefore, that was probably a different vein of loadstone, or infected with other mineral mixture, which the ancients commended for a purgative medicine, and ranked the same with the violentest kinds thereof; with *Hippophae*, *Cneoron*, and *Thymelæa*, as we find it in Hippocrates,* and might be somewhat doubtful, whether by the magnesian stone, he understood the loadstone; did not Achilles Statius define the same, the stone that loveth iron.

To this mineral condition belongeth what is delivered by some, that wounds which are made with weapons excited by the loadstone, contract a malignity, and become of more difficult cure; which, nevertheless, is not to be found in the incision of chirurgeons with knives, and lancets touched, which leave no such effect behind them. Hither must we also refer that affirmative, which says, the loadstone is poison; and therefore in the lists of poisons we find it in many authors. But this our experience cannot confirm, and the practice of the king of Zeilan[1] clearly contradicteth, who, as Gartias ab Horto, physician unto the Spanish viceroy, delivereth, hath all his meat served up in dishes of loadstone, and conceives thereby he preserveth the vigour of youth.

But surely from a magnetical activity must be made out what is let fall by Ætius, that a loadstone held in the hand of one that is podagrical, doth either cure or give great ease in the gout; or, what Marcellus Empericus affirmeth, that as an amulet it also cureth the headache: which are but additions unto its proper nature, and hopeful enlargements of its allowed attraction; for perceiving its secret power to draw magnetical bodies, men have invented a new attraction, to draw out the dolour and pain of any part. And from such grounds it surely became a philter, and was conceived a medicine of some venereal attraction; and therefore upon

---

* *De morbis internis.*   [1] *Zeilan.*] Ceylon.

this stone they graved the image of Venus, according unto that of Claudian, *Venerem magnetica gemma figurat*. Hither must we also refer what is delivered concerning its powder, to draw out of the body bullets and heads of arrows, and for the like intention is mixed up in plasters. Which course, although as vain and ineffectual it be rejected by many good authors, yet it is not methinks so readily to be denied, nor the practice of many physicians which have thus compounded plasters thus suddenly to be condemned, as may be observed in the *Emplastrum divinum Nicolai*, the *Emplastrum nigrum* of Augspurg, the *Opodeldoch* and *Attractivum* of Paracelsus, with several more in the dispensatory of Wecker, and practice of Sennertus. The cure also of *Hernia*, or ruptures in Pareus, and the method also of curation lately delivered by Daniel Beckerus,* and approved by the professors of Leyden, that is, of a young man of Spruceland, that casually swallowed a knife about ten inches long, which was cut out of his stomach, and the wound healed up. In which cure, to attract the knife to a convenient situation, there was applied a plaster made up with the powder of loadstone. Now this kind of practice Libavius, Gilbertus, and lately Swickardus,† condemn as vain, and altogether unuseful; because a loadstone in powder hath no attractive power, for in that form it amits its polary respects, and loseth those parts which are the rule of attraction.

Wherein, to speak compendiously, if experiment hath not deceived us, we first affirm that a loadstone in powder amits not all attraction; for if the powder of a rich vein be in a reasonable quantity presented toward the needle freely placed, it will not appear to be void of all activity, but will be able to stir it; nor hath it only a power to move the needle in powder and by itself, but this will it also do if incorporated and mixed with plasters, as we have made trial in the *Emplastrum de Minio*, with half an ounce of the mass mixing a dram of loadstone. For, applying the magdaleon[2] or roll unto the needle, it would both stir and attract it, not

* *De Cultrivoro Prussiaco*, 1636. † In his *Ars Magnetica*.

[2] *magdaleon or roll*.] An ancient word, of Hebrew origin, transmitted, through barbarous Greek, to barbarous Latin usage, denoting any kind of *emplastric* or other *pilulifiable* paste made up into cylindrical pills " or rolls."

equally in all parts, but more vigorously in some, according unto the mine of the stone more plentifully dispersed in the mass. And lastly, in the loadstone powdered, the polary respects are not wholly destroyed; for those diminutive particles are not atomical or merely indivisible, but consist of dimensions sufficient for their operations, though in obscurer effects. Thus, if unto the powder of loadstone or iron we admove the north pole of the loadstone, the powders or small divisions will erect and conform themselves thereto; but if the south pole approach they will subside, and inverting their bodies, respect the loadstone with the other extreme. And this will happen, not only in a body of powder together, but in any particle of dust divided from it.

Now, though we disavow not these plasters, yet shall we not omit two cautions in their use, that therein the stone be not too subtilely powdered, for it will better manifest its attraction in a more sensible dimension. That, where is desired a speedy effect, it may be considered whether it were not better to relinquish the powdered plasters, and to apply an entire loadstone unto the part; and though the other be not wholly ineffectual, whether this way be not more powerful, and so might have been in the cure of the young man delivered by Beckerus.

The last consideration concerneth magical relations; in which account we comprehend effects derived and fathered upon hidden qualities, specifical forms, antipathies and sympathies, whereof, from received grounds of art, no reasons are derived. Herein relations are strange and numerous, men being apt, in all ages, to multiply wonders, and philosophers dealing with admirable bodies, as historians have done with excellent men, upon the strength of their great achievements, ascribing acts unto them not only false, but impossible, and exceeding truth as much in their relations, as they have others in their actions. Hereof we shall briefly mention some delivered by authors of good esteem: whereby we may discover the fabulous inventions of some, the credulous supinity of others, and the great disservice unto truth by both; multiplying obscurities in nature, and authorising hidden qualities that are false; whereas wise men are ashamed there are so many true.[3]

[3] *true.*] Truly so called.—*Wr.*

And first, Dioscorides puts a shrewd quality upon it (and such as men are apt enough to experiment), who therewith discovers the incontinency of a wife, by placing the loadstone under her pillow, whereupon she will not be able to remain in bed with her husband. The same he also makes a help unto thievery. For thieves, saith he, having a design upon a house, do make a fire at the four corners thereof, and cast therein the fragments of loadstone, whence ariseth a fume that so disturbeth the inhabitants, that they forsake the house, and leave it to the spoil of the robbers. This relation, how ridiculous soever, hath Albertus taken up above a thousand years after, and Marbodeus, the Frenchman, hath continued the same in Latin verse, which, with the notes of Pictorius, is current unto our days. As strange must be the lithomancy or divination from this stone, whereby, as Tzetzes delivers, Helenus the prophet foretold the destruction of Troy. And the magic thereof not safely to be believed, which was delivered by Orpheus, that sprinkled with water, it will, upon a question, emit a voice not much unlike an infant. But, surely, the loadstone of Laurentius Guascus, the physician, is never to be matched, wherewith, as Cardan delivereth, whatsoever needles or bodies were touched, the wounds and punctures, made thereby, were never felt at all. And yet as strange is that which is delivered by some, that a loadstone, preserved in the salt of a *remora*, acquires a power to attract gold out of the deepest wells—certainly a studied absurdity, not casually cast out, but plotted for perpetuity—for the strangeness of the effect ever to be admired, and the difficulty of the trial, never to be convicted.

These conceits are of that monstrosity that they refute themselves in their recitements. There is another of better notice, and whispered through the world with some attention; credulous and vulgar auditors readily believing it, and more judicious and distinctive heads not altogether rejecting it. The conceit is excellent, and, if the effect would follow, somewhat divine, whereby we might communicate like spirits, and confer on earth, with Menippus in the moon. And this is pretended from the sympathy of two needles, touched with the same loadstone, and placed in the centre of two abecedary circles or rings, with letters described round about them, one friend keeping one, and another the other, and agreeing upon an hour wherein they will communicate. For then, saith tradition, at what distance of place soever, when one needle shall be removed unto any letter, the other, by a wonderful sympathy, will move unto the same. But herein I confess my experience can find no truth; for, having expressly framed two circles of wood, and, according to the number of the Latin letters, divided each into twenty-three parts, placing therein two stiles or needles composed of the same steel, touched with the same loadstone, and at the same point; of these two, whensoever I removed the one, although but at the distance of half a span, the other would stand like Hercules' pillars, and (if the earth stand still) have surely no motion at all. Now, as it is not possible that any body should have no boundaries, or sphere of its activity, so it is improbable it should effect that at distance, which nearer hand it cannot at all perform.[4]

[4] *Now as it is not possible, &c.*] But then itt is most wonderful that some things worke the same effect at distance that they doe conjoynd, as the powder of calcined Roman vitrioll strawd on a rag bloaded from a wounde heals the wounde as well and stanches the blood, as if itt were applyed to the wound. I have seen strange effects by itt.—*Wr.*

Sir Kenelm Digby, in *A late Discourse &c. touching the Cure of Wounds by the Powder of Sympathy*, p. 6, &c. relates the following incident, which happened to himself in France. Mr. James Howel (author of *Dendrologia* and other works), had received a very severe wound in his hand in attempting to part two friends who were fighting a duel. Having been requested to endeavour to heal the wound, Sir Kenelm consented, and thus narrates his proceeding:—" I asked him then for any thing that had the blood upon it, so he presently sent for his garter wherewith his hand was first bound, and having called for a bason of water as if I would wash my hands, I took a handful of powder of vitriol, which I had in my study, and presently dissolved it. As soon as the bloody garter was brought me I put it within the bason, observing in the interim what Mr. Howel did, who stood talking with a gentleman in a corner of my chamber, not regarding at all what I was doing; but he started suddenly, as if he had found some strange alteration in himself. I asked him what he ailed? 'I know not what ails me, but I find that I feel no more pain; methinks that a pleasing kind of freshness, as it were a wet cold napkin did spread over my hand, which hath taken away the inflammation that tormented me before:' I replied, 'Since that you feel already so good an effect of my medicament, I advise you to cast away all your plasters, only keep the wound clean, and in a moderate temper twixt heat and cold.' This was presently reported to the Duke of Buckingham, and a little after to the King, who were both very curious to know the circumstance of the

Again, the conceit is ill contrived, and one effect inferred, whereas the contrary will ensue; for, if the removing of one of the needles from A to B should have any action or influence on the other, it would not entice it from A to B, but repel it from A to Z; for needles excited by the same point of the stone do not attract, but avoid each other, even as these also do, when their invigorated extremes approach unto one another.

Lastly, were this conceit assuredly true, yet were it not

business, which was, that after dinner I took the garter out of the water, and put it to dry, but Mr. Howel's servant came running, that his master felt as much burning as ever he had done, if not more, for the heat was such as if his hands were twixt coals of fire: I answered, that although that happened at present, yet he should find ease in a short time; for I knew the reason of this new accident, and I would provide accordingly, for his master should be free from that inflammation, it may be, before he could possibly return unto him: but in case he found no ease, I wished him to come presently back again, if not, he might forbear coming. Thereupon he went, and at the instant I did put again the garter into the water, thereupon he found his master without any pain at all. To be brief, there was no sense of pain afterward; but within five or six days the wounds were cicatrized and entirely healed."

Dr. Bostock, in his remarks on the sympathetic powder, seems to have somewhat misstated the *modus operandi* laid down in the aforesaid treatise, which he justly characterises as "exemplifying admirably the mode of philosophising that was fashionable in the earlier part of the seventeenth century." He says, "Every one who is acquainted with the history of surgery is acquainted with the sympathetic powder, which, about the middle of the seventeenth century, engaged the notice and received the sanction of the most learned men of the age. This celebrated remedy derived its virtues not from its composition, but from the mode of its application, for it was not to be applied to the wound, but to the weapon by which the wound was inflicted; the wound was ordered to be merely closed up, and was taken no further care of. Most men of sense, indeed, ridiculed the proposal, but after being fully tried, it was found that the sympathetic mode of treating wounds was more successful than those plans which proceeded upon what were considered scientific principles; and it continued to gain ground in the public estimation, until at length some innovator ventured to try the experiment of closing up the wound without applying the sympathetic powder to the sword. Wiseman, who wrote about fifty or sixty years after the introduction of this mysterious operation by Sir Kenelm Digby, in describing the importance of keeping the divided parts in union, says, "for here nature will act her part, by the application of blood and nourishment to both sides indifferently, and finish the *coalities* without your further assistance. And this is that which gives such credit to the sympathetic powder."—*Elements of Physiology*, vol. i. p. 448.

a conclusion at every distance to be tried by every head; it being no ordinary or almanack business, but a problem mathematical, to find out the difference of hours in different places; nor do the wisest exactly satisfy themselves in all. For the hours of several places anticipate each other, according unto their longitudes, which are not exactly discovered of every place; and therefore the trial hereof, at a considerable interval, is best performed at the distance of the antœci—that is, such habitations as have the same meridian and equal parallel on different sides of the equator; or, more plainly, the same longitude, and the same latitude unto the south, which we have in the north. For, unto such situations, it is noon and midnight at the very same time.

And therefore, the sympathy of these needles is much of the same mould with that intelligence which is pretended from the flesh of one body transmuted by incision into another. For, if by the art of Taliacotius,* a permutation of flesh, or transmutation be made from one man's body into another, as, if a piece of flesh be exchanged from the bicipital muscle of either party's arm, and about them both an alphabet circumscribed, upon a time appointed, as some conceptions affirm, they may communicate at what distance soever. For, if the one shall prick himself in A, the other at the same time will have a sense thereof in the same part, and, upon inspection of his arm, perceive what letters the other points out in his. Which is a way of intelligence very strange, and would requite the lost art of Pythagoras, who could read a reverse in the moon.

Now this magnetical conceit, how strange soever, might have some original in reason; for men, observing no solid body whatsoever did interrupt its action, might be induced to believe no distance would terminate the same; and most, conceiving it pointed unto the pole of heaven, might also opinion that nothing between could restrain it. Whosoever was the author, the *Æolus* that blew it about was Famianus Strada, that elegant Jesuit, in his rhetorical prolusions, who chose out this subject to express the stile of Lucretius. But neither Baptista Porta, *De Furtivis Literarum notis*, Trithemius, in his *Steganography*, Selenus, in his *Cryptography*,

* *De Curtorum Chirurgia.*

nor *Nuncius inanimatus*,* make any consideration hereof, although they deliver many ways to communicate thoughts at distance. And this we will not deny may in some manner be affected by the loadstone, that is, from one room into another, by placing a table in the wall common unto both, and writing thereon the same letters one against another; for, upon the approach of a vigorous loadstone unto a letter on this side, the needle will move unto the same on the other. But this is a very different way from ours at present; and hereof there are many ways delivered, and more may be discovered, which contradict not the rule of its operations.

As for *Unguentum Armarium*, called also *Magneticum*, it belongs not to this discourse, it neither having the loadstone for its ingredient, nor any one of its actions; but supposed other principles, as common and universal spirits, which convey the action of the remedy unto the part, and conjoins the virtue of bodies far disjoined. But perhaps the cures it doth are not worth so mighty principles; it commonly healing but simple wounds, and such as, mundified and kept clean, do need no other hand than that of nature, and the balsam of the proper part. Unto which effect, there being fields of medicines, it may be a hazardous curiosity to rely on this; and, because men say the effect doth generally follow, it might be worth the experiment to try, whether the same will not ensue, upon the same method of cure, by ordinary balsams, or common vulnerary plasters.

Many other magnetisms may be pretended, and the like attractions through all the creatures of nature. Whether the same be verified in the action of the sun upon inferior bodies, whether there be Æolian magnets, whether the flux and reflux of the sea be caused by any magnetism from the moon, whether the like be really made out, or rather metaphorically verified in the sympathies of plants and animals, might afford a large dispute; and Kircherus, in his *Catena Magnetica*, hath excellently discussed the same; which work came late unto our hand, but might have much advantaged this discourse.[5]

Other discourses there might be made of the loadstone, as moral, mystical, theological; and some have handsomely

---

* By D. Goodwin, Bishop of Hereford.

[5] *Many other, &c.*] Added in the 2nd edition.

done them, as Ambrose, Austine, Gulielmus Parisiensis, and many more; but these fall under no rule, and are as boundless as men's inventions. And, though honest minds do glorify God hereby, yet do they most powerfully magnify him, and are to be looked on with another eye, who demonstratively set forth its magnalities; who not from postulated or precarious inferences entreat a courteous assent, but from experiments and undeniable effects enforce the wonder of its maker.

CHAPTER IV.

Of Bodies Electrical.

HAVING thus spoken of the loadstone and bodies magnetical, I shall, in the next place, deliver somewhat of electrical, and such as may seem to have attraction like the other. Hereof we shall also deliver what particularly spoken or not generally known is manifestly or probably true, what generally believed is also false or dubious. Now, by electrical bodies I understand, not such as are metallical, mentioned by Pliny and the ancients, for their *electrum* was a mixture made of gold, with the addition of a fifth part of silver—a substance now as unknown as true *aurichalcum*, or Corinthian brass, and set down among things lost by Pancirollus; nor by electric bodies do I conceive such only as take up shavings, straws, and light bodies (in which number the ancients only placed jet and amber); but such as, conveniently placed unto their objects, attract all bodies palpable whatsoever. I say conveniently placed, that is, in regard of the object, that it be not too ponderous, or any way affixed: in regard of the agent, that it be not foul or sullied, but wiped, rubbed, and excitated; in regard of both, that they be conveniently distant, and no impediment interposed. I say, all bodies palpable, thereby excluding fire, which indeed it will not attract, nor yet draw through it; for fire consumes its effluxions by which it should attract.

Now, although in this rank but two were commonly mentioned by the ancients, Gilbertus discovereth many more; as diamonds, sapphires, carbuncles, iris, opals, amethysts, beryl, crystal, Bristol stones, sulphur, mastic, hard wax, hard resin, arsenic, *sal-gemma,* roche alum, common glass, *stibium,* or glass of antimony. Unto these, Cabeus addeth white wax, *gum elemi, gum guaiaci, pix hispanica,* and *gypsum.* And unto these we add *gum animi, benjamin talcum,* china-dishes, *sandaraca,* turpentine, *styrax liquida,* and *carauna* dried into a hard consistence.[6] And the same attraction we find not only in simple bodies, but such as are much compounded: as in the *oxycroceum* plaster, and obscurely that *ad herniam* and *gratia Dei;* all which, smooth and rightly prepared, will discover a sufficient power to stir the needle, settled freely upon a well pointed pin; and so as the electric may be applied unto it without all disadvantage.

But the attraction of these electrics we observe to be very different. Resinous or unctuous bodies, and such as will flame, attract most vigorously, and most thereof without frication; as *animi, benjamin,* and most powerfully good hard wax, which will convert the needle almost as actively as the loadstone. And we believe that all, or most of this substance, if reduced to hardness, tralucency, or clearness, would have some attractive quality. But juices concrete, or gums easily dissolving in water, draw not at all; as *aloe, opium, sanguis draconis, lacca, galbanum, sagapenum.* Many stones also, both precious and vulgar, although terse and smooth, have not this power attractive: as emeralds, pearl, jaspis, cornelians, agate, heliotropes, marble, alabaster, touchstone, flint, and bezoar. Glass attracts but weakly, though clear; some slick[7] stones, and thick glasses indifferently; arsenic but weakly; so likewise glass of antimony; but *crocus metallorum*[8] not at all. Salts generally, but weakly; as *sal gemma,* alum, and also talc; not very discoverably by any frication; but, if gently warmed at the fire, and wiped with a dry cloth, they will better discover their electricities.

[6] *And unto these we add gum animi, &c.*] The author is perfectly correct in adding (evidently from his own experiments) these substances to the list of electrics. The "compounded bodies," which he next mentions, derive their electrical properties chiefly from the resin or wax which they contain.—*Br.*

[7] *slick.*] Smooth.

[8] *crocus metallorum.*] And yet (which is the more to be enquired) *crocus martis,* which hath much affinitye to, and his first original from iron, should in common reason attract more than any of the other.—*Wr.*

No metal attracts, nor animal concretion we know,[9] although polite and smooth; as we have made trial in elk's hoofs, hawks' talons, the sword of a sword-fish, tortoise-shells, sea-horse, and elephants' teeth, in bones, in hart's horn, and what is usually conceived unicorn's horn. No wood, though never so hard and polished, although out of some thereof electric bodies proceed; as ebony, box, *lignum vitæ*, cedar, &c. And, although jet and amber be reckoned among bitumens, yet neither do we find *asphaltum*, that is, bitumen of Judea, nor sea-coal, nor camphor, nor *mummia*, to attract, although we have tried in large and polished pieces. Now this attraction have we tried in straws and paleous bodies, in needles of iron equilibrated, powders of wood and iron, in gold and silver foliate; and not only in solid, but fluent and liquid bodies, as oils made both by expression and distillation, in water, in spirits of wine, vitriol, and *aqua fortis*.

But how this attraction is made, is not so easily determined: that it is performed by effluviums is plain, and granted by most; for electrics will not commonly attract, except they grow hot, or become perspirable. For if they be foul and obnubilated, it hinders their effluxion; nor if they be covered, though but with linen or sarsenet, or if a body be interposed, for that intercepts the effluvium. If also a powerful and broad electric of wax or *animi* be held over fine powder, the atoms or small particles will ascend most numerously unto it; and if the electric be held unto the light, it may be observed that many thereof will fly, and be as it were discharged from the electric,[1] to the distance

---

[9] *No metal attracts, nor animal concretion we know.*] Browne is in error respecting all the substances which he mentions in this paragraph, as well as in preceding and following ones, as not susceptible of electrical excitation; for all of them are in fact electrics. But as many among the number, especially the metals, require very perfect insulation, before they can be made to manifest electricity by friction, as many others, especially the true gums, the animal concretions, and the woods, require also to be made very dry; and as some further precautions are necessary in certain cases, in order to insure the success of the experiment, our author's failure, and consequent errors on this subject, are readily explained.—*Br.*

[1] *be as it were discharged from the electric.*] The true cause of this "projection of the atoms," is to be found in the law of electrical attraction and repulsion: *bodies similarly electrified, repel, and dissimilarly electri-*

sometimes of two or three inches. Which motion is performed by the breath of the effluvium issuing with agility; for as the electric cooleth, the projection of the atoms ceaseth.

The manner hereof Cabeus wittily attempteth, affirming that this effluvium attenuateth and impelleth the neighbour air, which returning home in a gyration, carrieth with it the obvious bodies unto the electric. And this he labours to confirm by experiments; for if the straws be raised by a vigorous electric, they do appear to wave and turn in their ascents. If, likewise, the electric be broad, and the straws light and chaffy, and held at a reasonable distance, they will not arise unto the middle, but rather adhere toward the verge or borders thereof. And, lastly, if many straws be laid together, and a nimble electric approach, they will not all arise unto it, but some will commonly start aside, and be whirled a reasonable distance from it. Now, that the air impelled returns unto its place in a gyration or whirling, is evident from the atoms or moats in the sun. For when the sun so enters a hole or window, that by its illumination the atoms or motes become perceptible, if then by our breath the air be gently impelled, it may be perceived that they will circularly return, and in a gyration,[2] unto their places again.

Another way of their attraction is also delivered; that is, by a tenuious emanation or continued effluvium, which after some distance retracteth into itself; as is observable in drops of syrups, oil, and seminal viscosities, which spun at length, retire into their former dimensions. Now these effluviums advancing from the body of the electric, in their return do carry back the bodies, whereon they have laid hold, within the sphere or circle of their continuities; and these they do not only attract, but with their viscous arms hold fast a good while after. And if any shall wonder why these effluviums issuing forth impel and protrude not the straw before they

---

fied, attract each other. The particles are first attracted by the excited electric, because they are in a dissimilar state of electricity to it; by contact with it, however, they acquire a similar state of electricity, and are, in consequence repelled from it.—*Br.*

[2] *gyration.*] The same gyration appears in thistledowne, and small feathers, and the smoke of a snuff, &c.—*Wr.*

can bring it back; it is because the effluvium, passing out in a smaller thread and more enlengthened filament, stirreth not the bodies interposed, but, returning unto its original, falls into a closer substance and carrieth them back unto itself. And this way of attraction is best received, embraced by Sir Kenelm Digby in his excellent treatise of bodies, allowed by Des Cartes in his Principles of Philosophy, as far as concerneth fat and resinous bodies, and with the exception of glass, whose attraction he also deriveth from the recess of its effluxion. And this in some manner the words of Gilbertus will bear. *Effluvia illa tenuiora concipiunt et amplectuntur corpora, quibus uniuntur, et electris tanquam extensis brachiis, et ad fontem propinquitate invalescentibus effluviis, deducuntur.* And if the ground were true, that the earth were an electric body, and the air but the effluvium thereof, we might have more reason to believe that from this attraction, and by this effluxion, bodies tended to the earth, and could not remain above it.[3]

Our other discourse of electricks concerneth a general opinion touching jet and amber, that they attract all light bodies, except *ocymum* or basil, and such as be dipped in oil or oiled; and this is urged as high as Theophrastus. But Scaliger acquitteth him; and had this been his assertion, Pliny would probably have taken it up, who herein stands out, and delivereth no more but what is vulgarly known. But Plutarch speaks positively in his *Symposiack's*, that amber attracteth all bodies, excepting basil and oiled substances. With Plutarch consent many authors, both ancient and modern; but the most inexcusable are Lemnius and Rueus: whereof the one, delivering the nature of minerals mentioned in Scripture, the infallible fountain of truth, confirmeth their virtues with erroneous traditions; the other, undertaking the occult and hidden miracles of nature, accepteth this for

---

[3] *And if the ground, &c.*] That there is a constant breathing of the earth every twelve houres, where itt may easily break forthe, as in the botome of the ocean, is more than probable by the rising of the seas every twelve houres, which wee call the flow, which when it is lifted up by the volubility of its nature, is apt to follow the leading of the moone, but is not raised by itt, because itt keeps a constant course, if there be no strong impediment, as well when she is under, as when above the earthe.—*Wr.*

one, and endeavoureth to allege a reason of that which is more than occult, that is, not existent.

Now herein, omitting the authority of others, as the doctrine of experiment hath informed us, we first affirm, that amber attracts not basil is wholly repugnant unto truth. For if the leaves thereof or dried stalks be stripped into small straws, they arise unto amber, wax, and other electricks, no otherwise than those of wheat and rye; nor is there any peculiar fatness or singular viscosity in that plant that might cause adhesion, and so prevent its ascension. But that jet and amber attract not straws oiled, is in part true and false; for, if the straws be much wet or drenched in oil, true it is that amber draweth them not, for then the oil makes the straw to adhere unto the part whereon they are placed, so that they cannot rise unto the attractor; and this is true, not only if they be soaked in oil, but spirits of wine or water. But if we speak of straws or festucous divisions lightly drawn over with oil, and so that it causeth no adhesion, or if we conceive an antipathy between oil and amber, the doctrine is not true; for amber will attract straws thus oiled, it will convert the needles of dials made either of brass or iron, although they be much oiled; for in these needles consisting free upon their centre, there can be no adhesion. It will likewise attract oil itself, and if it approacheth unto a drop thereof, it becometh[4] conical, and ariseth up unto it, for oil taketh not away his attraction, although it be rubbed over it. For if you touch a piece of wax, already excitated, with common oil, it will, notwithstanding, attract, though, not so vigorously as before; but if you moisten the same with any chemical oil, water, or spirits of wine, or only breathe upon it, it quite amits its attraction, for either its effluences cannot get through, or will not mingle with those substances.

It is likewise probable the ancients were mistaken concerning its substance and generation: they conceiving it a vegetable concretion made of the gums of trees, especially pine and poplar, falling into the water, and after, indurated or hardened, whereunto accordeth the fable of Phaeton's sisters. But surely the concretion is mineral, according as is delivered by Boëtius. For either it is found in mountains

[4] *it becometh.*] i. e. the oyle becometh.—*Wr.*

and mediterraneous parts, and so it is a fat and unctuous sublimation in the earth, concreted and fixed by salt and nitrous spirits wherewith it meeteth. Or else, which is most usual, it is collected upon the sea shore, and so it is a fat and bituminous juice coagulated by the saltness of the sea.[5]

[5] *It is likewise probable, &c.*] The whole progress of subsequent, and especially of recent observations and experiments on amber, has tended to show that the older was the more correct opinion; and that Sir Thomas concluded too hastily from its being found on the sea-shore, and even in deep mines, that its origin could not be vegetable. Brongniart and Leman (distinguished French mineralogists), both consider it a vegetable juice concreted—partly by the lapse of time—and modified by its subterraneous locality. It is found in the greatest abundance in beds of fossilized timber, at considerable depth, and beneath several other strata, near the coast of Prussia: it occurs there in the very midst of the timber—which appears to have produced it. Leman remarks, that a crust of dirt and other foreign substances, is often found on the surface of amber, like that which is contracted by vegetable gum in flowing over the bark of the tree, or falling on the ground. Specimens found on the sea-shore, or (occasionally) in alluvial deposits, are usually free from the crust. It is to be supposed that amber may have been the gum of a now extinct tree. This implied antiquity has been argued from the class of formations in which it is most copiously met with, and from the fact that the insects, &c. inclosed in it, are not the recent species, nor even analogous to those now existing in the same spot, tropical genera being found in the amber of northern latitudes. It may be admitted as probable, that we possess the ambers of several different trees: for very distinct varieties of it are known; one of which is noticed by Brongniart as destitute of the *succinic acid*, which he considers the chief criterion by which amber is distinguishable from *mellite*, and the fossilized resins, and from gum copal. Its original fluidity is unquestionable, from the delicacy of many species found in it.

The author of the article AMBER, in the *Encyc. Brit.* considers it rather likely to have been softened by the action of the sun than to have been ever liquid. One of the reasons adduced, seems to oppose rather than to support this opinion. "Drops of clear water are sometimes preserved in amber. These have doubtless been received into it while *soft*, &c." More probably when *fluid*. The same writer mentions an assertion of Girtanner, that amber is an "*animal* product—a sort of honey or wax formed by the red ant, *formica-rufa*." But after detailing some of Girtanner's observations, he represents his opinion as being that "amber is nothing but a *vegetable* oil, rendered concrete by the acid of ants." The article contains other incorrect statements;—that amber is the basis of *all* varnishes; and that "it seems generally agreed upon, that amber is a true bitumen of a fossil origin." This might be more generally the opinion when the article was first written—but is not so now; and therefore it ought not to have remained unaltered in the edition now publishing of the *Enc. Brit.*, in which the

Now, that salt spirits have a power to congeal and coagulate unctuous bodies, is evident in chymical operations; in the distillations of arsenick, sublimate, and antimony; in the mixture of oil of juniper with the salt and acid spirit of sulphur; for thereupon ensueth a concretion unto the consistence of birdlime; as also in spirits of salt, or *aqua fortis* poured upon oil of olive, or more plainly in the manufacture of soap. And many bodies will coagulate upon commixture, whose separated natures promise no concretion. Thus, upon a solution of tin by *aqua fortis*, there will ensue a coagulation, like that of whites of eggs. Thus, the volatile salt of urine will coagulate *aqua vitæ*,[6] or spirits of wine; and thus, perhaps, as Helmont excellently declareth, the stones or calculous concretions in kidney or bladder may be produced, the spirits or volatile salt of urine conjoining with the *aqua*

---

article appears nearly in its former state:—some paragraphs omitted, but no addition—no correction—no remodelling.

Patrin supposes it to be honey, gradually bitumenized by the action of certain *mineral* acids.

One of the most celebrated modern experimental philosophers, Sir David Brewster, from a series of experiments on the optical properties of amber, has arrived at a conclusion precisely in accordance with the opinion of the ancients, viz. that it is "beyond a doubt an *indurated vegetable juice;*" and he observes, "that the traces of a regular structure, indicated by its action upon polarised light, are not the effect of the ordinary laws of crystallisation by which *mellite* has been formed, but are produced by the same causes which influence the mechanical condition of gum arabic, and other gums which are known to be formed by the successive deposition and induration of vegetable fluids."

An interesting addition to the above authorities, in support of the vegetable origin of amber, occurs in a paper of Dr. Mac Culloch's, in the *Quarterly Journal of Science*, &c. vol. xvi. p. 41. His leading object is to point out the readiest mode of distinguishing those specimens of gum copal, animi, and perhaps other resins enclosing insects, which are sometimes offered for sale as amber. On the fact of insects being often found in amber, Dr. M. mainly insists, as the proof of its vegetable origin, especially when viewed in connection with similar enclosures in unfossilized resins. He proceeds to a chemical examination and comparison of amber with similar bodies, and ends by saying, "from these analogies we may, perhaps, safely conclude, that amber has been a vegetable resin converted to its present state during the same time and by the same causes which have converted common vegetable matter into jet, and, perhaps, ultimately into coal."

[6] *aqua vitæ.*] Some March beere or very stale wil turne *aqua vitæ* into the shape of whey.—*Wr.*

vitæ potentially lying therein; as he illustrateth from the distillation of fermented urine; from whence ariseth an *aqua vitæ* or spirit, which the volatile salt of the same urine will congeal, and finding an earthy concurrence, strike into a lapideous substance.

Lastly, we will not omit what Bellabonus, upon his own experiment, writ from Dantzick, unto Mellichius, as he hath left recorded in his chapter *De Succino*, that the bodies of flies, pismires, and the like, which are said ofttimes to be included in amber, are not real, but representative, as he discovered in several pieces broke for that purpose. If so, the two famous epigrams hereof in *Martial* are but poetical, the pismire of Brassavolus, imaginary, and Cardan's mausoleum for a fly, a mere fancy. But hereunto we know not how to assent, as having met with some whose reals make good their representments.[7]

---

[7] *representments.*] Avicen affirms that ambar appeares plentifully in hot countries (as the south parts of Arabia Felix, neare the sea), especially after great earthquakes, which makes good the assertion [that itt is most usually collected on the sea shore]. Whence itt is most probable that at the eruption thereof, itt might involve and consequently intumulate Martial's viper and Cardan's flye.— *W'r.*

The dean's fancy seems to have been running upon a mineral *rendered fluid by heat*; it might have occurred to him, that "Messrs. the viper and flye," would, in such a bath, have been more than *intumulated*;— they would have suffered *incineration!* There is, however, no accounting for the fables of antiquity, or the fancy of poets. The fabulous origin of amber, from the tears of the sister of Phaeton, lamenting his fate on the banks of Eridanus, is celebrated in Martial's Epigram on the bee in amber. But unfortunately for the poet, no authentic instance is said to have occurred of that insect having been found in amber. Sir Thomas, however, is quite correct in asserting the reality of man specimens of insects, &c. which have been found in it

CHAPTER V.

Compendiously of sundry other common tenets concerning minerals and terreous bodies, which, examined, prove either false or dubious.—That a diamond is softened or broken by the blood of a goat; that glass is poison, and that it is malleable; of the cordial quality of gold; that a pot full of ashes will contain as much water as it would without them; of white powder that kills without report; that coral is soft under water, but hardeneth in the air; that porcelain lies under the earth an hundred years in preparation; that a carbuncle gives a light in the dark; of the eagle stone; of fairy stones; with some others.

1. AND, first, we hear it in every mouth, and in many good authors read it, that a diamond, which is the hardest of stones, not yielding unto steel, emery, or any thing but its own powder, is yet made soft, or broke by the blood of a goat. Thus much is affirmed by Pliny, Solinus, Albertus, Cyprian, Austin, Isidore, and many christian writers: alluding herein unto the heart of man, and the precious blood of our Saviour, who was typified by the goat that was slain, and the scapegoat in the wilderness: and at the effusion of whose blood, not only the hard hearts of his enemies relented, but the stony rocks and vail of the temple were shattered. But this, I perceive, is easier affirmed than proved. For lapidaries, and such as profess the art of cutting this stone, do generally deny it; and they that seem to countenance it have in their deliveries so qualified it, that little from thence of moment can be inferred for it. For first, the holy fathers, without a further enquiry, did take it for granted, and rested upon the authority of the first deliverers. As for Albertus, he promiseth this effect, but conditionally, not except the goat drink wine, and be fed with *siler montanum, petroselinum,* and such herbs as are conceived of power to break the stone in the bladder. But the words of Pliny, from whom most likely the rest at first derived it, if strictly considered, do rather overthrow, than any way advantage this effect. His words are these: *Hircino rumpitur sanguine, nec aliter quàm recenti, calidoque macerata, et sic quoque multis ictibus, tunc etiam præterquam eximias incudes malleosque ferreos frangens.* That is, it is broken with goat's blood, but not except it be fresh and

warm, and that not without many blows, and then also it will break the best anvils and hammers of iron. And answerable hereto is the assertion of Isidore and Solinus. By which account, a diamond steeped in goat's blood rather increaseth in hardness, than acquireth any softness by the infusion, for the best we have are comminuible without it, and are so far from breaking hammers, that they submit unto pistillation, and resist not an ordinary pestle.⁸

Upon this conceit arose, perhaps, the discovery of another —that the blood of a goat was sovereign for the stone; as it stands commended by many good writers, and brings up the composition in the powder of Nicolaus,* and the electuary of the queen of Colein. Or rather, because it was found an excellent medicine for the stone, and its ability commended by some to dissolve the hardest thereof, it might be conceived by amplifying apprehensions to be able to break a diamond; and so it came to be ordered that the goat should be fed with saxifragous herbs, and such as are conceived of power to break the stone. However it were, as the effect is false in the one, so is it, surely, very doubtful in the other. For, although inwardly received, it may be very diuretic, and expulse the stone in the kidneys, yet how it should dissolve or break that in the bladder, will require a further dispute; and, perhaps, would be more reasonably tried by a warm injection thereof, than as it is commonly used. Wherein, notwithstanding, we should rather rely upon the urine in a castling's bladder, a resolution of crabs' eyes, or the second distillation of urine, as Helmont hath commended; or rather (if any such might be found) a chylifactory menstruum or digestive preparation, drawn from species or individuals whose stomachs peculiarly dissolve lapideous bodies.

2. That glass is poison, according unto common conceit, I know not how to grant. Not only from the innocency of

* *Pulvis Lithontripticus.*

⁵ 1. *And first, &c.*] Nothing can put Ross out of conceit with "the ancients." Though he admits the fact that diamonds are mastered by hammers, and not, as asserted by the ancients, softened by goat's blood; yet doth he not a whit the less believe this assertion as applied to *adamant*, of which, he says, there were divers kinds.—*Arcana*, p. 196.

its ingredients, that is, fine sand, and the ashes of glass-wort or fern, which in themselves are harmless and useful, or because I find it by many commended for the store, but also from experience, as having given unto dogs above a dram thereof, subtilely powdered in butter and paste, without any visible disturbance.[9]

The conceit is surely grounded upon the visible mischief of glass grossly or coarsely powdered, for that indeed is mortally noxious, and effectually used by some to destroy mice and rats; for, by reason of its acuteness and angularity, it commonly excoriates the parts through which it passeth, and solicits them unto a continual expulsion. Whereupon there ensue fearful symptoms, not much unlike those which attend the action of poison. From whence, notwithstanding, we cannot with propriety impose upon it that name, either by occult or elementary quality, which he that concedeth will much enlarge the catalogues or lists of poisons. For many things neither deleterious by substance or quality, are yet destructive by figure, or some occasional activity. So are leeches destructive, and by some accounted poison; not properly, that is, by temperamental contrariety, occult form, or so much as elemental repugnancy; but because, being inwardly taken, they fasten upon the veins and occasion an effusion of blood, which cannot be easily staunched. So a sponge is mischievous, not in itself, for in its powder it is harmless; but because, being received into the stomach it swelleth, and occasioning a continual distention, induceth a strangulation.[1] So pins, needles, ears of rye or barley may be poison.[2] So Daniel destroyed the

---

[9] *without any visible disturbance.*] Edit. 1646 adds, "And the trial thereof we the rather did make in that animal, because Grevinus, in his *Treatise of Poisons*, affirmeth that dogs are inevitably destroyed thereby."—p. 84.

[1] *So a sponge is mischievous, &c.*] As to a dog, soakt in butter or grease.—*Wr*.

[2] *ears of rye or barley, &c.*] A very remarkable and affecting proof of the truth of this observation occurred a few years ago in the family of the present Earl of Morley. His lordship's eldest son, Lord Boringdon, then in the twelfth year of his age, in the course of an evening walk with his father and brother, on the 17th of July, 1817, put an ear of rye into his mouth; and it appears that within a few seconds afterwards, it had become out of the power of man to save his life.

dragon by a composition of three things, whereof none was poison alone, nor properly altogether; that is, pitch, fat, and hair, according as is expressed in the history. " Then Daniel took pitch, and fat, and hair, and did seethe them together, and made lumps thereof; these he put in the dragon's mouth, and so he burst asunder."[3] That is, the fat and pitch being cleaving bodies, and the hair continually ex-

The lower part of the ear first entered the windpipe, and after the first fit of coughing, which lasted about five or six minutes, no more inconvenience was felt. He was about half a mile from home when the accident happened;—he walked gently home. Dr. Heath, who immediately saw him, gave him some bread, which he swallowed without difficulty. It was hoped that he had, in the field, unknowingly coughed up the corn, or that it had passed into the stomach. It appears that the ear of rye passed gently through the whole of the lungs without producing any great effect. It was at the very bottom of the lungs, where it ultimately lodged, that on the fourth day from the accident, it injured a vessel, and occasioned a hæmorrhage. In this situation it caused an abscess in the lower part of the lungs and liver, which terminated fatally on the 1st of November.

It will readily be supposed that nothing which medical skill could devise was omitted. Dr. Spurzheim and Dr. Roberton of Paris, Dr. Young and other distinguished medical men, assisted Dr. Heath. Not only the extreme rarity of the case, but the amiable character and high rank of the patient secured to him all that human ingenuity could effect. And it was a consolation to the family to ascertain, by subsequent investigation, that had the exact nature of the injury been known at the very first, no materially different treatment could have been adopted.

This account has been sketched from a highly interesting and very detailed narrative in MS. in the possession of the family, with which I have been favoured through the kind intervention of a friend.

[3] *Then Daniel took, &c.*] Ctesias makes mention of a horse-pismire (i. e. the bigger kind of them in hollow trees) which was fed by the magi till hee grew to such a vast bulke as to devour two pound of flesh a daye. This story might possibly relate to Daniel's dragon, which was before his time at least one hundred and ninety years. For hee wrote in the 94th Olympiade, whereas the captivitye was in the 43rd.—*Wr.*

The gravity of Sir Thomas's burlesque explanation of this apochryphal story (for he cannot for a moment be considered as speaking seriously) is happily imitated in the preceding note by the dean, whose delectable quotation from Ctesias (supported by a grave chronological computation) supplies the only point omitted by our author; viz., a conjecture as to the *species* of the creature who is said to have received, with so good a grace, the boluses of the prophet. Who will hesitate to admit the probability of the dean's suggestion, that the dragon of Daniel was no other than the horse-pismire of Ctesias?

timulating the parts, by the action of the one nature was provoked to expel, but by the tenacity of the other forced to retain; so that, there being left no passage in or out, the dragon brake in pieces. It must, therefore, be taken of grossly-powdered glass, what is delivered by Grevinus: and from the same must that mortal dysentery proceed which is related by Sanctorius. And in the same sense only shall we allow a diamond to be poison; and whereby, as some relate, Paracelsus himself was poisoned. So, even the precious fragments and cordial gems, which are of frequent use in physic, and in themselves confessed of useful faculties, received in gross and angular powders, may so offend the bowels, as to procure desperate languors, or cause most dangerous fluxes.

That glass may be rendered malleable and pliable unto the hammer many conceive, and some make little doubt, when they read in Dio, Pliny, and Petronius, that one unhappily effected it for Tiberius;[3] which, notwithstanding, must needs seem strange unto such as consider that bodies are ductile from a tenacious humidity, which so holdeth the parts together, that, though they dilate or extend, they part not from each other;—that bodies run into glass when the volatile parts are exhaled, and the continuating humour separated, the salt and earth (that is, the fixed parts) remaining;— and therefore vitrification maketh bodies brittle, as destroying the viscous humours which hinder the disruption of parts. Which may be verified even in the bodies of metals; for glass of lead or tin is fragile, when that glutinous sulphur hath been fired out which made their bodies ductile.

He that would most probably attempt it, must experiment upon gold, whose fixed and flying parts are so conjoined, whose sulphur and continuating principle is so united unto the salt, that some may be hoped to remain to hinder fragility after vitrification. But how to proceed, though after frequent corrosion, as that upon the agency of fire it should

---

[3] *one unhappily effected it, &c.*] *Unhappily*, because Tiberius put the artist to death for his performance. No explanation, however, is given by Dion Cassius of the mode in which he was said to have rendered whole a glass which he had broken.

not revive into its proper body before it comes to vitrify, will prove no easy discovery.[4]

3. That gold inwardly taken, either in substance, infusion, decoction, or extinction,[5] is a cordial of great efficacy, in sundry medical uses, although a practice much used, is also much questioned, and by no man determined beyond dispute.[6] There are, hereof, I perceive, two extreme opinions; some excessively magnifying it, and probably beyond its deserts; others extremely vilifying it, and perhaps below its demerits. Some affirming it a powerful medicine in many diseases; others averring that so used, it is effectual in none: and in this number are very eminent physicians, Erastus, Duretus, Rondeletius, Brassavolus, and many other; who, beside the strigments[7] and sudorous adhesions from men's hands, acknowledge that nothing proceedeth from gold in the usual decoction thereof. Now the capital reason that led men unto this opinion, was their observation of the inse-

[4] *no easy discovery.*] The two preceding paragraphs were added in the 2nd edition.

[5] *extinction.*] He refers probably to taking a liquid in which gold heated red hot has been extinguished.

[6] *That gold, &c.*] The whole of this examination of the question, how far gold is available as a medicine, is conducted with our author's usual acuteness and caution; and is remarkable as much for the candour with which he confesses his want of data whereby to determine the question, as for the extensive acquaintance he displays with what had been said by others. With all the advantages of subsequent experiment during nearly two centuries, it does not appear that this most precious metal has taken a prominent place among the medicines of the present day. Dr. Block, of Berlin, informs us, in his *Medicinische Bemerkungen*, that he has given, in obstinate constipations of the bowels, when unattended with pains or inflammation, not only pills of lead, but also of gold, with the best success, after every usual method has been resorted to in vain; whence it appeared to him that such remedies acted merely by their specific gravity. An eminent medical friend, of whom I have recently enquired, whether the chloride of gold is used in France, has favoured me with the following reply: "The chloride of gold has for several years past been used as a medicine in Paris, and its virtues much vaunted of by individuals for the cure of venereal and many other diseases; but it has not received corresponding support from French practitioners generally, and in this country I do not remember that it has been extensively tried in practice." The chloride of gold is the *red tincture of gold*, which was originally prepared by Glauber.

[7] *strigments.*] Scrapings. Here again is a coinage of the author's, for which he is his own sole authority.

parable nature of gold, it being excluded in the same quantity as it was received, without alteration of parts, or diminution of its gravity.

Now, herein to deliver somewhat, which in a middle way may be entertained: we first affirm, that the substance of gold is invincible by the powerfullest action of natural heat; and that not only alimentally in a substantial mutation, but also medicamentally in any corporeal conversion; as is very evident, not only in the swallowing of golden bullets, but in the lesser and foliate divisions thereof; passing the stomach and guts even as it doth the throat, that is, without abatement of weight or consistence; so that it entereth not the veins with those electuaries wherein it is mixed; but taketh leave of the permeant parts, at the mouths of the mesaraicks, or lacteal vessels, and accompanieth the inconvertible portion unto the siege. Nor is its substantial conversion expectable in any composition or aliment wherein it is taken. And therefore that was truly a starving absurdity which befel the wishes of Midas. And little credit there is to be given to the golden hen, related by Wendlerus. And so in the extinction of gold, we must not conceive it parteth with any of its salt or dissoluble principle thereby, as we may affirm of iron; for the parts thereof are fixed beyond division; nor will they separate upon the strongest test of fire. This we affirm of pure gold; for that which is current and passeth in stamp amongst us, by reason of its alloy, which is a proportion of silver or copper mixed therewith, is actually dequantitated by fire, and possibly by frequent extinction.

Secondly, although the substance of gold be not immuted, or its gravity sensibly decreased, yet that from thence some virtue may proceed either in substantial reception or infusion, we cannot safely deny. For possible it is that bodies may emit virtue and operation without abatement of weight; as is most evident in the loadstone, whose effluencies are continual and communicable without a minoration of gravity; and the like is observable in bodies electrical, whose emissions are less subtile. So will a diamond or sapphire emit an effluvium sufficient to move the needle or a straw, without diminution of weight. Nor will polished amber, although it send forth a gross and corporeal exhalement, be found a long time defective upon the exactest scales; which is more easily conceivable in a continued and tenacious effluvium, whereof a great part retreats into its body.

Thirdly, if amulets do work by emanations from their bodies, upon those parts whereunto they are appended, and are not yet observed to abate their weight; if they produce visible and real effects by imponderous and invisible emissions, it may be unjust to deny the possible efficacy of gold, in the non-omission of weight, or deperdition of any ponderous particles.[8]

Lastly, since *stibium*, or glass of antimony, since also its *regulus* will manifestly communicate unto water or wine a purging and vomitory operation, and yet the body itself, though after iterated infusions, cannot be found to abate either virtue or weight: we shall not deny but gold may do the like, that is, impart some effluences unto the infusion, which carry with them the separable subtilities thereof.[9]

---

[8] *Thirdly, if amulets, &c.*] This paragraph is so cautiously worded, by virtue of the little *if*, as to convey a proposition at once safe and undeniable. But, like many other cautious propositions, it says nothing. The questions remain, what amulets do "produce visible and real effects?"—whether these "work by emanations?"—and whether they do so without "abating their weight?" Though the Hon. Robt. Boyle was pleased to attribute the cure of an hæmorrhage to wearing "some moss from a dead man's skull," our readers will probably be inclined to indulge a good deal of scepticism as to the efficacy of such charms. Camphor, volatile alkali, pungent acids, &c. which are often used, and perhaps efficaciously, as repellents of contagion, can scarcely be termed *amulets;* and if they are so, they most certainly do not come within Sir Thomas's definition, as "not abating their weight by emanations." The Abbé Pluche speaks of the origin of amulets, properly so called, in his *Histoire du Ciel*, 12mo. tom. i. p. 360. See also a very curious little work on amulets, by Petr. Frid. Arpe, entitled *De prodigiosis Naturæ et Artis Operibus Talismanes et Amuleta dictis*, 12mo. *Hamburgi*, 1717.

[9] *Lastly, since* stibium, *&c.*] The *antimoniall cupp* was anciently in domestic medicine, on the double principle here stated, by which the metal, without losing its bulk, imparted to the wine poured into it the desired property. There occurs in the *Gentleman's Magazine* (vol. CII. pt. i. p. 581), a curious account of one of these "cupps." It is made of the *regulus of antimony*, cast in a mould; is about two inches high by about as many in diameter, and holds about four ounces; is contained in a leathern box; within are *written directions* for its use, prefaced by a full announcement of the "vertues of the cupp," together with some Latin and English verses. The process of preparing the cup for use

That therefore this metal thus received hath any undeniable effect, we shall not imperiously determine, although, beside the former experiments, many more may induce us to believe it. But, since the point is dubious and not yet authentically decided, it will be no discretion to depend on disputable remedies; but rather, in cases of known danger, to have recourse unto medicines of known and approved activity. For, beside the benefit accruing unto the sick, hereby may be avoided a gross and frequent error, commonly committed in the use of doubtful remedies conjointly with those which are of approved virtues, that is, to impute the cure unto the conceited remedy, or place it on that whereon they place their opinion; whose operation, although it be nothing, or its concurrence not considerable, yet doth it obtain the name of the whole cure, and carrieth often the honour of the capital energy, which had no finger in it.

Herein exact and critical trial should be made by public enjoinment, whereby determination might be settled beyond debate; for, since thereby not only the bodies of men, but great treasures might be preserved, it is not only an error of physics, but folly of state, to doubt thereof any longer.[1]

4. That a pot full of ashes will still contain as much water as it would without them, although by Aristotle in his problems taken for granted, and so received by most, is not effectable upon the strictest experiment I could ever make. For when the airy interstices are filled, and as much of the salt of the ashes as the water will imbibe is dissolved, there remains a gross and terreous portion at the bottom, which will possess a space by itself, according whereto, there will remain a quantity of water not receivable: so will it come to pass in a pot of salt, although decrepitated:[2] and so also in a pot of snow; for so much it will want in reception, as its solution taketh up, according unto the bulk whereof, there will remain a portion of water not to be admitted: so a

was either by letting wine stand for a certain time in it, or (if it was required to *antimonize* more wine than the cup would contain), by plunging the cup into the requisite quantity of wine. Regulus of antimony was also anciently used in the form of pills, which, it is asserted, were, by some frugal persons, *re-employed* as often as they could be recovered!

[1] *Herein, &c.*] Added in the 2nd edition.
[2] *decrepitated.*] Calcined till it has ceased to crackle.

glass stuffed with pieces of sponge will want about a sixth part of what it would receive without it : so sugar will not dissolve beyond the capacity of the water, nor a metal in *aqua fortis* be corroded beyond its reception ; and so a pint of salt of tartar, exposed unto a moist air until it dissolve, will make far more liquor, or, as some term it, oil, than the former measure will contain.

Nor is it only the exclusion of air by water, or repletion of cavities possessed thereby, which causeth a pot of ashes to admit so great a quantity of water, but also the solution of the salt of the ashes into the body of the dissolvent : so a pot of ashes will receive somewhat more of hot water than of cold, for the warm water imbibeth more of the salt ; and a vessel of ashes more than one of pin-dust or filings of iron; and a glass full of water will yet drink in a proportion of salt or sugar without overflowing.

Nevertheless, to make the experiment with most advantage, and in which sense it approacheth nearest the truth, it must be made in ashes thoroughly burnt and well reverberated by fire, after the salt thereof hath been drawn out by iterated decoctions. For then the body, being reduced nearer unto earth, and emptied of all other principles, which had former ingression unto it, becometh more porous, and greedily drinketh in water. He that hath beheld what quantity of lead the test of saltless ashes will imbibe, upon the refining of silver, hath encouragement to think it will do very much more in water.[3]

5. Of white powder, and such as is discharged without report,[4] there is no small noise in the world; but how far agreeable unto truth, few, I perceive, are able to determine. Herein therefore, to satisfy the doubts of some and amuse

---

[3] *Nevertheless, &c.*] Added in 2nd edition.

[4] *5 Of white powder, &c.*] The nearest approach to *white powder* is the *fulminating powder*, in which carbonate of potash is substituted for charcoal : the composition being three parts of nitre, two of carbonate of potash, and one of sulphur.—*Ure's Dictionary of Chemistry.*

But this detonates more loudly than gunpowder. The *error* which it was our author's object to correct here, was that of expecting an *effective* gunpowder (of whatever colour) which should be "without report." He justly observes, that, even admitting the probability of making a "white powder,"—"and such an one as may give no report,"—it would "be of little force, and the effects thereof no way to be feared."

the credulity of others, we first declare, that gunpowder consisteth of three ingredients, saltpetre, small-coal, and brimstone.⁵ Saltpetre, although it be also natural and found in several places, yet is that of common use an artificial salt, drawn from the infusion of salt earth, as that of stales, stables, dove-houses, cellars, and other covered places,⁶ where the rain can neither dissolve, nor the sun approach to resolve it : brimstone is a mineral body of fat and inflammable parts, and this is either used crude, and called *sulphur vive*, and is

⁵ *we first declare, &c.*] The account here given of gunpowder is upon the whole accurate; especially if we allow for the unsettled state of philosophical language at that time, which makes it sometimes difficult to feel assured of Sir Thomas's precise meaning. He was evidently aware of the necessity of employing *pure ingredients* in the composition of gunpowder; observing that "powder which is made of impure and greasy petre hath but a weak emission, and giveth a faint report;" and again, "that the best way to alter the noise and strength of the discharge, consists in the quality of the nitre." He assigns, with sufficient correctness, to its constituents their respective share in the general results, when he ascribes to the charcoal the "quick *accension* [ignition]" to the sulphur the "piercing and powerful firing," and to the nitre the "force and the report."—Modern experiment has shown that the detonation or explosion of gunpowder is attributable to the nitre, when combined with inflammable substances, viz. the sulphur and charcoal; and arises from the sudden extrication, by combustion, of nitrogen and carbonic acid gases, which expand to a volume about two thousand times greater than that originally occupied by the powder.— The opinions of Carden and Snellius, quoted by our author, as to the degree of expansion, are erroneous. In describing the mixture of the three ingredients of gunpowder, Sir Thomas has named proportions very different from those now adopted. Barrow informs us, that the Chinese soldiery make their gunpowder (for it is there the duty of every soldier to prepare his own) in the proportion of 50lbs. of nitre to 25lbs. each of sulphur and charcoal: but the modern practice is to employ about 75 of nitre and 15 (or 16) of charcoal to 10 (or 9) of sulphur; varying the relations between the two last, according as the object is to produce a powder of greater durability or of greater strength; more usually the sulphur has been increased, and the carbon lessened—in order to obtain a more lasting article, by a slight sacrifice of strength—which may readily be compensated by increasing the charge.

⁶ *Saltpetre, although it be also natural, &c.*] Native saltpetre, or nitre (*nitrate of potash*) occurs in crusts and capillary crystals, in Spain, France, Italy, and Hungary; in Arabia, Persia, and India; at the Cape of Good Hope, in the mountains of Kentucky, and near Lima in South America. But not being naturally produced in sufficient quantity, it is obtained artificially, in what are termed *nitre-beds*, as is described by Thenard (*Traité de Chimie*, ii. 57.)

of a sadder colour, or, after depuration, such as we have in magdaleons[7] or rolls, of a lighter yellow : small-coal[7] is known unto all, and for this use is made of sallow, willow, alder, hazel, and the like :—which three, proportionably mixed, tempered, and formed into granulary bodies, do make up that powder which is in use for guns.

Now all these, although they bear a share in the discharge, yet have they distinct intentions, and different offices in the composition. From brimstone proceedeth the piercing and powerful firing; for small-coal and petre together will only spit, nor vigorously continue the ignition. From small-coal ensueth the black colour and quick accension; for neither brimstone nor petre, although in powder, will take fire like small-coal, nor will they easily kindle upon the sparks of a flint; as neither will camphor, a body very inflammable; but small-coal is equivalent to tinder, and serveth to light the sulphur; it may also serve to diffuse the ignition through every part of the mixture; and being of more gross and fixed parts, may seem to moderate the activity of saltpetre, and prevent too hasty rarefaction.[8] From saltpetre proceedeth the force and the report; for sulphur and small-coal mixed will not take fire with noise or exilition,[9] and powder which is made of impure and greasy petre hath but a weak emission, and giveth a faint report. And therefore, in the three sorts of powder, the strongest containeth saltpetre, and the proportion thereof is about ten parts of petre unto one of coal and sulphur.

But the immediate cause of the report is the vehement commotion of the air, upon the sudden and violent eruption of the powder; for that being suddenly fired, and almost altogether, upon this high rarefaction requireth by many degrees a greater space than before its body occupied; but finding resistance, it actively forceth his way, and by concussion of the air occasioneth the report. Now with what

[7] *small-coal.*] The old term for charcoal. For *magdaleon*, see note at p 150.

[8] *it may also, &c.*] Added in 2nd edition. That charcoal serves as a diffusing medium to facilitate ignition is true ; but it is not easy to see how it can operate to "moderate the activity of saltpetre."

[9] *exilition.*] "The act of springing out suddenly." The present passage is Johnson's sole authority.

violence it forceth upon the air, may easily be conceived, if we admit, what Cardan affirmeth, that the powder fired doth occupy an hundred times a greater space than its own bulk; or rather what Snellius more exactly accounteth, that it exceedeth its former space no less than 12,500 times. And this is the reason not only of this fulminating report of guns, but may resolve the cause of those terrible cracks, and affrighting noises of heaven ;[1] that is, the nitrous and sulphureous exhalations, set on fire in the clouds; whereupon requiring a larger place, they force out their way, not only with the breaking of the cloud, but the laceration of the air about it. When, if the matter be spirituous, and the cloud compact, the noise is great and terrible: if the cloud be thin, and the materials weak, the eruption is languid, ending in coruscations and flashes without noise, although but at the distance of two miles ; which is esteemed the remotest distance of clouds.[2] And, therefore, such lightnings do seldom

[1] *And this is the reason, &c.*] In his comparison of gunpowder with lightning, our author proposes an opinion which was maintained by his great contemporary, Dr. Wallis ; who considered their effects so similar, that they might, without hesitation, be ascribed to the same cause. The discovery of electricity, and the identity of lightning with the electric fluid, was reserved for a century later :—but the philosophy of *sound* is substantially the same in both cases; for, although the *immediate* results of the ignition of gunpowder and of the discharge of electric fluid, are directly opposite,— being *rarefaction* in the one case, by the evolution of gases, and in the other *condensation* by the combination of other gases ; and although the *first* results on the surrounding atmosphere are also opposite,—the air in the latter case *advancing* in order to occupy the vacuum created by condensation, and in the former *retreating* in order to afford the space required by rarefaction ;—yet, the *subsequent* results in both cases are, alternate reactions of the particles of air, till its average density is regained. Hence it follows, that in both cases sound arises from the concussion, and consequent undulation (to use Professor Brande's term) occasioned by the respective explosion of gunpowder and of lightning.

If it be admitted, however, that the ideas of Sir Thomas on the point were not far from the truth ; it must, on the other hand, be confessed that he has clothed them in language not only unphilosophical, but most ambiguous, when he speaks of " the *breaking* of the clouds, and *laceration* of the air,"—and of " the *matter* being *spirituous,* and the clouds compact ; or " the clouds *thin* and the *materials weak.*"

[2] *the remotest distance of clouds.*] The average height of clouds scarcely exceeds a mile, or a mile and half. And many (especially

any harm; and, therefore also, it is prodigious to have thunder in a clear sky, as is observably recorded in some histories.³

From the like cause may also proceed subterraneous thunders and earthquakes, when sulphureous and nitrous veins being fired, upon rarefaction do force their way through bodies that resist them.⁴ Where, if the kindled matter be plentiful, and the mine close and firm about it, subversion of hills and towns doth sometimes follow: if scanty, weak, and the earth hollow, or porous, there only ensueth some faint concussion or tremulous and quaking motion. Surely, a main reason why the ancients were so imperfect in the doctrine of meteors, was their ignorance of gunpowder and fireworks, which best discover the causes of many thereof.⁵

Now, therefore, he that would destroy the report of powder, must work upon the petre; he that would exchange the colour, must think how to alter the small-coal; for the one, that is, to make white powder, it is surely many ways feasible: the best I know, is by the powder of rotten willows; spunk, or touch-wood prepared, might, perhaps, make it russet; and some, as Beringuccio affirmeth,* have promised to make it red: all which, notwithstanding, doth little con-

* In his *Pyrotechnia*.

thunder clouds), are suspended much lower; occasionally so low as apparently to touch the ground.

³ *and therefore, also, it is prodigious, &c.*] In the fall of meteoric stones, flashes of fire are seen proceeding from a cloud, and a loud rattling noise like thunder is heard. These circumstances, and the sudden stroke and detonation ensuing, long caused them to be confounded with an effect of lightning, and called thunderbolts. But one circumstance is enough to mark the difference: the flash and sound have been perceived occasionally to emanate from a *very small cloud* insulated in *a clear sky;* which never happens in a thunder storm, but which is undoubtedly intimately connected with their real origin.—*Herschel, Introductory Lecture,* p. 120.

⁴ *From the like cause, &c.*] Lemery, in the beginning of the eighteenth century, tried the following experiment. He mixed a considerable quantity of sulphur, and iron filings, with water, into a paste; enveloped it in a cloth, and buried it in the earth, which he rammed firmly about it. In a few hours the ground swelled and cracked, and sulphureous exhalations, accompanied with flame, made their appearance. In short he succeeded in producing, in miniature, an artificial volcano.

⁵ *thereof.*] This paragraph was added in the 2nd edition.

cern the report; for that, as we have showed, depends on another ingredient; and, therefore, also, under the colour of black, this principle is very variable; for it is made not only by willow, alder, hazel, &c., but some above all commend the coals of flax and rushes, and some also contend the same may be effected with tinder.

As for the other, that is, to destroy the report, it is reasonably attempted but two ways; either by quite leaving out, or else by silencing the saltpetre. How to abate the vigour thereof, or silence its bombulation, a way is promised by Porta, not only in general terms by some fat bodies, but in particular by borax and butter mixed in a due proportion; which, saith he, will so go off as scarce to be heard by the discharger; and indeed plentifully mixed, it will almost take off the report, and also the force of the charge. That it may be thus made without saltpetre, I have met with but one example, that is, of Alphonsus, Duke of Ferrara, who, in the relation of Brassavolus and Cardan,* invented such a powder as would discharge a bullet without report.

That therefore white powder there may be, there is no absurdity: that also such a one as may give no report we will not deny a possibility. But this, however contrived, either with or without saltpetre, will surely be of little force, and the effects thereof no way to be feared; for as it amits of report, so will it of effectual exclusion, and so the charge be of little force which is excluded. For this much is reported of that famous powder of Alphonsus, which was not of force enough to kill a chicken, according to the delivery of Brassavolus: *jamque pulvis inventus est qui glandem sine bombo projicit, nec tamen vehementer ut vel pullum interficere possit.*

It is not to be denied there are ways to discharge a bullet, not only with powder that makes no noise, but without any powder at all; as is done by water and wind-guns, but these afford no fulminating report, and depend on single principles. And even in ordinary powder there are pretended other ways to alter the noise and strength of the discharge; and the best, if not only way, consists in the quality of the nitre: for as for other ways which make either additions or altera-

* *De Examine Salium.*

tions in the powder or charge, I find therein no effect.⁶ That unto every pound of sulphur an adjection of one ounce of quicksilver, or unto every pound of petre, one ounce of *sal armoniac*, will much intend⁷ the force and consequently the report, as Beringuccio hath delivered, I find no success therein. That a piece of opium will dead the force and blow, as some have promised, I find herein no such peculiarity, no more than in any gum or viscose body; and as much effect there is to be found from scammony. That a bullet dipped in oil, by preventing the transpiration of air,⁸ will carry farther and pierce deeper, as Porta affirmeth, my experience cannot discern.⁹ That quicksilver is more destructive than shot, is surely not to be made out;¹ for it will scarce make any penetration, and discharged from a pistol will hardly pierce through a parchment. That vinegar, spirits of wine, or the distilled water of orange-peels, wherewith the powder is tempered, are more effectual unto the report than common water, as some do promise, I shall not affirm; but may assuredly more conduce unto the preservation and durance of the powder, as Cateneo* hath well observed.

That the heads of arrows and bullets have been discharged with that force, as to melt or grow red hot in their flight,² though commonly received, and taken up by Aristotle in his

---

* *Avertimenti intorno a un Bombardiero.*

⁶ *for other ways, &c.*] Quicklime, well dried and pulverized, is said, by the French translator of Henry's Epitome of Chemistry, to increase the explosive effect of gunpowder.

⁷ *intend.*] Make more intense.

⁸ *preventing the transpiration of air.*] Its *escape* between the bullet and the side of the barrel. The definition of the term by Johnson seems quite inapplicable to the present passage, though he cites it as his authority.

⁹ *That a bullet, &c.*] If the bullet, especially a tampin [*tampion*] thus dipt, doe fitt the peece, soe as to be ramd in; this a most certaine experiment, *mihi crede experto.*—*Wr.*

¹ *not to be made out.*] I believe that of Porta concerning quicksilver, yf hee bee rightly understood: but hee did wel to put itt in such obscure terms, least itt should prove too pernicious.—*Wr.*

² *That the heads of arrows and bullets, &c.*] If a ball strike a plate of iron, it will be broken in pieces, and the pieces often found in a nearly fused state. But this heat is generated by the percussion, not by the motion.

Meteors, is not so easily allowable by any who shall consider, that a bullet of wax will mischief without melting; that an arrow or bullet discharged against linen or paper does not set them on fire; and hardly apprehend how[3] an iron should grow red hot, since the swiftest motion at hand will not keep one red that hath been red by fire: as may be observed in swinging a red hot iron about, or fastening it into a wheel, which, under that motion, will sooner grow cold than without it. That a bullet also mounts upward upon the horizontal or point-blank discharge, many artists do not allow; who contend that it describeth a parabolical and bowing line by reason of its natural gravity inclining it always downward.[4]

But, beside the prevalence from saltpetre,[5] as master ingredient in the mixture, sulphur may hold a greater use in the composition, and further activity in the exclusion, than is by most conceived. For sulphur *vive* makes better powder than common sulphur, which nevertheless is of a quick accension. For small-coal, saltpetre, and camphor, made into powder will be of little force, wherein notwithstanding there wants not the accending ingredient. And camphor, though it flame well, yet will not flush so lively, or defecate saltpetre if you inject it thereon, like sulphur, as in the preparation of *sal prunellæ*. And, lastly, though many ways may be found to light this powder, yet is there none I know to make a strong and vigorous powder of saltpetre, without the admixtion of sulphur. Arsenic, red and yellow, that is orpiment and sandarach,[6] may, perhaps, do something, as being inflammable and containing sulphur in them; but containing also a salt,

---

[3] *and hardly apprehend how.*] "Neither will any readily apprehend how, &c."

[4] *That the heads, &c.*] Added in the 2nd edition.

[5] *prevalence, &c.*] Edit. 1646 reads, "prevalence to report from saltpetre by some antipathy or incummiscibility therewith upon the approach of fire."

[6] *sandarach.*] Nota differentiam inter Σανδαράκην et Σανδαράχην quam facili errore sed maximo vitæ periculo omittunt quidam medicastri: vide notas meas in voce apud eruditissim̄ m Gorrhæum. Cum κ scriptum, significat, *gummi Juniperi;* cum χ *auripigmentum;*—primum salutare: secundum deleterium. Σανδάραξ etiam est vernigo pictoris quam e gummi Juniperi conficiunt; Σανδαράκη autem est, aliis Corinthus, aliis Erithace, aliis Propolis, apum cibus, sed amari saporis, in favis reperitur scorsim a melle positus: Græci onomastici hic muti sunt.—*Wr.*

and mercurial mixtion, they will be of little effect; and white or crystalline arsenic of less, for that being artificial and sublimed with salt, will not endure flammation.

This antipathy or contention between saltpetre and sulphur upon an actual fire, in their complete and distinct bodies, is also manifested in their preparations, and bodies which invisibly contain them. Thus in the preparation of *crocus metallorum*, the matter kindleth and flusheth like gunpowder; wherein, not withstanding, there is nothing but antimony[7] and saltpetre. But this may proceed from the sulphur of antimony not enduring the society of saltpetre; for after three or four accensions, through a fresh addition of petre, the powder will flush no more, for the sulphur of the antimony is quite exhaled. Thus iron in *aqua fortis* will fall into ebullition, with noise and emication, as also a crass and fumid exhalation, which are caused from this combat of the sulphur of iron, which the acid and nitrous spirits of *aqua fortis*. So is it also in *aurum fulminans*, or powder of gold dissolved in *aqua regis*, and precipitated with oil of tartar, which will kindle without an actual fire, and afford a report like gunpowder; that is, not as Crollius* affirmeth, from any antipathy between *sal armoniac* and tartar, but rather between the nitrous spirits of *aqua regis*, commixed *per minima* with the sulphur of gold, as Sennertus hath observed.

6. That coral (which is a *lithophyton* or stone-plant, and groweth at the bottom of the sea) is soft under water, but waxeth hard in the air, although the assertion of Dioscorides, Pliny, and consequently Solinus, Isidore, Rueus, and many others,[8] and stands believed by most, we have some reason to doubt, especially if we conceive with common believers, a total softness at the bottom, and this induration to be singly made by the air, not only from so sudden a petrifaction and strange induration, not easily made out from the qualities of air, but because we find it rejected by experimental enquiries. Johannes Beguinus, in his chapter of the Tincture of Coral,

---

* *De Consensu Chymicorum.*

[7] *antimony.*] Sulphuret of antimony.
[8] *many others.*] Ovid. Met. xv. 46.

"Sic et *coralium* quo primum contigit auras,
Tempore durescit; mollis fuit herba sub undis."—*Jef.*

undertakes to clear the world of this error, from the express experiment of John Baptista de Nicole, who was overseer of the gathering of coral upon the kingdom of Tunis. "This gentleman," saith he, "desirous to find the nature of coral, and to be resolved how it groweth at the bottom of the sea, caused a man to go down no less than a hundred fathom, with express [direction] to take notice whether it were hard or soft in the place where it groweth. Who returning, brought in each hand a branch of coral, affirming it was as hard at the bottom as in the air where he delivered it. The same was also confirmed by a trial of his own, handling it a fathom under water before it felt the air." Boëtius, in his accurate tract *De Gemmis*, is of the same opinion, not ascribing its concretion unto the air, but the coagulating spirits of salt, and lapidifical juice of the sea, which entering the parts of that plant, overcomes its vegetability, and converts it into a lapideous substance. And this, saith he, doth happen when the plant is ready to decay; for all coral is not hard, and in many concreted plants some parts remain unpetrified, that is, the quick and livelier parts remain as wood, and were never yet converted. Now, that plants and ligneous bodies may indurate under water without approachment of air, we have experiment in coralline, with many coralloidal concretions; and that little stony plant, which Mr. Johnson nameth *hippuris coralloides*, and Gesner, *foliis mansu arenosis*, we have found in fresh water, which is the less concretive portion of that element. We have also with us the visible petrification of wood in many waters, whereof so much as is covered with water converteth into stone; as much as is above it and in the air, retaineth the form of wood, and continueth as before.[9]

Now, though[1] in a middle way we may concede, that some are soft, and others hard, yet, whether all coral were first a woody substance, and afterwards converted, or rather some thereof were never such, but from the sprouting spirit of salt were able even in their stony natures to ramify and send

[9] *and continueth, &c.*] Neere the banke of Harwel, two miles from Oxon, under a stile and bridge, is a draine or drill in a ditch, out of which I took diverse small stickes, some nearly incrustated, and some petrefied.—*Wr.*

[1] *Now, though, &c.*] Added in 3rd edit.

forth branches, as is observable in some stones, in silver and metallic bodies, is not without some question. And such at least might some of those be, which Fiaravanti observed to grow upon bricks at the bottom of the sea, upon the coast of Barbary.[2]

[2] 6. *That coral, &c.*] It must, in the very nature of things, be occasionally the fate of him who challenges the soundness of any received opinion—especially on subjects but little understood—to take his stand on ground not less hollow, and even to make his attack from a position equally untenable. Thus has it happened to our author in the present case. He justly denounces as erroneous the popular opinion, "that coral is soft under water, but waxeth hard in the air; but seems not in the slightest degree aware of that much graver error, then prevalent, that it belongs to the mineral or vegetable, instead of the animal kingdom. But in this he erred not only with the highest authorities, but with *all*, both prior to, and contemporary with him. Nor was the true nature of coral ascertained till long after him. Many of the older naturalists regarded it as a mere stone, a mineral taking somewhat the form a tree: others, and especially the early botanists, regarding its form rather than its material, pronounced it, without hesitation, a tree, duly provided with *root, trunk, branches, and twigs;* and having observed the exterior (and most recently deposited) layer to be softer than those beneath it, they called it the *bark*. In 1703, the Count Marsigli, having had the opportunity of remarking the coral at the surface of the sea, throwing out from various points its radiated and flower-like inhabitants, the *polypi*, he congratulated himself as having completed the plant by the discovery of its *flowers*. No one doubted this opinion, till Peyssonel distinguished himself by the discovery, but these *flowers* were in fact animals. But the truth was received reluctantly by the French naturalists, till Guettard and Jussieu, sent by the *Académie des Sciences*, confirmed and fully established the fact. We owe, however, to the naturalists of Italy, principally, our knowledge of the structure and physiology of coral, as well as of its mode of growth. A hasty sketch may not be unacceptable to the reader.

Each *coral* (that is, the entire habitation of *each* separate colony of *polypi*), is a kind of *shrub*, or *tree* in miniature, about eighteen inches igh, and one in diameter at the lower part of the *trunk*. Its base, by means of which, as by the *root*, the whole coral becomes firmly attached to the rock on which it grows, is spread out and flattened, like that of the larger *fuci*. At the height of a few inches from the base, the trunk throws out its *branches*, which again ramify into lesser ones, each terminated by a blunt, softer extremity.

In structure, as well as form, the coral bears a resemblance to wood: especially in its successive layers, which, viewed in section, exhibit concentric rings, less and less close to each other, as they are more distant from the centre, like those of the trunk of a tree. The outer layer, which like the *bark* is always softer than those beneath it, is in fact the living part of the coral. On its surface are dispersed, here and there, irregularly, tubercles, having their orifice divided into eight *radii;* each

7. We are not thoroughly resolved concerning porcelain[3] or china dishes, that, according to common belief they are made of earth, which lieth in preparation about an hundred years under ground; for the relations thereof are not only diverse but contrary, and authors agree not herein. Guido Pancirollus will have them made of egg-shells, lobster-shells, and gypsum laid up in the earth the space of eighty

tubercle being the mouth or entrance to the cell of a polype. This exterior surface or bark is longitudinally furrowed with *striæ*, occasioned by tubes or canals running along the branches, and filled with a milky fluid.

The reproduction or growth of coral is thus effected:—the egg is thrown out of the tubercle before described; it falls, an embryo drop of coral-jelly, and becomes agglutinated to the rock or other substance which receives it. It spreads out upon the surface thereof; and from its centre soon arises a tubercle, which at length, opens in the middle, and throws out its *tentacula* in search of nutriment, or for the purpose of respiration. Its growth becomes more and more rapid In its interior is secreted the calcareous material which becomes *coral*. Thus it shoots up and branches out, throwing out fresh polypi at various places. The extremities of its branches, being the points of recent formation, are always softer than the other parts; which may have led the erroneous supposition that it is soft under water, and hardens by exposure to the air.

The coral is supposed to attain its full growth in about ten years: and to lose gradually the brilliancy of its red colour by age.

It is found principally in the Mediterranean and Red Seas, at various depths from six to seven hundred feet below the surface of the sea.

The plant mentioned is probably a *chara* (*vulgaris* or *hispida*); but the crust is only a calcareous deposit.

That which our author calls *petrifaction* of wood, is in fact merely incrustation.

[3] *We are not, &c.*] This account of the Chinese method of making porcelain is accurate. As to the materials of which it was composed, Reaumur made some researches in the early part of the eighteenth century; the result of which was an opinion that true porcelain is made of two ingredients—the one capable of resisting the most violent heat that can be raised; while the other (which gives to porcelain its transparency) melts into glass. His conclusions were confirmed by a Father d'Entrecolles, a French missionary, in China, who sent, some time after, a memoir to the academy, describing the mode followed by the Chinese in the manufactory of their porcelain Two substances are employed by them, the one called *kaolin*, and the other *petunse*. It is now known that *kaolin* is what we call porcelain-clay, and that *petunse* is a fine white felspar. Felspar is fusible in a violent heat, but porcelain-clay is refractory in the highest temperatures that we have it in our power to produce in furnaces.

years: of the same affirmation is Scaliger, and the common opinion of most. Ramuzius, in his *Navigations*, is of a contrary assertion; that they are made out of earth, not laid under ground, but hardened in the sun and wind, the space of forty years. But Gonzales de Mendoza, a man employed into China from Philip the second, king of Spain, upon enquiry and ocular experience, delivered a way different from all these. For enquiring into the artifice thereof, he found they were made of a chalky earth; which, beaten and steeped in water, affordeth a cream or fatness on the top, and a gross subsidence at the bottom; out of the cream or superfluitance, the finest dishes, saith he, are made; out of the residence thereof, the coarser; which being formed, they gild or paint, and, not after an hundred years, but presently, commit unto the furnace. This, saith he, is known by experience, and more probable than what Odoardus Barbosa hath delivered, that they are made of shells, and buried under earth an hundred years. And answerable in all points hereto, is the relation of Linschotten, a diligent enquirer, in his Oriental Navigations. Later confirmation may be had from Alvarez the Jesuit, who lived long in those parts, in his relations of China: that porcelain vessels were made but in one town of the province of Chiamsi; that the earth was brought out of other provinces, but, for the advantage of water, which makes them more polite and perspicuous, they were only made in this; that they were wrought and fashioned like those of other countries, whereof some were tinted blue, some red, others yellow, of which colour only they presented unto the king.[4]

The latest account hereof may be found in the voyage of the Dutch ambassador, sent from Batavia unto the emperor of China, printed in French, 1665; which plainly informeth, that the earth, whereof porcelain dishes are made, is brought from the mountains of Hoang, and being formed into square loaves, is brought by water, and marked with the emperor's seal; that the earth itself is very lean, fine, and shining like sand; and that it is prepared and fashioned after the same manner which the Italians observe in the fine earthern vessels of Faventia or Fuenca; that they are so

---

[4] *Later confirmation, &c.*] Added in 2nd edition.

reserved concerning that artifice, that it is only revealed from father unto son; that they are painted with indigo,[5] baked in a fire for fifteen days together, and with very dry and not smoking wood: which when the author had seen, he could hardly contain from laughter at the common opinion above rejected by us.[6]

Now if any enquire, why, being so commonly made, and in so short a time, they are become so scarce, or not at all to be had; the answer is given by these last relators, that under great penalties it is forbidden to carry the first sort out of the country. And of those surely the properties must be verified, which by Scaliger and others are ascribed unto china dishes:—that they admit no poison, that they strike fire, that they will grow hot no higher than the liquor in them ariseth. For such as pass amongst us, and under the name of the finest, will only strike fire, but not discover aconite, mercury, or arsenic; but may be useful in dysenteries and fluxes beyond the other.

8.[7] Whether a carbuncle (which is esteemed the best and biggest of rubies) doth flame in the dark,[8] or shine like a coal in the night, though generally agreed on by common believers, is very much questioned by many. By Milius, who accounts it a vulgar error: by the learned Boëtius, who could not find it verified in that famous one of Rodolphus, which was as big as an egg, and esteemed the best in Europe. Wherefore, although we dispute not the possibility (and the like is said to have been observed in some

---

[5] *indigo.*] Cobalt?

[6] *The latest account, &c.*] Added in the 6th edition.

[7] § 8.] This, and the next paragraph, were added in the 2nd edition.

[8] *Whether a carbuncle, &c.*] That which Sir Thomas much doubted, has since been subjected to the test of repeated observation, and many very curious experiments, by which the phosphorescence of the diamond, sapphire, ruby, and topaz, as well as of many minerals and metals, and various other bodies, is fully established. Mr. Wedgewood has treated the subject at large in a paper in the 82nd volume of the *Philosophical Transactions*. This luminous property, which seems to be strictly phosphoric, is made apparent by subjecting the body in question to heat, in various ways. Several fluids (oils, spermaceti, butter, &c.) are luminous at or below the boiling point: minerals and other bodies become so by being sprinkled on a thick plate of iron, heated just below visible redness. The gems, and several of the harder minerals, emit their light upon attrition.

diamonds), yet, whether herein there be not too high an apprehension, and above its natural radiancy, is not without just doubt; however it be granted a very splendid gem, and whose sparks may somewhat resemble the glances of fire, and metaphorically deserve that name. And, therefore, when it is conceived by some, that this stone in the breastplate of Aaron respected the tribe of Dan, who burnt the city of Laish, and Sampson of the same tribe, who fired the corn of the Philistines, in some sense it may be admitted, and is no intolerable conception.

As for that Indian stone that shined so brightly in the night, and pretended to have been shown to many in the court of France, as Andreus Chioccus hath declared out of Thuanus, it proved but an imposture, as that eminent philosopher, Licetus,* hath discovered; and, therefore, in the revised editions of Thuanus it is not to be found. As for the phosphorus or Bononian stone,† which exposed unto the sun, and then closely shut up, will afterwards afford a light in the dark; it is of unlike consideration, for that requireth calcination or reduction into a dry powder by fire, whereby it imbibeth the light in the vaporous humidity of the air about it, and therefore maintaineth its light not long, but goes out when the vaporous vehicle is consumed.

9.[9] Whether the *ætites* or eagle-stone[1] hath that eminent property to promote delivery or restrain abortion, respectively applied to lower or upward parts of the body, we shall not discourage common practice by our question; but whether they answer the account thereof, as to be taken out of eagles' nests, co-operating in women into such effects, as they are conceived toward the young eagles; or whether the single signature of one stone included in the matrix and

* *De Quæsit. per Epistolas.* † *De Lapide Bononiense.*

[9] § 9.] This and the following paragraphs were first added in 3rd edition.

[1] *the ætites, or eagle-stone.*] A kind of hollow *geodes* of oxide of iron, often mixed with a larger or smaller quantity of *silex* and *alumina*, containing in their cavity some concretions, which rattle on shaking the stone. It is of a dull pale colour, composed of concentric layers of various magnitudes, of an oval or polygonal form, and often polished. Eagles were said to carry them to their nests, whence the name; and superstition formerly ascribed wonderful virtues to them.

belly of another, were not sufficient at first, to derive this virtue of the pregnant stone upon others in impregnation, may yet be farther considered. Many sorts there are of this rattling stone, beside the *geodes*, containing a softer substance in it. Divers are found in England, and one we met with on the sea shore, but because many of eminent use are pretended to be brought from Iceland, wherein are divers eyries of eagles; we cannot omit to deliver what we received from a learned person in that country.* *Ætites an in nidis aquilarum aliquando fuerit repertus, nescio. Nostra certe memoria, etiam inquirentibus non contigit invenisse, quare in fabulis habendum.*

10. Terrible apprehensions, and answerable unto their names, are raised of fairy stones and elves' spurs,[2] found commonly with us in stone, chalk, and marl-pits, which, notwithstanding, are no more than *echinometrites* and *belemnites*, the sea hedge-hog, and the dart-stone, arising from some siliceous roots, and softer than that of flint, the master-stone lying more regularly in courses, and arising from the primary and strongest spirit of the mine. Of the *echinites*, such as are found in chalk-pits are white, glassy, and built upon a chalky inside; some, of an hard and flinty substance, are found in stone-pits and elsewhere. Common opinion commendeth them for the stone, but are most practically used against films in horses' eyes.

11. Lastly, he must have more heads than Rome had hills, that makes out half of those virtues ascribed unto stones, and their not only medical, but magical properties, which are to be found in authors of great name. In Psellus, Serapion, Evax, Albertus, Aleazar, Marbodeus; in Maiolus, Rueus, Mylius, and many more.[3]

That *lapis lazuli* hath in it a purgative faculty we know; that bezoar is antidotal, *lapis judaicus* diuretical, coral ante-

* Theodore Jonas, Hitterdalæ pastor.

[2] *Terrible apprehensions, &c.*] Though he denounces the popular superstitions attached to these *fairy-stones, &c.* our author, in this paragraph, gives additional evidence that he had fallen into another error of his day, in confounding *fossils* with *minerals.—See Mr. Brayley's note*, p. 105.

[3] *many more.*] And above all Cardan in *De rariet.* ubique superstitiosissime.—*Wr.*

pileptical, we will not deny. That cornelians, jaspis, heliotropes, and blood-stones may be of virtue to those intentions they are employed, experience and visible effects will make us grant. But that an amethyst prevents inebriation; that an emerald will break if worn in copulation; that a diamond laid under the pillow, will betray the incontinency of a wife; that a sapphire is preservative against enchantments; that the fume of an agate will avert a tempest, or the wearing of a chrysophrase make one out of love with gold, as some have delivered, we are yet, I confess, to believe, and in that infidelity are likely to end our days. And therefore, they which, in the explication of the two beryls upon the ephods, or the twelve stones in the *rational* or breastplate[4] of Aaron, or those twelve which garnished the wall of the Holy City in the Apocalypse, have drawn their significations from such as these, or declared their symbolical verities from such traditional falsities, have surely corrupted the sincerity of their analogies, or misunderstood the mystery of their intentions.

Most men conceive that the twelve stones in Aaron's breastplate made a jewel surpassing any, and not to be paralleled; which, notwithstanding, will hardly be made out from the description of the text; for the names of the tribes were engraven thereon; which must notably abate their lustre. Besides, it is not clear made out that the best of gems, a diamond, was amongst them;[5] nor is it to be found in the list thereof, set down by the Jerusalem targum, wherein we find the darker stones of sardius, sardonynx, and jasper; and if we receive them under those names wherein they are usually described, it is not hard to contrive a more illustrious and splendent jewel. But being not ordained for mere lustre by diaphanous and pure tralucencies, their mys-

---

[4] *rational or breastplate.*] "Rationale *quoque judicii facies,*" &c. Exod. xxviii. 15.

[5] *not clear made out, &c.*] The doubt here intimated, whether the true diamond was among the stones of the breastplate, has been expressed by commentators, on the ground that it is too hard to be engraved. Calmet, in his figure of the Pectoral, omits it. Rosenmüller however asserts, on the testimony of Büsching, the existence of engraved diamonds of great antiquity. A diamond of sufficient size to admit the engraving, must have equaled the largest modern specimens. Like many other such questions, it admits of discussion, but not of solution.

terious significations became more considerable than their gemmary substances; and those, no doubt, did nobly answer the intention of the institutor. Beside, some may doubt whether there be twelve distinct species of noble tralucent gems in nature,[6] at least yet known unto us, and such as may not be referred unto some of those in high esteem among us, which come short of the number of twelve; which to make up, we must find out some others to match and join with the diamond, beryl, sapphire, emerald, amethyst, topaz, chrysolite, jacinth, ruby, and, if we may admit it in this number, the oriental granat.[7]

CHAPTER VI.

Of sundry tenets concerning vegetables or plants, which, examined, prove either false or dubious:—of mandrakes; that cinnamon, ginger, cloves, mace, are but the parts or fruits of the same tree: that miseltoe is bred upon trees, from seeds which birds let fall thereon; of the rose of Jericho, that flowereth every year upon Christmas Eve; of Glastonbury thorn; that Sferra Cavallo hath a power to break or loosen iron; that bays preserve from the mischief of lightning and thunder; that bitter almonds are preservatives against ebriety.

1. MANY molas and false conceptions there are of mandrakes.[8] The first, from great antiquity, conceiveth the root

---

[6] *whether there be twelve, &c.*] If we are to understand, by the terms "*noble* tralucent gems," those only which were formerly called *precious stones*, we shall scarcely enumerate more than two distinct species, viz., the diamond and sapphire; for the oriental ruby, amethyst, and topaz, are not distinct in species from the sapphire; and the crysoberyl and spinelle ruby, though distinct species, are inferior in hardness and brilliancy to stones of the first class. But if we extend our range, as Sir Thomas has done, to gems of lesser value, though we confine ourselves to such as are, scientifically speaking, distinct species, and so omit several of the most splendid and valuable, as being only varieties, we may still enlarge his list—for example: supposing his "chrysolite" to refer to the common chrysolite or *peridot*, and his "oriental granat" to be the *garnet*; we may add the *chrysoberyl*, or *oriental chrysolite*; the *almandine garnet*, or *carbuncle* of the ancients (which he seems to consider as only a ruby of greater size and beauty); the precious *tourmaline* (*lyncurium* of the ancients), and perhaps the *chrysopra e*; not to mention *opal* and *torquoise*.

[7] *Most men, &c.*] This whole paragraph was added in the 6th edition.

[8] *Many molas, &c.*] An excellent digest of the various and absurd

thereof resembleth the shape of man; which is a conceit not to be made out by ordinary inspection, or any other eyes, than such as, regarding the clouds, behold them in shapes conformable to pre-apprehensions.

Now, whatever encourageth the first invention, there have not been wanting many ways of its promotion. The first a *catechrestical* and far-derived similitude it holds with man; that is, in a bifurcation or division of the root into two parts, which some are content to call thighs; whereas, notwithstanding, they are ofttimes three, and when but two, commonly so complicated and crossed, that men, for this deceit, are fain to effect their design in other plants. And as fair a resemblance is often found in carrots, parsnips, briony, and many others. There are, I confess, divers plants which carry about them not only the shape of parts, but also of whole animals; but surely not all thereof, unto whom this conformity is imputed. Whoever shall peruse the signatures of Crollius, or rather the *Phytognomy* of Porta, and strictly observe how vegetable realities are commonly forced into animal representations, may easily perceive in very many, the semblance is but postulatory, and must have a more assimilating fancy than mine to make good many thereof.

Illiterate heads have been led on by the name, which, in the first syllable,* expresseth its representation; but other have better observed the laws of etymology, and deduced it from a word of the same language, because it delighteth to

---

* Μάνδρα, *spelunca*.

speculations and conjectures respecting the mandrake and its properties will be found in *Dr. Harris's Dictionary of the Natural History of the Bible*.

The Abbe Mariti, in his *Travels*, vol. ii. p. 195, thus describes the mandrake. "At the village of St. John, in the mountains, about six miles south-west from Jerusalem, this plant is found at present, as well as in Tuscany. It grows low like lettuce, to which its leaves have a great resemblance, except that they have a dark green colour. The flowers are purple, and the root is for the most part forked. The fruit, when ripe in the beginning of May, is of the size and colour of a small apple, exceedingly ruddy, *and of a most agreeable odour*. Our guide thought us fools for suspecting it to be unwholesome. He ate it freely himself; and it is generally valued by the inhabitants as exhilarating their spirits, and a provocative to venery."

grow in obscure and shady places; which derivation, although we shall not stand to maintain, yet the other seemeth answerable unto the etymologies of many authors, who often confound such nominal notations. Not to enquire beyond our own profession, the Latin physicians, which most adhered unto the Arabic way, have often failed herein; particularly Valescus de Taranta, a received physician, in whose *Philonium, or Medical Practice*, these may be observed: *Diarrhea*, saith he, *quia pluries venit in die*.[9] *Herisepela, quasi hærens pilis; emmorrohis, ab emach, sanguis, et morrohis, quod est cadere. Lithargia, à litos, quod est oblivio, et targus, morbus. Scotomia, à scotus, quod est videre, et mias, musca. Opthalmia, ab opus Græcè, quod est succus, et talmon quod est oculus. Paralisis, quasi læsio partis. Fistula, à fos sonns, et stolon quod est emissio, quasi emissio soni vel vocis.* Which are derivations as strange, indeed, as the other, and hardly to be paralleled elsewhere: confirming not only the words of one language with another, but creating such as were never yet in any.

The received distinction and common notation by sexes,[1] hath also promoted the conceit; for true it is, that herbalists, from ancient times, have thus distinguished them;

---

[9] *venit in die.*] Not unlike to that of εἰσαγωγή, which a wise man derived from (εἶσος and γωγους) or, as Calepin derives *aqua* from *à quà*, or as Minshew, *prospero* from *porro* and *spero*, where the long quantityes in the originals discover the follye of the derivations.—*Wr.*

[1] *The received distinction, &c.*] Nearly a century elapsed after this paragraph was written, before the distinction adverted to was well understood and explained. The real use of the *stamina* of plants, to fertilize the seed, though suspected by Ray and others, was not fully established till Linnæus, in 1732, published, in his *Fundamenta et Philosophia Botanica*, the results of his long and laborious consideration of the opinions which had preceded him, combined with his own patient and acute investigation of vegetable phenomena, put to the test of various ingenious experiments. He proved that "flowers are always furnished, either in the same individual, or two of the same species," with stamens and pistils,—the latter containing the seeds,—the former the pollen or dust which fertilizes and perfects it. These were therefore called the male and female parts of fructification; and in those orders in which one plant contains stamens only, and another only the pistil—the one was called the male, the other the female plant. This discovery he made the foundation of the artificial system, which, under the title of the *Linnæan system* of botany, became so universally popular.

naming that the male, whose leaves are lighter, and fruit and apples rounder; but this is properly no generative division, but rather some note of distinction in colour, figure, or operation. For though Empedocles* affirm, there is a mixed and undivided sex in vegetables, and Scaliger, upon Aristotle, doth favourably explain that opinion, yet will it not consist with the common and ordinary acceptation, nor yet with Aristotle's definition. For, if that be male which generates in another, that female which procreates in itself; if it be understood of sexes conjoined, all plants are female; and if of disjoined and congressive generation, there is no male or female in them at all.[2]

But the Atlas or main axis which supported this opinion, was daily experience, and the visible testimony of sense. For many there are, in several parts of Europe, who carry about roots and sell them unto ignorant people, which handsomely make out the shape of man or woman. But these are not productions of nature, but contrivances of art, as divers have noted, and Matthiolus plainly detected; who learned this way of trumpery from a vagabond cheater lying under his cure for the French disease. His words are these, and may determine the point: *Sed profecto vanum et fabulosum, &c.;* but this is vain and fabulous, which ignorant people and simple women believe; for the roots which are carried about by imposters to deceive unfruitful women, are made of the roots of canes, briony, and other plants; for in these, yet fresh and virent, they carve out the figures of men and women, first sticking therein the grains of barley or millet where they intend the hair should grow; then bury them in sand until the grains shoot forth their roots, which, at the longest, will happen in twenty days; they afterwards clip and trim those tender strings in the fashion of beards and other hairy teguments. All which, like other impostures, once discovered, is easily effected, and in the root of white briony may be practised every spring.

* *De Plantis.*

[2] *no male, &c.*] The name of male and female in plants is onlye tralatitious and similitudinarye, that which beares fruite beeing for distinction sake called female, and that which beares none the male.—*Wr.* See preceding note.

What is therefore delivered in favour thereof, by authors, ancient or modern,³ must have its root in tradition, imposture, far derived similitude, or casual and rare contingency. So may we admit of the epithet of Pythagoras, who calls it *anthropomorphus*,* and that of Columella, who terms it *semihomo*; more applicable unto the man-orchis, whose flower represents a man. Thus is Albertus to be received, when he affirmeth that mandrakes represent mankind, with the distinction of either sex.† Under these restrictions may those authors be admitted, which for this opinion are introduced by Drusius,⁴ nor shall we need to question the monstrous root of briony, described in Aldrovandus.‡

The second assertion concerneth its production.⁵ That it naturally groweth under gallowses and places of execution, arising from fat or urine that drops from the body of the

---

* *Orchis anthropomorphus, cujus icon in Kircheri Magia parastatica.*
† *De Mandragora.* ‡ *De Monstris.*

³ *What is therefore delivered, &c.*]

> Mark, how that rooted mandrake wears
> His human feet, his human hands!
> Oft, as his ghastly form he rears,
> Aghast the frighted plowman stands!
>   *Langhorne's Beeflower.*

⁴ *Drusius.*] Instead of the remaining part of the sentence, *Ed.* 1646 reads, "As David Camius, Moses filius Namanis, and Abenezra Hispanus."

⁵ *The second assertion, &c.*] Here again is our author the victim of the false philosophy of his age. The immortal Harvey, in his *De Generatione*, struck the first blow at the root of the irrational system called *æquivocal generation*, when he laid down his brief but most pregnant law, *omnia ex ovo*. But the belief transmitted from antiquity, that living beings generated spontaneously from putrescent matter, long maintained its ground; and a certain modification of it is even still advocated by some naturalists of the greatest acuteness. The first few pages of the volume entitled *Insect Transformations* (in the *Library of Entertaining Knowledge*), are occupied by a very interesting investigation of this subject.

In the midst of his errors, however, Sir Thomas makes a remark, which has been verified and confirmed by much more widely extended observation since, viz.: "that hogs, sheep, goats, hawks, hens, and others, have one peculiar and proper kind of vermin." A vast number of species of *pulex* and *pediculus* are now known; and I am not aware that any instance has occurred of the same species being parasitic on different animals.

dead; a story somewhat agreeable unto the fable of the serpent's teeth sowed in the earth by Cadmus; or rather, the birth of Orion, from the urine of Jupiter, Mercury, and Neptune. Now this opinion seems grounded on the former, that is, a conceived similitude it hath with man; and therefore from him, in some way, they would make out its production. Which conceit is not only erroneous in the foundation, but injurious unto philosophy in the superstruction; making putrefactive generations correspondent unto seminal productions, and conceiving in equivocal effects an univocal conformity unto the efficient. Which is so far from being verified of animals in their corruptive mutations into plants, that they maintain not this similitude in their nearer translation into animals. So when the ox corrupteth into bees, or the horse into hornets, they come not forth in the image of their originals. So the corrupt and excrementitious humours in man are animated into lice; and we may observe that hogs, sheep, goats, hawks, hens, and others, have one peculiar and proper kind of vermin; not resembling themselves according to seminal conditions, yet carrying a settled and confined habitude unto their corruptive originals. And therefore come not forth in generations erratical, or different from each other; but seem specifically and in regular shapes to attend the corruption of their bodies, as do more perfect conceptions the rule of seminal productions.

The third affirmeth the roots of mandrakes do make a noise, or give a shriek, upon eradication;[6] which is indeed ridiculous, and false below confute; arising, perhaps, from a small and stridulous noise, which being firmly rooted, it maketh upon divulsion of parts. A slender foundation for such a vast conception; for such a noise we sometimes observe in other plants, in parsnips, liquorice, eryngium, flags, and others.

The last concerneth the danger ensuing; that there follows an hazard of life to them that pull it up; that some

---

[6] *The third affirmeth, &c.*] To this Shakspeare alludes:—

......Wherefore should I curse them?
Would curses kill, as doth the mandrake's **groan,**
I would invent as bitter-searching terms,
As curs'd, as harsh, as horrible to bear.

evil fate pursues them, and they live not very long after. Therefore the attempt hereof, among the ancients, was not in ordinary way; but, as Pliny informeth, when they intended to take up the root of this plant, they took the wind thereof, and with a sword describing three circles about it, they digged it up, looking toward the west. A conceit, not only injurious unto truth, and confutable by daily experience, but somewhat derogatory unto the providence of God; that is, not only to impose so destructive a quality on any plant, but to conceive a vegetable, whose parts are useful unto many, should, in the only taking up, prove mortal unto any. To think he suffereth the poison of *Nubia** to be gathered, *napellus*, aconite, and *thora*, to be eradicated, yet this not to be moved. That he permitteth arsenic and mineral poisons to be forced from the bowels of the earth, yet not this from the surface thereof. This were to introduce a second forbidden fruit, and enhance the first malediction, making it not only mortal for Adam to taste the one, but capital unto his posterity to eradicate or dig up the other.

Now what begot, at least promoted, so strange conceptions, might be the magical opinion hereof; this being conceived the plant so much in use with Circe, and therefore named *Circæa*[7] (as Dioscorides and Theophrastus have delivered), which being the eminent sorceress of elder story, and by the magic of simples believed to have wrought many wonders, some men were apt to invent, others to believe any tradition or magical promise thereof.

Analogous relations concerning other plants, and such as are of near affinity unto this, have made its current smooth, and pass more easily among us. For the same effect is also delivered by Josephus concerning the root *baaras*; by Ælian, of *cynospastus*: and we read in Homer the very same opinion concerning *moly*:

Μῶλυ δέ μιν καλέουσι θεοί, χαλεπὸν δέ τ' ὀρύσσειν
Ἀνδράσι γε θνητοῖσι, θεοὶ δέ τε πάντα δύνανται.

The gods it *moly* call, whose root to dig away
Is dangerous unto man; but gods they all things may.

---

* *Granum Nubiæ*.

[7] *Circæa*.] Enchanter's nightshade.

Now parallels or like relations alternately relieve each other; when neither will pass asunder, yet are they plausible together; their mutual concurrences supporting their solitary instabilities.

Signaturists[8] have somewhat advanced it; who seldom omitting what ancients delivered, drawing into inference received distinctions of sex, not willing to examine its humane resemblance, and placing it in the form of strange and magical simples, have made men suspect there was more therein than ordinary practice allowed; and so became apt to embrace whatever they heard or read comformable unto such conceptions.

Lastly, the conceit promoteth itself: for concerning an effect whose trial must cost so dear, it fortifies itself in that invention; and few there are whose experiment it need to fear. For, what is most contemptible, although not only the reason of any head, but experience of every hand may well convict it, yet will it not by divers be rejected; for prepossessed heads will ever doubt it, and timorous beliefs will never dare to try it. So these traditions, how low and ridiculous soever, will find suspicion in some, doubt in others, and serve as tests or trials of melancholy and superstitious tempers for ever.

2. That cinnamon, ginger,[9] clove, mace, and nutmeg, are but the several parts and fruits of the same tree, is the common belief of those which daily use them; whereof to speak distinctly, ginger is the root of neither tree nor shrub, but of an herbaceous plant, resembling the water *fleur-de-lis*, as Garcias first described, or rather the common reed, as Lobelius since affirmed. Very common in many parts of India,[1] growing either from root or seed, which in December and

---

[8] *Signaturists.*] Those who hold the doctrine, that plants bear certain marks and *signatures*, indicative of their qualities or properties.

[9] *ginger.*] *Amomum Zingiber, L.* or *Zingiber officinalis.*

[1] *of India.*] And in Europe, too, for itt hath been of old, and is lately found in Austria, at the foote of the mount Cognamus: vide *Helym's Austria*, p. 74. Germanice. There are two kindes of itt, white and brown, which I suppose differ only in age. Itt is commonly brought to us from China: to them from some upper parts in Tartary: and therefore some call itt *Radix Scythica*: but this is an equivocall name, proper to *glycyrisa*, but applicable to ginger and rhubarbe, which both come also from thence. Offended with the earthynes of green ginger,

January they take up, and, gently dried, roll it up in earth, whereby occluding[2] the pores, they conserve the natural humidity, and so prevent corruption.

Cinnamon is the inward bark of a cinnamon tree,[3] whereof the best is brought from Zeilan; this freed from the outward bark, and exposed unto the sun, contracts into those folds wherein we commonly receive it. If it have not a sufficient insolation[4] it looketh pale, and attains not its laudable colour; if it be sunned too long, it suffereth a torrefaction, and descendeth somewhat below it.

Clove seems to be either the rudiment of a fruit,[5] or the fruit itself, growing upon the clove tree, to be found but in few countries. The most commendable is that of the isles of Molucca; it is first white, afterward green, which beaten down and dried in the sun, becometh black, and in the complexion we receive it.

Nutmeg is the fruit of a tree[6] differing from all these, and as Garcias describeth it, somewhat like a peach; growing in divers places, but fructifying in the isle of Banda. The fruit hereof consisteth of four parts; the first, or outward part, is a thick and carnous covering like that of a walnut; the

---

I causd choyce to bee made of the whitest; paring of the barke totally: then bruisd itt in a stone mortar into strings; then stewd itt on a gentle fire till the water was consumed from three pintes to a quarte (the pared ginger being but a quarter of a pound). When wee thought the vertue wholy extracted (which would have tincted a pottel of water sufficiently), streyning away the ginger with some pressure, gentlye, they boyled the water into a syrup, whose vertues are such, after a meale (the quantity of a spoonfull), as noe dredg. powders, or lozenges, can equall in four times soe much: for by a gentle mixture and fermentation, itt corrects all crude humors and flatulencyes, abates not the salivation, as all hot spices doe, and never heates further then stomache only.

[2] *occluding.*] Shutting up.

[3] *Cinnamon, &c.*] The bark of *Laurus Cinnamomum*. The perfection of this spice depends on the tree being at a fit age, and on the relative proportion of the inner part of the bark, which is the sweetest and most fragrant.

[4] *insolation.*] Exposure to the sun.

[5] *either the rudiment, &c.*] Cloves are the calyces, with the embryo seed, of *caryophyllus aromaticus*, beaten from the tree, just after the delicate peach-blossom-coloured flowers have faded. The pungent quality is lessened if the seed is suffered to become more mature.

[6] *Nutmeg, &c.*] This is an accurate description of the fruit of *myristaca moschata*, the nutmeg.

second, a dry and flosculous coat, commonly called mace; the third a harder tegument or shell, which lieth under the mace; the fourth, a kernel included in the shell, which is the same we call nutmeg. All which, both in their parts and order of disposure, are easily discerned in those fruits which are brought in preserves unto us.[7]

Now if, because mace and nutmegs proceed from one tree, the rest must bear them company, or because they are all from the East Indies, they are all from one plant, the inference is precipitous, nor will there such a plant be found in the herbal of nature.

3. That *viscus arboreus*, or, miseltoe, is bred upon trees from seeds, which birds, especially thrushes and ringdoves, let fall thereon, was the creed of the ancients, and is still believed among us, is the account of its production, set down by Pliny, delivered by Virgil, and subscribed by many more. If so, some reason must be assigned, why it groweth only upon certain trees, and not upon many whereon these birds do light. For as exotic observers deliver, it groweth upon almond trees, chesnut, apples, oaks, and pine trees. As we observe in England, very commonly upon apple, crabs, and whitethorn; sometimes upon sallow, hazel, and oak: rarely upon ash, limetree, and maple; never, that I could observe, upon holly, elm, and many more.[8] Why groweth it not in all countries and places where these birds are found? for so Brassavolus affirmeth, it is not to be found in the territory of Ferrara, and he was fain to supply himself from other parts of Italy. Why, if it ariseth from a seed, if sown will it not grow again, as Pliny affirmeth, and as by setting the berries thereof, we have in vain attempted its production? Why, if it cometh from seed that falleth upon the tree, groweth it often downwards, and puts forth under the bough, where seed can neither fall nor yet remain?[9] Hereof, beside some

[7] *in preserves, &c.*] Whereof my aunceint friend, Mr. Paul Clapham, sent me a pot of two pounds.—*Wr.*
Little did "my aunceint friend" suppose that his munificence would thus be immortalized!

[8] *rarely, &c.*] Ed. 1646 reads, "never upon bays, holly, ashes, elms, and many others."

[9] *under the bough, &c.*] This one objection is soe vigorous and clever, as cuts off the foolish assertion for ever.—*Wr.*
Yet is this apparently triumphant objection demolished, by the result

others, the Lord Verulam hath taken notice. And they surely speak probably who make it an arboreous excres-

of experiment, as will appear on reading the following very interesting passage, from the work of my old friend and fellow-citizen, Professor Lindley:—The seed of the miseltoe will germinate in any direction, either upwards, downwards, or laterally. The first movement made by this plant consists in an extension of its cauliculus, which derives its support from the cotyledons, and which terminates, at the radicular end, in a small green tubercle of a paler colour than the radicle itself. When the seed is fixed upon a branch by its natural glue, this incipient movement is effected at right angles with the branch; the young shoot is then curved backwards, and the radicular extremity descends to the surface of the branch, to which it adheres by expanding into a kind of disk. From this expansion the roots are emitted, and penetrate the interior of the branch whereon the seed of the miseltoe is fixed; its stem takes the direction above mentioned with reference to the centre of the branch on which it is fixed, and not with reference to the earth; so that with regard to the latter, it is sometimes ascending, sometimes descending, sometimes horizontal. The same phenomena occur if the germination takes place upon dead wood or inorganic substances: a number of seeds were glued to the surface of a cannon ball; all the radicles were directed towards the centre of the ball. Hence it is obvious that the tendency of the miseltoe is not towards the surface of its nutrition, but it obeys the attraction of the body upon which it grows. The miseltoe, which does not grow on the earth, obeys the attraction of any other body; while those plants which naturally grow in the earth obey no other attraction than that of the earth. Parasitical fungi, those which constitute mouldiness; aquatics, which originate on stones, all grow perpendicular to the body that produces them, and will therefore be placed in all kinds of positions with respect to the earth."

On the probable effect produced on the seeds by their passing through the stomachs of birds, Mr. Jesse has some observations in the second series of his *Gleanings*, p. 133. He had seen the young miseltoe cracking the bark of the hawthorn and sprouting out on the *under side* of the branch: as Sir Thomas observes. He asserts the miseltoe to abound in Herefordshire and Monmouthshire, where the miselthrush also abounds: while in Wiltshire and Devonshire both are less common. "Various attempts," he adds, "have been made by persons, with whom I am acquainted, to propagate the miseltoe, by depositing the seed between the forks of trees, and by inserting it in the bark, but the attempt has hitherto failed, as far as I can speak from my own observation. The seeds also of the ivy seldom grow, though planted with the greatest care, even under walls; yet if dropped by birds either upon or even in the crevices of walls, they will grow spontaneously and thrive luxuriantly. It is this circumstance which has led a friend of mine to suppose, and with some reason, that the seeds of the miseltoe and ivy must undergo some process, favourable to their germination, in passing through the stomach of birds."

cence,¹ or rather super-plant, bred of a viscous and superfluous sap, which the tree itself cannot assimilate; and therefore sprouteth not forth in boughs and surcles of the same shape, and similary unto the tree that beareth it, but in a different form, and secondary unto its specifical intention, wherein once failing, another form succeedeth, and in the first place that of miseltoe, in plants and trees disposed to its production. And therefore also, wherever it groweth, it is of constant shape, and maintains a regular figure; like other supercrescences, and such as living upon the stock of others are termed parasitical plants, as polypody, moss, the smaller capillaries, and many more. So that several regions produce several miseltoes: India one, America another, according to the law and rule of their degenerations.

Now what begot this conceit, might be the enlargement of some part of truth contained in its story. For certain it is, that some birds do feed upon the berries of this vegetable, and we meet in Aristotle with one kind of thrush called the miselthrush,* or feeder upon miseltoe.² But that which hath most promoted it is a received proverb, *turdus sibi malum cacat*, appliable unto such men as are authors of their own misfortune. For according unto ancient tradition and Pliny's relation, the bird, not able to digest the fruit whereon she

* ἐξοβόρος.

¹ *an arboreous excrescence.*] Arboreous excrescences of the oake are soe many as may raise the greatest wonder. Besides the gall, which is his proper fruite, hee shootes out oakerns, i. e. *ut nunc vocamus* (acornes) and oakes apples, and polypodye, and moss; five several sorts of excrescences.—*Wr.*

Is it not a greater wonder that the dean should have mistaken the gall for the fruit of the oak, and called the acorn an excrescence?

² *feeder upon miseltoe.*] Sir James Smith points out the distinctness of the miseltoe of the ancients, from ours, in the following passage:—
"*Loranthus europæus* seems to be the original, or most common miseltoe, ἐξος, of the Greeks, which grows usually on some kind of fir-tree. But our *viscum album* is likewise found in Greece, though rarely, growing on the oak; and this has been preferred from the most remote antiquity. Hence, when the superstitions of the east travelled westward, our Druids adopted a notion of the miseltoe of the oak being more holy or efficacious, in conjurations or medicine, than what any other tree afforded, the *loranthus*, or ordinary miseltoe, not being known here. This superstition actually remains, and a plant of *viscum* gathered from an oak is preferred by those who rely on virtues which, perhaps, never existed in any miseltoe whatever."

feedeth, from her inconverted muting ariseth this plant, of the berries whereof bird-lime is made, wherewith she is after entangled. But although proverbs be popular principles, yet is not all true that is proverbial; and in many thereof, there being one thing delivered and another intended, though the verbal expression be false, the proverb is true enough in the verity of its intention.

As for the magical virtues in this plant, and conceived efficacy unto veneficial intentions, it seemeth a pagan relick, derived from the ancient Druids, the great admirers of the oak, especially the miseltoe that grew thereon; which, according unto the particular of Pliny, they gathered with great solemnity. For after sacrifice, the priest, in a white garment, ascended the tree, cut down the miseltoe with a golden hook, and received it in a white coat; the virtue whereof was to resist all poisons, and make fruitful any that used it. Virtues not expected from classical practice; and did they fully answer their promise which are so commended, in epileptical intentions, we would abate these qualities. Country practice hath added another, to provoke the after-birth, and in that case the decoction is given unto cows. That the berries are poison, as some conceive, we are so far from averring, that we have safely given them inwardly, and can confirm the experiment of Brassavolus, that they have some purgative quality.

4. The rose of Jericho, that flourishes every year just about Christmas-eve, is famous in Christian reports; which, notwithstanding, we have some reason to doubt, and are plainly informed by Bellonius, it is but a monastical imposture, as he hath delivered, in his observations concerning the plants in Jericho. That which promoted the conceit, or perhaps begot its continuance, was a propriety in this plant; for, though it be dry, yet will it, upon imbibition of moisture,[3] dilate its leaves and explicate its flowers contracted and

---

[3] *imbibition of moisture.*] From this that is sayd touching imbibition of moysture, puts me in remembrance of a dry withy stake: which being robd of the barke a foote aboue ground, stood dead three years. In the third yeare, being come to rottenes, and the wood growing spungie, suckt up the moysture from the earthe, reviving the barke above, and then the tree, which grew greene againe with a large head, bigger then the plant to which itt was set. Soe there was a perfect greene withy, and yet noe roote, nor string of a roote, in the earthe below.—*Wr.*

seemingly dried up. And this is to be effected not only in the plant yet growing, but in some manner also in that which is brought exsuccous and dry unto us. Which quality being observed, the subtilty of contrivers did commonly play this show upon the eve of our Saviour's nativity; when by drying the plant again, it closed the next day, and so presented a double mystery, referring unto the opening and closing of the womb of Mary.[4]

There wanted not a specious confirmation from a text in Ecclesiasticus. *quasi palma exaltata sum in Cades, et quasi plantatio rosæ in Jericho:* "I was exalted like a palm-tree in Engaddi, and as a rose in Jericho." The sound whereof, in common ears, begat an extraordinary opinion of the rose of that denomination. But herein there seemeth a mistake: for, by the rose in the text, is implied the true and proper rose, as first the Greek, and ours accordingly, rendereth it. But that which passeth under this name, and by us is commonly called the rose of Jericho, is properly no rose, but a small thorny shrub or kind of heath, bearing little white flowers, far differing from the rose; whereof Bellonius, a very inquisitive herbalist, could not find any in his travels through Jericho. A plant so unlike a rose, it hath been mistaken by some good simplist for *amomum;* which truly understood, is so unlike a rose that, as Dioscorides delivers, the flowers thereof are like the white violet, and its leaves resemble briony.

Suitable unto this relation almost in all points is that of the thorn at Glastonbury,[5] and perhaps the daughter thereof;

---

[4] *referring unto, &c.*] Note this gross imposture.—*Wr.*

[5] *thorn at Glastonbury.*] A variety of the *cratægus oxyacanthæ*, whose usual period of flowering is May, whence its common name, Mayblossom. "Gilpin mentions that 'one of its progeny, which grew in the gardens at Bulstrode, had its flower-buds perfectly formed so early as the 21st December.' In the arboretum at the royal gardens, Kew, a similar thorn flowers at the same season. The belief, that certain trees put forth their flowers on Christmas-day, was not confined to the Glastonbury thorn. In the new forest at Cadenham, near Lyndhurst, an oak used to bud about that period; but the people, for two centuries, believed that it never budded all the year, except on Old Christmasday. The superstition was destroyed by careful investigation; and the circumstance is thus recorded in the Salisbury newspaper of January 10th, 1786:—'In consequence of a report that has prevailed in this county for upwards of two centuries, and which, by many, has been considered as a matter of faith, that the oak at Cadenham, in the new

herein our endeavours as yet have not attained satisfaction, and cannot therefore enlarge. Thus much in general we may observe, that strange effects are naturally taken for miracles by weaker heads, and artificially improved to that apprehension by wiser. Certainly many precocious trees, and such as spring in the winter, may be found in most parts of Europe, and divers also in England.* For most trees do

* Such a thorn there is in Parham-park, in Suffolk, and elsewhere. forest, shoots forth leaves on every Old Christmas-day, and that no leaf is ever to be seen on it either before or after that day, during the winter, a lady, who is now on a visit in this city, and who is attentively curious in every thing relative to art or nature, made a journey to Cadenham, on Monday the 3rd instant, purposely to enquire on the spot, about the production of this famous tree. On her arrival near it, the usual guide was ready to attend her; but on his being desired to climb the oak, and to search whether there were any leaves then on it, he said it would be to no purpose; but that if she would come on the Wednesday following, (Christmas-day,) she might certainly see thousands. However, he was prevailed upon to ascend, and on the first branch which he gathered appeared several fair new leaves, fresh sprouted from the buds, and nearly an inch and a half in length. It may be imagined that the guide was more amazed at this premature production than the lady, for, so strong was his belief in the truth of the whole tradition, that he would have pledged his life that not a leaf was to have been discovered on any part of the tree before the usual hour.'"

The preceding passage affords a good contrast to the following note, by Dean Wren, on the "Glastonbury thorn."

"—And the oake in the new forest. King James could not bee induced to beleeve the τὸ ὅτι of this, till Bishop Andrewes, in whose diocese the tree grew, caused one of his own chaplaines, a man of known integritye, to give a true information of itt, which he did: for upon the eve of the nativitye, he gathered about a [100] slips, with the leaves newly opened, which he stuck in claye in the bottom of long white boxes, and soe sent them post to the courte, where they deservedly raised not only admiration, but stopt the mouth of infidelitye and contradiction for ever. Of this I was both an eye-witness, and did distribute many of them to the great persons of bothe sexes in court and others, ecclesiastical persons. But in these last troublesome times, a divelish fellow (of Herostratus humour) having hewen itt round at the roote, made his last stroke on his own legg, whereof he died, together with the old wondrous tree: which now sprowtes up againe, and may renew his oakye age againe, yf some such envious chance doe not hinder or prevent itt: from which the example of the former villane may perchance deterr the attempte. This I thought to testifie to all future times, and therefore subscribe with the same hand through which those little oakye slips past." *Ita testor Chr. Wren, Dno Lanc-*

begin to sprout in the fall of the leaf or autumn, and if not kept back by cold and outward causes, would leaf about the solstice. Now if it happen that any be so strongly constituted, as to make this good against the power of winter, they may produce their leaves or blossoms in that season; and perform that in some singles, which is observable in whole kinds; as in ivy, which blossoms and bears at least twice a year, and once in the winter; as also in furze, which flowereth in that season.

5. That *ferrum equinum,* or *sferra cavallo,* hath a virtue attractive of iron,[6] a power to break locks and draw off the shoes of a horse that passeth over it; whether you take it for one kind of *securidaca,* or will also take in *lunaria,* we know it to be false, and cannot but wonder at Matthiolus, who upon a parallel in Pliny was staggered into suspension. Who notwithstanding in the imputed virtue to open things close and shut up, could laugh himself at that promise from the herb *Æthiopis* or *Æthiopian* mullein, and condemn the judgment of Scipio, who having such a pick-lock, would spend so many years in battering the gates of Carthage; which strange and magical conceit seems to have no deeper root in reason than the figure of its seed; for therein indeed it somewhat resembles a horse-shoe: which, notwithstanding, Baptista Porta hath thought too low a signification, and raised the same unto a lunary representation.

6. That bays will protect from the mischief of lightning and thunder, is a quality ascribed thereto, common with the fig-tree, eagle, and skin of a seal. Against so famous a quality, Vicomercatus produceth experiment of a bay-tree blasted in Italy. And therefore, although Tiberius for this intent did wear a laurel upon his temples, yet did Augustus take a more probable course, who fled under arches and hollow vaults for protection. And though Porta conceive, because in a streperous eruption it riseth against fire, it doth therefore resist lightning, yet is that no emboldening illation. And if we consider the threefold effect of Jupiter's trisulk, to burn, discuss,[7] and terebrate; and if that be true which

---

*celoto à sacris domesticis αὐτόπτης tunc: et Carolo Regi patrono opt. max*º. [*postea*] *ex* αὐτοποίᾳ *fidus assertor.*

[6] *That* ferrum equinum, *&c.*] Some species of *Hippocrepis?*

[7] *discuss.*] Dissipate.—*Wr.*

is commonly delivered, that it will melt the blade, yet pass the scabbard,—kill the child, yet spare the mother,—dry up the wine, yet leave the hogshead entire,[8]—though it favour

[8] *that it will melt, &c.*] This passage is strikingly illustrated by a very extraordinary case of lightning, related in the *London and Edinburgh Philosophical Magazine*, for Sept. 1832. Mr. and Mrs. Boddington, while seated in the barouche seat of their carriage, were struck senseless by a flash of lightning, which at the same time killed one of the horses, threw the post-boy to a considerable distance, and then entered the earth, making four large holes. The passage of the electric fluid is thus described:—"It struck Mrs. B'.s cotton umbrella, which was literally shivered to pieces, both the springs in the handle forced out, the wires that extended the whalebone broken, and the cotton covering rent into a thousand shreds. From the wires of the umbrella the fluid passed to the wire that was attached to the edge of her bonnet, the cotton-thread that was twisted round that wire, marking the place of entrance over the left eye, by its being burnt off from that spot all round the right side, crossing the back of the head and down into the neck above the left shoulder: the hair that came in contact with it was singed: it here made a hole through the handkerchief that was round her throat, and zigzagged along the skin of her neck to the steel busk of her stays, leaving a painful, but not deep, wound, and also affecting the hearing of the left ear. It entered the external surface of the busk:—this is clearly proved by the brown paper case in which it was inclosed, being perforated on the outside, and the busk itself fused for about a quarter of an inch on the upper surface, presenting a blistered appearance. Its passage down the busk could not be traced in any way; there was no mark whatever on the steel, nor was the paper that covered it discoloured or altered in the slightest degree: its exit at the bottom, however, was as clearly indicated as its entrance at the top: the steel was fused in the same manner, and the paper was perforated in the same way, but on the opposite side.

"There were marks of burning on the gown and petticoat above the steel; and the inside of the stays, and the garments under the stays, were pierced by the passage of the fluid to her thighs, where it made wounds on both; but that on the left so deep, and so near the femoral artery, that the astonishment is, that she escaped with life;—even as it was, the hæmorrhage was very great. Every article on which she sat was perforated to the cushion of the seat, the cloth of which was torn in a much more extensive way than the clothes; and the leather that covered the iron forced off in the same spot, clearly marking its egress at this place. In the case of Mr. B. the umbrella also was the conductor; it was made of silk, and was but little damaged; a small portion of the upper part only being torn where it joins the stick, and none of the springs or wires being displaced. The main force of the shock, however, appears to have passed down the handle to the left arm, though a portion of it made a hole through the brim of his hat, and burnt off all the hair that was below it together with the eye-brows and eye-lashes. The electric stream

the amulet, it may not spare us; it will be unsure to rely on any preservative, it is no security to be dipped in Styx, or clad in the armour of Ceneus. Now that beer, wine, and other liquors, are spoiled with lightning and thunder, we conceive it proceeds not only from noise and concussion of the air, but also noxious spirits which mingle therewith, and draw them to corruption; whereby they become not only dead themselves, but sometimes deadly unto others, as that which Seneca mentioneth; whereof whosoever drank, either lost his life or else his wits upon it.

7. It hath much deceived the hopes of good fellows, what is commonly expected of bitter almonds; and though in Plutarch confirmed from the practice of Claudius his physician, that antidote against ebriety hath commonly failed. Surely men much versed in the practice do err in the theory of inebriation; conceiving in that disturbance the brain doth only suffer from exhalations and vaporous ascensions from the stomach, which fat and oily substances may suppress; whereas the prevalent intoxication is from the spirits of drink dispersed into the veins and arteries; from whence by common conveyances they creep into the brain, insinuate into its ventricles, and beget those vertigoes accompanying

---

shattered the left hand, fused the gold shirt buttons, and tore the clothes in a most extraordinary manner, forcing parts of them, together with the buttons, to a considerable distance, and a deep wound was inflicted under its position on the wrist. The arm was laid bare to the elbow, which is presumed to have been at the moment very near his left waistcoat-pocket, in which there was a knife; this also was forced from its situation, and forced on the ground; a severe wound was made on his body, and every article of dress torn away as if it had been done by gunpowder. From the knife it passed to the iron of the seat, wounding his back, and setting fire to his clothes in its passage. Another portion descended to the right arm, which had hold of the lower part of the stick of the umbrella; was attracted by the sleeve-button, where it made a wound, but slight, compared to that on the left, passed down the arm (which it merely discoloured, and broke the skin of in two small places) to a gold pencil-case in the right waistcoat-pocket. The great coat he had on was torn to pieces, and the coat immediately above the waistcoat-pocket much rent; but the waistcoat itself was merely perforated; on the external part, where the discharge entered by a hole about the size of a pea, and on the inside by a similar hole at the other extremity of the pencil-case, where it passed out, setting fire to his trousers and drawers, and inflicting a deep wound round his back, the whole of which was literally flayed."

that perversion. And therefore the same effect may be produced by a glister; the head may be intoxicated by a medicine at the heel. So the poisonous bites of serpents, although on parts at distance from the head, yet having entered the veins, disturb the animal faculties, and produce the effects of drink, or poison swallowed. And so, as the head may be disturbed by the skin,[9] it may the same way be relieved; as is observable in balneations, washings, and fomentations, either of the whole body, or of that part alone.[1]

CHAPTER VII.[2]

Of some insects, and the properties of several plants:—of the death-watch; the presages drawn from oak-apple insects; whether all plants have seeds; whether the sap of trees runs to the ground in winter; of the effects of camphor; with many others.

1.[3] Few ears have escaped the noise of the death-watch, that is, the little clickling sound heard often in many rooms, somewhat resembling that of a watch; and this is conceived to be of an evil omen or prediction of some person's death: wherein notwithstanding there is nothing of rational presage or just cause of terror unto melancholy and meticulous heads. For this noise is made by a little sheathwinged grey insect,[4] found often in wainscot benches and wood-work in the summer. We have taken many thereof, and kept them in thin boxes, wherein I have heard and seen them

---

[9] *by the skin.*] Affections of the skin.—*Wr.*

[1] *that part alone.*] The most present way of bringing the drunken to the use of his senses, is to apply large sponges dipt in strong white wine vinegar, which a Doctor of Physic, of prime note and name, does assure mee is, upon manifold experience, found most true; yf they be for a while applied not to the head, but to the testicles.—*Wr.*

[2] *Chap.* VII.] A considerable portion of the contents of this chapter was added in the 2nd, 3rd, and 6th editions: the rest formed the conclusion of chap. VI. in the 1st edition, and was first made a separate chapter in the 2nd edition.

[3] § 1. Added in the 6th edition, as also the 7th paragraph: the intervening five, and the four succeeding ones, appeared first in the 2nd edition.

[4] *sheathwinged, &c.*] *Anobium tessellatum.*

work and knock with a little proboscis or trunk against the side of the box, like a *picus martius*, or woodpecker against a tree. It worketh best in warm weather, and for the most part giveth not over under nine or eleven strokes at a time. He that could extinguish the terrifying apprehensions hereof, might prevent the passions of the heart, and many cold sweats in grandmothers and nurses, who, in the sickness of children, are so startled with these noises.

2. The presage of the year succeeding, which is commonly made from insects or little animals in oak-apples, according to the kinds thereof, either maggot, fly or spider; that is, of famine, war, or pestilence; whether we mean that woody excrescence, which shooteth from the branch about May, or that round and apple-like accretion which groweth under the leaf about the latter end of summer, is, I doubt, too distinct, nor verifiable from event.

For flies and maggots are found every year, very seldom spiders: and Helmont affirmeth, he could never find the spider and the fly upon the same trees, that is the signs of war and pestilence, which often go together: beside, that the flies found were at first maggots, experience hath informed us; for keeping these excrescences, we have observed their conversions, beholding in magnifying glasses the daily progression thereof. As may be also observed in other vegetable excretions, whose maggots do terminate in flies of constant shapes; as in the nut-galls of the outlandish oak, and the mossy tuft of the wild briar; which having gathered in November, we have found the little maggots, which lodged in wooden cells all winter, to turn into flies in June.[5]

We confess the opinion may hold some verity in the analogy, or emblematical fancy. For pestilence is properly signified by the spider, whereof some kinds are of a very venomous nature; famine by maggots, which destroy the fruits of the earth; and war not improperly by the fly, if we rest in the fancy of Homer, who compares the valiant Grecian unto a fly.

Some verity it may also have in itself, as truly declaring the corruptive constitution in the present sap and nutrimental juice of the tree; and may consequently discover the

---

[5] *flies in June.*] Of the genus *Cynips*.

disposition of that year, according to the plenty or kinds of these productions. For if the putrefying juices of bodies bring forth plenty of flies and maggots, they give forth testimony of common corruption, and declare that the elements are full of the seeds of putrefaction, as the great number of caterpillars, gnats, and ordinary insects do also declare. If they run into spiders, they give signs of higher putrefaction, as plenty of vipers and scorpions are confessed to do; the putrefying materials producing animals of higher mischiefs, according to the advance and higher strain of corruption.[6]

3. Whether all plants have seed, were more easily determinable, if we could conclude concerning hartstongue,[7] fern, the capillaries, *lunaria*,[7] and some others. But whether those little dusty particles, upon the lower side of the leaves, be seeds and seminal parts; or rather, as it is commonly conceived, excremental separations; we have not as yet been able to determine by any germination or univocal production from them when they have been sowed on purpose; but having set the roots of hartstongue in a garden, a year or two after, there came up three or four of the same plants, about two yards distance from the first. Thus much we observe, that they seem to renew yearly, and come not fully out till the plant be in its vigour; and, by the help of magnifying glasses, we find these dusty atoms to be round at first, and fully representing seeds, out of which at last proceed little mites almost invisible; so that such as are old stand open, as being emptied of some bodies formerly included; which, though discernable in hartstongue, is more notoriously discoverable in some differences of brake or fern.

But exquisite microscopes and magnifying glasses have at last cleared this doubt, whereby also long ago the noble Fredericus Cæsius beheld the dusts of polypody as big as peppercorns; and as Johannes Faber testifieth, made draughts on paper of such kind of seeds, as big as his glasses represented them: and set down such plants under the classes of *herbæ tergifætæ*, as may be observed in his notable botanical tables.[8]

[6] *For if the putrefying, &c.*] See note at page 196.
[7] *hartstongue*, lunaria.] *Scolopendrium* and moonwort.
[8] *3. Whether all plants have seeds, &c.*] This doubt has been cleared

4. Whether the sap of trees runs down to the roots in winter, whereby they become naked and grow not; or whether they do not cease to draw any more, and reserve so much as sufficeth for conservation, is not a point indubitable.[9] For we observe, that most trees, as though they would be perpetually green, do bud at the fall of the leaf, although they sprout not much forward until the spring and warmer weather approacheth; and many trees maintain their leaves all winter, although they seem to receive very small advantage in their growth. But [that] the sap doth powerfully rise in the spring, to repair that moisture whereby they barely subsisted in the winter, and also to put the plant in a capacity of fructification,—he that hath beheld how many gallons of water may in a small time be drawn from a birch tree in the spring, hath slender reason to doubt.

5. That camphor eunuchates, or begets in men an impotency unto venery, observation will hardly confirm; and we have found it to fail in cocks and hens, though given for many days: which was a more favourable trial than that of Scaliger, when he gave it unto a bitch that was proud. For the instant turgescence is not to be taken off, but by medicines of higher natures; and with any certainty but one way that we know, which notwithstanding, by suppressing that natural evacuation, may incline unto madness, if taken in the summer.

6. In the history of prodigies we meet with many showers of wheat; how true or probable, we have not room to debate: only thus much we shall not omit to inform; that

---

up by the laborious investigations of subsequent botanists. Sir James Smith, in speaking of the *dorsal ferns*, remarks—"The production of perfect germinating seeds, contained in capsules, and consequently produced by impregnated *fertile flowers*, is as clear in ferns as in mosses."

[9] 4. *Whether the sap, &c.*] Du Petit Thouars supposes that the sap begins to move at the extremities of the branches before it stirs at the roots,—and this has been confirmed by experience. He theorises that the first budding in spring absorbs the sap from adjacent parts—which draw on those parts still further removed, and so on, till the whole mass of fluid is set in motion down to the roots. Dutrochet has formed a theory to account for the motion of vegetable fluids, by supposing galvanic action. See a curious account of his experiments and deductions, in *Lindley's Introd. to Botany*, p. 237, 238.

what was this year found in many places, and almost preached for wheat rained from the clouds, was but the seed of ivy-berries, which somewhat represent it; and though it were found in steeples and high places, might be conveyed thither, or muted out by birds; for many feed thereon, and in the crops of some we have found no less than three ounces.

7. That every plant might receive a name according unto the disease it cureth, was the wish of Paracelsus, a way more likely to multiply empiricks than herbalists: yet what is practised by many is advantageous unto neither; that is, relinquishing their proper appellations to re-baptize them by the name of saints, apostles, patriarchs, and martyrs, to call this the herb of John, that of Peter, this of James or Joseph, that of Mary or Barbara. For hereby apprehensions are made additional unto their proper natures; whereon superstitious practices ensue, and stories are framed accordingly, to make good their foundations.

8. We cannot omit to declare the gross mistake of many in the nominal apprehension of plants. To instance but in few. An herb, there is, commonly called *betonica*[1] *Pauli*, or *Paul's betony*; hereof the people have some conceit in reference to St. Paul; whereas, indeed, that name is derived from Paulus Ægineta, an ancient physician of Ægina, and is no more than speedwell, or fluellin. The like expectations are raised from *herba trinitatis*; which, notwithstanding, obtaineth that name from the figure of its leaves, and is one kind of liverwort, or *hepatica*. In *milium solis*, the epithet of the sun hath enlarged its opinion; which hath, indeed, no reference thereunto, it being no more than *lithospermon*, or *grummel*, or rather *milium soler*; which as Serapion from Aben Juliel hath taught us, because it grew plentifully in the mountains of Soler, received that appellation. In Jews' ears something is conceived extraordinary from the name, which is in propriety but *fungus sambucinus*, or an excrescence about the roots of elder, and concerneth not the nation of the Jews, but Judas Iscariot, upon a conceit he hanged on this tree; and is become a famous medicine in quinsies,[2] sore throats,[3]

---

[1] *betonica.*] *Pauli Ægineta betonica; nobis est* Flewellin.—*Wr.*
[2] *quinsies.*] *Lege* quinancyes.—*Wr.*
[3] *sore throats.*] A correspondent of the *Gentleman's Magazine,*

and strangulations,[4] ever since. And so are they deceived in the name of horse-radish, horse-mint, bull-rush, and many more: conceiving therein some prenominal consideration, whereas, indeed, that expression is but a Grecism, by the prefix of *hippos* and *bous*; that is, horse and bull, intending no more than great.[5] According whereto the great dock is called *hippolapathum*; and he that calls the horse of Alexander Great-head,[6] expresseth the same which the Greeks do in *Bucephalus*.

9. Lastly, many things are delivered and believed of other plants, wherein at least we cannot but suspend. That there is a property in basil to propagate scorpions, and that by the smell thereof they are bred in the brains of men, is much advanced by Hollerius, who found this insect in the brains of a man that delighted much in that smell. Wherein beside that we find no way to conjoin the effect unto the cause assigned; herein the moderns speak but timorously, and some of the ancients quite contrarily. For according unto Oribasius, physician unto Julian, the Africans, men best experienced in poisons, affirm, whosoever hath eaten basil, although he be stung with a scorpion, shall feel no pain thereby: which is a very different effect, and rather antidotally destroying, than seminally promoting its production.

That the leaves of *cataputia* or spurge, being plucked upward or downward, respectively perform their operations by

vol. lxxix. p. 38, relates a cure of sore throat by the use of sliced horse-radish—chewed, and then passed to the root of the tongue.

[4] *strangulations.*] *Supple* [inward].—*Wr.* i. e. *lege* 'inward strangulations.'

[5] *great.*] As is manifest in *Hipposelinum*, but especially in *hippoäetos*, the great eagle. *Hippelaphus, hippomœrathon,* Ἱππόγυποι, Ἱππομόμηκες, &c.—*Wr.*

To this list may be added horse-ant, bullhead, bullfinch, &c. But the prefix does not always mean "great." Evelyn says, that the horse-chestnut is so called because it cures horses and other cattle of coughs. And certainly both horse-chestnut and horse-radish are among the medicines used in farriery. Horse-beans, which are smaller than some other species, are so called because horses are fed with them:—horse-leeches, probably because they fasten on the legs of horses while drinking. Horse-hoe, through drawn by horses because it is *large*, owes its prefix to the former, not to the latter circumstance. Why is the epithet, *dog*, prefixed to the scentless violet and the wild rose?

[6] *Great-head.*] Or, as I knew a gallant horse, whom his lord called Club.—*Wr.*

purge or vomit, as some have written, and old wives still do preach, is a strange conceit, ascribing unto plants positional operations, and after the manner of the loadstone; upon the pole[7] whereof, if a knife be drawn from the handle unto the point, it will take up a needle; but if drawn again from the point to the handle, it will attract it no more.

That cucumbers are no commendable fruits; that being very waterish, they fill the veins with crude and windy serosities; that containing little salt or spirit, they may also debilitate the vital acidity, and fermental faculty of the stomach, we readily concede; but that they should be so cold, as be almost poison by that quality, it will be hard to allow, without the contradiction of Galen;* who accounteth them cold but in the second degree, and in that *classis* have most physicians placed them.[8]

That elder-berries are poison, as we are taught by tradition, experience will unteach us. And besides the promises of Blochwitius, the healthful effects thereof will convict us.

That an ivy cup will separate wine from water, if filled with both, the wine soaking through, but the water still remaining, as after Pliny many have averred, we know not how to affirm; who making trial thereof, found both the liquors to soak indistinctly through the bowl.[9]

That sheep do often get the rot, by feeding in boggy grounds where *ros solis*[1] groweth, seems beyond dispute.

* In his *Anatomia Sambuci*.

[7] *pole.*] Upon an armed stone there are two poles, one northe and the other southe. Now as the back of the knife layd on both these, being drawn from the southe to the northe, imprints the magneticall vertue, soe drawne back againe takes itt off.—*Wr.*

[8] *That cucumbers, &c.*] Added in the 2nd edition.

[9] *to soak indistinctly, &c.*] The fayling might bee by the weakenes of our racked wines.—*Wr.*

"Fixed or essential oils, or naphtha, and similar bodies, in mixture with water or aqueous solutions, in which they are not soluble, may be separated from the latter by a paper filter, previously moistened with pure water." *Faraday's Chemical Manipulation*, p. 241, No. 514.

[1] *ros solis.*] This plant (*drosera rotundifolia* and *longifolia*, the round and long leaved sundew, and the butterwort, and white rot, *pinguicula vulgaris*, and *hydrocotyle*), have been accused as the cause of dry rot; but they do not occur in every rotting soil. Various other causes have been assigned. But nothing seems so uniformly to occasion the

That this herb is the cause thereof, shepherds affirm and deny; whether it hath a cordial virtue by sudden refection, sensible experiment doth hardly confirm, but that it may have a balsamical and resumptive virtue, whereby it becomes a good medicine in catarrhs and consumptive dispositions, practice and reason conclude. That the lentous drops upon it are not extraneous, and rather an exudation from itself, than a rorid concretion from without; beside other grounds, we have reason to conceive: for having kept the roots moist and earthed in close chambers, they have, though in lesser plenty, sent out these drops as before.[2]

That *flos Africanus* is poison, and destroyeth dogs, in two experiments we have not found.[3]

That yew, and the berries[4] thereof, are harmless, we know.

That a snake will not endure the shade of an ash, we can deny.[5] Nor is it inconsiderable what is affirmed by Bellonius:[*] for if his assertion be true, our apprehension is often-

---

[*] Lib. 1. *Observat.*

disease as certain *paludal effluvia*, from whatever circumstances of locality of soil, or vegetation, such effluvia may be occasioned.

[2] *That sheep, &c.*] Added in the 3rd edition.

[3] *not found.*] There are diverse sorts of them. Some, by longe translations into our colder clymes, now grown harmlesse: as it happened in peaches, which in their original soyle were counted pernicious in an extreme degree of cold and moyst; but by transplantation and long mangonization among us, prove to bee beneficial to hot complexions: and with Spanish wine not much hurtful to any in a small quantitye.—*Wr.*

[4] *That yew, &c.*] I have often seen children eate them without hurt; but in hot countries the ixia grows to such a hight of clamminess, as cannot bee dissolved in the stomack.—*Wr.*

"Nihil æque facere ad viperæ morsum, quam taxi arboris succum.—*Sueion. Claud.* § 16.

"Cativulcus—taxo—se exanimavit."—*Cæsar. de Bell. Gall.* l. v. 31.

See an instance of two cows being killed by eating the leaves of yew, at High Lorton, Cumberland, in 1817. *Hampshire Chronicle*, Jan. 26, 1807.—"Three cows died a few days ago, at Drayton, in consequence of eating yew leaves."—*Evening Mail*, May 3rd, 1811.—"Two horses killed by eating yew in a close near Chelmsford; a great quantity being found in the stomachs of the dead animals. A filly was saved by powerful antidotes being quickly administered."—*Phil. Gazette*, Feb. 12, 1823.—*Jef.*

[5] *deny.*] Edit. 1646 and 1650 add here the following sentence:—"That cats have such delight in the herb *nepeta*, called therefore

times wide in ordinary simples, and in common use we mistake one for another. We know not the true thyme; the savory in our gardens is not that commended of old; and that kind of hyssop the ancients used, is unknown unto us, who make great use of another.

We omit to recite the many virtues and endless faculties ascribed unto plants, which sometimes occur in grave and serious authors; and we shall make a bad transaction for truth to concede a verity in half. To reckon up all, it were employment for Archimedes, who undertook to write the number of the sands. Swarms of others there are, some whereof our future endeavours may discover: common reason, I hope, will save us a labour in many, whose absurdities stand naked unto every eye; errors, not able to deceive the emblem of justice, and needing no Argus to descry them. Herein there surely wants expurgatory animadversions, whereby we might strike out great numbers of hidden qualities; and having once a serious and conceded list, we might, with more encouragement and safety, attempt their reasons.

cattaria, our experience cannot discover."—I have met with the probable reason for the suppression of this passage (3rd edit. 1658, and subsequent editions) in a letter from Dr. How to the author, dated 1655. "I have numbered, about two rootes of *nep*. in my garden, 16 cats, who never destroyed those plants, but have totally despoyled the neighbouring births in that bed to a yard's distance, rendring the place hard and smooth, like a walke with their frequent treddings."

THE THIRD BOOK:

THE PARTICULAR PART CONTINUED.

OF POPULAR AND RECEIVED TENETS CONCERNING ANIMALS.

CHAPTER I.

That an Elephant hath no joints, &c.

THE first shall be of the elephant, whereof there generally passeth an opinion it hath no joints:[6] and this absurdity is seconded with another, that, being unable to lie down, it sleepeth against a tree; which the hunters observing do saw

[6] *The first shall be of the elephant, &c.*] The "popular and received tenet" concerning this animal, which it is the main object of the chapter before us to refute, appears either to have been first delivered, or first recorded from tradition, by Ctesias the Cnidian, who is the earliest writer to whom I have been able to trace it; and who, according to Professor Schlegel, was the first among the Greeks who gave, from his own personal observation, a description of the elephant in any way copious, which was written about 380 A.C. The probability that Ctesias was the originator, or the first recorder, of this vulgar error, is confirmed by the circumstance that many idle tales, regarding other animals, appear to have been also first promulgated by him; and also by the fact, that Aristotle, in his details on the elephant, twice refutes the assertions of Ctesias, naming him; and when refuting this particular error, does so in such a manner, that although no name is given, his allusions, as Professor Schlegel has shown, can refer only to that writer. The absurdity respecting the elephant's posture in sleep and the consequent mode of capturing him, is also derived from Ctesias.

It is very true, therefore, that, the "conceit" in question "is not the daughter of later times, but an old and grey-headed error;" and it is also true that it is delivered as such by Aristotle. I have found it necessary, for reasons that will be evident in the course of these annotations,

it almost asunder; whereon the beast relying, by the fall of the tree falls also down itself, and is able to rise no more.

always to compare what our author has attributed to that philosopher, with the original statements made in his works; and as there are several curious points in the history of our knowledge respecting the elephant connected with the subject, and which contribute to elucidate Browne's remarks, I shall here introduce Aristotle's observations.

It will be proper to premise, however, that it has been shown by Professor Schlegel, in his learned and interesting *History of the Elephant and Sphinx*, (*Class. Journ.* vol. xxxi.), that the first battle between any of the nations of the western world and those of the eastern, in which elephants were used, was that of Arbela, and that some of these, taken by Alexander, and sent by him into Greece, were the first elephants seen in that country, and very probably the actual subjects of the admirable natural history of this animal contained in the works of Aristotle, which is manifestly, and indeed professedly, the result of frequent and minute actual examination of elephants of both sexes. And, "what he himself could not ascertain," as Professor Schlegel remarks, " viz. the beast's mode of life in his wild state, he doubtless ascertained from the Indian conductors who led the elephants." (Ib. p. 53.)

Aristotle, in the ninth chapter of his book, *On the Progressive Motion of Animals*, when showing that without inflexion there could be no progression, to which demonstration Browne's argument on the subject is greatly indebted (as he indeed indirectly acknowledges), has occasion to notice some partial exceptions to this rule, which he introduces thus: " It is possible, however, for the leg to be moved when not inflected, in the same manner as infants creep. And there is an ancient report of this kind about elephants, which is not true; for such animals as these are moved in consequence of an inflexion taking place either in their shoulders or hips. No animal, however, is capable of moving with a continued progressive motion, and with security, with its members straight; but it may be moved as they are in the *palæstræ*, who proceed on their knees through the dust."—*T. Taylor's Treatises of Aristotle on the Parts and Progressive Motion of Animals*, p. 181.

In the second book of his *History of Animals*, chap. i. when treating of the accordance of viviparous animals in general with each other, and with man, in configuration and in motions, the Stagyrite observes: "The legs, however, of other animals, as well the fore as the hind legs, have flexions contrary to each other, and to the flexions of the legs and arms of man, the elephant being excepted . . . . . What is asserted of the elephant, however, by some, is not true (i. e. that he cannot bend his legs, nor sit); for he can do both, except that he cannot, on account of his weight, at one and the same time, bend each fore leg, and recline on each side, but he can alone bend one leg, either the right or the left, and alone recline on one side, and in this manner he sleeps (leaning against some wall or tree). But he bends his hind legs in the

THAT AN ELEPHANT HATH NO JOINTS. 221

Which conceit is not the daughter of later times, but an old and grey-headed error, even in the days of Aristotle, as he delivereth in his book, *De Incessu Animalium*, and stands successively related by several other authors; by Diodorus Siculus, Strabo, Ambrose, Cassiodore, Solinus, and many more. Now, herein, methinks, men much forget themselves, not well considering the absurdity of such assertions.

For first, they affirm it hath no joints, and yet concede it walks and moves about;[7] whereby they conceive there may

same manner as men."—*Taylor's Translation of Aristotle's History of Animals*, p. 36.

In the latter passage, however, Aristotle, though he corrects the error of Ctesias in a satisfactory manner, appears, on another point, to be mistaken himself. For it would seem to imply that the elephant, having bent one fore-leg, cannot then bend the other so as to kneel with both—which is contrary to the fact. And, what is perhaps still more curious in the history of the subject, Mr. Taylor, in his concluding interpolation, has actually adopted a portion of the original error of Ctesias, to complete the sense of his author. Something, certainly, appears to be wanting, in order to complete the sense. But, that a statement by a writer who is never mentioned by Aristotle except for the purpose of refuting him, and which is in itself so well known to be untrue, should have been employed for the purpose, is very extraordinary. As the amplifications of Mr. Taylor's version of this passage also tend in some degree to obscure the sense, I will add the closer and more concise version of Du Val. "Flectunt autem crura, priora contrà, atque posteriora: et e contrario, quàm homo, membra inflectunt, excepto elephanto ..... Elephas non, ut aliqui retulerunt, agit: sed considendo crura inflectit, nequit tamen præ nimio pondere utrumque in latus equilibrio quodam vergere: sed aut lævo incubat, aut dextro, atque eo ipso habitu requiescit."—*Arist. Opera Omnia, curâ Du Val*, tom. i. p. 771, B.—*Br.*

[7] *For first, they affirm it hath no joints, &c.*] This argument of our author, showing, from reason, anatomy, and general analogy with other animals, the absurdity of the error he is refuting, is exceedingly logical and pertinent.

Ross, with his usual dogmatism, represents that "the doctor, prying too narrowly into the sayings of the ancients, reckoneth them amongst his *Vulgar Errors*, which being rightly understood, are no errors at all; as when they say the elephant hath no joynts, they meant their joynts were stiffe, and not so easily flexible as those of other animals." (*Arcan. Microc.* p. 152). But unfortunately for this explanation, Ctesias explicitly affirms, "that the elephant hath no joints in the bone of his leg," which fully justifies the importance given by Browne to the popular misrepresentation founded on the statement of that writer.

Robinson, by implication, condemns Browne for censuring the views of the ancients on this subject; observing, "*that elephants have no*

be a progression or advancement made in motion, without inflexion of parts. Now all progression or animal locomotion being (as Aristotle teaches) performed *tractu et pulsu*, that is by drawing on or impelling forward some part which was before in station, or at quiet,—where there are no joint or flexures, neither can there be the actions. And this is true, not only in quadrupeds, volatiles, and fishes, which have distinct and prominent organs of motion,—legs, wings, and fins, but in such also as perform their progression by the trunk,—as serpents, worms and leeches; whereof, though some want bones, and all extended articulations, yet have they arthritical analogies,* and, by the motion of fibrous and musculous parts, are able to make progression. Which to conceive in bodies flexible, and without all protrusion of parts, were to expect a race from Hercules' pillars or hope to behold the effects of Orpheus' harp, when trees found joints, and danced after his music.

Again, while men conceive they never lie down,[8] and enjoy not the position of rest ordained unto all pedestrious animals,

* Joint-like-parts.

joynts, though by some it be delivered in generall termes; yet was not their *Minerva* so dull, to except all; but did intend the *suffragineous* or *knee joynts* onely: without which there may be a progression in man; as upon stilts: by the sole motion of the hippe: in *quadrupedes*, as in full gallop." But though he proceeds to quote Cæsar as affirming such to be the case with the elk (*alces*), he adduces no facts whatever in contravention of Browne's representations and arguments; although, on the other hand, he has some good instances of animals to which station is rest, as many birds, and ordinarily horses also. Thus this commentator, in his defence of the ancients against our author, actually admits that they made the very statement which we have just seen to be that of Ctesias, the original promulgator of the story.—*Br.*

[8] *Again, while men conceive they never lie down.*] The argument contained in this and the following paragraph, is deserving of the same praise as has been awarded to the preceding direct argument on the necessity of the elephant having joints; that necessity being now shown, in an indirect manner, from the general necessity of change and alternation of posture in animals. But our author, from the deficiency of his knowledge both of the natural history and the anatomy of the elephant, happens not to have been aware that *station*, to it, is *rest* (except when greatly fatigued, or in great weakness from disease), as we have seen, when citing Robinson's animadversions, to be the case also with some other animals. From the construction of all the joints in the legs of this animal, and especially from that of the knee-joint,

hereby they imagine (what reason cannot conceive), that an animal of the vastest dimension and longest duration, should live in a continual motion, without that alternity and vicissitude of rest whereby all others continue; and yet must thus much come to pass, if we opinion they lie not down and enjoy no decumbence at all. For station is properly no rest, but one kind of motion, relating unto that which physicians (from Galen) do name extensive or tonical; that is, an extension of the muscles and organs of motion, maintaining the body at length, or in its proper figure.

Wherein although it seem to be unmoved, it is not without all motion; for in this position the muscles are sensibly extended, and labour to support the body; which, permitted unto its proper gravity, would suddenly subside and fall unto the earth; as it happeneth in sleep, diseases, and death. From which occult action and invisible motion of the muscles, in station (as Galen declareth), proceed more offensive lassi-

the elephant, when standing still, rests, as it were, upon four pillars, with scarcely any need of muscular exertion, and of none but what slight mental excitement can supply. Thus the elephant, which died some years since in the menagerie of the Jardin des Plantes, at Paris, was observed never to lie down, even in his last illness, until immediately before his death; and that which was so long exhibited at Exeter 'Change, London, and killed there in 1826, received 152 balls in almost every anterior part of his body, before he fell.

The following relation, however, is still more illustrative of the fact, that the elephant *rests* while *standing*; expecially when under any excitement. Mr. Corse (now Mr. Corse Scott), under whose direction the elephant hunters of Tiperah, in Bengal, were placed for several years, states, that it is always a good sign when an elephant lies down to sleep within a few months after he is taken; as it shows him to be of a good temper, not suspicious, but reconciled to his fate. "Elephants," he observes, "particularly goondahs (which are large male animals that have strayed from the woods and from the herds), have been known to *stand twelve months* at their pickets *without lying down to sleep*; though they sometimes take a short nap standing." *Obs. on the Manners, Habits, and Nat. Hist. of the Elephant—Phil. Trans.* 1799, p. 44.

From the observation of some remarkable case of this description, in a country where the rarity of the animal precluded the correction of the inference deduced from it, in addition perhaps to the "cylindrical composure of the legs," to which it is attributed by our author, the story of the want of knee-joints in the elephant, in all probability, must have originated.—*Br.*

tudes than from ambulation.[9] And therefore the tyranny of some have tormented men with long and enforced station; and though Ixion and Sisyphus, which always moved, do seem to have the hardest measure, yet was not Tityus favoured, that lay extended upon Caucasus, and Tantalus suffered somewhat more than thirst, that stood perpetually in hell. Thus Mercurialis, in his *Gymnastics*, justly makes standing one kind of exercise: and Galen, when we lie down, commends unto us middle figures, that is, not to lie directly, or at length, but somewhat inflected, that the muscles may be at rest; for such as he termeth *hypobolemaioi*, or figures of excess, either shrinking up or stretching out, are wearisome positions, and such as perturb the quiet of those parts. Now various parts do variously discover these indolent and quiet positions, some in right lines, as the wrists; some at right angles, as the cubit;[1] others at oblique angles, as the fingers and knees: all resting satisfied in postures of moderation, and none enduring the extremity of flexure or extension.[2]

Moreover, men herein do strangely forget the obvious relations of history, affirming they have no joints, whereas they daily read of several actions which are not performable without them. They forget what is delivered by Xiphilinus, and also by Suetonius, in the lives of Nero and Galba, that elephants have been instructed to walk on ropes, in public shows, before the people: which is not easily performed by man, and requireth not only a broad foot, but a pliable flexure of joints, and commandable disposure of all parts of progression. They pass by that memorable place in Curtius, concerning the elephant of King Porus; *Indus qui elephantem regebat, descendere cum ratus, more solito procumbere jussit*

---

[9] *From which, &c.*] N.B. *et cave!* The mischeef which cometh by standing long (as at studyes) appears in old age, by the swelling of the legs, and (ofttimes) the gout.—*Wr.*

Would not Darwin have said that this swelling was no other than the appetency of the leg towards an attainment of the columnar formation of the elephantine leg—an appetency excited by the stationary discipline of its studious owner, the dean?

[1] *cubit*] The fore-arm.

[2] *Now various parts, &c.*] This sentence was first added in the 2nd edit.

in genua, cæteri quoque (ita enim instituti erant) demisere corpora in terram. They remember not the expression of Osorius,* when he speaks of the elephant presented to Leo X.; *Pontificem ter genibus flexis, et demisso corporis habitu venerabundus salutavit.* But above all, they call not to mind that memorable show of Germanicus, wherein twelve elephants danced unto the sound of music, and after laid them down in the *tricliniums*, or places of festival recumbency.

They forget the etymology of the knee, approved by some grammarians.† They disturb the position of the young ones in the womb; which upon extension of legs is not easily conceivable, and contrary unto the general contrivance of nature. Nor do they consider the impossible exclusion thereof, upon extension and rigour of the legs.³

Lastly, they forget or consult not experience,⁴ whereof not

* *De rebus gestis Emanuelis.*   † Γόνυ from γωνία.

³ *They forget, &c.*] This paragraph was first added in the 2nd edit.

⁴ *they forget or consult not experience, &c.*] This will be the proper place to make a remark or two on the modern history and prevalence of this tale, that the legs of the elephant are devoid of joints. In the volume on the elephant, published in the *Menageries* of the *Library of Entertaining Knowledge*, are some quotations on the subject from early English works, for which the compiler of that volume is indebted to Steevens's notes on Shakspeare, though he does not acknowledge it. In a curious specimen of our early natural history, *The Dialogues of Creatures Moralyzed*, is mention, Steevens informs us, of "the *olefawnte* that *bowyth not the kneys.*" In the play of *All Fools*, 1605, occurs this passage: "I hope you are no *elephant*—you have *joints.*" Shakspeare, in his *Troilus and Cresside*, 1609, makes Ulysses say (act ii. sc. 3), "The elephant hath joints, but none for courtesy: his legs are legs for necessity, not for flexure." In *All's Lost by Lust*, 1633, a woman is said to be "stubborn as an *elephant's leg*—no bending in her." It will not follow from these expressions, that the authors of all the works in which they appear were actually believers in this story; nor could it be proved from them that it was generally believed at the times when they wrote: for, with respect to the three plays, the allusion may be regarded as founded only on the known prevalence, at some period, of the belief in question. Still, even these evince, at least, the former existence of the notion, as well as its extensive prevalence and popular currency. But the mention of it in *The Dialogues of Creatures Moralyzed*, shows it to have been a generally received opinion in this country at the date of their publication, early in the sixteenth century. Browne mentions it as a general opinion (the first edition of the *Vulgar Errors* being published in 1646, and the last in 1686), though he states it to be "at present well suppressed" in England by an elephant shown, "not many

many years past we have had the advantage in England, by an elephant shown in many parts thereof, not only in the posture of standing, but kneeling and lying down. Whereby, although the opinion at present be well suppressed, yet, from some strings of tradition, and fruitful recurrence of error, it is not improbable it may revive in the next generation again; this being not the first that hath been seen in England: for, besides some others, as Polydore Virgil relateth, Lewis the French king sent one to Henry III., and Emanuel of Portugal another to Leo X. into Italy, where, notwithstanding, the error is still alive and epidemical, as with us.

The hint and ground of this opinion might be, the gross and somewhat cylindrical composure of the legs, the equality and less perceptible disposure of the joints; especially in the former legs[5] of this animal; they appearing, when he standeth, like pillars of flesh, without any evidence of articulation. The different flexure and order of the joints might also countenance the same, being not disposed in the elephant as they

---

years past,"........." in many parts thereof, not only in the posture of standing, but kneeling and lying down." He expresses an apprehension, however, that it will revive again, citing the case of Italy, where, notwithstanding the opportunity of witnessing the habits of the animal, afforded by the elephant sent to Leo X., by Emanuel, King of Portugal, "the error," he observes, " is still alive and epidemical, as with us." And it remains, even to the present day, a " vulgar error" among the uneducated classes. It has long been the custom for the exhibitors of itinerant collections of wild animals, when showing the elephant, to mention the story of its having no joints, and its consequent inability to kneel; and they never fail to think it necessary to demonstrate its untruth by causing the animal to bend one of its fore-legs and to kneel also; but I never saw this done (and I have been present many times on such occasions), without observing that it was witnessed with astonishment and almost with incredulity, by several persons present, whether the exhibition has been in London or in a provincial town. We have thus an instance of an error of the grossest and most palpable description, and one which has often from time to time been refuted, respecting an animal which is not found in the countries in which that error has been entertained, prevailing for a period of at least 2,200 years, though for the last two centuries, to a greatly diminished extent. This is a fact which it will be well to bear in mind, in any enquiries respecting the probable truth of certain relations in natural history, which have at various periods, and among various nations, been generally received, but respecting the truth or falsity of which, we may not be in possession of decisive evidence.—*Br.*

[5] *former legs.*] Fore-legs: used in this case by Spenser.

CHAP. I.]   THAT AN ELEPHANT HATH NO JOINTS.   227

are in other quadrupeds, but carrying a nearer conformity unto those of man; that is, the bought[6] of the fore-legs, not directly backward, but laterally, and somewhat inward; but the hough or suffraginous flexure behind, rather outward: somewhat different unto many other quadrupeds,[7] as horses, camels,[8] deer, sheep, and dogs; for their fore-legs bend like our legs, and their hinder legs like our arms, when we move them to our shoulders. But quadrupeds oviparous, as frogs, lizards, crocodiles, have their joints and motive flexures more analogously framed unto ours: and some among viviparous, that is, such thereof as can bring their fore-feet and meat therein unto their mouths, as most can do, that have the clavicles or collar-bones, whereby their breasts are broader, and their shoulders more asunder; as the ape, the monkey, the squirrel, and some others.[9] If, therefore, any shall affirm the joints of elephants are differently framed from most of other quadrupeds, and more obscurely and grossly almost than any, he doth herein no injury unto truth.[1] But if, *à dicto secundùm quid ad dictum simpliciter*, he affirmeth also they have no articulations at all, he incurs the controlment of reason, and cannot avoid the contradiction also of sense.

As for the manner of their venation, if we consult historical experience, we shall find it to be otherwise than, as is commonly presumed, by sawing away of trees. The accounts whereof are to be seen at large at Johannes, Hugo,

[6] *the bought.*] The bend or flexure.
[7] *other quadrupeds.*] First edition added, "and such as can scratch the ear with the hinder foot."
[8] *camels.*] In the beginning of March, 1652-3, I saw a dromedary, which at the command of his master, by the word (busy) began to lye downe, first, by bending his fore-knees, and then the upper knee of the hinder legg, which is next the groine.—*Wr.*
[9] *some others.*] As mice sometimes, and dormice always, and among birds, the parat.—*Wr.*
[1] *If, therefore, any shall affirm, &c.*] There is some inaccuracy in this sentence: the joints of the elephant are framed upon the same general plan as those of other quadrupeds belonging to the same group of mammalia, and they certainly are *not* more obscurely and grossly formed than those of any others; having merely the variation of structure rendered necessary by the magnitude and the consequent weight of the animal, as we shall presently show; but being, at the same time, as admirably formed, and as exquisitely adapted to its particular exigencies, as those of any other creature whatever.—*Br.*

Edwardus Lopez, Garcias ab Horto, Cadamustus, and many more.

Other concernments there are of the elephant, which might admit of discourse. And if we should question the teeth of elephants,[2] that is, whether they be properly so termed, or might not rather be called horns,[3] it were no new enquiry of mine, but a paradox as old as Oppianus.* Whether, as Pliny and divers since affirm it, that elephants are terrified and make away upon the grunting of swine,[4] Garcias ab Horto may decide, who affirmeth upon experience, they enter their stalls, and live promiscuously in the woods of

* *Cygenet*, lib. 2.

[2] *elephants.*] There is another error concerning the teeth, which grow not, as most suppose, but as the tuskes of a boare proceed (like horns) from out the upper chawe, and soe bend up againe.—*Wr.*

[3] *might not rather be called horns.*] It is scarcely necessary to observe, that the tusks, as they are commonly called, of this animal, are truly *teeth*, being implanted in bones corresponding to those which carry the incisors of other animals : see *Cuvier, Règne Animal, édit. nouv.* tom. i. p. 237.—*Br.*

[4] *making away upon the grunting of swine.*] This aversion is alluded to in the following interesting passage from the *Menageries:* "But the elephant may be endued with this acute hearing, in addition to his exquisite touch, for the protection of the lesser animals from the accidents to which they would be subject from lying in his path. He has an extraordinary dislike to all small quadrupeds. Dogs running near him produce a great annoyance ; if a hare start from her cover, he is immediately alarmed ; and that pigs are his aversion, has been recorded by every naturalist, from Pliny to Buffon. It is even mentioned by Procopius, the historian of the Persian and Gothic wars, that, at the siege of Edessa, by Chosroes, King of Persia, in the time of Justinian, the besieged Greeks employed the cry of a pig to frighten from the walls the elephants of their enemy. The old naturalists explained this peculiarity by the doctrine of antipathies : in the same way that they affirmed that the elephant was fond of an ox, upon the principle of sympathies. It may appear something equally fanciful, to suggest the possibility that the elephant may dislike the smaller animals to come in his way from his instinctive disinclination to destroy them by an accidental tread. He always avoids a contest with inferior quadrupeds whenever he can ; and if a helpless living creature, such as an infant or a wounded man, lie in his way, he will move the object. The elephant is naturally gentle—anxious alone to procure his own food without molesting others. That he is so, is a merciful, as well as a wise dispensation. If he had possessed a ferocity equal to his power, he must have exterminated a very large part of the animal creation."—*Menageries,* vol. ii. p 69, 70.—*Br.*

Malavar. That the situation of the genitals is averse,[5] and their copulation like that which some believe of camels, as Pliny hath also delivered, is not to be received; for we have beheld that part in a different position; and their coition is made by supersaliency, like that of horses, as we are informed by some who have beheld them in that act. That some elephants have not only written whole sentences, as Ælian ocularly testifieth, but have also spoken, as Oppianus delivereth, and Christophorus à Costa particularly relateth,[6]—although it sound like that of Achilles' horse in Homer, we do not conceive impossible: nor, beside the affinity of reason in this animal, any such intolerable incapacity in the organs of divers quadrupeds, whereby they might not be taught to speak, or become imitators of speech, like birds.[7] Strange it is, how the curiosity of men, that

[5] *That the situation of the genitals, &c.*] Browne is quite correct in his statement of the manner in which coition is effected in the elephant; and from his mode of authenticating that statement, it might have been inferred, even in his time, that the notion of the modesty of the animal, or of its unwillingness or inability to continue its race in captivity, was merely a vulgar error; this, however, is not mentioned by our author.—*Br.*

[6] *have also spoken, as Oppianus delivereth, and Christophorus à Costa particularly relateth.*] In the volume on the elephant, in the *Library of Entertaining Knowledge*, before cited, occurs the following satisfactory explanation of this relation of Acosta:—" At Cochin, according to this writer, there was an elephant that worked at the port with all the skill of a human labourer. One day, when he was much fatigued, the governor of the port desired him to assist in launching a boat. The elephant refused; and the man of authority, having in vain employed all his caresses, commanded him to do it in the name of the King of Portugal. The loyal beast, it is added, instantly replied, ' I will, I will,' and performed his task. This story may explain some of the old fables of the elephant speaking; for, in the Malabar language, ' I will,' is expressed by ' hoo,'—a very natural sound for an elephant to make, not upon the invocation of the King of Portugal, but upon the more effectual stimulus of the blow which probably accompanied the utterance of the magical name."—*Menageries*, vol. ii. p. 154.—*Br.*

[7] *might not be taught to speak, &c.*] To expatiate on the futility of our author's reasoning, as to the probability of animals being taught to speak (to speak rationally, as he would seem to insinuate), is needless; but it will be proper to make a few remarks on the imperfect knowledge of his subject, which renders his reasoning futile. Like almost every other author who has written upon subjects connected with the instinct of brutes, he regards their *perceptive* faculties as lower degrees of *reason ;*

have been active in the instruction of beasts, has never fallen upon this artifice; and among those many paradoxical and unheard of imitations, should not attempt to make one speak. The serpent that spake unto Eve,[b] the dogs and cats that usually speak unto witches, might afford some encouragement. And since broad and thick chaps are required in birds that speak,[9] since lips and teeth are also organs of speech; from

mistaking the *analogical* relation to reason which they exhibit (using the term analogical in the same sense, *mutatis mutandis*, as that in which it has lately been employed in natural history, by Mr. W. S. Macleay), and by which they *represent* its attributes, for an *actual community of nature* with reason. The truth seems to be, with respect to the particular subject now before us, that brute animals, not having reason, and being consequently devoid of analytical thought, which is the activity of reason, are equally devoid of the means of uttering articulate speech, which is merely the exponent and vehicle of such thought in man. That this is the true nature of articulate speech, is proved by the fact, that those unfortunate individuals of the human race (of whom we may cite Peter, the wild boy, as an example), who have never been taught to *think*, and are devoid of reason, are equally devoid of the power of articulation, though their vocal organs are as perfect as those of educated men possessed of the full powers of speech. Some animals can be taught to produce sounds by their organs of voice, which closely resemble those of human speech; but sounds of this description can also be produced by inanimate machinery, as in the speaking *automata*, &c. of Kempelen and Kratzenstein; and such sounds, when uttered by animals, are indicative only of their own instinctive perceptions, like their ordinary inarticulate cries, and they are not indicative of these even in any greater degree than those cries are.

The only accurate view of the nature of the *analogue* of reason in brutes, with which I am acquainted, is contained in an enquiry into the nature of instinct, by Mr. John O. French, published in the first and second volumes of the *Zoological Journal*.

But, to proceed with our author, quadrupeds *have* been taught to "become imitators of speech like birds." Leibnitz has recorded the history of a dog, who had been taught, by the son of his master, a peasant in Saxony, to pronounce thirty different words. This fact may be regarded as throwing some degree of light upon, and rendering credible, many old relations of a similar kind, some long anterior to the time of our author. The substance of Leibnitz's account will be found in *Rees's Cyclopædia*, under the article DOG.—*Br.*

[b] *serpent, &c.*] See my notes at the very end, and on book v. c. 4.—*Wr.*

[9] *And since broad and thick chaps are required in birds that speak.*] An error is involved in this expression parallel to that popular one, which ascribes the ability of parrots to imitate the human voice, essentially to their broad and human-like tongue. Mr. Yarrell has remarked, in his *Memoir on the Organs of Voice in Birds*, that the raven, magpie,

these there is also an advantage in quadrupeds, and a proximity of reason in elephants and apes[1] above them all. Since also an echo will speak without any mouth at all,[2]

jay, and starling, produce a close imitation of the human voice with tongues long, slender, and horny. But the proper source of correction of both errors is the knowledge we now possess, that the organ of voice, in all birds, is the inferior *larynx*, situated at the bifurcation of the *trachea*, where the *bronchiæ* go off from it to the lungs, or in other words, *at the bottom of the windpipe;* the superior *larynx* or *glottis*, opening into the cavity of the mouth, being little more than a simple slit, giving utterance to the sounds produced below, or being at most one of the accessary organs for their regulation. The true cause of the accuracy with which the birds having "broad and thick chaps," especially the parrots, imitate speech, seems to be their accurate ear for sounds of every description, together with the arrangement and functions of the muscles of their organ of voice, giving them a greater compass of voice than other birds; by which means they are enabled to imitate any kind of sound they hear: for parrots, &c. it will be remembered, imitate the ticking of a clock, or the sharpening of a saw, or a whistled tune, as accurately as they do the voice itself.

This error, however, like the greater number of those entertained by our author himself, was an almost universal one, and continued to be so until the true nature and situation of the organs of voice in birds were first accurately shown by Cuvier, about the commencement of the present century. A summary view of the results of his investigation will be found near the end of the article, BIRDS, *Anatomy of*, in *Rees's Cyclopædia*, from the pen, we believe, of Professor Macartney, of Trinity College, Dublin, an accomplished comparative anatomist: and an excellent general account of the organs of voice in birds, illustrated by details and figures of them in many individual species, is given by Mr. Yarrell, in the paper before referred to, published in the *Transactions of the Linnæan Society*, vol. xvi. p. 305.—*Br.*

[1] *apes.*] In February, 1652-3 itt was constantly reported from some of the Portugal embassador's followers, that the present King of Spain had a baboone that went upright and spake many things: whether itt bee è *Satyrorum* or *Cynocephalorum genere* is not sayde. The way were to gain a pregnant female, and to traine the younge by language: they about Conge beleeve they can speake, but will not, fearing least soe they might be forced to labor. Sed de hujusmodi monstris, consule *Gassendum in Vitâ Pereskii*, p. 397, mira edisserentem.—*Wr.*

The author here falls into the still prevalent error, of attributing an extraordinary degree of sagacity to the apes, which, as has been observed by Cuvier (*Règne Anim.* tom. i. p. 88), do not in reality greatly surpass the dog in this respect, being chiefly indebted to their bodily conformation for the close resemblance of their gestures and actions to those of man.

It is almost needless to add, that Dean Wren's stories about apes speaking, or being taught to speak, are all futile and unfounded.—*Br.*

[2] *Since also an echo, &c.*] The "query of no great doubt," with

articulately returning the voice of man, by only ordering the vocal spirit in concave and hollow places; whether the musculous and motive parts about the hollow mouths of beasts may not dispose the passing spirit into some articulate notes, seems a query of no great doubt.[3]

CHAPTER II.

That the Horse hath no gall.

THE second assertion, that an horse hath no gall, is very general, nor only swallowed by the people and common farriers, but also received by good veterinarians, and some who have laudably discoursed upon horses. It seemeth also very ancient; for it is plainly set down by Aristotle; "an horse, and all solidungulous, or whole-hoofed animals, have no gall;"[4] and the same is also delivered by

which the chapter concludes, is certainly void of doubt; void, that is, of doubt that our author is wrong. It will be sufficient to observe, that an echo of human speech is merely a *reflection* of certain undulatory motions, previously impressed upon the air by the organs of speech, and that the reflected are *identical* with the original sounds, being in fact those very sounds merely caused to proceed in a new direction. The place of echo, therefore, has no share in the articulation of the sounds which are heard from it. Articulation, as before observed, is the result of analytical thought, which is peculiar to man; the brute animals which are taught to imitate it, merely frame sounds closely resembling those which they have heard from man; they never utter an original articulation of their own, whatever may be the mechanism of their organs of voice.—*Br.*

[3] *Since also, &c.*] First added in the 1st edit.

[4] *it is plainly set down by Aristotle, &c.*] It is evident, from an examination of the passage in Aristotle's *History of Animals* (lib. ii. cap. xv.) here referred to, that the word χολη is sometimes used by that author to denote the gall-bladder, and sometimes to denote the gall or bile itself, considered as one of the animal fluids. In the passage under consideration, it is used in the former sense, and thus understood, the assertion is strictly accurate. The gall-bladder is wanting in the horse and other solipedes. But while it is thus clear that the absence of *bile* in the horse is not affirmed by Aristotle, neither the passage itself, nor its context, prove him to have been aware of its presence; and there is some ground, therefore, for our author's animadversion. For while the bile itself in the stag and elephant is expressly alluded to, after the absence of the gall-bladder in those animals has been mentioned, that

Pliny,[5] which, notwithstanding, we find repugnant unto experience and reason. For first, it calls in question the providence or wise provision of nature, who, not abounding in superfluities, neither is deficient in necessities. Wherein nevertheless there would be a main defect, and her improvision justly accusable, if such a feeding animal, and so subject unto diseases from bilious causes, should want a proper conveyance for choler, or have no other receptacle for that humour than the veins and general mass of blood.

It is again controllable by experience,[6] for we have made some search and enquiry herein; encouraged by Absyrtus, a Greek author, in the time of Constantine, who, in his *Hippiatricks*, obscurely assigneth the gall a place in the liver; but more especially by Carlo Ruini, the Bononian, who, in his *Anatomia del Cavallo*, hath more plainly described it, and

of the horse, an animal, as we have seen, in the same predicament, is not mentioned or alluded to. At the same time, from an examination of the entire chapter, it would appear, I think, that the main subject being the gall-bladder as annexed or not to the liver, in various tribes of animals, the absence of the bile, in those described as devoid of that organ, is by no means intended to be expressly stated by the writer. —*Br.*

[5] *the same is also delivered by Pliny*] This is true: Pliny evidently borrowed his statement from the passage of Aristotle, considered above, and translating χολη by the Latin word, *fel*, applies that, as Aristotle does the former, sometimes to the gall-bladder, and sometimes to the fluid it contains.—*Hist. Nat.* lib. xi. cap. lxxiv.

A curious fact in the history of the subject appears from the notes of Hardouin, on this chapter of Pliny.—*Hist. Nat.* tom. i. p. 628. The absence of the gall-bladder in the solipedes was affirmed prior to Aristotle, by Ctesias, a circumstance which may assist, with some other correct statements now known to have been made by that writer (see notes on book ii. c. 8), to caution us from absolutely rejecting all his extraordinary relations; notwithstanding that (as we have seen in the notes on the preceding chapter) some of them are erroneous.—*Br.*

[6] *It is again controllable by experience.*] The contents of this paragraph evince our author's care to determine disputed points, and refute prevalent errors, by actual enquiry and observation. By a misconstruction of ancient authorities, he finds it believed that the bile is altogether absent in the horse; but, reason showing the improbability of this, and finding its presence affirmed by some authors, he dissects the liver and adjacent organs of that animal, in order to ascertain the fact. The vessel containing bile, which he discovered, is the hepatic duct, the dilatation of which, at its origin, in the horse and some other animals devoid of the gall-bladder, is so large as to form a sort of reservoir for the bile.—*Br.*

in a manner as I found it. For in the particular enquiry into that part, in the concave or sinuous part of the liver, whereabout the gall is usually seated in quadrupeds, I discover an hollow, long, and membraneous substance, of a pale colour without, and lined with choler and gall within, which part is by branches diffused into the lobes and several parcels of the liver; from whence receiving the fiery superfluity, or choleric remainder, by a manifest and open passage, it conveyeth it into the *duodenum* or upper gut, thence into the lower bowels; which is the manner of its derivation in man and other animals. And, therefore, although there be no eminent and circular follicle, no round bag or vesicle which long containeth this humour, yet is there a manifest receptacle and passage of choler from the liver into the guts; which, being not so shut up, or at least not so long detained, as it is in other animals, procures that frequent excretion, and occasions the horse to dung more often than many other, which, considering the plentiful feeding, the largeness of the guts and their various circumvolution, was prudently contrived by Providence in this animal. For choler is the natural glister, or one excretion whereby nature excludeth another, which descending daily into the bowels, extimulates those parts, and excites them unto expulsion. And, therefore, when this humour aboundeth or corrupteth, there succeeds, oft-times, a *cholerica passio*, that is a sudden and vehement purgation upward and downward: and when the passage of gall becomes obstructed, the body grows costive, and the excrements of the belly white; as it happeneth in the jaundice.

If any, therefore, affirm an horse hath no gall,[7] that is, no receptacle or part ordained for the separation of choler, or not that humour at all, he hath both sense and reason to oppose him. But if he saith it hath no bladder of gall, and

---

[7] *If any therefore affirm, &c.*] The concluding remarks on the subject appear to give a very just view of it, and partake of our author's logical acuteness. In the passage of Pliny, here alluded to (*Nat. Hist.* lib. xxxviii. cap. xl.), as is manifest from the entire contents of the chapter in which it occurs, the word *fel* means the bile itself; whereas, in the former citation from that writer, it means the receptacle for the bile, or gall-bladder. The two statements, therefore, are, in reality, in perfect harmony with each other.—*Br.*

such as is observed in many other animals, we shall oppose our sense if we gainsay him. Thus must Aristotle be made out when he denieth this part; by this distinction we may relieve Pliny of a contradiction, who, in one place affirming an horse hath no gall, delivereth yet in another, that the gall of an horse was accounted poison; and, therefore, at the sacrifices of horses in Rome, it was unlawful for the *flamen* to touch it. But with more difficulty, or hardly at all, is that reconcileable which is delivered by our countryman, and received veterinarian; whose words in his master-piece, and chapter of diseases from the gall, are somewhat too strict, and scarce admit a reconciliation. The fallacy, therefore, of this conceit, is not unlike the former, *à dicto secundùm quid ad dictum simpliciter* :—because they have not a bladder of gall, like those we usually observe in others, they have no gall at all; which is a paralogism not admittable—a fallacy that dwells not in a cloud, and needs not the sun to scatter it.

CHAPTER III.

That a Pigeon hath no gall.

The third assertion is somewhat like the second, that a dove or pigeon hath no gall, which is affirmed from very great antiquity: for, as Pierius observeth,[8] from this consideration the Egyptians did make it the hieroglyphic of meekness.[9] It hath been averred by many holy writers,

[8] *as Pierius observeth.*] In his *Hieroglyphica*, p. 221, B. 27; but he cites no authority for his assertion. See a remark on Pierius in note at p. 251-36.

[9] *of meekness.*] And not without excellent reason: for, whereas, all angry eruptions proceed from the more or less mixture of gall, not only in man, but other creatures; and that, when itt is seated in the liver, itt is the easier spread into all parts of the bodye, together with the blood, except he doe the more vigorously doe his office in the defæcation of the blood: it must of necessity thence follow, that where the gall is drainde from the blood by some other vessel than the liver, as by the gutts, from which itt is impossible to regurgitate into the blood, such creatures, and among them the dove especially, may be well sayd to have none in such a sense as is intended, i. e., whereby the vital parts should bee enflamed with such hot and fierye motions, as other creatures are, which have the *cisto*, or vesicle of gall in the liver, the *cordus*

commonly delivered by postillers and commentators; who, from the frequent mention of the dove in the Canticles, the precept of our Saviour, "to be wise as serpents and innocent as doves," and especially the appearance of the Holy Ghost in the similitude of this animal, have taken occasion to set down many affections of the dove, and, what doth most commend it is, that it hath no gall. And hereof have made use, not only minor divines, but Cyprian, Austin, Isidore, Beda, Rupertus, Jansenius, and many more.

Whereto, notwithstanding, we know not how to assent, it being repugnant unto the authority and positive determination of ancient philosophy. The affirmative of Aristotle, in his *History of Animals*, is very plain—*fel aliis ventri, aliis intestino jungitur*,—some have the gall adjoined to the guts; as the crow, the swallow, sparrow, and the dove; the same is also attested by Pliny, and not without some passion by Galen, who, in his book, *De Atra Bile*, accounts him ridiculous that denies it.

It is not agreeable to the constitution of this animal, nor can we so reasonably conceive there wants a gall; that is, the hot and fiery humour in a body so hot of temper, which phlegm or melancholy could not effect. Now, of what complexion it is, Julius Alexandrinus* declareth, when he affirmeth, that some, upon the use thereof, have fallen into fevers and quinsies. The temper of their dung and intestinal excretions do also confirm the same; which topically applied, become a *phœnigmus* or rubifying medicine, and are

* *Salubrium*, 31.

and *promus* of the blood; and by the accident of all those noxious humours which the second concoctions cannot mend: the sense, therefore, stands uncontrold, that the dove is, therefore, the embleme of meeknes, in that the gall (which begets those fiery motions in other creatures, by the neernes itt hathe to the principal enterails) is either none at all, or at least removed soe farr into the gutts, that it cannot produce such effects in her as in most other creatures itt dothe. So true is that maxime, in things of nature, *Idem est non esse et non apparere*: and *non operari* (heere) is as much as *non apparere*, and (by consequent) the same with *non esse*.—*Wr.*

The dean's ignorance of the true nature of bile is not to be wondered at; but it is very remarkable that he should have believed the Creator to have placed it, in any of his creatures, in such a situation as would prevent its exerting that influence which he had intended it to possess in the animal economy.

of such fiery parts, that, as we read in Galen, they have of themselves conceived fire, and burnt a house about them. And therefore, when, in the famine of Samaria (wherein the fourth part of a cab of pigeon's dung was sold for five pieces of silver), it is delivered by Josephus, that men made use hereof instead of common salt: although the exposition seem strange, it is more probable than many other. For, that it containeth very much salt, as besides the effects before expressed, is discernible by taste, and the earth of columbaries or dove-houses, so much desired in the artifice of saltpetre. And to speak generally, the excrement of birds hath more of salt and acrimony, than that of any other pissing animals. Now if, because the dove is of a mild and gentle nature, we cannot conceive it should be of an hot temper, our apprehensions are not distinct in the measure of constitutions, and the several parts which evidence such conditions. For the irascible passions do follow the temper of the heart, but the concupiscible distractions the *crasis* of the liver. Now, many have hot livers, which have but cool and temperate hearts; and this was probably the temper of Paris, a contrary constitution to that of Ajax, and both but short of Medea, who seemed to exceed in either.

Lastly, it is repugnant to experience; for anatomical enquiry discovereth in them a gall:[1] and that, according to the determination of Aristotle, not annexed unto the liver, but adhering unto the guts. Nor is the humour contained in smaller veins or obscurer capillations, but in a vesicle or little bladder, though some affirm it hath no bag at all. And therefore the hieroglyphic of the Egyptians, though allowable in the sense, is weak in the foundation: who, expressing meekness and lenity by the portrait of a dove with a tail erected, affirmed it had no gall in the inward parts, but only in the rump, and as it were out of the body.[2] And

[1] *anatomical enquiry discovereth, &c.*] It is now known that the gall-bladder does not exist in the dove: the vessel mentioned by our author is merely a dilation of the hepatic or of the hepatocystic duct, serving to contain the bile. This fact is in agreement with the statements of Aristotle and Pliny, which are cited in this and in the preceding page.—*Br.*

[2] *And therefore, &c.*] This statement is from Pierius, on the authority of Horapollo or Orus Apollo, in his *Hieroglyphica, curâ Pauw,* p. 105. See note 9, p. 251-3.

therefore also, if they conceived their gods were pleased with the sacrifice of this animal, as being without gall, the ancient heathens were surely mistaken in the reason, and in the very oblation. Whereas, in the holocaust or burnt-offering of Moses, the gall was cast away: for, as Ben Maimon instructeth, the inwards, whereto the gall adhereth, were taken out with the crop (according unto the law), which the priest did not burn, but cast unto the east; that is, behind his back, and readiest place to be carried out of the sanctuary. And if they also conceived that for this reason they were the birds of Venus, and, wanting the furious and discording part, were more acceptable unto the deity of love, they surely added unto the conceit; which was, at first, venereal, and in this animal may be sufficiently made out from that conception.

The ground of this conceit is partly like the former, the obscure situation of the gall, and out of the liver, wherein it is commonly enquired. But this is a very unjust illation, not well considering with what variety this part is seated in birds. In some, both at the stomach and the liver, as in the *capriceps*; in some at the liver only, as in cocks, turkeys, and pheasants; in others at the guts and liver, as in hawks and kites; in some at the guts alone, as crows, doves,[3] and many more. And these, perhaps, may take up all the ways of situation, not only in birds, but also other animals; for what is said of the anchovy—that (answerable unto its name*) it carrieth the gall in the head, is farther to be enquired. And though the discoloured particles in the skin of an heron be commonly termed gall, yet is not this animal deficient in that part, but containeth it in the liver. And thus, when it is conceived that the eyes of Tobias were cured by the gall of the fish *callionymus* or *scorpius marinus*, commended to that effect by Dioscorides, although that part were not in the liver, yet there were no reason to doubt that probability. And whatsoever animal it was, it may be received without exception, when it is delivered, the married couple, as a testimony of future concord, did cast the gall of the sacrifice behind the altar.

* Ἐγκρασίχολος.

[3] *doves.*] Sparows, swalows (as before).—*Wr.*

A strict and literal acception of a loose and tropical expression was a second ground hereof.[4] For while some affirmed it had no gall, intending only thereby no evidence of anger or fury; others have construed it anatomically, and denied that part at all. By which illation we may infer (and that from sacred text), a pigeon hath no heart; according to that expression, *Factus est Ephraim sicut columba seducta non habens cor.** And so, from the letter of Scripture, we may conclude it is no mild, but a fiery and furious animal, according to that of Jeremy,† *Facta est terra in desolationem, à facie iræ columbæ:* and again,‡ *revertamur ad terram nativitatis nostræ, à facie gladii columbæ.* Where, notwithstanding, the dove is not literally intended; but thereby may be implied the Babylonians, whose queen, Semiramis, was called by that name, and whose successors did bear the dove in their standard. So is it proverbially said, *Formicæ sua bilis inest, habet et musca splenem;* whereas we know philosophy doubteth these parts, nor hath anatomy so clearly discovered them in those insects.[5]

* Hosea vii.   † Cap. xxv. 38.   ‡ Cap. xlvi. 16.

[4] *A strict and literal acception, &c.*] This, and the concluding paragraph, furnish a very satisfactory explanation of the error discussed in the chapter; but it is probable that the absence of the gall-bladder in the dove, by being supposed to imply that of the bile itself, has also contributed to it.—*Br.*

See the English version of the passages referred to in Jeremiah.

[5] *doubteth these parts, &c.*] I doe believe that, as the gall has severall receptacles in severall creatures (as above is mentioned) soe there's scarce any creature but hath that emunctorye somewhere. What is the poyson in the tayle of the scorpion, and the sting raye or male thornback but his gall? And soe in hornets, bees, wasps, the same. What is the poyson in the tooth of serpents, and of the lamprey, and the *mus araneus*, and the tarantula, but the gall? which according to the condition and qualitye of the creature, as the spirits that accompany those ejaculations are more subtile, aerial, or fierye, soe they appeare more or lesse furious in their effects; whereas, those parts (by which they ejaculate this gall) being taken away, the other parts become not only edible and of high nourishment, as in the thornback and lamprey, and in the honey of the bee; but in some they become the most soveraigne antidotes, as in the flesh of vipers: nay, the very spirits of some of these being received into apte bodyes, in their full strength, imprint such an alexipharmacal or alexitarial virtue into those bodyes, against all poyson, as seemes almost miraculous, as in viper wine and oyle of scorpions.—*Wr.*

If, therefore, any affirm a pigeon hath no gall, implying no more thereby than the lenity of this animal, we shall not controvert his affirmation. Thus may we make out the assertions of ancient writers, and safely receive the expressions of divines and worthy fathers. But if, by a transition from rhetoric to logic, he shall contend it hath no such part or humour, he committeth an open fallacy, and such as was probably first committed concerning Spanish mares, whose swiftness tropically expressed from their generation by the wind, might after be grossly taken, and a real truth conceived in that conception.

CHAPTER IV.

That a Beaver, to escape the hunter, bites off his testicles or stones.

THAT a beaver, to escape the hunter, bites off his testicles or stones,[6] is a tenet very ancient; and hath had, thereby, advantage of propagation. For the same we find in the hieroglyphics of the Egyptians; in the Apologue of Æsop, an author of great antiquity, who lived in the beginning of the Persian monarchy, and in the time of Cyrus; the same is touched by Aristotle in his *Ethics*; but seriously delivered by Ælian, Pliny, and Solinus; the same we meet with in Juvenal, who by an handsome and metrical expression, more welcomely engrafts it into our junior memories;

―――― imitatus castora, qui se
Eunuchum ipse facit, cupiens evadere damno
Testiculorum, adeò medicatum intelligit inguen ;

it hath been propagated by emblems; and some have been

---

[6] *That a beaver, &c.*] The arrangement, conduct, and logic, of the entire train of arguments in this chapter, are equally admirable. It displays, also, extensive and accurate knowledge of natural history and comparative anatomy.

Ross, after himself delivering a tissue of gross errors relating to eunuchs, first repeats that of the beaver, as just refuted by our author; of course, *quoad* true testicles; and then, by a singular inconsistency contends, that Browne checks the ancients for this opinion without cause; and, after admitting the extirpated organs not to be true testicles, that, "if then, this be an error, it is nominal, not real."—*Arcan.* 117.—*Br.*

so bad grammarians as to be deceived by the name, deriving *castor à castrando;* whereas the proper Latin word is *fiber*,[7] and *castor* but borrowed from the Greek, so called *quasi γάστωρ,* that is, *animal ventricosum,* from his swaggy and prominent belly.

Herein, therefore, to speak compendiously, we first presume to affirm that, from a strict enquiry, we cannot maintain the evulsion or biting off any parts; and this is declarable from the best and most professed writers: for though some have made use hereof in a moral or tropical way, yet have the professed discoursers by silence deserted, or by experience rejected, this assertion. Thus was it in ancient times discovered, and experimentally refuted, by one Sestius, a physician, as it stands related by Pliny—by Dioscorides, who plainly affirms that this tradition is false—by the discoveries of modern authors, who have expressly discoursed hereon, as Aldrovandus, Matthiolus, Gesnerus, Bellonius[8]—by Olaus Magnus, Peter Martyr, and others, who have described the manner of their venations in America; they generally omitting this way of their escape, and have delivered several other, by which they are daily taken.

The original of the conceit was probably hieroglyphical, which after became mythological unto the Greeks, and so set down by Æsop; and by process of tradition, stole into a total verity, which was but partially true, that is, in its covert sense and morality. Now, why they placed this invention upon the beaver (beside the medicable and merchantable commodity of *castoreum,* or parts conceived to be bitten away), might be the sagacity and wisdom of that animal, which from the works it performs, and especially its artifice in building, is very strange, and surely not to be matched by any other. Omitted by Plutarch, *De Solertia Animalium,* but might have much advantaged the drift of that discourse.

If, therefore, any affirm a wise man should demean himself like the beaver, who, to escape with his life, contemneth

---

[7] *fiber.*] Which the Polonians by a more elegant name call *bi-fer, quasi animal biferum quod tam in terra quam in mari prædetur:* and from (*bifer*) wee call itt (corruptlye) bever.—*Wr.*

[8] *Bellonius.*] And particularly Baricellus, in his *Hortus Genialis,* p. 288.—*Wr.*

the loss of his genitals, that is, in case of extremity, not strictly to endeavour the preservation of all, but to sit down in the enjoyment of the greater good, though with the detriment and hazard of the lesser, we may hereby apprehend a real and useful truth. In this latitude of belief, we are content to receive the fable of Hippomanes, who redeemed his life with the loss of a golden ball; and, whether true or false, we reject not the tragedy of Absyrtus, and the dispersion of his members by Medea, to perplex the pursuit of her father. But if any shall positively affirm this act, and cannot believe the moral, unless he also credit the fable, he is surely greedy of delusion, and will hardly avoid deception in theories of this nature. The error, therefore, and alogy,[9] in this opinion, is worse than the last; that is, not to receive figures for realities, but expect a verity in apologues, and believe, as serious affirmations, confessed and studied fables.

Again, if this were true, and that the beaver, in chace, makes some divulsion of parts, as that which we call *castoreum*, yet are not the same to be termed testicles or stones; for these cods or follicles are found in both sexes, though somewhat more protuberant in the male. There is, hereto, no derivation of the seminal parts, nor any passage from hence, unto the vessels of ejaculation: some perforations only in the part itself, through which the humour included doth exudate, as may be observed in such as are fresh, and not much dried with age. And lastly, the testicles, properly so called, are of a lesser magnitude, and seated inwardly upon the loins:[1] and, therefore, it were not only a fruitless attempt, but impossible act, to eunuchate or castrate themselves; and might be an hazardous practice of art, if at all attempted by others.

Now, all this is confirmed from the experimental testimony of five very memorable authors;—Bellonius, Gesnerus, Amatus, Rondeletius, and Matthiolus,—who, receiving the hint hereof from Rondeletius, in the anatomy of two beavers, did find all true that had been delivered by him; whose words are these, in his learned book, *De Piscibus*:—*Fibri in inguinibus geminos tumores habent, utrinque unicum, ovi*

---

[9] *alogy.*] Unreasonableness, absurdity; from an old French word, *alogie*.

[1] *loins.*] Idem Baricellus (ut supra).—*Wr.*

anserini magnitudine; inter hos est mentula in maribus, in fœminis pudendum: hi tumores testes non sunt, sed folliculi membranâ contecti, in quorum medio singuli sunt meatus, è quibus exudat liquor pinguis et cerosus, quem ipse castor sæpe admoto ore lambit et exugit, postea veluti oleo, corporis paries oblinit. Hos tumores testes non esse hinc maximè colligitur, quòd ab illis nulla est ad mentulam via neque ductus quò humor in mentulæ meatum derivetur, et foras emittatur; præterea quòd testes intus reperiuntur, eosdem tumores moscho animali[2] *inesse puto, è quibus odoratum illud pus emanat.* Than which words there can be no plainer, nor more evidently discovering the impropriety of this appellation. That which is included in the cod or visible bag about the groin, being not the testicle or any spermatical part, but rather a collection of some superfluous matter deflowing from the body, especially the parts of nutrition, as unto their proper emunctories, and as it doth in musk and civet cats; though in a different and offensive odour; proceeding partly from its food—that being especially fish—whereof this humour may be a garous[3] excretion and olidous[4] separation.

Most, therefore, of the moderns, before Rondeletius, and all the ancients, excepting Sestius, have misunderstood this part, conceiving *castoreum* the testicles of the beaver; as Dioscorides, Galen, Ægineta, Ætius, and others have pleased to name it. The Egyptians also failed in the ground of their hieroglyphic, when they expressed the punishment of adultery by the beaver depriving himself of his testicles, which was amongst them the penalty of such incontinency.[5] Nor is Ætius, perhaps, too strictly to be observed, when he prescribeth the stones of the otter, or river-dog, as succedaneous unto *castoreum*. But most inexcusable of all, is Pliny; who having before him, in one place, the experiment of Sestius

---

[2] *moscho, &c.*] Hee means the civit cat.—*Wr.*

[3] *garous.*] Resembling *garum*, a pickle in which fish had been preserved.

[4] *olidous.*] Stinking.

[5] *ground of their hieroglyphic, &c.*]—Pierius (131, c.) is the authority for this explanation;—but he differs therein from Horapollo, who says, "quomodo hominem, qui sibi ipsi damni et perniciei autor sit."—*Hor. Hier.* p. 117. See note (9) at page 251-23.

against it, sets down in another, that the beavers of Pontus bite off their testicles; and in the same place affirmeth the like of the hyæna: which was indeed well joined with the beaver, as having also a bag in those parts; if, thereby, we understand the hyæna odorata, or civet cat, as is delivered and graphically described by Castellus.[6]*

Now, the ground of this mistake might be the resemblance and situation of these tumours about those parts, wherein we observe the testicles in other animals; which, notwithstanding, is no well-founded illation; for the testicles are defined by their office, and not determined by place or situation: they having one office in all, but different seats in many. For,—beside that no serpent or fishes oviparous, that neither biped nor quadruped oviparous,[7] have any exteriorly or prominent in the groin,—some also that are viviparous contain these parts within, as beside this animal, the elephant and the hedgehog.[8]

If any, therefore, shall term these testicles, intending metaphorically, and in no strict acception, his language is tolerable, and offends our ears no more than the tropical names of plants, when we read in herbals, of dogs, fox, and goat-stones. But if he insisteth thereon, and maintaineth a propriety in this language, our discourse hath overthrown his assertion, nor will logic permit his illation; that is, from things alike, to conclude a thing the same, and from an accidental convenience, that is, a similitude in place or figure, to infer a specifical congruity or substantial concurrence in nature.

* *Castellus de Hyæna Odorifera.*

[6] *Which was indeed, &c.*] First added in the 2nd edition.
[7] *quadruped oviparous.*] As the crocodile, which is both **quadruped** and oviparous, and next the tortoise.—*Wr.*
[8] *hedgehog.*] And the porcupine.—*Wr.*

CHAPTER V.

That a Badger hath the legs of one side shorter than of the other.

THAT a brock, or badger, hath the legs on one side shorter than of the other, though an opinion, perhaps, not very ancient, is yet very general; received not only by theorists and unexperienced believers, but assented unto by most who have the opportunity to behold and hunt them daily.[9] Which, notwithstanding, upon enquiry, I find repugnant unto the three determinators of truth—authority, sense, and reason. For first, Albertus Magnus speaks dubiously, confessing he could not confirm the verity hereof; but Aldrovandus plainly affirmeth there can be no such inequality observed: and for my own part, upon indifferent enquiry, I cannot discover this difference, although the regardable side be defined, and the brevity by most imputed unto the left.

Again, it seems no easy affront unto reason, and generally repugnant unto the course of nature; for if we survey the total set of animals, we may, in their legs, or organs of progression, observe an equality of length, and parity of numeration; that is, not any to have an odd leg, or the supporters and movers of one side not exactly answered by the other. Although the hinder may be unequal unto the fore and middle legs, as in frogs, locusts, and grasshoppers; or both unto the middle, as in some beetles and spiders, as is determined by Aristotle.* Perfect and viviparous quadrupeds, so standing in their position of proneness, that the opposite joints of neighbour legs consist in the same plane; and a line descending from their navel intersects at right angles the axis of the earth. It happeneth often, I confess, that a lobster hath the chely or great claw of one side longer than the other;[1] but this is not properly their leg, but a part of

* *De Incessu Animalium.*

[9] *assented unto, &c.*] The popular belief among the peasantry is, that, in running through a ploughed field, the animal always runs with his longer legs in the furrow.

[1] *a lobster, &c.*] This never happens, but when one is by chance wrung off, when they are young, by a bigger lobster, which growing out againe, can never reach the greatnes of the other: the fishermen finde

apprehension, and whereby they hold or seize upon their prey; for the legs and proper parts of progression are inverted backward, and stand in a position opposite unto these.

Lastly, the monstrosity is ill contrived, and with some disadvantage; the shortness being affixed unto the legs of one side, which might have been more tolerably placed upon the thwart or diagonal movers. For the progression of quadrupeds being performed *per diametrum*, that is, the cross legs moving or resting together, so that two are always in motion, and two in station at the same time,[2] the brevity had been more tolerable in the cross legs. For then the motion and station had been performed by equal legs; whereas, herein, they are both performed by unequal organs, and the imperfection becomes discoverable at every hand.

---

this continually to be true, and saye they seldome have a drafte of them, wherein some of them come not up thus grappled by the claw. I have often seene them brought up with half the claw newly nipt off, or else closed up againe with a cartilage, and sometimes with one only chlea, for soe itt should be written, cominge manifestly from χηλη, which signifies properly the tongs or pincher, the chlea of a lobster or of a crab.—*Wr.*

Upon this theory, the vulgar pronunciation, *cla,* is more correct than *claw.*

The dean assigns the true cause of that inequality often observed in the legs of crabs. But he is wrong in supposing the lost claw to have been bitten off by other crabs. There exists in this tribe (as well as in spiders and some other insects) a very curious provision, enabling the animal to throw off instantly a limb (or *antenna*) which has been so injured as to be useless; thus making way for the reproduction of the part. In the great majority of cases, the mutilation observed has resulted from the exercise of this power. See some curious instances detailed by Dr. Heineken, in the *Zoological Journal* (vol. iv. p. 285); and Dr. Mac Culloch's anatomical description of the process, in the 20th vol. of the *Journal of the Royal Institution.*

[2] *For the progression, &c.*] From this rule must be excepted the camel. "The mode of the camel's walk, as described by Aristotle (*Hist. Anim.* lib. ii. cap. i. p. 480, *Casaubon. Lugdun.* 1590), is, by raising the two legs of the same side, the one immediately after the other; not moving the legs diagonally, in the manner of most other quadrupeds."—*Rees's Cyclopædia,* article, CAMELUS.—*Br.*

CHAPTER VI.

That a Bear brings forth her Cubs informous or unshaped.

THAT a bear brings forth her young informous and unshapen, which she fashioneth after by licking them over, is an opinion not only vulgar, and common with us at present, but hath been of old delivered by ancient writers. Upon this foundation it was an hieroglyphic with the Egyptians;[3] Aristotle seems to countenance it; Solinus, Pliny, and Ælian, directly affirm it, and Ovid smoothly delivereth it;

> Nec catulus partu quem reddidit ursa recenti,
> Sed malè viva caro est, lambendo mater in artus
> Ducit, et in formam qualem cupit ipsa reducit.

Which, notwithstanding, is not only repugnant unto the sense of every one that shall enquire into it, but the exact and deliberate experiment of three authentic philosophers. The first, of Matthiolus in his *Comment on Dioscorides*, whose words are to this effect:—" In the valley of Anania, about Trent, in a bear which the hunters eventerated[4] or opened, I beheld the young ones with all their parts distinct, and not without shape, as many conceive—giving more credit unto Aristotle and Pliny, than experience and their proper senses." Of the same assurance was Julius Scaliger, in his *Exercitations; Ursam fœtus informes potius ejicere, quam parere, si vera dicunt, quos postea linctu effingat. Quid hujusce fabulæ authoribus fidei habendum, ex hac historia cognosces; in nostris alpibus venatores fœtam ursam cepêre, dissectâ eâ fœtus planè formatus intus inventus est.* And lastly, Aldrovandus, who from the testimony of his own eyes affirmeth, that in the cabinet of the senate of Bononia, there was preserved in a glass, a cub, taken out of a bear, perfectly formed, and complete in every part.

It is, moreover, injurious unto reason, and much impugneth

---

[3] *it was an hieroglyphic.*] Pierius, 131, c. and Horapollo, 117. See note 9, at page 251-53.

[4] *eventerated.*] Ript up, by opening the belly. Browne is the only authority given in Johnson.

the course and providence of nature, to conceive a birth should be ordained before there is a formation. For the conformation of parts is necessarily required, not only unto the pre-requisites and previous conditions of birth, as motion and animation, but also unto the parturition or very birth itself: wherein not only the dam, but the younglings play their parts, and the cause and act of exclusion proceedeth from them both. For the exclusion of animals is not merely passive like that of eggs, nor the total action of delivery to be imputed unto the mother,[5] but the first attempt beginneth from the infant, which, at the accomplished period, attempteth to change his mansion, and struggling to come forth, dilacerates and breaks those parts which restrained him before.

Besides (what few take notice of), men hereby do, in an high measure, vilify the works of God, imputing that unto the tongue of a beast, which is the strangest artifice in all the acts of nature; that is, the formation of the infant in the womb, not only in mankind, but all viviparous animals. Wherein the plastic or formative faculty, from matter appearing homogeneous, and of a similary substance, erecteth bones, membranes, veins, and arteries; and out of these contriveth every part in number, place, and figure, according to the law of its species: which is so far from being fashioned by any outward agent, that one omitted or perverted by a slip of the inward Phidias, it is not reducible by any other whatsoever: and therefore *Miré me plasmaverunt manus tuæ*, though it originally respected the generation of man, yet is it appliable unto that of other animals; who, entering the womb in bare and simple materials, return with distinction of parts, and the perfect breath of life. He that shall consider these alterations without, must needs conceive there have been strange operations within: which to behold, it were a spectacle almost worth one's being—a sight beyond all; except that man had been created first, and might have seen the show of five days after.

Now, as the opinion is repugnant both unto sense and

---

[5] *For the exclusion, &c.*] The fœtus *is* passive, and is expelled wholly by the efforts of the mother: a dead fœtus is as readily born as a living one; although a vulgar error prevails to the contrary.

reason, so hath it probably been occasioned from some slight ground in either. Thus in regard the cub comes forth involved in the *chorion*, a thick and tough membrane obscuring the formation, and which the dam doth after bite and tear asunder; the beholder at first sight conceives it a rude and informous lump of flesh, and imputes the ensuing shape unto the mouthing of the dam; which addeth nothing thereunto, but only draws the curtain, and takes away the vail which concealed the piece before. And thus have some endeavoured to enforce the same from reason; that is, the small and slender time of the bear's gestation, or going with her young; which lasting but a few days (a month some say), the exclusion becomes precipitous, and the young ones, consequently, informous,[6] according to that of Solinus, *Trigesimus dies*

[6] *informous.*] The *bearling*, though blind like most other *beastlings*, is not *informous*. It owes the discipline in question to that instinct which secures to the young of all animals, on their first appearance, the same species of maternal attention. Cuvier describes the cub of the black bear as measuring six or eight inches, devoid of teeth, covered with hairs, and having the eyes closed.

There is, however, another popular saying about the young of the bear which does not seem so easily disposed of;— its deriving nutriment from sucking its paws. The following graphic passage explains the fact. Speaking of a cub of the Norway bear, in the French Menagerie, Cuvier says, it "was particularly fond of sucking its paws, during which operation it always sent forth a uniform and constant murmur, something like the sound of a spinning-wheel. This appeared to be an imperious want with it, and it was surprising to observe the ardour with which it commenced the operation, and the enjoyment which it seemed to derive from it. The belief, which once so generally obtained, that these animals, during the season which they pass without eating, and surrounded by snows, support themselves by sucking their paws, seems not utterly without foundation. In truth, every natural action must have a tendency to some useful end, though it has not been observed that the bear extracts any thing from its paws by the act of suction. After all, it is more probable that bears lick their paws, as cats do, from a love of cleanliness, or merely in consequence of some pleasing sensation which nature has attached to the act, for inexplicable reasons, rather than for sustenance."—*Cuvier's Animal Kingdom, by Griffiths*, vol. ii. 220.—*Ed.*

The following note occurs in Dr. Richardson's account of the quadrupeds and birds collected in Captain Parry's second voyage to the Arctic Regions, published in the *Zoological Appendix* to the journal of that voyage, p. 290. "The female black or brown bears conceal their retreats with such care that they are extremely rarely killed when with young. Hence the ancients had an opinion that the bear brought forth

uterum liberat ursæ: unde evenit ut præcipitata fœcunditas informes creet partus. But this will overthrow the general method or nature in the works of generation. For therein the conformation is not only antecedent, but proportional unto the exclusion; and if the period of the birth be short, the term of conformation will be as sudden also. There may, I confess, from this narrow time of gestation, ensue a minority or smallness in the exclusion; but this, however, inferreth no informity, and it still receiveth the name of a natural and legitimate birth: whereas, if we affirm a total informity, it cannot admit so forward a term as an abortment,* for that supposeth conformation; so we must call this constant and intended act of nature, a slip or effluxion, that is, an exclusion before conformation,—before the birth can bear the name of the parent, or be so much as properly called an embryon.

CHAPTER VII.

Of the Basilisk.

MANY opinions are passant concerning the basilisk, or *little king* of serpents, commonly called the cockatrice; some affirming, others denying, most doubting the relation made hereof. What, therefore, in these uncertainties we may more safely determine; that such an animal there is, if we evade not the testimony of Scripture and human writers we cannot safely deny. So it is said, Psalm xci. *Super aspidem et basiliscum ambulabis,* wherein the vulgar translation retaineth the word of the Septuagint, using in other places the

* *Ἔκρυσις.*

unformed masses, and afterwards licked them into shape and life. Sir Thomas Browne cites many facts in opposition to this notion, some of which are quoted in *Shaw's Zoology* and similar and more recent facts are noticed in *Warden's Account of the United States,* vol. i. p. 195. After numerous enquiries amongst the Indians of Hudson's Bay, only one was found who had killed a pregnant bear. He stated that the den she had constructed was smaller than that usually made by the unimpregnated female."—*Br.*

Latin expression, *regulus;* as Proverbs xxiii. *Mordebit ut coluber, et sicut regulus venena diffundet:*[7] and Jeremy viii. *Ecce ego mittam vobis serpentes regulos, &c.*—that is, as ours translate it, "Behold I will send serpents, cockatrices among you, which will not be charmed, and they shall bite you." And as for human authors, or such as have discoursed of animals, or poisons, it is to be found almost in all: in Dioscorides, Galen, Pliny, Solinus, Ælian, Ætius, Avicen, Ardoynus, Grevinus, and many more. In Aristotle, I confess, we find no mention thereof, but Scaliger in his *Comment and Enumeration of Serpents* hath made supply; and in his *Exercitations* delivereth, that a basilisk was found in Rome, in the days of Leo the Fourth. The like is reported by Sigonius; and some are so far from denying one, that they have made several kinds hereof; for such is the *Catoblepas*[8] of Pliny conceived to be by some, and the *Dryinus* of Ætius by others.

But although we deny not the existence of the basilisk, yet, whether we do not commonly mistake in the conception hereof, and call that a basilisk which is none at all, is surely to be questioned. For certainly that, which, from the conceit of its generation, we vulgarly call a cockatrice, and wherein (but under a different name) we intend a formal identity and adequate conception with the basilisk, is not the basilisk of the ancients, whereof such wonders are delivered. For this of ours is generally described with legs, wings, a serpentine and winding tail, and a crest or comb somewhat like a cock. But the basilisk of elder times was a proper kind of serpent, not above three palms long,[9] as some account, and differenced

---

[7] *diffundet.*] Note the worde *diffundet*, which intimates a strange kind of poysoning (*undequâque*), most probably infecting the heart of him that approaches, by the breath drawne into the very heart immediately, then by the eye, which requires a longer way then the maner of infection is wont to take, killing in an instant, irrecoverablye, and diverse have perished by his spreading poyson in the dark holes, where they could never see the serpent. To which the story in Sennertus seems to add strong proofe.—*Wr.*

[8] *Catoblepas.*] This name is now appropriated to a genus containing the gnoo, and several species. The animal so called by Ælian is supposed by Cuvier to have been of this genus.

[9] *was a proper kind of serpent, &c.*] A distinction must be taken between the *basilisk* (or cockatrice) of Scripture, and that which is so called

from other serpents by advancing his head, and some white marks or coronary spots upon the crown, as all authentic writers have delivered.

Nor is this cockatrice only unlike the basilisk, but of no real shape in nature, and rather an hieroglyphical fancy, to express different intentions, set forth in different fashions.[1]

by modern naturalists; it seems most probable that the former was intended to denote the *naja* or *cobra capello* of the Portuguese.

Under the name of basilisk is at present designated a genus of reptiles, of the *saurian* order, which exhibit many affinities with the *iguanes* and *monitors*. No animal, perhaps, has been the subject of so great a number of prejudices as the one now under consideration. The most ancient authors have spoken of the basilisk as of a serpent which had the power of striking its victim dead by a single glance. Others have pretended that it could not exercise this faculty, unless it first perceived the object of its vengeance before it was itself perceived by it. It was also most absurdly imagined to proceed from the eggs of old cocks. Aldrovandus, and several other writers, have given figures of it. They have represented it with eight feet, a crown on the head, and a hooked and recurved beak. Pliny assures us that the serpent, named basilisk, has a voice so terrible, that it strikes terror into all other species—that it thus chases them from the spot which it inhabits, and of which it retains the sole and undisputed dominion. The name indeed, basilisk, in Greek, signifies royal. The fantastic forms and fabulous properties thus attributed to an animal which, most probably, never had an existence, rendered this name too celebrated for naturalists not to endeavour to apply it to another species, which accordingly they did. Seba figured a species of lizard, whose head is surmounted with projecting lines, and the back furnished with a broad vertical crest, which extends as far as over the tail, and which that author believed to be intended for the purposes of flight. He has designated it under the name of basilisk, or dragon of America, a flying amphibious animal. This is the animal which has subsequently been described in all works of natural history, under the name of basilisk.—*Cuvier's Animal Kingdom*, vol. ix. p. 226.

[1] *an hieroglyphical fancy, &c.*] This is also from Pierius (175, A.) The Bembine, or Isiac table, Dr. Young has shown to be the work of a Roman sculptor, imitating only the general style of the separate delineations of the Egyptian tablets. The inscriptions neither have any relation to the figures over which they are placed, nor form any connected sense of their own. It may be concluded, therefore, that although (presuming the imitation to be accurate) the Isiac table may be regarded as second-rate authority for the *delineation* of the separate figures and hieroglyphics it contains, it is devoid of all authority as showing their collocation.—EGYPT, *in Sup. to Ency. Brit.* 74. Isis is sometimes personified as a basilisk.—*Ib.* 58. Mneuis, as a basilisk and a tear.—*Ib.* 59, D. The asp and basilisk are both employed as the symbol of divinity.—*Ib.* 55.

Sometimes with the head of a man, sometimes with the head of an hawk, as Pierius hath delivered, and as with addition of legs, the heralds and painters still describe it. Nor was it only of old a symbolical and allowable invention, but is now become a manual contrivance of art and artificial imposture;

The *ibis*, mentioned in this chapter, is the hieroglyphic of the Egyptian god, Thoth, or Hermes, the secretary of Osiris.—*Ib.* 11.

With the exception of the basilisk, and perhaps the deer, not one of the animals named by Sir Thomas, as used hieroglyphically, is mentioned as an Egyptian hieroglyphic in Dr. Young's article, Egypt. Indeed, in my opinion, the others have the character of a spurious origin, having probably arisen towards the dark ages, when significations were *invented* for the ancient fables.

Nor are they, if we add to the exceptions "*le lézard*" (as the salamander), *les quadrupèdes à tête d'oiseau* (as the griffin), and "*le vipère*," either mentioned or figured by Champollion; but as the hieroglyphic texts present images of all kinds of natural objects, including mammalia, birds, reptiles, amphibia, fishes, and insects; and of the second class "*une foule*" (Champollion enumerating, among the eight hundred and sixty-four characters contained in those texts, thirty-four quadrupeds and fifty birds and their parts), it is probable that the *real* animals *may have been used* among the objects hieroglyphically employed; but the alleged grounds of their respective use are most likely erroneous. I should rather doubt, however, the use of the beaver, an animal scarcely likely to have been known to the Egyptians.

The *bear* may possibly be in the same predicament, especially as there appears to be no name for that animal in Egyptian for Champollion informs us, that the name for lion in that language (labo, laboi, or lifoi), is a compound word, meaning *valde hirsutus*, " et que c'est dans ce sens qu'on aurait aussi quelquefois appliqué ce nom à l'ours, dans la version Egyptienne des livres saints; *Apocalypse*, xiii. 2." This indicates that there was no name for the bear in Egyptian, as above noted, and if that were the case, it is clear there could be no hieroglyphic of it.

Browne's authority for the alleged Egyptian hieroglyphics he mentions in this book, are—Horapollo and Pierius—but principally the latter. From looking over Pierius, his explanations appear to be, perhaps always, fallacious; being founded on the misconception, before noted, as arising in the dark ages.

With respect to Horapollo, the following extract, from *Dr. Young's Discoveries in Hieroglyphical Literature*, will show the degree of reliance to be placed in him. After speaking of the traditional record of the true sense of the handled cross, he proceeds :—" We also find some imperfect hints of a partial knowledge of the sense of the hieroglyphics in the *puerile work* of Horapollo, which is much more like a collection of conceits and enigmas, than an explanation of a real system of serious literature; and while such scattered truths were confounded with a multitude of false assertions, it was impossible to profit by any of them, without some clue to assist us in the selection."

whereof, besides others, Scaliger hath taken notice: *Basilisci formam mentiti sunt vulgò gallinaceo similem, et pedibus binis;*[2] *neque enim absimiles sunt cæteris serpentibus, nisi macula quasi in vertice candida, unde illi nomen regium;* that is, "men commonly counterfeit the form of a basilisk with another like a cock and with two feet; whereas, they differ not from other serpents, but in a white speck upon their crown." Now, although in some manner it might be counterfeited in Indian cocks and flying serpents, yet is it commonly contrived out of the skins of thornbacks, skaits, or maids, as Aldrovand hath observed, and also graphically described in his excellent book of fishes, and for satisfaction of my own curiosity, I have caused some to be thus contrived out of the same fishes.

Nor is only the existency of this animal considerable, but many things delivered thereof, particularly its poison and its generation. Concerning the first, according to the doctrine of the ancients, men still affirm, that it killeth at a distance, that it poisoneth by the eye, and by priority of vision. Now, that deleterious it may be at some distance, and destructive without corporal contaction, what uncertainty soever there be in the effect, there is no high improbability in the relation. For if plagues or pestilential atoms have been conveyed in the air from different regions—if men at a distance have infected each other—if the shadows of some trees be noxious[3] —if torpedos deliver their opium at a distance, and stupify beyond themselves,[4] we cannot reasonably deny, that (beside

---

[2] *pedibus binis.*] As was that kept in the physick schooles in Oxon, of a most elegant forme, and as it seemes of a dusky, but transparent, substance, like glew, and as if shaped in a molde.—*Wr.*

[3] *if the shadows of some trees, &c.*] Later investigation has proved that the awful stories put forth in the latter end of the eighteenth century, of the poisonous character of the upas-tree, were impudent forgeries. For the assertion to which this passage alludes, viz., that its shadow is poisonous, there is certainly no foundation. In the island of Java, there are two trees which produce a very deadly poison; but the birds, nevertheless, perch on their branches in safety, and the natives collect their poisonous juices with impunity, and even wear a coarse stuff prepared from their bark.

[4] *at a distance, &c.*] The electrical shock of the torpedo, although it may be received without actual contact, cannot be communicated from a distance but by means of some conducting medium. Indeed, it is found that both the gymnote and torpedo are limited to precisely the

our gross and restrained poisons requiring contiguity unto their actions), there may proceed, from subtiler seeds, more agile emanations, which contemn those laws, and invade at distance unexpected.

That this venenation shooteth from the eye,[5] and that this

same conducting and non-conducting mediums as are met with in common electricity.

[5] *That this venenation, &c.*] Cuvier, on this point, makes the following observation in reference to the rattlesnake :—"It was for a long time believed it had the power of torpifying by its breath, and even of fascinating, that is, of forcing its prey, by its glance alone, to precipitate themselves into its mouth. It appears, however, that it is enabled to seize them only during those irregular movements which the fear of its aspect causes them to make."—See *Burton's Memoir on the Faculty of Fascination attributed to the Rattle-snake:* Philadel. 1796. But the subject is more fully adverted to in the following passage, in the supplementary observations on the Ophidians.

"It has been almost universally believed, that by certain special emanations, by the fear which they inspire, or even by a sort of magnetic or magic power, the serpents can stupify and fascinate the prey which they are desirous to obtain. Pliny attributes this kind of *asphyxia* to a nauseous vapour proceeding from these animals; an opinion which seems to receive confirmation from the facility with which, by the assistance of smell alone, the negroes and native Indians can discover serpents in the savannahs of America. Count de Lacépède seems inclined to adopt this notion in his History of Serpents.

"P. Kalm assures us, that being fixedly regarded by a serpent hissing, and darting its forked tongue out of its mouth, the squirrels are, as it were, constrained to fall from the summit of the trees into the mouth of the reptile, which swallows them up. According to the report of many travellers, one would think that by the effect of some charm, the *durissus* and *boïquira*, those redoubtable rulers of the steppes of America, possess the power of forcing their prey into their mouths. At their aspect, it is said, that hares, rats, frogs, and other reptiles, seem petrified with terror, and far from attempting to fly, will precipitate themselves upon the fate which awaits them. Even at a sufficient distance for escape, they are paralyzed by the sight of their tremendous foe, and deprived of all their faculties in a manner that appears wholly supernatural.

"But this fact, which is so interesting in animal physiology, is not only far from being clearly explained, but even far enough from being sufficiently demonstrated. Notwithstanding the ingenious conjectures of Sir Hans Sloane on this subject, the observations of Kalm, whose assertions were implicitly received by Linnæus; those of Lawson, Catesby, Brickel, Beverley, Bancroft, and Bartram; notwithstanding a work published *ex professo* on the matter, by Dr. Burton, of Philadelphia, and notwithstanding some recent accounts by Major Gordon, of this stupifying power in the serpents, which he attributes both to

way a basilisk may empoison—although thus much be not agreed upon by authors, some imputing it unto the breath, others unto the bite—it is not a thing impossible. For eyes receive offensive impressions from their objects, and may have influences destructive to each other. For the visible species of things strike not our senses immaterially, but streaming in corporal rays, do carry with them the qualities of the object from whence they flow, and the medium through which they pass. Thus, through a green or red glass, all things we behold appear of the same colours; thus sore eyes affect those which are sound, and themselves also by reflection, as will happen to an inflamed eye that beholds itself long in a glass; thus is fascination made out, and thus also it is not impossible, what is affirmed of this animal, the visible rays of their eyes carrying forth the subtilest portion of their poison, which received by the eye of man or beast, infecteth first the brain,[6] and is from thence communicated unto the heart.[7]

But lastly, that this destruction should be the effect of the first beholder, or depend upon priority of aspection, is a point not easily to be granted,[8] and very hardly to be made

---

the terror which they inspire, and to certain narcotic emanations from their bodies at particular times, it must be confessed that this subject is still liable to controversy, and still involved in a considerable degree of obscurity."—*Griffith's Cuvier*, ix. 311, 312. There is a very interesting lecture on this subject, in *Dr. Good's Book of Nature*, vol. ii. lec. 6.

[6] *brain.*] And why not by the smel rather, and from thence to the braine, as for the most part happens by contagion in time of the plague. Soe the poysonous breath of the basiliske, spreading far through the aire in those hot countryes of Africa, may easily surprise those that unawares come neer his denn.—*Wr.*

[7] *heart.*] But yf by the serpent's priority of vision, how comes itt to effect the eye first, but that coming unawares within the contagion of his deadly breath, a man is infected before he sees his mischeef. And which is most likely? by the poyson some smel immediately drawne to the harte with the pestilent air in those burning countryes; or by the eye into the braine, and thence to the harte, whereof noe man can justify the trueth, and may more justly bee denyed then granted, being farther fetcht, only infered by way of consequence to make good their assertion. Yf, then, the infection bee not received by the eye, as heere the learned Dr. [seems?] to opine, by what other way can it bee possibly received, but by the infected ayre immediately drawne into the heart? which I suppose the following discourse will cleere.—*Wr.*

[8] *not easily, &c.*] This velitation will [be] needles, yf as before, and

out upon the principles of Aristotle, Alhazen, Vitello, and others, who hold, that sight is made by reception, and not by extramission; by receiving the rays of the object into the eye, and not by sending any out. For hereby, although he behold a man first, the basilisk should rather be destroyed, in regard he first receiveth the rays of his antipathy and venomous emissions, which objectively move his sense; but how powerful soever his own poison be, it invadeth not the sense[9] of man, in regard he beholdeth him not. And therefore this conceit was probably begot by such as held the opinion of sight by extramission; as did Pythagoras, Plato, Empedocles, Hipparchus, Galen, Macrobius, Proclus, Simplicius, with most of the ancients, and is the postulate of Euclid in his *Opticks*, but now sufficiently convicted from observations of the dark chamber.[1]

As for the generation of the basilisk, that it proceedeth from a cock's egg, hatched under a toad or serpent, it is a conceit as monstrous[2] as the brood itself. For if we should

---

is most probable, wee conceive the infection of the basiliske to fasten upon the smel rather then the eye: both these senses, and indeed the five senses, being made by reception only, and not by extramission. Soe that his powerful poyson, which proceeds from his breath, rather then his eye, may invade the sense of smelling, and consequently destroy a man hereby; or may sudenly destroy the harte by drawing in that poysonous aire.— *Wr*.

[9] *sense.*] Eye.— *Wr*.

[1] *but now, &c.*] Instead of this concluding line (first added in the 2nd edit.), the following curious passage terminated the paragraph in the 1st edit. p. 120; "and of this opinion might they be, who from this antipathy of the basilisk and man, expressed first the enmity of Christ and Satan, and their mutual destruction thereby; when Satan, being elder than his humanity, beheld Christ first in the flesh, and so he was destroyed by the serpent; but elder than Satan in his divinity, and so beholding him first, he destroyed the old basilisk, and overcame the effect of his poison, sin, death, and hell."

On this passage, Dean Wren (who used the 1st edition) drily remarks:—"This argument is but symbolical, and concludes nothing."

[2] *a conceit as monstrous.*] At the end of the volume for 1710, of the *History of the French Royal Academy*, is a curious account, transmitted by M. Lapeyronie from Montpellier, of some "cock's eggs," which a farmer had brought to him, with the assurance that they were laid by a cock, and would be found to contain, instead of yolk, the embryo of a serpent. One of these eggs, opened in the presence of several *scavans*, was found devoid of yolk, but exhibiting a coloured particle in the

grant, that cocks growing old, and unable for emission, amass within themselves some seminal matter, which may after conglobate into the form of an egg, yet will this substance be unfruitful. As wanting one principle of generation, and a commixture of the seed of both sexes, which is required unto production, as may be observed in the eggs of hens not trodden, and as we have made trial in some which are termed cock's eggs. It is not indeed impossible, that from the sperm of a cock, hen, or other animal, being once in putrescence, either from incubation or otherwise, some generation may ensue; not univocal and of the same species, but some imperfect or monstrous production, even as in the body of man, from putrid humours and peculiar ways of corruption, there have succeeded strange and unseconded shapes of worms,[3] whereof we have beheld some ourselves, and read of others in medical observations. And so may strange and venomous serpents be several ways engendered; but that this generation should be regular, and always produce a basilisk, is beyond our affirmation, and we have good reason to doubt.

Again, it is unreasonable to ascribe the equivocancy of this form unto the hatching of a toad, or imagine that diversifies the production. For incubation alters not the species, nor if we observe it, so much as concurs either to the sex or colour: as appears in the eggs of ducks or partridges hatched under a hen, there being required unto their exclusion only a gentle and continued heat, and that not particular or confined unto the species or parent. So have I known the seed of silkworms hatched on the bodies of

centre, which was considered as the young serpent. The cock having been given up to M. Lapeyronie for dissection, the farmer very soon brought some more of these little eggs,—having discovered that they were laid by a hen! Anatomical figures accompany the paper.

The conceit, however, is not too monstrous for the belief of Al. Ross—who asks, "Why may not this serpent be ingendred of a cock's putrified seminal materials, being animated by his heat and incubation as well as other kinds of serpents are bred of putrified matter?"—*Arcana*, p. 146.

[3] *worms.*] Of which you may see the many strange and horrible shapes in *Parceus his Chirurgerye*, lib. xx. cap. iii. et iv. pp. 762-4.—**Wr.**

women:[4] and Pliny reports, that Livia, the wife of Augustus, hatched an egg in her bosom. Nor is only an animal heat required hereto, but an elemental and artificial warmth will suffice: for, as Diodorus delivereth, the Egyptians were wont to hatch their eggs in ovens, and many eye-witnesses confirm that practice unto this day. And, therefore, this generation of the basilisk seems like that of Castor and Helena; he that can credit the one, may easily believe the other; that is, that these two were hatched out of the egg which Jupiter, in the form of a swan, begat on his mistress Leda.

The occasion of this conceit might be an Egyptian tradition concerning the bird ibis, which after became transferred unto cocks. For an opinion it was of that nation, that the ibis,[5] feeding upon serpents,[6] that venomous food so inquinated their oval conceptions or eggs within their bodies, that they sometimes came forth in serpentine shapes, and therefore they always brake their eggs, nor would they endure the bird to sit upon them. But how causeless their fear was herein, the daily incubation of ducks, peahens, and many other testify; and the stork might have informed them; which bird they honoured and cherished, to destroy their serpents.

[4] *on the bodies of women.*] Betweene the breasts of a woman, rolled in fine lawne, and they are stronger then those hatcht in the cases, how warme soever kept. But itt must bee by election in virgin's breasts, *antequam sororiant, aut menstrua patiantur, nœ prorsus intereant, alioqui proditurœ feliciter.*—*Wr.*

[5] *ibis.*] Black ibis.—*Wr.*

[6] *serpents.*] Heer the learned author mistakes the story: for Tully, in the 2nd *De Natura Deorum* says, the Ægyptians justly honored the ibis; *quia pestem ab Ægypto avertunt quum serpentes volucros, Africo è Libyâ advertos, interficiant.* Soe farr were they from breaking their eggs, which had been to destroy the breed of those whom they honored. And what madnes had it been to honor the stork that destroyed the serpents and to destroy the ibides' eggs, by which creature (and not by the storke) those fiery flying serpents were destroyed. But mistake grew for want of right advertisement herein. For St. Hierom, that wel knew Egypt, tels us there were 2 kinds of the ibides: one coale black (and itt seemes pernicious some waye, and therefore hated by them), the other not much unlike the stork, though not the same. Soe that in honoring the second kinde, they might seem to honor the stork, which was (indeed) the right ibis, their preserver.—*Wr.*

That which much promoted it, was a misapprehension in Holy Scripture upon the Latin translation in Isa. li. *Ova aspidum ruperunt, et telas aranearum texuerunt, qui comedet de ovis eorum morietur, et quod confotum est, erumpet in regulum.* From whence, notwithstanding, beside the generation of serpents from eggs, there can be nothing concluded; and what kind of serpents are meant, not easy to be determined: for translations are very different: Tremellius rendering the asp *hæmorrhous*, and the regulus or basilisk, a viper; and our translation for the asp sets down a cockatrice in the text, and an adder in the margin.

Another place of Isaiah doth also seem to countenance it, chap. xiv.: *Ne læteris Philistæa, quoniam diminuta est virga percussoris tui; de radice enim colubri egredietur regulus, et semen ejus absorbens volucrem;* which ours somewhat favourably rendereth: "Out of the serpent's root shall come forth a cockatrice, and his fruit shall be a fiery flying serpent." But Tremellius, *è radice serpentis prodit hæmorrhous, et fructus illius prester volans;* wherein the words are different, but the sense is still the same; for therein are figuratively intended Uzziah and Ezechias; for though the Philistines had escaped the minor serpent, Uzziah, yet from his stock a fiercer snake should arise, that would more terribly sting them, and that was Ezechias.

But the greatest promotion it hath received from a misunderstanding of the hieroglyphical intention. For being conceived to be the lord and king of serpents, to awe all others, nor to be destroyed by any, the Egyptians hereby implied eternity, and the awful power of the supreme deity; and therefore described a crowned asp or basilisk upon the heads of their gods: as may be observed in the Bembine table,[7] and other Egyptian monuments.[8]

---

[7] *as may be observed, &c.*] This is from Pierius (141, B.) by whom a basilisk is figured from the Bembine, or Isiac table, as a serpent, with a crest, or crown, upon an obelisk, and having rudiments of wings and a long head and snout.

[8] *But, &c.*] This paragraph was first added in the 3rd edit.

CHAPTER VIII.

That a Wolf first seeing a man, begets a dumbness in him.

SUCH a story as the basilisk, is that of the wolf, concerning priority of vision, that a man becomes hoarse,[9] or dumb, if a wolf have the advantage first to eye him. And this is in plain language affirmed by Pliny: *In Italia, ut creditur, luporum visus est noxius, vocemque homini, quem priùs contemplatur, adimere;* so is it made out what is delivered by Theocritus, and after him by Virgil:

——— Vox quoque Mœrim
Jam fugit ipsa, lupi Mœrim videre priores.

And thus is the proverb to be understood, when, during the discourse, if the party or subject interveneth, and there ensueth a sudden silence, it is usually said, *lupus est in fabula.* Which conceit being already convicted, not only by Scaliger,[1] Riolanus, and others, but daily confutable almost everywhere out of England, we shall not further refute.

The ground, or occasional original hereof, was probably the amazement and sudden silence the unexpected appearance of wolves doth often put upon travellers; not by a supposed vapour, or venomous emanation, but a vehement fear, which naturally produceth obmutescence, and sometimes irrecoverable silence. Thus birds are silent in the presence of an hawk, and Pliny saith that dogs are mute in the shadow of an hyæna. But thus could not the mouths of worthy martyrs be silenced, who being exposed not only unto the eyes, but the merciless teeth of wolves, gave loud expressions of their faith, and their holy clamours[2] were heard as high as heaven.

[9] *that a man becomes hoarse.*] When any one becomes hoarse, the French say, *il a vu le loup.* See *Howell's Familiar Letters*, vol. iv. p. 52. See *Erasmi Colloquia, De Amicitiâ.*—*Jeff.*

Ross uses the *argumentum ad hominem* in this case: he says, "Dr. Browne did unadvisedly reckon this among his vulgar errors, for I believe he would find this no error, if he were suddenly surprised by a wolf, having no means to escape or save himself!"

[1] *Scaliger.*] *Exercitatione* 344.—*Wr.*

[2] *clamours.*] Shouts. Clamours is improper here, for 'twas not

That which much promoted it, beside the common proverb, was an expression in Theocritus, a very ancient poet, οὐ φθέγξῃ, Λύκον εἶδες, *Edere non poteris vocem, Lycus est tibi visus;* which Lycus was rival unto another, and suddenly appearing, stopped the mouth of his corrival. Now Lycus signifying also a wolf occasioned this apprehension; men taking that appellatively which was to be understood properly, and translating the genuine acception: which is a fallacy of equivocation, and in some opinions begat the like conceit concerning Romulus and Remus, that they were fostered by a wolf—the name of the nurse being Lupa—and founded the fable of Europa, and her carriage over the sea by a bull, because the ship or pilot's name was Taurus. And thus have some been startled at the proverb, *bos in lingua*, confusedly apprehending how a man should be said to have an ox in his tongue, that would not speak his mind; which was no more than that a piece of money had silenced him; for by the ox was only implied a piece of coin stamped with that figure, first current with the Athenians, and after among the Romans.[3]

CHAPTER IX.

Of the long life of the Deer.

THE common opinion concerning the long life of animals is very ancient, especially of crows, choughs, and deer, in moderate accounts exceeding the age of man, in some the days of Nestor, and in others surmounting the years of Artephius or Methuselah. From whence antiquity hath raised

---

feare of death that made them cry out at all; but an assured certainty of their neer approaching glorification made them kiss their persequutors, as promoters to eternity, and to sing in the midst of their torments aloud! Soe that, instead of "clamours," I put "shouts," wherewith they daunted those wolves, and made them stand amazed at their courage; which they concluded must needs proceed from the hope of something after death, to bee farr better then the present life, and by this meanes were many of them converted.—*Wr.*

[3] *first current with the Athenians, &c.*] Wherewith the embassadors stopt Demosthenes his mouth, that hee should not inveigh against their countrye.—*Wr.*

CHAP. IX.] OF THE LONG LIFE OF THE DEER. 263

proverbial expressions, and the real conception of their duration hath been the hyperbolical expression of many others. From all the rest we shall single out the deer, upon concession a long-lived animal, and in longevity by many conceived to attain unto hundreds; wherein, permitting every man his own belief, we shall ourselves crave liberty to doubt, and our reasons are these ensuing.

The first is that of Aristotle, drawn from the increment and gestation of this animal, that is, its sudden arrivance unto growth and maturity, and the small time of its remainder in the womb. His words in the translation of Scaliger are these—*De ejus vitæ longitudine fabulantur; neque enim aut gestatio aut incrementum hinnulorum ejusmodi sunt, ut præstent argumentum longævi animalis;* that is, "fables are raised concerning the vivacity[4] of deer, for neither are their gestation or increment such as may afford an argument of long life." And these, saith Scaliger, are good mediums conjunctively taken, that is, not one without the other. For of animals viviparous, such as live long go long with young, and attain but slowly to their maturity and stature. So the horse, that liveth about thirty, arriveth unto his stature about six years, and remaineth about ten months in the womb,—so the camel, that liveth unto fifty, goeth with young no less than ten months, and ceaseth not to grow before seven,—and so the elephant, that liveth an hundred, beareth its young above a year,[5] and arriveth unto perfection at twenty. On the contrary, the sheep and goat, which live but eight or ten years, go but five months,[6] and attain to their perfection at two years: and the like proportion is observable in cats, hares, and conies. And so the deer, that endureth the womb but eight months, and is complete at six years, from the course of nature we cannot expect to live an hundred, nor in any proportional allowance much

[4] *vivacity.*] i. e. long life. The passage is from the *Hist. Animal.* lib. vi. c. xxix.
[5] *above a year.*] The periods here assigned to the horse, camel, and elephant, are all shorter than the fact. That of the horse is twelve months, the camel eleven and a half, and the elephant twenty.
[6] *five months.*] The 1st of August was (of old) cal'd Lammas day, bycause the rams, going then to the flocks, made the fall of the lambs alwayes about the Nativitye; the 19th of December terminating the full time of gestation, i. e. five months, or twenty weeks.—*Wr.*

more than thirty. As having already passed two general motions observable in all animations, that is, its beginning and increase, and having but two more to run through, that is, its state and declination, which are proportionally set out by nature in every kind, and naturally proceeding admit of inference from each other.

The other ground that brings its long life into question, is the immoderate felicity, and almost unparalleled excess of venery, which every September may be observed in this animal, and is supposed to shorten the lives of cocks, partridges, and sparrows. Certainly a confessed and undeniable enemy unto longevity, and that not only as a sign in the complexional desire and impetuosity, but also as a cause in the frequent act, or iterated performance thereof. For though we consent not with that philosopher, who thinks a spermatical emission, unto the weight of one drachm, is equivalent unto the effusion of sixty ounces of blood, yet considering the exolution and languor ensuing that act in some—the extenuation and marcour in others, and the visible acceleration it maketh of age in most, we cannot but think it much abridgeth our days. Although we also concede that this exclusion is natural, that nature itself will find a way hereto without either act or object; and although it be placed among the six non-naturals, that is, such as, neither naturally constitutive, nor merely destructive, do preserve or destroy according unto circumstance; yet do we sensibly observe an impotency, or total privation thereof, prolongeth life; and they live longest in every kind that exercise it not at all. And this is true, not only in eunuchs by nature, but spadoes by art; for castrated animals, in every species, are longer lived than they which retain their virilities; for the generation of bodies is not merely effected, as some conceive of souls, that is, by irradiation, or answerably unto the propagation of light, without its proper diminution; but therein a transmission is made materially from some parts, with the idea of every one; and the propagation of one is, in a strict acception, some minoration of another. And, therefore, also, that axiom in philosophy, that the generation of one thing is the corruption of another, although it be substantially true concerning the form and matter, is also dispositively verified in the efficient or producer.

As for more sensible arguments, and such as relate unto experiment, from these we have also reason to doubt its age, and presumed vivacity; for where long life is natural, the marks of age are late; and when they appear, the journey unto death cannot be long. Now the age of the deer (as Aristotle long ago observed) is best conjectured by view of the horns and teeth. From the horns there is a particular and annual account unto six years, they arising first plain, and so successively branching; after which the judgment of their years, by particular marks, becomes uncertain. But when they grow old, they grow less branched, and first do lose their ἀμυντῆρες, or *propugnacula*, that is, their brow-antlers, or lowest furcations next the head; which, Aristotle saith, the young ones use in fight, and the old, as needless, have them not at all. The same may be also collected from the loss of their teeth, whereof in old age they have few or none before in either jaw. Now these are infallible marks of age, and when they appear, we must confess a declination; which notwithstanding (as men inform us in England, where observations may well be made), will happen between twenty and thirty. As for the bone, or rather induration of the roots of the arterial vein and great artery, which is thought to be found only in the heart of an old deer, and therefore becomes more precious in its rarity, it is often found in deer much under thirty, and we have known some affirm they have found it in one of half that age. And therefore, in that account of Pliny, of a deer with a collar about his neck, put on by Alexander the Great, and taken alive an hundred years after, with other relations of this nature, we much suspect imposture or mistake. And if we grant their verity, they are but single relations, and very rare contingencies in individuals, not affording a regular deduction upon the species. For though Ulysses' dog lived unto twenty, and the Athenian mule unto fourscore, yet do we not measure their days by those years, or usually say they live thus long. Nor can the three hundred years of John of times, or Nestor, overthrow the assertion of Moses,* or afford a reasonable encouragement beyond his septuagenary determination.

The ground and authority of this conceit was first hiero-

---

* Psalm xc.

glyphical, the Egyptians expressing longevity by this animal;[7] but upon what uncertainties, and also convincible falsities they often erected such emblems, we have elsewhere delivered. And if that were true which Aristotle * delivers of his time, and Pliny was not afraid to take up long after, the Egyptians could make but weak observations herein: for though it be said that Æneas feasted his followers with venison, yet Aristotle affirms that neither deer nor boar were to be found in Africa. And how far they miscounted the lives and duration of animals, is evident from their conceit of the crow, which they presume to live five hundred years; and from the lives of hawks, which (as Ælian delivereth) the Egyptians do reckon no less than at seven hundred.

The second, which led the conceit unto the Grecians, and probably descended from the Egyptians, was poetical; and that was a passage of Hesiod, thus rendered by Ausonius.

> Ter binos deciésque novem super exit in annos,
> Justa senescentûm quos implet vita virorum.
> Hos novies superat vivendo garrula cornix,
> Et quater egreditur cornicis sæcula cervus,
> Alipedem cervum ter vincit corvus.

> To ninety-six the life of man ascendeth,
> Nine times as long that of the chough extendeth,
> Four times beyond the life of deer doth go,
> And thrice is that surpassed by the crow.

So that, according to this account, allowing ninety-six for the age of man, the life of a deer amounts unto three thousand four hundred and fifty-six; a conceit so hard to be made out, that many have deserted the common and literal construction. So Theon, in Aratus, would have the number of nine not taken strictly, but for many years. In other opinions, the compute so far exceedeth the truth, that they have thought it more probable to take the word *genea*, that

---

* *Histor. Animal.* lib. viii.

[7] *was first hieroglyphical, &c.*] Obtained from Horapollo. The *antelope* is mentioned by Dr. Young, with the *bullock*, the *ram*, and the *tortoise*, as being sometimes representations of the things which they resemble, and sometimes having probably a metaphorical sense (*S. E. B. Egypt*, 75-78). Champollion mentions the gazelle, but not the deer.

is, a generation consisting of many years, but for one year, or a single revolution of the sun; which is the remarkable measure of time, and within the compass whereof, we receive our perfection in the womb. So that by this construction, the years of a deer should be but thirty-six, as is discoursed at large in that tract of Plutarch, concerning the cessation of oracles, and whereto in his discourse of the crow, Aldrovandus also inclineth. Others, not able to make it out, have rejected the whole account, as may be observed from the words of Pliny; *Hesiodus qui primus aliquid de longævitate vitæ prodidit, fabulosè (reor) multa de hominum ævo referens, cornici novem nostras attribuit ætates, quadruplum ejus cervis, id triplicatum corvis, et reliqua fabulosiùs de phœnice et nymphis.* And this, how slender soever, was probably the strongest ground antiquity had for this longevity of animals; that made Theophrastus expostulate with nature concerning the long life of crows; that begat that epithet of deer* in Oppianus, and that expression of Juvenal,

———Longa et cervina senectus.

The third ground was philosophical, and founded upon a probable reason in nature, that is, the defect of a gall: which part (in the opinion of Aristotle and Pliny), this animal wanted, and was conceived a cause and reason of their long life: according (say they) as it happeneth unto some few men, who have not this part at all. But this assertion is first defective in the verity concerning the animal alleged: for though it be true, a deer hath no gall in the liver like many other animals, yet hath it that part in the guts, as is discoverable by taste and colour: and therefore Pliny doth well correct himself, when, having affirmed before, it had no gall, he after saith, some hold it to be in the guts; and that for their bitterness, dogs will refuse to eat them. The assertion is also deficient in the verity of the induction or connumeration of other animals conjoined herewith, as having also no gall; that is, as Pliny accounteth, *equi, muli,* &c. Horses, mules, asses, deer, goats, boars, camels, dolphins, have no gall. In dolphins and porpoises I confess I could find no gall. But concerning horses, what truth there is

* Τετρακέρωτος.

herein we have declared before; as for goats, we find not them without it; what gall the camel hath, Aristotle declareth: that hogs also have it we can affirm; and that not in any obscure place, but in the liver, even as it is seated in man.[8]

That, therefore, the deer is no short-lived animal, we will acknowledge; that comparatively, and in some sense long-lived, we will concede; and thus much we shall grant, if we commonly account its days[9] by thirty-six or forty;[1] for thereby it will exceed all other cornigerous animals. But that it attaineth unto hundreds, or the years delivered by authors, since we have no authentic experience for it—since we have reason and common experience against it—since the grounds are false and fabulous which do establish it, we know no ground to assent.

Concerning deer, there also passeth another opinion, that the males thereof do yearly lose their pizzle: for men, observing the decidence of their horns, do fall upon the like conceit of this part, that it annually rotteth away, and successively reneweth again.[2] Now the ground hereof, was surely the observation of this part in deer after immoderate venery, and about the end of their rut, which sometimes becomes so relaxed and pendulous, it cannot be quite retracted: and being often beset with flies, it is conceived to rot, and at last to fall from the body. But herein experience will contradict us; for deer, which either die or are

---

[8] *Horses, &c.*] This statement is correct. It is asserted that the gall-bladder is common to all carnivorous animals possessing a liver, and that it seems to be wanting only in those which feed on vegetables alone. The gall-bladder is contained between the *peritonæum* and the liver.

[9] *days.*] Yeares.—*Wr.*

[1] *thirty-six or forty.*] A correct conclusion. Ross, however, is not inclined to give up the opinion of the "ancient sages," on "so weak grounds" as those advanced by Sir Thomas. His faith, however, might well admit such assertions as are here discussed; since he avowed his belief that old men may grow young again;—"that the decayed nature may be so renewed and repaired, as an old man may perform the function of a young man!"

[2] *this part, &c.*] Itt may sometimes rott, as the deers often doe; yf a sharpe and stervinge winter take them before they can repaire the strength lost by immoderate rutt: whence it seemes the terme (rott) first came: but that part wherein the rott always beginnes to appeare, is never renewed.—*Wr.*

killed at that time, or any other, are always found to have that part entire. And reason will also correct us; for spermatical parts, or such as are framed from the seminal principles of parents,[3] although homogeneous or similary, will not admit a regeneration; much less will they receive an integral restoration, which being organical and instrumental members, consist of many of those. Now this part, or animal of Plato, containeth not only sanguineous and reparable particles, but is made up of veins, nerves, arteries, and in some animals of bones;[4] whose reparation is beyond its own fertility, and a fruit not to be expected from the fructifying part itself. Which faculty, were it communicated unto animals whose originals are double, as well as unto plants whose seed is within themselves, we might abate the art of *Taliacotius*, and the new inarching of noses.[5] And therefore the fancies of poets have been so modest, as not to set down such renovations, even from the powers of their deities; for the mutilated shoulder of Pelops[6] was pieced out with ivory, and that the limbs of Hippolytus were set together, not regenerated by Æsculapius, is the utmost assertion of poetry.

[3] *such as are framed, &c.*] There seems some difficulty in determining the precise meaning of this phrase:—but Sir Thomas was not aware of what has been ascertained by the experiments of Bonnet and Spallanzani on snails and worms; and by those of Drs. Heineken and Mac Culloch on spiders and crabs; viz. that these comparatively imperfect animals have the wonderful power (not bestowed on those of far more complete organization) of reproducing parts of which they have been deprived—limbs, antennæ, and even the head.

[4] *bones.*] As in poll-cats and ferrets, which I caused to bee dissected, and found in one a bone as big as a walnut shaled.—*Wr.*

[5] *new inarching of noses.*] In the *Gents. Mag.* vol. 54, p. 891, is an account of this operation as performed in India, in 1792. An old work, entitled *Chirurgorum Comes*, 1687, concludes with an account of a similar operation, performed two hundred before, at Lausanne, by a surgeon named Greffonius, on a young woman. The physiological principles, on which this celebrated process has been successful, are discussed by Dr. Bostock, in his *Elementary System of Physiology*, vol. i. p. 450. Sir Kenelm Digby adds this marvellous assertion, that when a man, whose nose had been lost by extreme cold, was supplied with an artificial nose made of the flesh of some other person, " his new nose would putrify as soon as the person, out of whose substance it was taken, came to die!"

[6] *Pelops*] So Virgil;—Georgic. iii. 7:

Humeroque Pelops insignis eburno.

CHAPTER X.

That a Kingfisher, hanged by the bill, showeth where the wind lay.

THAT a kingfisher, hanged by the bill, showeth in what quarter the wind is, by an occult and secret propriety, converting the breast to that point of the horizon from whence the wind doth blow, is a received opinion, and very strange—introducing natural weathercocks, and extending magnetical positions as far as animal natures. A conceit supported chiefly by present practice, yet not made out by reason or experience.

Unto reason it seemeth very repugnant, that a carcass or body disanimated, should be so affected with every wind, as to carry a conformable respect and constant habitude thereto. For although in sundry animals we deny not a kind of natural meteorology or innate presention both of wind and weather, yet, that proceeding from sense receiving impression from the first mutation of the air, they cannot in reason retain that apprehension after death, as being affections which depend on life, and depart upon disanimation. And therefore with more favourable reason may we draw the same effect or sympathy upon the hedgehog, whose presention of winds is so exact, that it stoppeth the north or southern hole of its nest, according to the prenotion of these winds ensuing;[7] which some men observing, have been able to make predictions which way the wind would turn, and been esteemed hereby wise men in point of weather. Now this proceeding from sense in the creature alive, it were not reasonable to hang up an hedgehog dead, and to expect a conformable motion unto its living conversion. And though in sundry plants their virtues do live after death—and we know that scammony, rhubarb, and senna will purge without any vital assistance—yet in animals and sensible creatures, many actions are mixed, and depend upon their living form, as well as that of mistion; and though they wholly seem to retain unto the body, depart

---

[7] *whose presention of winds, &c.*] The popular belief of this "presention" (faculty of perceiving beforehand), in the hedgehog, seems to be without foundation.

upon disunion. Thus glow-worms alive project a lustre in the dark; which fulgour, notwithstanding, ceaseth after death; and thus the torpedo, which being alive stupifies at a distance, applied after death, produceth no such effect; which had they retained, in places where they abound they might have supplied opium,[8] and served as frontals in phrensies.

As for the experiment, we cannot make it out by any we have attempted; for if a single kingfisher be hanged up with untwisted silk in an open room, and where the air is free, it observes not a constant respect unto the mouth of the wind, but, variously converting, doth seldom breast it aright. If two be suspended in the same room, they will not regularly conform their breasts, but ofttimes respect the opposite points of heaven. And if we conceive that, for exact exploration, they should be suspended where the air is quiet and unmoved,—that, clear of impediments, they may more freely convert upon their natural verticity—we have also made this way of inquisition, suspending them in large and capacious glasses closely stopped; wherein nevertheless we observed a casual station, and that they rested irregularly upon conversion: wheresoever they rested, remaining inconverted; and possessing one point of the compass, whilst the wind, perhaps, had passed the two and thirty.

The ground of this popular practice might be the common opinion concerning the virtue prognostick of these birds; as also the natural regard they have unto the winds, and they unto them again; more especially remarkable in the time of their nidulation and bringing forth their young. For at that time, which happeneth about the brumal solstice, it hath been observed, even unto a proverb,[9] that the sea is calm, and the winds do cease, till the young ones are excluded, and forsake their nest; which floateth upon the sea, and by the roughness of winds, might otherwise be overwhelmed. But how far hereby to magnify their prediction we have no certain rule; for whether out of any particular prenotion they choose to sit at this time, or whether it be

---

[8] *opium.*] This term, used before (page 254) to express the stupifying effect of the gymnotic electricity, is, of course, employed figuratively.

[9] *proverb.*] Halcionian dayes, i. e. dayes of peace.— *Wr.*

thus contrived by concurrence of causes and providence of nature, securing every species in their production, is not yet determined.[1] Surely many things fall out by the design of the general motor and undreamt-of contrivance of nature which are not imputable unto the intention or knowledge of the particular actor. So, though the seminality of ivy be almost in every earth, yet that it ariseth and groweth not, but where it may be supported;[2] we cannot ascribe the same unto the distinction of the seed, or conceive any science therein which suspends and conditionates its eruption. So if, as Pliny and Plutarch report, the crocodiles of Egypt so aptly lay their eggs, that the natives thereby are able to know how high the flood will attain, it will be hard to make out how they should divine the extent of the inundation, depending on causes so many miles remote; that is, the measure of showers in Ethiopia; and whereof, as Athanasius in the *Life of Anthony* delivers, the devil himself upon demand could make no clear prediction. So are there likewise many things in nature which are the forerunners or signs of future effects,[3] whereto they neither concur in causality or prenotion, but are secretly ordered by the providence of causes and concurrence of actions collateral to their signations.

It was also a custom of old to keep these birds in chests, upon opinion that they prevented moths. Whether it were not first hanged up in rooms, to such effects, is not beyond all doubt; or whether we mistake not the posture of suspension, hanging it by the bill, whereas we should do it by the back, that by the bill it might point out the quarters of the wind; for so hath Kircherus described the orbis and the

---

[1] *not yet determined.*] All creatures know not only the meanes but the times of their preservation: and therefore that the halcyon knowing that at the winter solstice there is such a calm, chooseth that time to hatch his young, as the crowes did in 1652, when the mildnes of January was such, that they, supposing the spring was come on, did build their nests, and as I was credibly informed, some did hatche their broode.— *Wr.*

[2] *groweth not, but, &c.*] The ground affords a sufficient support for the purpose; for ivy will certainly grow where it has no other, and will cover the surface of the ground, growing among the herbage, and in some cases supplanting it.

[3] *So are there, &c.*] See an interesting chapter on prognostics in Forster's *Researches into Atmospheric Phænomena*, p. 128.

sea-swallow. But the eldest custom of hanging up these birds was founded upon a tradition, that they would renew their feathers every year as though they were alive: in expectation whereof, four hundred years ago, Albertus Magnus was deceived.[4]

CHAPTER XI.

Of Griffins.

THAT there are griffins in nature, that is, a mixed and dubious animal, in the forepart resembling an eagle, and behind the shape of a lion, with erected ears, four feet, and a long tail, many affirm, and most, I perceive, deny not.[5] The same is averred by Ælian, Solinus, Mela, and Herodotus—countenanced by the name sometimes found in Scripture, and was an hieroglyphic of the Egyptians.[6]

Notwithstanding we find most diligent enquirers to be of a contrary assertion. For beside that Albertus and Pliny have disallowed it, the learned Aldrovandus hath, in a large discourse rejected it; Matthias Michovius, who writ of those northern parts wherein men place these griffins, hath positively concluded against it; and, if examined by the doctrine of animals, the invention is monstrous, nor much inferior unto the figment of sphynx, chimæra, and harpies; for though there be some flying animals of mixed and participating natures,[7] that is, between bird and quadruped, yet are their

---

[4] *It was a custom, &c.*] First added in the 2nd edition.
[5] *That there are griffins, &c.*] Ross, as usual, defends the ancient opinion, at considerable length; and accounts for their not being now known to exist, by supposing them to have removed to places inaccessible to men, whereof he observes there are many such in the great and vast countries of Scythia, &c. &c.!—*Arcana*, p. 199.
[6] *and was an hieroglyphic, &c.*] Pierius (p. 233, E.), on the authority of the Isiac table; of which see note 1, at page 252.
[7] *of mixed and participating natures.*] Modern discovery has greatly added to our knowledge of those animals which form connecting links in the great chain. "There is nothing more wonderful and admirable in nature than this sort of connection between the classes, orders, groups, and genera of the animal kingdom. It is not a regular gradation of being, like the steps of a ladder, according to the Platonic system, nor do we think that it can be very easily reduced to any defi-

wings and legs so set together, that they seem to make each other, their being a commixion of both, rather than an adaptation or cement of prominent parts unto each other; as is observable in the bat, whose wings and fore-legs are contrived in each other. For though some species there be of middle and participating natures, that is, of bird and beast, as bats and some few others; yet are their parts so conformed and set together, that we cannot define the beginning or end of either; there being a commixion of both in the whole, rather than an adaptation or cement of the one unto the other.

Now for the word γρύψ or *gryps*, sometimes mentioned in Scripture, and frequently in human authors, properly understood it signifies some kind of eagle or vulture, from whence the epithet *grypus*, for an hooked or aquiline nose. Thus when the Septuagint makes use of this word,* Tremellius, and our translation, hath rendered it the ossifrage, which is one kind of eagle. And although the vulgar translation, and that annexed unto the Septuagint, retain the word *gryps*, which in ordinary and school construction is commonly rendered a griffin, yet cannot the Latin assume any other sense than the Greek, from whence it is borrowed. And though the Latin *gryphes* be altered somewhat by the addition of an *h*, or aspiration of the letter π, yet is not this unusual; so what the Greeks call τρόπαιον, the Latin will call *trophæum*; and that person, which in the gospel is named Κλέοπας, the Latins will render Cleophas. And therefore the quarrel of Origen was unjust, and his conception erroneous, when he conceived the food of griffins forbidden by the law of Moses;[8] that is, poetical animals, and things of no existence. And

* Lev. ii.

nite plan, notwithstanding the very ingenious and laudable attempts, in this way, of some recent naturalists. But we find in every class, and every order of animals, connecting links with all the other classes, and all the other orders. Somewhere or other, we are sure to find the existing bond of affinity. Thus we have flying mammalia, and walking birds—swimming birds, and flying fishes—in short, some out of each borrow the characters of others, and lose some of those peculiar to their own division."—*Cuvier*, by Griffith, vol. ix. p. 284.

[8] *Moses.*] The most learned among the Jews can give us noe certaine information concerning the names of animals, plants, mettals, vestments, or instruments, saith Gesner, in his learned book, *De Quadrupedibus*.—*Wr*.

therefore, when in the hecatombs and mighty oblations of the Gentiles, it is delivered they sacrificed *gryphes* or griffins, hereby we may understand some stronger sort of eagles. And therefore also, when it is said in Virgil, of an improper match, or Mopsus marrying Nysa, *Jungentur jam gryphes equis*, we need not hunt after other sense, than that strange unions shall be made, and different natures be conjoined together.

As for the testimonies of ancient writers, they are but derivative, and terminate all in one Aristeus, a poet of Proconesus, who affirmed that near the Arimaspi, or one-eyed nation, griffins defended the mines of gold. But this, as Herodotus delivereth, he wrote by hearsay; and Michovius, who had expressly written of those parts, plainly affirmeth, there is neither gold nor griffins in that country, nor any such animal extant; for so doth he conclude, *Ego vero contra veteres authores, gryphes nec in illa septentrionis, nec in aliis orbis partibus inveniri affirmârim.*

Lastly, concerning the hieroglyphical authority, although it nearest approach the truth, it doth not infer its existency. The conceit of the griffin, properly taken, being but a symbolical fancy, in so intolerable a shape including allowable morality. So doth it well make out the properties of a guardian, or any person entrusted; the ears implying attention—the wings, celerity of execution—the lion-like shape, courage and audacity—the hooked bill, reservance and tenacity. It is also an emblem of valour and magnanimity, as being compounded of the eagle and lion, the noblest animals in their kinds; and so is it appliable unto princes, presidents, generals, and all heroic commanders; and so is it also borne in the coat-arms of many noble families of Europe.

But the original invention seems to be hieroglyphical, derived from the Egyptians, and of an higher signification; by the mystical conjunction of hawk and lion, implying either the genial or the syderous sun, the great celerity thereof, and the strength and vigour in its operations: and therefore, under such hieroglyphics Osyris was described;[9] and in

---

[9] *by the mystical conjunction, &c.*] Most of the above statements are from Pierius; but he does not mention Osiris. Horapollo has **no** griffins. Plutarch says, that Osiris is typified by a hawk.—*Young, ut*

ancient coins we meet with griffins conjointly with Apollo's *tripodes* and chariot-wheels; and the marble griffins at St. Peter's in Rome, as learned men conjecture, were first translated from the temple of Apollo. Whether hereby were not also mystically implied the activity of the sun in Leo, the power of God in the sun, or the influence of the celestial Osyris, by Moptha, the genius of Nilus, might also be considered. And than the learned Kircherus, no man were likely to be a better Oedipus.[1]

CHAPTER XII.

Of the Phœnix.

THAT there is but one phœnix in the world, which after many hundred years burneth itself, and from the ashes thereof ariseth up another,[2] is a conceit not new or altogether popular, but of great antiquity; not only delivered by human authors, but frequently expressed also by holy writers: by Cyril, Epiphanius, and others; by Ambrose in his *Hexameron*, and Tertullian in his poem, *De Judicio Domini;* but more agreeably unto the present sense, in his excellent tract, *De Resurrectione Carnis; Illum dico alitem orientis peculiarem, de singularitate famosum, de posteritate monstruosum; qui semetipsum libenter funerans renovat, natali fine decedens, atque succedens iterum phœnix. Ubi jam nemo, iterum ipse; quia non jam, alius idem.* The Scripture also seems to favour it, particularly that of Job xxi. In the in-

---

sup. 45. "The pictorial delineation of Osiris has indifferently a human head or that of a hawk; but never that of any other animals."—*Ib.* 57. Champollion mentions these, as "*quadrupèdes à tête d'oiseau.*"—*Précis du Systême Hiéroglyphique*, &c. 1828, p. 305.

[1] *But the original, &c.*] First added in the 3rd edition.

[2] *That there is but one phœnix, &c.*] It is really amusing to observe the humorous obstinacy of honest master Ross in defending every thing, however absurd, which is derived from "the ancient sages." That the phœnix is but rarely seen he thinks no marvel; its instinct teaching it to keep out of the way of man, the great tyrant of the creatures;—"for had Heliogabalus, that Roman glutton, met with him, he had devoured him, though there were no more in the world!" —*Arcana*, p. 202.

terpretation of Beda, *Dicebam, in nidulo meo moriar, et sicut phœnix multiplicabo dies:* and Psalm xxxi. δίκαιος ὥσπερ φοῖνιξ ἀνθήσει, *vir justus ut phœnix florebit,* as Tertullian renders it, and so also expounds it in his book, before alleged.

All which notwithstanding, we cannot presume the existence of this animal, nor dare we affirm there is any phœnix in nature. For first, there wants herein the definitive confirmator and test of things uncertain, that is, the sense of man. For though many writers have much enlarged hereon, yet is there not any ocular describer, or such as presumeth to confirm it upon aspection. And therefore Herodotus, that led the story unto the Greeks, plainly saith, he never attained the sight of any, but only in the picture.

Again, primitive authors, and from whom the stream of relations is derivative, deliver themselves very dubiously; and, either by a doubtful parenthesis or a timorous conclusion, overthrow the whole relation. Thus Herodotus, in his *Euterpe,* delivering the story hereof, presently interposeth ἐμοὶ μὲν οὐ πιστὰ λέγοντες; that is, "which account seems to me improbable." Tacitus, in his *Annals,* affordeth a larger story, how the phœnix was first seen at Heliopolis, in the reign of Sesostris, then in the reign of Amasis, after in the days of Ptolemy, the third of the Macedonian race; but at last thus determineth, *sed antiquitas obscura, et nonnulli falsum esse hunc phœnicem neque Arabum è terris credidere.* Pliny makes yet a fairer story, that the phœnix flew into Egypt in the consulship of Quintus Plancius, that it was brought to Rome in the censorship of Claudius, in the eight hundredth year of the city, and testified also in their records; but after all concludeth, *Sed quæ falsa nemo dubitabit,* as we read it in the fair and ancient impression of Brixa, as Aldrovandus hath quoted it, and it is found in the manuscript copy, as Dalechampius hath also noted.[3]

Moreover, such as have naturally discoursed hereon, have so diversely, contrarily, or contradictorily, delivered themselves, that no affirmative from thence can reasonably be deduced; for most have positively denied it, and they which affirm and believe it, assign this name unto many, and mistake two or three in one. So hath that bird been taken for

---

[3] *as we read, &c.*] First added in 3rd edition.

the phœnix, which liveth in Arabia, and buildeth its nest with cinnamon; by Herodotus called *cinnamulgus*, and by Aristotle *cinnamomus;* and as a fabulous conceit is censured by Scaliger. Some have conceived that bird to be the phœnix, which by a Persian name with the Greeks is called *rhyntace;* but how they make this good, we find occasion of doubt, whilst we read in the life of Artaxerxes, that this is a little bird brought often to their tables, and wherewith Parysatis cunningly poisoned the queen. The *manucodiata*, or bird of paradise, hath had the honour of this name, and their feathers, brought from the Moluccas, do pass for those of the phœnix. Which, though promoted by rarity with us, the eastern travellers will hardly admit; who know they are common in those parts, and the ordinary plume of Janizaries among the Turks. And lastly, the bird *semenda* hath found the same appellation, for so hath Scaliger observed and refuted: nor will the solitude of the phœnix allow this denomination, for many there are of that species, and whose trifistulary bill and crany we have beheld ourselves. Nor are men only at variance in regard of the phœnix itself, but very disagreeing in the accidents ascribed thereto; for some affirm it liveth three hundred, some five, others six, some a thousand, others, no less than fifteen hundred years; some say it liveth in Æthiopia, others, in Arabia, some in Egypt, others, in India, and some in *Utopia*,—for such a one must that be which is described by Lactantius; that is, which neither was singed in the combustion of Phaeton, nor overwhelmed by the inundation of Deucalion.[4]

Lastly, many authors, who have discoursed hereof, have so delivered themselves, and with such intentions, that we cannot from thence deduce a confirmation. For some have written poetically, as Ovid, Mantuan, Lactantius, Claudian, and others. Some have written mystically, as Paracelsus in his book, *De Azoth*, or *De Ligno et Linea Vitæ;* and as several hermetical philosophers, involving therein the secret of their elixir, and enigmatically expressing the nature of their great work. Some have written rhetorically and con-

---

[4] *the combustion of Phaeton, &c.*] The combustion of Phaeton was but in Italy only, and Deucalion's flood only in Attick: both farr inoughe from Arabia or Ægypt; soe that the phœnix, yf any were, might live secure inoughe from those 2 mischeefs.—*Wr.*

cessively, not controverting, but assuming the question, which taken as granted advantaged the illation. So have holy men made use hereof as far as thereby to confirm the resurrection; for discoursing with heathens, who granted the story of the phœnix, they induced the resurrection from principles of their own, and positions received among themselves. Others have spoken emblematically and hieroglyphically; and so did the Egyptians, unto whom the phœnix was the hieroglyphic of the sun.[5] And this was probably the ground of the whole relation; succeeding ages adding fabulous accounts, which laid together built up this singularity, which every pen proclaimeth.

As for the texts of Scripture which seem to confirm the conceit, duly perpended they add not thereunto. For whereas, in that of Job, according to the Septuagint or Greek translation, we find the word phœnix, yet can it have no animal signification; for therein it is not expressed φοῖνιξ, but στέλεχος φοίνικος, the trunk of the palm-tree, which is also called phœnix, and therefore the construction will be very hard, if not applied unto some vegetable nature. Nor can we safely insist upon the Greek expression at all; for though the vulgar translates it *palma*, and some retain the word phœnix, others do render it by a word of a different sense: for so hath Tremellius delivered it; *Dicebam quòd apud nidum meum expirabo, et sicut arena multiplicabo dies;* so hath the Geneva and ours translated it, "I said I shall die in my nest, and shall multiply my days as the sand." As for that in the book of Psalms, *Vir justus ut phœnix*[6] *florebit*, as Epiphanius and Tertullian render it, it was only a mistake upon the homonymy* of the Greek word phœnix, which signifies also a palm-tree. Which is a fallacy of equivocation, from a community in name inferring a common nature, and whereby we may as firmly conclude, that *diaphœnicon*, a purging electuary, hath some part of the phœnix for its ingredient; which receiveth that name from dates,

* Consent of names.

[5] *have spoken, &c.*] From Pierius, whose authority is Pliny (lib. x. c. ii.); but Pliny does not allude to the *hieroglyphic*. It is also adduced from Horapollo, 49, 111.

[6] *ut phœnix.*] i. e. ut palma.—*Wr.*

or the fruit of the palm-tree, from whence, as Pliny delivers, the phœnix had its name.⁷

Nor do we only arraign the existence of this animal, but many things are questionable which are ascribed thereto, especially its unity, long life, and generation. As for its unity or conceit, there should be but one in nature, it seemeth not only repugnant unto philosophy, but also Holy Scripture; which plainly affirms, there went of every sort, two at least into the ark of Noah, according to the text, "Every fowl after his kind, every bird of every sort, they went into the ark, two and two of all flesh, wherein there is the breath of life; and they that went in, went in both male and female of all flesh." * It infringeth the benediction of God concerning multiplication. God blessed them, saying, "Be fruitful and multiply, and fill the waters in the seas, and let fowl multiply in the earth:" † and again, "Bring forth with thee every living thing, that they may breed abundantly in the earth, and be fruitful and multiply upon the earth;" ‡ which terms are not appliable unto the phœnix, whereof there is but one in the world, and no more now living than at the first benediction. For, the production of one being the destruction of another, although they produce and generate, they increase not, and must not be said to multiply, who do not transcend an unity.

As for longevity, that it liveth a thousand years or more; beside that from imperfect observations and rarity of appearance, no confirmation can be made, there may be probably a mistake in the compute. For the tradition being very ancient and probably Egyptian, the Greeks, who dispersed the fable, might sum up the account by their own numeration of years; whereas the conceit might have its original in times of shorter compute. For if we suppose our present calculation, the phœnix now in nature will be the sixth from the creation, but in the middle of its years; and, if the rabbins' prophecy§ succeed, shall conclude its days, not in its own, but the last and general flames, without all hope of reviviction.

* Gen. vii. † Gen. i. ‡ Gen. viii.
§ That the world should last but six thousand years.

⁷ *its name.*] *Phœnix dactylifera*, the date-palm.

Concerning its generation, that without all conjunction it begets and reseminates itself, hereby we introduce a vegetable production in animals, and unto sensible natures transfer the propriety of plants; that is, to multiply within themselves, according to the law of the creation, " Let the earth bring forth grass, the herb yielding seed, and the tree yielding fruit, whose seed is in itself." * Which is indeed the natural way of plants, who, having no distinction of sex, and the power of the species contained in every *individuum*, beget and propagate themselves without commixtion;[8] and therefore the fruits, proceeding from simpler roots, are not so unlike or distinguishable from each other as are the offsprings of sensible creatures and prolifications descending from double originals. But animal generation is accomplished by more, and the concurrence of two sexes is required to the constitution of one.[9] And therefore such as have no distinction of sex, engender not at all, as Aristotle conceives of eels[1] and testaceous animals.[2] And though plant-animals

* Gen. i.

[8] *having no distinction of sex, &c.*] In correction of this assertion see note 1, p. 194.

[9] *But animal generation, &c.*] Sir Everard Home first suspected, and then proved, that in a particular tribe of fishes, comprising the lamprey, the organs of both sexes are present in the same individual.—See *Phil. Trans.* 1815, part ii. p. 266.

[1] *eels.*] Aristotel's conceyte of eeles was not unlike that other of his, of the galaxia and of comets, whereof the knowlege then was small. But in the end of April, 1654, and after some firce storms, which they say make eeles wander, a large one was brought, out of which wee tooke neer (50) young eeles alive, each above 1 inche and a halfe long, of the bignes of a bristle, which moved as quick as the old one. From whence it appeares manifestly that they doe engender and become viviparous, contrary to the opinion of the world hitherto. Soe that now wee may conclude that the eele, as well as the viper, is vermiparou? and viviparous, and not only (as the *natrix*) oviparous. And in the Severne they finde clots of young lampreys, which they call elvers, a finger's length, white, as big as a wheete straw, 40 or more in a cluster, which I have found of a very pleasant taste, and are accompted daintyes. That which deceaved the world hitherto was, that the brood of the eele comes to life sooner then the spawne of any fish, bycause, being never severed from the *matrix*, till itt have life, itt is of soden growth, in which time the damm never ranges, and as soon as they are formed, are layd in bankes, or beds of mud, undiscernable.— *Wr.*

[2] *testaceous animals.*] They present examples of all the modes of generation. Several of them possess the faculty of self-impregnation,

do multiply, they do it not by copulation, but in a way analogous unto plants. So hermaphrodites, although they include the parts of both sexes, and may be sufficiently potent in either, yet unto a conception require a separated sex, and cannot impregnate themselves. And so also, though Adam included all human nature, or was (as some opinion) an hermaphrodite, yet had he no power to propagate himself; and therefore God said, "It is not good that man should be alone, let us make him an help meet for him;" that is, an help unto generation; for, as for any other help, it had been fitter to have made another man.

Now, whereas some affirm that from one phœnix there doth not immediately proceed another, but the first corrupteth into a worm, which after becometh a phœnix, it will not make probable this production. For hereby they confound the generation of perfect animals with imperfect—sanguineous with exsanguineous—vermiparous with oviparous; and erect anomalies, disturbing the laws of nature. Nor will this corruptive production be easily made out in most imperfect generations: for although we deny not that many animals are vermiparous, begetting themselves at a distance, and as it were at the second hand (as generally insects, and more remarkably butterflies and silkworms), yet proceeds not this generation from a corruption of themselves, but rather a specifical and seminal diffusion, retaining still the idea of themselves, though it act that part awhile, in other shapes. And this will also hold in generations equivocal, and such as are not begotten from parents like themselves; so from frogs corrupting, proceed not frogs again; so if there be anatiferous trees,[3] whose corruption breaks forth into bernacles, yet if they corrupt, they degenerate into maggots, which produce not them again. For this were a confusion of corruptive and seminal production, and a frustration of that seminal power committed to animals at the creation. The problem might have been spared, "Why we love not our lice as well as our children?" Noah's ark had been needless, the graves of animals would be the fruitfullest

others, although hermaphrodites, have need of a reciprocal intercourse. Many have the sexes separated. Some are oviparous, others viviparous.—*Griffith's Cuvier*, vol. xii. p. 4.

[3] *if there be, &c.*] See note at end of book iii.

womb; for death would not destroy, but empeople the world again.

Since, therefore, we have so slender grounds to confirm the existence of the phœnix,—since there is no ocular witness of it—since, as we have declared, by authors from whom the story is derived, it stands rather rejected—since they who have seriously discoursed hereof have delivered themselves negatively, diversely, or contrarily—since many others cannot be drawn into the argument as writing poetically, rhetorically, enigmatically, hieroglyphically—since Holy Scripture alleged for it, duly perpended, doth not advantage it;—and lastly, since so strange a generation, unity and long life, hath neither experience nor reason to confirm,—how far to rely on this tradition we refer unto consideration.

But surely they were not well-wishers unto parable[4] physic, or remedies easily acquired, who derived medicines from the phœnix, as some have done, and are justly condemned by Pliny; *Irridere est, vitæ remedia post millesimum annum reditura monstrare;* "It is a folly to find out remedies that are not recoverable under a thousand years," or propose the prolonging of life by that which the twentieth generation may never behold. More veniable is a dependence upon the philosopher's stone, potable gold, or any of those *arcanas* whereby Paracelsus, that died himself at forty-seven, gloried that he could make other men immortal.[5] Which, although extremely difficult, and *tantum non* infesible, yet are they not impossible, nor do they (rightly understood) impose any violence on nature. And therefore, if strictly taken for the phœnix, very strange[6] is that which is

---

[4] *parable.*] Easily obtained;—*parabiles.*

[5] *Paracelsus, &c.*] This is noe wonder in them that convert soules; but to make bodyes immortall argues him either of folly or falsehood, that yf he could, would not make demonstration upon himselfe of such an admirable skill, as would have advanced him to sitt next the greatest monarchs of the world. But itt seemes that bragg descended from him to all his disciples (the chymicks) among whom, scarce one of a 1000, but dyes a beggar.—*Wr.*

[6] *And therefore, &c.*] Itt seemes the learned man was staggerd at Plutarch's assertion, by mistaking the worde φοῖνιξ, which there signifies the *palm-tree* (not the bird soe much talkt off, but never seene as yet). Now itt is this φοῖνιξ, or palm-tree, whereof Plutarch speakes, whose fruite (sayth hee) is sweet, but breeds headach, which is most true of the dates, which they call dactylos: the Greekes cald it

delivered by Plutarch,* that the brain thereof is a pleasant bit, but that it causeth the headache. Which, notwithstanding, the luxurious emperor † could never taste, though he had at his table many a phœnicopterus, yet had he not one phœnix; for though he expected and attempted it, we read not in Lampridius that he performed it; and, considering the unity thereof, it was a vain design, that is, to destroy any species, or mutilate the great accomplishment of six days. And although some conceive—and it may seem true, that there is in man a natural possibility to destroy the world in one generation; that is, by a general conspire to know no woman themselves, and disable all others also,—yet will this never be effected. And therefore Cain, after he had killed Abel, were there no other woman living, could not have also destroyed Eve; which, although he had a natural power to effect, yet the execution thereof the providence of God would have resisted; for that would have imposed another creation upon him, and to have animated a second rib of Adam.

CHAPTER XIII.

Of Frogs, Toads, and Toad-stone.

CONCERNING the venomous urine of toads, of the stone in the toad's head,[7] and of the generation of frogs, concep-

---

* *De Sanitate Tuenda.* † *Heliogabalus.*

ἐγκέφαλον, and the Latines *cerebrum*, and wee the brain. But of this ridiculous mistake, and the occasion of itt, see that merie passage of Muret (lib. XII. cap. xii. *Variorum*), worth the view, which itt seemes this doctor had not read.—*Wr.*

A similar criticism occurs in the *Gentleman's Magazine* for 1820, p. 420. It is very singular that these critics, especially the dean, should not have remarked that Sir Thomas was perfectly aware of this homonymy, as he called it (page 279), and by the expression here used, "*if* strictly taken for the phœnix," he evidently means that it is *not* so to be taken, but to be understood as referring to the fruit of the palm-tree.

[7] *Concerning, &c.*] The story of the jewel in the toad's head, celebrated in Shakspeare, must be classed among fables. Toads have uniformly been considered objects of aversion, and very generally are believed to be venomous. On this point contrary opinions have been held even by naturalists of the present day. Cuvier expressly denies it; the

tions are entertained which require consideration. And first, that a toad pisseth, and this way diffuseth its venom,

English editors of *Cuvier's Animal Kingdom* discountenance, though they do not absolutely deny, the accusation (vol. ix. 451); observing that toads are *comparatively* harmless: that when surprised, they distil from the tubercles on the skin a white and fetid humour;—shoot a peculiar fluid from the *anus;* and attempt to bite. But their bite occasions no great inconvenience, merely producing at times a slight inflammation. They assert that neither the liquid ejaculated from the *anus*, nor that which oozes from the skin, is venomous; yet they admit that, when swallowed, these fluids have produced violent nausea, &c. M. Bosc asserts that the same symptoms will be occasioned by putting the hand to the nose after handling the toad. Schelhammer mentions a child which had a severe pustulory eruption from having had a toad held some minutes before its mouth. They describe the liquid as very bitter, acrid, and caustic. In the 64th vol. of *Tilloch's Philosophical Magazine*, there is a paper, by Mr. Fothergill, on the manners and habits of the toad, in which he professes to prove "not only its innocency, but its usefulness." He relates many observations, proving its utility as a destroyer of caterpillars, &c.;—but in *proof* of their harmlessness he only offers the following expression of his own opinion. "The writer hopes he has established the character of toads as to their usefulness; and that they are devoid of all poisonous or venomous qualities whatever, he is perfectly satisfied, from many years' observation and experience, having handled them in all directions, opened their mouths, and given them every opportunity and every provocation to exert their venomous powers, if possessed of any." In short, he believes them to be the most patient and harmless of all reptiles!

Dr. John Davy, in a paper read before the Royal Society, Dec. 22, 1825, asserts the accuracy of the ancient opinion, that the toad is poisonous, but he does not appear to have made any new discovery of importance, unless it be that the fluid, secreted on the back, and existing in the bile, the blood, and the urine of the animal, is *not injurious*, much less *fatal*, when absorbed and carried into circulation. Other naturalists have admitted the acrid nature of the fluid, and even, in certain cases, its deleterious effects when taken into the stomach, who maintain that it is not venomous. On the whole, Dr. Davy does not appear to have proved that the toad is to be classed among *venomous reptiles*, properly so called.

White says, "he well remembers the time, when a quack, at this village, ate a toad to make the country people stare." He mentioned, from undoubted authority, that "some ladies took a fancy to a toad, which they nourished summer after summer for many years, till he grew to a monstrous size, with the maggots which turn to flesh flies. The reptile used to come forth every evening from a hole under the garden steps, and was taken up, after supper, on the table to be fed. He fell a sacrifice at length to a tame raven."

The fluid, ejected from the *anus* of toads and frogs (especially *R. temporaria*), is not urine.

is generally received, not only with us, but also in other parts; for so hath Scaliger observed in his comment, *Aversum urinam reddere ob oculos persecutoris perniciosam ruricolis persuasum est ;* and Matthiolus hath also a passage, that a toad communicates its venom not only by urine, but by the humidity and slaver of its mouth ;[8] which, notwithstanding, strictly understood, may admit of examination : for some doubt may be made whether a toad properly pisseth, that is, distinctly and separately voideth the serous excretion ; for though not only birds, but oviparous quadrupeds and serpents have kidneys and ureters, and some fishes also bladders; yet for the moist and dry excretion they seem at last to have but one vent and common place of exclusion; and with the same propriety of language we may ascribe that action unto crows and kites. And this not only in frogs and toads, but may be enquired in tortoises: that is, whether that be strictly true, or to be taken for a distinct and separate miction,[9] when Aristotle affirmeth, that no oviparous animal, that is, which either spawneth or layeth eggs, doth urine, except the tortoise.

The ground or occasion of this expression might from hence arise, that toads are sometimes observed to exclude or spirt out a dark and liquid matter behind :[1] which we have observed to be true, and a venomous condition there may be perhaps therein; but some doubt there may be, whether this is to be called their urine, not because it is emitted aversely

[8] *not only by urine, &c.*] A strange and horrible example of this (toade killing by the mouth) there fel out in Dorset, not far from my habitation. A countrywoman, having the young sonne of a great person to nurse, willing to visit her reapers in the next field, but not willing to leave the childe alone in the house asleep, took itt with her ; and while shee distributed some drinke to the workers, layd the childe at the foote of a barley-cock : whome, when shee came to take up againe, shee found dade and swolen, and turning up the cloaths of the childe, found a huge toade hanging fast on the bellicock of the child, which the venomous beast had wholy swalowed, and by that quil diffused his deadly poison into all the vital parts of the infant; at which sight the poore woman fell distracted.— *Wr.*

[9] *miction.*] Not in Johnson : evidently a coinage from the Latin word, *mingo.*

[1] *behind.*] And I have often seen this spirting, which the vulgar rationally call pissing, though itt be not urine, but certainlye something anilogicall.-- *Wr.*

or backward by both sexes, but because it is confounded with the intestinal excretions and egestions of the belly; and this way is ordinarily observed, although possible it is that the liquid excretion may sometimes be excluded without the other.[2]

As for the stone commonly called the toad-stone, which is presumed to be found in the head of that animal, we first conceive it not a thing impossible; nor is there any substantial reason why, in a toad, there may not be found such hard and lapideous concretions: for the like we daily observe in the heads of fishes, as cods, carps, and perches; the like also in snails, a soft and exosseous animal, whereof in the naked and greater sort, as though she would requite the defect of a shell on their back, nature, near the head,[3] hath placed a flat white stone, or rather testaceous concretion: which, though Aldrovandus affirms, that after dissection of many he found but in some few, yet of the great grey snails[4] I have not met with any that wanted it; and the same indeed so palpable, that without dissection it is discoverable by the hand.

Again, though it be not impossible, yet it is surely very rare; as we are induced to believe from some enquiry of our own, from the trial of many who have been deceived, and the frustrated search of Porta, who, upon the explorement of many, could scarce find one. Nor is it only of rarity, but may be doubted whether it be of existency, or really any such stone in the head of a toad at all. For although lapidaries and questuary enquirers affirm it, yet the writers of minerals and natural speculators are of another belief: conceiving the stones, which bear this name,[5] to be a mineral

---

[2] *and this way is, &c.*] This sentence was first added in the 6th edit.

[3] *near the head.*] In the very same place on the top of the back, where the shell of the other snayle is fastened. — *Wr.*

[4] *grey snails.*] I have heard itt avowched by persons of great quality, contemporarye to the old Lord Burleigh, Lord Treasurer of Englande, that hee alwayes wore a blue ribbon (next his leg, garter-wise) studded (thick) with these shels of the grey snayles, to allaye the heate of the goute, and that hee profest that hee found manifest releef in itt; and that yf by chance hee lefte itt off, the paine would ever returne most vehementlye.— *Wr.*

[5] *this name.*] Toadstone, or *bufonite*, a species of *traprock*, called *amygdaloid*. It occurs in the traprock of Derbyshire, near Matlock.

concretion, not to be found in animals, but in fields. And therefore Boëtius refers it to *asteria* or some kind of *lapis stellaris*, and plainly concludeth, *reperiuntur in agris, quos tamen alii in annosis, ac qui diu in arundinetis, inter rubos sentesque delituerunt, bufonis capitibus generari pertinaciter affirmant.*

Lastly, if any such thing there be, yet must it not, for aught I see, be taken as we receive it, for a loose and moveable stone, but rather a concretion or induration of the crany itself; for being of an earthy temper, living in the earth, and as some say feeding thereon, such indurations may sometimes happen. Thus when Brassavolus after a long search had discovered one, he affirms it was rather the forehead bone petrified, than a stone within the crany; and of this belief was Gesner. Which is also much confirmed from what is delivered in Aldrovandus, upon experiment of very many toads, whose cranies or sculls in time grew hard and almost of a stony substance.[6] All which considered, we must with circumspection receive those stones which commonly bear this name, much less believe the traditions, that in envy to mankind they are cast out, or swallowed down by the toad;[7] which cannot consist with anatomy, and with the rest enforced this censure from Boëtius, *ab eo tempore pro nugis habui quod de bufonio lapide, ejúsque origine traditur.*

What therefore best reconcileth these divided determinations, may be a middle opinion; that of these stones some may be mineral, and to be found in the earth, some animal, to be met with in toads, at least by the induration of their cranies. The first are many and manifold, to be found in Germany and other parts; the last are fewer in number, and in substance not unlike the stones in crabs' heads. This is agreeable unto the determination of Aldrovandus,* and is also the judgment of the learned Spigelius† in his epistle unto Pignorius.[8]

But these toadstones, at least very many thereof, which are esteemed among us, are at last found to be taken not

* *De Mineral.* lib. iv.　　† *Musei Calceolariani*, sect. iii.

[6] *Which is also, &c.*] First in 2nd edition.

[7] *toad.*] See an account of a toad being found in a duck's egg. *Literary Panorama*, Aug. 1807, p. 1083.—*Jeff.*

[8] *What, therefore, &c.*] First in 2nd edition.

out of toads' heads, but out of a fish's mouth, being handsomely contrived out of the teeth of the *lupus marinus*, a fish often taken in our northern seas, as was publickly declared by an eminent and learned physician.* But, because men are unwilling to conceive so low of their toad-stones which they so highly value, they may make some trial thereof by a candent or red-hot iron applied unto the hollow and unpolished part thereof, whereupon, if they be true stones, they will not be apt to burn or afford a burnt odour, which they may be apt to do, if contrived out of animal parts or the teeth of fishes.[9]

Concerning the generation of frogs, we shall briefly deliver that account which observation hath taught us. By frogs I understand, not such as, arising from putrefaction, are bred without copulation, and because they subsist not long, are called *temporariæ*;[1] nor do I mean the little frog of an excellent parrot-green, that usually sits on trees and bushes, and is therefore called *ranunculus viridis*, or *arboreus*; but hereby I understand the aquatile or water-frog, whereof, in ditches and standing plashes, we may behold many millions every spring in England. Now these do not, as Pliny conceiveth, exclude black pieces of flesh, which after become frogs; but they let fall their spawn in the water, of excellent use in physic,[2] and scarce unknown unto any. In this spawn, of a lentous and transparent body, are to be discerned many specks, or little conglobations, which in a small time become of a deep black, a substance more

* Sir George Ent.

But these toad-stones, &c.] First in 6th edition.

[1] *temporaria.*] It is truly wonderful that Sir Thomas, who was not unacquainted with the generation of the frog, and who in this paragraph has correctly distinguished three species, the *temporaria*, or common garden-frog, the tree-frog, and the water-frog (the *esculenta*), should propose a position so gratuitous and absurd as that *one* of these species owes its origin to putrefaction.

[2] *spawn in the water, &c.*] The happiest experiment of this water, that I ever yet saw, was at Sir Thomas Coghil's, of Bletchington: where his eldest sonne, the squire (a widower) after a full liberal use of new claret in the must, for (5) continuate days fell into such an hæmorraghia at the nose, as by all applications inward and outward could not in 30 hours bee stopt; at last, sending for the surgeon, diverted itt by phlebotomy: the surgeon advisedly refusing to do itt, till he had given a scruple of diascordium in that water which saved it.—*Wr.*

compacted and terrestrious than the other; for it riseth not in distillation, and affords a powder when the white and aqueous part is exhaled. Now of this black or dusky substance is the frog at last formed; as we have beheld, including the spawn with water in a glass, and exposing it unto the sun. For that black and round substance, in a few days, began to dilate and grow longer, after awhile, the head, the eyes, the tail, to be discernible, and at last to become that which the ancients called *gyrinus*,[3] we a porwigle, or tadpole.[4] This in some weeks after becomes a perfect frog, the legs growing out before, and the tail wearing away, to supply the other behind; as may be observed in some which have newly forsaken the water; for in such, some part of the tail will be seen, but curtailed and short, not long and finny as before. A part provided them awhile to swim and move in the water, that is, until such time as nature excluded legs, whereby they might be provided not only to swim in the water, but

---

[3] *gyrinus*.] This is the name of a genus of beetles.

[4] *tadpole*.] Upon tryall I found that the tayle, after the space of a moone from the spawning, by degrees parted itt self into 2 legs, drawing dayly more and more till itt came to the vent of the belly. This experiment I made at Bishop's Fonntill, Wiltes, where having digd a new pond, in a fatty soil of white malme, upon the head of a strong spring (the midst of October, 1625), I let it rest till February following, at what time observing the banks full of spawne, I caused a bottomless tubb, perforated with small holes, to bee sett in the pond, into which I putt a great quantity of spawne, at the full of the moone watching itt every day till the next full moone in March: by which times the tayles being growne 2 inches (like the tayle of a bleake or small gogeon) began visibly to grow *bifide*, and after one weeke was perfectly shaped into 2 legs, by help whereof, they gott over the tub into the neighbor pond, where they became an excellent food for some store of trouts, which used to feed from my hand, and grew so large thereby, that one of them was full 22 inches fish between the head and the tayle; as some worthy friends yet living can well remember, being present both at the taking and the eating.

Since this observation of the fishye tayle of a frog *clearing* into 2 legs, I conceave that the Spaniards make a wholesome viand, and connt itt a dish fitt for a princes table: which putts mee in minde of a storye which I received from my brother, the new Lord Bp. of Elye, and Count Palatine: what time following (the then) Prince Charles into Spain by appointment, and were come into the porte at Laredo, they were invited by the governor to dinner, and at the second course had a dish of the hinder legs of *these* frogs fryed, as a dainty of more esteem with them then the patrich.—*Wr.*

move upon the land, according to the amphibious and mixt intention of nature, that is to live in both. So that whoever observeth the first progression of the seed before motion, or shall take notice of the strange indistinction of parts in the tadpole, even when it moveth about, and how successively the inward parts do seem to discover themselves, until their last perfection, may easily discern the high curiosity of nature in these inferior animals, and what a long line is run to make a frog.

And because many affirm and some deliver, that in regard it hath lungs and breatheth, a frog may be easily drowned, though the reason be probable, I find not the experiment answerable; for fastening one about a span under water, it lived almost six days. Nor is it only hard to destroy one in water, but difficult also at land: for it will live long after the lungs and heart be out; how long it will live in the seed, or whether the spawn of this year being preserved, will not arise into frogs in the next, might also be enquired: and we are prepared to try.[5]

CHAPTER XIV.

That a Salamander lives in the fire.

THAT a salamander is able to live in flames, to endure and put out fire, is an assertion, not only of great antiquity, but confirmed by frequent and not contemptible testimony. The Egyptians have drawn it into their hieroglyphicks,[6] Aristotle seemeth to embrace it; more plainly Nicander, Sarenus Sammonicus, Ælian, and Pliny, who assigns the cause of this effect: an animal (saith he) so cold, that it extinguisheth the fire like ice. All which notwithstanding, there is on the negative, authority and experience; Sextius a physician, as Pliny delivereth, denied this effect; Dioscorides affirmed it a point of folly to believe it; Galen, that it endureth the fire awhile, but in continuance is consumed therein. For expe-

---

[5] *Nor is it only, &c.*] First added in 5th edition.
[6] *The Egyptians, &c.*] So says Pierius (p. 162, H), but without authority. "*Le lézard*" is mentioned by Champollion as an Egyptian hieroglyphick.—*Précis*, p. 303.

rimental conviction, Matthiolus affirmeth, he saw a salamander burnt in a very short time; and of the like assertion is Amatus Lusitanus; and most plainly Pierius, whose words in his hieroglyphicks are these: " Whereas it is commonly said, that a salamander extinguisheth fire, we have found by experience, that it is so far from quenching hot coals, that it dyeth immediately therein." As for the contrary assertion of Aristotle, it is but by hearsay, ' as common opinion believeth,'—*Hæc enim (ut aiunt) ignem ingrediens eum extinguit;* and therefore, there was no absurdity in Galen, when as a septical medicine* he commended the ashes of a salamander; and magicians in vain, from the power of this tradition, at the burning of towns and houses expect a relief from salamanders.

The ground of this opinion might be some sensible resistance of fire observed in the salamander: which being, as Galen determineth, cold in the fourth, and moist in the third degree, and having also a mucous humidity above and under the skin, by virtue thereof it may awhile endure the flame; which being consumed it can resist no more. Such an humidity there is observed in newts or water-lizards, especially if their skins be perforated or pricked; thus will frogs and snails endure the flame; thus will whites of eggs, vitreous or glassy phlegm, extinguish a coal; thus are unguents made which protect awhile from the fire; and thus, beside the *Hirpini*, there are later stories of men that have passed untouched through the fire. And therefore some truth we allow in the tradition: truth according unto Galen, that it may for a time resist a flame, or, as Scaliger avers, extinguish or put out a coal; for thus much will many humid bodies perform: but that it perseveres and lives in that destructive element, is a fallacious enlargement. Nor do we reasonably conclude, because for a time it endureth fire, it subdueth and extinguisheth the same,—because by a cold and aluminous moisture it is able awhile to resist it, from a peculiarity of nature it subsisteth and liveth in it.

It hath been much promoted by stories of incombustible napkins and textures which endure the fire, whose materials are called by the name of salamander's wool. Which many

---

* A corruptive medicine, destroying the parts like arsenic.

too literally apprehending, conceive some investing part, or tegument of the salamander: wherein, beside that they mistake the condition of this animal (which is a kind of lizard, a quadruped corticated and depilous, that is, without wool, fur, or hair),[7] they observe not the method and general rule of nature; whereby all quadrupeds oviparous, as lizards, frogs, tortoises, chameleons, crocodiles, are without hair, and have no covering part or hairy investment at all. And if they conceive that, from the skin of the salamander, these incremable[8] pieces are composed, beside the experiments made upon the living, that of Brassavolus will step in, who, in the search of this truth, did burn the skin of one dead.

Nor is this salamander's wool desumed[9] from any animal, but a mineral substance, metaphorically so called from this received opinion. For (besides Germanicus's heart, and Pyrrhus's great toe, which would not burn with the rest of their bodies), there are, in the number of minerals, some bodies incombustible; more remarkably that which the ancients named *asbeston*,[1] and Pancirollus treats of in the chapter of *linum vivum*. Whereof by art were weaved napkins,[2] shirts, and coats, inconsumable by fire; and wherein

---

[7] *which is a kind of lizard, &c.*] *Lacerta Salamandra, Lin.* The salamanders constitute a separate group among the order *Batrachia*, of the class *Reptilia*:—divided into land and water salamanders; to the former of which belongs the Linnean salamander, and to the latter, the water-lizard, or *newt*. It is scarcely necessary to say that the fire story is a mere fable.

[8] *incremable*.] Incombustible.

[9] *desumed*.] Obtained, taken from.

[1] *asbeston*.] *Asbeston* is a mineral, of which there are five varieties;— 1. *Amianthus*, or *fibrous*. The ancients manufactured cloth of this; and several moderns have succeeded in doing the same. 2. *Common asbestus*. 3. *Mountain leather*, or when very thin, *mountain paper:* consists of fibrous parts so interwoven as to become tough. 4. *Mountain cork*, or *elastic asbestus:* resembles the preceding, but elastic. It swims on water; receives an impression from the nail; and is very tough. 5. *Mountain wood*, or *ligniform asbestus*, has the aspect of wood; internal lustre glimmering; soft, sectile, and tough. (*Ure*.)

Fibres of asbestus have been employed to make lamps.

It is not, however, absolutely indestructible by fire, though it long resists its action.

[2] *napkins*.] Sir Henrye Wooton (embassador att Venice almost twenty yeares) among many other choyce rarittyes had one of these

in ancient times, to preserve their ashes pure and without commixture, they burnt the bodies of kings. A napkin hereof Pliny reports that Nero had; and the like, saith Paulus Venetus, the emperor of Tartary sent unto Pope Alexander; and also affirms that in some part of Tartary there were mines of iron whose filaments were woven into incombustible cloth. Which rare manufacture, although delivered for lost by Pancirollus, yet Salmuth, his commentator, affirmeth, that one Podocaterus, a Cyprian, had showed the same at Venice; and his materials were from Cyprus, where indeed, Dioscorides placeth them; the same is also ocularly confirmed by Vives upon Austin, and Maiolus in his *Colloquies*. And thus in our days do men practise to make long-lasting snasts[3] for lamps out of *alumen plumosum;* and by the same we read in Pausanias, that there always burnt a lamp before the image of Minerva.

CHAPTER XV.

Of the Amphisbæna.

THAT the amphisbæna, that is, a smaller kind of serpent, which moveth forward and backward, hath two heads, or one at either extreme, was affirmed first by Nicander, and after by many others—by the author of the book, *De Theriaca ad Pisonem*, ascribed unto Galen; more plainly Pliny, *Geminum habet caput, tanquam parum esset uno ore effundi venenum;* but Ælian most confidently, who referring the conceit of *chimæra* and *hydra* unto fables, hath set down this as an undeniable truth.

Whereunto while men assent, and can believe a bicipitous conformation in any continued species, they admit a gemination of principal parts, not naturally discovered in any animal. True it is, that other parts in animals are not equal; for some make their progression with many legs, even to the number of an hundred, as *juli, scolopendræ,* or

---

napkins, which hee told mee hee could never gaine for moneye, till the Duke sent him that one for a new year's gifte.—*Wr.*

[3] *snasts.*] The burnt wicks of candles. A Norfolk provincialism. See *Forby's Vocab.*

such as are termed *centipedes;* some fly with two wings, as birds and many insects; some with four, as all farinaceous or mealy-winged animals, as butterflies and moths; all vaginipennous or sheath-winged insects, as beetles and dorrs; some have three testicles, as Aristotle speaks of the buzzard; and some have four stomachs, as horned and ruminating animals; but, for the principal parts, the liver, heart, and especially the brain, regularly they are but one in any kind of species whatsoever.

And were there any such species or natural kind of animal, it would be hard to make good those six positions of body, which according to the three dimensions are ascribed unto every animal; that is, *infra, supra, ante, retro, dextrorsum, sinistrorsum:* for if (as it is determined) that be the anterior and upper part wherein the senses are placed, and that the posterior and lower part which is opposite thereunto, there is no inferior or former part in this animal: for the senses being placed at both extremes, doth make both ends anterior, which is impossible, the terms being relative, which mutually subsist, and are not without each other. And therefore this duplicity was ill contrived, to place one head at both extremes, and had been more tolerable to have settled three or four at one. And, therefore, also, poets have been more reasonable than philosophers, and *Geryon* or *Cerberus* less monstrous than amphisbæna.

Again, if any such thing there were, it were not to be obtruded by the name of amphisbæna, or as an animal of one denomination; for properly that animal is not one, but multiplicious or many, which hath a duplicity or gemination of principal parts. And this doth Aristotle define, when he affirmeth a monster is to be esteemed one or many, according to its principle, which he conceived the heart; whence he derived the original of nerves, and thereto ascribed many acts which physicians assign unto the brain. And therefore, if it cannot be called one, which hath a duplicity of hearts in his sense, it cannot receive that appellation with a plurality of heads in ours. And this the practice of Christians hath acknowledged, who have baptized these geminous births and double connascencies, with several names, as conceiving in them a distinction of souls, upon the divided execution of their functions; that is, while one wept, the other laughing;

while one was silent, the other speaking; while one awaked, the other sleeping; as is declared by three remarkable examples in Petrarch, Vincentius, and the Scottish history of Buchanan.

It is not denied there have been bicipitous serpents with the head at each extreme, for an example hereof we find in Aristotle, and of the like form in Aldrovandus we meet with the icon of a lizard; and of this kind, perhaps, might that amphisbæna be, the picture whereof Cassianus Puteus showed unto the learned Faber.[4] Which double formations do often happen unto multiparous generations, more especially that of serpents; whose productions being numerous, and their eggs in chains or links together (which sometime conjoin and inosculate into each other), they may unite into various shapes, and come out in mixed formations. But these are monstrous productions, beside the intention of nature, and the statutes of generation, neither begotten of like parents, nor begetting the like again; but, irregularly produced, do stand as anomalies in the general book of nature. Which being shifts and forced pieces, rather than genuine and proper effects, they afford us no illation; nor is it reasonable to conclude from a monstrosity unto a species, or from accidental effects unto the regular works of nature.

Lastly, the ground of the conceit was the figure of this animal, and motion ofttimes both ways; for described it is to be like a worm, and so equally framed at both extremes, that at an ordinary distance it is no easy matter to determine which is the head; and therefore, some observing them to move both ways, have given the appellation of heads unto both extremes, which is no proper and warrantable denomination:[5] for many animals, with one head, do ordinarily perform both different and contrary motions; crabs move sideling, lobsters will swim swiftly backward, worms and leeches

[4] *and of this kind, &c.*] First in 3rd edition.
[5] *so equally framed, &c.*] This explanation is quite correct. The *amphisbæna* is characterized by the rings of square scales which surround its body, and by its tail, being nearly similar in form and size to the head, so that it is not easy at a glance to distinguish the one from the other, the eyes being remarkably small. They are not venomous; and have the power of moving both backwards and forwards—whence their name. It is very unaccountably spelt *amphisbæna*, in *Griffith's Cuvier*, and in *Gray's Synopsis*, at the end of the 9th vol. of that work

will move both ways, and so will most of those animals whose bodies consist of round and annulary fibres, and move by undulation; that is, like the waves of the sea, the one protruding the other, by inversion whereof they make a backward motion.

Upon the same ground hath arisen the same mistake concerning the scolopendra or hundred-footed insect, as is delivered by Rhodiginus from the scholiast of Nicander: *Dicitur à Nicandro,* ἀμφικαρὴς, *id est, dicephalus aut biceps fictum vero, quoniam retrorsum* (*ut scribit Aristotles*) *arrepit*, observed by Aldrovandus, but most plainly by Muffetus, who thus concludeth upon the text of Nicander: *Tamen pace tanti authoris dixerim, unicum illi duntaxat caput, licèt pari facilitate, prorsum capite, retrorsum ducente caudâ, incedat, quod Nicandro aliisque imposuisse dubito:* that is, under favour of so great an author, the scolopendra hath but one head, although with equal facility it moveth forward and backward, which I suspect deceived Nicander and others.

And therefore we must crave leave to doubt of this double-headed serpent until we have the advantage to behold, or have an iterated ocular testimony concerning such as are sometimes mentioned by American relators, and also such as Cassianus Puteus showed in a picture to Joannes Faber, and that which is set down under the name of *amphisbæna europæa*, in his learned discourse upon *Hernandez's History of America*.[6]

CHAPTER XVI.

That young Vipers force their way through the bowels of their Dam.

THAT the young vipers force their way through the bowels of their dam, or that the female viper, in the act of generation, bites off the head of the male, in revenge whereof the young ones eat through the womb and belly of the female, is a very ancient tradition; in this sense entertained in the hieroglyphicks of the Egyptians;[7] affirmed by Herodotus, Nicander, Pliny, Plutarch, Ælian, Jerome, Basil, Isidore;

---

[6] *And therefore, &c.*] First added in 6th edition.
[7] *in this sense, &c.*] Also from Pierius, 143, c. and Horapollo, 115.

seems countenanced by Aristotle and his scholar Theophrastus: from hence is commonly assigned the reason why the Romans punished parricides by drowning them in a sack with a viper. And so perhaps, upon the same opinion, the men of Melita, when they saw a viper upon the hand of Paul, said presently, without conceit of any other sin, "No doubt this man is a murderer, who, though he have escaped the sea, yet vengeance suffereth him not to live:" that is, he is now paid in his own way, the parricidous animal and punishment of murderers is upon him. And though the tradition were current among the Greeks, to confirm the same, the Latin name is introduced, *Vipera quasi vi pariat*. That passage also in the gospel, "O ye generation of vipers!" hath found expositions which countenance this conceit. Notwithstanding which authorities, transcribed relations and conjectures, upon enquiry we find the same repugnant unto experience and reason.[8]

And first, it seems not only injurious unto the providence of nature, to ordain a way of production which should destroy the producer, or contrive the continuation of the species by the destruction of the continuator, but it overthrows and frustrates the great benediction of God, " God blessed them, saying, be fruitful and multiply." Now, if it be so ordained that some must regularly perish by multiplication, and these be the fruits of fructifying in the viper, it cannot be said that God did bless, but curse, this animal; " Upon thy belly shalt thou go, and dust shalt thou eat all thy life," was not so great a punishment unto the serpent after the fall, as " increase, be fruitful, and multiply," was, before. This were to confound the maledictions of God, and translate the curse of the woman upon the serpent; that is, *in dolore paries*, " in sorrow shalt thou bring forth;" which, being proper unto the woman, is verified best in the viper, whose delivery is not only accompanied with pain, but also

---

[8] *and reason.*] Honest master Ross is very pertinacious in his opposition to the arguments of our author, as to the improbability and unreasonableness of the vulgar tenet respecting the viper—that it loses its own life in giving life to its progeny; and in some respects he opposes them with some plausibility. (See *Arcana*, page 149.) For there are not wanting parallels and well-authenticated cases in which the act of propagation is fatal: though in the present case it is not so.

with death itself. And lastly, it overthrows the careful course and parental provision of nature, whereby the young ones newly excluded are sustained by the dam, and protected until they grow up to a sufficiency for themselves. All which is perverted in this eruptive generation; for the dam being destroyed, the younglings are left to their own protection; which is not conceivable they can at all perform, and whereof they afford us a remarkable confirmance many days after birth: for the young ones, supposed to break through the belly of the dam, will, upon any fright, for protection run into it; for then the old one receives them in at her mouth, which way, the fright being past, they will return again;[9] which is a peculiar way of refuge, and although it

---

[9] *will upon any fright, &c.*] This is admitted to be true of the rattlesnake, but denied of the viper. I subjoin two passages from *Cuvier*, by Griffith, vol. ix. pp. 344, 356.

"The *crotali* are viviparous; at Martinique it is the general persuasion that the offspring are eaten by the vipers when they are very young, and a little after their birth. According to M. Palisot de Beauvois, this prejudice derives its origin from a fact wrongly interpreted. In the first journey made by this naturalist, in the country of the native *Tcharlokee*, he saw a *crotalus horridus* in a path, and approached it as softly as possible. At the moment when it was about to be struck, the animal agitated its rattles, opened a wide throat, and received into it five little ones, about as thick each as a goose-quill. But at the end of ten minutes, believing itself out of danger, it opened its mouth again and let the young ones out, which, however, entered there again, on the appearance of a new danger. M. Guillemart, a countryman of our own, has verified the same fact."

"In the fine days of early spring, the vipers may be seen basking in the morning sun, on little hills exposed to an eastern aspect, and they speedily occupy themselves in the great work of propagating their species. The act of generation takes a very long time in its accomplishment, and its result is the vivification of from twelve to twenty-five eggs, almost as large as those of wrens or titmice. These exclude the young, in the womb of the mother, and there they remain coiled up, and come to the length of three or four inches before they issue forth, which they generally do in the course of the fourth month after fecundation. Having thus, by a sort of parturition, quitted their mother, the young vipers, for some time after, carry with them the remains of the egg which enclosed them, and which then have the appearance of irregularly torn membranes. But from that time they are entirely strangers to the being which gave them birth, and do not seek refuge in her mouth, or the approach of danger, as the ancients erroneously imagined."

This resemblance of the remains of the egg which the young vipers

seem strange, is avowed by frequent experience and undeniable testimony.[1]

As for the experiment, although we have thrice attempted it, it hath not well succeeded; for though we fed them with milk, bran, cheese, &c. the females always died before the young ones were mature for this eruption; but rest sufficiently confirmed in the experiments of worthy enquirers. Wherein to omit the ancient conviction of Apollonius, we shall set down some few of modern writers. The first, of Amatus Lusitanus, in his comment upon Dioscorides, *Vidimus nos viperas prægnantes inclusas pixidibus parere, quæ*

---

carry about with them, to "irregularly torn membranes," may possibly have promoted the popular error under discussion. White has the following remarks.

"Though they are oviparous, yet they are viviparous also, hatching their young within their bellies, and then bringing them forth. Whereas snakes lay chains of eggs every summer in my melon-beds, in spite of all that my people can do to prevent them; which eggs do not hatch till the spring following, as I have often experienced. Several intelligent folks assure me that they have seen the viper open her mouth and admit her helpless young down her throat on sudden surprises, just as the female opossum does her brood into the pouch under her belly, upon the like emergencies; and yet the London viper-catchers insist on it, to Mr. Barrington, that no such thing ever happens."

"On August the 4th, 1775, we surprised a large viper, which seemed very heavy and bloated, as it lay in the grass basking in the sun. When we came to cut it up, we found that the abdomen was crowded with young, fifteen in number; the shortest of which measured full seven inches, and were about the size of full-grown earth-worms. This little fry issued into the world with the true viper-spirit about them, showing great alertness as soon as disengaged from the belly of the dam: they twisted and wriggled about, and set themselves up, and gaped very wide when touched with a stick, showing manifest tokens of menace and defiance, though as yet they had no manner of fangs that we could find, even with the help of our glasses."

"There was little room to suppose that this brood had ever been in the open air before; and that they were taken in for refuge, at the mouth of the dam, when she perceived that danger was approaching; because then probably we should have found them somewhere in the neck, and not in the abdomen."

[1] *undeniable testimony.*] Particularly by Scaliger, *Exercit.* 101, ἐξ αὐτοψία. The like is sayde of the weasel, that shee brings forth at the mouth, bycause they saw her remove her young ones with her mouth. And that Juno turned Galanthis, Alcmena's mayd, into a weasel, εἰς τὴν γαλῆν, bycause shee had cousened her with a lye, that her mistress was brought a bed.—*Wr.*

inde ex partu nec mortuæ, nec visceribus perforatæ manserunt. The second is that of Scaliger, *Viperas ab impatientibus moræ fœtibus numerosissimis rumpi atque interire, falsum esse scimus, qui in Vincentii Camerini circulatoris lignea theca vidimus enatas viperellas, parente salvâ.* The last, and most plain of Franciscus Bustamantinus, a Spanish physician of Alcala de Henares, whose words, in his third *De Animantibus Scripturæ*, are these: *Cùm verò per me et per alios hæc ipsa disquisissem servatâ viperina progenie, &c.* that is, when by myself and others, I had enquired the truth hereof, including vipers in a glass, and feeding them with cheese and bran, I undoubtedly found, that the viper was not delivered by the tearing of her bowels; but I beheld the young ones excluded by the passage of generation, near the orifice of the siege.[2] Whereto we might also add the ocular confirmation of Lacuna upon Dioscorides, Ferdinandus Imperatus, and that learned physician of Naples, Aurelius Severinus.[3]

Now, although the tradition be untrue, there wanted not many grounds which made it plausibly received. The first was, a favourable indulgence and special contrivance of nature, which was the conceit of Herodotus, who thus delivereth himself:—" Fearful animals, and such as serve for food, nature hath made more fruitful; but upon the offensive and noxious kind she hath not conferred fertility. So the hare, that becometh a prey unto man, unto beasts, and fowls of the air, is fruitful even to superfœtation; but the lion, a fierce and ferocious animal, hath young ones but seldom, and also but one at a time. Vipers indeed, although destructive, are fruitful; but, lest their numbers should increase, Providence hath contrived another way to abate it; for in copulation the female bites off the head of the male, and the young ones destroy the mother." But this will not consist with reason, as we have declared before. And if we more nearly consider the condition of vipers and noxious animals, we shall discover another higher provision of nature: how, although in their paucity she hath not abridged their malignity, yet hath she notoriously effected it by their secession or latitancy. For not

---

[2] *I undoubtedly found, &c.*] This is perfectly correct. See note 9, p. 299.

[3] *Whereto, &c.*] First added in 3rd edition.

only offensive insects, as hornets, wasps, and the like, but sanguineous corticated animals, as serpents, toads, and lizards, do lie hid and betake themselves to coverts in the winter. Whereby most countries enjoying the immunity of Ireland and Candy, there ariseth a temporal security from their venoms, and an intermission of their mischiefs, mercifully requiting the time of their activities.

A second ground of this effect was conceived, the justice of nature, whereby she compensates the death of the father by the matricide or murder of the mother; and this was the expression of Nicander. But the cause hereof is as improbable as the effect; and were indeed an improvident revenge in the young ones, whereby in consequence, and upon defect of provision, they must destroy themselves. And whereas he expresseth this decollation of the male by so full a term as ἀποκόπτειν, that is, to cut or lop off, the act is hardly conceivable; for the female viper hath but two considerable teeth, and those so disposed, so slender and needle-pointed, that they are apter for puncture than any act of incision. And if any like action there be, it may be only some fast retention or sudden compression in the *orgasmus* or fury of their lust, according as that expression of Horace is construed concerning Lydia and Telephus;

—— Sive puer furens,
Impressit memorem dente labris notam.

Others ascribe this effect unto the numerous conception of the viper; and this was the opinion of Theophrastus; who, though he denieth the exesion or forcing through the belly, conceiveth nevertheless that, upon a full and plentiful impletion there may, perhaps, succeed a disruption of the matrix, as it happeneth sometimes in the long and slender fish *acus*.*
Now, although in hot countries, and very numerous conceptions, in the viper or other animals, there may sometimes ensue a dilaceration of the genital parts, yet is this a rare and contingent effect, and not a natural and constant way of exclusion. For the wise Creator hath formed the organs of animals unto their operations, and in whom he ordaineth a

---

* Needle-fish; found sometimes upon the sea-shore, consisting of four lines unto the vent, and six from thence unto the head.

numerous conception, in them he hath prepared convenient receptacles, and a suitable way of exclusion.

Others do ground this disruption upon their continued or protracted time of delivery, presumed to last twenty days; whereat, excluding but one a day, the latter brood, impatient, by a forcible proruption anticipate their period of exclusion; and this was the assertion of Pliny, *Cæteri tarditatis impatientes prorumpunt latera, occisâ parente;* which was occasioned upon a mistake of the Greek text in Aristotle, τίκτει δὲ ἐν μιᾷ ἡμέρᾳ καθ' ἕν, τίκτει δὲ πλείω ἢ εἴκοσιν, which are literally thus translated, *Parit autem unâ die secundùm unum, parit autem plures quàm viginti,* and may be thus Englished: "She bringeth forth in one day, one by one, and sometimes more than twenty:" and so hath Scaliger rendered it, *Sigillatim parit, absolvit unâ die, interdum plures quàm viginti;* but Pliny, whom Gaza followeth, hath differently translated it, *Singulos diebus singulis parit, numero fere viginti;* whereby he extends the exclusion unto twenty days, which in the textuary sense is fully accomplished in one.

But what hath most advanced it, is a mistake in another text of Aristotle, which seemeth directly to determine this disruption, τίκτει μικρὰ ἐχίδεια ἐν ὑμέσιν, αἳ περιῤῥήγνωνται τριταῖοι, ἐνίοτε δὲ καὶ ἔσωθεν διαφαγόντα αὐτὰ ἐξέρχεται, which Gaza hath thus translated: *Parit catulos obvolutos membranis, quæ tertio die rumpuntur, evenit interdum ut qui in utero adhuc sunt abrosis membranis prorumpant.* Now herein probably Pliny, and many since have been mistaken; for the disruption of the membranes or skins, which include the young ones, conceiving a dilaceration of the matrix and belly of the viper; and concluding, from a casual dilaceration, a regular and constant disruption.

As for the Latin word, *vipera,* which in the etymology of Isidore promoteth this conceit, more properly it may imply *vivipera.*[4] For whereas other serpents lay eggs,[5] the viper excludeth living animals; and though the *cerastes* be also viviparous, and we have found formed snakes in the belly of the *cæcilia* or slow-worm, yet may the viper emphatically

---

[4] *As for the Latin word, &c.*] The correct derivation of the word is here assigned.

[5] *eggs.*] That the eele is *vivipara,* see my demonstrative note 1, supra, p. 281.

bear the name For the notation or etymology is not of necessity adequate unto the name; and therefore, though animal be deduced from *anima*, yet are there many animations beside, and plants will challenge a right therein as well as sensible creatures.

As touching the texts of Scripture, and compellation of the Pharisees by "generation of vipers," although constructions be made hereof conformable to this tradition, and it may be plausibly expounded, that out of a viperous condition they conspired against their prophets and destroyed their spiritual parents; yet (as Jansenius observeth) Gregory and Jerome do make another construction; apprehending thereby what is usually implied by that proverb, *Mali corvi, malum ovum;* that is, "of evil parents, an evil generation," a posterity not unlike their majority, of mischievous progenitors a venomous and destructive progeny.

And lastly, concerning the hieroglyphical account, according to the vulgar conception set down by Orus Apollo, the authority thereof is only emblematical; for were the conception true or false, to their apprehensions it expressed filial impiety:[6] which strictly taken, and totally received for truth, might perhaps begin, but surely promote this conception.

More doubtful assertions have been raised of no animal than the viper, as we have dispersedly noted; and Francisco Redi hath amply discovered in his noble observations of vipers:[7] from good reasons and iterated experiments affirming, that a viper containeth no humour, excrement, or part which, either drank or eat, is able to kill any; that the *remorsores* or dog-teeth, are not more than two in either sex; that these teeth are hollow, and though they bite and prick therewith, yet are they not venomous, but only open a way and entrance unto the poison, which notwithstanding is not poisonous except it touch or attain unto the blood; and that there is no other poison in this animal, but only that almost insipid liquor like oil of almonds, which stagnates in the sheaths and cases that cover the teeth; and that this pro-

---

[6] *it expressed filial impiety.*] Correct, so far as the vulgar conception set down by Orus Apollo, 115. See Champollion, *Précis,* p. 303.

[7] *Francisco Redi, &c.*] Redi's experiments, as detailed in this paragraph, have been confirmed by later observations.

ceeds not from the bladder of gall, but is rather generated in the head, and perhaps demitted and sent from thence into these cases by salival conduits and passages, which the head communicateth unto them.[8]

CHAPTER XVII.

That Hares are both male and female.

THE double sex of single hares, or that every hare is both male and female, beside the vulgar opinion, was the affirmative of Archelaus, of Plutarch, Philostratus, and many more. Of the same belief have been the Jewish rabbins. The same is likewise confirmed from the Hebrew word, * which, as though there were no single males of that kind, hath only obtained a name of the feminine gender. As also from the symbolical foundation of its prohibition in the law,† and what vices therein it figured; that is, not only pusillanimity and timidity from its temper, feneration[9] or usury from its fœcundity and superfetation, but from this mixture of sexes, unnatural venery and degenerous effemination.[1] Nor are there hardly any who either treat of mutation or mixtion of sexes, who have not left some mention of this point; some speaking positively, others dubiously, and most resigning it unto the enquiry of the reader. Now hereof to speak distinctly, they must be male and female by mutation and succession of sexes, or else by composition, mixture, or union thereof.

As for the mutation of sexes, or transition into one another, we cannot deny it in hares, it being observable in man. For hereof, beside Empedocles or Tiresias, there are not a few examples: and though very few, or rather none which have emasculated or turned women, yet very many, who from an esteem or reality of being women, have infallibly proved men.

* Arnabeth. † Levit. ii.

[8] *More doubtful, &c.*] This paragraph was first added in 6th edition.
[9] *feneration.*] Usury.
[1] *Of the same belief, &c.*] This passage was first added in **the 3rd** edition.

Some at the first point of their menstruous eruptions; some in the day of their marriage; others many years after, which occasioned disputes at law, and contestations concerning a restore of the dowry. And that not only mankind, but many other animals, may suffer this transexion, we will not deny, or hold it at all impossible; although I confess, by reason of the postick and backward position of the feminine parts in quadrupeds, they can hardly admit the substitution of a protrusion effectual unto masculine generation, except it be in retromingents, and such as couple backward.

Nor shall we only concede the succession of sexes in some, but shall not dispute the transition of reputed species in others; that is, a transmutation, or (as Paracelsians term it) transplantation of one into another. Hereof in perfect animals of a congenerous seed, or near affinity of natures, examples are not unfrequent, as in horses, asses, dogs, foxes, pheasants, cocks, &c., but in imperfect kinds, and such, where the discrimination of sex is obscure, these transformations are more common, and in some within themselves without commixion, as particularly in caterpillars or silkworms, wherein there is a visible and triple transfiguration. But in plants, wherein there is no distinction of sex, these transplantations are conceived more obvious than any; as that of barley into oats, of wheat into darnel; and those grains which generally arise among corn, as cockle, *aracus*, *ægilops*, and other degenerations, which come up in unexpected shapes, when they want the support and maintenance of the primary and master-forms. And the same do some affirm concerning other plants in less analogy of figures; as the mutation of mint into cresses, basil into serpoil, and turnips into radishes. In all which, as Severinus* conceiveth, there may be equivocal seeds and hermaphroditical principles, which contain the radicality and power of different forms; thus in the seed of wheat their lieth obscurely the seminality of darnel, although in a secondary or inferior way, and at some distance of production; which, nevertheless, if it meet with convenient promotion, or a conflux and conspiration of causes more powerful than the other, it then beginneth to edify in chief, and contemning the superintendent form, produceth the signatures of itself.

* *In Idea Medicinæ Philosophicæ.*

Now therefore, although we deny not these several mutations, and do allow that hares may exchange their sex,[2] yet this we conceive doth come to pass but sometimes, and not in that vicissitude or annual alternation as is presumed: that is, from imperfection to perfection, from perfection to imperfection; from female unto male, from male to female again, and so in a circle to both, without a permansion in either. For beside the inconceivable mutation of temper, which should yearly alternate the sex, this is injurious unto the order of nature, whose operations do rest in the perfection of their intents, which, having once attained, they maintain their accomplished ends, and relapse not again into their progressional imperfections. So if, in the minority of natural vigour, the parts of seminality take place, when upon the increase or growth thereof the masculine appear, the first design of nature is achieved, and those parts are after maintained.

But surely it much impeacheth this iterated transexion of hares, if that be true which Cardan and other physicians affirm, that transmutation of sex is only so in opinion; and that these transfeminated persons were really men at first, although succeeding years produced the manifesto or evidence of their virilities: which, although intended and formed, was not at first excluded; and that the examples hereof have undergone no real or new transexion, but were androgynally born, and under some kind of hermaphrodites. For though Galen do favour the opinion, that the distinctive parts of sexes are only different in position, that is inversion or protrusion, yet will this hardly be made out from the anatomy of those parts; the testicles being so seated in the female, that they admit not of protrusion, and the neck of the matrix wanting those parts which are discoverable in the organ of virility.

The second, and most received acception is, that hares are male and female by conjunction of both sexes, and such as are found in mankind, poetically called hermaphrodites; supposed to be formed from the equality, or *non victorie* of

[2] *sex.*] Why may not the sex *seem* to change in hares rather than in men? Frequent storyes wee have of some taken for maydes till ripe age or marriage have discovered the instruments of the male to have been but hidden.—*Wr.*

either seed; carrying about them the parts of man and woman although with great variety in perfection, site, and ability, not only as Aristotle conceived, with a constant impotency in one, but as later observers affirm, sometimes with ability of either venery. And therefore the providence of some laws have thought good, that at the years of maturity they should elect one sex, and the errors in the other should suffer a severer punishment. Whereby, endeavouring to prevent incontinency, they unawares enjoined perpetual chastity; for being executive in both parts, and confined unto one, they restrained a natural power, and ordained a partial virginity. Plato, and some of the rabbins, proceeded higher, who conceived the first man an hermaphrodite; and Marcus Leo, the learned Jew, in some sense hath allowed it; affirming that Adam in one *suppositum*, without division, contained both male and female. And therefore, whereas it is said in the text, that "God created man in his own image, in the image of God created he him, male and female created he them:" applying the singular and plural unto Adam, it might denote, that in one substance, and in himself he included both sexes, which was after divided, and the female called woman. The opinion of Aristotle extendeth farther, from whose assertion all men should be hermaphrodites; for affirming that women do not spermatize, and confer a place or receptacle rather than essential principles of generation, he deductively includes both sexes in mankind; for from the father proceed not only males and females, but from him also must hermaphroditical and masculo-feminine generations be derived, and a commixion of both sexes arise from the seed of one. But the schoolmen have dealt with that sex more hardly than any other; who, though they have not much disputed their generation, yet have they controverted their resurrection, and raised a query, whether any at the last day should arise in the sex of women; as may be observed in the supplement of Aquinas.

Now, as we must acknowledge this androgynal* condition in man, so can we not deny the like doth happen in beasts. Thus do we read in Pliny, that Nero's chariot was drawn by four hermaphroditical mares; and Cardan affirms, he also beheld one at Antwerp. And thus may we also concede, that

* Consisting of man and woman.

hares have been of both sexes, and some have ocularly confirmed it; but that the whole species or kind should be bisexous or double-sexed, we cannot affirm, who have found the parts of male and female respectively distinct and single in any wherein we have enquired; and the like success had Bacchinus in such as he dissected.* And whereas it is conceived, that being an harmless animal, and delectable food unto man, nature hath made them with double sexes, that actively and passively performing, they might more numerously increase, we forget an higher providence of nature whereby she especially promotes the multiplication of hares, which is by superfetation; that is, a conception upon a conception, or an improvement of a second fruit before the first be excluded; preventing hereby the usual intermission and vacant time of generation, which is very common and frequently observable in hares, mentioned long ago by Aristotle, Herodotus, and Pliny; and we have often observed, that after the first cast, there remain successive conceptions, and other younglings very immature, and far from their term of exclusion.

Nor need any man to question this in hares, for the same we observe doth sometime happen in women: for although it be true, that upon conception the inward orifice of the matrix exactly closeth, so that it commonly admitteth nothing after, yet falleth it out sometime, that in the act of coition, the avidity of that part dilateth itself, and receiveth a second burden; which if it happen to be near in time unto the first, they do commonly both proceed unto perfection, and have legitimate exclusions, periodically succeeding each other: but if the superfetation be made with considerable intermission, the latter most commonly proves abortive; for the first being confirmed, engrosseth the aliment from the other. However, therefore, the project of Julia seems very plausible, and that way infallible, when she received not her passengers before she had taken in her lading, yet was there a fallibility therein; nor indeed any absolute security in the policy of adultery after conception: for the matrix (which some have called another animal within us, and which is not subjected unto the law of our will), after reception of its proper tenant, may yet receive a strange and spurious inmate: as is con-

* *Bacch. de Hermaphroditis.*

firmable by many examples in Pliny; by Larissæa in *Hippocrates*, and that merry one in Plautus urged also by Aristotle; that is, of Iphicles and Hercules, the one begat by Jupiter, the other by Amphitryon upon Alcmæna; as also in those superconceptions, where one child was like the father, the other like the adulterer; the one favoured the servant, the other resembled the master.

Now the grounds that begat, or much promoted the opinion of a double sex in hares, might be some little bags or tumours, at first glance representing stones or testicles, to be found in both sexes about the parts of generation; which men observing in either sex, were induced to believe a masculine sex in both. But to speak properly, these are no testicles or parts official unto generation, but glandulous substances that seem to hold the nature of emunctories. For herein may be perceived slender perforations, at which may be expressed a black and fæculent matter. If therefore from these, we shall conceive a mixtion of sexes in hares, with fairer reason we may conclude it in beavers; whereof both sexes contain a double bag or tumour in the groin, commonly called the cod of castor, as we have delivered before.

Another ground were certain holes or cavities observable about the siege; which being perceived in males, made some conceive there might be also a feminine nature in them. And upon this very ground, the same opinion hath passed upon the hyæna, and is declared by Aristotle, and thus translated by Scaliger: *Quòd autem aiunt utriusque sexus habere genitalia, falsum est; quod videtur esse fœmineum sub cauda, est simile figurâ fœminino, verùm pervium non est;* and thus is it also in hares, in whom these holes, although they seem to make a deep cavity, yet do they not perforate the skin, nor hold a community with any part of generation; but were (as Pliny delivereth) esteemed the marks of their age, the number of those deciding their number of years. In which opinion what truth there is we shall not contend; for if in other animals there be authentic notations, if the characters of years be found in the horns of cows, or in the antlers of deer; if we conjecture the age of horses from joints in their docks, and undeniably presume it from their teeth, we cannot affirm, there is in this conceit any affront unto nature; although, whoever enquireth shall find no assurance therein.

The last foundation was retromingency or pissing backward; for men observing both sexes to urine backward, or aversely between their legs, they might conceive there was a feminine part in both; wherein they are deceived by the ignorance of the just and proper site of the pizzle, or part designed unto the excretion of urine: which in the hare holds not the common position, but is aversely seated, and in its distention inclines unto the coccyx or scut. Now from the nature of this position, there ensueth a necessity of retrocopulation,[3] which also promoteth the conceit: for some observing them to couple without ascension, have not been able to judge of male or female, or to determine the proper sex in either. And to speak generally, this way of copulation is not appropriate unto hares, nor is there one, but many ways of coition, according to divers shapes and different conformations. For some couple laterally or sidewise, as worms: some circularly or by complication, as serpents: some pronely, that is, by contaction of the ventral parts in both, as apes, porcupines, hedgehogs, and such as are termed *mollia*, as the cuttle-fish and the purple; some mixtly, that is, the male ascending the female, or by application of the ventral parts of the one, unto the postick parts of the other, as most quadrupeds: some aversely, as all crustacious animals, lobsters, shrimps, and crevises, and also retromingents, as panthers, tigers, and hares.[4] This is the constant law of their coition, this they observe and transgress not: only the vitiosity of man hath acted the varieties hereof; nor content with a digression from sex or species, hath in his own kind run through the anomalies of venery; and been so bold, not only to act, but represent to view, the irregular ways of lust.

[3] *retrocopulation.*] Which is true in lions alsoe, and partlye in dogs.—*Wr.*

[4] *hares.*] Hares and lions: which I sawe at the tower, and remember itt is specified expresly by Aristotle of them.—*Wr.*

CHAPTER XVIII.

That Moles are blind.

THAT moles are blind and have no eyes,[5] though a common opinion, is received with much variety; some affirming only they have no sight, as Oppianus, the proverb *talpa cæcior*, and the word σπαλαχία, or *talpitas*, which in Hesychius is made the same with *cæcitas;* some that they have eyes, but no sight, as the text of Aristotle seems to apply; some neither eyes nor sight, as Albertus, Pliny, and the vulgar opinion; some both eyes and sight, as Scaliger, Aldrovandus, and some others. Of which opinions, the last, with some restriction, is most consonant unto truth; for that they have eyes in their head, is manifested unto any that wants them not in his own; and are discoverable, not only in old ones, but as we have observed in young and naked conceptions, taken out of the belly of the dam. And he that exactly enquires into the cavity of their cranies, may perhaps discover

---

[5] *That moles are blind, &c.*] The eyes of the mole are so extremely minute, and so perfectly hid in its hair, that it is not wonderful if careless and casual observers have pronounced it blind.—Still less is it wonderful, that so absurd a personage as Alexander Ross, should have declared them to be but "forms of eyes," given by nature "rather for ornament than use; as wings are given to the ostrich, which never flies, and a long tail to the rat, which serves for no other use but to be catched sometimes by it!"—*Arc.* 151.

"It appears," however, observe the editors of *Cuvier's Animal Kingdom*, "that this animal was not known to the ancients, who have been very wrongfully accused of having fallen into the gross error of supposing that the mole had no eyes. Aristotle, it is true, in two places of his *History of Animals*, repeats this assertion. But the researches of modern times have ascertained that this illustrious naturalist was perfectly right in refusing the organs of vision to the mole of his native country, to the σκαλαξ or ασκαλαξ, of ancient Greece. There does, in fact, exist, in that country, a little subterraneous animal totally deprived of sight: naturalists have only recently become acquainted with it, and have designated it under the appellation of the *rat-mole*. They have been obliged to confess, after many ages of injustice towards the ancients, that these last had truth altogether on their side, with regard to the mole known in Greece, and had correctly observed, that this animal was not only completely blind, but did not possess even *the smallest* rudiment of an external eye."--Vol. ii. p. 197.

some propagation of nerves communicated unto these parts. But that the humours, together with their coats, are also distinct (though Galen seem to affirm it), transcendeth our discovery; for separating these little orbs, and including them in magnifying glasses, we discerned no more than Aristotle mentions, τῶν ὀφθαλμῶν μέλαινα, that is, a black humour, nor any more if they be broken. That therefore they have eyes, we must of necessity affirm; but that they be comparatively incomplete, we need not to deny: so Galen affirms the parts of generation in women are imperfect, in respect of those of men, as the eyes of moles in regard of other animals: so Aristotle terms them πηρουμένους, which Gaza translates *oblæsos*, and Scaliger by a word of imperfection, *inchoatos*.

Now as that they have eyes is manifest unto sense; so that they have sight, not incongruous unto reason; if we call not in question the providence of this provision, that is, to assign the organs, and yet deny the office; to grant them eyes, and withhold all manner of vision. For as the inference is fair, affirmatively deduced from the action to the organ, that they have eyes because they see; so is it also from the organ to the action, that they have eyes, therefore some sight designed, if we take the intention of nature in every species, and except the casual impediment, or morbosities in individuals. But as their eyes are more imperfect than others, so do we conceive of their sight or act of vision, for they will run against things, and huddling forwards fall from high places. So that they are not blind, nor yet distinctly see; there is in them no cecity, yet more than a cecutiency; they have sight enough to discern the light, though not perhaps to distinguish of objects or colours; so are they not exactly blind, for light is one object of vision. And this (as Scaliger observeth) might be as full a sight as nature first intended, for living in darkness under the earth, they had no further need of eyes than to avoid the light; and to be sensible whenever they lost that darkness of earth, which was their natural confinement. And therefore, however translators do render the word of Aristotle or Galen, that is *imperfectos, oblæsos,* or *inchoatos*, it is not much considerable; for their eyes are sufficiently begun to finish this action, and competently perfect for this imperfect vision.

And lastly, although they had neither eyes nor sight, yet could they not be termed blind. For blindness being a privative term unto sight,[6] this appellation is not admittible in propriety of speech, and will overthrow the doctrine of privations; which presuppose positive forms or habits, and are not indefinite negations, denying in all subjects, but such alone wherein the positive habits are in their proper nature, and placed without repugnancy. So do we improperly say a mole is blind, if we deny it the organs or a capacity of vision from its created nature; so when the text of John had said, that person was blind from his nativity, whose cecity our Saviour cured, it was not warrantable in Nonnus to say he had no eyes at all, as in the judgment of Heinsius, he describeth in his paraphrase; and as some ancient fathers affirm, that by this miracle they were created in him. And so though the sense may be accepted, that proverb must be candidly interpreted, which maketh fishes mute; and calls them silent which have no voice in nature.

Now this conceit is erected upon a misapprehension or mistake in the symptoms of vision; men confounding abolishment, diminution, and depravement, and naming that an abolition of sight, which indeed is but an abatement. For if vision be abolished, it is called *cæcitas*, or blindness; if depraved, and receive its objects erroneously, hallucination; if diminished, *hebetudo visus, caligatio,* or dimness. Now instead of a diminution or imperfect vision in the mole, we affirm an abolition or total privation; instead of a caligation or dimness, we conclude a cecity or blindness. Which hath been frequently inferred concerning other animals. So some affirm the water-rat is blind, so Sammonicus and Nicander do call the *mus araneus*, the shrew or ranney,[7] blind. And because darkness was before light, the Egyptians worshipped the same. So are *cæciliæ* or slow-worms accounted blind:[8] and the like we affirm proverbially of the

---

[6] *a private term unto sight.*] "A term expressing privation of sight."

[7] *ranney.*] This is the very word, *araneus;* castinge away the first *a*, and turning the Latine termination of *eus* into our English form.—*Wr.*

[8] *So some affirm, &c.*] Erroneously.—Neither the water-rat, the shrew, nor the slow-worm is blind. The eyes of the former are very small, and (especially in the shrew) much concealed by fur. Bewick

beetle; although their eyes be evident, and they will fly against lights, like many other insects; and though also Aristotle determines, that the eyes are apparent in all flying insects, though other senses be obscure, and not perceptible at all. And if from a diminution we may infer a total privation, or affirm that other animals are blind which do not acutely see, or comparatively unto others, we shall condemn unto blindness many not so esteemed; for such as have corneous or horny eyes, as lobsters and crustaceous animals, are generally dim-sighted; all insects that have *antennæ*, or long horns to feel out their way, as butterflies and locusts; or their fore-legs so disposed, that they much advance before their heads, as may be observed in spiders; and if the eagle were judge, we might be blind ourselves. The expression therefore of Scripture in the story of Jacob, is surely without circumspection : " And it came to pass, when Jacob was old and his eyes were dim," *quando caligarunt oculi*, saith Jerome and Tremellius, which are expressions of diminution, and not of absolute privation.

Other concerns there are of moles, which, though not commonly opinioned, are not commonly enough considered: as the peculiar formation of their feet, the slender *ossa jugalia*, and dog-teeth, and how hard it is to keep them alive out of the earth. As also the ferity and voracity of these animals; for though they be contented with roots, and stringy parts of plants, or worms under ground, yet when they are above it, they will sometimes tear and eat one another, and in a large glass wherein a mole, a toad, and a viper were inclosed, we have known the mole to dispatch them, and to devour a good part of them both.[9]

says, that the water-shrew (*Sorex fodiens*) is called in Lincolnshire the *blind mouse*. The slow-worm is more commonly called the *blind-worm*, *Anguis fragilis*.

[9] *Other concerns, &c.*] This paragraph first added in 6th edition.

CHAPTER XIX.

That Lampreys have many eyes.

WHETHER lampreys have nine eyes, as is received, we durst refer it unto Polyphemus, who had but one to judge it. An error concerning eyes, occasioned by the error of eyes; deduced from the appearance of divers cavities or holes on either side,[1] which some call eyes that carelessly behold them; and is not only refutable by experience, but also repugnant unto reason. For, beside the monstrosity they fasten unto nature, in contriving many eyes, who hath made but two unto any animal, that is, one of each side, according to the division of the brain; it were a superfluous inartificial act to place and settle so many in one plane; for the two extremes would sufficiently perform the office of sight without the help of the intermediate eyes, and behold as much as all seven joined together. For the visible base of the object would be defined by these two; and the middle eyes, although they behold the same thing, yet could they not behold so much thereof as these; so were it no advantage unto man to have a third eye between those two he hath already; and the fiction of Argus seems more reasonable than this; for though he had many eyes, yet were they placed in circumference and positions of advantage, and so are they placed in several lines in spiders.

Again, these cavities which men call eyes are seated out of the head, and where the gills of other fish are placed; containing no organs of sight, nor having any communication with the brain. Now all sense proceeding from the brain, and that being placed (as Galen observeth) in the upper part of the body, for the fitter situation of the eyes, and conveniency required unto sight; it is not reasonable to imagine that they are anywhere else, or deserve that name which are seated in other parts. And therefore, we relinquish as fabulous what is delivered of *sternophthalmi*, or men with

---

[1] *holes on either side.*] These are the bronchial apertures, of which the lamprey has seven on each side.—It has two eyes; but it is remarkable that there are no *holes* in the skin, but only transparent round spots, over the eyes.

eyes in their breast; and when it is said by Solomon, "A wise man's eyes are in his head," it is to be taken in a second sense, and affordeth no objection. True it is, that the eyes of animals are seated with some difference, but in sanguineous animals in the head, and that more forward than the ear or hole of hearing. In quadrupeds, in regard of the figure of their heads, they are placed at some distance; in latirostrous and flat-billed birds they are more laterally seated; and therefore, when they look intently they turn one eye upon the object; and can convert their heads to see before and behind, and to behold two opposite points at once. But at a more easy distance are they situated in man, and in the same circumference with the ear; for if one foot of the compass be placed upon the crown, a circle described thereby will intersect, or pass over both the ears.

The error in this conceit consists in the ignorance of these cavities, and their proper use in nature; for this is a particular disposure of parts, and a peculiar conformation whereby these holes and sluices supply the defect of gills, and are assisted by the conduit in the head; for, like cetaceous animals and whales, the lamprey hath a *fistula*, spout or pipe at the back part of the head, whereat it spurts out water. Nor is it only singular in this formation, but also in many other; as in defect of bones, whereof it hath not one, and for the spine or backbone, a cartilaginous substance without any spondyles, processes, or protuberance whatsoever. As also in the provision which nature hath made for the heart; which in this animal is very strangely secured, and lies immured in a cartilage or gristly substance. And lastly, in the colour of the liver; which is in the male of an excellent grass-green, but of a deeper colour in the female, and will communicate a fresh and durable verdure.

CHAPTER XX.

That Snails have two eyes.

WHETHER snails have eyes some learned men have doubted.[2] For Scaliger terms them but imitations of eyes, and Aristotle upon consequence denieth them, when he affirms that testaceous animals have no eyes.[3] But this now seems sufficiently asserted by the help of exquisite glasses, which discover those black and atramentous spots or globules to be their eyes.[4]

[2] *Whether snails, &c.*] The snayle hath but 3 senses, that is, the touch, the smell. and the tast; he sees not, he hears not. The touch is principally in his hornes; the smel and taste in his mouth, in which I found he hath a little black toung not bigger then a hair, with which he frets herbes, bread, and all things that he fastens upon for foode, as I once made a visible and certaine experiment.—*Br.*

[3] *Aristotle, &c.*] Mr. E. W. Brayley, jun., in a very elaborate and highly interesting paper, in the second volume of the *Zoological Journal*, has very successfully advocated this opinion of the great father of zoology; and after detailing the various opinions (or rather enquiries) of the most able modern naturalists, he concludes by stating his opinion that Aristotle was right in believing that *all* the testaceous molusca are without the organ and sense of sight, and that the feelers of snails are only organs endued with the most delicate sense of touch and feeling. In a note, however, Mr. Brayley suggests that as they are certainly capable of conveying to the *sensorium* a perception of those *vibrations of air*, which impart to more perfect animals the sense of *sound*, so they may also "convey a perception of those *undulations of the luminiferous ether*, which (adopting the Huygenian undulatory theory of light, as revived and explained by Dr. T. Young), enable those animals which possess true eyes to enjoy the sense of *vision!*"

[4] *But this now seems, &c.*] This sentence was substituted, in the 6th edition, for the following passage. "And for my own part, after much enquiry, I am not satisfied that these are eyes, or that those black and atramentous spots which seem to represent them are any ocular realities: for if any object be presented unto them, they will sometimes seem to decline it, and sometimes run against it; if also these black extremities, or presumed eyes be clipped off, they will notwithstanding make use of their protrusions or horns, and poke out their way as before: again, if they were eyes or instruments of vision, they would have their originals in the head, and from thence derive their motive and optic organs, but their roots and first extremities are seated low upon the sides of the back, as may be perceived in the whiter sort of snails when they retract them."

That they have two eyes is the common opinion; but if they have two eyes, we may grant them to have no less than four, that is, two in the larger extensions above, and two in the shorter and lesser horns below; and this number may be allowed in these inferior and exsanguineous animals,[5] since we may observe the articulate and latticed eyes in flies, and nine in some spiders: and in the great phalangium spider of America, we plainly number eight.

But in sanguineous animals, quadrupeds, bipeds, or man, no such number can be regularly verified, or multiplicity of eyes confirmed; and therefore what hath been under this

[5] *and this number may be allowed, &c.*] This remark, in the 6th edition, supplies the place of the following:—the succeeding paragraph which also occurs in all the earlier editions, was omitted in the 6th— " which will be monstrous and beyond the affirmation of any.

"Now the reason why we name these black strings eyes, is because we know not what to call them else, and understand not the proper use of that part, which indeed is very obscure, and not delivered by any, but may probably be said to assist the protrusion and retraction of their horns, which being a weak and hollow body, require some inward establishment to confirm the length of their advancement, which we observe they cannot extend without the concurrence hereof; for if with your finger you apprehend the top of the horn, and draw out this black and membranous emission, the horn will be excluded no more; but if you clip off the extremity, or only singe the top thereof with *aqua fortis*, or other corrosive water, leaving a considerable part behind, they will nevertheless exclude the horns, and therefore explorate their way as before; and indeed the exact sense of these extremities is very remarkable, for if you dip a pen in aqua fortis, oil of vitriol, or turpentine, and present it towards these points, they will at a reasonable distance decline the acrimony thereof, retiring or distorting them to avoid it; and this they will nimbly perform, if objected to the extremes, but slowly or not at all if approached unto their roots."

The various readings given in this and the preceding note, prove that the earlier opinions of Sir Thomas were more in conformity with the sagacious assertion of the great naturalist of antiquity,—and, I may add, with the conclusions which the investigation of Sir Everard Home, and other distinguished naturalists, have recently led them to form. The paper by Mr. Brayley, referred to in note 3, p. 318, will be found to contain a detailed and very interesting account of those investigations.

Sir E. Home has pointed out the mistake of Swammerdam, whose microscopic examinations led him to consider the black *rete mucosum*, at the point of the horn, as *nigrum pigmentum*, and a pellucid part which he found there, as the *cornea*. Sir Thomas was probably misled by similar investigations, or he might have seen Swammerdam's work, which appeared in Dutch some years before the sixth edition of the *Vulgar Errors.*

kind delivered, concerning the plurality, paucity, or anomalous situation of eyes, is either monstrous, fabulous, or under things never seen, includes good sense or meaning. And so may we receive the figment of Argus, who was an hieroglyphick of heaven, in those centuries of eyes expressing the stars, and their alternate wakings, the vicissitude of day and night. Which strictly taken cannot be admitted, for the subject of sleep is not the eye, but the common sense, which once asleep, all eyes must be at rest. And therefore what is delivered as an emblem of vigilancy, that the hare and lion do sleep with one eye open, doth not evince they are any more awake than if they were both closed. For the open eye beholds in sleep no more than that which is closed, and no more one eye in them than two in other animals that sleep with both open, as some by disease, and others naturally, which have no eyelids at all.

As for Polyphemus, although the story be fabulous, the monstrosity is not impossible. For the act of vision may be performed with one eye, and in the deception and fallacy of sight, hath this advantage of two, that it beholds not objects double,[6] or sees two things for one. For this doth happen when the axis of the visive cones, diffused from the object, fall not upon the same plane, but that which is conveyed into one eye, is more depressed or elevated than that which enters the other. So if, beholding a candle, we protrude either upward or downward the pupil of one eye, the object will appear double; but if we shut the other eye, and behold it with one, it will then appear but single, and if we adduce the eye unto either corner, the object will not duplicate, for in that position the axis of the cones remains in the same plane, as is demonstrated in the optics and delivered by Galen, in his tenth, *De usu partium*.

Relations also there are of men that could make themselves invisible, which belongs not to this discourse, but may

---

[6] *it beholds not objects double.*] In connection with this very curious question of single vision with two eyes, Dr. Wollaston read a short paper to the R. S. in February, 1824, on *semi-decussation* of the optic nerves. A subject to which he had been led by a singular species of blindness which had affected him—in which he had suffered a temporary loss of sight on the left side only of *both eyes*. See *Quarterly Journal*, vol. xvii. p. 227.

serve as notable expressions of wise and prudent men, who so contrive their affairs, that although their actions be manifest, their designs are not discoverable. In this acception there is nothing left of doubt, and Giges ring remaineth still amongst us, for vulgar eyes behold no more of wise men than doth the sun; they may discover their exterior and outward ways, but their interior and inward pieces he only sees, that sees into their beings.

CHAPTER XXI.

That the Chameleon lives only upon air.

CONCERNING the Chameleon,[7] there generally passeth an opinion that it liveth only upon air, and is sustained by no other aliment. Thus much is in plain terms affirmed by Solinus, Pliny, and others, and by this periphrasis is the same described by Ovid.[8] All which notwithstanding, upon enquiry I find the assertion mainly controvertible, and very much to fail in the three inducements of belief.

And first for its verity, although asserted by some, and traditionally delivered by others, yet is it very questionable.

---

[7] *Concerning the Chameleon, &c.*] It is singular that Sir Thomas has not mentioned the vulgar opinion that this reptile undergoes frequent changes of colour according to that of the bodies near it. He has assigned *some* probable grounds for its being supposed to feed on air, viz. its powers of abstinence and its faculty of self-inflation. It lives on insects, which it catches by means of its long gluey tongue, and crushes between its jaws. It has been ascertained by careful experiment that the chameleon can live without eating for four months. It can inflate, not only its lungs but its whole body, including even the feet and tail. The frequent variations of colour observed in the chameleon are by no means determined by those of surrounding objects. They depend on the volition of the animal, or the state of its feelings, on its good or bad health, and are, besides, subordinate to climate, age, and sex. A. Ross so resolutely withstands the Doctor's arguments against the common opinion, as even to assert that flies are eaten by the chameleon, "rather out of wantonness or for physic." He adverts indeed to the fact, only as giving a reason for the animal being provided with digestive organs; but says that the slime on the tongue is not intended for catching the flies, but for destroying serpents, on whose approach the chameleon drops some of the slime on the head of the serpent, which presently dies.

[8] *Ovid.*] See *Metam.* l. xv. fab. 4. l. 411.

For beside Ælian, who is seldom defective in these accounts, Aristotle, distinctly treating hereof, hath made no mention of this remarkably propriety, which either suspecting its verity, or presuming its falsity, he surely omitted; for that he remained ignorant of this account, it is not easily conceivable, it being the common opinion, and generally received by all men. Some have positively denied it, as Augustinus, Niphus, Stobæus, Dalechampius, Fortunius Licetus, with many more; others have experimentally refuted it, as namely Johannes Landius, who in the relation of Scaliger, observed a chameleon to lick up a fly from his breast. But Bellonius* hath been more satisfactorily experimental, not only affirming they feed on flies, caterpillars, beetles, and other insects, but upon exenteration he found these animals in their bellies; whereby we might also add the experimental decisions of the worthy Peireschius and learned Emanuel Tizzanius, in that chameleon which had been often observed to drink water, and delight to feed on meal-worms. And although we have not had the advantage of our own observation, yet we have received the like confirmation from many ocular spectators.

2. As touching the verisimility or probable truth of this relation, several reasons there are which seem to overthrow it. For first, there are found in this animal, the guts, the stomach, and other parts official unto nutrition; which, were its aliment the empty reception of air, their provisions had been superfluous. Now the wisdom of nature abhorring superfluities, and effecting nothing in vain, unto the intention of these operations, respectively contriveth the organs, and therefore where we find such instruments, we may with strictness expect their actions, and where we discover them not, we may with safety conclude the non-intention of their operations. So when we perceive that bats have teats, it is not unreasonable to infer they suckle their younglings with milk; but whereas no other flying animal hath these parts, we cannot from them expect a viviparous exclusion, but either a generation of eggs, or some vermiparous separation, whose navel is within itself at first, and its nutrition after not connexedly depending of its original.

* *Comment in Ocell. Lucan.*

Again, nature is so far from leaving any one part without its proper action, that she ofttimes imposeth two or three labours upon one, so the pizzle in animals is both official unto urine and to generation; but the first and primary use is generation, for some creatures enjoy that part which urine not. So the nostrils are useful both for respiration and smelling; but the principal use is smelling, for many have nostrils which have no lungs, as fishes, but none have lungs or respiration, which have not some show or some analogy of nostrils. Thus we perceive the providence of nature, that is, the wisdom of God, which disposeth of no part in vain, and some parts unto two or three uses, will not provide any without the execution of its proper office, nor where there is no digestion to be made, make any parts inservient to that intention.

Beside the remarkable teeth, the tongue of this animal is a second argument to overthrow this aërial nutrication; and that not only in its proper nature, but also its peculiar figure. For of this part, properly taken, there are two ends; that is, the formation of the voice and the execution of taste; for the voice, it can have no office in chameleons, for they are mute animals; as, beside fishes, are most other sorts of lizards.

As for their taste, if their nutriment be air, neither can it be an instrument thereof; for the body of that element is ingustible, void of all sapidity, and, without any action of the tongue, is by the rough artery or weazand conducted into the lungs. And therefore Pliny much forgets the strictness of his assertion, when he alloweth excrements unto that animal, that feedeth only upon air; which notwithstanding, with the urine of an ass, he commends as a magical medicine upon our enemies.

The figure of the tongue seems also to overthrow the presumption of this aliment, which, according to exact delineation, is in this animal peculiar, and seemeth contrived for prey. For in so little a creature it is at the least a palm long, and being itself very slow in motion, hath in this part a very great agility; withal its food being flies, and such as suddenly escape, it hath in the tongue a mucous and slimy extremity, whereby upon a sudden emission it inviscates and tangleth those insects. And therefore some have thought its name not unsuitable unto its nature; the nomination in Greek* is a little lion; not so much for the resemblance of shape, as affinity of condition; that is, for vigilancy in its prey, and sudden rapacity thereof, which it performeth not like the lion with its teeth, but a sudden and unexpected ejaculation of the tongue. This exposition is favoured by some, especially the old gloss upon Leviticus, whereby in the translation of Jerome and the Septuagint this animal is forbidden; whatever it be, it seems as reasonable as that of Isidore, who derives this name, *à camelo et leone*, as presuming herein resemblance with a camel.[9]

3. As for the possibility hereof, it also is not unquestionable, and wise men are of opinion the bodies of animals cannot receive a proper aliment from air: for, beside that, taste being (as Aristotle terms it) a kind of touch, it is required the aliment should be tangible and fall under the palpable affections of touch; beside also that there is some sapor in all aliments, as being to be distinguished and judged by the gust, which cannot be admitted in air; beside these, I say, if we consider the nature of aliment, and the proper use of air in respiration, it will very hardly fall under the name hereof, or properly attain the act of nutrication.

And first, concerning its nature, to make a perfect nutrition into the body nourished, there is required a transmutation of the nutriment. Now where this conversion or aggeneration[1] is made, there is also required in the aliment

* χαμαιλέων.

[9] *camel.*] In the first edition he goes on thus:—" For this derivation offendeth the rules of etymology, wherein indeed the notation of names should be orthographical, not exchanging diphthongs for vowels, or converting consonants into each other." But notwithstanding this observation, he has spelled the word *camelon* in every edition. Dean Wren criticised the spelling, and noticed its inconsistency with the above remark of that author, who was probably induced, in every edition subsequent to the first, to suppress the observation, lest he might seem to condemn himself.

[1] *aggeneration.*] Generic assimilation. Johnson defines this, " the state of growing or uniting to another body." Webster defines it, " the state of growing to another." Both definitions are erroneous, or liable at least to be misunderstood. They would apply to the attachment of parasitic plants. Certainly they do not express the signification in

a familiarity of matter, and such a community or vicinity unto a living nature, as by one act of the soul may be converted into the body of the living, and enjoy one common soul: which cannot be effected by air, it concurring only with our flesh in common principles, which are at the largest distance from life, and common also unto inanimated constitutions. And therefore, when it is said by Fernelius, and asserted by divers others, that we are only nourished by living bodies, and such as are some way proceeding from them, that is, the fruits, effects, parts, or seeds thereof, they have laid out an object very agreeable unto assimilation; for these indeed are fit to receive a quick and immediate conversion, as holding some community with ourselves, and containing approximate dispositions unto animation.

Secondly (as is argued by Aristotle against the Pythagoreans), whatsoever properly nourisheth before its assimilation, by the action of natural heat it receiveth a corpulency or incrassation progressional unto its conversion; which notwithstanding, cannot be effected upon air, for the action of heat doth not condense but rarify that body, and by attenuation disposeth it for expulsion rather than for nutrition.

Thirdly (which is the argument of Hippocrates), all aliment received into the body, must be therein a considerable space retained, and not immediately expelled. Now air, but momentally remaining in our bodies, it hath no proportionable space for its conversion, not only of length enough to refrigerate the heart, which having once performed, lest being itself heated again it should suffocate that part, it maketh no stay, but hasteth back the same way it passed in.

Fourthly, the use of air attracted by the lungs, and without which there is no durable continuation in life, is not the nutrition of parts, but the contemperation and ventilation of that fire always maintained in the forge of life; whereby, although in some manner it concurreth unto nu-

which the word is used in the present passage. It is here meant to express the transmutation of that which is eaten, from its own nature, into that of the animal receiving it. It becomes *assimilated, generically,* to the nature of that animal.

trition, yet can it not receive the proper name of nutriment. And therefore by Hippocrates* it is termed *alimentum non alimentum*, a nourishment and no nourishment. That is, in a large acception, but not in propriety of language; conserving the body, not nourishing the same, nor repairing it by assimilation, but preserving it by ventilation; for thereby the natural flame is preserved from extinction, and so the *individuum* supported in some way like nutrition.

And though the air so entereth the lungs, that by its nitrous spirit it doth affect the heart and several ways qualify the blood; and though it be also admitted into other parts, even by the meat we chew, yet that it affordeth a proper nutriment alone, is not easily made out.[2]

Again, some are so far from affirming the air to afford any nutriment, that they plainly deny it to be any element, or that it entereth into mixed bodies as any principle in their compositions, but performeth other offices in the universe; as to fill all vacuities about the earth or beneath it, to convey the heat of the sun, to maintain fires and flames, to serve for the flight of volatiles, respiration of breathing animals, and refrigeration of others. And although we receive it as an element, yet, since the transmutation of elements and simple bodies is not beyond great question; since also it is no easy matter to demonstrate that air is so much as convertible into water; how transmutable it is into flesh, may be of deeper doubt.[3]

And although the air attracted may be conceived to nourish the invisible flame of life, inasmuch as common and culinary flames are nourished by the air about them, we make some doubt whether air is the pabulous supply of fire, much less that flame is properly air kindled. And the same before us hath been denied by the Lord of Verulam, in his tract of *Life and Death:* and also by Dr. Jordan, in his book of mineral waters. For that which substantially maintaineth the fire is the combustible matter in the kindled body, and not the ambient air, which affordeth exhalation to

* *De Alimento.*

[2] *And though, &c.*] This paragraph was altered in 6th edition.
[3] *Again, &c.*] This paragraph first added in 2nd edition.

its fuliginous atoms, nor that which causeth the flame properly to be termed air, but rather, as he expresseth it, the accension of fuliginous exhalations, which contain an unctuosity in them, and arise from the matter of fuel; which opinion will salve many doubts, whereof the common conceit affordeth no solution.

As first, how fire is stricken out of flints? that is, not by kindling the air from the collision of two hard bodies; for then diamonds should do the like better than flints; but rather from sulphureous,[4] inflamed, and even vitrified effluviums and particles, as hath been observed of late. The like, saith Jordan, we observe in canes, and woods[5] that are unctuous and full of oil, which will yield fire[6] by frication or collision, not by kindling the air about them, but the inflammable oil within them. Why the fire goes out without air? that is, because the fuliginous exhalations, wanting evaporation, recoil upon the flame and choke it, as is evident in cupping-glasses, and the artifice of charcoals, where, if the air be altogether excluded, the fire goes out. Why some lamps included in close bodies have burned many hundred years, as that discovered in the sepulchre of Tullia, the sister of Cicero, and that of Olibius many years after, near Padua? because, what ever was their matter, either a preparation of gold or *naptha*, the duration proceeded from the purity of their oil, which yielded no fuliginous exhalations to suffocate the fire; for if air had nourished the flame, it had not continued many minutes, for it would have been spent and

---

[4] *sulphureous.*] Itt is manifest to sense, that in the collision of the steele and the flint there is a sulphureous odour, which thoughe but fainte (in regard of the small splinters from whence it comes) yet to an acute and unobstructed braine is plainly perceptible.—*Wr.* See note at page 102.

[5] *saith Jordan, &c.*] Dr. Jordan's observation appears to have been an anticipation of Sir H. Davy's, who having been informed that two pieces of bonnet cane rubbed together produced a faint light, examined the phænomenon, and found that all canes of this kind "when briskly rubbed together, produced sparks of white light. The luminous appearance was much more vivid on collision. When the canes were violently struck together, sparks nearly as vivid as those from the gun-lock were produced." The cause he ascertained to be that the *epidermis* of the cane was composed chiefly of *silica*.—*Br.*

[6] *fire.*] And with the fire a smel as of oylye substance fired.—*Wr.*

wasted by the fire.⁷ Why a piece of flax will kindle, although it touch not the flame? because the fire extendeth further than indeed it is visible, being at some distance from the wick, a pellucid and transparent body, and thinner than the air itself. Why metals, in their liquation, although they intensely heat the air above their surface, arise not yet into a flame, nor kindle the air about them? because their sulphur is more fixed, and they emit not inflammable exhalations. And lastly, why a lamp or candle burneth only in the air about it, and inflameth not the air at a distance from it? because the flame extendeth not beyond the inflammable effluence, but closely adheres unto the original of its inflammation; and therefore it only warmeth, not kindleth the air about it. Which notwithstanding it will do, if the ambient air be impregnate with subtle inflammabilities, and such as are of quick accension, as experiment is made in a close room, upon an evaporation of spirits of wine and camphor; as subterraneous fires do sometimes happen,⁸ and as Creusa and Alexander's boy in the bath were set on fire by *naptha*.

⁷ *Why some lamps, &c.*] For a curious discussion on these marvellous lamps, see *Ozanam's Philosophical Recreations*, by Hutton, vol. i. p. 496.

⁸ *as subterraneous fires do sometimes happen.*] This remark, and indeed the whole of Browne's enquiries and observations in the two preceding paragraphs, respecting the nature of flame, very naturally remind us of one of the most splendid (because most useful) achievements of modern science—Sir Humphrey Davy's invention of the safety-lamp, for the purpose of obviating those " subterraneous" explosions which had previously occurred with destructive frequency, in the working of our collieries.

The causes and character of these terrific explosions, the means used in the early part of the present century to induce the efforts of scientific men to discover a remedy, and the perfect success which attended those of Sir Humphrey for that purpose, form the subject of a detailed and most interesting narrative in the 11th chapter of *Dr. Paris's Life of Sir H. Davy.*

The carburetted hydrogen given out by coal, and found frequently in vast masses in the crevices, or fissures, which are opened in working the mines, forms by combination with atmospheric air that inflammable gas, technically called *fire-damp*. The manner in which this gas explodes, is thus graphically described by Dr. Paris:—"On the approach of a candle, it is in an instant kindled; the expanding fluid drives before it a roaring whirlwind of flaming air, which tears up every thing in its progress, scorching some of the miners to a cinder, and burying others under enormous ruins shaken from the roof; when thundering to the

Lastly, the element of air is so far from nourishing the body, that some have questioned the power of water; many shafts, it converts the mine, as it were, into an enormous piece of artillery, and wastes its fury in a discharge of thick clouds of coal-dust, stones, and timber, together with the limbs and mangled bodies of men and horses."—Vol. ii. p. 63.

A society was established on the 1st of October, 1813, at Bishop-Wearmouth, by Sir Ralph Milbanke, Dr. Gray (afterwards Bishop of Bristol), and other gentlemen, "for preventing accidents in coal-mines," which obtained the patronage of the Bishop of Durham, the Duke of Northumberland, and other noblemen and gentlemen. This society established a correspondence with others, and at length, through the chairman, Dr. Gray, engaged Sir Humphrey Davy in the investigation. He soon ascertained, by experiment on *fire-damp*, that it is a combination of hydrogen and carbon: that it will not explode if mixed with less than six times, nor more than fourteen times its volume of atmospheric air;—that an *explosive mixture* of gas, admitted into a vessel having apertures only above and below, *merely enlarges* the light, and then gradually *extinguishes it without* explosion:—that the explosive gas will not explode in a tube less than one-eighth of an inch in diameter: —and that red hot charcoal *does not explode*, but gives light in the explosive gas. On these principles various lamps were constructed by Sir Humphrey, which were perfectly safe: but their light was extinguished when the air became so polluted with fire-damp as to be explosive. It remained then for him (as Dr. Paris observes), after having disarmed the fire-damp of its terror, to enlist it into his service.—"The simple means by which this was effected are as interesting as their results are important. He had previously arrived at the fact, that wire-gauze might be substituted as air-feeders to the lamp, in the place of his tubes or safety canals: but not until the lapse of several weeks, did the happy idea of constructing the lamp entirely of wire gauze occur to him:—the history of this elaborate enquiry affords a striking proof of the inability of the human mind to apprehend simplicities, without a process of complication, which works as the grappling machinery of truth. His original lamp, with tubes or canals, as already described, was perfectly safe in the most explosive atmosphere, but its light was necessarily extinguished by it; whereas in the wire-gauze cage, the fire-damp itself continues to burn, and thus to afford to the miner a useful light, while he is equally secured from the fatal effects of explosion.

"Nothing now remained but to ascertain the degree of fineness which the wire-gauze ought to possess in order to form a secure barrier against the passage of flame. For this purpose, Davy placed his lighted lamps in a glass receiver, through which there was a current of air which passed into the lamp more or less explosive, and caused it to change rapidly or slowly at pleasure, so as to produce all possible varieties of inflammable and explosive mixtures: and he found that iron wire-gauze, composed of wires from one fortieth to one sixtieth of an inch in diameter, and

conceiving it enters not the body in the power of aliment, or that from thence there proceeds a substantial supply. For beside that some creatures drink not at all; even unto ourselves, and more perfect animals, though many ways assistant thereto, it performs no subtantial nutrition, serving for refrigeration, dilution of solid aliment, and its elixation[9] in the stomach; which from thence, as a vehicle, it conveys through less accessible cavities, and so in a rorid substance through the capillary cavities, into every part; which having performed, it is afterward excluded by urine, sweat, and serous separations. And this opinion surely possessed the ancients for when they so highly commended that water which is suddenly hot and cold, which is without all savour, the lightest, the thinnest, and which will soonest boil beans or peas, they had no consideration of nutrition;[1] whereunto had they had respect, they would have surely commended gross and turbid streams, in whose confusion at least, there might be contained some nutriment; and not jejune or limpid water, nearer the simplicity of its element. Although, I confess, our clearest waters, and such as seem simple unto sense, are much compounded unto reason, as may be observed in the evaporation of large quantities of water, wherein beside a terreous residence, some salt is also found, as is also observable in rain water; which appearing pure and empty, is full of seminal principles, and carrieth vital atoms of plants and animals in

containing twenty-eight wires, or seven hundred and eighty-four apertures to the inch, was safe under all circumstances, in atmospheres of this kind: and he consequently employed that material in guarding lamps for the coal-mines, where, in January, 1816, they were immediately adopted, and have long been in general use."—Vol. ii. pp. 97-9.

Such is a rapid and very slight sketch of the history of a discovery which (to use Dr. P.'s words), "whether considered in relation to its scientific importance, or to its great practical value, must be regarded as one of the most splendid triumphs of human genius. It was the fruit of elaborate experiment and close induction: chance, or accident, which comes in for so large a share of the credit of human invention, has no claim to prefer upon this occasion: step by step may he be followed throughout the whole progress of his research, and so obviously does the discovery of each new fact spring from those that preceded it, that we never for a moment lose sight of our philosopher, but keep pace with him during the whole of his enquiry."

[9] *elixation.*] Boiling or stewing.
[1] *nutrition.*] But only of puritye for refreshing the harte.—*Wr.*

it, which have not perished in the great circulation of nature; as may be discovered from several insects generated in rain water from the prevalent fructification of plants thereby; and (beside the real plant of Cornerius*) from vegetable figurations, upon the sides of glasses, so rarely delineated in frosts.[2]

All which considered, severer heads will be apt enough to conceive the opinion of this animal, not much unlike that of the *astomi*, or men without mouths, in Pliny; suitable unto the relation of the mares in Spain, and their subventaneous conceptions from the western wind; and in some way more unreasonable than the figment of Rabican, the famous horse in *Ariosto*, which being conceived by flame and wind, never tasted grass, or fed on any grosser provender than air; for this way of nutrition was answerable unto the principles of his generation. Which being not airy, but gross and seminal in the chameleon, unto its conservation there is required a solid pasture, and a food congenerous unto the principles of its nature.

The grounds of this opinion are many: the first observed by Theophrastus, was the inflation or swelling of the body made in this animal upon inspiration or drawing in its breath: which people observing, have thought it to feed upon air. But this effect is rather occasioned upon the greatness of its lungs, which in this animal are very large, and by their backward situation afford a more observable dilatation; and though their lungs be less, the like inflation is observable in toads, but especially in sentortoises.[3]

A second is the continual hiation or holding open its mouth, which men observing, conceive the intention thereof to receive the aliment of air; but this is also occasioned by the greatness of its lungs; for repletion whereof, not having a sufficient or ready supply by its nostrils, it is enforced to dilate and hold open the jaws.

The third is the paucity of blood observed in this animal, scarce at all to be found but in the eye, and about the heart;

* *Zibavius*, tom. iv. *Chym*.

[2] *Although, I confess, &c.*] This sentence was first added in 2nd edition.

[3] *but especially in sentortoises.*] These gentry were first mentioned in the 6th edition.

which defect being observed, inclined some into thoughts, that the air was a sufficient maintenance for these exsanguinous parts. But this defect, or rather paucity of blood, is also agreeable unto many other animals, whose solid nutriment we do not controvert; as may be observed in other sorts of lizards, in frogs, and divers fishes; and therefore an horse-leech will not readily fasten upon every fish; and we do not read of much blood that was drawn from frogs by mice, in that famous battle of Homer.[4]

The last and most common ground which begat or promoted this opinion is, the long continuation hereof without any visible food, which some observing, precipitiously conclude they eat not any at all. It cannot be denied it is (if not the most of any) a very abstemious animal, and such as by reason of its frigidity, paucity of blood, and latitancy in the winter (about which time the observations are often made), will long subsist without a visible sustentation. But a like condition may be also observed in many other animals; for lizards and leeches,[5] as we have made trial, will live some months without sustenance; and we have included snails in glasses all winter, which have returned to feed again in the spring. Now these, notwithstanding, are not conceived to pass all their lives without food: for so to argue is fallacious, and is moreover sufficiently convicted by experience. And therefore probably other relations are of the same verity, which are of the like affinity; as is the conceit of the *rhintace* in Persia, the *canis levis* of America, and the *manucodiata* or bird of paradise in India.

[4] *that famous battle of Homer.*] This passage was but a friske of his stile.—*Wr.*

[5] *leeches.*] Leeches are kept by all apothecaryes in glasses of water, without any other nourishment; which can bee little, or none at all. The often change of the water serving for two intentions, and both contrary to the worke of nourishment; viz., first to preserve itt from putrefaction, which is the principal aliment which they sucke from thick and muddye standing waters; and secondly, to cleanse them from that venome, which they had formerlye contracted, which nothing could soe properly or speedily effect as the dailye supply of fresh cleere water; by which consequentially they become the more hungry, and apte to catche holde, and to holde the faster when they are on: evident arguments that from the pure water alone they drew no aliment, but fedd on that store which they had formerlye contracted in putrified standing waters.—*Wr.*

To assign a reason of this abstinence in animals, or declare how, without a supply, there ensueth no destructive exhaustion, exceedeth the limits and intention of my discourse. Fortunius Licetus, in his excellent tract, *De his qui diu vivunt sine alimento*, hath very ingeniously attempted it; deducing the cause hereof from an equal conformity of natural heat and moisture, at least no considerable exuperancy in either; which concurring in an unactive proportion, the natural heat consumeth not the moisture (whereby ensueth no exhaustion) and the condition of natural moisture is able to resist the slender action of heat, (whereby it needeth no reparation), and this is evident in snakes, lizards, snails, and divers insects, latitant many months in the year; which being cold creatures, containing a weak heat in a crass or copious humidity, do long subsist without nutrition: for, the activity of the agent being not able to over-master the resistance of the patient, there will ensue no deperdition. And upon the like grounds it is, that cold and phlegmatic bodies, and (as Hippocrates determineth) that old men will best endure fasting. Now the same harmony and stationary constitution, as it happeneth in many species, so doth it fall out sometimes in individuals. For we read of many who have lived long time without aliment; and beside deceits and impostures, there may be veritable relations of some, who without a miracle, and by peculiarity of temper, have far out-fasted Elias. Which notwithstanding, doth not take off the miracle; for that may be miraculously effected in one, which is naturally causable in another. Some naturally living unto an hundred; unto which age others, notwithstanding, could not attain without a miracle.[6]

[5] *Which notwithstanding, &c.*] This sentence first added in 2nd edition.

[6] *miracles.*] The reader will have remarked in the course of this chapter, some false positions and unphilosophical observations, into which the author was led by the ignorance which at that time existed of some of those laws which modern discoveries have established in chemistry and physics; more especially with reference to the components of air, and the nature of combustion.

CHAPTER XXII.

That the Ostrich digesteth iron.

THE common opinion of the Ostrich, Struthiocamelus or Sparrow Camel, conceives that it digesteth iron, and this is confirmed by the affirmations of many: besides swarms of others, Rhodiginus in his prelections taketh it for granted, Johannes Langius in his epistles pleadeth experiment for it; the common picture also confirmeth it, which usually describeth this animal with an horseshoe in its mouth. Notwithstanding upon inquiry we find it very questionable, and the negative seems most reasonably entertained, whose verity indeed we do the rather desire, because hereby we shall relieve our ignorance of one occult quality, for in the list thereof it is accounted, and in that notion imperiously obtruded upon us. For my part, although I have had the sight of this animal, I have not had the opportunity of its experiment, but have received great occasion of doubt from learned discourses thereon.

For Aristotle and Oppianus, who have particularly treated hereof, are silent in this singularity, either omitting it as dubious, or as the comment saith, rejecting it as fabulous. Pliny, speaking generally, affirming only the digestion is wonderful in this animal; Ælian delivereth that it digested stones without any mention of iron; Leo Africanus, who lived in those countries wherein they most abound, speaketh diminutively, and but half way into this assertion, *Surdum ac simplex animal est, quicquid invenit, absque delectu, usque ad ferrum devorat;* Fernelius in his second *De Abditis rerum causis*, extenuates it, and Riolanus in his comment thereof positively denies it. Some have experimentally refuted it, as Albertus Magnus, and most plainly Ulysses Aldrovandus, whose words are these, *Ego ferri frusta devorare, dum Tridenti essem, observavi, sed quæ incocta rursus excerneret*, that is, "at my being at Trent, I observed the ostrich to swallow iron, but yet to exclude it undigested again."[7]

---

[7] *and most plainly, &c.*] But though Aldrovandus saw this *once*, "one swallow makes not a summer," says Master Ross, "who fully believes the iron to be digested; he is satisfied that even in that one

Now beside experiment, it is in vain to attempt against it by philosophical argument, it being an occult quality, which contemns the law of reason, and defends itself by admitting no reason at all. As for its possibility we shall not at present dispute; nor will we affirm that iron ingested, receiveth in the stomach of the ostrich no alteration at all; but if any such there be, we suspect this effect rather from some way of corrosion than any of digestion; not any liquid reduction or tendence to chylification by the power of natural heat, but rather some attrition from an acid and vitriolous humidity in the stomach, which may absterse and shave the scorious parts thereof. So rusty iron crammed down the throat of a cock, will become terse and clear again in its gizzard. So the counter, which, according to the relation of Amatus, remained a whole year in the body of a youth, and came out much consumed at last, might suffer this diminution rather from sharp and acid humours, than the strength of natural heat, as he supposeth. So silver swallowed and retained for some time in the body will turn black, as if it had been dipped in aqua fortis, or some corrosive water, but lead will remain unaltered, for that metal containeth in it a sweet salt or sugar, whereby it resisteth ordinary corrosion, and will not easily dissolve even in aqua fortis. So when for medical uses we take down the filings of iron or steel, we must not conceive it passeth unaltered from us, for though the grosser parts be excluded again, yet are the dissoluble parts extracted, whereby it becomes effectual in deoppila-

---

instance the stomach suckt something out of it!" The ostrich is naturally herbivorous; but though vegetable matter constitutes the basis of its food, and though it is often seen pasturing in the south of Africa, it is yet so voracious, and its senses of taste and smell are so obtuse, that it devours animal and mineral substances indiscriminately, until its enormous stomach is completely full. It swallows without any choice, and merely as it were for ballast, wood, stones, grass, iron, copper, gold, lime, or, in fact, any other substance equally hard, indigestible, and deleterious. The powers of digestion in this bird are certainly very great, but their operation is confined to matters of an alimentary character. But copper, far from being converted into nutriment, acts upon its stomach like poison, and nails very frequently pierce its coats and membranes. Vaillant mentions that one of these birds died in consequence of having devoured an immense quantity of quick lime.—*Cuvier.* In *Loudon's Magazine of Natural History*, No. 6, p. 62, is a relation of an ostrich having been killed by swallowing glass.

tions,[8] and therefore for speedier operation we make extinctions, infusions, and the like, whereby we extract the salt and active parts of the medicine, which being in solution, more easily enter the veins. And this is that the chemists mainly drive at in the attempt of their *Aurum Potabile*, that is, to reduce that indigestible substance into such a form as may not be ejected by siege, but enter the cavities, and less accessible parts of the body, without corrosion.

The ground of this conceit is its swallowing down fragments of iron, which men observing, by a froward illation, have therefore conceived it digesteth them, which is an inference not to be admitted, as being a fallacy of the consequent, that is, concluding a position of the consequent, from the position of the antecedent. For many things are swallowed by animals rather for condiment, gust or medicament, than any substantial nutriment. So poultry, and especially the turkey, do of themselves take down stones, and we have found at one time in the gizzard of a turkey no less than seven hundred. Now these rather concur unto digestion, than are themselves digested, for we have found them also in the guts and excrements; but their descent is very slow, for we have given them stones and small pieces of iron, which eighteen days after we have found remaining in the gizzard; and therefore the experiments of Langius and others might be fallible, whilst after the taking they expected it should come down within a day or two after. Thus also we swallow cherry stones, but void them unconcocted, and we usually say they preserve us from surfeit, for being hard bodies they conceive a strong and durable heat in the stomach, and so prevent the crudities of their fruit: and upon the like reason do culinary operators observe, that flesh boils best when the bones are boiled with it. Thus dogs will eat grass, which they digest not; thus camels to make the water sapid, do raise the mud with their feet; thus horses will knable[9] at walls, pigeons delight in salt stones; rats will gnaw iron, and Aristotle saith the elephant swalloweth stones; and thus may also the ostrich swallow iron, not as

---

[8] *deoppilations.*] Clearing away obstructions.

[9] *knable.*] "Probably to be found no where else," says Johnson. "than in this passage." Very probably; the fact is, that it is a frequent Norfolk vulgarization of the word *nibble*.

his proper aliment, but for the ends above expressed, and even as we observe the like in other animals.

And whether these fragments of iron and hard substances swallowed by the ostrich have not also that use in their stomachs which they have in other birds, that is, in some way to supply the use of teeth, by commolition, grinding and compressing of their proper aliment, upon the action of the strongly conformed muscles of the stomach, as the honoured Dr. Harvey discourseth, may also be considered.[1]

What effect therefore may be expected from the stomach of an ostrich by application alone to further digestion in ours beside the experimental refute of Galen, we refer it unto considerations above alleged. Or whether there be any more credit to be given unto the medicine of Ælian, who affirms, the stones they swallow have a peculiar virtue for the eyes, than that of Hermolaus and Pliny drawn from the urine of this animal,—let them determine who can swallow so strange a transmission of qualities, or believe that any bird or flying animal doth separately and distinctly urine beside the bat.

That therefore an ostrich will swallow and take down iron is easily to be granted; that oftentimes it passes entire away, if we admit of ocular testimony, is not to be denied. And though some experiment may also plead that sometimes they are so altered as not to be found or excluded in any discernible parcels, yet whether this be not effected by some way of corrosion, from sharp and dissolving humidities, rather than any proper digestion, chylifactive mutation, or alimental conversion, is with good reason doubted.[2]

CHAPTER XXIII.

Of the Unicorn's horn.

GREAT account and much profit is made of unicorn's horn, at least of that which beareth the name thereof; wherein notwithstanding, many, I perceive, suspect an im-

[1] *And whether, &c.*] This paragraph first added in third edition.
[2] *That therefore, &c.*] This paragraph was first added in second edition.

posture, and some conceive there is no such animal extant.³ Herein, therefore, to draw up our determinations: beside the several places of Scripture mentioning this animal (which some may well contend to be only meant of the rhinoceros) we are so far from denying there is any unicorn at all, that we affirm there are many kinds thereof. In the number of quadrupeds, we will concede no less than five; that is, the Indian ox, the Indian ass, the rhinoceros, the oryx, and that which is more eminently termed *monoceros* or *unicornis*. Some in the list of fishes; as that described by Olaus, Albertus, and others; and some unicorns we will allow even among insects, as those four kinds of nasicornous beetles, described by Muffetus.

Secondly, although we concede there be many unicorns, yet are we still to seek; for whereunto to affix this horn in question, or to determine from which thereof we receive this magnified medicine, we have no assurance, or any satisfactory decision. For although we single out one, and eminently thereto assign the name of the unicorn, yet can we

³ *some conceive, &c.*] Some information, on this much debated subject, was obtained by M. Rüppell, in Kordofan, where the unicorn was said to be known, and to bear the name of millekma. Persons of various conditions in life agreed to the statement, that the millekma was of a reddish colour, of the size of a small horse, of the slender make of a gazelle, and furnished with a long, straight, slender horn in the male, which was wanting in the female. Some added that it had divided hoofs, while others declared it to be single-hoofed. According to these statements it inhabits the deserts of the south of Kordofan, is uncommonly fleet, and comes only occasionally to the Koldagi slave mountain on the borders of Kordofan. Three several Arabs asserted to M. Rüppell that they had themselves seen the animal in question; and one of his slaves from Koldagi, on seeing the antelopes brought from the desert of Korti, gave, of his own free motion, a description of the millekma, exactly coinciding with the notices afterwards obtained by the traveller.

The unicorn of Scripture, however, which is there spoken of as an animal of great size and strength, is probably one of the species of two-horned rhinoceros. Mr. Burchell has described one in the *Bulletin des Sciences, Juin,* 1817. In the 15th number of the *Missionary Sketches,* published by the London Missionary Society, is a description, accompanied by a wood-cut, of a species shot in South Africa—the head of which is preserved in the museum of the society, Old Jewry, London: which seems, on account of its great size, strength, and ferocity, and of the extraordinary length of its anterior horn, not unlikely to have been the unicorn of Scripture.

not be secure what creature is meant thereby, what constant shape it holdeth, or in what number to be received. For as far as our endeavours discover, this animal is not uniformly described, but differently set forth by those that undertake it. Pliny affirmeth it is a fierce and terrible creature; Vartomannus, a tame and mansuete animal; those which Garcias ab Horto described about the Cape of Good Hope, were beheld with heads like horses; those which Vartomannus beheld, he described with the head of a deer; Pliny, Ælian, Solinus, and after these from ocular assurance, Paulus Venetus affirmeth the feet of the unicorn are undivided, and like the elephants; but those two which Vartomannus beheld at Mecca were, as he describeth, footed like a goat. As Ælian describeth, it is in the bigness of an horse: as Vartomannus, of a colt; that which Thevet speaketh of was not so big as an heifer; but Paulus Venetus affirmeth they are but little less than elephants. Which are discriminations very material, and plainly declare, that under the same name authors describe not the same animal: so that the unicorn's horn of one, is not that of another, although we proclaim an equal virtue in all.

Thirdly, although we were agreed what animal this was, or differed not in its description yet would this also afford but little satisfaction; for the horn we commonly extol is not the same with that of the ancients. For that, in the description of Ælian and Pliny, was black; this which is showed amongst us is commonly white, none black; and of those five which Scaliger beheld, though one spadiceous, or of a light red, and two inclining to red, yet was there not any of this complexion among them.

Fourthly, what horns soever they be which pass amongst us, they are not surely the horns of any one kind of animal, but must proceed from several sorts of unicorns. For some are wreathed, some not: that famous one which is preserved at St. Denis, near Paris, hath wreathy spires, and cochleary turnings about it, which agreeth with the description of the unicorn's horn in Ælian. Those two in the treasure of St. Mark are plain and best accord with those of the Indian ass, or the descriptions of other unicorns: that in the repository of the Elector of Saxony is plain and not hollow, and is believed to be a true land unicorn's horn. Albertus

Magnus describeth one ten feet long, and at the base about thirteen inches compass: and that of Antwerp, which Goropius Becanus describeth, is not much inferior unto it; which best agree unto the descriptions of the sea-unicorns; for these, as Olaus affirmeth, are of that strength and bigness, as to be able to penetrate the ribs of ships. The same is more probable, because it was brought from Iceland, from whence, as Becanus affirmeth, three other were brought in his days: and we have heard of some which have been found by the sea-side, and brought unto us from America. So that, while we commend the unicorn's horn, and conceive it peculiar but unto one animal, under apprehension of the some virtue we use very many, and commend that effect from all, which every one confineth unto some one he hath either seen or described.

Fifthly, although there be many unicorns, and consequently many horns, yet many there are which bear that name, and currently pass among us, which are no horns at all. Such are those fragments and pieces of *lapis ceratites*, commonly termed *cornu fossile*, whereof Boëtius had no less than twenty several sorts presented him for unicorn's horns. Hereof, in subterraneous cavities, and under the earth, there are many to be found in several parts of Germany, which are but the lapidescencies and petrifactive mutations of hard bodies: sometimes of horn, of teeth, of bones, and branches of trees, whereof there are some so imperfectly converted, as to retain the odour and qualities of their originals, as he relateth of pieces of ash and walnut. Again, in most, if not all, which pass amongst us, and are extolled for precious horns, we discover not an affection common unto other horns; that is, they mollify not with fire, they soften not upon decoction or infusion, nor will they afford a jelly or mucilaginous concretion in either; which notwithstanding we may effect in goat's horns, sheep's, cow's, and hart's horn; in the horn of the rhinoceros, the horn of the *pristis*, or sword-fish.[4] Nor do they become friable or easily powder-

---

[4] *an affection common unto other horns, &c.*] It would appear that Browne had confounded true horn (which is composed of coagulated albumen, with a little gelatin, and about a half per cent. of phosphate of lime), with hart's horn, and others of a similar nature, intermediate between bone and horn.

able by philosophical calcination, that is, from the vapour or steam of water, but split and rift contrary to other horns. Briefly, many of those commonly received, and whereof there be so many fragments preserved in England, are not only no horn, but a substance harder than a bone, that is, parts of the tooth of a morse or sea-horse: in the midst of the solider part containing a curdled grain, which is not to be found in ivory. This, in northern regions, is of frequent use for hafts of knives or hilts of swords, and being burnt, becomes a good remedy for fluxes; but antidotally used, and exposed for unicorn's horn, it is an insufferable delusion, and with more veniable deceit it might have been practised in hart's horn.

The like deceit may be practised in the teeth of other sea animals; in the teeth also of the hippopotamus, or great animal which frequenteth the river Nilus: for we read that the same was anciently used instead of ivory, or elephant's tooth. Nor is it to be omitted, what hath been formerly suspected, but now confirmed by Olaus Wormius, and Thomas Bartholinus, and others, that those long horns, preserved as precious rarities in many places, are but the teeth of narwhals, to be found about Iceland, Greenland, and other northern regions, of many feet long, commonly wreathed, very deeply fastened in the upper jaw, and standing directly forward, graphically described in Bartholinus,[*] according unto one sent from a bishop of Iceland, not separated from the crany. Hereof Mercator hath taken notice in his description of Iceland: some relations hereof there seem to be in Purchas, who also delivereth, that the horn at Windsor was in his second voyage brought hither by Forbisher. These, before the northern discoveries, as unknown rarities, were carried by merchants into all parts of Europe; and though found on the sea-shore, were sold at very high rates; but are now become more common, and probably in time will prove of little esteem; and the bargain of Julius the Third be accounted a very hard one, who stuck not to give many thousand crowns for one.

Nor is it great wonder we may be so deceived in this, being daily gulled in the brother antidote, bezoar; whereof

---

[*] *De Unicornu.*

though many be false, yet one there passeth amongst us of more intolerable delusion, somewhat paler than the true stone, and given by women in the extremity of great diseases, which, notwithstanding is no stone, but seems to be the stony seed of some *lithospermum* or greater grumwell; or the *lobus echinatus* of Clusius, called also the bezoar nut; for being broken, it discovereth a kernel of a leguminous smell and taste, bitter like a lupine, and will swell and sprout if set in the ground, and therefore more serviceable for issues, than dangerous and virulent diseases.[5]

Sixthly, although we were satisfied we had the unicorn's horn, yet were it no injury unto reason to question the efficacy thereof, or whether those virtues pretended do properly belong unto it. For what we observed (and it escaped not the observation of Paulus Jovius many years past), none of the ancients ascribed any medicinal or antidotal virtue unto the unicorn's horn; and that which Ælian extolleth, who was the first and only man of the ancients who spake of the medical virtue of any unicorn, was the horn of the Indian ass; whereof, saith he, the princes of those parts make bowls and drink therein, as preservatives against poison, convulsions, and the falling sickness. Now the description of that horn is not agreeable unto that we commend; for that (saith he) is red above, white below, and black in the middle; which is very different from ours, or any to be seen amongst us. And thus, though the description of the unicorn be very ancient, yet was there of old no virtue ascribed unto it; and although this amongst us receive the opinion of the same virtue, yet is it not the same horn whereunto the ancients ascribed it.

Lastly, although we allow it an antidotal efficacy, and such as the ancients commended, yet are there some virtues ascribed thereto by moderns not easily to be received; and it hath surely fallen out in this, as other magnified medicines, whose operations, effectual in some diseases, are presently extended unto all. That some antidotal quality it may have, we have no reason to deny; for since elk's hoofs and horns are magnified for epilepsies, since not only the

---

[5] *The like deceit, &c.*] These two paragraphs were first added in the 2nd edition.

bone in the hart, but the horn of the deer is alexipharmical,* and ingredient into the confection of hyacinth, and the electuary of Maximilian, we cannot without prejudice except against the efficacy of this. But when we affirm it is not only antidotal to proper venoms, and substances destructive by qualities we cannot express; but that it resisteth also sublimate, arsenick, and poisons which kill by second qualities, that is, by corrosion of parts; I doubt we exceed the properties of its nature, and the promises of experiment will not secure the adventure. And therefore in such extremities, whether there be not more probable relief from fat and oily substances, which are the open tyrants over salt and corrosive bodies, than precious and cordial medicines which operate by secret and disputable properties; or whether he that swallowed lime, and drank down mercury water, did not more reasonably place his cure in milk, butter, or oil, than if he had recurred unto pearl and bezoar, common reason at all times, and necessity in the like case, would easily determine.

Since therefore, there be many unicorns; since that whereto we appropriate a horn is so variously described, that it seemeth either never to have been seen by two persons, or not to have been one animal; since though they agreed in the description of the animal, yet is not the horn we extol the same with that of the ancients; since what horns soever they be that pass among us, they are not the horns of one, but several animals: since many in common use and high esteem are no horns at all; since if they were true horns, yet might their virtues be questioned; since though we allowed some virtues, yet were not others to be received; with what security a man may rely on this remedy, the mistress of fools hath already instructed some, and to wisdom (which is never too wise to learn), it is not too late to consider.

* Expulsive of poisons.

CHAPTER XXIV.

That all Animals of the Land are in their kind in the Sea.

THAT all animals of the land are, in their kind, in the sea, although received as a principle, is a tenet very questionable, and will admit of restraint. For some in the sea are not to be matched by any enquiry at land, and hold those shapes which terrestrious forms approach not; as may be observed in the moon-fish, or *orthragoriscus*, the several sorts of rays, torpedos, oysters, and many more; and some there are in the land which were never maintained to be in the sea, as panthers, hyænas, camels, sheep, moles, and others, which carry no name in icthyology, nor are to be found in the exact descriptions of Rondeletius, Gesner, or Aldrovandus.

Again, though many there be which make out their nominations, as the hedgehog, sea serpents, and others; yet are there also very many that bear the name of animals at land, which hold no resemblance in corporal configuration; in which account, we compute *vulpecula, canis, rana, passer, cuculus, asellus, turdus, lepus, &c.* Wherein while some are called the fox, the dog, the sparrow or frog fish, and are known by common names with those at land; yet as their describers attest, they receive not these appellations from a total similitude in figure, but any concurrence in common accidents, in colour, condition or single conformation. As for sea-horses, which much confirm this assertion, in their common descriptions,[6] they are but *grotesco* delineations, which fill up empty spaces in maps, and mere pictorial inventions, not any physical shapes: suitable unto those which (as Pliny delivereth) Praxiteles long ago set out in the temple of Domitius. For that which is commonly called a sea-horse, is properly called a *morse*, and makes not out

[6] *descriptions.*] But Scaliger, in his 187th exercitation, relates a particular description of them, and that 2 of them having got from the Portugals (watching at Capo Viride in the mouth of Gambra) as soone as they sawe the men returne to the long boote, set upon them most fiercely, and were not driven away with blowes; but as despairinge of doing any hurt to the men.—*Wr.*

that shape. That which the ancients named *hippocampus*, is a little animal about six inches long, and not preferred beyond the class of insects.[7] That which they termed *hippopotamus*, an amphibious animal, about the river Nile, so little resembleth an horse, that, as Matthiolus observeth, in all except the feet it better makes out a swine. That which they termed a lion, was but a kind of lobster; that which they called the bear, was but one kind of crab; and that which they named *bos marinus*, was not as we conceive a fish resembling an ox, but a skait or thornback, so named from its bigness, expressed by the Greek word *bous*, which is a prefix of augmentation to many words in that language.

And therefore, although it be not denied that some in the water do carry a justifiable resemblance to some at land, yet are the major part which bear their names, unlike; nor do they otherwise resemble the creatures on earth, than they on earth the constellations which pass under animal names in heaven; nor the dog-fish at sea much more make out the dog of the land, than that his cognominal or namesake in the heavens. Now if from a similitude in some, it be reasonable to infer a correspondence in all, we may draw this analogy of animals upon plants; for vegetables there are which carry a near and allowable similitude unto animals.* We might also conclude that animal shapes were generally made out in minerals: for several stones there are that bear their names in relation to animals or their parts, as *lapis anguinus, conchites, echinites, encephalites, ægophthalmus*, and many more; as will appear in the writers of minerals, and especially in Boëtius and Aldrovandus.

Moreover, if we concede that the animals of one element might bear the names of those in the other, yet in strict reason the watery productions should have the prenomination, and they of the land rather derive their names than nominate those of the sea; for the watery plantations were first existent, and as they enjoyed a priority in form, had

* *Fab. Column. de stirp. rarioribus, Orchis, Cercopithecophora, Anthropophora.*

[7] *not preferred, &c.*] A mistake. The hippocampus is one of the osseous fishes, belonging to the tribe called, by Cuvier, *lophobranches:—syngnathus hippocampus,* Lin.; but now constituted a distinct genus, *hippocampus vulgaris.*

also in nature precedent denominations; but falling not under that nomenclature of Adam, which unto terrestrious animals assigned a name appropriate unto their natures, from succeeding spectators they received arbitrary appellations, and were respectively denominated unto creatures known at land, who in themselves had independent names, and not to be called after them which were created before them.

Lastly, by this assertion we restrain the hand of God,[8] and abridge the variety of the creation, making the creatures of one element, but an acting over those of another, and conjoining as it were the species of things which stood at distance in the intellect of God, and though united in the chaos, had several seeds of their creation. For although in that indistinguished mass all things seemed one, yet separated by the voice of God, according to their species, they came out in incommunicated varieties, and irrelative seminalities, as well as divided places, and so although we say the world was made in six days, yet was there as it were a world in every one, that is, a distinct creation of distinguished creatures; a distinction in time of creatures divided in nature, and a several approbation and survey in every one.

CHAPTER XXV.[9]

Concerning the common course of our Diet, in making choice of some animals, and abstaining from eating others.

WHY we confine our food unto certain animals, and totally reject some others, how these distinctions crept into several nations, and whether this practice be built upon solid reason, or chiefly supported by custom or opinion, may admit consideration.

For first, there is no absolute necessity to feed on any, and if we resist not the stream of authority, and several deductions from Holy Scripture, there was no sarcophagy* before

* Eating of flesh.

[8] *we restrain the hand of God.*] This is a greate inconsequent, for both baboons and tritons imitate the shape of man, without disparagement to him, or (the Creator) Him that made man.—*Wr.*

[9] This chapter was new in 2nd edition.

the flood, and without the eating of flesh, our fathers, from vegetable aliments, preserved themselves unto longer lives than their posterity by any other. For whereas it is plainly said, "I have given you every herb which is upon the face of all the earth, and every tree; to you it shall be for meat:"—presently after the deluge, when the same had destroyed or infirmed[1] the nature of vegetables, by an expression of enlargement it is again delivered, "Every moving thing that liveth shall be meat for you; even as the green herb have I given you all things."

And therefore, although it be said that Abel was a shepherd, and it be not readily conceived the first man would keep sheep, except they made food thereof; great expositors will tell us, that it was partly for their skins wherewith they were clothed, partly for their milk whereby they were sustained, and partly for sacrifices, which they also offered.

And though it may seem improbable that they offered flesh yet ate none thereof, and Abel can hardly be said to offer the firstlings of his stock, and the fat or acceptable part, if men used not to taste the same, whereby to raise such distinctions; some will confine the eating of flesh unto the line of Cain, who extended their luxury, and confined not unto the rule of God. That if at any time the line of Seth ate flesh, it was extraordinary, and not only at their sacrifices; or else, as Grotius hinteth, if any such practice there were, it was not from the beginning, but from that time when the ways of men were corrupted, and whereof it is said, that the wickedness of man's heart was great; the more righteous part of mankind probably conforming unto the diet prescribed in Paradise, and the state of innocency; and yet however the practice of man conformed, this was the injunction of God, and might be therefore sufficient, without the food of flesh.

That they fed not on flesh, at least the faithful party, before the flood, may become more probable, because they refrained the same for some time after. For so it was generally delivered of the golden age and reign of Saturn, which is conceived the time of Noah, before the building of Babel.

[1] *infirmed.*] What scriptural evidence have we that the flood had "impaired the properties" of the vegetables which had been and still remained as food for man?

And he that considereth how agreeable this is unto the traditions of the Gentiles; that that age was of one tongue; that Saturn devoured all his sons but three; that he was the son of Oceanus and Thetis; that a ship was his symbol; that he taught the culture of vineyards, and the art of husbandry, and was therefore described with a sickle, may well conceive these traditions had their original in Noah. Nor did this practice terminate in him, but was continued at least in many after; as (beside the Pythagoreans of old, and Banyans now in India, who, upon single opinions refrain the food of flesh) ancient records do hint or plainly deliver; although we descend not so low as that of Asclepiades delivered by Porphyrius,* that men began to feed on flesh in the reign of Pygmaleon, brother of Dido, who invented several torments to punish the eaters of flesh.

Nor did men only refrain from the flesh of beasts at first, but, as some will have it, beasts from one another. And if we should believe very grave conjectures, carnivorous animals now were not flesh devourers then, according to the expression of the divine provision for them; "To every beast of the earth, and to every fowl of the air, I have given every green herb for meat, and it was so." And is also collected from the store laid up in the ark, wherein there seems to have been no fleshy provision for carnivorous animals. For of every kind of unclean beast there went but two into the ark, and therefore no stock of flesh to sustain them many days, much less almost a year.

But whenever it be acknowledged that men began to feed on flesh, yet how they betook themselves after to particular kinds thereof, with rejection of many others, is a point not clearly determined. As for the distinction of clean and unclean beasts, the original is obscure, and salveth not our practice. For no animal is naturally unclean, or hath this character in nature, and therefore whether in this distinction there were not some mystical intention; whether Moses, after the distinction made of unclean beasts, did not name these so before the flood by anticipation; whether this distinction before the flood were not only in regard of sacrifices, as that delivered after was in regard of food (for many were

---

* περὶ ἀποχῆς.

clean for food, which were unclean for sacrifice), or whether the denomination were but comparative, and of beasts less commodious for food, although not simply bad, is not yet resolved.

And as for the same distinction in the time of Moses, long after the flood, from thence we hold no restriction, as being no rule unto nations beside the Jews, in dietetical consideration or natural choice of diet, they being enjoined or prohibited certain foods upon remote and secret intentions. Especially thereby to avoid community with the Gentiles upon promiscuous commensality, or to divert them from the idolatry of Egypt, whence they came, they were enjoined to eat the gods of Egypt in the food of sheep and oxen. Withal in this distinction of animals the consideration was hieroglyphical, in the bosom and inward sense implying an abstinence from certain vices symbolically intimated from the nature of those animals, as may be well made out in the prohibited meat of swine, cony, owl, and many more.

At least the intention was not medical, or such as might oblige unto conformity, or imitation: for some we refrain which that law alloweth, as locusts and many others; and some it prohibiteth, which are accounted good meat in strict and medical censure, as (beside many fishes which have not fins and scales) the swine, cony, and hare, a dainty dish with the ancients; as is delivered by Galen, testified by Martial, as the popular opinion implied that men grew fair by the flesh thereof, by the diet of Cato, that is, hare and cabbage, and the *jus nigrum*,* or black broth of the Spartans, which was made with the blood and bowels of an hare.

And if we take a view of other nations we shall discover that they refrained many meats upon like considerations. For in some the abstinence was symbolical: so Pythagoras enjoined abstinence from fish, that is, luxurious and dainty dishes; so, according to Herodotus, some Egyptians refrained swine's flesh, as an impure and sordid animal, which whoever but touched was fain to wash himself.

Some abstained superstitiously or upon religious considerations: so the Syrians refrained fish and pigeons; the

---

* *Inter quadrupedes mattya prima lepus.*

Egyptians of old, dogs, eels, and crocodiles, though Leo Africanus delivers that many of late do eat them with good gust; and Herodotus also affirmeth that the Egyptians of Elephantina (unto whom they were not sacred) did eat thereof in elder times; and writers testify that they are eaten at this day in India and America. And so, as Cæsar reports,* unto the ancient Britains it was piaculous[2] to taste a goose, which dish at present no table is without.

Unto some nations the abstinence was political, and for some civil advantage: so the Thessalians refrained storks, because they destroyed their serpents; and the like in sundry animals is observable in other nations.

And under all these considerations were some animals refrained: so the Jews abstained from swine at first symbolically, as an emblem of impurity, and not fear of the leprosy, as Tacitus would put upon them. The Cretians superstitiously, upon tradition that Jupiter was suckled into that country by a sow. Some Egyptians politically, because they supplied the labour of plowing by rooting up the ground. And upon like considerations, perhaps, the Phœnicians and Syrians fed not on this animal; and, as Solinus reports, the Arabians also and Indians. A great part of mankind refraining one of the best foods, and such as Pythagoras himself would eat; who, as Aristoxenus records,† refused not to feed on pigs.

Moreover, while we single out several dishes, and reject others, the selection seems but arbitrary, or upon opinion; for many are commended and cried up in one age, which are decried and nauseated in another. Thus, in the days of Maecenas, no flesh was preferred before young asses; which notwithstanding became abominable unto succeeding appetites. At the table of Heliogabalus the combs of cocks were an esteemed service; which country stomachs will not admit at ours. The *sumen*, or belly and dugs of swine with pig, and sometimes beaten and bruised unto death; the womb of the same animal, especially that was barren, or else had cast her young ones, though a tough and membranous part, was magnified by Roman palates; whereunto

---

* Lib. v. *De Bello Gall.*   † *Aul. Gell.* lib. **iv.**

[2] *piaculous.*] Requiring expiation.

nevertheless, we cannot persuade our stomachs. How *alec*, *muria*, and *garum*, would humour our gust I know not; but surely few there are that could delight in their *cyceon*, that is, the common draught of honey, cheese, parched barley-flower, oil, and wine; which notwithstanding was a commended mixture, and in high esteem among them. We mortify ourselves with the diet of fish, and think we fare coarsely if we refrain from the flesh of other animals. But antiquity held another opinion hereof; when Pythagoras, in prevention of luxury, advised not so much as to taste of fish. Since the Rhodians were wont to call them clowns that eat flesh; and since Plato, to evidence the temperance of the noble Greeks before Troy, observed, that it was not found they fed on fish, though they lay so long near the Hellespont, and it was only observed in the companions of Menelaus,* that, being almost starved, they betook themselves to fishing about Pharos.

Nor will (I fear) the attest or prescript of philosophers and physicians be a sufficient ground to confirm or warrant common practice, as is deducible from ancient writers, from Hippocrates, Galen, Simeon, Sethi, and the latter tracts of Nonnus† and Castellanus.‡ So Aristotle and Albertus commend the flesh of young hawks; Galen§ the flesh of foxes about autumn, when they feed on grapes; but condemneth quails; and ranketh geese but with ostriches: which, notwithstanding, present practice and every table extolleth. Men think they have fared hardly, if in times of extremity they have descended so low as dogs: but Galen delivereth,‖ that young, fat, and gelded, they were the food of many nations: and Hippocrates¶ ranketh the flesh of whelps with that of birds, who also commends them against the spleen, and to promote conception. The opinion in Galen's time, which Pliny also followeth, deeply condemneth horse-flesh, and conceived the very blood thereof destructive; but no diet is more common among the Tartars, who also drink their blood. And though this may only seem an adventure of northern stomachs, yet as Herodotus tells us, in the hotter clime of Persia the same was a convivial dish,

* *Odyss.* iv. † Non. *De Re Cibaria.* ‡ Cast. *De Esu Carnium.*
§ Gal. *Alim. sac.* lib. iii.
‖ Gal. *Simpl. fac.* lib. iii. ¶ Hip. *De Morbis de supersit.*

and solemnly eaten at the feasts of their nativities; whereat they dressed whole horses, camels, and asses, contemning the poverty of Grecian feasts, as unfurnished of dishes sufficient to fill the bellies of their guests.

Again, while we confine our diet in several places, all things almost are eaten, if we take in the whole earth;[3] for that which is refused in one country is accepted in another, and in the collective judgment of the world, particular distinctions are overthrown. Thus were it not hard to show, that tigers, elephants, camels, mice, bats, and others, are the food of several countries; and Lerius, with others, delivers, that some Americans eat of all kinds, not refraining toads and serpents; and some have run so high, as not to spare the flesh of man; a practice inexcusable, nor to be drawn into example, a diet beyond the rule and largest indulgence of God.

As for the objection against beasts and birds of prey it acquitteth not our practice, who observe not this distinction in fishes, nor regard the same in our diet of pikes, perches, and eels; nor are we excused herein, if we examine the stomachs of mackerels, cods, and whitings. Nor is the foulness of food sufficient to justify our choice: for (beside that their natural heat is able to convert the same into laudable aliment) we refuse not many whose diet is more impure than some which we reject; as may be considered in hogs, ducks, puets, and many more.

[3] *all things almost are eaten, &c.*] This chapter, which exhibits all the characteristic acuteness of our author, and has afforded opportunity for the display of his extensive and very curious reading, reminds me of a passage in *Burchell's Southern Africa*, vol. ii. p. 33, to which I refer the reader.

I remember an amusing illustration of the adage, that one man's food is another's poison, in an incident of which I was a witness. Some years ago, visiting France in company with a Scotch gentleman, we sat down to dinner, just after our landing, at a *table d'hôte*, at Dieppe. Among the dishes which had been provided to suit the nationality of British visitors, was some "*ros bif;*" a lean square lump of beef roasted to the consistence of mahogany, served up with thin sour gravy. My Scotch friend, after vainly endeavouring to feed on the French dishes, was introduced to the beef. Its toughness he might have endured; but the thin sour gravy was too much! He turned to me with a face of absolute despair, exclaiming, "*I'll certainly be starved in this country.*" Milk and eggs were the only food I could prevail on him to taste.

Thus we perceive the practice of diet doth hold no certain course nor solid rule of selection or confinement; some in an indistinct voracity eating almost any; others out of a timorous pre-opinion refraining very many. Wherein, indeed, necessity, reason, and physic, are the best determinators. Surely many animals may be fed on, like many plants; though not in alimental, yet medical considerations: whereas, having raised antipathies by pre-judgment or education, we often nauseate proper meats, and abhor that diet which disease or temper requireth.

Now, whether it were not best to conform unto the simple diet of our forefathers; whether pure and simple waters were not more healthful than fermented liquors; whether there be not an ample sufficiency without all flesh, in the food of honey, oil, and the several parts of milk; in the variety of grains, pulses, and all sorts of fruits, since either bread or beverage may be made almost of all; whether nations have rightly confined unto several meats; or whether the common food of one country be not more agreeable unto another; how indistinctly all tempers apply unto the same, and how the diet of youth and old age is confounded; were considerations much concerning health, and might prolong our days, but not this discourse.

CHAPTER XXVI.[4]

Of the Spermaceti Whale.

WHAT *spermaceti* is, men might justly doubt, since the learned Hofmannus, in his work of thirty years,[*] saith plainly, *Nescio quid sit*. And therefore need not wonder at the variety of opinions; while some conceived it to be *flos maris;* and many, a bituminous substance floating upon the sea.

That it was not the spawn of the whale, according to vulgar conceit or nominal appellation, philosophers have always doubted, not easily conceiving the seminal humour of animals should be inflammable or of a floating nature.

[*] *De Medicamentis Officin.*

[4] *Chap.* xxvi.] This chapter was first added in 3rd edition.

That it proceedeth from the whale, beside the relation of Clusius and other learned observers, was indubitably determined, not many years since, by a *spermaceti* whale, cast on our coast of Norfolk;* which, to lead on further enquiry, we cannot omit to inform. It contained no less than sixty feet in length, the head somewhat peculiar, with a large prominency over the mouth; teeth only in the lower jaw, received into fleshy sockets in the upper. The weight of the largest about two pounds; no gristly substances in the mouth, commonly called whale-bones; only two short fins seated forwardly on the back; the eyes but small; the pizzle large and prominent. A lesser whale of this kind, above twenty years ago, was cast upon the same shore.†

The description of this whale seems omitted by Gesner, Rondeletius, and the first editions of Aldrovandus; but described in the Latin impression of Pareus, in the *Exoticks* of Clusius, and the *Natural History* of Nirembergius; but more amply in the icons and figures of Johnstonus.

Mariners (who are not the best nomenclators) called it a *jubartas*, or rather *gibbartas*. Of the same appellation we meet with one in Rondeletius, called by the French, *gibbar*, from its round and gibbous back. The name, *gibbarta*, we find also given unto one kind of Greenland whales; but this of ours seemed not to answer the whale of that denomination, but was more agreeable unto the *trumpo* or *spermaceti* whale,[5] according to the account of our Greenland describers in Purchas; and maketh the third among the eight remarkable whales of that coast.

Out of the head of this whale, having been dead divers days and under putrefaction, flowed streams of oil and *spermaceti*, which was carefully taken up and preserved by the coasters. But upon breaking up, the magazine of *spermaceti* was found in the head, lying in folds and courses, in the bigness of goose-eggs, encompassed with large flaky substances,

* Near Wells.   † Near Hunstanton.

trumpo *or* spermaceti *whale.*] The *cachalot macrocephalus*. The upper part of its enormous head, as here described, is filled with an oil, called (very absurdly) *spermaceti*, which fixes when it cools, assuming a consistence like that of the pulp of a water-melon, and when completely concrete, it is crystallized and brilliant.

as large as a man's head, in form of honeycombs, very white and full of oil.

Some resemblance or trace hereof there seems to be in the *physiter* or *capidolio* of Rondeletius; while he delivers, that a fatness, more liquid than oil, runs from the brain of that animal; which being out, the relicks are like the scales of *Sardinos* pressed into a mass; which melting with heat, are again concreted by cold. And this many conceive to have been the fish which swallowed Jonas; although, for the largeness of the mouth, and frequency in those seas, it may possibly be the *lamia*.

Some part of the *spermaceti* found on the shore was pure, and needed little depuration; a great part mixed with fœtid oil, needing good preparation, and frequent expression, to bring it to a flaky consistency. And not only the head, but other parts contained it. For the carnous parts being roasted the oil dropped out, an axungious[6] and thicker part subsiding; the oil itself contained also much in it, and still after many years some is obtained from it.

Greenland enquirers seldom meet with a whale of this kind; and therefore it is but a contingent commodity, not reparable from any other. It flameth white and candent like camphor, but dissolveth not in *aqua fortis* like it. Some lumps containing about two ounces, kept ever since in water, afford a fresh and flosculous smell. Well prepared and separated from the oil, it is of a substance unlikely to decay, and may outlast the oil required in the composition of Matthiolus.

Of the large quantity of oil, what first came forth by expression from the *spermaceti* grew very white and clear, like that of almonds or *ben*. What came by decoction was red. It was found to spend much in the vessels which contained it; it freezeth or coagulateth quickly with cold, and the newer soonest. It seems different from the oil of any other animal, and very much frustrated the expectation of our soap-boilers, as not incorporating or mingling with their lyes. But it mixeth well with painting colours, though hardly drieth at all. Combers of wool made use hereof, and country people for cuts, aches, and hard tumours. It may prove of good

---

[6] *axungious.*] Fatty. From *axungia*.

medical use, and serve for a ground in compounded oils and balsams. Distilled, it affords a strong oil, with a quick and piercing water. Upon evaporation it gives a balsam, which is better performed with turpentine distilled with *spermaceti*.

Had the abominable scent permitted, enquiry had been made into that strange composure of the head, and hillock of flesh about it. Since the workmen affirmed they met with *spermaceti* before they came to the bone, and the head yet preserved seems to confirm the same. The sphincters inserving unto the *fistula* or spout, might have been examined, since they are so notably contrived in other cetaceous animals; as also the *larynx* or throttle, whether answerable unto that of dolphins and porpoises in the strange composure and figure which it maketh. What figure the stomach maintained in this animal of one jaw of teeth, since in porpoises, which abound in both, the ventricle is trebly divided, and since in that formerly taken nothing was found but weeds and a *loligo*. The heart, lungs, and kidneys, had not escaped; wherein are remarkable differences from animals of the land: likewise what humour the bladder contained, but especially the seminal parts, which might have determined the difference of that humour from this which beareth its name.

In vain it was to rake for ambergriese[7] in the paunch of this leviathan, as Greenland discoverers, and attests of experience dictate that they sometimes swallow great lumps thereof in the sea; insufferable foetor denying that enquiry: and yet if, as Paracelsus encourageth, ordure makes the best musk, and from the most foetid substances may be drawn the most odoriferous essences; all that had not Vespasian's nose * might boldly swear here was a subject fit for such extractions.

* *Cui odor lucri ex re qualibet.*

[7] *ambergriese.*] This substance is excrement hardened by disease, and mixed with undigested aliment: found in lumps in the intestines.

CHAPTER XXVII.

Compendiously of the musical note of Swans before their death; that the flesh of Peacocks corrupteth not; that they are ashamed of their legs; that Storks will only live in republicks and free states; of the noise of a Bittern by putting the bill in a reed; that Whelps are blind nine days; of the antipathy between a Toad and a Spider, a Lion and a Cock; that an Earwig hath no wings; of Worms; that Flies make that humming noise by their mouths or wings; of the Tainct or small Red Spider; of the Glow-worm; of the providence of Pismires in biting off the ends of corn.

1. AND first, from great antiquity, and before the melody of Syrens, the musical note of swans hath been commended, and that they sing most sweetly before their death: for thus we read in Plato, that from the opinion of *Metempsychosis*, or transmigration of the souls of men into the bodies of beasts most suitable unto their human condition, after his death Orpheus the musician became a swan; thus was it the bird of Apollo, the god of music, by the Greeks; and an hieroglyphick of music among the Egyptians,[*] from whom the Greeks derived the conception;—hath been the affirmation of many Latins, and hath not wanted assertors almost from every nation.

All which notwithstanding, we find this relation doubtfully received by Ælian, as an hearsay account by Bellonius, as a false one by Pliny, expressly refuted by Myndius in *Athenæus*, and severely rejected by Scaliger; whose words unto Cardan are these: *De cygno verò cantu suavissimo quem cum parente mendaciorum Græcia jactare ausus es, ad Luciani tribunal apud quem novi aliquid dicas, statuo.* Authors also that countenance it, speak not satisfactorily of it: some affirming they sing not till they die; some that they sing, yet die not. Some speak generally, as though this note were in all; some but particularly, as though it were only in some; some in places remote, and where we can have no trial of it; others in places where every experience can refute it; as

---

[*] *an hieroglyphick, &c.*] In Horapollo. Neither Dr. Young nor Champollion speaks of it, though the latter mentions, as represented in hieroglyphicks, "many web-footed birds."—*Br.*

Aldrovandus upon relation delivered concerning the music of the swans on the river of Thames, near London.

Now that which countenanceth and probably confirmeth this opinion, is the strange and unusual conformation of the windpipe, or vocal organ [9] in this animal; observed first by Aldrovandus, and conceived by some contrived for this intention. For in its length it far exceedeth the gullet, and hath in the chest a sinuous revolution, that is, when it ariseth from the lungs it ascendeth not directly unto the throat, but de-

---

[9] *conformation of the windpipe, &c.*] The vast variety which exists, in quality and extent of tone, as well as in diversity of modulation in the cry and song of birds, arises from a corresponding variety in the structure of their organs of voice. This curious subject has been investigated with much diligence and ingenuity by various ornithologists; especially by Dr. Latham some years ago, and more recently by Mr. Yarrell. Their papers, in the *Linnæan Transactions*, vols. iv. xv. and xvi., will afford much gratification to those readers who feel an interest in the subject. From the examination of these naturalists, it appears, that much of the strength, as well as perfection, of the song of birds, is attributable to the number and size of the muscles of the larynx. Those of the singing birds are the most numerous of any; and in the *nightingale* are stronger than in any other bird of the same size. The power and depth of tone in some birds will be found to increase with the elongation of the tube. On which principle it is, that the difference of the vocal powers of the mute swan and hooper, or wild swan, must be explained. The more complicated the structure of the tube, the more disagreeable the sound of the voice; the simple forms belonging to the most delightful of our singing birds. Again, shrill notes are produced by short tubes (as in the case of the *singing birds*), and deep tones by long tubes (as in the *waders* and *swimmers*). The substance of the tube itself is also to be considered: birds possessing strong and broad cartilages, or bony rings, have monotonous and loud voices, while the more slender rings allow a corresponding variety in the scale of tone. Mr. Yarrell concludes his second paper with the following observation:—" It will perhaps be objected, that the utmost extent of motion which birds appear to possess the power of exercising, over the various parts of their organ of voice, seems insufficient to account for the effects produced; but it may in answer be urged, that the closest examination or most scientific demonstration of the *chordæ vocales* and muscles in man, with all the auxiliary appendages, afford but an imperfect illustration of the varied and extraordinary powers of the human voice." It need scarcely be observed, that the peculiarity noticed by our author in the tracheæ of the wild swan, has nothing to do with any extraordinary powers of submersion: but is the occasion of the shrill, piercing, and harsh note which has obtained from him the name of the whistler or hooper; an appellation far more applicable than that of the "musical" swan, for which he is indebted to fabulous antiquity.

scending first into a capsulary reception of the breast-bone, by a serpentine and trumpet recurvation it ascendeth again into the neck, and so by the length thereof a great quantity of air is received, and by the figure thereof a musical modulation effected. But to speak indifferently, this formation of the weazand[1] is not peculiar unto the swan, but common also unto the *platea* or shovelard, a bird of no musical throat; and, as Aldrovandus confesseth, may thus be contrived in the swan to contain a larger stock of air, whereby being to feed on weeds at the bottom, they might the longer space detain their heads under water. But were this formation peculiar, or had they unto this effect an advantage from this part, yet have they a known and open disadvantage from another, that is, a flat bill. For no latirostrous[2] animal (whereof nevertheless there are no slender numbers), were ever commended for their note, or accounted among those animals which have been instructed to speak.

When therefore, we consider the dissension of authors, the falsity of relations, the indisposition of the organs, and the immusical note of all we ever beheld or heard of, if generally taken, and comprehending all swans, or of all places, we cannot assent thereto. Surely he that is bit with a *tarantula*, shall never be cured by this music; and with the same hopes we expect to hear the harmony of the spheres.

2. That there is a special propriety in the flesh of peacocks roasted or boiled, to preserve a long time incorrupted, hath been the assertion of many; stands yet confirmed by Austin, *De civitate Dei;* by Gygas Sempronius in Aldrovandus; and the same experiment we can confirm ourselves, in the brawn or fleshy parts of peacocks so hanged up with thread, that they touch no place whereby to contract a moisture; and hereof we have made trial both in summer and winter. The reason, some, I perceive, attempt to make out from the siccity and dryness of its flesh, and some are content to rest in a secret propriety hereof. As for the siccity[3] of the flesh, it is more remarkable in other animals; as

---

[1] *weazand.*] Winde-pipe.—*Wr.*
[2] *latirostrous.*] Broad or shovel-beaked.—*Wr.*
[3] *siccity.*] There is a siccity which is joynd more with **rarifye:** and another which approaches nearer to solidity; and of this kind are these 5 mentioned, especially 1, 3, 5. But the siccity of the peacock

eagles, hawks, and birds of prey. That it is a propriety or agreeable unto none other, we cannot, with reason, admit; for the same preservation, or rather incorruption, we have observed in the flesh of turkeys, capons, hares, partridges, venison, suspended freely in the air, and after a year and a half, dogs have not refused to eat them.[4]

As for the other conceit, that a peacock is ashamed when he looks on his legs, as is commonly held, and also delivered by Cardan; beside what hath been said against it by Scaliger; let them believe that hold specifical deformities, or that any part can seem unhandsome to their eyes, which hath appeared good and beautiful unto their Maker's. The occasion of this conceit might first arise from a common observation, that when they are in their pride, that is advance their train, if they decline their neck to the ground, they presently demit, and let fall the same: which indeed they cannot otherwise do; for contracting their body, and being forced to draw in their fore-parts, to establish their hinder in the elevation of their train, if the fore-parts depart and incline to the ground, the hinder grow too weak, and suffer the train to fall. And the same in some degree is also observable in turkeys.

3. That storks are to be found, and will only live in republicks or free states, is a petty conceit to advance the opinion of popular policies, and from antipathies in nature to disparage monarchical government. But how far agreeable unto truth, let them consider who read in Pliny, that among the Thessalians, who were governed by kings, and much abounded with serpents, it was no less than capital to kill a

---

is accompanyed with an unwonted rarity, as appeares by his fethers, the largest and lightest of any other bird under heaven, which argues the drines of his natural temper, *in extremo siccitatis;* to which you may joyne the beauty of his colors, the whitenes, softnes, and tendernes of the pith in his wing and tayle fethers, proceeding (at a yard length) out of a quil, not an inche long, and soe thin and tender, that for want of substance and strength, are not so useful as a crowe's quil.—*Wr.*

[4] *the same preservation, &c.*] "My pendent pantry, made of deal and fine fly wire, and suspended in the great walnut tree, proves an incomparable preservative for meat against flesh-flies. The flesh, by hangin in a brisk current of air, becomes dry on the surface, and keeps till it i tender without tainting."—*Rev. G. White's MSS. Jesse's 2nd Gleaning* p. 171.

stork; that the ancient Egyptians honoured them, whose government was from all times monarchical; that Bellonius affirmeth men make them nests in France;[5] that relations make them common in Persia, and the dominions of the great Turk; and lastly, how Jeremy the prophet delivered himself* unto his countrymen, whose government was at that time monarchical;—" the stork in the heaven knoweth her appointed times; the turtle, crane, and swallow, observe the time of their coming; but my people know not the judgments of the Lord;"—wherein, to exprobrate their stupidity, he induceth the providence of storks. Now if the bird had been unknown, the illustration had been obscure, and the exprobration not so proper.

4. That a bittern maketh that mugient[6] noise, or as we term it, bumping, by putting its bill into a reed, as most believe, or as Bellonius and Aldrovandus conceive, by putting the same in mud or water, and after awhile retaining the air by suddenly excluding it again, is not so easily made out. For my own part, though after diligent enquiry, I could never behold them in this motion. Notwithstanding, by others whose observations we have expressly requested, we are informed that some have beheld them making this noise on the shore, their bills being far enough removed from reed or water; that is, first strongly attracting the air, and unto a manifest distention of the neck, and presently after with great contention and violence excluding the same again. As for what others affirm, of putting their bill in water or mud, it is also hard to make out. For what may be observed from any that walketh the fens, there is little intermission, nor any observable pause, between the drawing in and sending forth of their breath. And the expiration or breathing forth doth not only produce a noise, but the inspiration or haling

---

* Jer. viii. 7.

[5] *men make them nests, &c.*] "There is a rich hospital at Fez, in Morocco, for the purpose of *assisting and nursing sick cranes and storks, and of burying them when dead.* They hold that storks are human beings in that form, from some distant islands."—*Queen Bee*, iii. 18.—*Jeff.*

[6] *mugient.*] Bellowing, or rather braying, like an asse: for soe his compound name (in the Greeke) signifies ὀνοκρόταλος, i.e. the harrishe noyse of an asse.—*Wr.*

in of the air, affordeth a sound that may be heard almost a flight-shot.⁷

Now the reason of this strange and peculiar noise, is deduced from the conformation of the windpipe, which in this bird is different from other volatiles.⁸ For at the upper extreme it hath no fit *larynx* or throttle to qualify the sound, and at the other end, by two branches deriveth itself into the lungs. Which division consisteth only of semicircular fibres, and such as attain but half way round the part: by which formation they are dilatable into larger capacities, and are able to contain a fuller proportion of air; which being with violence sent up the weazand, and finding no resistance by the *larynx*, it issueth forth in a sound like that from caverns, and such as sometimes subterraneous eruptions from hollow rocks afford.⁹ As Aristotle observeth in a problem :* and

† Sect. xv.

⁷ *but the inspiration, &c.*] The screaming of parrots is said to be effected by inspiration as well as expiration.

⁸ *Now the reason, &c.*] See note on the organs of voice in birds, p. 358. The same contradiction of the common notion is given (from personal experience) by Rev. S. Fovargue, in his *New Catalogue of Vulgar Errors*, pp. 19, 20, 21. He gives, at the same time, a pleasant account of the cunning with which the bittern attempts to deceive his pursuer, when escape is impossible—after relating that he had heard a bittern utter this peculiar cry, and on repairing to the spot whence the sound proceeded, found that it was covered with coarse grass, where there were no reeds—he proceeds thus :—

"When the aforesaid bittern rose up, I shot, and wounded him slightly, and marked him down again in the same kind of grass or short mowed flags. As the grass was not higher than one's shoes, and it was wounded, I was in hopes of having the pleasure of seeing him lie on the ground very plain. However, I let my pointer go first, knowing that he would stand at the place. Accordingly he made a dead point at it. I came up as silent as possible, to take a view of it, but to my great surprise, nothing was to be seen.

"There was indeed something which appeared long, like two green weeds lying among the grass, and there was something like a large spot of dried grass or flags a little before them.

"While I was looking at the place, the dog, being out of patience, seized hold of this phænomenon, which proved to be no other than the bittern itself. Those things which seemed to be green weeds, were its legs extended at the full length, behind the bird, as it lay quite flat upon its belly; and that broad spot of brown or dried grass, was the body, with the wings extended to their full stretch, quite flat upon the ground, which, I believe, formed as complete a *deceptio visus* as any thing in nature."

⁹ *being with violence, &c.*] Yf you observe the geese in their lowd

is observable in pitchers, bottles, and that instrument which Aponensis upon that problem describeth, wherewith in Aristotle's time gardeners affrighted birds.

Whether the large perforations of the extremities of the weazand, in the abdomen, admitting large quantity of air within the cavity of its membranes, as it doth in frogs, may not much assist this mugiency or boation, may also be considered. For such as have beheld them making this noise out of the water, observe a large distention in their bodies; and their ordinary note is but like that of a raven.

5. That whelps are blind nine days, and then begin to see,[1] is the common opinion of all, and some will be apt enough to descend upon oaths upon it. But this I find not answerable unto experience, for upon a strict observation of many, I have scarce found any that see the ninth day, few before the twelfth, and the eyes of some not open before the fourteenth day. And this is agreeable unto the determination of Aristotle, who computeth the time of their *anopsy* or non-vision by that of their gestation. For some, saith he, do go with their young the sixth part of a year, two days over or under, that is, about sixty days or nine weeks; and the whelps of these see not till twelve days. Some go the fifth part of a year, that is seventy-one days; and these, saith he, see not before the fourteenth day. Others do go the fourth part of the year, that is, three whole months;[2] and these, saith he, are without sight no less than seventeen days.[3] Wherein although the accounts be different, yet doth the least thereof exceed the term of nine days, which is so generally received. And this compute of Aristotle doth generally overthrow the common cause alleged for this effect,

call (which is hearde very far) you shall observe a stronge commotion of their lungs, rising to the bottom of the neck.— *Wr.*

[1] *begin to see.*] Itt is probable, in hot, they saw after 9 dayes; in our clymate perhaps not till 12.— *Wr.*

[2] *three whole months.*] i. e. 91 dayes.— *Wr.*

[3] *seventeen days.*] 'Tis observable that the soonest bred see soonest: and the reason is naturall. The acceleration of the birthe and sighte from one and the same cause; viz. the activity of the spirits in the braine, which in some kinde of dogs is seen much more than in others: and in all the lesser kinds more then the greater: in these, the spirits (of the whelps) being drowned in a loade of fat and fleshe, which afterwards growing dryer, gives them leave to put forthe the spirits to an highth o-strength, though not of such nimbleness as in the lesser kindes.— *Wr.*

that is, a precipitation or over-hasty exclusion before the birth be perfect, according unto the vulgar adage, *Festinans canis cæcos parit catulos:* for herein the whelps of longest gestation are also the latest in vision. The manner hereof is this: at the first littering their eyes are fastly closed, that is, by coalition or joining together of the eyelids, and so continue until about the twelfth day; at which time they begin to separate, and may be easily divelled⁴ or parted asunder; they open at the inward *canthus* or greater angle of the eye, and so by degrees dilate themselves quite open: an effect very strange, and the cause of much obscurity, wherein as yet men's enquiries are blind, and satisfaction not easily acquirable. Whatever it be, thus much we may observe, those animals are only excluded without sight which are multiparous and multifidous, that is, which have many at a litter, and have also their feet divided into many portions. For the swine, although multiparous, yet being bisulcous, and only cloven-hoofed, is not excluded in this manner, but farrowed with open eyes as other bisulcous animals.

6. The antipathy between a toad and a spider, and that they poisonously destroy each other, is very famous, and solemn stories have been written of their combats, wherein most commonly the victory is given unto the spider. Of what toads and spiders it is to be understood would be considered. For the *phalangium* and deadly spiders are different from those we generally behold in England. However, the verity hereof, as also of many others, we cannot but desire; for hereby we might be surely provided of proper antidotes in cases which require them. But what we have observed herein, we cannot in reason conceal; who having in a glass included a toad with several spiders, we beheld the spiders, without resistance to sit upon his head and pass over all his body; which at last upon advantage he swallowed down, and that in few hours, unto the number of seven.⁵

⁴ *divelled.*] Pulled asunder.
⁵ *seven.*] This is a remarkable experiment, whereon wee maye conclude against the old deception.—*Wr.*

Erasmus tells a ridiculous story of a monk found asleep on his back, with a toad squatted upon his mouth. The brethren carefully conveying the body, placed it immediately under the web of a spider, who instantly descended upon, and at length *slew* the toad, and delivered the monk from an ugly death.

And in the like manner will toads also serve bees, and are accounted enemies unto their hives.[6]

7. Whether a lion be also afraid of a cock, as is related by many, and believed by most, were very easy in some places to make trial. Although how far they stand in fear of that animal we may sufficiently understand from what is delivered by Camerarius, whose words in his *Symbola* are these; *Nostris temporibus in aula serenissimi Principis Bavariæ, unus ex leonibus miris saltibus in vicinam cujusdam domus aream sese dimisit, ubi gallinaceorum cantum aut clamores nihil reformidans, ipsos, una cum pluribus gallinis devoravit.* That is, "in our time in the court of the Prince of Bavaria, one of the lions leaped down into a neighbour's yard, where, nothing regarding the crowing or noise of the cocks, he eat them up with many other hens."[7] And therefore a very unsafe defensative it is against the fury of this animal (and surely no better than virginity or blood royal), which Pliny* doth place in cock broth: for herein, saith he, whoever is anointed (especially if garlick be boiled therein), no lion or panther will touch him. But of an higher nature it were, and more exalted antipathy, if that were certain which Proclus delivers, that solary demons, and such as appear in the shape of lions, will disappear and vanish if a cock be presented upon them.[8]

8. It is generally conceived an earwig hath no wings, and is reckoned amongst impennous[9] insects by many: but he that

* *De sacrificiis et magia.*

[6] *hives.*] Which the bees (who of all creatures have the most accurate smell) soone perceive, and are poisoned with itt. That they never gather of more then one and the same flower in kinde, is manifest *ad oculum:* that by only flying swift by over many they discerne that one kind, are arguments of their exquisite smell.— *Wr.*

[7] *nothing regarding, &c.*] The learned and reverend Bishop Andrewes was desirous to try this upon a young lyon, to whome hee cast in a younge cock, whom (as he was crowing) the lyon seized on (as a cat on a mouse) and tare him and eate him up. Hee related this to mee for information against the fabulous conceyte, anno 1620, at his own table.— *Wr.*

Ross, rather than give up the old belief, accounts for the story told of the Prince of Bavaria's lion, by supposing it must have been mad! The bishop did not probably dream of such a solution.

[8] *But of an higher nature, &c.*] This sentence first added in 2nd edit.
[9] *impennous.*] Wingless.

shall narrowly observe them, or shall with a needle put aside the short and sheathy cases on their back, may extend and draw forth two wings of a proportionable length for flight, and larger than in many flies. The experiment of Pennius is yet more perfect, who with a brush or bristle so pricked them as to make them fly.

9. That worms are exsanguinous animals,[1] and such as have no blood at all, is the determination of philosophy, the general opinion of scholars, and I know not well how to dissent from thence myself. If so, surely we want a proper term whereby to express that humour in them which so strictly resembleth blood; and we refer it unto the discernment of others what to determine of that red and sanguinous humour, found more plentifully about the torquis or carneous circle of great worms in the spring, affording in linen or paper an indiscernible tincture from blood. Or wherein that differeth from a vein, which in an apparent blue runneth along the body, and if dextrously pricked with a lance emitteth a red drop, which pricked on either side, it will not readily afford.

In the upper parts of worms, there are likewise found certain white and oval glandulosities, which authors term eggs, and in magnifying glasses they also represent them; how properly, may also be enquired; since, if in them there be distinctions of sexes, these eggs are to be found in both. For in that which is presumed to be their coition, that is, their usual complication, or lateral adhesion above the ground, dividing suddenly[2] with two knives the adhering parts of both, I have found these eggs in either.

10. That flies, bees, &c. do make that noise or humming sound by their mouth, or as many believe, with their wings only, would be more warily asserted, if we consulted the

---

[1] *That worms are, &c.*] They are not so. Sir Everard Home, in his 13th lecture on *Comparative Anatomy*, illustrated by the exquisite pencil of Bauer, shows that the earth-worm is provided with a central artery, with six bags or cells on each side, filled with red blood; thereby proving the accuracy of Sir Thomas's own examination.

[2] *dividing.*] Itt seemes to have been in the very instant of coition, when the male emptyes himself of them, and was imparted before the full impletion of the female.— *Wr.*

The dean's remark proves him unacquainted with the mode of propagation in the worm. See Sir E. Home's 13th lecture.

determination of Aristotle, who as in sundry other places, so more expressly in his book of respiration, affirmeth this sound to be made by the illision of an inward spirit upon a pellicle or little membrane about the precinct or pectoral division of their body. If we also consider that a bee or fly, so it be able to move the body, will buzz, though its head be off; that it will do the like if deprived of wings,[3] reserving the head, whereby the body may be the better moved; and that some also which are big and lively will hum without either head or wing.

Nor is it only the beating upon this little membrane by the inward and connatural spirit, as Aristotle determines, or the outward air, as Scaliger conceiveth, which affordeth this humming noise, but most of the other parts may also concur hereto: as will be manifest, if while they hum we lay our finger on the back or other parts, for thereupon will be felt a serrous or jarring motion, like that which happeneth while we blow on the teeth of a comb through paper; and so, if the head or other parts of the trunk be touched with oil, the sound will be much impaired, if not destroyed; for those being also dry and membranous parts, by attrition of the spirit do help to advance the noise. And therefore also the sound is strongest in dry weather, and very weak in rainy seasons, and towards winter; for then the air is moist, and the inward spirit growing weak, makes a languid and dumb allision upon the parts.

11. There is found in the summer a kind of spider called a tainct, of a red colour, and so little of body that ten of the largest will hardly outweigh a grain; this by country people is accounted a deadly poison unto cows and horses; who, if they suddenly die, and swell thereon, ascribe their death hereto, and will commonly say, they have licked a tainct. Now to satisfy the doubts of men, we have called this tradition unto experiment; we have given hereof unto dogs, chickens, calves, and horses, and not in the singular number; yet never could find the least disturbance ensue. There must be therefore other causes enquired of the sudden death

---

[3] *that it will do the like, &c.*] This is not accurate. Dr. Geer tried it and found the sound continued, when the stumps of the wings remained, whose vibration occasioned the sound: but it ceased when he perfected the experiment by entirely removing the wings.

and swelling of cattle; and perhaps this insect is mistaken, and unjustly accused for some other. For some there are which from elder times have been observed pernicious unto cattle, as the *buprestis*, or burstcow, the *pityocampe* or *eruca pinuum*, by Dioscorides, Galen, and Ætius, the *staphilinus* described by Aristotle and others, or those red phalangious spiders like *cantharides*, mentioned by Muffetus. Now, although the animal may be mistaken, and the opinion also false, yet in the ground and reason which makes men most to doubt the verity hereof, there may be truth enough, that is, the inconsiderable quantity of this insect. For that a poison cannot destroy in so small a bulk, we have no reason to affirm. For if, as Leo Africanus reporteth, the tenth part of a grain of the poison of *nubia** will dispatch a man in two hours; if the bite of a viper and sting of a scorpion is not conceived to impart so much; if the bite of an asp will kill within an hour, yet the impression scarce visible, and the poison communicated not ponderable; we cannot as impossible reject this way of destruction, or deny the power of death in so narrow a circumscription.

12. Wondrous things are promised from the glow-worm;[4] from thence perpetual lights are pretended, and waters said to be distilled which afford a lustre in the night; and this is asserted by Cardan, Albertus, Gaudentinus, Mizaldus, and many more. But hereto we cannot with reason assent; for the light made by this animal depends much upon its life. For when they are dead they shine not, nor always while they live; but are obscure or light, according to the protrusion of their luminous parts, as observation will instruct us. For this flammeous light is not over all the body, but only visible on the inward side, in a small white part near the tail. When this is full and seemeth protruded, there ariseth a flame of a circular figure and emerald green colour; which is discernible in any dark place in the day; but when it falleth and seemeth contracted, the light disappeareth, and the colour of

* *Granum Nubiæ.*

[4] *glow-worm.*] There is a glow-fly as well as a glow-worm. One of them flew about my face as I sate in my chamber at Bletchington, Oxon. Junio ineunte, 1650. See the particular narration in my notes on the *Lorde Verulam's Naturall Historye*, p. 180.—*Wr.*

The male glow-worm is winged.

the part only remaineth. Now this light, as it appeareth and disappeareth in their life, so doth it go quite out at their death; as we have observed in some, which preserved in fresh grass have lived and shined eighteen days: but as they declined, and the luminous humour dried, their light grew languid, and at last went out with their lives. Thus also the torpedo, which, alive, hath a power to stupify at a distance, hath none upon contraction being dead, as Galen and Rondeletius particularly experimented. And this hath also disappointed the mischief of those intentions, which study the advancement of poisons; and fancy destructive compositions from asp's or viper's teeth, from scorpion's or hornet's stings.[5] For these amit their efficacy in the death of the individual,

---

[5] *And this hath also disappointed, &c.*] The sting being secured from the bodye of a waspe as itt hung on the finger, turnd itt selfe and rann (up to the roots) into the finger, and caused a very dolorous and greate impostume. And one was bit by the head of a snake, after 6 hours' amputation whereof hee was never totally cured to his death: *me teste oculato.* Whether there may be destructive compositions made of those parts is uncertain: thus far itt is improbable; bycause the teeth of vipers and stings of scorpions are but the outward instrumentall partes through which the poysonous spirit of those venemous creatures is ejaculated by them while they live: but being dead, there is no such active quality in those parts more then anye other, and that the poyson consistes in the vital spirits is manifest, for that wee see the vipers drownd in a sack butt, infuse their spirit into the wine, making itt become an excellent antedote: the great quantitye of wine overcoming the small quantitye of the poyson which comes from them. The like may bee sayde of the vertue which together with the spirits of the scorpion, drownd in oyle, is imprinted on the oyle, makinge itt the only cure of the scorpion's stinge: whereof the reason is manifest. Oyle by nature, abates, and duls, and retundes the fiercenes and spreadinge of poyson injected into us by venemous creatures, where we may come to apply itt: but being dull of itt selfe, and not able to follow the swift spreading of the scorpions poyson, thro soe small a puncture, as soone as itt is felt, followes the poyson injected by the same waye; and soe making way for the oyle, wherein itt is caryed, caryes the balme that kils and deades the killing poyson before itt can seise on our vitall spirits to destroy them. And noe doubt but the oyle, wherein hornets are drowned, would cure their punctures alsoe; a thing worthe the tryall.— *Wr.*

It is not the case that the poison of serpents is only fatal when infused by the living reptile.—As is proved by the well-known fact that several individuals successively met their death by wearing a boot into the inside of which it was afterwards found the fang of a rattlesnake had stuck fast, so as to wound the leg when drawn on.

and act but dependently on their forms. And thus far also those philosophers concur with us, which held the sun and stars were living creatures, for they conceived their lustre depended on their lives, but if they ever died, their light must also perish.

It were a notable piece of art to translate the light from the Bononian stone into another body; he that would attempt to make a shining water from glow-worms, must make trial when the splendent part is fresh and turgid. For even from the great American glow-worms, and flaming flies, the light declineth as the luminous humour drieth.[6]

Now whether the light of animals, which do not occasionally shine from contingent causes, be not of kin unto the light of heaven; whether the invisible flame of life received in a convenient matter, may not become visible, and the diffused æthereal light make little stars by conglobation in idoneous parts of the *compositum;* whether also it may not have some original in the seed and spirit analogous unto the element of stars, whereof some glimpse is observable on the little refulgent humour, at the first attempts of formation; philosophy may yet enquire.[7]

True it is, that a glow-worm will afford a faint light, almost a day's space, when many will conceive it dead; but this is a mistake in the compute of death, and term of disanimation; for indeed, it is not then dead, but if it be distended will slowly contract itself again, which when it cannot do, it ceaseth to shine any more. And to speak strictly, it is no easy matter to determine the point of death in insects and creatures who have not their vitalities radically confined unto one part; for they are not dead when they cease to move or afford the visible evidences of life; as may be observed in flies, who when they appear even desperate and quite forsaken of their forms, by virtue of the sun or warm ashes will be revoked unto life, and perform its functions again.

Now whether this lustre, awhile remaining after death, dependeth not still upon the first impression, and light communicated or raised from an inward spirit, subsisting awhile in a moist and apt recipient, nor long continuing in this, or

---

[6] *It were a notable piece, &c.*] This paragraph was first added in 6th edition.

[7] *Now whether, &c.*] This paragraph was first added in 3rd edition.

the more remarkable Indian glow-worm; or whether it be of another nature, and proceedeth from different causes of illumination; yet since it confessedly subsisteth so little a while after their lives, how to make perpetual lights, and sublunary moons thereof as is pretended, we rationally doubt, though not so sharply deny, with Scaliger and Muffetus.⁸

13. The wisdom of the pismire is magnified by all, and in the panegyricks of their providence we always meet with this. That to prevent the growth of corn which they store up, they bite off the end thereof;⁹ and some have conceived that from hence they have their name in Hebrew;* from

* *Namalh à Namal circumcidit.*

⁸ *Now whether this lustre, &c.*] This paragraph was first added in 3rd edition.

⁹ *they bite off the end, &c.*] A more satisfactory and interesting solution of this question cannot be given, than is contained in the following quotation from one of the most interesting works on natural history in our language. "When we find the writers of all nations and ages unite in affirming, that, having deprived it of the power of vegetating, ants store up grain in their nests, we feel disposed to give larger credit to an assertion, which at first sight seems to savour more of fact than of fable, and does not attribute more sagacity and foresight to these insects than in other instances they are found to possess. Writers in general, therefore, who have considered this subject, and some even of very late date, have taken it for granted that the ancients were correct in this notion. But when observers of nature began to examine the manners and economy of these creatures more narrowly, it was found, at least with respect to the European species of ants, that no such hoards of grain were made by them, and, in fact, that they had no magazines in their nests in which provisions of any kind were stored up. It was therefore surmised that the ancients, observing them carry about their *pupa*, which in shape, size, and colour, not a little resemble a grain of corn, and the ends of which they sometimes pull open to let out the inclosed insect, mistook the one for the other, and this action for depriving the grain of the *corculum*. Solomon's lesson to the sluggard has been generally adduced as a strong confirmation of the ancient opinion: it can, however, only relate to the species of a warm climate, the habits of which are probably different from those of a cold one;—so that his words, as commonly interpreted, may be perfectly correct and consistent with nature, and yet be not at all applicable to the species that are indigenous to Europe. But I think, if Solomon's words are properly considered, it will be found that this interpretation has been fathered upon them, rather than fairly deduced from them. He does not affirm that the ant which he proposes to his sluggard as an example, laid up in her magazines stores of grain: 'Go to the ant, thou sluggard, consider her ways and be wise; which having neither captain, overseer, or ruler, prepares her bread in the summer, and gathers her food in the

whence ariseth a conceit that corn will not grow if the extremes be cut or broken. But herein we find no security to prevent its germination; as having made trials in grains, whose ends cut off have notwithstanding suddenly sprouted, and according to the law of their kinds; that is, the roots of barley and oats at contrary ends, of wheat and rye at the same. And therefore some have delivered that after rainy weather they dry these grains in the sun: which if effectual, we must conceive to be made in a high degree and above the progression of malt; for that malt will grow, this year hath informed us, and that unto a perfect ear.

And if that be true which is delivered by many, and we shall further experiment, that a decoction of toad-stools if poured upon earth, will produce the same again; if sow-thistles will abound in places manured with dung of hogs, which feed much upon that plant; if horse-dung reproduceth oats; if winds and rains will transport the seminals of plants; it will not be easy to determine where the power of generation ceaseth. The forms of things may lie deeper than we conceive them; seminal principles may not be dead in the divided atoms of plants; but wandering in the ocean of nature, when they hit upon proportionable materials, may unite and return to their visible selves again.

But the prudence of this animal is by gnawing, piercing, or otherwise, to destroy the little nib or principle of germination. Which, notwithstanding is not easily discoverable; it being no ready business to meet with such grains in ant-hills; and he must dig deep, that will seek them in the winter.[1]

harvest.' These words may very well be interpreted simply to mean, that the ant, with commendable prudence and foresight, makes use of the proper seasons to collect a supply of provisions sufficient for her purposes. There is not a word in them implying that she stores up grain or other provision. She prepares her bread and gathers her food, —namely, such food as is suited to her—in summer and harvest,—that is, when it is most plentiful,—and thus shows her wisdom and prudence by using the advantages offered to her. The words thus interpreted, which they may be without any violence, will apply to our European species as well as to those that are not indigenous."—*Kirby and Spence, Introd. to Entomology,* vol. ii. p. 45—47.

[1] *And if that be true, &c.*] These two concluding paragraphs were first added in 3rd edition.

CHAPTER XXVIII.[2]

That the Chicken is made out of the yolk of the Egg; that Snakes sting; of the Tarantula; the Lamb of Tartary; the swiftness of Tigers; with sundry queries.

THAT a chicken is formed out of the yolk of the egg, was the opinion of some ancient philosophers. Whether it be not the nutriment of the pullet may also be considered; since umbilical vessels are carried unto it; since much of the yolk remaineth after the chicken is formed; since in a chicken newly hatched the stomach is tinged yellow, and the belly full of yolk, which is drawn in at the navel or vessels towards the vent, as may be discerned in chickens within a day or two before exclusion.

Whether the chicken be made out of the white, or that be not also its aliment, is likewise very questionable; since an umbilical vessel is derived unto it; since after the formation and perfect shape of the chicken, much of the white remaineth.

Whether it be not made out of the *grando*, gallature, germ or tred of the egg, as Aquapendente informeth us, seemeth to many of doubt: for at the blunter end it is not discovered after the chicken is formed; by this also the yolk and white are continued, whereby it may continually receive its nutriment from them both.

Now, that from such slender materials nature should effect this production, it is no more than is observed in other animals; and, even in grains, and kernels, the greatest part is but the nutriment of that generative particle, so disproportionable unto it.

A greater difficulty, in the doctrine of eggs, is, how the sperm of the cock prolificates and makes the oval conception fruitful, or how it attaineth unto every egg, since the vitellary or place of the yolk is very high; since the ovary or part where the white involveth it, is in the second region of the matrix, which is somewhat long and inverted; since also a cock will in one day fertilate the whole racemation

---

[2] *Chap.* xxviii.] This chapter was added in 2nd edition, except two paragraphs, one added in 3rd and the other in the 6th edition.

or cluster of eggs, which are not excluded in many weeks after.

But these at last, and how in the *cicatricula* or little pale circle, formation first beginneth, how the *grando* or tredle are but the poles and establishing particles of the tender membranes, firmly conserving the floating parts in their proper places, with many other observables, that ocular philosopher and singular discloser of truth, Dr. Harvey, hath discovered in that excellent discourse of generation, so strongly erected upon the two great pillars of truth, experience and solid reason.[3]

That the sex is discernible from the figure of eggs, or that cocks or hens proceed from long or round ones, as many contend, experiment will easily frustrate.

The Egyptians observed a better way, to hatch their eggs in ovens, than the Babylonians, to roast them at the bottom of a sling, by swinging them round about till heat from motion had concocted them; for that confuseth all parts without any such effect.

Though slight distinction be made between boiled and roasted eggs, yet is there no slender difference, for the one is much drier than the other; the egg expiring less in the elixation or boiling; whereas in the assation or roasting it will sometimes abate a drachm, that is, threescore grains in weight. So a new-laid egg will not so easily be boiled

---

[3] *But these at last, &c.*] The great principle of Harvey, "*omnia ex ovo*," has received splendid confirmation from the labours of Hunter, Malpighi, and Dutrochet, but still more from the recent investigations and discoveries of Sir E. Home, who has given, in his 14th lecture, a detailed account of the progressive changes of the egg during incubation; illustrated by exquisite microscopical figures. He has ascertained that the moleculi or *cicatricula*, exists both in mammalia and birds, and that in the latter it becomes, after impregnation, the embryo; which is nourished both by the yolk and the white. Sir Thomas seems, in one of his observations, to confound the *grandines*, or *chalazæ* (which are two knotty bodies, proceeding from the two ends of the yolk) with the *molecule*, a round milk-white spot on the surface of the yolk-bag, surrounded with white concentric circles. The fact which he notices of the whole cluster of eggs being fertilized at once, is a case somewhat analogous to that of quadrupeds which produce several young at a birth with one impregnation: the case of the *aphides* is still more remarkable, in which this is the fact not only with the eggs of the individual, but with those of its offspring to the ninth generation.

hard, because it contains a greater stock of humid parts, which must be evaporated before the heat can bring the inexhalable parts into consistence.[4]

Why the hen hatcheth not the egg in her belly, or maketh not at least some rudiment thereof within herself by the natural heat of inward parts, since the same is performed by incubation from an outward warmth after?[5] Why the egg is thinner at one extreme? Why there is some cavity or emptiness at the blunter end?[6] Why we open them at that part? Why the greater end is first excluded? Why some eggs are all red, as the kestrils; some only red at one end, as those of kites and buzzards? Why some eggs are not oval but round, as those of fishes, &c.—are problems whose decisions would too much enlarge this discourse.

That snakes and vipers do sting or transmit their mischief by the tail, is a common expression not easily to be justified, and a determination of their venoms unto a part, wherein we could never find it; the poison lying about the teeth, and communicated by bite, in such as are destructive. And therefore, when biting serpents are mentioned in the Scripture, they are not differentially set down from such as mischief by stings; nor can conclusions be made conformable to this opinion, because, when the rod of Moses was turned into a serpent, God determinatively commanded him to take up the same by the tail.

Nor are all snakes of such empoisoning qualities as common opinion presumeth; as is confirmable from the

---

[4] *So a new-laid egg, &c.*] This is not the received theory of the coagulation of albumen. "Cohesive attraction is the real cause of the phænemenon. In proportion as the temperature rises, the particles of water and albumen recede from each other, their affinity diminishes, and then the albumen precipitates. However, by uniting albumen with a large quantity of water, we diminish its coagulating property to such a degree, that heat renders the solution merely opalescent. A new-laid egg yields a soft coagulum by boiling; but when, by keeping, a portion of the water has transuded so as to leave a void space within the shell, the concentrated albumen affords a firm coagulum."—*Ure.*

[5] *Why the hen, &c.*] She does "make some rudiment," viz. the molecule, which, however, without impregnation, would not become a chick by the process of incubation.

[6] *Why there is some cavity, &c.*] It contains air, by which, in the earlier stages, the blood of the chick is aerated.

ordinary green snake with us, from several histories of domestic snakes, from ophiophagous nations, and such as feed upon serpents.[7]

Surely the destructive delusion, of Satan in this shape, hath much enlarged the opinion of their mischief. Which, notwithstanding, was not so high with the heathens, in whom the devil had wrought a better opinion of this animal, it being sacred unto the Egyptians, Greeks, and Romans, and the common symbol of sanity. In the shape whereof, Æsculapius, the god of health, appeared unto the Romans, accompanied their embassadors to Rome from Epidaurus, and the same did stand in the Tiberine isle upon the temple of Æsculapius.

Some doubt many have of the *tarantula*, or poisonous spider of Calabria, and that magical cure of the bite thereof by music. But since we observe that many attest it from experience; since the learned Kircherus hath positively averred it, and set down the songs and tunes solemnly used for it; since some also affirm the *tarantula* itself will dance upon certain strokes, whereby they set their instruments against its poison, we shall not at all question it.[8]

Much wonder is made of the *borametz*,[9] that strange

---

[7] *from ophiophagous, &c.*] But the venomous serpents are eaten as well as the harmless —— indeed the poison itself may be swallowed with impunity. Its fatality is evolved only on its entering into the circulation through a wound.

[8] *Some doubt many have, &c.*] The effects ascribed to its wounds, and their wonderful cures have long been celebrated: but after all there seems to have been more of fraud than of truth in the business; and the whole evil appears to consist in swelling and inflammation. Dr. Clavitio submitted to be bitten by this animal, and no bad effects ensued; and the Count de Borch, a Polish nobleman, bribed a man to undergo the same experiment, in whom the only result was a swelling in the hand, attended by intolerable itching. The fellow's sole remedy was a bottle of wine, which charmed away all his pain, without the aid of "pipe and tabor."— *K. and Sp.* i. 128.

[9] *the borametz.*] *Polypodium borametz*, L. Mirbel (in the 8vo. edition of *Buffon*, by Sonnini) calls it *polyp. chinois.* Jussieu gives the following account of it under the article, BAROMETZ.

" Cette espèce de polypode de Tartarie, *polypodium borametz*, L., présente dans la disposition de ses parties une forme singulière. Sa tige, longue d'environ un pied et dans une direction horizontale, est portée sur quatre ou cinq racines qui la tiennent élevée hors de terre. Sa surface est couverte d'un duvet assez long, soyeux et d'une couleur

plant-animal or vegetable lamb of Tartary, which wolves delight to feed on, which hath the shape of a lamb, affordeth a bloody juice upon breaking, and liveth while the plants be consumed about it. And yet if all this be no more, than the shape of a lamb in the flower or seed, upon the top of the stalk, as we meet with the forms of bees, flies, and dogs in some others; he hath seen nothing that shall much wonder at it.

It may seem too hard to question the swiftness of tigers, which hath therefore given names unto horses, ships, and rivers, nor can we deny what all have thus affirmed; yet cannot but observe, that Jacobus Bontius, late physician at Java in the East Indies, as an ocular and frequent witness, is not afraid to deny it; to condemn Pliny who affirmeth it; and that indeed it is but a slow and tardigradous animal, preying upon advantage, and otherwise may be escaped.

Many more there are whose serious enquiries we must request of others, and shall only awake considerations, whether that common opinion that snakes do breed out of the back or spinal marrow of man, doth build upon any constant root or seed in nature; or did not arise from contingent generation, in some single bodies remembered by Pliny or others, and might be paralleled since in living corruptions of the guts and other parts; which regularly proceed not to putrefactions of that nature.

Whether the story of the remora be not unreasonably amplified;[1] whether that of bernacles and goose-trees be not too much enlarged;[2] whether the common history of bees

---

jaune dorée. Ainsi conformée, elle ressemble à la toison d'un agneau de Scythie, et on la trouve, ainsi citée dans les contes fabuleux imaginés sur quelques singularités du règne végétal."—*Dictionnaire des Sciences Naturelles*, vol. iv. p. 85.

Ross contends stoutly for the literal verity of this pleasant story; and utterly rejects the sceptical explanations proposed by Sir Thomas.

[1] *amplified.*] Alluding probably to the absurd story of a vessel in full sail being stopt by one of these singular little fishes adhering to it.

[2] *too much enlarged.*] The natural history of the *lepas anatifera*, or bernacle, is too well understood, to render it necessary to say a syllable in refutation of the old story of its producing geese. It may be allowed, however, to notice the fact (discovered by Sir E. Home, and illustrated by highly magnified figures in his *Comparative Anatomy*) that this is one of the self-impregnating animals.

will hold, as large accounts have delivered; whether the brains of cats be attended with such destructive malignities, as Dioscorides and others put upon them?

As also whether there be not some additional help of art, unto the numismatical and musical shells, which we sometimes meet with in conchylious collections among us?

Whether the fasting spittle of man be poison unto snakes and vipers, as experience hath made us doubt? Whether the nightingale's sitting with her breast against a thorn, be any more than that she placeth some prickles on the outside of her nest, or roosteth in thorny prickly places, where serpents may least approach her; whether mice[3] may be bred by putrefaction as well as univocal production, as may be easily believed, if that receipt to make mice out of wheat will hold, which Helmont* hath delivered. Whether quails from any idiosyncracy or peculiarity of constitution, do innocuously feed upon hellebore, or rather sometime but medically use the same; because we perceive that stares, which are commonly said harmlessly to feed on hemlock, do not make good the tradition; and he that observes what vertigoes, cramps and convulsions follow thereon in these animals, will be of our belief.

* *Helm. Imago Fermenti, &c.*

[3] *Whether mice, &c.*] Ross's note on this doubt cannot be omitted. "So he may doubt whether in cheese and timber, worms are generated; or if beetles and wasps in cow's dung; or if butter-flies, locusts, grasshoppers, shell-fish, snails, eels, and such like, be procreated of putrified matters, which is apt to receive the form of that creature to which it is by formative power disposed. To question this, is to question reason, sense, and experience. If he doubts of this, let him go to Egypt, and there he will find the fields swarming with mice begot of the mud of Nylus, to the great calamity of the inhabitants. What will he say to those rats and mice, or little beasts resembling mice found generated in the belly of a woman dissected after her death, of which Lemnius is a witness? I have seen one whose belly, by drinking of puddle water, was swelled to a vast capacity, being full of small toads, frogs, evets [water-lizards] and such vermin usually bred in putrified water."—P. 155.

THE FOURTH BOOK:

THE PARTICULAR PART CONTINUED.

OF MANY POPULAR AND RECEIVED TENETS CONCERNING MAN.

CHAPTER I.

That only Man hath an erect figure.

THAT only man hath an erect figure, and for to behold and look up toward heaven, according to that of the poet:[1]

> Pronaque cum spectant animalia cætera terram,
> Os homini sublime dedit, cœlumque tueri
> Jussit, et erectos ad sydera tollere vultus,

is a double assertion, whose first part may be true if we take erectness strictly, and so as Galen hath defined it, for they only, saith he, have an erect figure, whose spine and thighbone are carried in right lines, and so indeed, of any we yet know, man only is erect.[2] For the thighs of other animals do stand at angles with their spine, and have rectangular positions in birds, and perfect quadrupeds. Nor doth the

---

[1] *the poet.*] Ovid. Met. i. 84. See also Cicero, De Nat. Deor. ii. 56.
[2] *man only is erect.*] But itt is most evident that baboones and apes doe not only .... as a man, but goe as erect also.—*Wr.*
    This is incorrect. Man alone, unquestionably, is constructed for an erect position. The apes, which resemble him in their conformation more closely than any other animals, are incapable of attaining a perfectly erect attitude, and though they occasionally assume a position nearly so, yet even this they cannot long retain. Their narrowness of pelvis, the configuration of their thighs and lower extremities, the situation of their flex or muscles, and the want of muscular calves and buttocks, constitute together an incapacity for perfect or continued verticity of attitude in the *quadrimana*.

frog, though stretched out, or swimming, attain the rectitude of man, or carry its thigh without all angularity. And thus is it also true, that man only sitteth, if we define sitting to be a firmation of the body upon the *ischias;* wherein, if the position be just and natural, the thigh-bone lieth at right angles to the spine, and the leg-bone or *tibia* to the thigh. For others, when they seem to sit, as dogs, cats, or lions, do make unto their spine acute angles with their thigh, and acute to the thigh with their shank. Thus is it likewise true, what Aristotle allegeth in that problem, why man alone suffereth pollutions in the night, because man only lieth upon his back,—if we define not the same by every supine position, but when the spine is in rectitude with the thigh, and both with the arms lie parallel to the horizon, so that a line through their navel will pass through the zenith and centre of the earth. And so cannot other animals lie upon their backs, for though the spine lie parallel with the horizon, yet will their legs incline, and lie at angles unto it. And upon these three divers positions in man, wherein the spine can only be at right lines with the thigh, arise those remarkable postures, prone, supine, and erect, which are but differenced in situation, or angular postures upon the back, the belly, and the feet.

But if erectness be popularly taken, and as it is largely opposed unto proneness, or the posture of animals looking downwards, carrying their venters or opposite part of the spine directly towards the earth, it may admit of question. For though in serpents and lizards we may truly allow a proneness, yet Galen acknowledgeth that perfect quadrupeds, as horses, oxen, and camels, are but partly prone, and have some part of erectness; and birds, or flying animals, are so far from this kind of proneness, that they are almost erect; advancing the head and breast in their progression, and only prone in the act of volitation or flying; and if that be true which is delivered of the penguin or *anser Magellanicus,* often described in maps about those straits, that they go erect like men, and with their breast and belly do make one line perpendicular unto the axis of the earth, it will almost make up the exact erectness of man.* Nor will that insect come very

---

* Observe also the *Urias Bellonii* and *Mergus major.*

short, which we have often beheld, that is, one kind of locust which stands not prone, or a little inclining upward, but in a large erectness, elevating always the two fore legs, and sustaining itself in the middle of the other four; by zoographers called *mantis,* and by the common people of Provence, Prega Dio, the prophet and praying locust, as being generally found in the posture of supplication, or such as resembleth ours, when we lift up our hands to heaven.

As for the end of this erection, to look up toward heaven, though confirmed by several testimonies, and the Greek etymology of man, it is not so readily to be admitted; and, as a popular and vain conceit, was anciently rejected by Galen, who in his third *De usu partium,* determines that man is erect, because he was made with hands, and was therewith to exercise all arts, which in any other figure he could not have performed, as he excellently declareth in that place, where he also proves that man could have been made neither quadruped nor centaur.[3]

And for the accomplishment of that intention, that is, to look up and behold the heavens, man hath a notable disadvantage in the eyelid, whereof the upper is far greater than the lower, which abridgeth the sight upwards contrary to those of birds, who herein have the advantage of man; insomuch that the learned Plempius[*] is bold to affirm, that if he had had the formation of the eyelids, he would have contrived them quite otherwise.[4]

The ground and occasion of that conceit was a literal apprehension of a figurative expression in Plato, as Galen thus delivers: to opinion that man is erect to look up and behold heaven, is a conceit only fit for those that never saw the fish *uranoscopus,*[5] that is, the beholder of heaven, which

[*] *Ophthalmographia.*

[3] *man could have been, &c.*] Why not as well as an ape, if that reason be good; for an ape uses his hand as well as man, and yett hee is *quadrupes* too.—*Wr.* Incorrect again. Apes cannot use their hands *as well as man,* because destitute of the facility which man possesses for the free use of his hands and arms, in the erect position, and because of the superior mechanical adaptation of the human hand to the exercise of the arts and occupations of life. The opinion quoted by our author that man could not become quadruped, is incontrovertible.

[4] *And for the accomplishment, &c.*] This paragraph first added in 2nd edition.

[5] *to opinion, &c.*] This is a poore cavil, or the end of mans lookinge

hath its eyes so placed, that it looks up directly to heaven, which man doth not, except he recline, or bend his head backward; and thus to look up to heaven agreeth not only unto man but asses; to omit birds with long necks, which look not only upward, but round about at pleasure; and therefore men of this opinion understood not Plato when he saith, that man doth *sursum aspicere;* for thereby was not meant to gape, or look upward with the eye, but to have his thoughts sublime, and not only to behold, but speculate their nature with the eye of the understanding.[6]

Now although Galen in this place makes instance but in one, yet are there other fishes whose eyes regard the heavens, as plane and cartilaginous fishes, as pectinals, or such as have their bones made literally like a comb, for when they apply themselves to sleep or rest upon the white side, their eyes on the other side look upward toward heaven. For birds, they generally carry their heads erected like a man, and have advantage in their upper eyelid, and many that have long necks, and bear their heads somewhat backward, behold far more of the heavens, and seem to look above the equinoctial circle; and so also in many quadrupeds, although their progression be partly prone, yet is the sight of their eye direct, not respecting the earth but heaven, and makes an higher arch of latitude than our own. The position of a frog with his head above water exceedeth these; for therein he seems to behold a large part of the heavens, and the acies of his eye to ascend as high as the tropic; but he that hath beheld the posture of a bittern will not deny that it beholds almost the very zenith.[7]

upward is not the same with *uranoscopus,* to which the same is equivocal, bycause this posture, being always at the botom, hee lookes alwayes upwards, not to heaven, but as watching for his foode flooting over his head; the question then is, not whether any other creatures have the head erect as man, but whether to the same ende.—*Wr.*

[6] *understood not Plato, &c.*] This is too pedanticall and captious: for Plato sayd plainlye, *Astronomiæ causa datos esse homini oculos,* but not to other creatures, though they have their heads more erect than bee, and far better sight.—*Wr.*

[7] *the posture of a bittern, &c.*] Which proceeds from his timorous and jealous nature, holding his head at hight, for discovery, not enduring any man to come neere: his neck is stretch out, but his bill stands like the cranes, hernshawes, &c.—*Wr.*

CHAPTER II.

That the Heart is on the left side.

THAT the heart of man is seated in the left side is an asseveration, which, strictly taken, is refutable by inspection, whereby it appears the base and centre thereof is in the midst of the chest; true it is, that the mucro or point thereof inclineth unto the left, for by this position it giveth way unto the ascension of the midriff, and by reason of the hollow vein could not commodiously deflect unto the right. From which diversion, nevertheless, we cannot so properly say 'tis placed in the left, as that it consisteth in the middle, that is, where its centre riseth; for so do we usually say a gnomon[8] or needle is in the middle of a dial, although the extremes may respect the north or south, and approach the circumference thereof.

The ground of this mistake is a general observation from the pulse or motion of the heart, which is more sensible on this side; but the reason hereof is not to be drawn from the situation of the heart, but the site of the left ventricle wherein the vital spirits are laboured, and also the great artery that conveyeth them out, both which are situated on the left. Upon this reason epithems or cordial applications are justly applied unto the left breast, and the wounds under the fifth rib may be more suddenly destructive, if made on the sinister side, and the spear of the soldier that pierced our Saviour is not improperly described, when painters direct it a little towards the left.

The other ground is more particular and upon inspection; for in dead bodies, especially lying upon the spine, the heart doth seem to incline upon the left; which happeneth not from its proper site, but besides its sinistrous gravity, is drawn that way by the great artery, which then subsideth and haleth the heart unto it; and thereof strictly taken, the heart is seated in the middle of the chest, but after a care-

---

[8] *gnomon.*] There is not the same reason of a *gnomon* and a needle. This is ever in the midst, but a gnomon stands on the substilar line, which declines east or west, as the place does, wherein 'tis drawne.—*Wr.*

less and inconsiderate inspection, or according to the readiest sense of pulsation, we shall not quarrel if any affirm it is seated towards the left. And in these considerations must Aristotle be salved, when he affirmeth the heart of man is placed in the left side, and thus in a popular acception may we receive the periphrasis of Persius, when he taketh the part under the left pap for the heart,* and if rightly apprehended, it concerneth not this controversy, when it is said in Ecclesiastes, the heart of a wise man is in the right side, but that of a fool in the left; for thereby may be implied, that the heart of a wise man delighteth in the right way, or in the path of virtue; that of a fool in the left, or road of vice, according to the mystery of the letter of Pythagoras, or that expression in Jonah, concerning sixscore thousand, that could not discern between their right hand and their left, or knew not good from evil.[9]

That assertion also that man proportionally hath the largest brain,[1] I did I confess somewhat doubt, and conceived it might have failed in birds, especially such as having little bodies, have yet large cranies, and seem to contain much brain, as snipes, woodcocks, &c. But upon trial I find it very true. The brains of a man, Archangelus and Bauhinus observe to weigh four pounds, and sometimes five and a half. If therefore a man weigh one hundred and forty pounds, and his brain but five, his weight is twenty seven times as much as his brain, deducting the weight of that five pounds which is allowed for it. Now in a snipe, which weighed four ounces two drachms, I find the brains to weigh but half a drachm, so that the weight of the body, allowing for the brain, exceeded the weight of the brain sixty-seven times and a half.

More controvertible it seemeth in the brains of sparrows, whose cranies are rounder, and so of larger capacity; and most of all in the heads of birds, upon the first formation in the egg, wherein the head seems larger than all the body,

* *Lava in parte mamillæ.*

[9] *for thereby, &c.*] This concluding part of the sentence was first added in 2nd edition.

[1] *man hath, &c.*] This is most especially true when spoken of "*the hemispheres of the brain,*" that is, of that part of this organ which serves as the principal instrument of the intellectual operations.—See *Cuvier,* by *Griffith,* i. 86.

and the very eyes almost as big as either. A sparrow in the total we found to weigh seven drachms and four and twenty grains, whereof the head a drachm, but the brain not fifteen grains, which answereth not fully the proportion of the brain of man; and therefore it is to be taken of the whole head with the brains, when Scaliger* objected that the head of a man is the fifteenth part of his body, that of a sparrow scarce the fifth.[2]

CHAPTER III.

That Pleurisies are only on the left side.

That pleurisies are only on the left side, is a popular tenet not only absurd but dangerous: from the misapprehension hereof men omitting the opportunity of remedies, which otherwise they would not neglect. Chiefly occasioned by the ignorance of anatomy, and the extent of the part affected, which in an exquisite pleurisy is determined to be the skin or membrane which investeth the ribs, for so it is defined, *inflammatio membranæ costas succingentis;* an inflammation, either simple, consisting only of an hot and sanguineous affluxion, or else denominable from other humours, according to the predominancy of melancholy, phlegm, or choler. The membrane thus inflamed, is properly called *pleura*, from whence the disease hath its name; and this investeth not only one side, but over-spreadeth the cavity of the chest, and affordeth a common coat unto the parts contained therein.

Now therefore the *pleura* being common unto both sides, it is not reasonable to confine the inflammation unto one, nor strictly to determine it is always in the side; but sometimes before and behind, that is, inclining to the spine or breast-bone, for thither this coat extendeth, and therefore with equal propriety we may affirm that ulcers of the lungs, or apostems of the brain, do happen only in the left side, or that ruptures are confinable unto one side; whereas the peritonæum or rim of the belly may be broke, or its perforations relaxed in either.

---

* *Histor. Animal.* lib. 1.

[2] *More controvertible, &c.*] This paragraph first added in 2nd edition.

CHAPTER IV.

Of the Ring-finger.

AN opinion there is, which magnifies the fourth finger of the left hand; presuming therein a cordial relation, that a particular vessel, nerve, vein, or artery, is conferred thereto from the heart, and therefore that especially hath the honour to bear our rings. Which was not only the Christian practice in nuptial contracts, but observed by heathens, as Alexander ab Alexandro, Gellius, Macrobius and Pierius have delivered, as Levinus Lemnius hath confirmed, who affirms this peculiar vessel to be an artery, and not a nerve, as antiquity hath conceived it; adding moreover that rings hereon peculiarly affect the heart; that in lipothymies or swoonings he used the frication of this finger with saffron and gold; that the ancient physicians mixed up their medicines herewith; that this is seldom or last of all affected with the gout, and when that becometh nodous, men continue not long after. Notwithstanding all which, we remain unsatisfied, nor can we think the reasons alleged sufficiently establish the pre-eminency of this finger.

For first, concerning the practice of antiquity, the custom was not general to wear their rings either on this hand or finger; for it is said, and that emphatically in Jeremiah, *si fuerit Jeconias filius Joachim regis Judæ annulus in manu dextrâ meâ, inde evellam eum:* "though Coniah the son of Joachim king of Judah, were the signet on my right hand, yet would I pluck thee thence." So is it observed by Pliny, that in the portraits of their gods, the rings were worn on the finger next the thumb;[3] that the Romans wore them also upon their little finger, as Nero is described in Petronius: some wore them on the middle finger, as the ancient Gauls and Britons; and some upon the forefinger, as is deducible from Julius Pollux, who names that ring, *corianos.*

---

[2] *finger next the thumb.*] Rings were formerly worn upon the thumb; as appears from the portraits of some of our English monarchs. Nieuhoff mentions that the old viceroy of Canton wore an ivory ring on his thumb, "as an emblem signifying the undaunted courage of the Tartar people.'—*Embassy to China*, p. 45.

Again, that the practice of the ancients had any such respect of cordiality or reference unto the heart, will much be doubted, if we consider their rings were made of iron :[4] such was that of Prometheus, who is conceived the first that brought them in use. So, as Pliny affirmeth, for many years the senators of Rome did not wear any rings of gold,[5] but the slaves wore generally iron rings until their manumission or preferment to some dignity. That the Lacedemonians continued their iron rings unto his days, Pliny also delivereth, and surely they used few of gold; for beside that Lycurgus prohibited that metal, we read in Athenæus, that,

[4] *will much be doubted, &c.*] Yet Pliny says, *etiam nunc sponsæ annulus ferreus mittitur, isque sine gemmâ.*—*Nat. Hist.* l. xxxiii. cap. 1.
 At Silchester in Hampshire (the *Vindonum* of the Romans), was found an iron ring, with a singular-shaped key attached to it; now in the possession of Mrs. Keep, at the farm-house, where I saw it, June 26, 1811.—*Jeff.*
[5] *the senators, &c.*] Juvenal, comparing the extravagance of his own times with those of the old Romans, has *annulus in digito non ferreus.*—*Sat.* xi. 129. Kennet observes that the Roman knights were allowed a gold ring, and a horse at the public charge, hence *eques auratus.*—*Roman Antiquities.* Tacitus says, *De Mor. German.* s. 31 :—Fortissimus quisque (Cattorum) ferreum insuper annulum (ignominiosum id genti) velut vinculum gestat, donec se cæde hostis absolvet." Among the Eastern nations also was the ring worn as a badge of slavery.—See *Lowth*, note on Isa. xlix. 23.—*Jeff.*
 We may add that rings were frequently used by medical practitioners, as charms and talismans, against all sorts of calamities inflicted by all kinds of beings :—Hippocrates and Galen both enjoin on physicians the use of rings. See a curious paper on this subject in the *Archæologia*, vol. xxi. p. 119.
 Patriotism has, in our own days, induced the exchange of gold for iron rings. The women of Prussia, in 1813, offered up their wedding-rings upon the altars of their country, and the government, in exchange, distributed iron rings with this inscription, "I exchange gold for iron."
 Rings however have not only been deemed badges of slavery, but very anciently and far more generally they denoted authority and government. Pharaoh in committing that of Egypt to Joseph gave him his ring—so Ahasuerus to Mordecai. With great probability has it been conjectured, that, in conformity with the Scriptural examples of this ancient usage, the Christian church afterwards adopted the ring in marriage, as a symbol of the authority which the husband gave the wife over his household, and over the " worldly goods" with which he endowed her; accompanying it, in many of the early Catholic rituals, with the betrothing or earnest penny, which was deposited either in the bride's right hand, or in a purse brought by her for the purpose.

having a desire to gild the face of Apollo, they enquired of the oracle where they might purchase so much gold; and were directed unto Crœsus King of Lydia.

Moreover, whether the ancients had any such intention, the grounds which they conceived in vein, nerve or artery, are not to be justified, nor will inspection confirm a peculiar vessel in this finger. For as anatomy informeth, the *basilica* vein dividing into two branches below the cubit, the outward sendeth two surcles unto the thumb, two unto the forefinger, and one unto the middle finger in the inward side; the other branch of the basilica sendeth one surcle unto the outside of the middle finger, two unto the ring, and as many unto the little fingers; so that they all proceed from the basilica, and are in equal numbers derived unto every one. In the same manner are the branches of the axillary artery distributed into the hand: for below the cubit it divideth into two parts, the one running along the radius, and, passing by the wrist or pulse, is at the fingers subdivided into three branches; whereof the first conveyeth two surcles unto the thumb, the second as many to the forefinger, and the third one unto the middle finger, and the other or lower division of the artery descendeth by the *ulna*, and furnisheth the other fingers; that is the middle with one surcle, and the ring and little fingers with two. As for the nerves, they are disposed much after the same manner, and have their original from the brain, and not the heart, as many of the ancients conceived,[6] which is so far from affording nerves unto other parts, that it receiveth very few itself from the sixth conjugation, or pair of nerves in the brain.

Lastly, these propagations being communicated unto both hands, we have no greater reason to wear our rings on the left, than on the right; nor are there cordial considerations in the one, more than the other. And therefore when Forestus for the stanching of blood makes use of medical applications unto the fourth finger, he confines not that practice unto the left, but varieth the side according to the nostril bleeding. So in fevers, where the heart primarily suffereth, we apply medicines unto the wrists of either arms; so we touch the pulse of both, and judge of the affections of the

[6] *as many of the ancients conceived.*] With whom Ross, as usual, is disposed to agree.—See *Arcana Microcosmi*, p. 35.

heart by the one as well as the other. And although in dispositions of liver or spleen, considerations are made in phlebotomy respectively to their situation; yet when the heart is affected, men have thought it as effectual to bleed on the right as the left; and although also it may be thought a nearer respect is to be had of the left, because the great artery proceeds from the left ventricle, and so is nearer that arm, it admits not that consideration. For under the channel-bones the artery divideth into two great branches, from which trunk or point of division, the distance unto either hand is equal, and the consideration also answerable.

All which with many respective niceties, in order unto parts, sides, and veins, are now become of less consideration, by the new and noble doctrine of the circulation of the blood.[7]

And therefore Macrobius, discussing the point, hath alleged another reason; affirming that the gestation of rings upon this hand and finger, might rather be used for their conveniency and preservation, than any cordial relation. For at first (saith he) it was both free and usual to wear rings on either hand; but after that luxury increased, when precious gems and rich insculptures were added, the custom of wearing them on the right hand was translated unto the left; for, that hand being less employed, thereby they were best preserved. And for the same reason, they placed them on this finger: for the thumb was too active a finger, and is commonly employed with either of the rest; the index or forefinger was too naked whereto to commit their precosities, and hath the tuition of the thumb scarce unto the second joint: the middle and little finger they rejected as extremes, and too big or too little for their rings, and of all choose out the fourth, as being least used of any, as being guarded on either side, and having in most this peculiar condition, that it cannot be extended alone and by itself, but will be accompanied by some finger on either side.[8] And to this opinion assenteth Alexander ab Alexandro, *annulum nuptialem prior ætas in sinistrâ ferebat, crediderim nè attereretur.*

[7] *All which, &c.*] First added in 6th edition.
[8] *and having, &c.*] This is not true.—*Wr.*
But indeed, Mr. Dean, it *is* true. The *annularis* is the *only* finger in the human hand, not possessed of the power of separate movement.

Now that which begat or promoted the common opinion, was the common conceit that the heart was seated on the left side; but how far this is verified, we have before declared. The Egyptian practice hath much advanced the same, who unto this finger derived a nerve from the heart; and therefore the priest anointed the same with precious oils before the altar. But how weak anatomists they were, which were so good embalmers, we have already showed. And though this reason took most place, yet had they another which more commended that practice: and that was the number whereof this finger was an hieroglyphick. For by holding down the fourth finger of the left hand, while the rest were extended, they signified the perfect and magnified number of six. For as Pierius hath graphically declared, antiquity expresed numbers by the fingers of either hand: on the left they accounted their digits and articulate numbers unto an hundred; on the right hand hundreds and thousands; the depressing this finger, which in the left hand implied but six, in the right indigitated six hundred. In this way of numeration, may we construe that of Juvenal concerning Nestor.

——————— Qui pertot sæcula mortem
Distulit, atque suos jam dextrâ computat annos.

And however it were intended, in this sense it will be very elegant what is delivered of wisdom, Prov. iii. "Length of days in her right hand, and in her left hand riches and honour."

As for the observation of Lemnius, an eminent physician, concerning the gout, however it happened in his country, we may observe it otherwise in ours; that is, chiragrical persons do suffer in this finger as well as in the rest, and sometimes first of all, and sometimes nowhere else. And for the mixing up medicines herewith, it is rather an argument of opinion than any considerable effect; and we as highly conceive of the practice in *diapalma;* that is, in the making of that plaster to stir it with the stick of a palm.

CHAPTER V.

Of the Right and Left Hand.

It is also suspicious, and not with that certainty to be received, what is generally believed concerning the right and left hand; that men naturally make use of the right,[9] and that the use of the other is a digression or aberration from that way which nature generally intendeth. We do not deny that almost all nations have used this hand, and ascribed a pre-eminence thereto: hereof a remarkable passage there is in Genesis: "And Joseph took them both, Ephraim in his right hand towards Israel's left hand, and Manasses in his left hand towards Israel's right hand. And Israel stretched out his right hand and laid it upon Ephraim's head, who was the younger, and his left hand upon Manasses' head, guiding his hand wittingly, for Manasses was the first-born. And when Joseph saw that his father laid his right hand upon the head of Ephraim, it displeased him, and he held up his father's hand to remove it from Ephraim's head unto Manasses' head; and Joseph said, Not so my father, for this is the first-born: put thy right hand upon his head." The like appeareth from the ordinance of Moses in the consecration of their priests: "Then shalt thou kill the ram, and take of his blood, and put it upon the tip of the right ear of Aaron, and upon the tip of the right ear of his sons, and upon the thumb of the right hand, and upon the great toe of the right foot, and sprinkle the blood on the altar round about." That the Persians were wont herewith to plight their faith, is testified by Diodorus; that the Greeks and Romans made use hereof, beside the testimony of divers authors, is evident from their custom of discumbency at their meals, which was upon their left side, for so their right was free, and ready for all service. As also from the conjunction of the right hands and not the left, observable in the Roman medals of

---

[9] *men naturally, &c.*] Cann this be denyed? or yf there be some exceptions, i. e. aberrations from the generall rule, doe they not the more confirme itt? *Omnis exceptio stabilit regulam in non exceptis*, is an axiome invincible.—*Wr.*

concord. Nor was this only in use with divers nations of men, but was the custom of whole nations of women; as is deducible from the Amazons in the amputation of their right breast, whereby they had the freer use of their bow. All which do seem to declare a natural preferment[1] of the one unto motion before the other; wherein notwithstanding, in submission to future information, we are unsatisfied unto great dubitation.

For first, if there were a determinate prepotency in the right, and such as ariseth from a constant root in nature, we might expect the same in other animals, whose parts are also differenced by dextrality: wherein notwithstanding we cannot discover a distinct and complying account; for we find not that horses, bulls, or mules, are generally stronger on this side. As for animals whose forelegs more sensibly supply the use of arms, they hold, if not an equality in both, a prevalency ofttimes in the other, as squirrels, apes, and monkeys; the same is also discernible in parrots, who feed themselves more commonly by the left leg; and men observe that the eye of a tumbler is biggest, not constantly in one, but in the bearing side.

That there is also in men a natural prepotency in the right, we cannot with constancy affirm,[2] if we make observation in children; who, permitted the freedom of both, do ofttimes confine unto the left,[3] and are not without great difficulty restrained from it. And therefore this prevalency

---

[1] *natural preferment.*] Ed. 1646 has "naturall preheminency and preferment." — On which Dean Wren says, "Granting this natural preeminencye, confirmed by Scripture soe evidentlye, all the rest is but velitation : for that which God and nature call right, must in reason bee soe cald : and whatsoever varys from thence is an aberration from them bothe."

[2] *That there is, &c.*] Alex. Ross asserts roundly, that Scripture, general consent, experience, and reason, unite in ascribing superior dignity, agility, and strength, to the right side ; "because" (says he), "on the right side is the liver, the *cistern of blood*," &c. &c. — *Arcana*, p. 153.

[3] *do ofttimes, &c.*] This vitiosity proceeds from the maner of gestation : servants and nurses usually carry them on their left arme, soe that the child cannot use its right, and being accustomed to the left, becomes left handed. But among the Irishe, who cary their children astride their neckes, you shall rarely see one left-handed of either sex. — *Wr.*

is either uncertainly placed in the laterality, or custom determines its indifferency. Which is the resolution of Aristotle, in that problem which enquires why the right side, being better than the left, is equal in the senses; because, saith he, the right and left do differ by use and custom, which have no place in the senses. For right and left, as parts inservient unto the motive faculty, are differenced by degrees from use and assuefaction, according whereto the one grows stronger and ofttimes bigger than the other. But in the senses it is otherwise; for they acquire not their perfection by use or custom, but at the first we equally hear, and see with one eye, as well as with another. And therefore, were this indifferency permitted, or did not constitution, but nature, determine dextrality, there would be many more Scevolas than are delivered in story; nor needed we to draw examples of the left from the sons of the right hand, as we read of seven thousand in the army of the Benjamites.* True it is, that although there be an indifferency in either, or a prevalency indifferent in one, yet is it most reasonable for uniformity and sundry respective uses, that men should apply themselves to the constant use of one;[4] for there will otherwise arise anomalous disturbances in manual actions, not only in civil and artificial, but also in military affairs, and the several actions of war.

Secondly, the grounds and reason alleged for the right are not satisfactory, and afford no rest in their decision. Scaliger, finding a defect in the reason of Aristotle, introduceth one of no less deficiency himself; *ratio materialis* (saith he) *sanguinis crassitudo simul et multitudo*, that is, the reason of the vigour of this side is the crassitude and plenty of blood; but this is not sufficient; for the crassi-

* *Benjamin Filius Dextræ.*

[4] *the constant, &c.*] Wise men count them unlucky that use the left hand, as going contrary to the generall course of nature in all places of the world and all times since the creation. And although the heathen drew a superstitious conceyte from don † first on the left side rather then the right, yet that sprang from an apprehension of disorder in soe doing, and consequentlye (as they thought) unlucky, as in that of Augustus, *Lærum sibi prodidit cultrum præpostere indutum quo die militari tumultu afflictus.*—*Wr.*

† Some omission or error here.

tude or thickness of blood affordeth no reason why one arm should be enabled before the other, and the plenty thereof, why both not enabled equally. Fallopius is of another conceit, deducing the reason from the *azygos*, or *vena sine pari*, a large and considerable vein arising out of the *cava* or hollow vein, before it enters the right ventricle of the heart, and placed only in the right side. But neither is this persuasory; for the *azygos* communicates no branches unto the arms or legs on either side, but disperseth into the ribs on both, and in its descent doth furnish the left emulgent with one vein, and the first vein of the loins on the right side with another; which manner of derivation doth not confer a peculiar addition unto either. Cælius Rhodiginus, undertaking to give a reason of ambidexters and left-handed men, delivereth a third opinion: men, saith he, are ambidexters, and use both hands alike, when the heat of the heart doth plentifully disperse into the left side, and that of the liver into the right, and the spleen be also much dilated; but men are left-handed whenever it happeneth that the heart and liver are seated on the left side, or when the liver is on the right side, yet so obducted and covered with thick skins that it cannot diffuse its virtue into the right. Which reasons are no way satisfactory, for herein the spleen is unjustly introduced to invigorate the sinister side, which being dilated it would rather infirm and debilitate. As for any tunicles or skins which should hinder the liver from enabling the dextral parts, we must not conceive it diffuseth its virtue by mere irradiation, but by its veins and proper vessels, which common skins and teguments cannot impede. And for the seat of the heart and liver in one side, whereby men become left-handed, it happeneth too rarely to countenance an effect so common; for the seat of the liver on the left side is monstrous, and rarely to be met with in the observations of physicians. Others, not considering ambidexters and left-handed men, do totally submit unto the efficacy of the liver; which, though seated on the right side, yet by the subclavian division doth equidistantly communicate its activity unto either arm; nor will it salve the doubts of observation; for many are right-handed whose livers are weakly constituted, and many use the left in whom that part is strongest; and we observe in apes and other animals, whose liver is in the right, no regular prevalence therein.

And therefore the brain, especially the spinal marrow, which is but the brain prolonged, hath a fairer plea hereto; for these are the principles of motion, wherein dextrality consists, and are divided within and without the crany. By which division transmitting nerves respectively unto either side, according to the indifferency or original and native prepotency, there ariseth an equality in both, or prevalency in either side. And so may it be made out, what many may wonder at, why some most actively use the contrary arm and leg; for the vigour of the one dependeth upon the upper part of the spine, but the other upon the lower.

And therefore many things are philosophically delivered concerning right and left, which admit of some suspension. That a woman upon a masculine conception advanceth her right leg,[5] will not be found to answer strict observation. That males are conceived in the right side of the womb, females in the left, though generally delivered, and supported by ancient testimony, will make no infallible account; it happening ofttimes that males and females do lie upon both sides, and hermaphrodites, for aught we know, on either. It is also suspicious what is delivered concerning the right and left testicle, that males are begotten from the one and females from the other.[6] For though the left seminal vein proceedeth from the emulgent, and is therefore conceived to carry down a serous and feminine matter; yet the seminal arteries which send forth the active materials, are both derived from the great artery. Beside, this original of the left vein was thus contrived to avoid the pulsation of the great artery, over which it must have passed to attain unto the testicle. Nor can we easily infer such different effects from the diverse situation of parts which have one end and office; for in the kidneys, which have one office, the right is seated lower than the left, whereby it lieth free, and giveth way unto the liver. And therefore also that way which is

That a woman, &c.] This instance is most true, as I have often tryed upon wager, whereas they sodenlye rise from their seate, yf both feete be free.—*Wr.*

[6] *That males, &c.*] All this while hee does not disprove this: and the reason is as good as 'tis manifest.—*Wr.*

delivered for masculine generation, to make a strait ligature about the left testicle, thereby to intercept the evacuation of that part, deserveth consideration. For one sufficeth unto generation, as hath been observed in semicastration, and ofttimes in carnous ruptures. Beside, the seminal ejaculation proceeds not immediately from the testicle, but from the spermatick glandules; and therefore Aristotle affirms (and reason cannot deny) that although there be nothing diffused from the testicles, an horse or bull may generate after castration; that is, from the stock and remainder of seminal matter, already prepared and stored up in the prostates or glandules of generation.

Thirdly, although we should concede a right and left in nature, yet in this common and received account we may err from the proper acception: mistaking one side for another;[7] calling that in man and other animals the right which is the left, and that the left which is the right, and that in some things right and left, which is not properly either.

For first, the right and left are not defined by philosophers according to common acception, that is, respectively from one man unto another, or any constant site in each: as though that should be the right in one, which upon confront or facing, stands athwart or diagonally unto the other, but were distinguished according to the activity and predominant locomotion upon either side. Thus Aristotle, in his excellent tract, *De Incessu Animalium*, ascribeth six positions unto animals, answering the three dimensions, which he determineth not by site or position unto the heavens, but by the faculties and functions; and these are *imum summum, ante retro, dextra et sinistra;* that is the superior part, where the aliment is received, that the lower extreme, where it is last expelled; so he termeth a man a plant inverted; for he supposeth the root of a tree the head or upper part thereof, whereby it receiveth its aliment, although therewith it respects the centre of the earth, but with the other the

---

[7] *mistaking one side, &c.*] Wee take that to be right and lefte which God and nature call soe: and all other reasons are frivolous. Vide Luke i. 11; Gal. ii. 9. Let itt be noted that God cals the left hand the side hand, i. e. *beside* the right hand, to which he gives in that very place, the name of δέξια, ut Ps. xc. v. 7, ἐκ τοῦ κλίτους σου χιλιὰς, καὶ μυριὰς ἐκ δεξιῶν σου. κλίτος autem, ut norunt eruditi, proprie significat declinationem a recto, et hic, a rectâ.— *Wr.*

zenith; and this position is answerable unto longitude. Those parts are anterior and measure profundity, where the senses, especially the eyes, are placed, and those posterior which are opposite hereunto. The dextrous and sinistrous parts of the body make up the latitude, and are not certain and inalterable like the other; for that, saith he, is the right side, from whence the motion of the body beginneth, that is the active or moving side; but that the sinister which is the weaker or more quiescent part. Of the same determination were the Platonicks and Pythagoreans before him; who, conceiving the heavens an animated body, named the east the right or dextrous part, from whence began their motion; and thus the Greeks, from whence the Latins have borrowed their appellations, have named this hand δέξια, denominating it not from the site, but office, from δέχομαι capio, that is, the hand which receiveth, or is usually employed in that action.

Now upon these grounds we are most commonly mistaken, defining that by situation which they determined by motion; and giving the term of right hand to that which doth not properly admit it. For first, many in their infancy are sinistrously disposed, and divers continue all their life Ἀριστεροὶ, that is, left-handed, and have but weak and imperfect use of the right: now unto these, that hand is properly the right, and not the other esteemed so by situation.[8] Thus may Aristotle be made out, when he affirmeth the right claw of crabs and lobsters is biggest, if we take the right for the most vigorous side, and not regard the relative situation: for the one is generally bigger than the other, yet not always upon the same side. So may it be verified, what is delivered by Scaliger in his *Comment*, that palsies do oftenest happen upon the left side, if understood in this sense; the most vigorous part protecting itself, and protruding the matter upon the weaker and less resistive side. And

[8] *that hand is properly, &c.*] This exception is soe far from destroying the generall rule, that itt rather confirms itt. For the most parte of all men in all nations of the world are right-handed, and in those that use the lefte hand, the righte hand keepes the name; how should hee else bee distinguished from all men that are right-handed. And thoughe the left hand bee as useful to some as the right to all others, yet itt is still their left hand; and by that name they are distinguisht, and cald left-handed men.—*Wr.*

thus the law of commonwealths, that cut off the right hand of malefactors, if philosophically executed, is impartial; otherwise the amputation not equally punisheth all.

Some are Ἀμφιδέξιοι, that is, ambidextrous or right-handed on both sides; which happeneth only unto strong and athletical bodies, whose heat and spirits are able to afford an ability unto both. And therefore Hippocrates saith, that women are not ambidextrous, that is, not so often as men; for some are found which indifferently make use of both. And so may Aristotle say, that only men are ambidextrous; of this constitution was Asteropæus in *Homer*, and Parthenopeus, the Theban captain, in *Statius*: and of the same do some conceive our father Adam to have been, as being perfectly framed, and in a constitution admitting least defect. Now in these men the right hand is on both sides, and that is not the left which is opposite unto the right, according to common acception.

Again,[9] some are Ἀμφαριστεροὶ, as Galen hath expressed it; that is, ambilevous or left-handed on both sides; such as with agility and vigour have not the use of either; who are not gymnastically composed, nor actively use those parts. Now in these there is no right hand: of this constitution are many women, and some men, who, though they accustom themselves unto either hand, do dextrously make use of neither. And therefore, although the political advice of Aristotle be very good, that men should accustom themselves to the command of either hand; yet cannot the execution or performance thereof be general: for though there be many found that can use both, yet will there divers remain that can strenuously make use of neither.

Lastly, these lateralities in man are not only fallible, it relatively determined unto each other, but made in reference unto the heavens and quarters of the globe: for those parts

---

[9] *Again, &c.*] In the use of string instruments both hands are dextrously used, yet the easiest and slowest parte is alwayes put on the lefte side; bycause all men use it soe: and excepting the harpe, there is scarce any string instrument to fit both hands, or the virginals, harpsicords, organs, which have all their ground from the harpe, layd along as it were in those instruments and supplied with keys (as that by the fingers) by which they are mediately made to speake as the harpe by the fingers immediately.—*Wr.*

are not capable of these conditions in themselves, nor with any certainty respectively derived from us, nor from them to us again. And first, in regard of their proper nature, the heavens admit not these sinister and dexter respects, there being in them no diversity or difference, but a simplicity of parts and equiformity in motion continually succeeding each other; so that from what point soever we compute, the account will be common unto the whole circularity. And therefore though it be plausible, it is not of consequence hereto what is delivered by Solinus; that man was therefore a microcosm or little world, because the dimensions of his positions were answerable unto the greater. For as in the heavens the distance of the north and southern pole, which are esteemed the superior and inferior points, is equal unto the space between the east and west, accounted the dextrous and sinistrous parts thereof, so is it also in man; for the extent of his fathom or distance betwixt the extremity of the fingers of either hand upon expansion, is equal unto the space between the sole of the foot and the crown. But this doth but petitionarily infer a dextrality in the heavens, and we may as reasonably conclude a right and left laterality in the ark or naval edifice of Noah. For the length thereof was thirty cubits, the breadth fifty, and the height or profundity thirty: which well agreeth unto the proportion of man; whose length, that is, a perpendicular from the vertex unto the sole of the foot, is sextuple unto his breadth, or a right line drawn from the ribs of one side to another, and decuple unto his profundity, that is, a direct line between the breast-bone and the spine.

Again, they receive not these conditions with any assurance or stability from ourselves. For the relative foundations, and points of denomination, are not fixed and certain, but variously designed according to imagination. The philosopher accounts that east from whence the heavens begin their motion. The astronomer, regarding the south and meridian sun, calls that the dextrous part of heaven which respecteth his right hand; and that is the west. Poets, respecting the west, assign the name of right unto the north which regardeth their right hand; and so must that of Ovid be explained, *utque, duæ dextrâ zonæ, totidémque sinistrâ.*

But augurs, or soothsayers, turning their face to the east, did make the right in the south;[1] which was also observed by the Hebrews and Chaldeans.* Now if we name the quarters of heaven respectively unto our sides, it will be no certain or invariable denomination. For, if we call that the right side of heaven which is seated easterly unto us when we regard the meridian sun, the inhabitants beyond the equator and southern tropick, when they face us, regarding the meridian, will contrarily define it; for unto them, the opposite part of heaven will respect the left, and the sun arise to their right.

And thus have we at large declared, that although the right be most commonly used, yet hath it no regular or certain root in nature. Since it is not confirmable from other animals: since in children it seems either indifferent or more favourable in the other; but more reasonable for uniformity in action, that men accustom unto one: since the grounds and reasons urged for it do not sufficiently support it; since, if there be a right and stronger side in nature, yet may we mistake in its denomination; calling that the right which is the left, and the left which is the right. Since some have one right, some both, some neither. And lastly, since these affections in man are not only fallible in relation unto one another, but made also in reference unto the heavens, they being not capable of these conditions in them-

---

* Psalm lxxxix. 13.

[1] *But augurs, &c.*] But Pomponius Lætus (in *De Auguribus*) sayes, if the *augur versus orientem sedebat, tenens dextrâ lituum*, i. e., *curvum baculum, quo in cœlo regiones dividit et quæ auguria conveniunt prædicit: si læva fuerint, fælicia pronunciat;* not bycause what comes to our left hand comes from the right hand of the gods, as some would say, but, sayes he, *quia a læva parte septentrio est; pars n. illa orbis, quia altior est prospera putatur; et a dextrâ parte meridies, quia depressior infelix*. And this reason is not particular, but generall, and such as prevailes all the other of philosophers, astronomers, or poets which respect their owne artes more then the nobler scite of the world. Whose longitude, that is the greatest distance, is accounted from east to west, which are every where round the world. But the latitude, which is the least distance, is counted from the æquator to each pole. And bycause the northerne in all respects of habitation, religion, learning, artes, government, wealth, honor, and all relations to heaven is infinitely more noble, and withall the higher parte of the world: therefore, 'tis justly cald the *right side* of the world.— *Wr*.

selves, nor with any certainty from us, nor we from them again.

And therefore what admission we owe unto many conceptions concerning right and left, requireth circumspection. That is, how far we ought to rely upon the remedy in Kiranides, that is, the left eye of an hedgehog fried in oil to procure sleep, and the right foot of a frog in a deer's skin for the gout; or, that to dream of the loss of right or left tooth presageth the death of male or female kindred, according to the doctrine of Artemidorus. What verity there is in that numeral conceit in the lateral division of man by even and odd, ascribing the odd unto the right side, and even unto the left; and so, by parity or imparity of letters in men's names to determine misfortunes on either side of their bodies; by which account in Greek numeration, Hephæstus or Vulcan was lame in the right foot, and Annibal lost his right eye. And lastly, what substance there is in that auspicial principle, and fundamental doctrine of ariolation, that the left hand is ominous, and that good things do pass sinistrously upon us, because the left hand of man respected the right hand of the gods, which handed their favours unto us.[2]

[2] *unto us.*] This chapter is very characteristic of our author. It displays remarkably the great pains he frequently bestows on the elucidation of lesser points, and the quaint and varied illustration which his extensive and curious reading enabled him to supply. The closing paragraph may serve to exemplify this latter remark: while the former is justified, not only by individual passages in the chapter, but by its great length, and by the care and argumentative precision with which he successively examines the various opinions, more or less absurd, which have been expressed on this *most momentous* topic, — summing up at the close, by a detail of the several reasons for his conclusion thereon.

Brande's Journal notices (vol. ii. page 423) a discourse by Signor Zecchinelli, on the reason of the prevalent custom of using the right in preference to the left hand. His theory is, first, that it was obviously necessary,—in order to avoid (what our author more felicitously terms) "anomalous discordances in manual actions,"—that one hand should obtain a general preference to the other. The next question was,— which to prefer? The Signor decides that mankind must have discovered that the left hand, from its anatomical connection with the most vital and important parts of the animal economy, could not be the one preferred. "For it must have been observed, that when the left arm is long used, or violently exercised, the left side also of the chest is put more or less in motion, and a consequent and corresponding obstacle produced not only to the free emission of the blood from the heart, but

CHAPTER VI.

On Swimming and Floating.

THAT men swim naturally, if not disturbed by fear; that men being drowned and sunk do float the ninth day, when their gall breaketh; that women drowned swim prone, but men supine, or upon their backs, are popular affirmations whereto we cannot assent. And first that man should swim naturally, because we observe it is no lesson unto other animals, we are not forward to conclude; for other animals swim in the same manner as they go, and need no other way of motion for natation in the water, than for progression upon the land. And this is true, whether they move *per latera*, that is, two legs of one side together, which is tolutation or ambling, or *per diametrum*, lifting one foot before, and the cross foot behind, which is succussation or trotting; or whether, *per frontem*, or *quadratum*, as Scaliger terms it, upon a square base, the legs of both sides moving together, as frogs and salient animals, which is properly called leaping. For by these motions they are able to support and impel themselves in the water, without alteration in the stroke of their legs, or position of their bodies.

But with man it is performed otherwise: for in regard of site he alters his natural posture and swimmeth prone, whereas he walketh erect.[3] Again, in progression, the arms move parallel to the legs, and the arms and legs unto each other; but in natation they intersect and make all sorts of angles.

---

also to its progress through the *aorta* and its ramifications." The editor goes on to observe, that the prevalence of the arterial system in the left side of the body renders this opinion quite plausible: and the painful sensations we experience, when we agitate greatly the left arm, or attempt to run while carrying a weight in the left hand, proves in a certain manner the truth of Signor Z.'s assertion.

Dr. A. Clarke, on Gen. xlviii. 18, remarks, that "the right hand of God," in the heavens, expresses the place of the most exalted dignity. But among the Turks, and in the north of China, the left hand is most honourable.

[3] *he alters, &c.*] "This is no reason," says Ross; "for man alters his natural posture when he crawls; will it follow, therefore, that this motion is not natural to man?"—See *Arcana,* p. 155.

And lastly, in progressive motion, the arms and legs do move successively, but in natation both together; all which aptly to perform, and so as to support and advance the body, is a point of art, and such as some in their young and docile years could never attain. But although swimming be acquired by art, yet is there somewhat more of nature in it than we observe in other habits, nor will it strictly fall under that definition; for once obtained, it is not to be removed; nor is there any who from disuse did ever yet forget it.

Secondly, that persons drowned arise and float the ninth day, when their gall breaketh, is a questionable determination both in the time and cause. For the time of floating, it is uncertain, according to the time of putrefaction, which shall retard or accelerate according to the subject and season of the year; for as we observed, cats and mice will arise unequally, and at different times, though drowned at the same. Such as are fat do commonly float soonest, for their bodies soonest ferment, and that substance approacheth nearest unto air: and this is one of Aristotle's reasons why dead eels will not float, because saith he, they have but slender bellies and little fat.

As for the cause, it is not so reasonably imputed unto the breaking of the gall as the putrefaction or corruptive fermentation of the body, whereby the unnatural heat prevailing, the putrefying parts do suffer a turgescence and inflation and becoming aery and spumous affect to approach the air, and ascend unto the surface of the water; and this is also evidenced in eggs, whereof the sound ones sink, and such as are addled swim, as do also those which are termed *hypenemia* or wind eggs, and this is also a way to separate seeds, whereof such as are corrupted and sterile swim, and this agreeth not only unto the seeds of plants locked up and capsulated in their husks, but also unto the sperm and seminal humour of man, for such a passage hath Aristotle upon the inquisition and test of its fertility.

That the breaking of the gall is not the cause hereof, experience hath informed us. For opening the abdomen, and taking out the gall in cats and mice, they did notwithstanding arise. And because we had read in Rhodiginus of a tyrant, who to prevent the emergency of murdered bodies, did use to cut off their lungs, and found men's minds possessed with this reason, we committed some unto the water without lungs, which notwithstanding floated with the others; and to complete the experiment, although we took out the guts and bladder, and also perforated the cranium, yet would they arise, though in a longer time. From these observations in other animals, it may not be unreasonable to conclude the same in man, who is too noble a subject on whom to make them expressly, and the casual opportunity too rare almost to make any. Now if any shall ground this effect from gall or choler, because it is the highest humour, and will be above the rest, or being the fiery humour, will readiest surmount the water, we must confess in the common putrescence it may promote elevation, which the breaking of the bladder of gall, so small a part in man, cannot considerably advantage.

Lastly, that women drowned float prone, that is, with their bellies downward, but men supine or upward, is an assertion wherein the ὅτι or point itself is dubious, and, were it true, the reason alleged for it is of no validity. The reason yet current was first expressed by Pliny, *veluti pudori defunctorum parcente natura*, nature modestly ordaining this position to conceal the shame of the dead, which hath been taken up by Solinus, Rhodiginus, and many more. This indeed (as Scaliger termeth it) is *ratio civilis non philosophica*, strong enough for morality or rhetoricks, not for philosophy or physicks. For first, in nature the concealment of secret parts is the same in both sexes, and the shame of their reveal equal: so Adam upon the taste of the fruit was ashamed of his nakedness as well as Eve. And so likewise in America and countries unacquainted with habits, where modesty conceals these parts in one sex, it doth it also in the other, and therefore had this been the intention of nature, not only women but men also had swimmed downwards; the posture in reason being common unto both, where the intent is also common.

Again, while herein we commend the modesty, we condemn the wisdom of nature: for that prone position we make her contrive unto the women, were best agreeable unto the man, in whom the secret parts are very anterior and more discoverable in a supine and upward posture; and therefore Scaliger declining this reason, hath recurred unto another from the difference of parts in both sexes; *Quod ventre vasto* *sunt mulieres plenoque intestinis, itaque minus impletur et subsidet, inanior maribus quibus nates præponderant;* if so, then men with great bellies will float downward, and only *Callipygæ,* and women largely composed behind, upward. But anatomists observe, that to make the larger cavity for the infant, the haunch-bones in women, and consequently the parts appendent, are more protuberant than they are in men. They who ascribe the cause unto the breasts of women, take not away the doubt, for they resolve not why children float downward, who are included in that sex, though not in the reason alleged. But hereof we cease to discourse, lest we undertake to afford a reason of the golden tooth,* that is, to invent or assign a cause, when we remain unsatisfied or unassured of the effect.

That a mare will sooner drown than a horse, though commonly opinioned, is not I fear experienced; nor is the same observed in the drowning of whelps and kitlings. But that a man cannot shut or open his eyes under water, easy experiment may convict. Whether cripples and mutilated persons, who have lost the greatest part of their thighs, will not sink but float, their lungs being abler to waft up their bodies, which are in others overpoised by the hinder legs; we have not made experiment. Thus much we observe, that animals drown downwards, and the same is observable in frogs, when the hinder legs are cut off; but in the air most seem to perish headlong from high places: however Vulcan thrown from heaven be made to fall on his feet.[4]

CHAPTER VII.

That Men weigh heavier dead than alive, and before meat than after.

THAT men weigh heavier dead than alive, if experiment hath not failed us, we cannot reasonably grant.[5] For though

* Of the cause whereof much dispute was made, and at last proved an imposture.

[4] *That a mare, &c.*] This paragraph added in 2nd edition.
[5] *That men weigh heavier, &c.*] What shall be said of the man who can use such an argument as the following: — "Why doth a man fall down in his sleep, who stood upright when he was awake, if he be

the trial hereof cannot so well be made on the body of man, nor will the difference be sensible in the debate of scruples or drachms, yet can we not confirm the same in lesser animals, from whence the inference is good, and the affirmative of Pliny saith, that it is true in all. For exactly weighing and strangling a chicken in the scales, upon an immediate ponderation, we could discover no sensible difference in weight, but suffering it to lie eight or ten hours, until it grew perfectly cold, it weighed most sensibly lighter; the like we attempted and verified in mice, and performed their trials in scales that would turn upon the eighth or tenth part of a grain.

Now whereas some allege that spirits are lighter substances, and naturally ascending, do elevate and waft the body upward, whereof dead bodies being destitute contract a greater gravity; although we concede that spirits are light, comparatively unto the body, yet that they are absolutely so, or have no weight at all, we cannot readily allow. For since philosophy affirmeth that spirits are middle substances between the soul and body, they must admit of some corporeity, which supposeth weight or gravity. Beside in carcasses warm, and bodies newly disanimated, while transpiration remaineth, there do exhale and breathe out vaporous and fluid parts, which carry away some power of gravitation. Which though we allow we do not make answerable unto living expiration, and therefore the chicken or mice were not

not heavier than he was?"—*Ross, Arcana*, p. 100. Truly we may say, "Every man is not a proper champion for truth, nor fit to take up the gauntlet in the cause of verity!"—*Rel. Med.* p. 9.

The result of modern investigation seems to confirm the opinion so preposterously advocated by Ross; at least it shows that the specific gravity of the human body is in reality greater after death than it was while living. Dalton, in an interesting paper on the *Effects of Atmospheric Pressure on the Animal Frame*, published in the 10th vol. of the *Manchester Memoirs*, thus sums up: "Upon the whole I am inclined to believe the true explanation of the difficulty will be found in this, that the whole substance of the body is pervious to air, and that a considerable portion of it constantly exists in the body during life subject to increase and diminution according to the pressure of the atmosphere, in the same manner as it exists in water, and further, that when life is extinct, this air in some degree escapes, and renders the parts specifically heavier than when the vital functions were in a state of activity."

so light being dead, as they would have been after ten hours kept alive, for in that space a man abateth many ounces; nor if it had slept, for in that space of sleep, a man will sometimes abate forty ounces: nor if it had been in the middle of summer, for then a man weigheth some pounds less than in the height of winter, according to experience, and the statick aphorisms of Sanctorius.

Again, whereas men affirm they perceive an addition of ponderosity in dead bodies, comparing them usually unto blocks and stones, whensoever they lift or carry them; this accessional preponderancy is rather in appearance than reality. For being destitute of any motion, they confer no relief unto the agents or elevators, which make us meet with the same complaints of gravity in animated and living bodies, where the nerves subside, and the faculty locomotive seems abolished, as may be observed in the lifting or supporting of persons inebriated, apoplectical, or in lipothymies and swoonings.

Many are also of opinion, and some learned men maintain, that men are lighter after meals than before, and that by a supply and addition of spirits obscuring the gross ponderosity of the aliment ingested; but the contrary hereof we have found in the trial of sundry persons in different sex and ages. And we conceive men may mistake, if they distinguish not the sense of levity unto themselves, and in regard of the scale, or decision of trutination.[6] For after a draught of wine, a man may seem lighter in himself from sudden reflection, although he be heavier in the balance, from a corporal and ponderous addition; but a man in the morning is lighter in the scale, because in sleep some pounds have perspired; and is also lighter unto himself, because he is refected.

And to speak strictly, a man that holds his breath is weightier while his lungs are full, than upon expiration. For a bladder blown is weightier than one empty; and if it contain a quart, expressed and emptied it will abate about a quarter of a grain. And therefore we somewhat mistrust the experiment of a pumice-stone taken up by Montanus, in his comment upon Avicenna, where declaring how the rarity of parts, and numerosity of pores, occasioneth a lightness in

---

[6] *trutination.*] The act of weighing in scales; from *trutina.*

bodies, he affirms that a pumice-stone powdered is lighter than one entire; which is an experiment beyond our satisfaction; for, beside that abatement can hardly be avoided in the trituration, if a bladder of good capacity will scarce include a grain of air, a pumice of three or four drachms, cannot be presumed to contain the hundredth part thereof; which will not be sensible upon the exactest beams we use. Nor is it to be taken strictly, what is delivered by the learned Lord Verulam, and referred unto further experiment; that a dissolution of iron in *aqua fortis*, will bear as good weight as their bodies did before, notwithstanding a great deal of waste by a thick vapour that issueth during the working; for we cannot find it to hold either in iron or copper, which is dissolved with less ebullition; and hereof we made trial in scales of good exactness; wherein if there be a defect, or such as will not turn upon quarter grains, there may be frequent mistakes in experiments of this nature. That also may be considered which is delivered by Hamerus Poppius, that antimony calcined or reduced to ashes by a burning glass, although it emit a gross and ponderous exhalation, doth rather exceed than abate its former gravity.[7] Nevertheless, strange it is, how very little and almost insensible abatement there will be sometimes in such operations, or rather some increase, as in the refining of metals, in the test of bone-ashes, according to experience: and in a burnt brick, as Monsieur de Calve,* affirmeth. Mistake may be made in this way of trial; when the antimony is not weighed immediately upon the calcination, but permitted the air, it imbibeth the humidity thereof, and so repaireth its gravity.

CHAPTER VIII.

That there are several passages for Meat and Drink.

THAT there are different passages for meat and drink, the meat or dry aliment descending by the one, the drink or

* *Des Pierres.*

[7] *that antimony, &c.*] This is like that other refuted **before, that a** pumice powdered weighs heavier then before.—*Wr.*

moistening vehicle by the other, is a popular tenet in our days, but was the assertion of learned men of old. For the same was affirmed by Plato, maintained by Eustathius in Macrobius, and is deducible from Eratosthenes, Eupolis and Euripides. Now herein men contradict experience, not well understanding anatomy, and the use of parts. For at the throat there are two cavities or conducting parts; the one the *œsophagus* or gullet, seated next the spine, a part official unto nutrition, and whereby the aliment both wet and dry is conveyed unto the stomach; the other (by which 'tis conceived the drink doth pass) is the weazand, rough artery, or wind-pipe, a part inservient to voice and respiration; for thereby the air descendeth into the lungs, and is communicated unto the heart. And therefore, all animals that breathe or have lungs, have also the weazand; but many have the gullet or feeding channel, which have no lungs or windpipe; as fishes which have gills, whereby the heart is refrigerated; for such thereof as have lungs and respiration, are not without the weazand, as whales and cetaceous animals.

Again, beside these parts destined to divers offices, there is a peculiar provision for the wind-pipe, that is, a cartilagineous flap upon the opening of the larynx or throttle, which hath an open cavity for the admission of the air; but lest thereby either meat or drink should descend, Providence hath placed the *epiglottis, ligula,* or flap like an ivy leaf, which always closeth when we swallow, or when the meat and drink passeth over it into the gullet. Which part although all have not that breathe, as all cetaceous and oviparous animals, yet is the weazand secured some other way; and therefore in whales that breathe, lest the water should get into the lungs, an ejection thereof is contrived by a *fistula* or spout at the head. And therefore also, though birds have no *epiglottis*, yet can they so contract the rim or chink of their *larynx*, as to prevent the admission of wet or dry ingested; either whereof getting in, occasioneth a cough, until it be ejected. And this is the reason why a man cannot drink and breathe at the same time; why, if we laugh while we drink, the drink flies out at the nostrils; why, when the water enters the weazand, men are suddenly drowned; and thus must it be understood, when we read of one that died by the seed of a grape,* and another by an hair in milk.⁸

Now if any shall affirm, that some truth there is in the assertion, upon the experiment of Hippocrates, who, killing an hog after a red potion, found the tincture thereof in the larynx; if any will urge the same from medical practice, because in affections both of lungs and weazand, physicians make use of syrups, and lambitive medicines;⁹ we are not averse to acknowledge, that some may distil and insinuate into the wind-pipe, and medicines may creep down, as well as the rheum before them: yet to conclude from hence, that air and water have both one common passage, were to state the question upon the weaker side of the distinction, and from a partial or guttulous irrigation to conclude a total descension.

CHAPTER IX.

Of Saluting upon Sneezing.

CONCERNING Sternutation or Sneezing, and the custom of saluting or blessing upon that motion, it is pretended, and generally believed, to derive its original from a disease, wherein sternutation proved mortal, and such as sneezed, died. And this may seem to be proved from Carolus Sigonius, who in his History of Italy, makes mention of a pestilence in the time of Gregory the Great, that proved pernicious and deadly to those that sneezed. Which notwithstanding will not sufficiently determine the grounds hereof, that custom having an elder era than this chronology affordeth.

---

* Anacreon the Poet, if the story be taken literally.

⁸ *by an hair in milk.*] And a woman in Knowle, Wiltes, by a piece of the great tendon in a neck of veale (which is commonly cald the Halifax) which getting sodenly within the larinx chokt her.—*Wr.* See my note relating the death of Lord Boringdon, at p. 168.

⁹ *syrups.*] In a dangerous catharr, the end of giving syrupes is, that sliding downe with the rheumes, they may both abate and correct the cold crude salt corroding qualityes of rheumes: and withall by the heat of the ingredients, and the balmy benigne quality of sugar, att once arme and warme the lungs, and withall thicken the rheum that fals, that itt may bee more easily expectorated.—*Wr.*

For although the age of Gregory extend above a thousand, yet is this custom mentioned by Apuleius, in the fable of the fuller's wife, who lived three hundred years before; by Pliny in that problem of his, *cur sternutantes salutantur;* and there are also reports that Tiberius the emperor, otherwise a very sour man, would perform this rite most punctually unto others, and expect the same from others unto himself. Petronius Arbiter, who lived before them both, and was proconsul of Bithynia in the reign of Nero, hath mentioned it in these words, *Gyton collectione spiritûs plenus, ter continuò ità sternutavit, ut grabatum concuteret, ad quem motum Eumolpus conversus, Salvere Gytona jubet.* Cœlius Rhodiginus hath an example hereof among the Greeks far ancienter than these, that is, in the time of Cyrus the younger, when consulting about their retreat, it chanced that one among them sneezed, at the noise whereof the rest of the soldiers called upon Jupiter Soter. There is also in the Greek *Anthology* a remarkable mention hereof in an epigram, upon one Proclus; the Latin whereof we shall deliver, as we find it often translated.

> Non potis est Proclus digitis emungere nasum,
>   Namq; est pro nasi mole pusilla manus :
> Non vocat ille Jovem sternutans, quippe nec audit
>   Sternutamentum, tam procul aure sonat.

> Proclus with his hand his nose can never wipe,
>   His hand too little is his nose to gripe ;
> He sneezing calls not *Jove*, for why? he hears
>   Himself not sneeze, the sound's so far from's ears.

Nor was this only an ancient custom among the Greeks and Romans, and is still in force with us, but is received at this day in remotest parts of Africa.[1] For so we read in Codignus,* that upon a sneeze of the Emperor of Monomotapa, there passed acclamations successive through the city; and as remarkable an example there is of the same custom, in the remotest parts of the East, recorded in the travels of Pinto.

But the history will run much higher, if we should take in the rabbinical account hereof, that sneezing was a mortal

---

* *De rebus Abassinorum.*

[1] *Africa.*] And in Otaheite.—*Jeff.*

sign even from the first man, until it was take noff by the special supplication of Jacob. From whence, as a thankful acknowledgment, this salutation first began, and was after continued by the expression of *Tobim Chaiim*, or *vita bona*, by standers by, upon all occasion of sneezing.²

Now the ground of this ancient custom was probably the opinion the ancients held of sternutation,³ which they generally conceived to be a good sign or a bad, and so upon this motion accordingly used a *salve* or Ζεῦ σῶσον, as a gratulation for the one, and a deprecation for the other. Now of the ways whereby they enquired and determined its signality; the first was natural, arising from physical causes, and consequences oftentimes naturally succeeding this motion, and so it might be justly esteemed a good sign; for sneezing being properly a motion of the brain, suddenly expelling through the nostrils what is offensive unto it, it cannot but afford some evidence of its vigour, and therefore, saith Aristotle,* they that hear it, προσκυνοῦσιν ὡς ἱερόν, "honour it as somewhat sacred," and a sign of sanity in the diviner part, and this he illustrates from the practice of physicians, who in persons near death, do use sternutatories, or such medicines as provoke unto sneezing, when if the faculty awaketh, and sternutation ensueth, they conceive hopes of life, and with gratulation receive the signs of safety.† And so is it also of good signality, according to that of Hippocrates, that sneezing cureth the hiccough, and is profitable unto women in hard labour, and so is it good in lethargies, apoplexies, catalepsies, and comas. And in this natural way is it sometime likewise of bad effects or signs, and may give hints of deprecation; as in diseases of the chest, for therein Hippocrates condemneth it as too much exagitating; in the beginning of catarrhs, according unto Avicenna, as hindering concoction; in new and tender conceptions, as Pliny observeth, for then it endangers abortion.

The second way was superstitious and augurial, as Cœlius

---

* *Problems*, sect. 33. † 2 Kings iv. 35.

² *And as remarkable, &c.*] This sentence and the following paragraph were added in 3rd edition.

³ *sternutation.*] Physitians generallye define itt to be the trumpet of nature upon the ejection of a noxious vapour from the braine, and therefore saye rightly itt is *bonum signum malæ causæ, sc. depulsæ.*—*Wr.*

Rhodiginus hath illustrated in testimonies as ancient as Theocritus and Homer; as appears from the Athenian master, who would have retired because a boatman sneezed; and the testimony of Austin, that the ancients were wont to go to bed again if they sneezed while they put on their shoe. And in this way it was also of good and bad signification; so Aristotle hath a problem, why sneezing from noon unto midnight was good, but from night to noon unlucky. So Eustathius upon Homer observes, that sneezing to the left hand was unlucky, but prosperous unto the right; so, as Plutarch relateth, when Themistocles sacrificed in his galley before the battle of Xerxes, and one of the assistants upon the right hand sneezed, Euphrantides, the soothsayer, presaged the victory of the Greeks, and the overthrow of the Persians.

Thus we may perceive the custom is more ancient than commonly conceived, and these opinions hereof in all ages, not any one disease, to have been the occasion of this salute and deprecation. Arising at first from this vehement and affrighting motion of the brain, inevitably observable unto the standers by; from whence some finding dependent effects to ensue, others ascribing hereto as a cause what perhaps but casually or inconnexedly succeeded, they might proceed unto forms of speeches, felicitating the good, or deprecating the evil to follow.

CHAPTER X.

That Jews Stink.

THAT Jews stink[4] naturally, that is, that in their race and nation there is an evil savour, is a received opinion we know

[4] *That Jews stink.*] The Jews anxiously observing the prohibited eating of blood keepe their flesh covered with onyons and garleek till itt putrifie, and contracte as bad a smell as that of rottenes from those strong sawces; and soe by continual use thereof emit a loathsom savour, as Mr. Fulham experimented in Italye at a Jewish meeting, with the hazard of life, till he removed into the fresh air. *Teste ipso fide dignissimo.*— *Wr.*

Howell, in a letter written to Lord Clifford, in reply to his enquiries respecting the Jews, does not hesitate to adopt the common opinion as one so well known as to need no proof. "As they are," says he, "the

not how to admit, although we concede many questionable points, and dispute not the verity of sundry opinions which are of affinity hereto. We will acknowledge that certain odours attend on animals, no less than certain colours; that pleasant smells are not confined unto vegetables, but found in divers animals, and some more richly than in plants; and though the problem of Aristotle enquires why no animal smells sweet beside the pard, yet later discoveries add divers sorts of monkeys, the civet cat and gazela, from which our musk proceedeth. We confess that beside the smell of the species there may be individual odours, and every man may have a proper and peculiar savour, which although not perceptible unto man, who hath this sense but weak, is yet sensible unto dogs, who hereby can single out their masters in the dark. We will not deny that particular men have sent forth a pleasant savour, as Theophrastus and Plutarch report of Alexander the Great, and Tzetzes and Cardan do testify of themselves. That some may also emit an unsavoury odour, we have no reason to deny; for this may happen from the quality of what they have taken, the fœtor whereof may discover itself by sweat and urine, as being unmasterable by the natural heat of man, not to be dulcified by concoction beyond an unsavoury condition; the like may come to pass from putrid humours, as is often discoverable in putrid and malignant fevers; and sometime also in gross and humid bodies even in the latitude of sanity, the natural heat of the parts being insufficient for a perfect and thorough digestion, and the errors of one concoction not rectifiable by another. But that an unsavoury odour is gentilitious or national unto the Jews, if rightly understood, we cannot well concede, nor will the information of reason or sense induce it.

For first, upon consult of reason, there will be found no easy assurance to fasten a material or temperamental propriety upon any nation; there being scarce any condition (but what depends upon clime) which is not exhausted or obscured from the commixture of introvenient nations either by commerce or conquest; much more will it be difficult to

most contemptible people, and have a kind of fulsome scent, no better than a stink, that distinguisheth them from others, so they are the most timorous people on earth, &c."—*Familiar Letters*, book i. § 6, letter xv. p. 252.

make out this affection in the Jews; whose race however pretended to be pure, must needs have suffered inseparable commixtures with nations of all sorts; not only in regard of their proselytes, but their universal dispersion; some being posted from several parts of the earth, others quite lost, and swallowed up in those nations where they planted. For the tribes of Reuben, Gad, part of Manasses and Naphthali, which were taken by Assur, and the rest at the sacking of Samaria, which were led away by Salmanasser into Assyria, and after a year and a half arrived at Arsereth, as is delivered in Esdras; these I say never returned,[5] and are by the Jews as vainly expected as their Messias. Of those of the tribe of Judah and Benjamin, which were led captive into Babylon by Nebuchadnezzar, many returned under Zorobabel; the rest remained, and from thence long after, upon invasion of the Saracens, fled as far as India; where yet they are said to remain but with little difference from the Gentiles.

[5] *For the tribes, &c.*] The subsequent history of the ten tribes, who were carried into captivity at the fall of Samaria, has ever remained and must remain a matter of conjecture.—It is, however, most probable that our author's supposition is correct. Dr. Claudius Buchanan is satisfied "that the greater part of the ten tribes, which now exist, are to be found in the countries of their first captivity." In support of which opinion he cites the following passage from a speech of King Agrippa to the Jews, in the reign of Vespasian;—"What, do you stretch your hopes beyond the river Euphrates?—Do any of you think that your fellow-tribes will come to your aid out of *Adiabene*? Besides, if they would come, the Parthian will not permit it."—*Joseph. de Bell.* lib. ii. c. 28,—a proof, as the Dr. remarks, that the ten tribes were still in captivity, in Media, under the Persian princes, during the 1st century of the Christian era, 700 years after their transplantation. Again he adduces a passage from Jerome, written in the 5th century, in his notes on Hosea;—"unto this day the ten tribes are subject to the kings of the Persians, *nor* has *their* captivity ever been loosed." He says also, "the ten tribes inhabit at this day the cities and mountains of the Medes," tom. vi. p. 80. To this day, continues Dr. B., no family, Jew or Christian, is permitted to leave the Persian territories without the king's permission.—See Dr. Claudius Buchanan's *Christian Researches in Asia*, p. 239.

The Samaritan traditions, however, might lead to the opinion that a considerable remnant of the Israelites avoided captivity, and were left on the soil of Palestine. The singular fact that they have preserved the Mosaic law in the ruder and more ancient character, strongly confirms this hypothesis, which derives additional support also from various other considerations.—See *History of the Jews* (*Fam. Lib.*), ii. 10.

The tribes that returned to Judea, were afterward widely dispersed; for beside sixteen thousand which Titus sent to Rome under the triumph of his father Vespasian, he sold no less than an hundred thousand for slaves. Not many years after, Adrian the emperor, who ruined the whole country, transplanted many thousands into Spain, from whence they dispersed into divers countries, as into France and England, but were banished after from both. From Spain they dispersed into Africa, Italy, Constantinople, and the dominions of the Turk, where they remain as yet in very great numbers. And if (according to good relations), where they may freely speak it, they forbear not to boast that there are at present many thousand Jews in Spain, France, and England, and some dispensed withal even to the degree of priesthood; it is a matter very considerable, and could they be smelled out, would much advantage, not only the church of Christ, but also the coffers of princes.[6]

Now having thus lived in several countries, and always in subjection, they must needs have suffered many commixtures; and we are sure they are not exempted from the common contagion of venery contracted first from Christians. Nor are fornications unfrequent between them both; there commonly passing opinions of invitement, that their women desire copulation with them rather than their own nation, and affect Christian carnality above circumcised venery. It being therefore acknowledged that some are lost, evident that others are mixed, and not assured that any are distinct, it will be hard to establish this quality upon the Jews, unless we also transfer the same unto those whose generations are mixed, whose genealogies are Jewish, and naturally derived from them.

Again, if we concede a national unsavouriness in any people, yet shall we find the Jews less subject hereto than any, and that in those regards which most powerfully concur to such effects, that is, their diet and generation. As for their diet, whether in obedience unto the precepts of reason, or the injunctions of parsimony, therein they are very tem-

---

[6] *The tribes, &c.*] The subject of this paragraph is fully treated in the course of the *History of the Jews*, referred to in the preceding note: the last chapter of which gives a very elaborate and careful estimate of the present number of Jews in various countries.

perate, seldom offending in ebriety or excess of drink, nor erring in gulosity or superfluity of meats; whereby they prevent indigestion and crudities,⁷ and consequently putrescence of humours. They have in abomination all flesh maimed, or the inwards any way vitiated, and therefore eat no meat but of their own killing. They observe not only fasts at certain times, but are restrained unto very few dishes at all times; so few, that whereas S. Peter's sheet will hardly cover our tables, their law doth scarce permit them to set forth a lordly feast; nor any way to answer the luxury of our times, or those of our forefathers. For of flesh their law restrains them many sorts, and such as complete our feasts; that animal, *propter convivia natum,** they touch not, nor any of its preparations or parts, so much in respect at Roman tables, nor admit they unto their board, hares, conies, herons, plovers, or swans. Of fishes they only taste of such as have both fins and scales, which are comparatively but few in number; such only, saith Aristotle, whose egg or spawn is arenaceous: whereby are excluded all cetaceous and cartilagineous fishes; many pectinal, whose ribs are rectilineal; many costal, which have their ribs embowed; all spinal, or such as have no ribs, but only a backbone, or somewhat analogous thereto, as eels, congers, lampreys; all that are testaceous, as oysters, cockles, wilks, scollops, muscles; and likewise all crustaceous, as crabs, shrimps, and lobsters. So that, observing a spare and simple diet, whereby they prevent the generation of crudities; and fasting often, whereby they might also digest them; they must be less inclinable unto this infirmity than any other nation, whose proceedings are not so reasonable to avoid it.

As for their generations and conceptions (which are the purer from good diet), they become more pure and perfect by the strict observation of their law; upon the injunctions whereof, they severely observe the times of purification, and avoid all copulation, either in the uncleanness of themselves,

---

* *Quanti est gula, quæ sibi totos ponit apros! Animal propter convivia natum.*

⁷ *indigestion and crudities.*] This crudity of indigestion is soe cleerly discernable in the breath of children; that hee who comes fasting into a great schoole shall soone perceave itt, to his smell, most odious.—*Wr.*

or impurity of their women. A rule, I fear, not so well observed by Christians; whereby not only conceptions are prevented, but if they proceed, so vitiated and defiled, that durable inquinations remain upon the birth. Which, when the conception meets with these impurities, must needs be very potent; since in the purest and most fair conceptions, learned men derive the cause of pox and meazles, from principles of that nature; that is, the menstruous impurities in the mother's blood, and virulent tinctures contracted by the infant, in the nutriment of the womb.

Lastly, experience will convict it; for this offensive odour is no way discoverable in their synagogues where many are,[8] and by reason of their number could not be concealed: nor is the same discernible in commerce or conversation with such as are cleanly in apparel, and decent in their houses. Surely the Viziers and Turkish bashas are not of this opinion; who, as Sir Henry Blunt informeth, do generally keep a Jew of their private council. And were this true, the Jews themselves do not strictly make out the intention of their law, for in vain do they scruple to approach the dead, who livingly are cadaverous, or fear any outward pollution, whose temper pollutes themselves. And lastly, were this true, yet our opinion is not impartial; for unto converted Jews who are of the same seed, no man imputeth this unsavoury odour; as though aromatized by their conversion, they lost their scent with their religion, and smelt no longer than they savoured of the Jew.

Now the ground that begat or propagated this assertion, might be the distasteful averseness of the Christian from the Jew, upon the villany of that fact, which made them abominable and stink in the nostrils of all men. Which real practice and metaphorical expression did after proceed into a literal construction; but was a fraudulent illation; for such an evil savour their father Jacob acknowledged in himself, when he said his sons had made him stink in the land, that is, to be abominable unto the inhabitants thereof.* Now how dangerous it is in sensible things to

* Gen. xxxiv.

[8] *many are.*] See the evidence hereof, p. 413, undeniably proceed.—*Wr.*

use metaphorical expressions unto the people, and what absurd conceits they will swallow in their literals, an impatient[9] example we have in our own profession; who having called an eating ulcer by the name of a wolf, common apprehension conceives a reality therein, and against ourselves ocular affirmations are pretended to confirm it.

The nastiness of that nation, and sluttish course of life, hath much promoted the opinion, occasioned by their servile condition at first, and inferior ways of parsimony ever since; as is delivered by Mr. Sandys; they are generally fat, saith he, and rank of the savours which attend upon sluttish corpulency.[1] The epithets assigned them by ancient times, have also advanced the same; for Ammianus Marcellinus describeth them in such language, and Martial more ancient, in such a relative expression sets forth unsavoury Bassa.

> Quod jejunia sabbatariorum
> Mallem, quàm quod oles, olere, Bassa.

From whence, notwithstanding, we cannot infer an inward imperfection in the temper of that nation; it being but an effect in the breath from outward observation, in their strict and tedious fasting; and was a common effect in the breaths of other nations, became a proverb among the Greeks* and the reason thereof begot a problem in Aristotle.†

Lastly, if all were true, and were this savour conceded, yet are the reasons alleged for it no way satisfactory. Hucherius,† and after him Alsarius Crucius,‡ imputes this effect unto their abstinence from salt or salt meats;[2] which how to make good in the present diet of the Jews, we know not; nor shall we conceive it was observed of old, if we consider they seasoned every sacrifice and all oblations whatsoever; whereof we cannot deny a great part was eaten by the priests. And if the offering were of flesh, it

* Νηστείας ὄζειν. *Jejunia olere.*   † *De Sterilitate.*
‡ *Cruc. Med. Epist.*

[9] *impatient.*] *Lege* insufferable.—*Wr.*
[1] *rank, &c.*] Which Mr. Fulham confirmd as above, p. 413. This is enonghe, leaving the cause to further inquisition.—*Wr.*
[2] *salt meats.*] Which they supply with onyons and garlick, ut supra —*Wr.*

was salted no less than thrice, that is, once in the common chamber of salt, at the footstep of the altar, and upon the top thereof, as is at large delivered by Maimonides. Nor, if they refrained all salt, is the illation very urgent: for many there are not noted for ill odours,[3] which eat no salt at all; as all carnivorous animals, most children, many whole nations, and probably our fathers after the creation; there being indeed, in every thing we eat, a natural and concealed salt,[4] which is separated by digestions, as doth appear in our tears, sweat, and urines, although we refrain all salt, or what doth seem to contain it.

Another cause is urged by Campegius, and much received by Christians; that this ill savour is a curse derived upon them by Christ, and stands as a badge or brand of a generation that crucified their *Salvator*. But this is a conceit without all warrant, and an easy way to take off dispute in what point of obscurity soever. A method of many writers, which much depreciates the esteem and value of miracles; that is, therewith to salve not only real verities, but also non-existencies. Thus have elder times not only ascribed the immunity of Ireland from any venomous beast unto the staff or rod of Patrick, but the long tails of Kent unto the malediction of Austin.[5]

Thus therefore, although we concede that many opinions are true which hold some conformity unto this, yet in assenting hereto many difficulties must arise; it being a

[3] *not noted, &c.*] This is contraryed by experience. Supra, p. 413.—*Wr.*

[4] *salt.*] The earthy being separated, leaves the other sweet, not salt. But the many circulations of them acquiring saltnes from the naturall heate, send out that unnecessary saltnes in sweat, and teares, and urine, and generally in salivation.—*Wr.*

[5] *long tails of Kent.*] Bailey gives the following notice of these gentry:—"The Kentish men are said to have had long tails for some generations; by way of punishment, as some say, for the Kentish Pagans abusing Austin the monk and his associates, by beating them, and opprobriously tying fish-tails to their backsides; in revenge of which, such appendants grew to the hind parts of all that generation. But the scene of this lying wonder was not in Kent, but in Carne, in Dorsetshire, many miles off. Others again say it was for cutting off the tail of St. Thomas of Canterbury's horse, who, being out of favour with King Henry II. riding towards Canterbury upon a poor sorry horse, was so served by the common people.

dangerous point to annex a constant property unto any nation, and much more this unto the Jew; since their quality is not verified by observation;[6] since the grounds are feeble that should establish it; and lastly, since if all were true, yet are the reasons alleged for it of no sufficiency to maintain it.

CHAPTER XI.

Of Pigmies.

BY pigmies we understand a dwarfish race of people, or lowest diminution of mankind, comprehended in one cubit, or as some will have it, in two foot or three spans; not taking them single, but nationally considering them, and as they make up an aggregated habitation. Whereof, although affirmations be many, and testimonies more frequent than in any other point which wise men have cast into the list of fables, yet that there is, or ever was such a race or nation, upon exact and confirmed testimonies, our strictest enquiry receives no satisfaction.[7]

I say "exact testimony," first, in regard of the authors from whom we derive the account; for, though we meet herewith in Herodotus, Philostratus, Mela, Pliny, Solinus, and many more, yet were they derivative relators, and the primitive author was Homer; who, using often similes, as well to delight the ear, as to illustrate his matter, in the third of his Iliads, compareth the Trojans unto cranes, when they descend against the pigmies; which was more largely set out by Oppian, Juvenal, Mantuan, and many poets since, and being only a pleasant figment in the fountain, became a solemn story in the stream, and current still among us.

[6] *not verifiable, &c.*] It is, ut supra, p. 413.—*Wr.*

[7] *By pigmies, &c.*] Ross contends,—as he almost invariably does—for the truth of the old saying. He argues that "it stands with reason there should be such, that God's wisdom might be seen in all sorts of magnitudes; for if there have been giants, why not also pigmies, nature being as propense to the least, as to the greatest magnitude." He adduces the testimony of Buchanan, who, speaking of the isles of Scotland, amongst the rest sets down the Isle of Pigmies.

Again,[8] many professed enquirers have rejected it. Strabo, an exact and judicious geographer, hath largely condemned it as a fabulous story. Julius Scaliger, a diligent enquirer, accounts thereof but as a poetical fiction. Ulysses Aldrovandus, a most exact zoographer, in an express discourse hereon, concludes the story fabulous, and a poetical account of Homer; and the same was formerly conceived by Eustathius, his excellent commentator. Albertus Magnus, a man ofttimes too credulous, herein was more than dubious; for he affirmeth if any such dwarfs were ever extant, they were surely some kind of apes; which is a conceit allowed by Cardan,[9] and not esteemed improbable by many others.

There are, I confess, two testimonies, which from their authority, admit of consideration. The first of Aristotle,* whose words are these, ἔστι δὲ ὁ τόπος, &c. That is, *Hic locus est quem incolunt pygmæi, non enim id fabula est, sed pusillum genus ut aiunt.* Wherein indeed Aristotle plays the Aristotle, that is, the wary and evading assertor; for though with *non est fabula* he seems at first to confirm it, yet at the last he claps in *ut aiunt*, and shakes the belief he put before upon it. And therefore, I observe Scaliger hath not translated the first; perhaps supposing it surreptitious or unworthy so great an assertor. And truly for those books of animals, or work of eight hundred talents, as Athenæus terms it, although ever to be admired, as containing most excellent truths, yet are many things therein delivered upon relation, and some repugnant unto the history of our senses; as we are able to make out in some, and Scaliger hath observed in many more, as he hath freely declared in his comment upon that piece.

The second testimony is deduced from Holy Scripture,† thus rendered in vulgar translation: *Sed et Pygmæi qui erant in turribus tuis, pharetras suas suspenderunt in muris*

---

* *Hist. Animal.* lib. viii.   † Ezek. xxvii. 12.

[8] *Again.*] This paragraph is taken almost verbatim from Cardan in the place cited below.—*Wr.*

[9] *Cardan.*] Rightly does he quote Cardan, who in the 8th book, *De Varietate,* cap. xl. p. 527, approves of Strabo's judgement of Homer's fiction: and concludes they were mistaken, being noe other then apes.—*Wr.*

tuis per gyrum; from whence notwithstanding we cannot infer this assertion. For, first, the translators accord not, and the Hebrew word *gammadim* is very variously rendered. Though Aquila, Vatablus, and Lyra will have it *pygmei*, yet in the Septuagint it is no more than watchmen, and so in the Arabic and High Dutch. In the Chaldee, Cappadocians; in Symmachus, Medes; and in the French, those of Gamad. Theodotion of old, and Tremellius of late, have retained the textuary word, and so have the Italian, Low Dutch, and English translators; that is, the men of Arvad were upon thy walls round about, and the Gammadims were in thy towers. Nor do men only dissent in the translation of the word, but in the exposition of the sense and meaning hereof; for some by Gammadims understand a people of Syria, so called from the city Gamala;* some hereby understand the Cappadocians, many the Medes; and hereof Forerius hath a singular exposition, conceiving the watchmen of Tyre might well be called pigmies, the towers of that city being so high, that unto men below they appeared in a cubital stature. Others expounded it quite contrary to common acception, that is, not men of the least, but of the largest size; so doth Cornelius construe *pygmæi*, or *viri cubitales*, that is, not men of a cubit high, but of the largest stature, whose height like that of giants, is rather to be taken by the cubit than the foot; in which phrase we read the measure of Goliah, whose height is said to be six cubits and a span. Of affinity hereto is also the exposition of Jerom; not taking pigmies for dwarfs, but stout and valiant champions; not taking the sense of πυγμή, which signifies the cubit measure, but that which expresseth pugils, that is, men fit for combat and the exercise of the fist. Thus can there be no satisfying illation from this text, the diversity or rather contrariety of expositions and interpretations, distracting more than confirming the truth of the story.[1]

Again, I say, exact testimonies, in reference unto cir-

---

* See Mr. Fuller's excellent description of Palestine.

[1] *story.*] The least I suppose that ever was seen and lived long, was Lucius Augustus his dwarfe, who was *bypedali minor, librarum septendecim, sed vocis immensæ.*—*Suetonius in Octavio,* § 53. Certainly few apes come under this hight.

cumstantial relations so diversely or contrarily delivered. Thus the relation of Aristotle placeth them above Egypt towards the head of the Nile in Africa. Philostratus affirms they are about Ganges in Asia, and Pliny in a third place, that is, Gerania in Scythia; some write they fight with cranes, but Menecles, in Athenæus, affirms they fight with partridges; some say they ride on partridges, and some on the backs of rams.

Lastly, I say, confirmed testimonies; for though Paulus Jovius delivers there are pigmies beyond Japan, Pigafeta, about the Moluccas, and Olaus Magnus placeth them in Greenland, yet wanting frequent confirmation in a matter so confirmable, their affirmation carrieth but slow persuasion, and wise men may think there is as much reality in the pigmies of Paracelsus,* that is, his non-adamical men, or middle natures betwixt men and spirits.

There being thus no sufficient confirmation of their verity, some doubt may arise concerning their possibility, wherein, since it is not defined in what dimensions the soul may exercise her faculties, we shall not conclude impossibility, or that there might not be a race of pigmies, as there is sometimes of giants. So may we take in the opinion of Austin, and his comment Ludovicus.[2] But to believe they should be in the stature of a foot or span, requires the preaspection of such a one as Philetas, the poet, in Athenæus, who was fain to fasten lead unto his feet, lest the wind should blow him away; or that other in the same author, who was so little *ut ad obolum accederet;* a story so strange, that we might herein excuse the printer, did not the account of Ælian accord unto it, as Casaubon hath observed in his learned animadversions.

Lastly, if any such nation there were, yet it is ridiculous what men have delivered of them; that they fight with cranes upon the backs of rams or partridges; or what is delivered by Ctesias, that they are negroes in the midst of India, whereof the king of that country entertaineth three

---

* By pigmies intending fairies and other spirits about the earth; as by nymphs and salamanders, spirits of fire and water.—*Lib. de Pygmæis, Nymphis, &c.*

[2] *Ludovicus.*] Lud. Vives.

thousand archers for his guard, which is a relation below the tale of Oberon; nor could they better defend him than the emblem saith, they offended Hercules whilst he slept, that is, to wound him no deeper than to awake him.

CHAPTER XII.

Of the Great Climacterical Year, that is, Sixty-three.

CONCERNING the eyes of the understanding, and those of the sense, are differently deceived in their greatest objects. The sense apprehending them in lesser magnitudes than their dimensions require; so it beholdeth the sun, the stars, and the earth itself. But the understanding quite otherwise; for that ascribeth unto many things far larger horizons than their due circumscriptions require, and receiveth them with amplifications which their reality will not admit. Thus hath it fared with many heroes and most worthy persons, who, being sufficiently commendable from true and unquestionable merits, have received advancement from falsehood and the fruitful stock of fables. Thus hath it happened unto the stars, and luminaries of heaven; who, being sufficiently admirable in themselves, have been set out by effects, no way dependent on their efficiencies, and advanced by amplifications to the questioning of their true endowments. Thus is it not improbable it hath also fared with number, which though wonderful in itself, and sufficiently magnifiable from its demonstrable affections, hath yet received adjections from the multiplying conceits of men, and stands laden with additions which its equity will not admit.

And so perhaps hath it happened unto the numbers seven and nine, which multiplied into themselves do make up sixty-three, commonly esteemed the great climacterical of our lives. For the days of men are usually cast up by septenaries, and every seventh year conceived to carry some altering character with it, either in the temper of body, mind, or both. But among all other, three are most remarkable, that is, seven times seven, or forty-nine; nine times nine, or eighty-one; and seven times nine, or the year of sixty-three, which is conceived to carry with it the most considerable fatality, and consisting of both the other numbers, was apprehended to comprise the virtue of either, is therefore expected and entertained with fear, and esteemed a favour of fate to pass it over; which, notwithstanding, many suspect to be but a panic terror, and men to fear they justly know not what, and to speak indifferently I find no satisfaction, nor any sufficiency in the received grounds to establish a rational fear.

Now herein to omit astrological considerations (which are but rarely introduced), the popular foundation whereby it hath continued, is first, the extraordinary power and secret virtue conceived to attend these numbers, whereof we must confess there have not wanted, not only especial commendations, but very singular conceptions. Among philosophers, Pythagoras seems to have played the leading part, which was long after continued by his disciples, and the Italick school. The philosophy of Plato, and most of the Platonists, abounds in numeral considerations. Above all, Philo, the learned Jew, hath acted this part even to superstition, bestowing divers pages in summing up every thing, which might advantage this number. Which, notwithstanding, when a serious reader shall perpend, he will hardly find any thing that may convince his judgment, or any further persuade than the lenity of his belief, or prejudgment of reason inclineth.[3]

For first, not only the numbers seven and nine, from considerations abstruse have been extolled by most, but all or most of the other digits have been as mystically applauded. For the numbers one and three have not been only admired by the heathens, but from adorable grounds, the unity of God, and mystery of the Trinity admired by many Christians. The number four stands much admired, not only in the quaternity of the elements (which are the principles of bodies), but in the letters of the name of God (which in the Greek, Arabian, Persian, Hebrew, and Egyptian, consisteth of that number), and was so venerable among the Pytha-

---

[3] *Which, notwithstanding, &c.*] The excellent Bishop Hall sums up in the following brief and pious exclamation:—" Away with all niceties of Pythagorean calculations; all numbers are alike to me, save those which God himself hath chalked out to us!"—*Bp. Hall's Works*, p. 510.

goreans, that they swore by the number four.[4] That of six hath found many leaves in its favour; not only for the days of the creation, but its natural consideration, as being a perfect number, and the first that is completed by its parts, that is the sixth, the half, and the third, 1, 2, 3, which drawn into a sum make six. The number of ten hath been as highly extolled, as containing even, odd, long, plain, quadrate, and cubical numbers; and Aristotle observed with admiration, that Barbarians, as well as Greeks, did use a numeration unto ten, which being so general was not to be judged casual, but to have a foundation in nature. So that not only seven and nine, but all the rest have had their eulogies, as may be observed at large in Rhodiginus, and in several writers since; every one extolling number, according to his subject, and as it advantaged the present discourse in hand.

Again, they have been commended, not only from pretended grounds in nature, but from artificial, casual, or fabulous foundations: so have some endeavoured to advance their admiration, from the nine muses, from the seven wonders of the world, from the seven gates of Thebes; in that seven cities contended for Homer, in that there are seven stars in Ursa minor, and seven in Charles's wain, or Plaustrum of Ursa major. Wherein indeed, although the ground be natural, yet, either from constellations or their remarkable parts, there is the like occasion to commend any other number; the number five from the stars in Sagitta, three from the girdle of Orion, and four from Equiculus, Crusero, or the feet of the Centaur; yet are such as these clapped in by very good authors, and some not omitted by Philo.

Nor are they only extolled from arbitrary and poetical grounds, but from foundations and principles, false or dubious. That women are menstruant and men pubescent at the year of twice seven is accounted a punctual truth; which period nevertheless we dare not precisely determine, as having observed a variation and latitude in most, agreeable unto the

---

[4] *four.*] 5: for the dimensions of man, dilated into a *pentalpha.*—*Wr.*
It is not a little singular that, in this enumeration, the author of the *Quincunx* should have omitted the number five.

heat of clime or temper; men arising variously unto virility, according to the activity of causes that promote it. *Sanguis menstruosus ad diem, ut plurimum, septimum durat,* saith Philo: which notwithstanding is repugnant unto experience, and the doctrine of Hippocrates; who in his book, *de diæta,* plainly affirmeth, it is thus but with few women, and only such as abound with pituitous and watery humours.

It is further conceived to receive addition, in that there are seven heads of Nile; but we have made manifest elsewhere,[5] that by the description of geographers, they have been sometime more,[6] and are at present fewer; in that there were seven wise men of Greece; which though generally received, yet having enquired into the verity thereof we cannot so readily determine it: for in the life of Thales, who was accounted in that number, Diogenes Laertius plainly saith, *Magna de eorum numero discordia est,* some holding but four, some ten, others twelve, and none agreeing in their names, though according in their number. In that there are just seven[7] planets or errant stars in the lower orbs of heaven; but it is now demonstrable unto sense, that there are many more, as Galileo* hath declared; that is, two more in the orb of Saturn, and no less than four or more in the sphere of Jupiter. And the like may be said of the Pleiades or seven stars, which are also introduced to magnify this number; for whereas, scarce discerning six, we account them seven, by his relation, there are no less than forty.[8]

That the heavens are encompassed with seven circles,[9] is also the allegation of Philo; which are, in his account, the

* *Nuncius Syderus.*

[5] *elsewhere.*] See book vi. c. 8.

[6] *more.*] Honterus reckoned of old, noe fewer then 16; whereof now the slime of Nilus (since itt was banked in divers places) hath obstructed eleven.—*Wr.*

[7] *seven.*] Yf the sun be sett in the center of the universe fixte and immoveable, as the Copernicans contend, then there are but 5 primarye planets as they call them. For the moon they say is a secondary planet, and the earthe another.—*Wr.* We must suspect an error in this note.

[8] *forty.*] Discernable by a good telescope.—*Wr.*

[9] *seven circles.*] The 2 pole circles are in effect but as one, to this intention: likewise the 2 tropicks: let the æquator bee a thirde: the zodiack, a fourth: the horison a fifth; the colure of solstice (i. e. the meridian) a sixte: and the æquinoctial colure a seventhe.—*Wr.*

arctick, antarctick, the summer and winter tropicks, the equator, zodiack, and the milky circle; whereas by astronomers they are received in greater number. For though we leave out the lacteous circle (which Aratus, Geminus (and Proclus, out of him), hath numbered among the rest), yet are there more by four than Philo mentions; that is, the horizon, meridian, and both the colures; circles very considerable, and generally delivered, not only by Ptolemy, and the astronomers since his time, but such as flourished long before, as Hipparchus and Eudoxus. So that, for ought I know, if it make for our purpose, or advance the theme in hand, with equal liberty we may affirm there were seven sibyls, or but seven signs in the zodiack circle of heaven.

That verse in Virgil, translated out of Homer,* *O térque quatérque beati* (that is, as men will have it, seven times happy), hath much advanced this number in critical apprehensions. Yet is not this construction so indubitably to be received, as not at all to be questioned: for, though Rhodiginus, Beroaldus, and others, from the authority of Macrobius, so interpret it, yet Servius, his ancient commentator, conceives no more thereby than a finite number for indefinite, and that no more is implied than often happy. Strabo, the ancientest of them all, conceives no more, by this in Homer, than a full and excessive expression; whereas, in common phrase and received language, he should have termed them thrice happy, herein, exceeding that number, he called them four times happy, that is, more than thrice. And this he illustrates by the like expression of Homer, in the speech of Circe, who, to express the dread and terror of the ocean, sticks not unto the common form of speech in the strict account of its reciprocations, but largely speaking, saith, it ebbs and flows no less than thrice a day, *terque die revomit fluctus, iterúmque resorbet*. And so when 'tis said by Horace, *felices ter et amplius*, the exposition is sufficient, if we conceive no more than the letter fairly beareth, that is, four times, or indefinitely more than thrice.

But the main considerations, which most set off this number, are observations drawn from the motions of the moon supposed to be measured by sevens; and the critical

* Τρὶς μάκαρες Δαναοὶ καὶ τετράκις.

or decretory days[1] dependent on that number. As for the motion of the moon, though we grant it to be measured by sevens, yet will not this advance the same before its fellow numbers; for hereby the motion of other stars are not measured, the fixed stars by many thousand years; the sun by 365 days, the superior planets by more, the inferior by somewhat less. And if we consider the revolution of the first moveable, and the daily motion from east to west common unto all the orbs, we shall find it measured by another number, for being performed in four and twenty hours, it is made up of four times six: and this is the measure and standard of other parts of time, of months, of years, olympiads, lustres, indictions of cycles, jubilees, &c.

Again, months are not only lunary, and measured by the moon, but also solary, and determined by the motion of the sun; that is the space wherein the sun doth pass thirty degrees of the ecliptick. By this month Hippocrates* computed the time of the infant's gestation in the womb; for nine times thirty, that is, 270 days, or complete nine months, make up forty weeks, the common compute of women. And this is to be understood, when he saith, two days make the fifteenth, and three the tenth part of the month. This was the month of the ancient Hebrews, before their departure out of Egypt;[2] and hereby the compute will fall out right, and the account concur, when in one place it is said, the

---

* *De Octomestri Partu.*

[1] *decretory days.*] Dayes of 24 houres are properly the measure to which wee reduce months and yeares. The rest are not reduced to dayes but years: saving, that in the compute of the æquinoctial procession caused by the Julian excess, wee accompt the thirty-third bissextile daye supernumerary, and to bee rejected. Likewise in the decennovall cycles. The true cycle of the moon is 6939 dayes, 16 houres, $\frac{595}{1080}$ moments. The Dionysian Paschal cycle of 19 years, cald the golden number, is 6939 dayes, 18 hours: the difference is 1 hour, and 485 moments, which in 16 cycles, or every 304 yeares makes almost a day of the moones anticipation. Of these dayes, since the Nicene council, we must accompt noe less then 4; and of the 5th a 3rd parte: by which the vernall full moone, cald the *Terminus Paschalis*, does now anticipate in the Julian kalender. And this is that which the great Scaliger cals, προήγησιν σηληνιακήν.— *Wr.*

[2] *Egypt.*] For they used the Ægyptian yeare of months, cald *annus canicularis*, from the sun's revolution to the rising of the doggstar.— *Wr.*

waters of the flood prevailed an hundred and fifty days, and in another it is delivered, that they prevailed from the seventeenth day of the second month, unto the seventeenth day of the seventh. As for hebdomadal periods or weeks, although in regard of their sabbaths they were observed by the Hebrews, yet it is not apparent the ancient Greeks or Romans used any; but had another division of their months into ides, nones, and calends.

Moreover, months, howsoever taken, are not exactly divisible into septenaries or weeks, which fully contain seven days; whereof four times do make completely twenty-eight. For, beside the usual or calendary month, there are but four considerable:[3] the month of peragration, of apparition, of consecution, and the medical or decretorial month; whereof some come short, others exceed this account. A month of peragration is the time of the moon's revolution from any part of the zodiack unto the same again, and this containeth but twenty-seven days, and about eight hours: which cometh short to complete the septenary account. The month of consecution, or as some will term it, of progression, is the space between one conjunction of the moon with the sun unto another; and this containeth twenty-nine days and an half; for the moon returning unto the same point wherein it was kindled by the sun, and not finding it there again (for in the meantime, by its proper motion it hath passed through two signs[4]), it followeth after, and attains the sun in the space of two days and four hours more, which added unto the account of peragration, make twenty-nine days and an half; so that this month exceedeth the latitude of septenaries, and the fourth part comprehendeth more than seven days. A month of apparition is the space wherein the moon appeareth (deducting three days wherein it commonly disappeareth, and, being in combustion with the sun, is presumed of less activity), and this containeth but twenty-six days and twelve hours. The medical month not much exceedeth this, consisting of twenty-six days and twenty-two hours, and is made up out of all the other months. For if, out of twenty-nine

---

[3] *considerable.*] Considerable lunar months.—*Wr.*

[4] *signs.*] This was a mistake in the learned author; for the moon goes but one signe in 2 dayes and a half. And how could the sun get through a whole signe in 27 days 8 hours?—*Wr.*

and an half, the month of consecution, we deduct three days of disappearance, there will remain the month of apparition twenty-six days and twelve hours: whereto if we add twenty-seven days and eight hours, the month of peragration, there will arise fifty-three days and ten hours, which divided by two, makes twenty-six days and twenty-two hours; called by physicians the medical month; introduced by Galen against Archigenes for the better compute of decretory or critical days.

As for the critical days (such I mean wherein upon a decertation between the disease and nature, there ensueth a sensible alteration, either to life or death), the reasons thereof are rather deduced from astrology than arithmetic: for, accounting from the beginning of the disease, and reckoning on unto the seventh day, the moon will be in a tetragonal or quadrate aspect,[5] that is, four signs removed from that wherein the disease began; in the fourteenth day it will be in an opposite aspect; and at the end of the third septenary, tetragonal again; as will most graphically appear in the figures of astrologers, especially Lucas Gauricus, *De diebus decretoriis*.

Again (beside that, computing by the medical month, the first hebdomade or septenary consists of six days, seventeen hours and an half, the second happeneth in thirteen days and eleven hours, and the third but in the twentieth natural day),—what Galen first, and Abenezra since observed, in his tract of *Critical Days*, in regard of eccentricity and the epicycle or lesser orb wherein it moveth,—the motion of the moon is various and unequal, whereby the critical account

---

[5] *aspect.*] Aspect is a certaine distance of the planets wherein they are supposed to hinder or promote the effects which they usually produce in the signes, and in the bodily parts subject to them; according to which aception, conjunction cannot bee properly cald an aspect, though of all other postures in heaven to us it bee the strongest, bycause the planets, however distant in altitude immensely, yet conveye their force conjoyntlye with greater power. Of other aspects, some are cald happye, as the Trigon: first, bycause when planets are 4 signes distant, they are in signs of like nature, agreeinge in the same active and passive qualityes. Next, Sextile, which is of signes agreeing in one qualitye, and disagreeing in another. But quadrate and opposite are in signes of contrarye qualityes, and by their jarringe beames infest each other, and are therefore cald (not without great reason in nature) malefic.— *Wr.*

must also vary. For though its middle motion be equal, and of thirteen degrees, yet in the other it moveth sometimes fifteen, sometimes less than twelve. For, moving in the upper part of its orb, it performeth its motion more slowly than in the lower; insomuch that, being at the height, it arriveth at the tetragonal and opposite sign sooner, and the critical day will be in six and thirteen; and being at the lowest, the critical account will be out of the latitude of seven, nor happen before the eighth or ninth day. Which are considerations not to be neglected in the compute of decretory days, and manifestly declare that other numbers must have a respect herein as well as seven and fourteen.

Lastly, some things to this intent are deduced from Holy Scripture; thus is the year of jubilee introduced to magnify this number, as being a year made out of seven times seven; wherein notwithstanding there may be a misapprehension; for this ariseth not from seven times seven, that is, forty-nine, but was observed the fiftieth year, as is expressed, "And you shall hallow the fiftieth year, a jubilee shall that fiftieth year be unto you." Answerable whereto is the exposition of the Jews themselves, as is delivered by Ben-Maimon; that is, the year of jubilee cometh not into the account of the years of seven, but the forty-ninth is the release, and the fiftieth the year of jubilee. Thus is it also esteemed no small advancement unto this number, that the genealogy of our Saviour is summed up by fourteen, that is, this number doubled, according as is expressed, Matt. i. So all the generations, from Abraham to David, are fourteen generations; and from David unto the carrying away into Babylon, are fourteen generations; and from the carrying away into Babylon unto Christ, are fourteen generations. Which nevertheless must not be strictly understood as numeral relations require: for from David unto Jeconiah are accounted by Matthew but fourteen generations; whereas according to the exact account in the History of Kings, there were at least seventeen; and three in this account, that is, Ahazias, Joas, and Amazias, are left out. For so it is delivered by the evangelist,—"And Joram begat Ozias:" whereas in the regal genealogy there are three successions between: for Ozias or Uzziah was the son of Amazias, Amazias of Joas, Joas of Azariah, and Azariah of Joram; so that in strict account, Joram was the *abavus* or grandfather twice removed, and not the father of Ozias. And these two omitted descents made a very considerable measure of time in the royal chronology of Judah; for though Azariah reigned but one year, yet Joas reigned forty, and Amazias no less than nine and twenty. However therefore these were delivered by the evangelist, and carry (no doubt) an incontrollable conformity unto the intention of his delivery;[6] yet are they not appliable unto precise numerality, nor strictly to be drawn unto the rigid test of numbers.

Lastly, though many things have been delivered by

[6] *However, therefore, &c.*] Whether this omission originated with the Evangelist, or existed in the Jewish registers, from which he copied, must ever remain the subject of conjecture; as well as the probable motive of the omission, in either case. That such publicly recognised tables of descent existed, even to the time of Jesus Christ, we know from Josephus, *De Vita Sua*, p. 998, D.; and that Matthew would use them, cannot be deemed unlikely. The most probable ground for supposing the omission of these three kings in the public tables, is the curse denounced, on account of Ahab's awful idolatry, against his family (into which Joram married), even to the third or fourth generation. If however it be thought improbable that such hiatus existed in the public genealogies, it must then be attributed to the Evangelist himself. Nor will this perhaps be deemed an inadmissible hypothesis, if we fully consider the circumstances. The sole object which he had in view in giving such a genealogy, was to prove that Jesus Christ, whom he was about to proclaim to the Jews as their Messiah, was indeed descended from the stock of David, answering — in this important respect — the prophetic description of him; a proof which the omission of several names would in no degree affect. Now, as Matthew was addressing Jews, it is very likely that he would resort to a method usually adopted among them (probably for the facility of recollection which it afforded); viz. that of dividing the genealogy into classes, if possible of *equal extent*. The threefold state of the Jews, *first*, under patriarchs, prophets, and judges, *then* under kings, and *lastly* under princes and priests, rendered such a classification additionally proper. The reign of David, and the Babylonish captivity, presented the most obvious points of division: but when thus divided, the classes were of *unequal extent;* the second containing too many names for the narrator's purpose. In order to make it equal to the others, he may therefore be supposed to have adopted the direct expedient of omitting the three names in question. Of which practice he had several examples, to justify him, in the Jewish Scriptures, particularly in Ezra vii. 2; where six generations are omitted at once. Nor does the literal incorrectness of the phrase "Joram begat Ozias," afford a valid objection: this term being applied not only to immediate, but to more remote, descendants. See Jer. xxxix.

authors concerning number, and they transferred unto the advantage of their nature, yet are they ofttimes otherwise to be understood than as they are vulgarly received in active and casual considerations; they being many times delivered hieroglyphically, metaphorically, illustratively, and not with reference unto action or causality. True it is, that God made all things in number, weight, and measure, yet nothing by them or through the efficacy of either. Indeed our days, actions, and motions being measured by time (which is but motion measured), whatever is observable in any falls under the account of some number; which notwithstanding cannot be denominated the cause of those events. So do we unjustly assign the power of action even unto time itself, nor do they speak properly who say that time consumeth all things; for time is not effective, nor are bodies destroyed by it, but from the action and passion of their elements in it; whose account it only affordeth, and measuring out their motion informs us in the periods and terms of their duration, rather than effecteth or physically produceth the same.

A second consideration, which promoteth this opinion, are confirmations drawn from writers who have made observations, or set down favourable reasons for this climacterical year; so have Henricus Ranzovius,* Baptista Codronchus,† and Levinus Lemnius‡ much confirmed the same, but above all, that memorable letter of Augustus sent unto his nephew Caius, wherein he encourageth him to celebrate his nativity, for he had now escaped sixty-three, the great climacterical and dangerous year unto man. Which notwithstanding, rightly perpended, it can be no singularity to question it, nor any new paradox to deny it.

For first, it is implicitly, and upon consequence denied by Aristotle in his Politicks, in that discourse against Plato, who measured the vicissitude and mutation of states, by a periodical fatality of number. Ptolemy, that famous mathematician, plainly saith, he will not deliver his doctrines by parts and numbers, which are ineffectual, and have not the nature of causes. Now by these numbers, saith Rhodiginus and Mirandula, he implieth climacterical years, that is, septenaries and novenaries set down by the bare observation of

* *De Annis Climactericis.*   † *De Occultis Naturæ Miraculis.*
‡ *Bel.* lib. v.

numbers. Censorinus, an author of great authority and sufficient antiquity, speaks yet more amply in his book, *De Die Natali*, wherein, expressly treating of climacterical days, he thus delivereth himself:—"Some maintain that seven times seven, that is forty-nine, is most dangerous of any other, and this is the most general opinion: others unto seven times seven add nine times nine, that is, the year of eighty-one, both which, consisting of square and quadrate numbers, were thought by Plato and others to be of great consideration: as for this year of sixty-three, or seven times nine, though some esteem it of most danger, yet do I conceive it less dangerous than the other; for though it containeth both numbers above named, that is, seven and nine, yet neither of them square or quadrate; and as it is different from them both, so is it not potent in either." Nor is this year remarkable in the death of many famous men. I find indeed, that Aristotle died this year; but he, by the vigour of his mind, a long time sustained a natural infirmity of stomach; so that it was a greater wonder he attained unto sixty-three, than that he lived no longer. The psalm of Moses hath mentioned a year of danger differing from all these; and that is, ten times seven or seventy; for so it is said, the days of man are threescore and ten.[7] And the very same is affirmed by Solon, as Herodotus relates in a speech of his unto Crœsus, *Ego annis septuaginta humanæ vitæ modum definio*: and surely that year must be of greatest danger which is the period of all the rest; and fewest safely pass through that which is set as a bound for few or none to pass. And therefore, the consent of elder times settling their conceits upon climacters, not only differing from this of ours, but one another, though several nations and ages do fancy unto themselves different years of danger, yet every one expects the same event, and constant verity in each.

Again, though Varro divided the days of man into five portions, Hippocrates into seven,[8] and Solon into ten, yet

[7] *The psalm of Moses, &c.*] Psalm xc.

[8] *Hippocrates into seven.*] Proclus also divided them into seven ages, each supposed to be under distinct planetary influence. The first four years he called the age of *infancy*; the second *childhood*, to 14; third, *adolescence* or *youthhood*, to 22; fourth, *young manhood*, to 42; fifth, *mature manhood*, to 56; sixth, *old age*, to 68; seventh, *decrepit age*, to 88. All beyond that age he considers to be a second infancy.

probably their divisions were to be received with latitude, and their considerations not strictly to be confined unto their last unities. So when Varro extendeth *Pueritia* unto fifteen, *Adolescentia* unto thirty, *Juventus* unto thirty-five, there is a latitude between the terms or periods of compute, and the verity holds good in the accidents of any years between them. So when Hippocrates divideth our life into seven degrees or stages, and maketh the end of the first seven, of the second fourteen, of the third twenty-eight, of the fourth thirty-five, of the fifth forty-seven, of the sixth fifty-six, and of the seventh, the last year, whenever it happeneth; herein we may observe, he maketh not his divisions precisely by seven and nine, and omits the great climacterical: beside there is between every one at least the latitude of seven years, in which space or interval, that is either in the third or fourth year, whatever falleth out is equally verified of the whole degree, as though it had happened in the seventh. Solon divided it into ten septenaries, because in every one thereof, a man received some sensible mutation; in the first is dedentition or falling of teeth, in the second pubescence, in the third the beard groweth, in the fourth strength prevails, in the fifth maturity for issue, in the sixth moderation of appetite, in the seventh prudence, &c. Now herein there is a tolerable latitude, and though the division proceed by seven, yet is not the total verity to be restrained unto the last year, nor constantly to be expected the beard should be complete at twenty-one, or wisdom acquired just in forty-nine; and thus also, though seven times nine contain one of those septenaries, and doth also happen in our declining years, yet might the events thereof be imputed unto the whole septenary, and be more reasonably entertained with some latitude, than strictly reduced unto the last number, or all the accidents from fifty-six imputed unto sixty-three.

Thirdly, although this opinion may seem confirmed by observation, and men may say it hath been so observed, yet we speak also upon experience, and do believe that men from observation will collect no satisfaction. That other years may be taken against it, especially if they have the advantage to precede it, as sixty against sixty-three, and sixty-three against sixty-six. For fewer attain to the latter than the former, and so surely in the first septenary do most die, and probably also in the very first year, for all that ever lived were in the account of that year, beside the infirmities that attend it are so many, and the body that receives them so tender and inconfirmed, we scarce count any alive that is not past it.

Fabritius Paduanius,* discoursing of the great climacterical, attempts a numeration of eminent men who died in that year, but in so small a number as not sufficient to make a considerable induction. He mentioneth but four, Diogenes Cynicus, Dionysius Heracleoticus, Xenocrates Platonicus, and Plato. As for Dionysius, as Censorinus witnesseth, he famished himself in the eighty-second year of his life; Xenocrates, by the testimony of Laertius, fell into a cauldron, and died the same year, and Diogenes the cynick, by the same testimony, lived almost unto ninety. The date of Plato's death is not exactly agreed on, but all dissent from this which he determineth. Neanthes, in Laertius, extendeth his days unto eighty-four, Suidas unto eighty-two, but Hermippus defineth his death in eighty-one; and this account seemeth most exact, for if, as he delivereth, Plato was born in the eighty-eighth olympiad, and died in the first year of the 108th, the account will not surpass the year of eighty-one, and so in his death he verified the opinion of his life, and of the life of man, whose period, as Censorinus recordeth, he placeth in the quadrate of nine, or nine times nine, that is, eighty-one; and therefore, as Seneca delivereth, the magicians, at Athens, did sacrifice unto him, as declaring in his death somewhat above humanity, because he died in the day of his nativity, and without deduction justly accomplished the year of eighty-one. Bodin,† I confess, delivers a larger list of men that died in this year; *Moriuntur innumerabiles anno sexagesimo tertio, Aristotles, Chrysippus, Bocatius, Bernardus, Erasmus, Lutherus, Melancthon, Sylvius, Alexander, Jacobus Sturmius, Nicolaus Cusanus, Thomas Linacer, eodem anno Cicero cæsus est.* Wherein, beside that it were not difficult to make a larger catalogue of memorable persons that died in other years, we cannot but doubt the verity of his induction. As for Sylvius and Alexander, which of that name he meaneth I know not, but for Chrysippus, by the testimony of Laertius,

* *De catena temporis.* † *Method. His.*

he died in the 73rd year, Bocatius in the 62nd, Linacer the 64th, and Erasmus exceeded 70, as Paulus Jovius hath delivered in his elegy of learned men; and as for Cicero, as Plutarch in his life affirmeth, he was slain in the year of 64, and therefore sure the question is hard set, and we have no easy[9] reason to doubt, when great and entire authors shall introduce injustifiable examples, and authorize their assertions by what is not authentical.

Fourthly, they which proceed upon strict numerations, and will by such regular and determined ways measure out the lives of men, and periodically define the alterations of their tempers, conceive a regularity in mutations, with an equality in constitutions, and forget that variety which physicians therein discover; for seeing we affirm that women do naturally grow old before men, that the cholerick fall short in longevity of the sanguine, that there is *senium ante senectum*, and many grow old before they arrive at age, we cannot affix unto them all one common point of danger, but should rather assign a respective fatality unto each; which is concordant unto the doctrine of the numerist, and such as maintain this opinion, for they affirm that one number respecteth men, another women; as Bodin, explaining that of Seneca, *Septimus quisque annus ætati signum imprimit*, subjoins, *hoc de maribus dictum oportuit, hoc primum intueri licet, perfectum numerum, id est, sextum fœminas, septenarium mares immutare*.

Fifthly, since we esteem this opinion to have some ground in nature, and that nine times seven revolutions of the sun imprint a dangerous character on such as arrive unto it, it will leave some doubt behind, in what subjection hereunto were the lives of our forefathers presently after the flood, and more especially before it, who, attaining unto 8 or 900 years, had not their climacters computable by digits, or as we do account them, for the great climacterical was past unto them before they begat children, or gave any testimony of their virility, for we read not that any begat children before the age of sixty-five.[1] And this may also afford a

---

[9] *easy.*] Small.—*Wr.*

[1] *not that any, &c.*] This is true of all the patriarchs before the flood, whose long life needed noe hastening of progenye; the delay whereof might be a concurrent cause of their longævitye. For,

hint to enquire what are the climacters of other animated creatures, whereof the life of some attains not so far as this of ours, and that of others extends a considerable space beyond it.

Lastly, the imperfect accounts that men have kept of time, and the difference thereof, both in the same and diverse commonweaths, will much distract the certainty of this assertion. For though there were a fatality in this year, yet divers were, and others might be, out in their account, aberring several ways from the true and just compute; and calling that one year which perhaps might be another.

For first, they might be out in the commencement or beginning of their account; for every man is many months elder than he computeth. For although we begin the same from our nativity, and conceive that no arbitrary, but natural term of compute, yet for the duration of life or existence, we are liable in the womb unto the usual distinctions of time, and are not to be exempted from the account of age and life, where we are subject to diseases, and often suffer death. And therefore Pythagoras, Hippocrates, Diocles, Avicenna, and others, have set upon us numeral relations and temporal considerations in the womb; not only affirming the birth of the seventh month to be vital, that of the eighth mortal, but the progression thereto to be measured by rule, and to hold a proportion unto motion and formation. As what receiveth motion in the seventh, to be perfected in triplicities; that is, the time of conformation unto motion is double, and that from motion unto the birth, treble; so what is formed the thirty-fifth day, is moved the seventieth, and born the two

---

doubtless such as was their longævitye, such in proportion wee must think their strengthe, and such the degrees by which they grew unto itt. To the forbearance from mariage we may add their detestation of polygamye, to which doubtless our Saviour gives that testimony.—Matth. xx. 8. From the beginninge itt was not soe, that is, no one of the patriarchs used polygamy till Lamech, the 9th from Adam, almost 900 years after the creation, thereby justly reproaching the incontinency of after ages, not only for their præcipitation, but the lustful desire of change without sufficient cause, viz., the adultery of the wife, whose life being taking off by the law, lefte the man free to marrye againe. That therefore we read not of the antideluvian fathers begetting children before 65 is true of all; for Lamech begat not Noah till his 182nd yeare. But after the flood, to repeople the world, all the patriarchs till Terah begat children before 35, which is but halfe of the former time of 65 yeares.— *Wr.*

hundred and tenth day. And therefore if any invisible causality there be, that after so many years doth evidence itself at sixty-three, it will be questionable whether its activity only set out at our nativity, and begin not rather in the womb, wherein we place the like considerations. Which doth not only entangle this assertion, but hath already embroiled the endeavours of astrology in the erection of schemes, and the judgment of death or diseases; for being not incontrollably determined at what time to begin, whether at conception, animation, or exclusion (it being indifferent unto the influence of heaven to begin at either), they have invented another way, that is, to begin *ab hora quæstionis*, as Haly, Messahallach, Ganivetus, and Guido Bonatus, have delivered.

Again, in regard of the measure of time by months and years, there will be no small difficulty; and if we shall strictly consider it, many have been and still may be, mistaken. For neither the motion of the moon, whereby months are computed, nor of the sun, whereby years are accounted, consisteth of whole numbers, but admits of fractions and broken parts, as we have already declared concerning the moon. That of the sun consisteth of three hundred and sixty-five days, and almost six hours, that is, wanting eleven minutes; which six hours, omitted, or not taken notice of, will, in process of time, largely deprave the compute; and this is the occasion of the bissextile or leap-year, which was not observed in all times, nor punctually in all commonwealths; so that in sixty-three years there may be lost almost eighteen days, omitting the intercalation of one day every fourth year, allowed for this quadrant, or six hours supernumerary. And though the same were observed, yet to speak strictly, a man may be somewhat out in the account of his age at sixty-three; for although every fourth year we insert one day, and so fetch up the quadrant, yet those eleven minutes whereby the year comes short of perfect six hours will, in the circuit of those years, arise unto certain hours, and in a larger progression of time unto certain days. Whereof at present we find experience in the calendar we observe. For the Julian year of three hundred and sixty-five days being eleven minutes larger than the annual revolution of the sun, there will arise an anticipation in the equinoxes; and as Junctinus computeth,*2 in every 136th year they will anticipate almost one day. And therefore those ancient men and Nestors of old times, which yearly observed their nativities, might be mistaken in the day; nor is that to be construed without a grain of salt, which is delivered by Moses : [3] " At the end of four hundred years, even the self-same day, all the host of Israel went out of the land of Egypt." For in that space of time the equinoxes had anticipated, and the eleven minutes had amounted far above a day. And this compute rightly considered will fall fouler on them who cast up the lives of

* *Comment. in Sphæram Job. de Sacro Bosco.*

[2] *as Junctinus computeth.*] See a short but an exact discussion of this *in calce libri*, and Junctinus his error.— *Wr.*

The following is the " discussion" at the end of the dean's copy, but it seems more appropriate to place it here.—*Ed.*

Quantitas anni	Maxima	365d.	5h.	56'	57"	nunquam assurgit ad 57'.
	Minima	365	5	44	38	nunquam deficit ad 44'
	Media, seu communis	365	5	49	0	alii addunt 15' 46"

Cum igitur annus Julianus supponatur, superaddere quotannis 10' 48", necesse est, ut quolibet bissexto, æquinoctia retrocedant in diebus Julianis 43' et 12" adeo ut in 134 annis, rotrocedant 24h. 6' 52" et in 1644 (post Christum) annis 12d. 7h. 52' 22". Ita a correcto kalendario (44 annis ante c. n.), ad annum presentem, 1652, retrocesserunt 12d. 17h. 13' 22". Supine igitur numeravit author è Junctino : in annis 136, retrocedere æquinoctia, diem integrum fere, cum præter integrum diem, colligantur totidem annis 1h. 26' 24". Alphonsini dicunt in 400 annis æquinoctia retrocedere 3 dies fere, quod proxime accedit ad priorem calculum, si num addas (ad annos Christi elapsos sc. 1652), annos a correcto kalendario ad Christum natum, sc. 44, fiunt anni 1696 : in quibus habemus quater 3 dies, et quæ excurrunt 96 dierum minuta : sc. 17' et 26". Per utrumque calculum, si 33us quilibet bissextus abjiciatur, manebunt æquinoctia in sedibus suis in futurum. Sed 12 dies qui ex eo excessu creverunt, optime et sine tumultu eximentur e mensibus dierum (31) duplus annis sequentibus ; sc. ex Martio, Maio, Julio, Augusto, Octobri et Decembri ; et sic duæ anni medietates facient paria fere. Nam communibus annis currunt ab æquinoctio verno ad autumnale 186d. 8h. 8', ab autumnali ad vernum 178d. 21h. 47'.— *Wr.*

[3] *which is delivered by Moses.*] Moses accounted by the old Ægyptian yeare, wherein he was most skilfull : and the Ægyptian yeare was a yeare of days without any intercalation. Soe that the head of the yeare was vagrant, but the accompt of dayes most exact, insomuch that the best astronomers to this day use that yeare in their accompts : by which they measure the Julian yeares. Soe then, his mention of the Julian excesse of 11 minutes yearlye is $\dot{\alpha}\pi\rho o\sigma\delta\iota \acute{o}\rho\nu\sigma o\nu$. For Moses did not use the Julian yeare, which had its original from the Ægyptian yeares 1454 yeares after.— *Wr.*

kingdoms, and sum up their duration by particular numbers; as Plato first began, and some have endeavoured since by perfect and spherical numbers, by the square and cube of seven, and nine, and twelve, the great number of Plato. Wherein indeed Bodin* hath attempted a particular enumeration; but (beside the mistakes committable in the solary compute of years), the difference of chronology disturbs the satisfaction and quiet of his computes; some adding, others detracting, and few punctually according in any one year; whereby indeed such accounts should be made up, for the variation in an unit destroys the total illation.

Thirdly, the compute may be unjust, not only in a strict acception, of few days or hours, but in the latitude also of some years; and this may happen from the different compute of years in divers nations, and even such as did maintain the most probable way of account: their year being not only different from one another, but the civil and common account disagreeing much from the natural year, whereon the consideration is founded. Thus from the testimony of Herodotus, Censorinus, and others, the Greeks observed the lunary year, that is, twelve revolutions of the moon, 354 days; but the Egyptians, and many others, adhered unto the solary account, that is, 365 days, that is, eleven days longer. Now hereby the account of the one would very much exceed the other: a man in the one would account himself sixty-three, when one in the other would think himself but sixty-one; and so, although their nativities were under the same hour, yet did they at different years believe the verity of that which both esteemed affixed and certain unto one. The like mistake there is in a tradition of our days; men conceiving a peculiar danger in the beginning days of May, set out as a fatal period unto consumptions and chronical diseases; wherein, notwithstanding, we compute by calendars not only different from our ancestors but one another, the compute of the one anticipating that of the other; so that while we are in April, others begin May, and the danger is past unto one, while it beginneth with another.

Fourthly, men were not only out in the number of some days, the latitude of a few years, but might be wide by

---

* *Matt. Histor.*

whole olympiads and divers decads of years. For as Censorinus relateth, the ancient Arcadians observed a year of three months, the Carians of six, the Iberians of four; and as Diodorus and Xenophon *de Æquivocis* allege, the ancient Egyptians have used a year of three, two, and one menth: so that the climacterical was not only different unto those nations, but unreasonably distant from ours; for sixty-three will pass in their account, before they arrive so high as ten in ours.

Nor, if we survey the account of Rome itself, may we doubt they were mistaken, and if they feared climacterical years, might err in their numeration. For the civil year, whereof the people took notice, did sometimes come short, and sometimes exceed the natural. For according to Varro, Suetonius, and Censorinus, their year consisted first of ten months; which comprehend but 304 days, that is, sixty-one less than ours containeth; after by Numa or Tarquin, from a superstitious conceit of imparity, were added fifty-one days, which made 355, one day more than twelve revolutions of the moon. And thus a long time it continued, the civil compute exceeding the natural; the correction whereof, and the due ordering of the leap-year was referred unto the Pontifices; who either upon favour or malice, that some might continue their offices a longer or shorter time, or from the magnitude of the year, that men might be advantaged, or endamaged in their contracts, by arbitrary intercalations, depraved the whole account. Of this abuse Cicero accused Verres, which at last proceeded so far, that when Julius Cæsar came unto that office, before the redress hereof he was fain to insert two intercalary months unto November and December, when he had already inserted twenty-three days unto February; so that the year consisted of 445 days; a quarter of a year longer than that we observed; and though at the last the year was reformed, yet in the mean time they might be out wherein they summed up climacterical observations.

Lastly, one way more there may be of mistake, and that not unusual among us, grounded upon a double compute of the year; the one beginning from the 25th of March, the other from the day of our birth, unto the same again, which is the natural account. Now hereupon many men frequently miscast their days; for in their age they deduce the account not from the day of their birth, but the year of our Lord, wherein they were born. So a man that was born in January, 1582, if he live to fall sick in the latter end of March, 1645, will sum up his age, and say I am now sixty-three, and in my climacterical and dangerous year; for I was born in the year 1582, and now it is 1645, whereas indeed he wanteth many months of that year, considering the true and natural account unto his birth; and accounteth two months for a year: and though the length of time and accumulation of years do render the mistake insensible; yet is it all one, as if one born in January, 1644, should be accounted a year old the 25th of March, 1645.[4]

All which perpended, it may be easily perceived with what insecurity of truth we adhere unto this opinion; ascribing not only effects depending on the natural period of time, unto arbitrary calculations, and such as vary at pleasure; but confirming our tenets by the uncertain account of others and ourselves, there being no positive or indisputable ground where to begin our compute. That if there were, men have been several ways mistaken; the best in some latitude, others in greater, according to the different compute of divers states, the short and irreconcilable years of some, the exceeding error in the natural frame of others, and the lapses and false deductions of ordinary accountants in most.

Which duly considered, together with a strict account and critical examen of reason, will also distract the witty determinations of astrology. That Saturn, the enemy of life, comes almost every seventh year, unto the quadrate or malevolent place; that as the moon about every seventh day arriveth unto a contrary sign, so Saturn, which remaineth about as many years as the moon doth days in one sign, and holdeth the same consideration in years as the moon in days, doth cause these periculous periods. Which together with other planets, and profection of the horoscope, unto the seventh house, or opposite signs every seventh year, oppresseth

[4] *should be accounted a year old, &c.*] Whereas, if born on the first of January, 1644, he would be only 85 days old on the 25th of March, that being the first day of the year 1645: still more strange does it sound, to assert that on the 24th of March, 1645, he would be **a year** older than on the 25th March of the same year.

living natures, and causeth observable mutations in the state of sublunary things.

Further satisfaction may yet be had from the learned discourse of Salmasius* lately published, if any desire to be informed how different the present observations are from those of the ancients; how every one hath different climactericals; with many other observables, impugning the present opinion.⁵

CHAPTER XIII.

Of the Canicular or Dog-days.

WHEREOF to speak distinctly.—Among the southern constellations, two there are which bear the name of the dog; the one in sixteen degrees of latitude, containing on the left thigh a star of the first magnitude, usually called Procyon or Anticanis, because say some it riseth before the other; which if truly understood, must be restrained unto those habitations, who have elevation of pole above thirty-two degrees. Mention thereof there is in Horace,† who seems to mistake or confound the one with the other; and after him in Galen, who is willing the remarkablest star of the other should be called by this name; because it is the first that ariseth in the constellation; which notwithstanding, to speak strictly, it is not; unless we except one of the third magnitude in the right paw, in his own and our elevation, and two more on his head in and beyond the degree of sixty. A second and more considerable one there is, and neighbour unto the other, in forty degrees of latitude, containing eighteen stars, whereof that in his mouth, of the first magnitude, the Greeks

---

* *De Annis Climactericis.*
† *Jam Procyon fuerit et stella vesani Leonis.*

⁵ *Which duly, &c.*] The two concluding paragraphs were added in 2nd edition.

I subjoin several references here transcribed from a copy belonging to my late friend Rev. Jos. Jefferson; which may be useful to others, though I have not had opportunity to avail myself of them. See *Pluche*, i. 266.—Vid. *J. F. Ringelbergii Lucubrationes de Annis Climactericis*, p. 548.—Concerning an "odd number," see *Stopford's Pagano-Papismus*, p. 262.—*Jeff.*

call Σείριος, the Latins *canis major*, and we emphatically the dog-star.

Now from the rising of this star, not cosmically, that is, with the sun, but heliacally, that is, its emersion from the rays of the sun, the ancients computed their canicular days; concerning which, there generally passeth an opinion, that during those days all medication or use of physick is to be declined, and the cure committed unto nature. And therefore as though there were any feriation[6] in nature or *justitiums*[7] imaginable in professions, whose subject is natural, and under no intermissive, but constant way of mutation, this season is commonly termed the physician's vacation, and stands so received by most men. Which conceit, however general, is not only erroneous but unnatural, and subsisting upon foundations either false, uncertain, mistaken, or misapplied, deserves not of mankind that indubitable assent it findeth.[8]

For first, which seems to be the ground of this assertion, and not to be drawn into question, that is, the magnified quality of this star, conceived to cause or intend the heat of this season, whereby these days become more observable than the rest, we find that wiser antiquity was not of this opinion. For, seventeen hundred years ago it was a vulgar error rejected by Geminus, a learned mathematician, in his Elements of Astronomy, wherein he plainly affirmeth, that common opinion made that a cause, which was at first observed but as a sign; the rising and setting both of this star and others being observed by the ancients, to denote and testify certain points of mutation, rather than conceived to induce or effect the same. For our fore-fathers, saith he, observing the course of the sun, and marking certain muta-

---

[6] *feriation.*] Vacations.   [7] *justitiums.*] Probably, *statute laws.*

[8] *there generally passeth, &c.*] In the present day, it is difficult to believe that so absurd a position could have obtained general credence, even among the ignorant, much more that it could have exercised any influence on medical science. Yet that Sir Thomas knew it to have that influence in his day, is evident not only from the present, but especially from the concluding paragraph of this chapter. Nor is his estimate of the evil resulting from such a "vulgar error in practice" less forcibly proved by the pains, ingenuity, and labour, with which he attacks it, and from the great length to which his very judicious investigation of the subject is here carried.

tions to happen in his progress through particular parts of the zodiack, they registered and set them down in their parapegmes, or astronomical canons; and being not able to design these times by days, months, or years (the compute thereof, and the beginning of the year being different, according unto different nations), they thought best to settle a general account unto all, and to determine these alterations by some known and invariable signs; and such did they conceive the rising and setting of the fixed stars; not ascribing thereto any part of causality, but notice and signification. And thus much seems implied in that expression of Homer, when speaking of the dog-star he concludeth, κακόν δέ τε σῆμα τέτυκται, *Malum autem signum est;* the same, as Petavius observeth, is implied in the word of Ptolemy, and the ancients, περὶ ἐπισημωσιῶν, that is, of the signification of stars. The term of Scripture also favours it; as that of Isaiah, *Nolite timere à signis cœli,* and that in Genesis, *ut sint in signa et tempora,* let there be lights in the firmament, and let them be for signs and for seasons.

The primitive and leading magnifiers of this star were the Egyptians, the great admirers of dogs in earth and heaven; wherein they worshipped Anubis or Mercurius, the scribe of Saturn, and counsellor of Osyris, the great inventor of their religious rites, and promoter of good unto Egypt, who was therefore translated into this star; by the Egyptians called Sothis, and Siris by the Ethiopians, from whence that Sirius or the dog-star had its name is by some conjectured.[9]

And this they looked upon, not with reference unto heat, but celestial influence upon the faculties of man, in order to religion and all sagacious invention, and from hence derived the abundance and great fertility of Egypt, the overflow of Nilus happening about the ascent hereof; and therefore, in hieroglyphical monuments, Anubis is described with a dog's head, with a crocodile between his legs, with a sphere in his hand, with two stars, and a water-pot standing by him, implying thereby the rising and setting of the dog-star, and the inundation of the river Nilus.

But if all were silent, Galen hath explained this point

---

[9] *The primitive, &c.*] This paragraph was added in 2nd edition; the next paragraph was added in the 3rd edition.

CHAP. XIII.] THE CANICULAR OR DOG-DAYS. 449

unto the life; who expounding the reason why Hippocrates declared the affections of the year by the rising and setting of stars; it was, saith he, because he would proceed on signs and principles best known unto all nations; and upon his words in the first of the epidemicks, *In Thaso autumno circa equinoctium et sub virgilias pluviæ erant multæ,* he thus enlargeth. If, saith he, the same compute of times and months were observed by all nations, Hippocrates had never made any mention either of *arcturus, pleiades,* or the dog-star, but would have plainly said, in Macedonia, in the month *Dion,*[1] thus or thus was the air disposed. But for as much as the month *Dion* is only known unto the Macedonians, but obscure unto the Athenians and other nations, he found more general distinctions of time, and instead of naming months, would usually say, at the equinox, the rising of the *pleiades,* or the dog-star; and by this way did the ancients divide the seasons of the year, the autumn, winter, spring, and summer. By the rising of the *pleiades* denoting the beginning of summer, and by that of the dog-star the declination thereof. By this way Aristotle, through all his books of animals, distinguisheth their times of generation, latitancy, migration, sanity, and venation; and this were an allowable way of compute, and still to be retained, were the site of the stars as inalterable, and their ascents as invariable, as primitive astronomy conceived them; and therefore though Aristotle frequently mentioneth this star, and particularly affirmeth that fishes in the Bosphorus are best catched from the arise of the dog-star, we must not conceive the same a mere effect thereof; nor though Scaliger from hence be willing to infer the efficacy of this star, are we induced hereto, except (because the same philosopher affirmeth, that tunny is fat about the rising of the *pleiades,* and departs upon *arcturus,* or that most insects are latent from the setting of the seven stars), except, I say, he give us also leave to infer that these particular effects and alterations proceed from those stars, which were indeed but designations of such quarters and portions of the year, wherein the same were observed. Now what Pliny affirmeth of the orix, that it seemeth to adore this star, and taketh notice thereof by voice and sternuta-

---

[1] *Dion.*] Itt is Dius, not Dion.—*Wr.*

tion, until we be better assured of its verity, we shall not salve the sympathy.

Secondly, what slender opinion the ancients held of the efficacy of this star, is declarable from their compute; for as Geminus affirmeth, and Petavius, his learned commentator, proveth, they began their account from its heliacal emersion, and not its cosmical ascent. The cosmical ascension of a star we term that, when it ariseth together with the sun, or the same degree of the ecliptick wherein the sun abideth; and that the heliacal, when a star which before for the vicinity of the sun was not visible, being further removed, beginneth to appear. For the annual motion of the sun from west to east being far swifter than that of the fixed stars, he must of necessity leave them on the east while he hasteneth forward, and obscureth others to the west, and so the moon which performs its motion swifter than the sun (as may be observed in their conjunctions and eclipses), gets eastward out of his rays, and appears when the sun is set.[2] If therefore the dog-star had this effectual heat which is ascribed unto it, it would afford best evidence thereof, and the season would be most fervent, when it ariseth in the probablest place of its activity, that is, the cosmical ascent; for therein it ariseth with the sun, and is included in the same irradiation. But the time observed by the ancients was long after this ascent, and in the heliacal emersion, when it becomes at greatest distance from the sun, neither rising with it nor near it; and therefore had they conceived any more than a bare signality in this star, or ascribed the heat of the season thereunto, they would not have computed from its heliacal ascent, which was of inferior efficacy; nor imputed the vehemency of heat unto those points wherein it was more remiss, and where with less probability they might make out its action.

Thirdly, although we derive the authority of these days from observations of the ancients, yet are our computes very different, and such as confirm not each other. For whereas

---

[2] *the moon, &c.*] This is obscurely saydo. Nor though the moon gets eastward of the sonne, i. e., to speak properly, appears on the east from the new to the full, yet from the full to the new shee appears west of him, which is nothing else but that going throughe the twelve times for his once, she must of necessity seeme sometimes eastward o him, and sometimes west, according to the diurnal motion.— *Wr.*

they observed it heliacally, we seem to observe it cosmically, for before it ariseth heliacally, unto our latitude, the summer is even at an end. Again, we compute not only from different ascents, but also from diverse stars; they from the greater dog-star, we from the lesser;[3] they from Orion's, we from Cephalus's dog; they from Sirius, we from Crocyon; for the beginning of the dog-days with us is set down the 19th of July, about which time the lesser dog-star ariseth with the sun, whereas the star of the greater dog ascendeth not until after that month. And this mistake will yet be larger, if the compute be made stricter, and as Dr. Bainbrigge,[*] late professor of astronomy in Oxford, hath set it down, who in the year 1629 computed, that in the horizon of Oxford, the dog-star arose not before the fifteenth day of August, when in our almanack accounts those days are almost ended. So that the common and received time not answering the true compute, it frustrates the observations of ourselves; and being also different from the calculations of the ancients, their observations confirm not ours, nor ours theirs, but rather confute each other.

Nor will the computes of the ancients be so authentic unto those who shall take notice how commonly they applied the celestial descriptions of other climes unto their own, wherein the learned Bainbrigius justly reprehendeth Manilius, who transferred the Egyptian descriptions unto the Roman account, confounding the observation of the Greek and Barbarick spheres.[4]

Fourthly (which is the argument of Geminus), were there any such effectual heat in this star, yet could it but weakly

---

[*] *Bainb. Canicularis.*

[3] *the lesser, &c.*] The observation of the dog-star's rising came from the Ægyptians at Alexandria, lying under 30 degrees, where when the sun comes to the tropicks in the [....] degree of Cancer, both the dog-stars rise with him together, begin to increase the heate, which afterwards the sun coming towards Leo doubles, soe that they esteeme not of that heate from the dog-star's rise alone, but from their conjoynt rising with the sun in Leo. But the principall observation of the dog-star rising was from the course of their yeare, which they therefore cald Ἔτος κυνικὸν, as beginning always from the first cosmical rising of the dog-star.— *Wr.*

[4] *And this mistake, &c.*] The conclusion of this paragraph, with the next, were first added in 3rd edition.

evidence the same in summer, it being about 40 degrees distance from the sun, and should rather manifest its warming power in the winter, when it remains conjoined with the sun in its hybernal conversion. For about the 29th of October, and in the 16th of Scorpius, and so again in January, the sun performs his revolution in the same parallel with the dog-star. Again, if we should impute the heat of this season unto the co-operation of any stars with the sun, it seems more favourable for our times to ascribe the same unto the constellation of Leo. Where besides that the sun is in his proper house, it is conjoined with many stars, whereof two of the first magnitude, and in the 8th of August is corporally conjoined with Basiliscus, a star of eminent name in astrology, and seated almost in the ecliptick.

Fifthly, if all were granted, that observation and reason were also for it, and were it an undeniable truth that an effectual fervour proceedeth from this star, yet would not the same determine the opinion now in question, it necessarily suffering such restrictions as to take off general illations. For first, in regard of different latitudes, unto some the canicular days are in the winter; as unto such as have no latitude, but live in a right sphere, that is, under the equinoctial line, for unto them it ariseth when the sun is about the tropick of Cancer, which season unto them is winter,[5] and the sun remotest from them. Nor hath the same position in the summer, that is, in the equinoctial points, any advantage from it, for in the one point the sun is at the meridian before the dog-star ariseth; in the other the star is at the meridian before the sun ascendeth.

Some latitudes have no canicular days at all; as namely all those which have more than seventy-three degrees of northern elevation; as the territory of Nova Zembla, part of Greenland, and Tartary, for unto that habitation the dog-star is invisible, and appeareth not above the horizon.

Unto such latitudes wherein it ariseth, it carrieth a various and very different respect: unto some it ascendeth when summer is over, whether we compute heliacally or cosmi-

[5] *winter.*] They have two winters, viz. when the sonne is in either tropick, in which respect yf there be any difference in the temper, itt is when the sonne enters the midst of ♑, and by his eccentricity is nearer to the earth there then when he is in Cancer.—*Wr.*

cally; for, though unto Alexandria it ariseth in Cancer, yet it ariseth not unto Biarmia cosmically before it be in Virgo, and heliacally about the autumnal equinox. Even unto the latitude of fifty-two, the efficacy thereof is not much considerable, whether we consider its ascent, meridian, altitude, or abode above the horizon. For it ariseth very late in the year, about the eighteenth of Leo, that is, the 31st of July. Of meridian altitude it hath but 23 degrees, so that it plays but obliquely upon us, and as the sun doth about the 23rd of January. And lastly, his abode above the horizon is not great; for in the eighteenth of Leo, the 31st of July, although they arise together, yet doth it set above five hours before the sun, that is, before two o'clock, after which time we are more sensible of heat than all the day before.

Secondly, in regard of the variation of the longitude of the stars, we are to consider (what the ancients observed not), that the site of the fixed stars is alterable, and that since elder times they have suffered a large and considerable variation of their longitudes. The longitude of a star, to speak plainly, is its distance from the first point of numeration toward the east; which first point unto the ancients was the vernal equinox. Now by reason of their motion from west to east, they have very much varied from this point. The first star of Aries, in the time of Meton, the Athenian, was placed in the very intersection, which is now elongated and removed eastward twenty-eight degrees; insomuch that now the sign of Aries possesseth the place of Taurus, and Taurus that of Gemini. Which variation of longitude must very much distract the opinion of the dog-star;[6] not only in our days, but in times before and after; for since the world began it hath arisen in Taurus, and if the world last, may have its ascent in Virgo; so that we must place the canicular days, that is, the hottest time of the year, in the spring in the first age, and in the autumn in ages to come.

Thirdly, the stars have not only varied their longitudes,

---

[6] *of the dog-star.*] Not only of the dogg-star, but of all the imaginary houses of the astrologers, and consequently all that heathenish structure of the fortitude, detriments, aspects, triciplicityes, and such ridiculous stuff, utterly dasht, and confounded, and condemned of late by all the learned astronomers: *Tycho, pluries;* Kepler, expresly in *Cometæ anni* 1618; and Longomontany *ubique.*—*Wr.*

whereby their ascents have altered, but have also changed their declinations, whereby their rising at all, that is their appearing, hath varied. The declination of a star we call its distance from the equator.[7] Now though the poles of the world and the equator be immoveable, yet because the stars in their proper motions from west to east do move upon the poles of the eclipstick, distant twenty-three degrees and an half from the poles of the equator, and describe circles parallel not unto the equator, but the eclipstick; they must be, therefore, sometimes nearer, sometimes removed further from the equator. All stars that have their distance from the eclipstick northward not more than twenty-three degrees and an half (which is the greatest distance of the eclipstick from the equator) may in progression of time have declination southward, and move beyond the equator; but if any star hath just this distance of twenty-three and an half (as hath *Capella* on the back of *Ericthonius*) it may hereafter move under the equinoctial; and the same will happen respectively unto stars which have declination southward. And therefore many stars may be visible in our hemisphere which are not so at present; and many which are at present, shall take leave of our horizon, and appear unto southern habitations. And therefore the time may come that the dog-star may not be visible in our horizon, and the time hath been when it hath not showed itself unto our neighbour latitudes. So that canicular days there have been none, nor shall be; yet certainly in all times some season of the year more notably hot than other.

Lastly, we multiply causes in vain; and for the reason hereof we need not have recourse unto any star but the sun, and continuity of its action. For the sun ascending into the northern signs, begetteth first a temperate heat in the air; which by his approach unto the solstice he intendeth, and by continuation increaseth the same even upon declination. For running over[8] the same degrees again, that is, in *Leo*, which he hath done in *Taurus*, in July which he did in May; he augmenteth the heat in the latter which he began in the first; and easily intendeth the same by continuation which

[7] *equator.*] Equinoctial.

[8] *For running over.*] In those four signes, Taurus, Gemini, Cancer, Leo, they have a continual summer, hottest *in extremis*.—**Wr.**

was well promoted before. So is it observed, that they which dwell between the tropicks and the equator have their second summer hotter and more maturative of fruits than the former.

So we observe in the day[9] (which is a short year[1]), the greatest heat about two in the afternoon, when the sun is past the meridian (which is his diurnal solstice), and the same is evident from the thermometer or observations of the weatherglass. So are the colds of the night sharper in the summer about two or three after midnight, and the frosts in winter stronger about those hours. So likewise in the year we observe the cold to augment, when the days begin to increase, though the sun be then ascensive and returning from the winter tropick. And therefore if we rest not in this reason for the heat in the declining part of summer, we must discover freezing stars that may resolve the latter colds of winter; which whoever desires to invent, let him study the stars of Andromeda, or the nearer constellation of Pegasus, which are about that time ascendant.

It cannot therefore seem strange, or savour of singularity, that we have examined this point, since the same hath been already denied by some; since the authority and observations of the ancients, rightly understood, do not confirm it; since our present computes are different from those of the ancients, whereon notwithstanding they depend; since there is reason against it, and if all were granted, yet must it be maintained with manifold restraints, far otherwise than is received. And lastly, since from plain and natural principles the doubt may

---

[9] *day.*] Every day is an emblem of the yeare; and therein the sun hath his declination, or distance from the meridian, as from the æquator, his solstice in itt, as in the tropicks; and his different altitudes or azimuths every moment.—*Wr.*

[1] *short year.*] 'Tis seemingly strange, but most true, that they who lye betweene the æquator and the tropic, have a hotter summer than they that lye under the æquator: suppose under 12 degrees north or south: bycause with them sommer is twice doubled in 3 months; having the sonn twice over their heads in that space: whereas they under the æquator have him twice, but in 6 months distance, and 2 winters between. For the distance of the son from the center in his auge at summer is 1210 semidiameters of the earth: but his nearest distance is never above 1122, every semidiameter containing $7159\frac{1}{4}$ of our miles.—*Wr.*

be fairly salved, and not clapt up from petitionary foundations and principles unestablished.

But that which chiefly promoted the consideration of these days, and medically advanced the same, was the doctrine of Hippocrates, a physician of such repute that he received a testimony from a Christian that might have been given unto Christ.* The first in his book, *De aere, aquis, et locis, syderum ortu, &c.* That is, we are to observe the rising of stars, especially the dog-star, *arcturus*, and the setting of the *pleiades*, or seven stars. From whence notwithstanding we cannot infer the general efficacy of these stars, or co-efficacy particular in medications. Probably expressing no more hereby than if he should have plainly said, especial notice we are to take of the hottest time in summer, of the beginning of autumn and winter; for by the rising and setting of those stars were these times and seasons defined. And therefore subjoins this reason, *quoniam his temporibus morbi finiuntur,* because at these times diseases have their ends, as physicians well know, and he elsewhere affirmeth, that seasons determine diseases, beginning in their contraries; as the spring the diseases of autumn, and the summer those of winter. Now (what is very remarkable) whereas in the same place he adviseth to observe the times of notable mutations, as the equinoxes and the solstices, and to decline medication ten days before and after; how precisely soever canicular cautions be considered, this is not observed by physicians, nor taken notice of by the people. And indeed should we blindly obey the restraints both of physicians and astrologers, we should contract the liberty of our prescriptions, and confine the utility of physic unto a very few days. For, observing the dog-days, and as is expressed, some days before, likewise ten days before, and after the equinoctial and solstitial points, by this observation alone are exempted an hundred days. Whereunto if we add the two Egyptian days in every month,[2] the interlunary and plenilunary exemptions, the eclipses of sun and moon, conjunctions and oppositions planetical, the houses of planets, and the site of the luminaries under the signs (wherein some would induce a

---

* *Qui nec fallere potest nec falli.*

[2] *the two Egyptian days, &c.*] Futilissimæ observationes.—*Wr.*

restraint of purgation or phlebotomy), there would arise above an hundred more; so that of the whole year the use of physic would not be secure much above a quarter. Now as we do not strictly observe these days, so need we not the other;[3] and although consideration be made hereof, yet must we prefer the nearer indication before those which are drawn from the time of the year, or other celestial relations.

The second testimony is taken out of the last piece of his age, and after the experience[4] (as some think) of no less than an hundred years, that is, his *Book of Aphorisms*, or short and definitive determinations in physick. The aphorism alleged is this, *Sub Cane et ante Canem difficiles sunt purgationes*. *Sub Cane et Anticane*, say some, including both the dog-stars, but that cannot consist with the Greek, 'ἀπὸ κύνα καὶ πρὸ κυνὸς, nor had that criticism been ever omitted by Galen. Now how true this sentence was in the mouth of Hippocrates, and with what restraint it must be understood by us, will readily appear from the difference between us both in circumstantial relations.

And first, concerning his time and chronology; he lived in the reign of Artaxerxes Longimanus, about the 82nd olympiad, 450 years before Christ, and from our times above two thousand. Now since that time, as we have already declared, the stars have varied their longitudes, and having made large progressions from west to east, the time of the dog-star's ascent must also very much alter; for it ariseth later now in the year than it formerly did in the same latitude, and far later unto us who have a greater elevation, for in the days of Hippocrates this star ascended in Cancer, which now ariseth in Leo, and will in progression of time arise in Virgo; and therefore, in regard of the time wherein he lived, the aphorism was more considerable in his days than in ours, and in times far past than present, and in his country than ours.

The place of his nativity was Coos, an island in the Myrtoan sea, not far from Rhodes, described in maps by the name of Lango, and called by the Turks, who are masters

---

[3] *other.*] i. e. canicular.

[4] *experience.*] Experience of 100 yeares infers he lived at least 120 in all.—*Wr.*

thereof, Stancora, according unto Ptolemy, of northern latitude, 36 degrees. That he lived and writ in these parts is not improbably collected from the epistles that passed betwixt him and Artaxerxes, as also between the citizens of Abdera and Coos, in the behalf of Democritus; which place being seated, from our latitude of 52, 16 degrees southward, there will arise a different consideration, and we may much deceive ourselves, if we conform the ascent of stars in one place unto another, or conceive they arise the same day of the month in Coos and in England; for, as Petavius computes, in the first Julian year, at Alexandria, of latitude 31, the star arose cosmically in the twelfth degree of Cancer, heliacally the 26th; by the compute of Geminus, about this time at Rhodes, of latitude 37, it ascended cosmically the 16th of Cancer, heliacally the first of Leo; and about that time at Rome, of latitude 42, cosmically the 22nd of Cancer, and heliacally the first of Leo; for unto places of greater latitude it ariseth ever later, so that in some latitudes the cosmical ascent happeneth not before the twentieth degree of Virgo, ten days before the autumnal equinox, and if they compute heliacally, after it in Libra.

Again, should we allow all, and only compute unto the latitude of Coos, yet would it not impose a total omission of physick: for if in the hottest season of that clime, all physick were to be declined, then surely in many other none were to be used at any time whatsoever; for unto many parts, not only in the spring and autumn, but also in the winter, the sun is nearer than unto the clime of Coos in the summer.

The third consideration concerneth purging medicines, which are at present far different from those implied in this aphorism, and such as were commonly used by Hippocrates. For three degrees we make of purgative medicines; the first thereof is very benign, not far removed from the nature of aliment, into which, upon defect of working, it is ofttimes converted, and in this form do we account manna, cassia, tamarinds, and many more, whereof we find no mention in Hippocrates. The second is also gentle, having a familiarity with some humour, into which it is but converted if it fail of its operation; of this sort are aloe, rhubarb, senna, &c. whereof also few or none were known unto Hippocrates. The third is of a violent and venomous quality, which, frustrate of its action, assumes as it were the nature of poison, such as *scammoneum, colocynthis, elaterium, euphorbium, tithymallus, laureola, peplum,* &c. Of this sort Hippocrates made use even in fevers, pleurisies, and quinsies; and that composition is very remarkable which is ascribed unto Diogenes in Ætius,* that is, of pepper, sal-ammoniac, euphorbium, of each an ounce, the doses whereof four scruples and an half, which whosoever should take, would find in his bowels more than a canicular[5] heat, though in the depth of winter. Many of the like nature may be observed in Ætius, or in the book *De Dinamidiis,* ascribed unto Galen, which is the same *verbatim* with the other.

Now in regard of the second, and especially the first degree of purgatives, the aphorism[6] is not of force, but we may safely use them, they being benign and of innoxious qualities; and therefore Lucas Gauricus, who hath endeavoured with many testimonies to advance this consideration, at length concedeth that lenative physick may be used, especially when the moon is well affected in Cancer, or in the watery signs. But in regard of the third degree, the aphorism is considerable; purgations may be dangerous, and a

* *Tetrab.* lib. i. Serm. 3.

[5] *canicular.*] Such as is the heate of the dog-dayes in the hottest countreyes, where the dog-star sheweth his force most.—*Wr.*

[6] *aphorism.*] Aphorisme is a general rule grounded upon reason, ratified by experience; but in this place he gives this name to that received opinion, that during the dog-dayes all physicke is to be declined; not bycause itt was grounded upon truthe, but bycause itt was generally *supposed* to bee soe; the ground whereof relating to those countreyes onlye which lye under the torrid zone, hee refutes in this chapter most judiciouslye, and determines the state of the question most excellentlye in the two following periods in four propositions or conclusions. First, that in preventinge there is no use of that rule, for that noe wise man will defer the physick till the dog-dayes, having fitter times in the spring, and the fall, wherein to take such physick with greater advantage. Second, that the heate of the dog-dayes in our clymates is not soe greate as that of the torrid zone in their spring. Third, that in chronical diseases physick may safely bee deferred till those dayes bee over. Fourth, that the strength of the aphorisme is grounded cheefly upon a point of wisdom; that itt must needs bee dangerous to adde-fire to fire, i. e. when the bodye is overheated in the dog-dayes to adde the heat and acrimony of purging medicines, but yet where the case is desperate, as in sharpe fits, wisdom must give way to necessity; *better purge than dye.*—*Wr.*

memorable example there is in the medical epistles of Crucins, of a Roman prince that died upon an ounce of *diaphœnicon* taken in this season; from the use whereof we refrain not only in hot seasons, but warily exhibit it at all times in hot diseases; which when necessity requires, we can perform more safely than the ancients, as having better ways of preparation and correction, that is, not only by addition of other bodies, but separation of noxious parts from their own.

But besides these differences between Hippocrates and us, the physicians of these times and those of antiquity, the condition of the disease and the intention of the physician hold a main consideration in what time and place soever. For physick is either curative or preventive; preventive we call that which by purging noxious humours, and the causes of diseases, preventeth sickness in the healthy, or the recourse[7] thereof in the valitudinary; this is of common use at the spring and fall, and we commend not the same at this season.[8] Therapeutick or curative physick we term that which restoreth the patient unto sanity, and taketh away diseases actually affecting. Now of diseases some are chronical and of long duration, as quartan agues, scurvy, &c., wherein, because they admit of delay, we defer the cure to more advantageous seasons; others we term acute, that is, of short duration and danger, as fevers, pleurisies, &c., in which, because delay is dangerous, and they arise unto their state before the dog-days determine, we apply present remedies according unto indications, respecting rather the acuteness[9] of the disease, and precipitancy[1] of occasion, than the rising or setting of the stars, the effects of the one being disputable, of the other assured and inevitable.

And although astrology may here put in, and plead the secret influence of this star; yet Galen in his comment makes

---

[7] *recourse.*] Recurrence.

[8] *at this season.*] That is during the dog-days.—*Wr.*

[9] *acuteness.*] i. e., the sharp and fierce condition of the disease, admitting noe delay of any requisite helpe in physic.—*Wr.*

[1] *precipitancy.*] Precipitancy is properly the swift motion of a man falling headlong, hence itt signifies the soden passings of occasions in diseases, which once let passe can never be redeemed, and by those means endanger the life of the patient, by suffering the disease (which might have been timely prevented) to get such a masterye as noe physick can quell.—*Wr.*

no such consideration, confirming the truth of the aphorism from the heat of the year, and the operation of medicines exhibited. In regard that bodies, being heated by the summer, cannot so well endure the acrimony of purging medicines and because upon purgations contrary motions ensue, the heat of the air attracting the humours outward, and the action of the medicine retracting the same inward. But these are readily salved in the distinctions before alleged, and particularly in the constitution of our climate, and divers others, wherein the air makes no such exhaustion of spirits, and in the benignity of our medicines, whereof some in their own nature, others well prepared, agitate not the humours, nor make a sensible perturbation.

Nor do we hereby reject or condemn a sober and regulated astrology; we hold there is more truth therein, than in astrologers; in some more than many allow, yet in none so much as some pretend. We deny not the influence of the stars, but often suspect the due application thereof; for though we should affirm that all things were in all things, that heaven were but earth celestified, and earth but heaven terrestrified, or that each part above had an influence upon its divided affinity below; yet how to single out these relations,* and duly to apply their actions, is a work ofttimes to be effected by some revelation, and Cabala from above, rather than any philosophy or speculation here below. What power soever they have upon our bodies, it is not requisite they should destroy our reasons, that is, to make us rely on the strength of nature, when she is least able to relieve us; and when we conceive the heaven against us, to refuse the assistance of the earth created for us. This were to suffer from the mouth of the dog above, what others do from the teeth of the dogs below; that is, to be afraid of their proper remedy, and refuse to approach any water,[2] though that hath often proved a cure unto their disease.[3] There is

* Hic labor, hoc opus est.

[2] *refuse to approach any water.*] The horror of water in this disease, though a very general, is not an invariable symptom, even in the human subject.

[3] *hath often proved a cure, &c.*] "Morin relates the case of a young woman, twenty years old, who, labouring under symptoms of hydrophobia, was plunged into a tub of water, with a bushel of salt dissolved in it,

in wise men a power beyond the stars; and Ptolemy encourageth us, that by foreknowledge we may evade their actions; for, being but universal causes, they are determined by particular agents; which being inclined, not constrained, contain within themselves the casting act, and a power to command the conclusion.

Lastly, if all be conceded, and were there in this aphorism an unrestrained truth, yet were it not reasonable from a caution to infer a non-usance or abolition, from a thing to be used with discretion, not to be used at all. Because the apostle bids us beware of philosophy, heads of extremity will have none at all; an usual fallacy in vulgar and less distinctive brains, who having once overshot the mean, run violently on, and find no rest but in the extremes.[4]

---

and was harassed with repeated dippings till she became insensible, and was at the point of death, when she was still left in the tub sitting against its sides. In this state, we are told, she was at length fortunate enough to recover her senses: when, much to her own astonishment, as well as that of the bystanders, she found herself capable of looking at the water, and even of drinking it without choaking."—*Good's Study of Medicine*, iii. 362.

Dr. Good enumerates a variety of modes of treatment which have been adopted, and medicines which have been prescribed, with most uncertain and only occasional success.

An American plant (*Scutellaria lateriflora*, or *Virginian scullcap*) has been used with great success by several American practitioners: and so powerful has been its influence, that it has been made the subject of a separate publication by Dr. Spalding, of New York, in 1819. It appears to have been discovered by a Dr. Lawrence Van Derveer, of New Jersey, who used it successfully in hydrophobia, as early as 1773. From him the remedy was communicated through his son to other practitioners: and was very extensively used at the date of Dr. Spalding's pamphlet. It is taken in a decoction of the dried plant; a tea-spoonful and a half to a quart of boiling water:—the patient taking half a pint of this infusion, morning and night.

Dr. S. states that the *scutellaria* has been given to more than 850 persons bitten by animals believed to be rabid, and that in only three instances had hydrophobic symptoms supervened, and in each of these cases the quantity of the plant actually taken had been very inconsiderable. It had also been given to more than 1,100 animals under similar circumstances, and with nearly equal success.

[4] *extremes.*] This censure fitlye reaches all clymats of the worlde and all times for a prudent caution. For as in the state of corrupted nature, this fallacy is (more than epidemical, that is) universall: soe (to the comforte of the worlde) being once swalowed, and put in practise, itt

Now hereon we have the longer insisted, because the error is material, and concerns ofttimes the life of man; an error, to be taken notice of by state, and provided against by princes who are of the opinion of Solomon, that their riches consist in the multitude of their subjects. An error worse than some reputed heresies; and of greater danger to the body, than they unto the soul; which whosoever is able to reclaim, he shall save more in one summer, than Themison* destroyed in any autumn; he shall introduce a new way of cure, preserving by theory, as well as practice, and men not only from death, but from destroying themselves.

* A physician. *Quot Themison ægros autumno occiderit uno.*—*Juvenal.* never failes to pay the practisers in fine with their owne coigne, **viz.** destruction and ruin.— *Wr.*

END OF VOL. I.

Volume II

CONTENTS OF VOL. II.

PSEUDODOXIA EPIDEMICA, Books V. to VII.

THE FIFTH BOOK; *the particular part continued. Of many things questionable as they are commonly described in pictures. Of many popular customs, &c.*

Chap. 1.	Of the picture of the pelican..	Page 1
Chap. 2.	Of the picture of dolphins	4
Chap. 3.	Of the picture of a grasshopper	6
Chap. 4.	Of the picture of the serpent tempting Eve	9
Chap. 5.	Of the picture of Adam and Eve with navels	14
Chap. 6.	Of the pictures of the Jews and Eastern nations, at their feasts, especially our Saviour at the Passover	17
Chap. 7.	Of the picture of our Saviour with long hair	26
Chap. 8.	Of the picture of Abraham sacrificing Isaac	28
Chap. 9.	Of the picture of Moses with horns	29
Chap. 10.	Of the scutcheons of the twelve tribes of Israel	32
Chap. 11.	Of the pictures of the sibyls	38
Chap. 12.	Of the picture describing the death of Cleopatra	39
Chap. 13.	Of the pictures of the nine worthies	42
Chap. 14.	Of the picture of Jephthah sacrificing his daughter	47
Chap. 15.	Of the picture of John the Baptist in a camel's skin	50
Chap. 16.	Of the picture of St. Christopher	52
Chap. 17.	Of the picture of St. George	54
Chap. 18.	Of the picture of St. Jerome	56
Chap. 19.	Of the pictures of mermaids, unicorns, and some others	59
Chap. 20.	Of the hieroglyphical pictures of the Egyptians	65
Chap. 21.	Of the picture of Haman hanged	69
Chap. 22.	Of the picture of God the Father; of the sun, moon, and winds, with others	72
Chap. 23.	Compendiously of many popular customs, opinions, &c.: viz. of an hare crossing the high-way; of the ominous appearing of owls and ravens; of the falling of salt; of breaking the egg-shell; of the true lovers' knot; of the cheek burning or ear tingling; of speaking under the rose; of smoke following the fair; of sitting cross-legged; of hair upon moles; of the set time of paring of nails; of lions' heads upon spouts and cisterns; of the saying, ungirt, unblest; of the sun dancing on Easter-day; of the silly-how; of being drunk once a month; of the appearing of the devil with a cloven hoof.	79
Chap. 24.	Of popular customs, opinions, &c.; of the prediction of the year ensuing from the insects in oak apples; that children would naturally speak Hebrew; of refraining to kill swallows; of lights burning dim at the apparition of spirits; of the wearing of coral; of Moses' rod in the discovery of mines; of discovering doubtful matters by book or staff	91

THE SIXTH BOOK; *the particular part continued. Of popular and received tenets, cosmographical, geographical, and historical.*

Chap. 1.	Concerning the beginning of the world, that the time thereof is not precisely known, as commonly it is presumed	103
Chap. 2.	Of men's enquiries in what season or point of the Zodiack it began, that, as they are generally made, they are in vain, and as particularly, uncertain	119
Chap. 3.	Of the divisions of the seasons and four quarters of the year, according unto astronomers and physicians; that the common compute of the ancients, and which is still retained by some, is very questionable	122

Chap. 4.	Of some computation of days, and deductions of one part of the year unto another	Page 127
Chap. 5.	A digression of the wisdom of God in the site and motion of the sun	130
Chap. 6.	Concerning the vulgar opinion, that the earth was slenderly peopled before the flood	136
Chap. 7.	Of east and west	153
Chap. 8.	Of the river Nilus	163
Chap. 9.	Of the Red Sea	176
Chap. 10.	Of the blackness of negroes	180
Chap. 11.	Of the same	192
Chap. 12.	A digression concerning blackness	197
Chap. 13.	Of gypsies	204
Chap. 14.	Of some others	207

THE SEVENTH BOOK: *the particular part concluded. Of popular and received tenets, chiefly historical and some deduced from the Holy Scriptures.*

Chap. 1.	That the forbidden fruit was an apple	210
Chap. 2.	That a man hath one rib less than a woman	214
Chap. 3.	Of Methuselah	216
Chap. 4.	That there was no rainbow before the flood	219
Chap. 5.	Of Shem, Ham, and Japheth	222
Chap. 6.	That the tower of Babel was erected against a second deluge	225
Chap. 7.	Of the mandrakes of Leah	227
Chap. 8.	Of the three kings of Collein	232
Chap. 9.	Of the food of John Baptist, locusts and wild honey	234
Chap. 10.	That John the Evangelist should not die	235
Chap. 11.	Of some others more briefly	241
Chap. 12.	Of the cessation of oracles	243
Chap. 13.	Of the death of Aristotle	246
Chap. 14.	Of the wish of Philoxenus to have the neck of a crane	252
Chap. 15.	Of the lake Asphaltites	255
Chap. 16.	Of divers other relations: viz. of the woman that conceived in a bath; of Crassus that never laughed but once; that our Saviour never laughed; of Sergius the Second, or Bocca di Porco; that Tamerlane was a Scythian shepherd	259
Chap. 17.	Of some others: viz. of the poverty of Belisarius; of *fluctus decumanus*, or the tenth wave; of Parisatis that poisoned Statira by one side of a knife; of the woman fed with poison, that should have poisoned Alexander: of the wandering Jew; of pope Joan; of friar Bacon's brazen head that spoke; of Epicurus	267
Chap. 18.	More briefly of some others: viz. that the army of Xerxes drank whole rivers dry; that Hannibal eat through the Alps with vinegar; of Archimedes his burning the ships of Marcellus; of the Fabii that were all slain; of the death of Æschylus; of the cities of Tarsus and Anchiale built in one day; of the great ship Syracusia or Alexandria; of the Spartan boys	276
Chap. 19.	Of some relations whose truth we fear	284

PSEUDODOXIA EPIDEMICA.

THE FIFTH BOOK:

THE PARTICULAR PART CONTINUED.

OF MANY THINGS QUESTIONABLE AS THEY ARE COMMONLY DESCRIBED IN PICTURES; OF MANY POPULAR CUSTOMS, ETC.

CHAPTER I.

Of the Picture of the Pelican.

AND first, in every place we meet with the picture of the pelican, opening her breast with her bill, and feeding her young ones with the blood distilled from her. Thus is it set forth not only in common signs, but in the crest and scutcheon of many noble families; hath been asserted by many holy writers, and was an hieroglyphick of piety and pity among the Egyptians; on which consideration they spared them at their tables.[1]

[1] *And first, &c.*] These singular birds are said to fish in companies: they form a circle on the water, and having by the flapping of their huge wings, driven the terrified fish towards the centre, they suddenly dive all at once as by consent, and soon fill their immense pouches with their prey. In order subsequently to disgorge the contents, in feeding their young, they have only to press the pouch on their breast. This operation may very probably have given rise to the fable, that the pelican opens her breast to nourish her young.

As to its hieroglyphical import, Horapollo says that it was used among the Egyptians as an emblem of folly; on account of the little care it takes to deposit its eggs in a safe place. He relates that it buries them in a hole; that the natives, observing the place, cover it with dry cow's dung, to which they set fire. The old birds immediately endeavouring to extinguish the fire with their wings, get them burnt, and so are easily caught.—*Horap. Hierogl. cura Pauw,* 4to. Traj. ad Rh. 1727, **pp. 67, 68.**

Notwithstanding, upon enquiry we find no mention hereof in ancient zoographers, and such as have particularly discoursed upon animals, as Aristotle, Ælian, Pliny, Solinus, and many more; who seldom forget proprieties of such a nature, and have been very punctual in less considerable records. Some ground hereof I confess we may allow, nor need we deny a remarkable affection in pelicans toward their young; for Ælian, discoursing of storks, and their affection toward their brood, whom they instruct to fly, and unto whom they redeliver up the provision of their bellies, concludeth at last, that herons and pelicans do the like.

As for the testimonies of ancient fathers, and ecclesiastical writers, we may more safely conceive therein some emblematical, than any real story: so doth Eucherius confess it to be the emblem of Christ. And we are unwilling literally to receive that account of Jerom, that perceiving her young ones destroyed by serpents, she openeth her side with her bill, by the blood whereof they revive and return unto life again. By which relation they might indeed illustrate the destruction of man by the old serpent, and his restorement by the blood of Christ: and in this sense we shall not dispute the like relations of Austin, Isidore, Albertus, and many more; and under an emblematical intention, we accept it in coat-armour.

As for the hieroglyphick of the Egyptians, they erected the same upon another consideration, which was parental affection; manifested in the protection of her young ones, when her nest was set on fire. For as for letting out her blood, it was not the assertion of the Egyptians, but seems translated unto the pelican from the vulture, as Pierius hath plainly delivered. *Sed quòd pelicanum (ut etiam aliis plerisque persuasum est) rostro pectus disseccantem pingunt, ita ut suo sanguine filios alat, ab Ægyptiorum historia valde alienum est, illi enim vulturem tantùm id facere tradiderunt.*

And lastly, as concerning the picture, if naturally examined, and not hieroglyphically conceived, it containeth many improprieties, disagreeing almost in all things from the true and proper description. For, whereas it is commonly set forth green or yellow, in its proper colour it is inclining to white, excepting the extremities or tops of the wing feathers, which are brown. It is described in the bigness of a hen, whereas it approacheth and sometimes exceedeth the magnitude of a swan.[2] It is commonly painted with a short bill; whereas that of the pelican[3] attaineth sometimes the length of two spans. The bill is made acute or pointed at the end, whereas it is flat and broad,[4] though somewhat inverted at the extreme. It is described like *fissipedes*, or birds which have their feet or claws divided: whereas it is palmipedous, or fin-footed, like swans and geese, according to the method of nature in latirostrous or flat-billed birds, which being generally swimmers, the organ is wisely contrived unto the action, and they are framed with fins or oars upon their feet, and therefore they neither light, nor build on trees, if we except cormorants, who make their nests like herons. Lastly, there is one part omitted more remarkable than any other; that is, the chowle or crop adhering unto the lower side of the bill, and so descending by the throat; a bag or sachel very observable, and of a capacity almost beyond credit; which, notwithstanding, this animal could not want; for therein it receiveth oysters, cockles, scollops, and other testaceous animals, which being not able to break, it retains them until they open, and vomiting them up, takes out the meat contained. This is that part preserved for a rarity, and wherein (as Sanctius delivers) in one dissected, a negro child was found.

A possibility there may be of opening and bleeding their breast, for this may be done by the uncous and pointed extremity of their bill; and some probability also that they sometimes do it for their own relief, though not for their

[2] *whereas it approacheth, &c.*] This bird, says Buffon, would be the largest of water-birds, were not the body of the albatross more thick, and the legs of the flamingo so much longer. It is sometimes six feet long from point of bill to end of tail, and twelve feet from wing-tip to wing-tip.

[3] *that of the pelican.*] This description of the authors agrees (*per omnia*) with that live pellican, which was to bee seen in King-street, Westminster, 1647, from whence (doubtles) the author maketh this relation ἐξ αὐτοψία.—*Wr.*

[4] *flat and broad.*] From hence itt is that many ancients call this bird the shoveller: and the Greeks derive πελεκᾶν from πελεκᾶν, to wound as with an axe, which suites with the shape of his beake in length and breadthe like a rooting axe, *per omnia.*—*Wr.*

But the term *shoveller* is now applied to a species of duck; *Anas clypeata.*

young ones; that is, by nibbling and biting themselves on the itching part of their breast, upon fulness or acrimony of blood. And the same may be better made out, if (as some relate) their feathers on that part are sometimes observed to be red and tinctured with blood.[5]

CHAPTER II.

Of the Picture of Dolphins.

THAT dolphins are crooked, is not only affirmed by the hand of the painter, but commonly conceived their natural and proper figure, which is not only the opinion of our times, but seems the belief of elder times before us. For, beside the expressions of Ovid and Pliny, the portraits in some ancient coins are framed in this figure, as will appear in some thereof in Gesner, others in Goltsius, and Lævinus Hulsius in his description of coins from Julius Cæsar unto Rodolphus the second.

Notwithstanding, to speak strictly, in their natural figure they are straight, nor have their spine convexed, or more considerably embowed, than sharks, porpoises,[6] whales, and

---

[5] *A possibility, &c.*] This paragraph was first added in 6th edition.

[6] *porpoises.*] Reade porkpisces. The porkpisce (that is the dolphin hath his name from the hog hee resembles in convexity and curvitye of his backe, from the head to the tayle: nor is hee otherwise curbe, then as a hog is: except that before a storme, hee tumbles just as a hog runs. That which I once saw, cutt up in Fish-street, was of this forme and above five foote longe: his skin not skaly, but smoothe and black, like bacon in the chimney: and his bowels in all points like a hog: and yf instead of his four fins you imagine four feete, hee would represent a black hog (as it were) sweal'd alive.—*Wr.*

This creature, so graphically described by the dean, is probably the common dolphin,—*Delphinus Delphis;* but the porpoise is a different animal, *Delphis phocæna,* now constituted a distinct genus. Ray, however, says that the porpoise is the dolphin of the ancients. The following passage from his *Philosophical Letters,* p. 46, corroborates the dean's proposed etymology. It occurs in a letter to Dr. Martin Lister, May 7, 1669. " Totum corpus copiosâ et densâ pinguedine (piscatores *blubber* vocant), duorum plus minus digitorum crassitie undique integebatur, immediate sub cute, et supra carnem musculosam sita, ut in porcis; ob quam rationem, et quod porcorum grunnitum quadantenus imitetur, *porpesse*,—i. e. *porcum piscem,* dictum eum existimo."

other cetaceous animals, as Scaliger plainly affirmeth; *Corpus habet non magis curvum quàm reliqui pisces.* As ocular enquiry informeth; and as, unto such as have not had the opportunity to behold them, their proper portraits will discover in Rondeletius, Gesner, and Aldrovandus. And as indeed is deducible from pictures themselves; for though they be drawn repandous, or convexedly crooked in one piece, yet the dolphin that carrieth Arion[7] is concavously inverted, and hath its spine depressed in another. And answerably hereunto may we behold them differently bowed in medals, and the dolphins of Tarus and Fulius do make another flexure from that of Commodus and Agrippa.[8]

And therefore what is delivered of their incurvity, must either be taken emphatically, that is, not really, but in appearance; which happeneth when they leap above water and suddenly shoot down again: which is a fallacy in vision, whereby straight bodies in a sudden motion protruded obliquely downward appear to the eye crooked; and this is the construction of Bellonius: or, if it be taken really, it must not universally and perpetually; that is, not when they swim and remain in their proper figures, but only when they leap, or impetuously whirl their bodies any way; and this is the opinion of Gesnerus. Or lastly, it may be taken neither really nor emphatically, but only emblematically; for being the hieroglyphick of celerity,[9] and swifter than other animals,

---

[7] *yet the dolphin that carrieth Arion.*] "The Persian authors of high antiquity say, that the *delfin* will take on his back persons in danger of being drowned, from whence comes the fable of Arion. The word is derived from דלף *stillare, fluere*, delf; because the dolphin was considered as the king of the sea, and Neptune a monarch represented under the image of this fish. Dolphins were the symbols of maritime towns and cities. See Spanheim, 4to. 141, ed. 1671."—*Dr. S. Weston's Specimen of the Conformity of the European with the Oriental Languages, &c.* 8vo. 1803, pp. 75, 76. See also *Alciati Emblem.* xc.

[8] *And answerably, &c.*] First added in 3rd edition.

[9] *the hieroglyphick of celerity.*] Sylvanus Morgan in his *Sphere of Gentry* (fol. 1661), p. 69, says that the dolphin is the hieroglyphick of society! "there being no fish else that loves the company of men."

"Some authors, more especially the ancients, have asserted that dolphins have a lively and natural affection towards the human species, with which they are easily led to familiarize. They have recounted many marvellous stories on this subject. All that is known with certainty is, that when they perceive a ship at sea, they rush in a crowd

men best expressed their velocity by incurvity, and under some figure of a bow; and in this sense probably do heralds also receive it, when, from a dolphin extended, they distinguish a dolphin embowed.

And thus also must that picture be taken of a dolphin clasping an anchor;[1] that is, not really, as is by most conceived out of affection unto man, conveying the anchor unto the ground; but emblematically, according as Pierius hath expressed it, the swiftest animal conjoined with that heavy body, implying that common moral, *festina lentè*: and that celerity should always be contempered with cunctation.

CHAPTER III.

Of the Picture of a Grasshopper.

THERE is also among us a common description and picture of a grasshopper, as may be observed in the pictures of emblematists, in the coats of several families, and as the word *cicada* is usually translated in dictionaries. Wherein to speak strictly, if by this word grasshopper, we understand that animal which is implied by τέττιξ with the Greeks, and by *cicada* with the Latins, we may with safety affirm the picture is widely mistaken, and that for aught enquiry can inform, there is no such insect in England.[2] Which how

before it, surround it, and express their confidence by rapid, varied, and repeated evolutions, sometimes bounding, leaping, and manœuvering in all manner of ways; sometimes performing complicated circumvolutions, and exhibiting a degree of grace, agility, dexterity, and strength, which is perfectly astonishing. Perhaps however they follow the track of vessels with no other view than the hopes of preying on something that may fall from them."—*Cuvier, by Griffith.*

[1] *a dolphin clasping an anchor.*] The device of the family of Manutius, celebrated as learned printers at Venice and Rome. See *Alciati Emblem.* cxliv.

[2] *no such insect in England.*] It is perfectly true that, till recently, no species of the true Linnæan Cicadæ (*Tettigonia*, Fab.) had been discovered in Great Britain. About twenty years since, I had the pleasure of adding this classical and most interesting genus to the British Fauna. Having, about that time, engaged Mr. Daniel Bydder (a weaver in Spitalfields, and a very enthusiastic entomologist) to collect for me in the New Forest, Hampshire, I received from him thence

paradoxical soever, upon a strict enquiry, will prove undeniable truth.

For first, that animal which the French term *sauterelle*, we a grasshopper, and which under this name is commonly described by us, is named "Ακρις by the Greeks, by the Latins *locusta*, and by ourselves in proper speech a locust; as in the diet of John Baptist, and in our translation, " the locusts have no king, yet go they forth all of them by bands."* Again, between the *cicada* and that we call a grasshopper the differences are very many, as may be observed in themselves, or their descriptions in Matthiolus, Aldrovandus, and Muffetus. For first, they are differently cucullated or capuched upon the head and back, and in the *cicadæ* the eyes are more prominent: the locusts have *antennæ* or long horns before, with a long falcation or forcipated tail behind: and being ordained for saltation, their hinder legs do far exceed the other. The locust or our grasshopper hath teeth, the *cicada* none at all; nor any mouth, according unto Aristotle.[3] The *cicada* is most upon trees; and lastly, the

* Proverbs xxx.

many valuable insects from time to time, and at length, to my surprise and great satisfaction, a pair of CICADÆ! Mr. John Curtis (since deservedly well known as the author of *British Entomology*) was then residing with me as draughtsman; and no doubt our united examinations were diligently bestowed to find the little stranger among the described species of the continent; but in vain. I quite forget whether we bestowed a MS. name; probably not; as scarcely hoping that the first species discovered to be indigenous, would also prove to be peculiar to our country, and be distinguished by the national appellation of *Cicada* ANGLICA. Yet so it has proved: Mr. Samouelle, I believe, first gave it that name; and Mr. Curtis has given an exquisite figure, and full description of it, in the 9th vol. of his *British Entomology*, No. 392. I cannot however speak in so high terms of his account of its original discovery. I cannot understand why he has thus drily noticed it: " *C. Anglica* was first discovered in the New Forest about twenty years ago." I should have supposed that it might have given him some pleasure to attach to his narrative the name of an old friend, from whom he had received early and valuable assistance, and to whom he was indebted for his acquaintance with the art he has so long and so successfully pursued. At all events he ought to have recorded the name of the poor man by whose industry and perseverance the discovery was effected.

[3] *The locust, &c.*] Both the *locustæ* and *cicadæ* are furnished with teeth—if by that term we are to understand *mandibulæ* and *maxillæ*. But in *cicadæ* they are not so obvious; being enclosed in the labium. This conformation probably led Aristotle to say they had no mouth.

frittinnitus, or proper note thereof, is far more shrill than that of the locust, and its life so short in summer, that for provision it needs not have recourse unto the providence of the pismire in winter.

And therefore where the cicada must be understood, the pictures of heralds and emblematists are not exact, nor is it safe to adhere unto the interpretation of dictionaries, and we must with candour make out our own translations; for in the plague of Egypt, Exodus x., the word Ἀκρίς is translated a locust, but in the same sense and subject, Wisdom xvi., it is translated a grasshopper; " for them the bitings of grasshoppers and flies killed;" whereas we have declared before the cicada hath no teeth, but is conceived to live upon dew; and the possibility of its subsistence is disputed by Licetus. Hereof I perceive Muffetus hath taken notice, dissenting from Langius and Lycosthenes, while they deliver the *cicadæ* destroyed the fruits in Germany, where that insect is not found, and therefore concludeth, *Tam ipsos quàm alios deceptos fuisse autumo, dum locustas cicadas esse vulgari errore crederent.*

And hereby there may be some mistake in the due dispensation of medicines desumed from this animal, particularly of *diatettigon*, commended by Ætius, in the affections of the kidneys. It must be likewise understood with some restriction what hath been affirmed by Isidore, and yet delivered by many, that cicades are bred out of cuckoo-spittle or woodsear, that is, that spumous frothy dew or exudation, or both, found upon plants, especially about the joints of lavender and rosemary, observable with us about the latter end of May. For here the true cicada is not bred; but certain it is, that out of this, some kind of locust doth proceed, for herein may be discovered a little insect of a festucine or pale green, resembling in all parts a locust, or what we call a grasshopper.[4]

---

[4] *cicades are bred, &c.*] Here is another error. The froth spoken of is always found to contain the *larva* of a little skipping insect, frequently mis-called a *cicada*, but properly *cercopis;* allied in form to *cicada*, and of the same order, viz., *homoptera*, but very distinct in generic character, and especially without the power of sound. It has no great resemblance to *locustæ*, which belong to a distinct order, viz., *orthoptera*.

Lastly, the word itself is improper, and the term grasshopper not appliable unto the cicada; for therein the organs of motion are not contrived for saltation, nor have the hinder legs of such extension, as is observable in salient animals, and such as move by leaping. Whereto the locust is very well conformed, for therein the legs behind are longer than all the body, and make at the second joint acute angles, at a considerable advancement above their backs.

The mistake therefore with us might have its original from a defect in our language, for having not the insect with us, we have not fallen upon its proper name, and so make use of a term common unto it and the locust; whereas other countries have proper expressions for it. So the Italian calls it *cicada*, the Spaniard *cigarra*, and the French *cigale*; all which appellations conform unto the original, and properly express this animal. Whereas our word is borrowed from the Saxon gærsthoop, which our forefathers, who never beheld the cicada, used for that insect which we yet call a grasshopper.[5]

CHAPTER IV.

Of the Picture of the Serpent tempting Eve.

IN the picture of paradise, and delusion of our first parents, the serpent is often described with human visage,[6] not unlike unto Cadmus or his wife in the act of their metamorphosis. Which is not a mere pictorial contrivance or invention of the picturer, but an ancient tradition and conceived reality, as it stands delivered by Beda and authors of some antiquity,[7]

[5] *Whereas our word, &c.*] This sentence was first added in 6th edition.

[6] *visage.*] See Munster's Hebrew Bible, where in the letter which begins the first Ψ the serpent is made with a Virgin's face.— *Wr.*

In Munster's Hebrew and Latin Bible (Basil, 1535, *ex Off. Bebeliana*), at the commencement of the Psalms, is the initial letter B, which is a wood-cut of Adam, Eve, and the serpent between them, with the face of a virgin.

[7] *antiquity.*] See vol. i. p. 57, where he quotes Basil saying, that the serpent went upright and spake. 'Tis probable (and thwarteth noe truth) that the serpent spake to Eve. Does not the text expressly saye soe? The devil had as much power then as now, and yf now he can take upon him the forme of an angel of light, why not then the face of a humane creature as well as the voice of man ?— *Wr.*

that is, that Satan appeared not unto Eve in the naked form of a serpent, but with a virgin's head, that thereby he might become more acceptable, and his temptation find the easier entertainment. Which nevertheless is a conceit not to be admitted, and the plain and received figure is with better reason embraced.

For first, as Pierius observeth from Barcephas, the assumption of human shape had proved a disadvantage unto Satan, affording not only a suspicious amazement in Eve,[8] before the fact, in beholding a third humanity beside herself and Adam, but leaving some excuse unto the woman, which afterward the man took up with lesser reason, that is, to have been deceived by another like herself.

Again, there is no inconvenience in the shape assumed, or any considerable impediment that it might disturb that performance in the common form of a serpent. For whereas it is conceived the woman must needs be afraid thereof, and rather fly than approach it, it was not agreeable unto the condition of paradise and state of innocency therein; if in that place, as most determine, no creature was hurtful or terrible unto man, and those destructive effects they now discover succeeded the curse, and came in with thorns and briars; and therefore Eugubinus (who affirmeth this serpent was a basilisk) incurreth no absurdity, nor need we infer that Eve should be destroyed immediately upon that vision. For noxious animals could offend them no more in the garden than Noah in the ark; as they peaceably received their names, so they friendly possessed their natures, and were their conditions destructive unto each other, they were not so unto man, whose constitutions then were antidotes, and needed not fear poisons; and if (as most conceive) there

[8] *Eve.*] Eve might easier entertaine a suspicious amazement to heare a serpent speake in a humane voyce, than to heare a humane voyce in a humane shape; nor was itt more wonder for Sathan to assume one than both. It suited better with his crafte to deliver his wile by a face suitable to the voice of man, and since we believe the one, we may without error believe the other. But itt is safest to believe what we finde recorded of the human voyce, and leave the other to Him who thought not fit to reveale any more. Wee see the fathers differ in opinion, and there is enough on either side to refute the scorne of Julian, who payd deare inoughe for his atheistical, or rather anti-theisticall blasphemye.—*Wr.*

were but two created of every kind, they could not at that time destroy either man or themselves, for this had frustrated the command of multiplication, destroyed a species, and imperfected the creation; and therefore also if Cain were the first man born, with him entered, not only the act, but the first power of murder, for before that time neither could the serpent nor Adam destroy Eve, nor Adam and Eve each other, for that had overthrown the intention of the world, and put its creator to act the sixth day over again.

Moreover, whereas in regard of speech, and vocal conference with Eve, it may be thought he would rather assume an human shape and organs, than the improper form of a serpent, it implies no material impediment. Nor need we to wonder how he contrived a voice out of the mouth of a serpent, who hath done the like out of the belly of a Pythonissa, and the trunk of an oak, as he did for many years at Dodona.

Lastly, whereas it might be conceived[9] that an human

---

[9] *conceived*.] Itt might wel bee conceived (and soe it seemes itt was) oy St. Basil, that a virgin's head (hee does not saye a humane shape) was fittest for this intention of speakinge, itt being most probable Eve would be more amazed to heare such a creature as a serpent speake with a humane voyce, then to heare a human voyce passe through the mouth of a virgin face. To hear a voice without a head must needs (as the subtile serpent knew full well) have started in Eve either the supposition of a causeles miracle, or the suspition of an imposture; therefore to cut off those scruples, which might have prevented and frustrated his ayme, 'tis most probable the subtile tempter assumed the face as well as the voice of a virgin to conveigh that temptation which he supposed Eve would greedily entertain.

Julius Scaliger, that magazin of all various learninge, in his 183rd exercitation and 4th section, speaking of certaine strange kinds of serpents, reports that in Malabar, there are serpents 8 foote long, of a horrible aspect, but harmless unless they bee provoked. These he cals boy-lovers (pæderotas) for that they will for manye houres together stand bolt upright gazing on the boyes at their sportes, never offring to hurte any of them.

These, saithe he, while they glide on the ground are like other serpents or eeles (like conger eeles), but raising themselves upright they spread themselves into such a corpulent breadthe, that had they feet they would seeme to be men, and therefore he cals them by a coigned name, ἐγχελανθρώπους, eele-like men, though hee might more properly call them ὀφιανθρώπους, dragon-like men. Now though we can yeeld noe greater beleefe to this story then the Portuguez that traffique thither deserve, yet bycause the world owes many excellent discoveryes

shape was fitter for this enterprise, it being more than probable she would be amazed to hear a serpent speak; some

of hidden truths to his indefatigable diligence and learned labors, seldome taxed for fabulous assertions, why may we not think that itt was this kinde of serpent, whose shape Satan assumed when he spake to Eve.* For since Moses tels us that God permitted the serpent to deceive our grandmother by faigning the voyce of man, wee may reasonably acquit St. Basil of error, or offring violence to trueth, that hee tooke it as granted by a paritye of like reason, that the serpent would rather assume such a face and appearance of humane forme as might sute with a humane voyce, at least would frame a humane visage as well as a human tounge, which is but a parte in the head of man, for which the head (rather then for any other sense) seemes to have been made by God, that the spirits of men (which till they discover themselves by language cannot bee understood) might by the benefit of this admirable instrument, have mutual commerce and intelligence, and conveighe their inwarde conceptions each to other. Surely yf every such a strange serpent as this which Scaliger describes were scene in the world, we must perforce grant that they are some of that kinde which God at first created soe, and that Satan subtily choose to enter into that kinde which before the curse naturally went upright (*as they say the basiliske now does*) and could soe easily, soe nearly represent the appearance and show of man not only in gate but in voyce as the Scripture speakes. That they have no feete makes soe much the more for the conjecture, and that however itt seemes this kinde of serpent (which Satan used as an instrument of his fraud) did originally goe upwright, and can yet frame himselfe into that posture, yet by God's just doome is now forced to creep on his belly in the duste; where though they strike at our heele, they are liable to have their heade bruised and trampled on by the foote of man.— *Wr.*

In one of the illustrations to Cædmon's Paraphrase, mentioned p. 14, I find the serpent standing "bolt upright," receiving his sentence, and another figure of him lying on the ground, do indicate his condemnation to subsequent *reptility*. Some critics have complained of the painters for representing him without feet in his interview with Eve, whereas, say they, his creeping on his belly was inflicted on him as a punishment. Had those critics been acquainted with Professor Mayer's assertion, that rudimental feet are found in almost all the serpent tribe, they would doubtless have regarded it as a confirmation of their opinion, and would have contended that these imperfect and unserviceable rudiments of feet were all the traces left to them of those locomotive powers which this, as well as other vertebrated animals, had originally enjoyed.

Dr. Adam Clarke gives a very long and elaborate article on the temptation of Eve. His opinion is that the tempter was an *ape;* he builds

---

* See what I noted long since on Gen. iii. 14, to this purpose in the Geneva Bible.

conceive she might not yet be certain that only man was privileged with speech, and being in the novity of the creation, and inexperience of all things, might not be affrighted to hear a serpent speak. Besides, she might be ignorant of their natures, who was not versed in their names, as being not present at the general survey of animals when Adam assigned unto every one a name concordant unto its nature.

his hypothesis on the fact that the Hebrew word (*nachash*, Gen. iii. 1) is nearly the same with an Arabic word, signifying an *ape* and THE DEVIL! He thus sums up: "In this account we find, 1. That whatever this *nachash* was, he stood at the *head* of all inferior animals for wisdom and understanding. 2. That he *walked erect*, for this is necessarily implied in his punishment—*on thy belly* (i. e. on all fours) *shalt thou go*. 3. That he was *endued with the gift of speech*, for a conversation is here related between him and the woman. 4. That he was also endued with the *gift of reason*, for we find him reasoning and disputing with Eve. 5. That these things were *common to this creature*, the woman no doubt having often seen him walk erect, talk, and reason, and therefore she testifies no kind of surprise when he accosts her in the language related in the text." Granting, for a moment, the Doctor's five positions, I would ask, does he mean that the ape is a creature which *now* answers the description? Most certainly it does not, any more than the serpent. If on the other hand he means that the creature, through whom Satan tempted Eve, had *previously* possessed those advantages, but *lost them* as a punishment of that offence, then why not suppose it to have been a serpent, or any other creature, as well as the ape? The theory itself stultifies any attempt to discover the tempter among creatures *now* in existence, because we are required to suppose their nature and habits to have totally changed. The serpent certainly has one claim, which the ape has not, namely, that its present mode of going is (in accordance with the Scriptural description) *on its belly;* which, with deference to the learned Doctor, "going on all fours" is not, unless he can justify what he in fact says, that *quadrupeds* and *reptiles* move alike! Moreover, his selection is specially unfortunate in this very respect, that of all animals the ape *now* approaches most nearly to the human mode of walking, and exhibits therefore the most incomplete example of the fulfilment of the curse—"*on thy belly shalt thou go*."

Hadrian Beverland, in his *Peccatum Originale*, 12mo. 1676, has published his strange speculations as to the NATURE of the temptation, to which our mother yielded. But after all, neither as one point nor another, which has not been clearly revealed, shall we be likely either to obtain or communicate any useful information. The indulgence of a prurient and speculative imagination on points which, not having been disclosed, cannot be discovered, and the knowledge of which would serve no good purpose, were far better restrained. We know, alas, that what constituted sin originally, has ever been and ever will be its heinous feature in the sight of the Great Lawgiver—viz., disobedience to his known and understood commands.

Nor is this only my opinion, but the determination of Lombard and Tostatus, and also the reply of Cyril unto the objection of Julian, who compared this story unto the fables of the Greeks.

CHAPTER V.

Of the Picture of Adam and Eve with Navels.

ANOTHER mistake there may be in the picture of our first parents, who after the manner of their posterity are both delineated with a navel; and this is observable not only in ordinary and stained pieces, but in the authentic draughts of Urbin, Angelo, and others.[1] Which notwithstanding cannot be allowed, except we impute that unto the first cause, which we impose not on the second, or what we deny unto Nature, we impute unto naturity itself, that is, that in the first and most accomplished piece, the Creator affected superfluities, or ordained parts without use or office.[2]

[1] *and others.*] It is observable in the rude figures of Adam and Eve, among the illuminations of Cædmon's *Metrical Paraphrase of Scripture History*, engraved in the 24th vol. of the *Archæologia*. But worse mistakes have been committed in depicting "our first parents." In the gallery of the convent of Jesuits, at Lisbon, there is a fine picture of Adam in paradise, dressed (*qu. after the fall?*) in blue breeches with silver buckles, and Eve with a striped petticoat. In the distance appears a procession of capuchins bearing the cross.

[2] *Which notwithstanding, &c.*] It seems to have been the intention of our author, in this somewhat obscure sentence, to object, that, in supposing Adam to have been formed with a navel, we suppose a superfluity in that which was produced by nature (*naturity*), while in nature herself we affirm there is nothing superfluous, or useless. It is, however, somewhat hazardous to pronounce that useless whose office may not be very obvious to us. Who will venture to point out the office of the *mammæ* in the male sex? or to say wherefore some of the serpent tribes are provided with the rudiments of feet which can scarcely, if at all, be of any use to them?—a fact which has been asserted recently by a German naturalist of distinction, Dr. Mayer, as the result of long and very extensive anatomical examination of the principal families of the serpents. He thereon proposes a new division of the order,—into PHÆNOPTERA, those snakes whose rudimental feet are externally visible, and comprising *Boa, Python, Eryx, Clothonia,* and *Tortrix;* CRYPTOPODA, in which the bony rudiments are entirely concealed beneath the skin, containing *Anguis, Typhlops,* and *Amphisbæna;* and CHONDROPODA and

For the use of the navel is to continue the infant unto the mother, and by the vessels thereof to convey its aliment and sustentation. The vessels whereof it consisteth, are the umbilical vein, which is a branch of the porta, and implanted in the liver of the infant; two arteries likewise arising from the iliacal branches, by which the infant receiveth the purer portion of blood and spirits from the mother; and lastly, the *urachos* or ligamental passage derived from the bottom of the bladder, whereby it dischargeth the waterish and urinary part of its aliment. Now upon the birth, when the infant forsaketh the womb, although it dilacerate, and break the involving membranes, yet do these vessels hold, and by the mediation thereof the infant is connected unto the womb, not only before, but awhile also after the birth. These therefore the midwife cutteth off, contriving them into a knot close unto the body of the infant; from whence ensueth that tortuosity or complicated nodosity we usually call the navel; occasioned by the colligation of vessels before mentioned. Now the navel being a part, not precedent, but subsequent unto generation, nativity, or parturition, it cannot be well imagined at the creation or extraordinary formation of Adam, who immediately issued from the artifice of God; nor also that of Eve, who was not solemnly begotten, but suddenly framed, and anomalously proceeded from Adam.

And if we be led into conclusions that Adam had also this

APODA, in which the rudiments are scarcely, or not at all, observable.—*Nova Acta Acad. Cæsar. Naturæ Curiosorum*, tom. xii. p. 2.

Respecting the singular subject of discussion in this chapter; it appears to me that not only Adam and Eve, but all species, both of the animal, vegetable, and mineral kingdoms, were created at once in their perfect state, and therefore all exhibiting such remaining traces of a less perfect state, as those species, in their maturity, retain. If so, Adam was created with the marks of an earlier stage of existence, though he had never passed through that stage.

Sir Thomas's opinion is cited and adopted by Dr. John Bulwer, in his most curious work, entitled *Anthropometamorphosis: Man Transformed: or the Artificial Changling, Historically Presented*, &c. 4to. 1653, p. 401. In the same work (p. 492), Dr. B. also discusses at some length Sir Thomas's chapter on pigmies (c. xi. book IV.). — See *Rel. Med.*, where Adam is called "the man without a navel." Ross deems the part in question to have been intended by the Creator merely for ornament; in support of which opinion he cites Canticles vii. 2!!

part, because we behold the same in ourselves, the inference is not reasonable; for if we conceive the way of his formation, or of the first animals, did carry in all points a strict conformity unto succeeding productions, we might fall into imaginations that Adam was made without teeth; or that he ran through those notable alterations in the vessels of the heart, which the infant suffereth after birth: we need not dispute whether the egg or bird were first; and might conceive that dogs were created blind, because we observe they are littered so with us. Which to affirm, is to confound, at least to regulate creation unto generation, the first acts of God, unto the second of nature; which were determined in that general indulgence, increase and multiply, produce or propagate each other; that is, not answerably in all points, but in a prolonged method according to seminal progression. For the formation of things at first was different from their generation after; and although it had nothing to precede it, was aptly contrived for that which should succeed it. And therefore though Adam were framed without this part, as having no other womb than that of his proper principles, yet was not his posterity without the same; for the seminality of his fabrick contained the power thereof; and was endued with the science of those parts whose predestinations upon succession it did accomplish.

All the navel, therefore, and conjunctive part we can suppose in Adam, was his dependency on his Maker, and the connexion he must needs have unto heaven, who was the Son of God. For, holding no dependence on any preceding efficient but God, in the act of his production there may be conceived some connexion, and Adam to have been in a momental navel with his Maker.[3] And although from his carnality and corporal existence, the conjunction seemeth no nearer than of causality and effect; yet in his immortal and diviner part he seemed to hold a nearer coherence, and an umbilicality even with God himself. And so indeed although the propriety of this part be found but in some animals, and many species there are which have no navel at all; yet is there one link and common connexion, one general ligament, and

[3] *in a momental navel with his Maker.*] Momental; *important.* "Substantially (or in an important sense), in a state of connexion with his Maker."

necessary obligation of all whatever unto God. Whereby, although they act themselves at distance, and seem to be at loose, yet do they hold a continuity with their Maker. Which catenation or conserving union, whenever his pleasure shall divide, let go, or separate, they shall fall from their existence, essence, and operations; in brief, they must retire unto their primitive nothing, and shrink into their chaos again.

They who hold the egg was before the bird, prevent this doubt in many other animals, which also extendeth unto them. For birds are nourished by umbilical vessels, and the navel is manifest sometimes a day or two after exclusion. The same is probable in all oviparous exclusions, if the lesser part of eggs must serve for the formation, the greater part for nutriment. The same is made out in the eggs of snakes; and is not improbable in the generation of porwiggles or tadpoles, and may be also true in some vermiparous exclusions: although (as we have observed in the daily progress in some) the whole maggot is little enough to make a fly, without any part remaining.[4]

CHAPTER VI.

Of the Pictures of the Jews and Eastern Nations, at their Feasts, especially our Saviour at the Passover.

CONCERNING the pictures of the Jews, and eastern nations at their feasts, concerning the gesture of our Saviour at the passover, who is usually described sitting upon a stool or bench at a square table, in the midst of the twelve, many make great doubt; and (though they concede a table gesture) will hardly allow this usual way of session.[5]

Wherein, restraining no man's enquiry, it will appear that accubation, or lying down at meals, was a gesture used by very many nations. That the Persians used it, beside the

[4] *They who hold, &c.*] This paragraph was first added in the 2nd edition.

[5] *session.*] See Fenelon's Letter to the French Academy, § 8, p. 231. Glasg. 1750.—*Jeff.* I give this reference, though I have not been able to avail myself of it.

testimony of humane writers, is deducible from that passage in Esther:* "That when the king returned into the place of the banquet of wine, Haman was fallen upon the bed whereon Esther was." That the Parthians used it, is evident from Athenæus, who delivereth out of Possidonius, that their king lay down at meals on an higher bed than others.⁶ That Cleopatra thus entertained Anthony, the same author manifesteth, when he saith, she prepared twelve tricliniums. That it was in use among the Greeks, the word *triclinium* implieth, and the same is also declarable from many places in the *Symposiacks* of Plutarch. That it was not out of fashion in the days of Aristotle, he declareth in his *Politicks;* when among the institutionary rules of youth, he adviseth they might not be permitted to hear iambicks and tragedies before they were admitted unto discumbency or lying along with others at their meals. That the Romans used this gesture at repast, beside many more, is evident from Lipsius, Mercurialis, Salmasius, and Ciaconius, who have expressly and distinctly treated hereof.

Now of their accumbing places, the one was called *stibadion* and *sigma*, carrying the figure of an half-moon, and of an uncertain capacity, whereupon it received the name of *hexaclinon, octoclinon*, according unto that of Martial—

> Accipe Lunatâ scriptum testudine sigma:
> Octo capit, veniat quisquis amicus erit.

Hereat in several ages the left and right hand were the principal places, and the most honourable person, if he were not master of the feast, possessed one of those rooms. The other was termed *triclinium*, that is, three beds about a table, as may be seen in the figures thereof, and particularly in the *Rhamnusian triclinium*, set down by Mercurialis.† The customary use hereof was probably deduced from the frequent use of bathing, after which they commonly retired to bed, and refected themselves with repast; and so that custom by degrees changed their cubiculary beds into discubitory, and introduced a fashion to go from the baths unto these.

As for their gesture or position, the men lay down leaning

* Esther vii.   † *De Arte Gymnastica.*

⁶ *That the Persians, &c.*] This sentence was first added in the 2nd edition.

on their left elbow, their back being advanced by some pillow or soft substance; the second lay so with his back towards the first, that his head attained about his bosom;[7] and the rest in the same order. For women, they sat sometimes distinctly with their sex, sometimes promiscuously with men, according to affection or favour, as is delivered by Juvenal.

Gremio jacuit nova nupta mariti.

And by Suetonius, of Caligula, that at his feasts he placed his sisters, with whom he had been incontinent, successively in order below him.

Again, as their beds were three, so the guests did not usually exceed that number in every one, according to the ancient laws, and proverbial observations to begin with the Graces, and make up their feasts with the Muses; and therefore it was remarkable in the Emperor Lucius Verus, that he lay down with twelve, which was, saith Julius Capitolinus, *præter exempla majorum*, not according to the custom of his predecessors, except it were at public and nuptial suppers. The regular number was also exceeded in the last supper, whereat there were no less than thirteen, and in no place fewer than ten, for as Josephus delivereth, it was not lawful to celebrate the passover with fewer than that number.[8]

Lastly, for the disposing and ordering of the persons; the first and middle beds were for the guests, the third and lowest for the master of the house and his family, he always lying in the first place of the last bed, that is, next the middle bed, but if the wife or children were absent, their rooms were supplied by the *umbræ*, or hangers on, according to that of Juvenal.[9]

—— Locus est et pluribus umbris.

For the guests, the honourablest place in every bed was the first, excepting the middle or second bed, wherein the most honourable guest of the feast was placed in the last place,

---

[7] *bosom.*] See note 4, p. 23.

[8] *The regular number, &c.*] This sentence first added in 2nd edition.

[9] *Juvenal.*] (Not Juvenal, but Horace), *Epist.* lib. i. 8. l. 28. See also *Hor. Sat.* ii. 8, 22: "— quos Mæcenas adduxerat umbras," — "Porro et conviva ad cœnam dicitur σκιὰν suum adducere, cum amicum aliquem non invitatum secum adducit."—*Plut.* 7, 6.

because by that position he might be next the master of the feast.* For the master lying in the first of the last bed, and the principal guest in the last place of the second, they must needs be next each other, as this figure doth plainly declare, and whereby we may apprehend the feast of Perpenna made unto Sertorius, described by Sallustius, whose words we shall thus read with Salmasius: *Igitur discubuere, Sertorius inferior in medio lecto, supra Fabius; Antonius in summo; Infra scriba Sertorii Versius; alter scriba Mecænas in imo, medius inter Tarquitium et dominum Perpennam.*

[Diagram of triclinium seating arrangement, with labels including *Locus Summus*, *Supra*, *Medius*, *Ultimus Honoratissimus*, *Infra*, *L. Fabius (Locus Vacuus) Sertorius*, *Medius Lectus*, *Versius*, *Ultimus Infra*, *(Locus Vacuus) Summus Lectus*, *Medius*, *Antonius*, *Primus Locu. seu Summus Supra*, *Perpenna Dominus*, *Locus Summus seu Domini Supra*, *Mecænas Imus Lectus*, *Medius*, *Tarquitius*, *Ultimus*.]

At this feast there were but seven, the middle places of the highest and middle bed being vacant, and hereat was Sertorius the general, and principal guest slain; and so may we make out what is delivered by Plutarch in his life, that lying on his back and raising himself up, Perpenna cast him-

* *Jul. Scalig. Familiarum Exercitationum Problema* 1.

self upon his stomach, which he might very well do, being master of the feast, and lying next unto him; and thus also from this tricliniary disposure, we may illustrate that obscure expression of Seneca; that the north wind was in the middle, the north-east on the higher side, and the north-west on the lower. For as appeareth in the circle of the winds, the north-east will answer the bed of Antonius, and the north-west that of Perpenna.

That the custom of feasting upon beds was in use among the Hebrews, many deduce from Ezekiel,* "Thou sattest upon a stately bed, and a table prepared before it." The custom of discalceation or putting off their shoes at meals, is conceived to confirm the same; as by that means keeping their beds clean; and therefore they had a peculiar charge to eat the passover with their shoes on; which injunction were needless, if they used not to put them off. However it were in times of high antiquity, probable it is that in after ages they conformed unto the fashions of the Assyrians and eastern nations, and lastly of the Romans, being reduced by Pompey unto a provincial subjection.[1]

That this discumbency at meals was in use in the days of our Saviour, is conceived probable from several speeches of his expressed in that phrase, even unto common auditors, as Luke xiv.: *Cum invitatus fueris ad nuptias, non discumbas in primo loco;* and, besides many more, Matthew xxiii., when reprehending the Scribes and Pharisees, he saith, *Amant protoclisias, id est, primos recubitus in cœnis, et protocathedrias, sive, primas cathedras, in synagogis;* wherein the terms are very distinct, and by an antithesis do plainly distinguish the posture of sitting, from this of lying on beds. The consent of the Jews with the Romans in other ceremonies and rites of feasting makes probable their conformity in this. The Romans washed, were anointed, and wore a cenatory garment: and that the same was practised by the Jews, is deducible from that expostulation of our Saviour with Simon,† that he washed not his feet, nor anointed his head with oil; the common civilities at festival entertainments: and that expression of his concerning the cenatory or wedding gar-

---

* Ezek. xxiii.   † Luke vii.

However it were, &c.] This sentence was first added in 2nd edition

ment;* and as some conceive of the linen garment of the young man, or St. John; which might be the same he wore the night before at the last supper.[2]

That they used this gesture at the passover, is more than probable from the testimony of Jewish writers, and particularly of Ben-Maimon recorded by Scaliger, *De Emendatione temporum.* After the second cup according to the institution, the son asketh, what meaneth this service?† then he that maketh the declaration, saith, how different is this night from all other nights; for all other nights we wash but once, but this night twice; all other we eat leavened or unleavened bread, but this only leavened; all other we eat flesh roasted, boiled, or baked, but this only roasted; all other nights we eat together lying or sitting, but this only lying along. And this posture they used as a token of rest and security which they enjoyed, far different from that at the eating of the passover in Egypt.

That this gesture was used when our Saviour eat the passover, is not conceived improbable from the words whereby the Evangelists express the same, that is, ἀναπίπτειν, ἀνακεῖσθαι, κατακεῖσθαι, ἀνακλιθῆναι, which terms do properly signify this gesture, in Aristotle, Athenæus, Euripides, Sophocles, and all humane authors; and the like we meet with in the paraphrastical expression of Nonnus.

Lastly, if it be not fully conceded, that this gesture was used at the passover, yet that it was observed at the last supper seems almost incontrovertible: for at this feast or cenatory convention, learned men make more than one supper, or at least many parts thereof. The first was that legal one of the passover, or eating of the paschal lamb with bitter herbs, and ceremonies described by Moses.‡ Of this it is said, "Then when the even was come, he sat down with the twelve."§ This is supposed when it is said, that the supper being ended, our Saviour arose, took a towel and washed the disciples' feet. The second was common and domestical, consisting of ordinary and undefined provisions; of this it may be said, that our Saviour took his garment, and sat down again, after he had washed the disciples' feet, and performed

* Matt. xxii.   † Exod. xii.   ‡ Matt. xxvi.   § John xiii.

[2] *the consent of the Jews, &c.*] First added in 2nd edition.

the preparative civilities of suppers; at this 'tis conceived the sop was given unto Judas, the original word implying some broth or decoction, not used at the passover. The third or latter part was eucharistical, which began at the breaking and blessing of the bread, according to that of Matthew, "And as they were eating, Jesus took bread and blessed it."

Now although, at the passover or first supper, many have doubted this reclining posture, and some have affirmed that our Saviour stood, yet that he lay down at the other, the same men have acknowledged, as Chrysostom,* Theophylact, Austin, and many more. And if the tradition will hold, the position is unquestionable; for the very *triclinium* is to be seen at Rome, brought thither by Vespasian, and graphically set forth by Casalius.³

Thus may it properly be made out, what is delivered, John xiii.; *Erat recumbens unus ex discipulis ejus in sinu Jesu quem diligebat;* "Now there was leaning on Jesus' bosom one of his disciples whom Jesus loved;" which gesture will not so well agree unto the position of sitting, but is natural, and cannot be avoided in the laws of accubation.⁴ And the

De Veterum Ritibus.

³ *Lastly, if it be not, &c.*] This and the next paragraph were first added in the 2nd edition.

⁴ *which gesture, &c.*] I am not aware whether our author had any authority for saying that "the back was advanced by some pillow or soft substance." If it was so, John could not very conveniently have leaned back upon the bosom of his master. It seems probable that each person lay at an acute angle with the line of the table (as seems implied in the following quotation), in which case the head of John, as our author observes, p. 19, would have attained to about his master's bosom. It must also (as it seems to me) be supposed that the table was scarcely, if at all, higher than the level of the couch. I subjoin Godwin's description of the table, &c. "The table being placed in the middest, round about the table were certain beds, sometimes two, sometimes three, sometimes more, according to the number of the guests; upon these they lay down in manner as followeth: each bed contained three persons, sometimes more,—seldom or never *more* (qu. *fewer?*) If one lay upon the bed, then he rested the upper part of his body upon the left elbow, the lower part lying at length upon the bed: but if many lay on the bed, then the uppermost did lie at the bed's head, laying his feet behinde the second's back: in like manner the third or fourth did lye, each resting his head in the other's bosome. Thus John leaned on *Jesus' bosom.*"—*Moses and Aaron,* p. 93, 4to. 1667.

very same expression is to be found in Pliny, concerning the emperor Nerva and Veiento whom he favoured; *Cœnabat Nerva cum paucis, Veiento recumbebat propius atque etiam in sinu;* and from this custom arose the word ἐπιστήθιος, that is, a near and bosom friend. And therefore Casaubon* justly rejecteth Theophylact;[5] who not considering the ancient manner of decumbency, imputed this gesture of the beloved disciple unto rusticity, or an act of incivility. And thus also, have some conceived it may be more plainly made out what is delivered of Mary Magdalen, that she " stood at Christ's feet behind him weeping, and began to wash his feet with tears, and did wipe them with the hairs of her head."† Which actions, if our Saviour sat, she could not perform standing, and had rather stood behind his back than at his feet. And therefore it is not allowable, what is observable in many pieces, and even of Raphael Urbin, wherein Mary Magdalen is pictured before our Saviour washing his feet on her knees, which will not consist with the strict description and letter of the text.

Now, whereas this position may seem to be discountenanced by our translation, which usually renders it sitting, it cannot have that illation: for the French and Italian translations, expressing neither position of session nor recubation, do only say that he placed himself at the table; and when ours expresseth the same by sitting, it is in relation unto our custom, time, and apprehension. The like upon occasion is not unusual: so when it is said, Luke iv., πτύξας τὸ βιβλίον, and the Vulgate renders it, *cum plicâsset librum*, ours translateth it, he shut or closed the book; which is an expression proper unto the paginal books of our times, but not so agreeable unto volumes or rolling books, in use among the Jews, not only in elder times, but even unto this day. So when it is said, the Samaritan delivered unto the host twopence

* *Not. in Evang.* † Luke vii.

[5] *Theophylact.*] Theophylact, bishop of Bulgary, lived 930th yeare of Christe, in which time the empire being translated into Germanye, and the maner of lying at all meales translated into the maner of sitting, which was most used among the northern nations, gave the bishop occasion to taxe the Jewish and Roman forme of lying as uncouth and uncivil: every nation preferring their owne customes, and condemning all other as barbarians.—*Wr.*

for the pro ision of the Levite, and when our Saviour agreed with the labourers for a penny a day, in strict translation it should be seven-pence halfpenny, and is not to be conceived our common penny, the sixtieth part of an ounce. For the word in the original is δηνάριον, in Latin *denarius*, and with the Romans did value the eighth part of an ounce, which, after five shillings the ounce, amounteth unto seven-pence halfpenny of our money.

Lastly, whereas it might be conceived that they ate the passover, standing rather than sitting, or lying down, according to the institution, Exodus xii., "Thus shall you eat with your loins girded, your shoes on your feet, and your staff in your hand;" the Jews themselves reply, this was not required of succeeding generations, and was not observed but in the passover of Egypt. And so also many other injunctions were afterward omitted: as the taking up of the paschal lamb from the tenth day, the eating of it in their houses dispersed, the striking of the blood on the door-posts, and the eating thereof in haste; solemnities and ceremonies primitively enjoined, afterward omitted; as was also this of station: for the occasion ceasing, and being in security, they applied themselves unto gestures in use among them.

Now in what order of recumbency Christ and the disciples were disposed, is not so easily determined. Casalius, from the Lateran *triclinium*, will tell us, that there being thirteen, five lay down in the first bed, five in the last, and three in the middle bed; and that our Saviour possessed the upper place thereof. That John lay in the same bed seems plain, because he leaned on our Saviour's bosom. That Peter made the third in that bed, conjecture is made, because he beckoned unto John, as being next him, to ask of Christ who it was that should betray him? That Judas was not far off, seems probable, not only because he dipped in the same dish, but because he was so near that our Saviour could hand the sop unto him.[6]

[6] *Now in what order, &c.*] This paragraph was added in 2nd edit.

CHAPTER VII.

Of the Picture of our Saviour with Long Hair.

ANOTHER picture there is of our Saviour described with long hair,[7] according to the custom of the Jews, and his description sent by Lentulus unto the senate.[8] Wherein

[7] *Another picture, &c.*] A very beautiful head of our Saviour has recently been engraved in *mezzotint*, by J. Rogers. It is a copy from a gem, said to have been executed by order of Tiberius Cæsar, and subsequently sent to Pope Innocent VIII. by the emperor of the Turks as a ransom for his brother.

Another error has been noticed by some commentators in representing our Lord with a crown of long thorns, whereas it is supposed to have been made of the *acanthus*, or bears-foot, a prickly plant, very unlike a thorn. See Dr. Adam Clarke, *in loc.*

[8] *his description sent by Lentulus, &c.*] Or rather said to have been sent by Lentulus, &c.; for this letter is now known to have been a forgery. The supposed author was a Roman governor of Syria; of whom it was pretended that he was a follower of our Lord, and that he gave a description of his person in a letter to the senate. This was however obviously insupposable at a period when the governors of provinces addressed the emperor, and no longer the senate; to say nothing of the style, which is by no means Augustan. The fact is, as has been remarked to me, that when publick opinion had been made up as to the probable appearance of our Lord's person, this letter comes out to settle the point. In No. 7026-4 of the Harleian MSS. is preserved a copy of this letter, on vellum, in the beautiful handwriting of the celebrated German dwarf Math. Buchinger, which he sent to his patron, Lord Oxford. It contains also a portrait agreeing with the description given in the letter. This letter has been translated into English, and occurs, *Christ. Mag.* 1764, p. 455, and other places.

Perhaps the most celebrated of the reputed original portraits of the Redeemer is that said to have been received by Abgarus, king of Edessa, mentioned by Evagrius. Eusebius gives a letter sent by the said Abgar to Jesus Christ, professing the conviction which the Redeemer's miracles had wrought in his mind of the divine character of our Lord, and entreating him to come to Edessa and cure a disease under which the king had long laboured;—together with our Lord's answer, declining to come, but promising to send a disciple to heal the king. For these letters see Hone's *Apocryphal New Testament.* In his *Every-Day Book*, Jan. 13th, he gives a wood-cut of the portrait. In the *London Literary Gazette* of Nov. 29, 1834, is a much better account of the circumstance, in a review of *Baron Hubboff's History of Armenia*, published by the Oriental Translation Society. I subjoin his account of the picture. "Abgar sent a painter to take the likeness of th s Saviour,

indeed the hand of the painter is not accusable, but the judgment of the common spectator: conceiving he observed this fashion of his hair, because he was a Nazarite; and confounding a Nazarite by vow, with those by birth or education.

The Nazarite by vow is declared, Numbers vi.; and was to refrain three things, drinking of wine, cutting the hair, and approaching unto the dead; and such an one was Sampson. Now that our Saviour was a Nazarite after this kind, we have no reason to determine; for he drank wine, and was therefore called by the Pharisees a wine-bibber; he approached also the dead, as when he raised from death Lazarus, and the daughter of Jairus.

The other Nazarite was a topical appellation, and appliable unto such as were born in Nazareth, a city of Galilee, and in the tribe of Napthali. Neither, if strictly taken, was our Saviour in this sense a Nazarite, for he was born in Bethlehem in the tribe of Judah; but might receive that name because he abode in that city, and was not only conceived therein, but there also passed the silent part of his life after his return from Egypt; as is delivered by Matthew, "And he came and dwelt in a city called Nazareth, that it might be fulfilled which was spoken by the prophet, he shall be called a Nazarene." Both which kinds of Nazarites, as they are distinguishable by Zain, and Tsade in the Hebrew, so in the Greek, by Alpha and Omega: for, as Jansenius observeth,* where the votary Nazarite is mentioned, it is written, Ναζαραῖος, as Levit. vi. and Lament. iv. Where it

* *Jans. Concordia Evangelica.*

if he would not vouchsafe to visit Edessa. The painter made many vain attempts to draw a correct likeness of our Saviour. But Jesus, being willing to satisfy the desire of King Abgar, took a clean handkerchief and applied it to his countenance. In that same hour, by a miraculous power, his features and likeness were represented on the handkerchief." The picture thus miraculously produced, is said to have been the means of delivering the city from the siege laid to it by Chosroes, the Persian, 500 years afterwards. Thaddeus went to Edessa after Christ's ascension and healed Abgar.

See also *Mr. W. Huttman's Life of Christ*, where will be found a copious account of the portrait of Jesus Christ, published in prints, coins, &c. Mr. Huttman spells the name of the king of Edessa, *Agbar*.

is spoken of our Saviour, we read it, Ναζωραῖος, as in Matthew, Luke, and John; only Mark, who writ his gospel at Rome, did Latinize and wrote it Ναζαρηνός.

CHAPTER VIII.

Of the Picture of Abraham sacrificing Isaac.

IN the picture of the immolation of Isaac, or Abraham sacrificing his son, Isaac is described as a little boy;[9] which notwithstanding is not consentaneous unto the authority of expositors, or the circumstance of the text. For therein it is delivered that Isaac carried on his back the wood for the sacrifice, which being an holocaust or burnt-offering to be consumed unto ashes, we cannot well conceive a burthen for a boy; but such a one unto Isaac, as that which it typified was unto Christ, that is, the wood or cross whereon he suffered, which was too heavy a load for his shoulders, and was fain to be relieved therein by Simon of Cyrene.[1]

Again he was so far from a boy, that he was a man grown, and at his full stature, if we believe Josephus, who placeth him in the last of adolescency, and makes him twenty-five years old. And whereas in the vulgar translation he is termed *puer*,[2] it must not be strictly apprehended (for that

---

[9] *as a little boy.*] More absurd representations have been made of this event. Bourgoanne notices a painting in Spain where Abraham is preparing to shoot Isaac with a pistol! Phil. Rohr (*Pictor Errans*) mentions one in which Abraham's weapon was a sword.

[1] *too heavy a load, &c.*] Some painters have accordingly represented Christ and Simon of Cyrene as both employed in carrying the cross. Some have supposed, as Lipsius notices, that only a part (probably the transverse portion) of the cross was borne by our Lord.—*Lipsii Opera*, vol. iii. p. 658.

[2] *puer.*] In the Greeke the word [παῖς] is ambiguous and, as wee say, *polysen on*, signifying diverselye according to the subject to which it relates: as when it relates to a lord and master it signifies a servant, and is to bee soe translated: where itt relates to a father itt signifyes a sonne. The old translation is therefore herein faulty, which takes the word in the prime grammatical sense for a child, which is not always true. In the 4th cap. of the Acts, vers. 25, itt renders Δαβιδ τοῦ παιδός σου, David pueri tui, and in the 27th, παῖδά σου Ἰησοῦν puerum tuum

age properly endeth in puberty, and extendeth but unto fourteen), but respectively unto Abraham, who was at that time above six score. And therefore also herein he was not unlike unto him, who was after led dumb unto the slaughter, and commanded by others, who had legions at command; that is, in meekness and humble submission. For had he resisted, it had not been in the power of his aged parent to have enforced; and many at his years have performed such acts, as few besides at any. David was too strong for a lion and a bear; Pompey had deserved the name of Great; Alexander of the same cognomination was generalissimo of Greece; and Annibal, but one year after, succeeded Asdrubal in that memorable war against the Romans.

CHAPTER IX.

Of the Picture of Moses with Horns.

In many pieces, and some of ancient bibles, Moses is described with horns.[3] The same description we find in a silver medal; that is, upon one side Moses horned, and on the reverse the commandment against sculptile images. Which is conceived to be a coinage of some Jews, in derision of Christians, who first began that portrait.[4]

The ground of this absurdity was surely a mistake of the Hebrew text, in the history of Moses when he descended from the mount, upon the affinity of *kæren* and *karan*, that is, an horn, and to shine, which is one quality of horn. The vulgar translation conforming unto the former; *Ignorabat quòd cornuta esset facies ejus.** *Qui videbant faciem Mosis esse cornutam.* But the Chaldee paraphrase, translated by Paulus Fagius, hath otherwise expressed it: *Moses nesciebat*

* Exod. xxxiv. 29, 30.

Iesum, in both places absurdly: which Beza observed and corrected; rendering the first by the word servant, and the later by the word sonne rightlye and learnedlye.—*Wr.*

[3] *In many pieces, &c.*] And in Michael Angelo's Statue of Moses in St. Peter's at Rome.

[4] *The same description, &c.*] This sentence was first added in 2nd edition.

*quòd multus esset splendor gloriæ vultus ejus. Et viderunt filii Israel quòd multa esset claritas gloriæ faciei Mosis.*⁵ The expression of the Septuagint is as large, δεδόξασται ἡ ὄψις τοῦ χρώματος τοῦ προσώπου, *Glorificatus est aspectus cutis, seu coloris faciei.*

And this passage of the Old Testament is well explained by another of the New; wherein it is delivered, that "they could not stedfastly behold the face of Moses,"* διὰ τὴν δόξαν τοῦ προσώπου, that is, for the glory of his countenance. And surely the exposition of one text is best performed by another;⁶ men vainly interposing their constructions, where the Scripture decideth the controversy. And therefore some have seemed too active in their expositions, who in the story of Rahab the harlot, have given notice that the word also signifieth an hostess; for in the epistle to the Hebrews, she is plainly termed πόρνη,⁷ which signifies not an hostess, but a pecuniary and prostituting harlot,† a term applied unto Lais by the Greeks, and distinguished from ἑταίρα, or *amica*, as may appear in the thirteenth of Athenæus.

And therefore more allowable is the translation of Tre-

* 2 Cor. iii. 13.
† What kind of harlot she was, read *Camar. de Vita Eliæ.*

⁵ *But the Chaldee, &c.*] First added in 2nd edition.
⁶ *another.*] This is a golden rule, as necessary as infallible.— *Wr.*
⁷ *in the epistle, &c.*] Dr. Adam Clarke (on Joshua ii. 2), admitting that πόρνη generally signifies a prostitute, contends nevertheless that it might not have been used in that sense here: he asks why the derived meaning of the word, from πορνάω, to sell, may not have reference to *goods*, as well as to *person?* In that sense he observes the Chaldee Targum understood the word, and in their translation gave it accordingly the meaning of a *tavern keeper*. He concludes rather a long article by saying, "it is most likely that she was a single woman, or widow, who got her bread honestly, by keeping a house of entertainment for strangers." He proceeds however in this criticism, on a principle which he has elsewhere laid down, "that the writers of the New Testament scarcely ever quote the Old Testament, but from the Septuagint translation;" thus he contents himself with a rabbinical version of the LXX— and to that interpretation would bind the apostle.

Dr. Gill notices the rabbinical authorities in favour of the interpretation adopted by Dr. Clarke, but remarks that the Jews commonly take Rahab to be a harlot; and that generally speaking, in those times and countries such as kept public houses were prostitutes. He notices the Greek version and decidedly leans to the usual acceptation of the term.

mellius, *quod splendida facta esset cutis faciei ejus;* or as Estius hath interpreted it, *facies ejus erat radiosa,* his face was radiant, and dispersing beams like many horns and cones about his head; which is also consonant unto the original signification, and yet observed in the pieces of our Saviour, and the Virgin Mary, who are commonly drawn with scintillations, or radiant halos about their head; which, after the French expression, are usually termed the glory.

Now if, besides this occasional mistake, any man shall contend a propriety in this picture, and that no injury is done unto truth by this description, because an horn is the hieroglyphick of authority, power, and dignity, and in this metaphor is often used in Scripture; the piece I confess in this acception is harmless and agreeable unto Moses; and, under such emblematical constructions, we find that Alexander the Great, and Attila king of the Huns, in ancient medals are described with horns. But if from the common mistake, or any solary consideration, we persist in this description, we vilify the mystery of the irradiation, and authorize a dangerous piece, conformable unto that of Jupiter Ammon; which was the sun, and therefore described with horns, as is delivered by Macrobius; *Hammonem quem Deum solem occidentem Libyes existimant, arietinis cornibus fingunt, quibus id animal valet, sicut radiis sol.* We herein also imitate the picture of Pan, and pagan emblem of nature. And if (as Macrobius and very good authors concede) Bacchus (who is also described with horns), be the same deity with the sun; and if (as Vossius well contendeth)* Moses and Bacchus were the same person; their descriptions must be relative, or the tauricornous picture of the one, perhaps the same with the other.[8]

* *De Origine Idololatriæ.*

[8] *any solary consideration.*] *Solary,* 'relating to the sun.'—The Hebrew word used in this passage signifies *to shoot forth,* and may be applied perhaps to rays of light, as well as to horns. Bp. Taylor, in his *Holy Dying,* p. 17, describes the rising sun, as "peeping over the eastern hills, *thrusting out his golden horns,* &c."—*Jeff.*

CHAPTER X.

Of the Scutcheons of the Twelve Tribes of Israel.

WE will not pass over the scutcheons of the tribes of Israel, as they are usually described in the maps of Canaan and several other pieces; generally conceived to be the proper coats, and distinctive badges of their several tribes. So Reuben is conceived to bear three bars wave, Judah a lion rampant, Dan a serpent nowed, Simeon a sword impale, the point erected, &c.* The ground whereof is the last benediction of Jacob, wherein he respectively draweth comparisons from things here represented.

Now herein although we allow a considerable measure of truth, yet whether, as they are usually described, these were the proper cognizances, and coat-arms of the tribes; whether in this manner applied, and upon the grounds presumed, material doubts remain.

For first, they are not strictly made out from the prophetical blessing of Jacob; for Simeon and Levi have distinct coats, that is, a sword, and the two tables, yet are they by Jacob included in one prophecy; " Simeon and Levi are brethren, instruments of cruelty are in their habitations." So Joseph beareth an ox, whereof notwithstanding there is no mention in this prophecy; for therein it is said, " Joseph is a fruitful bough, even a fruitful bough by a well;" by which repetition are intimated the two tribes descending from him, Ephraim and Manasses; whereof notwithstanding Ephraim only beareth an ox. True it is, that many years after, in the benediction of Moses, it is said of Joseph, " His glory is like the firstlings of his bullock:" and so we may concede, what Vossius learnedly declareth, that the Egyptians represented Joseph in the symbol of an ox; for thereby was best implied the dream of Pharaoh, which he interpreted, the benefit by agriculture, and provident provision of corn which he performed; and therefore did Serapis bear a bushel upon his head.

Again, if we take these two benedictions together, the resemblances are not appropriate, and Moses therein con-

* Gen. xlix.

CHAP. X.] THE SCUTCHEONS OF THE TWELVE TRIBES.   33

forms not unto Jacob; for that which in the phophecy of Jacob is appropriated unto one, is in the blessing of Moses made common unto others. So, whereas Judah is compared unto a lion by Jacob, Judah is a lion's whelp, the same is applied unto Dan by Moses, " Dan is a lion's whelp, he shall leap from Bashan;" and also unto Gad, " he dwelleth as a lion."

Thirdly, if a lion were the proper coat of Judah, yet were it not probably a lion rampant, as it is commonly described, but rather couchant or dormant, as some heralds and rabbins do determine, according to the letter of the text, *Recumbens dormisti ut leo*, " He couched as a lion, and as a young lion, who shall rouse him?"

Lastly, when it is said, " Every man of the children of Israel shall pitch by his own standard, with the ensign of their father's house;"* upon enquiry what these standards and ensigns were, there is no small incertainty, and men conform not unto the prophecy of Jacob. Christian expositors are fain herein to rely upon the rabbins, who notwithstanding are various in their traditions, and confirm not these common descriptions. For as for inferior ensigns, either of particular bands or houses, they determine nothing at all; and of the four principal or legionary standards, that is, of Judah, Reuben, Ephraim, and Dan (under every one whereof marched three tribes), they explain them very variously. Jonathan, who compiled the *Targum*, conceives the colours of these banners to answer the precious stones in the breastplate, and upon which the names of the tribes were engraven.† So the standard for the camp of Judah was of three colours, according unto the stones, chalcedony, sapphire, and sardonyx; and therein were expressed the names of the three tribes, Judah, Issachar, and Zabulon; and in the midst thereof was written, " Rise up, Lord, and let thy enemies be scattered; and let them that hate thee, flee before thee:‡ in it was also the portrait of a lion. The standard of Reuben was also of three colours, sardine, topaz, and amethyst; therein were expressed the names of Reuben, Simeon, and Gad, in the midst was written, " Hear, O Israel, the Lord

* Num. ii.
† The like also P. Fagius upon the Targum or Chaldee Paraphrase of Onkelos, Num. i.   ‡ Num. x.

our God, the Lord is one;"* therein was also the portraiture of a hart. But Abenezra and others, beside the colours of the field, do set down other charges, in Reuben's the form of a man or mandrake, in that of Judah a lion, in Ephraim's an ox, in Dan's the figure of an eagle.

And thus indeed the four figures in the banners of the principal squadrons of Israel, are answerable unto the cherubims in the vision of Ezekiel;† every one carrying the form of all these. As for the likeness of their faces, they four had the likeness of the face of a man, and the face of a lion on the right side, and they four had the face of an ox on the left side, they four had also the face of an eagle. And conformable hereunto the pictures of the evangelists (whose gospels are the Christian banners) are set forth with the addition of a man or angel, an ox, a lion, and an eagle. And these symbolically represent the office of angels and ministers of God's will, in whom is required understanding as in a man, courage and vivacity as in the lion, service and ministerial officiousness as in the ox, expedition or celerity of execution as in the eagle.[9]

* Deut. vi. † Ezek. i.

[9] *eagle.*] The reasons which the fathers give of these emblems is excellent and proper. St. Matthew insists on those prophecyes in Christ, and therefore hath an angel, as itt were revealing those things to him. St. Marke insists most upon his workes of wonder and miracles, and therefore hathe the lyon of Judah by him. St. Luke is most copious in those storyes which set forthe his passive obedience, and therefore hathe the beast of sacrifice by him. And lastly, St. John, whose gospel sores like the eagle up to heaven, and expresses the divinity of Christe in such a sublime manner above all the rest, hath therefore that bird set by him. They were shortly, but excellently expresst by these four emblems at the pedestal of Prince Henrye's pillar, each of them in a scroll uttering these four wordes, which make up a verse. *Expecto*, by the angel, *impavidus*, by the lion, *patienter*, by the oxe, *dum renovabor*, by the eagle.—*Wr.*

The dean's exposé reminds us of that of Victorinus, Bishop of Petau, mentioned by Dr. Clarke (in his *Concise View of the Succession of Sacred Literature*, &c., p. 199, vol. i.). In his Comment on the 4th chap. of Rev. v. 6, 7, the bishop remarks:—"The four living creatures are the four gospels. The *lion* denotes MARK, in whom the voice of a *lion*, roaring in the wilderness, is heard; *the voice of one that crieth in the wilderness, &c.* MATTHEW, who has the resemblance of a *man*, endeavours to show us the family of Mary, from whom Christ took flesh; he speakes of him as a man; *the book of the generations, &c.* LUKE,

CHAP. X.]   THE SCUTCHEONS OF THE TWELVE TRIBES.   35

From hence, therefore, we may observe that these descriptions, the most authentic of any, are neither agreeable unto one another, nor unto the scutcheons in question. For though they agree in Ephraim and Judah, that is, the ox and the lion, yet do they differ in those of Dan and Reuben, as far as an eagle is different from a serpent, and the figure of a man, hart, or mandrake, from three bars wave. Wherein notwithstanding we rather declare the incertainty of arms in this particular,[1] than any way question their antiquity; for

who relates the priesthood of Zecharias offering sacrifice for the people, &c., has the resemblance of a *calf*. JOHN, like an eagle with outstretched wings soaring aloft, speaks concerning the WORD OF GOD, &c." But here we find various opinions; for while St. Jerome, in his Commentary on Matthew, and Gregory in his 4th Homily on Ezekiel, give the same version as Victorinus, St. Augustine assigns the man to Mark, and the lion to Matthew. And the dean, in the preceding note, follows those who regard Matthew's man to have been an angel.

[1] *the incertainty of arms in this particular.*] Not a few of our antiquarian writers, theologians, as well as heralds, have been anxious to trace the origin of heraldry to the Bible. Bishop Hall, in his *Impresse of God*, says, "If the testament of the patriarchs had as much credit as antiquity, all the patriarchs had their armes assigned them by Jacob: Judah a *lyon*, Dan a *serpent*, Nepthali *an hinde*, Benjamin *a wolf*, Joseph *a bough*, and so of the rest." *Works*, fol. 1648, p. 406, E.

In Mr. Jefferson's copy occurs the following MS. note. "Sir John Prestwick, in his MS. history of the noble family of Chichester, derives the practice of heraldry from Gen. i. 14. 'Let them be for *signs*,'— which he refers to *heraldic signs*."

Sylvanus Morgan begins with the creation; "deducing from the principles of nature" his *Sphere of Gentry*, which he divides into four books, the first entitled Adam's shield, or nobility native; the 2nd, Joseph's coat, or nobility dative, &c. In the latter he gives a curiously engraven representation, and a description of Joseph's whole achievement; his coat being *per fesse imbatled Argent and Gules out of a Well a Tree growing Proper, ensigned with a Helmet of a Knight thereon, out of a crown Mural Gules, a Wheatsheaf Or ;* his Mantles being of three sorts: the outmost being that of the *gown*, being cloth of gold lined with *Ermine, Erminees, Erminois,* and *Erminets ;* the next being that of the *Cloak*, accompanying him in all his adversities, being lined *Vaire, Vairy,* and *Cuppa ;* the outside *Purple:* the third being the *Mantle* for his funeral, being mantled *Sable,* lined *Argent ;* his Motto, *Nec Sorti nec Fato :* having his wife's armes in an In-Escutcheon, she being the daughter and heir of Potiphar, Prince and Priest of *On :* his Sword and Girdle on the left side. Thus he is a publick person, conferring honours by *Nobility Dative* to his brethren ! !"—*Sphere of Gentry,* book ii. p. 72. Alas! for poor Joseph's coat of many colours, to be thus blazoned!

Master Morgan, in setting forth the Camp of Israel seemeth not

hereof more ancient examples there are than the scutcheons of the tribes, if Osyris, Mizraim, or Jupiter the Just, were the son of Cham; for of his two sons, as Diodorus delivereth, the one for his device gave a dog, the other a wolf. And, beside the shield of Achilles, and many ancient Greeks, if we receive the conjecture of Vossius, that the crow upon Corvinus' head was but the figure of that animal upon his helmet, it is an example of antiquity among the Romans.

But more widely must we walk if we follow the doctrine of the Cabalists, who in each of the four banners inscribe a letter of the tetragrammaton, or quadriliteral name of God; and mysterizing their ensigns, do make the particular ones of the twelve tribes, accommodable unto the twelve signs in the zodiac, and twelve months in the year; but the tetrarchical or general banners of Judah, Reuben, Ephraim, and

less exactly informed as to the precise bearing of each tribe (*Ibid.* p. 78).

  JUDAH bare Gules, a *Lyon* couchant or,   East.
  ZABULUN's black *Ship's* like to a man of warr.
  ISSACHAR's *Asse* between two burthens girt,
  As DAN's *Sly Snake* lies in a field of vert.   North.
  ASHUR with azure a *Cup of Gold* sustains,
  And NEPTHALI's *Hind* trips o'er the flowry plains.
  EPHRAIM's strong *Ox* lyes with the couchant *Hart*, West.
  MANASSEH's *Tree* its branches doth impart.
  BENJAMIN's *Wolfe* in the field gules resides,
  REUBEN's field argent and blew *Barrs Waved* glides. South.
  SIMEON doth beare the *Sword:* and in that manner
  GAD having pitched his Tent sets up his *Banner.*

Unfortunately, however, as our author shrewdly remarks, the "descriptions" of the *conoscenti* are not "agreeable unto one another." Andrew Favine, in his *Theater of Honor and Knighthood*, fol. 1623. p. 4, perfectly agrees with Morgan as to the antiquity of *armes and blazons*, which he does not hesitate to say "have been in use from the creation of the world." But when he descends to particulars, their disagreement is instantly apparent. To say nothing of *tinctures*, half the *bearings* are different. Favine makes Judah's lyon *rampant* instead of *couchant;* Reuben bears an *armed man*, instead of the *bars wavy;* in Ephraim's standard he omits the *hart;* to Simeon he assigns *two* swords instead of *one;* to Gad a *sword* instead of a *banner;* (though I suspect the *description* of Morgan intended a sword, but the artist, misunderstanding his doggrel, has drawn a banner); to Manasseh a *crowned sceptre* instead of a *tree;* and to Dan, *ears of corn* instead of a *cup of gold*.

CHAP. X.] THE SCUTCHEONS OF THE TWELVE TRIBES. 37

Dan,[2] unto the signs of Aries, Cancer, Libra, and Capricornus;* that is, the four cardinal parts of the zodiack and seasons of the year.[3]

* *Recius de Calesti Agricultura*, lib. iv.

[2] *do make the particular ones, &c.*] Browne most probably alludes to the opinion of Kircher on this point. But several other writers have taken pains to establish the same theory. General Vallancy, in his chapter on the astronomy of the ancient Irish; i. e., *Collectanea de Rebus Hibernicis*, vol. vi. ch. ix.) proposes a scheme, which Dr. Hales has adopted, with some alterations, in his *Chronology*, vol. ii. At still greater length has Sir Wm. Drummond investigated the subject, in a paper on Gen. xlix. in the *Classical Journal*, vol. iii. p. 387. But here again the authorities are at issue. Sir William thus arranges his Zodiack:—Reuben, *Aquarius*; Simeon and Levi, *Pisces*; Judah, *Leo*; Zebulun, *Capricorn*; Issachar, *Cancer*; Dan, *Scorpius*; Gad, *Aries*; Asher, *Libra*; Napthali, *Virgo*; Joseph, *Taurus*; Benjamin, *Gemini*; Manasseh, *Sagittarius*. General Vallancy on the other hand assigns to Simeon and Levi the sign *Gemini*, to Zebulun, *Cancer*; to Issacher, *Taurus*; to Napthali, *Aries*; to Joseph, *Virgo*; and to Benjamin, *Capricorn*; omitting Gad, Asher, and Manasseh. Dr. Hales also omits Manasseh, but places Gad in *Pisces*, Asher in *Virgo*, and Joseph in *Sagittarius*. There are other variations. Some have given Levi *an open bough*. The banner of Gad, which in Morgan bears a lion, is also given *green*, and without any device. Reuben has sometimes a mandrake, instead of the *bars* or the *armed man*. Dan's serpent is sometimes *nowed*, sometimes *curled*. Manasseh has sometimes an ox, and Ephraim an unicorn or a bough. But enough of this. Further examination of the various fanciful speculations of critics and antiquaries, whether heraldic or astronomical, will only confirm our author's conclusion, " of the incertainty of arms," and the irreconcilable discrepancy of those who have written on the subjects of the present chapter:— *quot homines, tot sententiæ*; and how should it be otherwise in a case where nothing can be known, and any thing may therefore be conjectured? Before I close this note, however, I must be allowed to protest against Sir Wm. Drummond's mode of conducting his enquiry. With a view of enhancing the probability of his favourite theory, he commences by endeavouring to prove that the patriarchs were tinctured with polytheism, and addicted to divination and astrology; and arrives, in the space of half a dozen sentences, at the absurd and revolting conclusion, that Jacob was an astrologer, who believed himself under the influence of the planet Saturn! To what lengths will not some men go in support of a favourite hypothesis, however fanciful! What would be our feelings of indignation against him who should demolish the classical remains of Grecian antiquity, to make way for the vagaries of modern architecture? Less deep by far, than when we are asked to sacrifice the hallowed and beautiful simplicity of Scripture narrative to the base figments of rabbinical tradition, or the gratuitous assumptions of such critics as Sir Wm. Drummond.

[3] *But more widely, &c.*] First added in 2nd edition.

CHAPTER XI.

Of the Pictures of the Sybils.

THE pictures of the sybils are very common, and for their prophecies of Christ in high esteem with Christians; described commonly with youthful faces, and in a defined number. Common pieces making twelve, and many precisely ten; observing therein the account of Varro, that is, *Sibylla Delphica, Erythræa, Samia, Cumana, Cumæa,* or *Cimmeria, Hellespontiaca, Libyca, Phrygia, Tiburtina, Persica.* In which enumeration I perceive learned men are not satisfied, and many conclude an irreconcilable incertainty; some making more, others fewer, and not this certain number. For Suidas, though he affirm that in divers ages there were ten, yet the same denomination he affordeth unto more; Boysardus, in his tract of *Divination,* hath set forth the icons of these ten, yet addeth two others, *Epirotica* and *Ægyptia;* and some affirm that prophesying women were generally named sybils.

Others make them fewer: Martianus Capella two; Pliny and Solinus three; Ælian four; and Salmasius in effect but seven. For discoursing thereof in his *Plinian Exercitations,* he thus determineth; *Ridere licet hodiernos pictores, qui tabulas proponunt Cumanæ, Cumææ et Erythrææ, quasi trium diversarum sibyllarum; cùm una eademque fuerit Cumana, Cumæa, et Erythræa, ex plurium et doctissimorum authorum sententia.* Boysardus gives us leave to opinion there was no more than one; for so doth he conclude, *In tanta scriptorum varietate liberum relinquimus lectori credere, an una et eadem in diversis regionibus peregrinata, cognomen sortita sit ab iis locis ubi oracula reddidisse comperitur, an plures extiterint:* and therefore not discovering a resolution of their number from pens of the best writers, we have no reason to determine the same from the hand and pencil of painters.

As touching their age, that they are generally described as young women, history will not allow; for the sybil whereof Virgil speaketh, is termed by him *longæva sacerdos,* and Servius, in his comment, amplifieth the same. The other, that sold the books unto Tarquin, and whose history is plainer than any, by Livy and Gellius is termed *anus*; that is, properly no woman of ordinary age, but full of years, and in the days of dotage, according to the etymology of Festus,* and consonant unto the history, wherein it is said, that Tarquin thought she doted with old age. Which duly perpended, the *licentia pictoria* is very large; with the same reason they may delineate old Nestor like Adonis, Hecuba with Helen's face, and time with Absolom's head. But this absurdity that eminent artist, Michael Angelo, hath avoided, in the pictures of the Cumean and Persian Sybils, as they stand described from the printed sculptures of Adam Mantuanus.[4]

CHAPTER XII.

Of the Picture describing the death of Cleopatra.

THE picture concerning the death of Cleopatra, with two asps or venomous serpents unto her arms or breasts, or both, requires consideration:[5] for therein (beside that this variety

* *Anus, quasi* Ανούς, *sine mente.*

[4] *Mantuanus.*] On the subject of this chapter, the origin of the Sybils, see the Abbé Pluche, *Hist. du Ciel*, vol. i. p. 263.—*Jeff.*

[5] *The picture, &c.*] "An ancient encaustic picture of Cleopatra has lately been discovered, and detached from a wall, in which it had been hidden for centuries, and supposed to be a real portrait, painted by a Greek artist. It is done on blue slate. The colouring is fresh, very like life. She is represented applying the aspic to her bosom." *Extract from a Letter from Paris; Phil. Gaz.* Nov. 27, 1822.—*Jeff.*

The preceding notice refers in all probability to the painting which was afterwards brought over to England by its possessor, Signor Micheli, who valued it at £10,000. He caused an engraving of it to be executed, which I have had an opportunity of seeing, in the hands of R. R. Reinagle, Esq., R.A. by whose kindness I have also been favoured with the following very full and interesting history and description of this curious work of art, in compliance with my request:

"17, Fitzroy Square, Dec. 2, 1834.

"Sir,—The painting was done on a species of black slaty marble—was broken in two or three places. It was said by the Chev. Micheli, the proprietor, who brought it from Florence to this country, that it had been found in the recesses of a great wine cellar, where other fragments of antiquity had been deposited. That it was in a very thick case of wood nearly mouldered away. That it got into a broker's hands, by the major domo of the house or palace where it was discovered, having sold a parcel of

is not excusable) the thing itself is questionable; nor is it insignificant lumber, so called, in which this painting was found. It was generally incrusted with a sort of tartar and decomposed varnish, which was cleared off by certain eminent chemists of Florence. Parts of the colouring were scraped off and analysed by three or four persons. Formal attestations were made by them before the constituted authorities, and the documents had the stamps of authorized bodies and signatures. The colours were found to be all mineral, and few in number. The red was the *synopia* of Greece; another laky red, put over the red mantle Cleopatra wore, was of a nature not discovered;— it had the look of Venetian glazed red lake, of the crimson colour;— the white was a *calx*, but I forget of what nature;—the yellow was of the nature of Naples yellow—it seemed a vitrification; there was also yellow ochre;—the black was charcoal. The green curtain was esteemed *terra verd* of Greece, passed over with some unknown enriching yellow colour. The hair was deep auburn colour, and might be mangenese;— the curls, elaborately made out, were finished hair by hair, with vivid curved lines on the lighted parts, of the bright yellow golden colour. The necklace consisted of various stones set in gold: the amulet was of gold, and a chain twice or thrice round her right wrist. She wore a crown with radiating points, and jewels between each;—also a forehead jewel, with a large pearl at the four corners, worn lozengeways on her forehead; part of her front hair was plaited, and two plaits where brought round the neck, and tied in a knot of the hair;—the red mantle was fastened on both shoulders—no linen was seen. She held the asp in her left hand: it was of a green colour, and rather large. Its head was fanciful, and partook of the whims of sculptors, both ancient and modern, resembling the knobhead and pouting mouth of the dolphin. While writhing, it seems as if preparing to give a second bite; two minute indents of the fangs were imprinted on the inside of the left breast, and a drop or two of blood flowed. Cleopatra was looking upwards; a shuddering expression from quivering lips, and heavy tears falling down her cheeks, gave the countenance a singular effect; her right hand was falling from the wrist as if life were departing and convulsion commencing. The composition of the figure was erect and judiciously disposed for the confined space it was placed in. The proportion of the picture was about two feet nine inches, and narrow, like that sized canvass which artists in England call a *kitcat*. On decomposing the colours, the learned men of Florence and of Paris were fully persuaded that it was an encaustic painting; wax and resinous gum were distinctly separated. The whole picture presented the strongest signs of antiquity; but whether it is a real antique, remains still a doubt on many minds. It was attributed to Timomachus, an artist of great eminence and a traveller, who lived at the court of Augustus Cæsar. He followed the encaustic style of Apelles, and with him died or faded away that difficult art. The picture was painted (as is surmised) by the above-named Greek artist, from memory (for he had seen Cleopatra often), to supply her place in the triumph of Augustus, when he celebrated his Egyptian victories over Anthony and Cleopatra. She, by

indisputably certain what manner of death she died.[6] Plutarch, in the life of Anthony, plainly delivereth, that no man knew the manner of her death; for some affirmed she perished by poison, which she always carried in a little hollow comb, and wore it in her hair. Beside, there were never any asps discovered in the place of her death; although two of her maids perished also with her; only it was said, two small and almost insensible pricks were found upon her arm; which was all the ground that Cæsar had to presume the manner of her death. Galen, who was contemporary unto Plutarch, delivereth two ways of her death; that she killed herself by the bite of an asp, or bit an hole in her arm and poured poison therein. Strabo, that lived before them both, hath also two opinions; that she died by the bite of an asp, or else a poisonous ointment.

We might question the length of the asps, which are some-

her desperate resolution, deprived him of the honour of exposing her person to the gaze of the Roman people. The picture was said to have been taken, as a precious relic of art, by Constantine to Byzantium, afterwards named Constantinople, and restored to Rome on the return of his successors to the ancient seat of government. Among the very many things in and relating to art, this picture was overlooked, and remained in the deep dark recesses of the wine cellar. The Chevalier Micheli carried it back to Italy, when he left England, about two years ago. What has become of it since I know not.

"The title of the print is as follows:—'Cleopatra, Queen of Egypt. The original, of which the present plate is a faithful representation, is the only known and hitherto discovered specimen of ancient Greek painting. It has given rise to the most learned enquiries both in Italy and France, and been universally admitted by cognoscenti, assisted by actual analysis of the colours, to be an encaustic painting. The picture is attributed to Timomachus, and supposed to have been painted by him for his friend and patron, Augustus Cæsar, 33 years before Christ, to adorn the triumph that celebrated his Egyptian victories over Anthony and Cleopatra, as a substitute for the beautiful original, of whom he was disappointed by the heroic death she inflicted on herself. This plate is dedicated to the virtuosi and lovers of refined art in the British empire by the author, who is also the possessor of this inestimable relic of Grecian art.'

"I remain your very obedient servant.
"To Mr. S. Wilkin. "R. R. REINAGLE."

[6] *the thing itself, &c.*] The painters have however this justification, that they follow authorities. "Cæsar, from the two small pricks presumed the manner of her death." Suetonius and Eutropius mention one asp; Horace, Virgil, Florus, and Propertius, two.—*Ross* and *Jeff.*

times described exceeding short; whereas the *chersæa*, or land-asp, which most conceive she used, is above four cubits long. Their number is not unquestionable; for whereas there are generally two described, Augustus (as Plutarch relateth) did carry in his triumph the image of Cleopatra, but with one asp unto her arm. As for the two pricks, or little spots in her arm, they infer not their plurality; for like the viper the asp hath two teeth, whereby it left this impression, or double puncture behind it.

And lastly, we might question the place; for some apply them unto her breast, which notwithstanding will not consist with the history, and Petrus Victorius hath well observed the same. But herein the mistake was easy, it being the custom in capital malefactors to apply them unto the breast; as the author *De Theriaca ad Pisonem*, an eye-witness hereof in Alexandria, where Cleopatra died, determineth; "I beheld," saith he, "in Alexandria, how suddenly these serpents bereave a man of life; for when any one is condemned to this kind of death, if they intend to use him favourably, that is, to despatch him suddenly, they fasten an asp unto his breast, and bidding him walk about, he presently perisheth thereby."

CHAPTER XIII.

Of the Pictures of the Nine Worthies.

THE pictures of the nine worthies[7] are not unquestionable, and to critical spectators may seem to contain sundry improprieties. Some will enquire why Alexander the Great is described upon an elephant:[8] for we do not find he used that animal in his armies, much less in his own person; but

---

[7] *the nine worthies.*] Namely, Joshua, Gideon, Sampson, David, Judas Maccabæus, Alexander the Great, Julius Cæsar, Charlemagne, and Godfrey of Boulogne.

[8] *Some will enquire, &c.*] Ross suggests that "this picture hath reference to that story of the elephant in Philostratus (lib. i. c. 61), which from Alexander to Tiberius, lived three hundred and fifty years. This huge elephant, Alexander, after he had overcome Porus, dedicated to the sun, in these words, Ἀλέξανδρος ὁ Διὸς τὸν Αἴαντα τῷ ἡλίῳ; for he gave to this elephant the name of Ajax, and the inhabitants so honoured this beast, that they beset him round with garlands and ribbons.—*Arcana*, p. 160.

his horse is famous in history, and its name alive to this day.⁹ Beside, he fought but one remarkable battle wherein there were any elephants, and that was with Porus, king of India, in which notwithstanding, as Curtius, Arrianus, and Plutarch report, he was on horseback himself. And if because he fought against elephants he is with propriety set upon their backs, with no less (or greater) reason is the same description agreeable unto Judas Maccabeus, as may be observed from the history of the Maccabees, and also unto Julius Cæsar, whose triumph was honoured with captive elephants, as may be observed in the order thereof set forth by Jacobus Laurus.* And if also we should admit this description upon an elephant, yet were not the manner thereof unquestionable, that is, in his ruling the beast alone; for beside the champion upon their back, there was also a guide or ruler which sat more forward to command or guide the beast. Thus did King Porus ride when he was overthrown by Alexander; and thus are also the towered elephants described, Maccabees ii. 6. Upon the beasts¹ there were strong towers of wood, which covered every one of them, and were girt fast unto them by devices; there were also upon every one of them thirty-two strong men, beside the Indian that ruled them.

Others will demand, not only why Alexander upon an elephant, but Hector upon an horse; whereas his manner of fighting, or presenting himself in battle, was in a chariot,²

* *In Splendore Urbis Antiquæ.*

⁹ *but his horse, &c.*] There is an engraving of Alexander on *Bucephalus*, from an antique statue, without stirrups, in the *Youth's Magazine*, for May, 1820.—*Jeff.*

¹ *upon the beasts.*] Yf wee reckon but 300lb. weight for every man and his armour and weapons (which is the lowest proportion), and allowing for the tower and harnessing but 5 or 600lb. more, the burthen of each elephant cannot be esteemed less than 10,100lb. weight; which is a thing almost incredible: for, 4,000lb. or 5,000lb. is the greatest loade that 8 or 10 strong horses are usually put to drawe.—*Wr.*

² *chariot.*] The use of chariots and (in warr) of iron, and in private travayle of lighter substance is as olde as Jacob, as appeares Gen. xlv. 27. And in Gen. xiv. 7, the text sayes, that Pharoah had in his army 600 chosen chariots, besides all the chariots of Ægypt. Now the former of these two storyes was 500 yeares before the Trojan war, and the later 300.—*Wr.*

as did the other noble Trojans, who, as Pliny affirmeth, were the first inventors thereof. The same way of fight is testified by Diodorus, and thus delivered by Sir Walter Raleigh: "Of the vulgar, little reckoning was made, for they fought all on foot, slightly armed, and commonly followed the success of their captains, who rode not upon horses, but in chariots drawn by two or three horses." And this was also the ancient way of fight among the Britons, as is delivered by Diodorus, Cæsar, and Tacitus; and there want not some who have taken advantage hereof, and made it one argument of their original from Troy.

Lastly, by any man versed in antiquity, the question can hardly be avoided, why the horses of these worthies, especially of Cæsar, are described with the furniture of great saddles and stirrups; for saddles, largely taken, though some defence there may be, yet that they had not the use of stirrups, seemeth of lesser doubt; as Pancirollus hath observed, as Polydore Virgil and Petrus Victorius have confirmed,* expressly discoursing hereon; as is observable from Pliny, and cannot escape our eyes in the ancient monuments, medals, and triumphant arches of the Romans. Nor is there any ancient classical word in Latin to express them. For *staphia*, *stapes*, or *stapeda*, is not to be found in authors of this antiquity. And divers words which may be urged of this signification, are either later, or signified not thus much in the time of Cæsar. And therefore, as Lipsius observeth, lest a thing of common use should want a common word, Franciscus Philelphus named them *stapedas*, and Bodinus Subiecus, *pedanos*. And whereas the name might promise some antiquity, because among the three small bones in the auditory organ, by physicians termed *incus*, *malleus* and *stapes*, one thereof from some resemblance doth bear this name; these bones were not observed, much less named by Hippocrates, Galen, or any ancient physician. But as Laurentius observeth, concerning the invention of the *stapes* or stirrup-bone, there is some contention between Columbus and Ingrassias; the one of Sicilia, the other of Cremona, and both within the compass of this century.

The same is also deducible from very approved authors.

* *De Inventione Rerum, Variæ Lectiones.*

CHAP. XIII.] OF THE PICTURES OF THE NINE WORTHIES. 45

Polybius, speaking of the way which Annibal marched into Italy, useth the word βεβημάτισται, that is, saith Petrus Victorius, it was stored with devices for men to get upon their horses, which assents were termed *bemata*, and in the life of Caius Gracchus, Plutarch expresseth as much. For endeavouring to ingratiate himself with the people, besides the placing of stones at every mile's end, he made at nearer distances certain elevated places and scalary ascents, that by the help thereof they might with better ease ascend or mount their horses. Now if we demand how cavaliers, then destitute of stirrups, did usually mount their horses, as Lipsius informeth, the unable and softer sort of men had their ἀναβοχεῖς, or *stratores*, which helped them upon horseback, as in the practice of Crassus, in Plutarch, and Caracalla, in Spartianus, and the later example of Valentinianus, who because his horse rose before, that he could not be settled on his back, cut of the right hand of his strator. But how the active and hardy persons mounted, Vegetius* resolves us, that they used to vault or leap up, and therefore they had wooden horses in their houses and abroad, that thereby young men might enable themselves in this action; wherein by instruction and practice they grew so perfect, that they could vault up on the right or left, and that with their sword in hand, according to that of Virgil,—

> Poscit equos atque arma simul, sultúque superbus
> Emicat.

And again,—

> Infrænant alii currus, et corpora saltu
> Injiciunt in equos.

So Julius Pollux adviseth to teach horses to incline, dimit, and bow down their bodies, that their riders may with better ease ascend them. And thus may it more causally be made out what Hippocrates affirmeth of the Scythians, that using continual riding they were generally molested with the *sciatica* or hip gout. Or what Suetonius delivereth of Germanicus, that he had slender legs, but increased them by riding after meals; that is, the humours descending upon

* *De re Milit.*

their pendulosity, they having no support or suppedaneous stability.³

Now if any shall say that these are petty errors and minor lapses, not considerably injurious unto truth, yet is it neither reasonable nor safe to contemn inferior falsities, but rather as between falsehood and truth there is no medium, so should they be maintained in their distances; nor the contagion of the one approach the sincerity of the other.

---

³ *Or what Suetonius, &c.*] Hippocrates observes, that the Scythians, who were much on horseback, were troubled with defluxions and swellings in their legs, occasioned by their dependent posture, and the want of something to sustain their feet. Had stirrups been known, this inconvenience could not have been urged, and on this fact, together with other arguments, Berenger much relies in his opinion that stirrups were not known to the ancients. See his *History and Art of Horsemanship*, 2 vols. 4to. Montfaucon attributes this ignorance to the absence of saddles, and to the impossibility of attaching stirrups to the horse-cloths, or *ephippia*, which were anciently used for saddles.

Beckman, in his chapter on *stirrups* (*History of Inventions and Discoveries*, vol. ii. 270), among other authorities, refers to the present chapter *in the French translation*. Nothing, he says, resembling stirrups, remains in ancient works of art or coins. Xenophon, in his chapter on horsemanship, makes no mention of them. Stone mounting-steps, he observes, were not only used among the Romans, but are still to be found even in England. Victorious generals used to compel the vanquished even of the highest rank, to stoop that they might mount by stepping on their backs. He mentions some spurious inscriptions and coins which exhibit the stirrup. He names Mauritius as the first writer who has expressly mentioned it, in the sixth century, and from Eustathius it appears that even in the 12th century, the use of stirrups had not become common.

"Abdallah's friend found him with his foot in the stirrup, just mounting his camel." *Sale's Koran, Prelim. Disc.* p. 29. Abdallah lived in the sixth century.—*Jeff.*

"*Stirops.* From the old English *astige* or *stighe*, to ascend or mount up, and *ropes;* being first devised with cords or *ropes*, before they were made with leather and iron fastened to it." *Verstegan,* p. 209. "To have *styed* up from the very centre of the earth." *Bishop Hall's Contemplations on the Ascension,* vol. ii. p. 285. *Hinc Stigh-ropes.*—*Jeff.*

According to Sir John Carr's "*Caledonian Sketches,*" in his account of a male equipage, that island is not yet "a land of bridles and saddles."—*Mo. Rev. Sep.* 1809.—*Jeff.*

CHAPTER XIV.

Of the Picture of Jephthah Sacrificing his Daughter.

THE hand of the painter confidently setteth forth the picture of Jephthah in the posture of Abraham, sacrificing his only daughter. Thus is it commonly received, and hath had the attest of many worthy writers. Notwithstanding, upon enquiry we find the matter doubtful, and many upon probable grounds to have been of another opinion; conceiving in this oblation not a natural but a civil kind of death, and a separation only unto the Lord. For that he pursued not his vow unto a literal oblation, there want not arguments both from the text and reason.[4]

For first, it is evident that she deplored her virginity, and not her death: "Let me go up and down the mountains and bewail my virginity, I and my fellows."

Secondly, when it is said, that Jephthah did unto her according unto his vow, it is immediately subjoined, *et non*

---

[4] *For that he pursued not, &c.*] The observations of Dr. Adam Clarke on this very interesting question, are so spirited and satisfactory, that I must insert them. Judg. xi. 31.—"The translation of which, according to the most accurate Hebrew scholars, is this—' I will consecrate it to the Lord; OR, I will offer it for a burnt-offering:' that is, ' if it be a thing fit for *a burnt-offering*, it shall be made one : if fit *for the service of God*, it shall be consecrated to him.' That conditions of this kind must have been implied in the vow is evident enough : to have been made without them it must have been the vow of a *heathen* or a *madman*. If a *dog* had met him, this could not have been made a *burnt-offering:* and if his neighbour's or friend's *wife, son*, or *daughter*, &c. had been returning from a visit to his family, his vow gave him no right over them. Besides, *human sacrifices* were ever an abomination to the Lord ; and this was one of the grand reasons why God drave out the Canaanites, &c. because they offered their sons and daughters to Moloch, in the fire ; i. e. made burnt-offerings of them, as is generally supposed. That Jephthah was a deeply pious man, appears in the whole of his conduct ; and that he was well acquainted with the *law of Moses,*—which prohibited such sacrifices, and stated what was to be offered in sacrifice,—is evident enough from his expostulation with the king and people of Ammon, verse 14 to 27. Therefore it must be granted that he never made that rash vow which several suppose he did ; nor was he capable, if he had, of executing it in that most shocking manner which some Christian writers (tell it not in Gath) have contended for. He could not commit a crime which himself had just now been an executor of God's justice to punish in others."

cognovit virum, and she knew no man; which, as immediate in words, was probably most near in sense unto the vow.

Thirdly, it is said in the text, that the daughters of Israel went yearly to talk with the daughter of Jephthah four days in the year; which had she been sacrificed they could not have done: for whereas the word is sometime translated to lament, yet doth it also signify to talk or have conference with one, and by Tremellius, who was well able to judge of the original, it is in this sense translated: *Ibant filiæ Israelitarum, ad confabulandum cum filia Jepththaci, quatuor diebus quotannis:* and so it is also set down in the marginal notes of our translation. And from this annual concourse of the daughters of Israel, it is not improbable in future ages the daughter of Jephthah came to be worshipped as a deity, and had by the Samaritans an annual festivity observed unto her honour, as Epiphanius hath left recorded in the heresy of the Melchisedecians.

It is also repugnant unto reason; for the offering of mankind was against the law of God, who so abhorred human sacrifice, that he admitted not the oblation of unclean beasts, and confined his altars but unto few kinds of animals, the ox, the goat, the sheep, the pigeon, and its kinds. In the cleansing of the leper, there is, I confess, mention made of the sparrow; but great dispute may be made whether it be properly rendered. And therefore the Scripture with indignation ofttimes makes mention of human sacrifice among the Gentiles; whose oblations scarce made scruple of any animal, sacrificing not only man, but horses, lions, eagles; and though they come not into holocausts, yet do we read the Syrians did make oblations of fishes unto the goddess Derceto. It being therefore a sacrifice so abominable unto God, although he had pursued it, it is not probable the priests and wisdom of Israel would have permitted it; and that not only in regard of the subject or sacrifice itself, but also the sacrificator, which the picture makes to be Jephthah, who was neither priest, nor capable of that office; for he was a Gileadite, and as the text affirmeth, the son also of an harlot. And how hardly the priesthood would endure encroachment upon their function, a notable example there is in the story of Ozias.

Secondly, the offering up of his daughter was not only

unlawful and entrenched upon his religion, but had been a course that had much condemned his discretion; that is, to have punished himself in the strictest observance of his vow, when as the law of God had allowed an evasion; that is, by way of commutation or redemption, according as is determined, Levit. xxvii. Whereby if she were between the age of five and twenty, she was to be estimated but at ten shekels, and if between twenty and sixty, not above thirty. A sum that could never discourage an indulgent parent; it being but the value of a servant slain; the inconsiderable salary of Judas; and will make no greater noise than three pounds fifteen shillings with us. And therefore their conceit is not to be exploded, who say that from the story of Jephthah's sacrificing his own daughter, might spring the fable of Agamemnon, delivering unto sacrifice his daughter Iphigenia, who was also contemporary unto Jephthah; wherein to answer the ground that hinted it, Iphigenia was not sacrificed herself, but redeemed with an hart, which Diana accepted for her.[5]

Lastly, although his vow run generally for the words, "Whatsoever shall come forth, &c.," yet might it be restrained in the sense, for whatsoever was sacrificeable and justly subject to lawful immolation; and so would not have sacrificed either horse or dog, if they had come out upon him. Nor was he obliged by oath unto a strict observation of that which promissorily was unlawful; or could he be qualified by vow to commit a fact which naturally was abominable. Which doctrine had Herod understood, it might have saved John Baptist's head, when he promised by oath to give unto Herodias whatsoever she would ask; that is, if it were in the compass of things which he could lawfully grant. For his oath made not that lawful which was illegal before; and if it were unjust to murder John, the supervenient oath did not extenuate the fact, or oblige the juror unto it.[6]

Now the ground at least which much promoted the opinion, might be the dubious words of the text, which contain the sense of his vow; most men adhering unto

[5] *Iphigenia, &c.*] So the son of Idomeneus, on whose fate there is an interesting scene in *Fenelon's Telemachus*, book v.—*Jeff.*

[6] *Lastly, although his vow, &c.*] First added in 2nd edition.

their common and obvious acception. "Whatsoever shall come forth of the doors of my house, shall surely be the Lord's, and I will offer it up for a burnt-offering." Now whereas it is said, *Erit Jehovæ, et offeram illud holocaustum*, the word signifying both *et* and *aut*, it may be taken disjunctively; *aut offeram*, that is, it shall either be the Lord's by separation, or else, an holocaust by common oblation; even as our marginal translation advertiseth, and as Tremellius rendereth it, *Erit inquam Jehovæ, aut offeram illud holocaustum*. And, for the vulgar translation, it useth often *et* where *aut* must be presumed, as Exod. xxi.; *Si quis percusserit patrem et matrem*, that is, not both, but either. There being therefore two ways to dispose of her, either to separate her unto the Lord, or offer her as a sacrifice, it is of no necessity the latter should be necessary; and surely less derogatory unto the sacred text and history of the people of God must be the former.

CHAPTER XV.

Of the Picture of John the Baptist in a Camel's Skin.

THE picture of John the Baptist in a camel's skin is very questionable,[7] and many I perceive have condemned it.

---

[7] *in a camel's skin, &c.*] Ross, as usual, supports the opinion which Browne attacks. "It was fit the Baptist, who came to preach repentance for sin, should wear a garment of skins, which was the first clothes that Adam wore after he had sinned; for his fig-leaves were not proper, and this garment also showed both his poverty and humility. For as great men wear rich skins and costly furs, he was contented with a camel's skin. By this garment also he shows himself to be another Elijah (2 Kings i.), who did wear such a garment, and to be one of those of whom the apostle speaks, who went about in skins, of whom the world was not worthy. Neither was it unuseful in John's time, and before, to wear skins; for the prophets among the Jews, the philosophers among the Indians, and generally the Scythians did wear skins; hence by Claudian they are called *pellita juventus*. Great commanders also used to wear them; as Hercules the lion's skin, Acestes the bear's, Camilla the tiger's. John's garment, then, of camel's hair, was not, as some fondly conceit, a sackcloth or camblet, but a skin with the hair on it."

This is quaint and lively enough; but the most competent autho-

The ground or occasion of this description are the words of the Holy Scripture, especially of Matthew and Mark (for Luke and John are silent herein); by them it is delivered, "his garment was of camel's hair, and he had a leather girdle about his loins." Now here it seems the camel's hair is taken by painters for the skin or pelt with the hair upon it. But this exposition will not so well consist with the strict acception of the words; for Mark i., it is said, he was, ἐνδεδυμένος τρίχας καμήλου, and Matthew iii., εἶχε τὸ ἔνδυμα ἀπὸ τριχῶν καμήλου, that is, as the vulgar translation, that of Beza, that of Sixtus Quintus, und Clement the Eighth, hath rendered it, *vestimentum habebat è pilis camelinis;* which is, as ours translateth it, a garment of camel's hair; that is, made of some texture of that hair, a coarse garment, a cilicious or sackcloth habit, suitable to the austerity of his life,—the severity of his doctrine, repentance,—and the place thereof, the wilderness,—his food and diet, locusts and wild honey.ᵇ Agreeable unto the example of Elias,* who is said to be *vir pilosus*, that is, as Tremellius interprets, *Veste villosâ cinctus*, answerable unto the habit of the ancient prophets, according to that of Zachary: "In that day the prophets shall be ashamed, neither shall they wear a rough garment to deceive;"† and suitable to the cilicious and hairy vests of the strictest orders of friars, who derive the institution of their monastic life from the example of John and Elias.

As for the wearing of skins, where that is properly intended, the expression of the Scripture is plain; so is it said, Heb. xi., they wandered about ἐν αἰγείοις δέρμασιν, that is, in goat's skins; and so it is said of our first parents, Gen. iii., That God made them χιτῶνας δερματίνους, *vestes pelliceas*, or coats of skins;" which though a natural habit unto all, before the invention of texture, was something more unto Adam, who had newly learned to die; for unto him a garment from the dead was but a dictate of death, and an habit of mortality.

* 2 Kings iii. 18. † Zach. xiii.

rities agree with our author in supposing John's garment to have been made of a coarse sort of camel's hair camblet, or stuff: and Harmer has given several instances of such an article being worn.

ᵇ *his food, &c.*] See book vii. ch. ix.

Now if any man will say this habit of John was neither of camel's skin, nor any coarse texture of its hair, but rather some finer weave of camelot, grograin, or the like, inasmuch as these stuffs are supposed to be made of the hair of that animal, or because that Ælian affirmeth that camel's hair of Persia is as fine as Milesian wool, wherewith the great ones of that place were clothed; they have discovered an habit not only unsuitable unto his leathern cincture, and the coarseness of his life, but not consistent with the words of our Saviour, when reasoning with the people concerning John, he saith, "What went you out into the wilderness to see? A man clothed in soft raiment? Behold, they that wear soft raiment, are in king's houses."

CHAPTER XVI.

Of the Picture of St. Christopher.

THE picture of St. Christopher, that is, a man of a giant-like stature, bearing upon his shoulders our Saviour Christ, and with a staff in his hand, wading through the water, is known unto children, common over all Europe, not only as a sign unto houses, but is described in many churches,[9] and stands Colossus-like in the entrance of *Notre Dame* in Paris.[1]

Now from hence common eyes conceive an history suitable unto this description, that he carried our Saviour in his minority over some river of water; which notwithstanding we cannot at all make out. For we read not thus much in any good author, nor of any remarkable Christopher, before the reign of Decius, who lived two hundred and fifty years after Christ. This man indeed, according unto history, suffered as a martyr in the second year of that emperor, and in the Roman calendar takes up the 21st of July.

[9] *is known unto children, &c.*] This gigantic saint is not so general an acquaintance in our nurseries, &c. as he seems to have been in days of yore. An amusing account of one of the ecclesiastical figures of him, just as here described, may be found in the *Gent.'s Mag.* for Oct. 1803.

[1] *Notre Dame.*] Also in the cathedral of Christ's Church, Canterbury.—*Jeff.*

The ground that begat or promoted this opinion, was first the fabulous adjections of succeeding ages unto the veritable acts of this martyr, who in the most probable accounts was remarkable for his staff, and a man of a goodly stature.

The second might be a mistake or misapprehension of the picture, most men conceiving that an history, which was contrived at first but as an emblem or symbolical fancy; as from the annotations of Baronius upon the Roman martyrology, Lipellous,* in the life of St. Christopher, hath observed in these words: *Acta S. Christopheri à multis depravata inveniuntur: quod quidem non aliunde originem sumpsisse certum est, quàm quòd symbolicas figuras imperiti ad veritatem successu temporis transtulerint: itaque cuncta illa de Sancto Christophero pingi consueta, symbola potiùs quàm historiæ alicujus existimandum est esse expressam imaginem;* that is, "the acts of St. Christopher are depraved by many: which surely began from no other ground than that in process of time unskilful men translated symbolical figures unto real verities: and therefore what is usually described in the picture of St. Christopher, is rather to be received as an emblem, or symbolical description, than any real history." Now what emblem this was, or what its signification, conjectures are many; Pierius hath set down one, that is, of the disciple of Christ; for he that will carry Christ upon his shoulders, must rely upon the staff of his direction, whereon if he firmeth himself he may be able to overcome the billows of resistance, and in the virtue of this staff, like that of Jacob, pass over the waters of Jordan. Or otherwise thus: he that will submit his shoulders unto Christ, shall by the concurrence of his power increase into the strength of a giant; and being supported by the staff of his Holy Spirit, shall not be overwhelmed by the waves of the world, but wade through all resistance.

Add also the mystical reasons of this portrait alleged by Vida and Xerisanus; and the recorded story of Christopher, that before his martyrdom he requested of God, that wherever his body were, the places should be freed from pestilence and mischiefs, from infection. And therefore his picture or portrait was usually placed in public ways, and at

* *Lip. De Vitis Sanctorum.*

the entrance of towns and churches, according to the received distich:² *

Christophorum videas, postea tutus eris.

CHAPTER XVI.

Of the Picture of St. George.

THE picture of St. George killing the dragon, and as most ancient draughts do run, with the daughter of a king standing by, is famous amongst Christians. And upon this description dependeth a solemn story, how by this achievement he redeemed a king's daughter: which is more especially believed by the English, whose protector he is; and in which form and history, according to his description in the English college at Rome, he is set forth in the icons or cuts of martyrs by Cevalerius, and all this according to the Historia Lombardica, or golden legend of Jacobus de Voragine.³ Now of what authority soever this piece be amongst us, it is I perceive received with different beliefs: for some believe the person and the story; some the person, but not the story; and others deny both.⁴

* *Anton. Castellionæ Antiquitates Mediolanenses*

² *Add also the mystical, &c.*] First added in 3rd edition.
³ *and all this, &c.*] First added in 2nd edition.
⁴ *some believe the person, &c.*] Dr. Pettingal published a dissertation to prove both the person and the story to be fabulous, and the device of the order to be merely emblematical: and Dr. Byron wrote an essay (in verse) to prove that St. Gregory the Great, and not St. George, was the guardian saint of England. Against these two, and other writers on the same side, Dr. S. Pegge drew up a paper which appeared in the 5th vol. of the *Archæologia:* vindicating the honor of the patron saint of these realms, and *of that society;* asserting that he was a Christian saint and martyr—George of Cappadocia; and distinct from the Arian bishop George of Alexandria, with whom Dr. Reynolds had identified him. In this paper Dr. Pegge has not mentioned the present chapter, which in all probability only attracted his notice some years after.—In his (posthumous work called) *Anonymiana,* No. 54, he says, that " the substance of Pettingal's dissertation on the original of the equestrian figure of St. George (which the learned author supposes to be all emblematical) and of the Garter, may be found in *Browne's Vulgar Errors.*"

Browne, however, it must be observed, is of the same opinion as Dr.

That such a person there was, we shall not contend: for besides others, Dr. Heylin hath clearly asserted it in his *History of St. George*. The indistinction of many in the community of name, or the misapplication of the acts of one unto another, hath made some doubt thereof. For of this name we meet with more than one in history, and no less than two conceived of Cappadocia. The one an Arian, who was slain by the Alexandrians in the time of Julian; the other a valiant soldier and Christian martyr, beheaded in the reign of Dioclesian. This is the George conceived in this picture, who hath his day in the Roman calendar, on whom so many fables are delivered, whose story is set forth by Metaphrastes, and his miracles by Turonensis.

As for the story depending hereon, some conceive as lightly thereof, as of that of Perseus and Andromeda, conjecturing the one to be the father of the other; and some too highly assert it. Others with better moderation, do either entertain the same as a fabulous addition unto the true and authentic story of St. George,[5] or else, we conceive the literal acception to be a misconstruction of the symbolical expression; apprehending a veritable history, in an emblem or piece of Christian poesy. And this emblematical construction hath been received by men not forward to extenuate

Pegge as to the reality of St. George, his identity with George of Cappadocia, and his distinctness from the Arian bishop. All these parties are agreed in declining assent to the dragon part of the story.

It is very probable that Sir Thomas was led partly by his residence at Norwich, to investigate the story of St. George, who is a personage of no small importance there. Pegge mentions the guild of St. George in that city (in his paper in the Archæologia), but he was probably not aware that there has been from time immemorial, on ["Lord] Mayor's Day" at Norwich, an annual pageant, the sole remnant of St. George's guild, in which an immense dragon, horrible to view, with hydra head, and gaping jaws and wings, and scales bedecked in gold and green, is carried about by a luckless wight, whose task it is, the live-long-day, by string and pulley from within, to ope and shut the monster's jaws, by way of levying contributions on the gaping multitude, especially of *youthful* gazers, with whom it is matter of half terror, half joy, to pop a half-penny into the opened mouth of SNAP (so is he called), whose bow of thanks, with long and forked tail high waved in air, acknowledges the gift. Throughout the rest of the year, fell *Snap* lives on the forage of that memorable day: quietly reposing in the hall of his conqueror's sainted brother, St. Andrew, where the civic feast is held.

[5] *some conceive, &c.*] First added in 2nd edition.

the acts of saints: as, from Baronius, Lipellous the Carthusian hath delivered in the life of St. George; *Picturam illam St. Georgii quâ effingitur eques armatus, qui hastæ cuspide hostem interficit, juxta quem etiam virgo posita manus supplices tendens ejus explorat auxilium, symboli potiùs quàm historiæ alicujus censenda expressa imago. Consuevit quidem ut equestris militiæ miles equestri imagine referri.* That is, the picture of St. George, wherein he is described like a cuirassier or horseman completely armed, &c. is rather a symbolical image, than any proper figure.[6]

Now in the picture of this saint and soldier, might be implied the Christian soldier, and true champion of Christ: A horseman armed *cap à pié*, intimating the *panoplia* or complete armour of a Christian combating with the dragon, that is, with the devil, in defence of the king's daughter, that is, the Church of God.[7] And therefore although the history be not made out, it doth not disparage the knights and noble order of St. George: whose cognisance is honourable in the emblem of the soldier of Christ, and is a worthy memorial to conform unto its mystery. Nor, were there no such person at all, had they more reason to be ashamed, than the noble order of Burgundy, and knights of the golden fleece; whose badge is a confessed fable.[8]

CHAPTER XVIII.

Of the Picture of Jerome.

THE picture of Jerome usually described at his study, with a clock hanging by, is not to be omitted; for though the meaning be allowable, and probable it is that industrious father did not let slip his time without account, yet must not

[6] *the picture, &c.*] First added in 2nd edition.

[7] *Church of God.*] Or rather the soule, for soe in the picture and story shee is called [*psyche*] that is the soul of man, which in a specificall sense is endeed every Christian soule, and comprehensively may signifye, the Church of God.—*Wr.*

[8] *fable.*] Borowed from that old storye of the Argo-nauts, or Argo-knights, as wee may call them, though the golden fleece be a meer romance.—*Wr.*

perhaps that clock he set down to have been his measure thereof. For clocks[9] or automatous organs, whereby we now distinguish of time, have found no mention in any ancient writers, but are of late invention, as Pancirollus observeth. And Polydore Virgil, discoursing of new inventions whereof the authors are not known, makes instance in clocks and guns. Now Jerome is no late writer, but one of the ancient fathers, and lived in the fourth century, in the reign of Theodosius the first.

It is not to be denied that before the days of Jerome there were horologies, and several accounts of time; for they measured the hours not only by drops of water in glasses called *clepsydræ*, but also by sand in glasses called *clepsammia*. There were also from great antiquity, scioterical or sun-dials, by the shadow of a stile or *gnomon* denoting the hours of the day; an invention ascribed unto Anaximenes by Pliny. Hereof a memorable one there was in Campus Martius, from an obelisk erected, and golden figures placed horizontally about it; which was brought out of Egypt by Augustus, and described by Jacobus Laurus.* And another of great antiquity we meet with in the story of Ezechias; for so it is delivered in 2 Kings, xx.: "That the Lord brought the shadow backward ten degrees by which it had gone down in the dial of Ahaz." That is, say some, ten degrees, not lines; for the hours were denoted by certain divisions or steps in the dial, which others distinguished by lines, according to that of Persius,—

> Stertimus indomitum quod despumare Falernum
> Sufficiat, quintâ dum linea tangitur umbra.

That is, the line next the meridian, or within an hour of noon.

* A peculiar description and particular construction hereof out of R. Chomer, is set down, *Curios. de Caffarel.* chap. ix.

[9] *clocks.*] The ancient pictures of St. Hierom were naked, on his knees, in a cave, with an hour-glasse and a scull by him, intimating his indefatigable continuance in prayers and studye while hee lived in the cave at Bethleem. But the later painters at Rome, bycause hee had been senator and of a noble familye, picture him in the habit of the cardinals, leaning on his arm at a desk in study with a clock hanging by him, and his finger on a scull: and this they take to bee a more proper symbol of the cardinal eminencye.—*Wr.*

Of later years there succeeded new inventions, and horologies composed by trochilick or the artifice of wheels; whereof some are kept in motion by weight, others perform without it. Now as one age instructs another, and time, that brings all things to ruin, perfects also every thing; so are these indeed of more general and ready use than any that went before them. By the water-glasses the account was not regular; for from attenuation and condensation, whereby that element is altered, the hours were shorter in hot weather than in cold, and in summer than in winter. As for scioterical dials, whether of the sun or moon, they are only of use in the actual radiation of those luminaries, and are of little advantage unto those inhabitants, which for many months enjoy not the lustre of the sun.

It is, I confess, no easy wonder how the horometry of antiquity discovered not this artifice, how Architas, that contrived the moving dove, or rather the helicosophy of Archimides, fell not upon this way. Surely as in many things, so in this particular, the present age hath far surpassed antiquity; whose ingenuity hath been so bold not only to proceed below the account of minutes, but to attempt perpetual motions;[1] and engines whose revolutions (could their substance answer the design) might out-last the exemplary mobility, and out-measure time itself. For such a one is that mentioned by John Dee, whose words are these, in his learned preface unto Euclid: "By wheels, strange works and incredible are done: a wondrous example was seen in my time in a certain instrument, which, by the inventor and artificer was sold for twenty talents of gold; and then by chance had received some injury, and one Janellus of Cremona did mend the same, and presented it unto the emperor Charles the Fifth. Jeronymous Cardanus can be my witness, that therein was one wheel that moved at such a rate, that in seven thousand years only his own period should be finished; a thing almost incredible, but how far I keep within my bounds many men yet alive can tell."

[1] *perpetual motions.*] John Romilly, a celebrated watchmaker, born at Geneva, wrote a letter on the impossibility of perpetual motion.—*Jeff.*

CHAPTER XIX.

Of the Pictures of Mermaids, Unicorns, and some others.

FEW eyes have escaped the pictures of mermaids ;[2] that is, according to Horace's monster, with a woman's head

[2] *mermaids.*] The existence of mermaids has been so generally ridiculed, and high authorities have so repeatedly denounced as forgeries, delusions, or travellers' wonders, the detailed narratives and exhibited specimens of these sea-nymphs, that it must be a Quixotic venture to say a word in their defence. Yet am I not disposed to give up their cause as altogether hopeless. I cannot admit the probability of a belief in them having existed from such remote antiquity, and spread so widely, without *some foundation* in truth. Nor can I consent to reject *en masse* such a host of delightfully pleasant stories as I find recorded of these *daughters of the sea* (as Illiger call the Dugongs), merely because it is the fashion to decry them. I must be allowed, then, to hold my opinion in abeyance for further evidence. Unconvinced even by Sir Humphry Davy's grave arguments to prove that such things cannot be, and undismayed by his asserted detection of the apes and salmon in poor Dr. Philip's "undoubted original," I persist in expecting one day to have the pleasure of beholding—A MERMAID !

But what is a mermaid? Aye, there is the very *gist* of the question. Cicero little dreamt of his classical rule being degraded by application to such a discussion as the present ; but I shall nevertheless endeavour to avail myself of his maxim ;—*Omnis disputatio debet a definitione proficisci.* What is a mermaid ? Not the fair lady of the ocean, admiring herself in a hand-mirror, and bewitching the listener by her song ;—not the *triton*, dwelling in the ocean-cave, and sounding his conch-like cornet or trumpet ;—not the *bishop-frocked* creature of Rondeletius ; nor Aldrovandus' *mer-devil*, with his horns and face of fury ; nor the howling and tempest-stirring *monsters* of Olaus Magnus—not, in short, the creature of poetry or fiction : but a most supposable, and probably often seen, though hitherto undescribed, species of the *herbivorous cetacea* (the seals and lamantins), more approaching, in several respects, the human configuration, than any species we know.

Let us hear and examine Sir Humphry's arguments against the probability of such a discovery. He says, that "a *human* head, *human* hands, and *human* mammæ, are wholly inconsistent with a *fish's* tail." In one sense this is undeniable ;—viz.—since *homo sapiens* is (begging Lord Monboddo's pardon) an *incaudate* animal,—it follows that the head, hands, and *mammæ* of any creature furnished also with a tail, could not be *human :* and so, conversely, the tail of such a creature could not be a *fish's* tail. But this is a truism, only to be paralleled by the exclamation attributed by Peter Pindar to Sir Joseph Banks, when he had boiled the fleas and found they did not turn red,—"*Fleas* are not *lobsters !* &c." Davy's was not a nominal objection, a mere play upon

above, and fishy extremity below; and these are conceived to answer the shape of the ancient sirens that attempted

words: he goes on to say, "the human head is adapted for an erect posture, and in such a posture an animal with a fish's tail could not swim." The head of *our mermaid*, however, may more strongly *resemble* the human head, than any described animal of its tribe, and yet preserve at the same time the power which they all have, of raising the head perpendicularly out of the water while swimming, as Sir Humphry himself probably did, when he was mistaken by the fair ladies of Caithness for a mermaid! Cuvier remarks, moreover, that the tails of these herbivorous cetacea differ from those of fish in their greater adaptation to maintain an erect posture. Sir Humphry proceeds—"A creature with lungs must be on the surface several times in a day; and the sea is an inconvenient breathing place!" I must take the liberty of confronting this most singular observation with a much greater authority. Cuvier says (and surely Sir Humphry must have for the moment forgotten), that the *cetacea*, though constantly residing in the sea, "as they respire by lungs, are obliged to rise frequently to the surface to take in fresh supplies of air." What is to be said of a naturalist who argues against the possibility of any creature provided with lungs residing in the sea, in the face of so important an example of the fact as we have in the entire class of cetacea? What would Cuvier, with all his readiness to do homage to genius in any man, and especially in so splendid an instance as Davy, what must he have thought, had he read his preceding remarks? *Magnus aliquando dormitat Homerus!*

It is the more remarkable, as Sir Humphry actually mentions some species of this very tribe as having probably given rise to some of the stories about mermaids. And as to *mammæ* and *hands*, to which he also objects if in company with the fish's tail, we must here again have recourse to the protection of Cuvier against our mighty assailant. "The first family" (herbivorous cetacea), says Cuvier, "frequently emerge from the water to seek for pasture on the shore. They have two mammæ on the breast, and hairs like mustachios, two circumstances which, when they raise the anterior part of the body above water, give them some resemblance to men and women, and have probably occasioned those fables of the ancients concerning Tritons and Syrens. Vestiges of claws may be discovered on the edges of their fins, which they use with dexterity in creeping, and carrying their little ones. This has given rise to a comparison of these organs with hands, and hence these animals have been called manatis" (or *lamantins*).

Thus I have sketched the sort of creature which may be supposed to exist: nor can I deem it unreasonable to expect such a discovery, though Davy, after saying, "It doubtless might please God to make a mermaid; but I do not believe God ever did make one:"—somewhat arrogantly pronounces that "such an animal, if created, could not long exist, and, with scarce any locomotive powers, would be the prey of other fishes formed in a manner more suited to their element."

It is singular that a writer in the *Enc. Metropolitana* should have con

upon Ulysses. Which notwithstanding were of another description, containing no fishy composure, but made up of man and bird: the human mediety variously placed not only above, but below, according unto Ælian, Suidas, Servius, Boccatius, and Aldrovandus, who hath referred their description unto the story of fabulous birds; according to the description of Ovid, and the account thereof in Hyginus, that they were the daughters of Melpomene, and metamorphosed into the shape of man and bird by Ceres.

And therefore these pieces, so common among us, do rather derive their original, or are indeed the very descriptions of Dagon, which was made with human figure above, and fishy shape below: whose stump, or, as Tremellius and our margin render it, whose fishy part only remained, when the hands and upper part fell before the ark. Of the shape of Artergates, or Derceto, with the Phœnicians, in whose

cluded a long and amusing article with the marginal note, "mermaids impossible animals;" supported solely by the very extraordinary arguments of Sir Humphry.

Those who are desirous of seeing an enumeration of all the supposed mermaids and monsters, which have at various times amused the public, may refer to the article just quoted, and to a miscellaneous volume, entitled the *Working Bee*, published by Fisher and Co., Newgate-street, in which is an *Historical Memoir of Syrens or Mermaids*.

In explanation of one or two allusions in my preceding remarks, I may just mention that in the *Evangelical Magazine*, for Sept. 1822, is inserted part of a letter from the Rev. Dr. Philip, dated Cape Town, April 20th, 1822. The Dr. says, he had just seen a mermaid, then exhibiting in that town. The head is about the size of a baboon's, thinly covered with black hair; a few hairs on the upper lip. The forehead low, but with better proportioned and more like human features than any of the baboons. The ears, nose, lips, chin, breasts, fingers, and nails, resemble the human subject. Eight *incisores*, four *canine*, eight *molares*. The animal, though shrunk, is about three feet long; its resemblance to a man having ceased immediately under the *mammæ*. On the line of separation, and immediately under the breast, are two fins. Below, it resembles a salmon. It is covered with scales—but which on the upper part are scarcely perceptible: it was caught somewhere on the north of China by a fisherman, who sold it for a trifle. At Batavia it was bought by Capt. Eades, in whose possession it then was. This very specimen Davy pronounced to be composed of the head and bust from two apes, fastened to the tail of the kipper salmon,—*salmo salar*.

He also notices another instance of a supposed mermaid, seen off the coast of Caithness, which turned out to have been a gentleman bathing. He is asserted to have intended *himself*. See his *Salmonia*.

fishy and feminine mixture, as some conceive, were implied the moon and the sea, or the deity of the waters; and therefore, in their sacrifices, they made oblation of fishes. From whence were probably occasioned the pictures of Nereides and Tritons among the Grecians, and such as we read in Macrobius, to have been placed on the top of the temple of Saturn.

We are unwilling to question the royal supporters of England, that is, the approved descriptions of the lion and the unicorn. Although, if in the lion the position of the pizzle be proper, and that the natural situation, it will be hard to make out their retrocopulation, or their coupling and pissing backward, according to the determination of Aristotle; all that urine backward do copulate πυγηδὸν, *clunatim*, or aversely, as lions, hares, lynxes.

As for the unicorn, if it have the head of a deer and the tail of a boar, as Vertomannus describeth it, how agreeable it is to this picture every eye may discern. If it be made bisulcous or cloven-footed, it agreeth unto the description of Vertomannus, but scarce of any other; and Aristotle supposeth that such as divide the hoof, do also double the horn; they being both of the same nature, and admitting division together. And lastly, if the horn have this situation and be so forwardly affixed, as is described, it will not be easily conceived how it can feed from the ground; and therefore we observe that nature, in other cornigerous animals, hath placed the horns higher and reclining, as in bucks; in some inverted upwards, as in the rhinoceros, the Indian ass, and unicornous beetles; and thus have some affirmed it is seated in this animal.

We cannot but observe that in the picture of Jonah and others, whales are described with two prominent spouts on their heads; whereas indeed they have but one in the forehead, and terminating over the windpipe.[3] Nor can we overlook the picture of elephants with castles on their backs, made in the form of land castles, or stationary fortifications, and answerable unto the arms of Castile, or Sir John Old-

---

[3] *two prominent points, &c.*] The cetacea have all two spiracles, but on some they are considerably remote from each other, in others close together, and in some so near that they seem to **unite in one and** the same opening.

castle; whereas the towers they bore were made of wood, and girt unto their bodies, as is delivered in the books of Maccabees, and as they were appointed in the army of Antiochus.

We will not dispute the pictures of retiary spiders, and their position in the web, which is commonly made lateral, and regarding the horizon, although, if observed, we shall commonly find it downward, and their heads respecting the centre. We will not controvert the picture of the seven stars; although if thereby be meant the Pleiades, or sub-constellation upon the back of Taurus, with what congruity they are described, either in site or magnitude, in a clear night an ordinary eye may discover from July unto April. We will not question the tongues of adders and vipers, described like an anchor, nor the picture of the fleur-de-lis: though how far they agree unto their natural draughts, let every spectator determine.

Whether the cherubims about the ark be rightly described in the common picture,* that is, only in human heads, with two wings, or rather in the shape of angels or young men, or somewhat at least with feet, as the Scripture seems to imply. Whether the cross seen in the air by Constantine, were of that figure wherein we represent it, or rather made out of X and P, the two first letters of Χριστός. Whether the cross of Christ did answer the common figure; whether so far advanced above his head; whether the feet were so disposed, that is, one upon another, or separately nailed, as some with reason describe it, we shall not at all contend. Much less whether the house of Diogenes were a tub framed of wood, and after the manner of ours, or rather made of earth, as learned men conceive, and so more clearly make out that expression of Juvenal.† We should be too critical to question the letter Y, or bicornous element of Pythagoras, that is, the making of the horns equal;[7] or the left less than the right, and so destroying the symbolical intent of the

* 2 Chron. iii. 13. † —— Dolia magni non ardent Cynici, &c.

[7] *the letter Y, &c.*] An allusion to this letter, in Dr. Donne's sermon on "Where your treasure is, there will your heart be also," is mentioned by Dr. Vicesimus Knox in his 38th Winter Evening; with some excellent observations on the style of the old sermon writers. —*Jeff.*

figure; confounding the narrow line of virtue with the larger road of vice, answerable unto the narrow door of heaven, and the ample gates of hell, expressed by our Saviour, and not forgotten by Homer in that epithet of Pluto's house.[5]*

Many more there are whereof our pen shall take notice, nor shall we urge their enquiry; we shall not enlarge with what incongruity, and how dissenting from the pieces of antiquity, the pictures of their gods and goddesses are described, and how hereby their symbolical sense is lost; although herein it were not hard to be informed from Phornutus,† Fulgentius,‡ and Albricus.§ Whether Hercules be more properly described strangling than tearing the lion, as Victorius hath disputed; nor how the characters and figures of the signs and planets be now perverted, as Salmasius hath learnedly declared. We will dispense with bears with long tails, such as are described in the figures of heaven; we shall tolerate flying horses, black swans, hydras, centaurs, harpies, and satyrs, for these are monstrosities, rarities, or else poetical fancies,[6] whose shadowed moralities require their substantial falsities. Wherein indeed we must not deny a liberty; nor is the hand of the painter more restrainable than the pen of the poet. But where the real works of nature, or veritable acts of story are to be described, digressions are abberrations; and art being but the imitator or secondary representor, it must not vary from the verity of the example, or describe things otherwise than they truly are, or have been. For hereby introducing false ideas of things, it perverts and deforms the face and symmetry of truth.

* Ἐυρυπυλῆς.
† *Phornut. De Natura Deorum.*
‡ *Fulg. Mythologia.*
§ *Albric. De Deorum Imaginious.*

[5] *Whether the cherubims, &c.*] This paragraph first added in 2nd edition.

[6] *flying horses, &c.*] Modern discoveries have lessened this list. The black swan, though *rara avis*, is no longer a poetical fancy. There was a time when the camelopard was deemed imaginary.

CHAPTER XX.

Of the Hieroglyphical Pictures of the Egyptians.

CERTAINLY of all men that suffered from the confusion of Babel, the Egyptians found the best evasion; for, though words were confounded, they invented a language[7] of things, and spake unto each other by common notions in nature. Whereby they discoursed in silence, and were intuitively understood from the theory of their expresses. For they assumed the shapes of animals common unto all eyes, and by their conjunctions and compositions[8] were able to communicate their conceptions unto any that coapprehended the syntaxes of their natures. This many conceive to have been the primitive way of writing, and of greater antiquity than letters; and this indeed might Adam well have spoken, who understanding the nature of things, had the advantage of natural expressions. Which the Egyptians but taking upon trust, upon their own or common opinion, from conceded mistakes they authentically promoted errors; describing in their hieroglyphicks creatures of their own invention, or from known and conceded animals, erecting significations not inferible from their natures.[9]

[7] *a language.*] A common language might possibly bee framed which all should understand under one character, in their own tongue, as well as all understand in astronomy the 12 signes, the 7 planets, and the several aspects; or in geometry, a triangle, a rhombe, a square, a parallelogram, a helix, a decussation, a cross, a circle, a sector, and such like very many: or the Saracenicall and algebraick characters in arithmetick, or the notes of weight among physitians and apothecaryes: or lastly, those marks of punctuations and qualityes among grammarians in Hebrew under, in Arabick above, the words. To let pass Paracelsus his particular marks, and the common practice of all trades.—*Wr.*

[8] *by their conjunctions, &c.*] More clearly, " by the conjunction and composition of those shapes of animals, &c."

[9] *Which the Egyptians, &c.*] How little, alas, do we know of the picture-writing of the Egyptians, even after all the profound researches of Young, Champollion, Klaproth, Akerblad, De Sacy, and others: and how little (we may perhaps add) can we hope ever to see effected. We are told by Clemens Alexandrinus (and subsequent researches have done little more than enable us to comprehend his meaning) that the Egyp-

And first, although there were more things in nature, than words which did express them, yet even in these mute and tians used three modes of writing ;—the *epistolographic* (called *demotic* by Herodotus and Diodorus, and *enchorial* in the Rosetta inscription), the *hieratic* (employed by the sacred scribes), and the *hieroglyphick*,— consisting of the *kuriologic* (subsequently termed *phonetic*) and the *symbolic*, of which there are several kinds ;—one representing objects *properly*, another *metaphorically*, a third *enigmatically*. The great discovery made by Dr. T. Young, from the Rosetta inscription, was that *some* of the hieroglyphs were the *signs of sounds*, each hieroglyph signifying the first letter of the Egyptian name of the object represented. Supposing *all* their picture-writing to be symbolical, then it would be manifestly impossible to hope to read it. For example, we are *told* that the figure of a *bee* expressed the idea of *royalty ;* but who could have *guessed* this ? Supposing on the other hand that the hieroglyphs were *entirely phonetic* (which was not the case, nor can we possibly ascertain in what proportion they were so), supposing them also to be certain and determinate signs of sounds, one and the same sign always employed to represent one and the same sound ;—supposing in short that " we could spell syllables and distinguish words with as much certainty and precision as if they had been written in any of the improved alphabets of the west, there would yet always remain one difficulty over which genius itself could not triumph ; namely, to discover the signification of the words, when it is not known by tradition or otherwise :"—when the original language has long since utterly vanished ;—and when the only instrument left wherewith we can labour (the Coptic) is but the mutilated and imperfect fragment of an extinct language, itself when living the remnant only of that elder form of speech which we are seeking to decypher ; but of which, alas ! through so imperfect a medium, but slight traces and lineaments can be here and there faintly reflected. The article, EGYPT, in the *Sup.* to *Ency. Brit.* and HIEROGLYPHICKS, in *Ency. Metrop.* together with articles in the 45th and 57th vols. of the *Edinburgh Review*, will give those disposed to go further into the subject a full and interesting view of all that has hitherto been effected in this most difficult, if not hopeless, field of labour.

But our author's special object in this chapter is to bring against the Egyptians the twofold charge ; first, of " describing in their hieroglyphicks creatures of their own inventions ;" and secondly, of " erecting, from known and conceded animals, significations not inferible from their natures." No charge, however, can be fairly entertained till it has been proved ;—and it would be no easy matter to show that many of the monsters enumerated, were really Egyptian : .... " Considering how absurdly and monstrously complicated the Egyptian superstitions really were, it becomes absolutely essential to separate that which is most fully established or most generally admitted, from the accidental or local varieties, which may have been exaggerated by different authors into established usages of the whole nation, and still more from those which have been the fanciful productions of their own inventive faculties."—*Dr. Young*, EGYPT, *Sup. Ency. Brit.* iv. 43.

silent discourses, to express complexed significations, they took a liberty to compound and piece together creatures of allowable forms into mixtures inexistent. Thus began the descriptions of griffins, basilisks, phœnix, and many more; which emblematists and heralds have entertained with significations answering their institutions; hieroglyphically adding martegres, wivernes, lion-fishes, with divers others. Pieces of good and allowable invention unto the prudent spectator, but are looked on by vulgar eyes as literal truths or absurd impossibilities; whereas indeed they are commendable inventions, and of laudable significations.

Again, beside these pieces fictitiously set down, and having no copy in nature, they had many unquestionably drawn, of inconsequent signification, nor naturally verifying their intention. We shall instance but in few, as they stand recorded by Orus. The male sex they expressed by a vulture,[1] because of vultures all are females, and impregnated by the wind; which authentically transmitted hath passed many pens, and became the assertion of Ælian, Ambrose, Basil, Isidore, Tzetzus, Philes, and others. Wherein notwithstanding what injury is offered unto the creation in this confinement of sex, and what disturbance unto philosophy in the concession of windy conceptions, we shall not here declare. By two drachms they thought it sufficient to signify an heart;[2] because the heart at one year weigheth two drachms, that is, a quarter of an ounce, and unto fifty years annually increaseth the weight of one drachm, after which in the same proportion it yearly decreaseth; so that the life of a man doth not naturally extend above an hundred. And this

---

The authors on whom Browne relies, especially Pierius, are by no means to be received without the caution expressed in the foregoing quotation.

[1] *The male sex, &c.*] See *Pierius Hieroglyphica*, fol. 1626, lxxiii. c. 1, 4. *Horapollo* (4to. curâ *Pauw*), No. 12.

[2] *By two drachms, &c.*] Pierius says that the Egyptians used the vulture to symbolize two drachms, or a heart; and he gives other reasons for the adoption of the symbol, though he deems that mentioned by Browne the most probable (Ibid. l. xviii. c. 20). Horapollo says, they used the vulture to represent two drachms, because unity was expressed by two lines; and, unity being the beginning of numbers, most fitly doth its sign express a vulture, because, like unity, it is *singly* the author of its own increase (Ibid. No. 12).

was not only a popular conceit, but consentaneous unto the physical principles, as Hernius hath accounted it.*

A woman that hath but one child, they express by a lioness; for that conceiveth but once.[3] Fecundity they set forth by a goat, because but seven days old it beginneth to use coition.[4] The abortion of a woman they describe by an horse kicking a wolf; because a mare will cast her foal if she tread in the track of that animal.[5] Deformity they signify by a bear;[6] and an unstable man by a hyæna,[7] because that animal yearly exchangeth its sex. A woman delivered of a female child they imply by a bull looking over his left shoulder;[8] because if in coition a bull part from a cow on that side, the calf will prove a female.[9]

All which, with many more, how far they consent with truth we shall not disparage our reader to dispute; and though some way allowable unto wiser conceits who could distinctly receive their significations, yet carrying the majesty of hieroglyphicks, and so transmitted by authors, they crept

* In his *Philosophia Barbarica*.

[3] *A woman, &c.*] *Pierius*, lib. i. c. 14, *Horapollo*, No. 82.
[4] *Fecundity, &c.*] *Pierius*, lib. x. c. 10, *Horapollo*, No. 48.
[5] *The abortion, &c.*] *Pierius*, lib. xi. c. 9, *Horapollo*, No. 45. Whether the tracke of the wolfe will cause abortion in a mare is hard to bee knowne: but the mare does soe little feare the wolfe, that (as I have heard itt from the mouth of a gentleman, an eye-witness of what he related) as soone as shee perceaves the wolfe to lye in watch for her young foale, she will never cease hunting with open mouth till shee drive him quite away: the wolfe avoyding the gripe of her teeth, as much as the stroke of her heeles: and to make up the probability hereof, itt is certaine that a generous horse will fasten on a dog with his teeth, as fell out anno 1653, in October, at Bletchinden (Oxon), a colt being bated by a mastive (that was set on by his master to drive him out of a pasture) tooke up the dog in his teeth by the back, and rann away with him, and at last flinging him over his head lefte the dog soe bruised with the gripe and the fall, that hee lay half dead; but the generous colte leapt over the next hedge, and ran home to his own pasture unhurt.—*Wr.*

[6] *Deformity, &c.*] *Pierius*, l. xi. c. 42. *Horapollo*, No. 83, says, "Hominem, qui initio quidem informis natus sit, sed postea formam acceperit, innuunt depicta ursa prægnante."

[7] *an unstable, &c.*] *Pierius*, l. xi. c. 24, *Horapollo*, No. 69.

[8] *A woman, &c.*] *Pierius*, l. iii. c. 6. *Horapollo*, who adds also the converse of the proposition, No. 43.

[9] *female.*] I have heard this avowed by auncient grave farmers.— **Wr.**

into a belief with many, and favourable doubt with most. And thus, I fear, it hath fared with the hieroglyphical symbols of Scripture; which, excellently intended in the species of things sacrificed, in the prohibited meats, in the dreams of Pharaoh, Joseph, and many other passages, are ofttimes racked beyond their symbolizations, and enlarged into constructions disparaging their true intentions.[1]

CHAPTER XXI.[2]

Of the Picture of Haman Hanged.

IN common draughts, Haman is hanged by the neck upon an high gibbet, after the usual and now practised way of suspension: but whether this description truly answereth the original, learned pens consent not, and good grounds

---

[1] *intentions.*] Ross despatches the 16th, 17th, 18th, 19th and 20th chapters in the following summary remarks:—

"In some subsequent chapters the doctor questions the pictures of St. Christopher carrying Christ over the river: of St. George on horseback killing the dragon; of St. Jerom with a clock hanging by; of mermaids, unicorns, and some others; with some hieroglyphick pictures of the Egyptians. In this he doth *luctari cum larvis*, and with Æneas in the poet, *Irruit et frustra ferro diverberat umbras.* He wrestles with shadows; for he may as well question all the poetical fictions, all the sacred parables, all tropical speeches; also escutcheons, or coats of arms, signs hanging out at doors—where he will find blue boars, white lions, black swans, double-headed eagles, and such like, devised only for distinction. The like devices are in military ensigns. Felix, Prince of Salernum, had for his device a tortoise with wings, flying, with this motto, *amor addidit*; intimating, that love gives wings to the slowest spirits. Lewis of Anjou, King of Naples, gave for his device, a hand out of the clouds, holding a pair of scales, with this motto, *Æqua durant semper.* Henry the First, of Portugal, had a flying horse for his device. A thousand such conceits I could allege, which are symbolical, and therefore it were ridiculous to question them, if they were historical. As for the cherubims, I find four different opinions. 1. Some write they were angels in the form of birds. 2. Aben Ezra thinks the word cherub signifieth any shape or form. 3. Josephus will have them to be winged animals, but never seen by any. 4. The most received opinion is, that they had the shape of children; for *rub* in Hebrew, and *rabe* in Chaldee, signifieth a child; and *che*, as: so then, cherub signifieth as a child, and it is most likely they were painted in this form."

[2] *Chap.* xxi.] The whole chapter first added in 6th edition.

there are to doubt. For it is not easily made out that this was an ancient way of execution in the public punishment of malefactors among the Persians, but we often read of crucifixion in their stories. So we find that Orostes, a Persian governor, crucified Polycrates the Samian tyrant. And hereof we have an example in the life of Artaxerxes, King of Persia (whom some will have to be Ahasuerus in this story), that his mother, Parysatis, flayed and crucified her eunuch. The same also seems implied in the letters patent of King Cyrus: *Omnis qui hanc mutaverit jussionem, tollatur lignum de domo ejus, et erigatur, et configatur in eo.**

The same kind of punishment was in use among the Romans, Syrians, Egyptians, Carthaginians, and Grecians. For though we find in Homer that Ulysses in a fury hanged the strumpets of those who courted Penelope, yet it is not so easy to discover that this was the public practice or open course of justice among the Greeks.

And even that the Hebrews used this present way of hanging, by illaqueation or pendulous suffocation, in public justice and executions, the expressions and examples in Scripture conclude not, beyond good doubt.

That the King of Hai was hanged, or destroyed by the common way of suspension, is not conceded by the learned Masius in his comment upon that text; who conceiveth thereby rather some kind of crucifixion, at least some patibulary affixion after he was slain, and so represented unto the people until toward the evening.

Though we read in our translation that Pharaoh hanged the chief baker, yet learned expositors understand hereby some kind of crucifixion, according to the mode of Egypt, whereby he exemplarily hanged out till the fowls of the air fed on his head or face, the first part of their prey being the eyes. And perhaps according to the signal draught hereof in a very old manuscript of Genesis, now kept in the Emperor's library at Vienna, and accordingly set down by the learned Petrus Lambecius, in the second tome of the description of that library.

When the Gibeonites hanged the bodies of those of the

---

* In Ezra vi.

house of Saul, thereby was intended some kind of crucifying,[3] according unto good expositors, and the vulgar translation; *crucifixerunt eos in monte coram domino.* Nor only these, mentioned in Holy Scripture, but divers in human authors, said to have suffered by way of suspension or crucifixion might not perish by immediate crucifixion;[4] but however otherwise destroyed, their bodies might be afterward appended or fastened unto some elevated engine, as exemplary objects unto the eyes of the people. So sometimes we read of the crucifixion of only some part, as of the heads of Julianus and Albinus, though their bodies were cast away.[5] Besides, all crosses or engines of crucifixion were not of the ordinary figure, nor compounded of transverse pieces, which make out the name, but some were simple, and made of one *arrectarium* serving for affixion or infixion, either fastening or piercing through; and some kind of crucifixion is the setting of heads upon poles.

That legal text which seems to countenance the common way of hanging, if a man hath committed a sin worthy of death, and they hang him on a tree,* is not so received by Christian and Jewish expositors. And, as a good annotator of ours† delivereth, out of Maimonides: the Hebrews understand not this of putting him to death by hanging, but of hanging a man after he was stoned to death, and the manner is thus described; after he is stoned to death they fasten a piece of timber in the earth, and out of it there cometh a piece of wood, and then they tie both his hands one to another, and hang him unto the setting of the sun.

* Deut. xxi. † Ainsworth.

[3] *the Gibeonites, &c.*] The Jews, as is just afterwards remarked, inflicted the infamy (rather than punishment) of hanging *after* death. And so might these Gibeonites. But they were not Israelites, as Rev. T. H. Horne has observed, but Canaanites, and probably retained their own laws. See his section on the punishments mentioned in Scripture; *Introduction, &c.* part ii. ch. iii. §iv.

[4] *Nor only, &c.*] This sentence is inserted, in MS. SLOAN. 1827, instead of the following: "Many, both in Scripture and human writers, might be said to be crucified, though they did not perish immediately by crucifixion."

[5] *cast away.*] The succeeding sentence was added from MS. SLOAN. 1827.

Beside, the original word, *hakany,* determineth not the doubt. For that by lexicographers or dictionary interpreters, is rendered suspension and crucifixion, there being no Hebrew word peculiarly and fully expressing the proper word of crucifixion, as it was used by the Romans; nor easy to prove it the custom of the Jewish nation to nail them by distinct parts unto a cross, after the manner of our Saviour crucified; wherein it was a special favour indulged unto Joseph to take down the body.

Lipsius lets fall a good caution to take off doubts about suspension delivered by ancient authors, and also the ambiguous sense of κρεμάσαι among the Greeks. *Tale apud Latinos ipsum suspendere, quod in crucem referendum moneo juventutem;* as that also may be understood of Seneca, *Latrocinium fecit aliquis, quid ergo meruit? ut suspendatur.* And this way of crucifying he conceiveth to have been in general use among the Romans, until the latter days of Constantine, who in reverence unto our Saviour abrogated that opprobrious and infamous way of crucifixion. Whereupon succeeded the common and now practised way of suspension.

But long before this abrogation of the cross, the Jewish nation had known the true sense of crucifixion: whereof no nation had a sharper apprehension, while Adrian crucified five hundred of them every day, until wood was wanting for that service. So that they which had nothing but 'crucify' in their mouths, were therewith paid home in their own bodies; early suffering the reward of their imprecations, and properly in the same kind.

CHAPTER XXII.[6]

Of the Picture of God the Father; of the Sun, Moon, and Winds, with others.

THE picture of the Creator, or God the Father, in the shape

---

[6] *Chap.* xxii.] The first and second subjects of this chapter were Nos. 14 and 15, of chapter xxii. in editions 1672 and 1686. There they were obviously out of their place, occurring in the midst of a very different class of observations. I have therefore removed them: and having found (in No. 1827 of the Sloanian MSS. in the British Museum) some

of an old man, is a dangerous piece,[7] and in this fecundity of sects may revive the *anthropomorphites*.* Which although maintained from the expression of Daniel, "I beheld where the ancient of days did sit, whose hair of his head was like the pure wool;" yet may it be also derivative from the hieroglyphical description of the Egyptians; who to express their eneph or Creator of the world, described an old man in a blue mantle, with an egg in his mouth, which was the emblem of the world. Surely those heathens, that notwithstanding the exemplary advantage in heaven, would endure no pictures of sun or moon, as being visible unto all the world, and needing no representation, do evidently accuse the practice of those pencils that will describe invisibles. And he that challenged the boldest hand unto the picture of an echo, must laugh at this attempt, not only in the description of invisibility, but circumscription of ubiquity, and fetching under lines incomprehensible circularity.

The pictures of the Egyptians were more tolerable, and in their sacred letters more veniably expressed the apprehension of divinity. For though they implied the same by an eye upon a sceptre, by an eagle's head, a crocodile and the like, yet did these manual descriptions pretend no corporal representations, nor could the people misconceive the same unto real correspondencies. So, though the cherub carried some apprehension of divinity, yet was it not conceived to be the shape thereof; and so perhaps, because it is metaphorically predicated of God that he is a consuming fire, he may be harmlessly described by a flaming representation.

* Certain hereticks who ascribed human figure unto God, after which they conceived he created man in his likeness.

additional instances of mistakes in "pictural draughts," I have formed the two transplanted numbers, together with the hitherto unpublished matter, into a new chapter.

[7] *piece.*] This is a very just and worthy censure, and well followed with scorne in the close of this paragraph. St. Paul saw things in a vision which himself could not utter: and therefore they are verye bold with God, who dare to picture him in any shape visible to the eye of mortality, which Daniel himself behelde not, but in a rapture and an extatical vision: unlesse they can answere that staggering question, "To what will you liken me?"—*Wr.*

St. Avgustine censures this impropriety; Ep. cxxii.

Yet if, as some will have it, all mediocrity of folly is foolish, and because an unrequitable evil may ensue, an indifferent convenience must be omitted, we shall not urge such representments; we could spare the Holy Lamb for the picture of our Saviour, and the dove or fiery tongues to represent the Holy Ghost.

2. The sun and moon are usually described with human faces; whether herein there be not a Pagan imitation, and those visages at first implied Apollo and Diana, we may make some doubt; and we find the statue of the sun was framed with rays about the head, which were the indeciduous and unshaven locks of Apollo. We should be too iconomical* to question the pictures of the winds, as commonly drawn in human heads, and with their cheeks distended; which notwithstanding we find condemned by Minutius, as answering poetical fancies, and the Gentile description of Æolus, Boreas, and the feigned deities of winds.

3.[8] In divers pieces, and that signal one of Testa,[9] describing Hector dragged by Achilles about the walls of Troy, we find him drawn by cords or fastenings about both his ancles; which notwithstanding is not strictly answerable unto the account of Homer, concerning this act upon Hector, but rather applicable unto that of Hippothous drawing away the body of Patroclus, according to the expression of Homer:

> Hippothous pede trahebat in forti pugna per acrem pugnam.
> Ligatum loro ad malleolum circa tendines.—*Hom. Il.* xvii. 289.

---

* Or quarrelsome with pictures. Dion. Ep. 7, a, *ad Policar. et Pet. Hall. not. in vit. S. Dionys.*

[8] § 3.] The rest of this chapter is now first printed;—from MS. SLOAN· 1827, 3;—where it is thus prefaced:—" Though some things we have elsewhere delivered of the impropriety, falsity, or mistakes, in pictural draughts, yet to awaken your curiosity, these may be also considered. —In divers pieces, &c."

[9] *Testa.*] Pietro Testa, a painter of Lucca and Rome, drowned 1632, in the Tyber, endeavouring to save his hat, which had been blown off by a gust of wind.—*Gr.*

For that act performed by Achilles upon Hector is more particularly described:

> Amborum retro pedum perforavit tendines
> Ad talum usque a calce, bubulaque innexuit lora
> De curruque ligavit; caput vero trahi sivit.—*Hom. Il.* xxii. 396.

So that he bound not these ties about his feet, but made a perforation behind them, through which he ran the thongs, and so dragged him after his chariot: which was not hard to effect; the strength of those tendons being able to hold in that tracture; and is a common way practised by butchers, thus to hang their sheep and oxen.[1]

This, though an unworthy act, and so delivered by Homer, yet somewhat retaliated the intent of Hector himself towards the body of Patroclus, the intimate of Achilles; and stands excused by Didymus upon the custom of the Thessalians, to drag the body of the homicide unto the grave of their slain friends; and the example of Simon the Thessalian, who thus dealt with the body of Eurodamus, who had before slain his brother.

4. But, not to amuse you with pictures derived from Gentile histories, the draught of Potiphar's lady lying on a bed, and drawing Joseph unto her, seems additional unto the text, nor strictly justifiable from it; wherein it is only said, that, after some former temptation, when Joseph came home to despatch or order his affairs, and there was no man of the house then within, or with him, that she laid hold of his garment and said, "lye with me," without such apt preparations either of nakedness, or being in her bed, or the like opportunities, which pictures thereof have described.

5. The picture of Moses, praying between Hur and Aaron, seems to have miscarried in some draughts; while some omit the rod which he should hold up in his hand; and others describe him on his knees, with his hands supported by them: whereas it is plainly said in the text, that, when Moses was weary of standing, he sat down upon the rock. And therefore, for the whole process, and full representation, there must be more than one draught; the one representing him

[1] *oxen.*] In the royal library at Turin is a curious volume, containing the *Iliad*, illustrated by the monks. One of the illuminations represents the burial of Hector, and a train of Benedictines assisting in the funeral ceremony.

in station, the other in session, another in genuflexion. And though in this piece Aaron is allowed to be present on the hill at Rephidim, yet may he also challenge a place in the other piece of mount Sinai (wherein he is often omitted), according to the command of God unto Moses: "Thou shalt come up, thou *and Aaron with thee;* but let not the priests nor the people break through, to come up unto the Lord."

6. The picture of Jael nailing the head of Sisera unto the ground, seems questionable in some draughts; while Sisera is made to lie in a prone posture, and the nail driven into the upper part of the head; whereas it is plainly delivered that Jael struck the nail through his temples, and fastened him to the ground: and which was the most proper and penetrable part of the skull; such as a woman's hand might pierce, driving a large nail through, and longer than the breadth of a head, according to the description,—that she took no ordinary nail, but such as fastened her tent, and pierced his head, and the ground under it.

7. An improper spectacle at a feast, and very incongruous unto the birth-day of a prince, a time of pardon and relaxation, was the head of John the Baptist. More properly, in the noble picture thereof, the hand of Reuben hath left out the person of Herodias, who was not in the room, agreeably unto the delivery of St. Mark; that, after Herod had promised to grant her daughter whatever she would ask, she went out to enquire of her mother, Herodias, what she should demand. And that Salome, or her daughter, brought in the head of John unto Herod, as he was sitting at the table, though it well sets off the picture, is not expressed in the text; wherein it is only said that she brought it unto her mother.

8. That King Ahasuerus feasted apart from the queen, is confirmable from Scripture account. Whether the queen were present at the fatal feast of Belshazzar seems of greater doubt; forasmuch as it is said in the text, that, upon the fright and consternation of the king, when none of the Chaldeans could read the hand-writing on the wall, the queen came in, and recommended Daniel unto him. But if it be only meant and understood of the queen-mother, the draught may hold, and the *licentia pictoria* not culpable in that notable piece of Tintoret or Bassano describing the feast of

Belshazzar, wherein the queen is placed at the table with the king.

9. Though some hands have failed, yet the draught of St. Peter in the prison is properly designed by Rubens, sleeping between two soldiers, and a chain on each arm; and so illustrateth the text, that is, with two chains fastened unto his arms, and the one arm of each of the soldiers, according to the custom of those times, to fasten the prisoner unto his guard or keeper; and after which manner St. Paul is conceived to have had the liberty of going about Rome.

10. In the picture of our Saviour sleeping in the ship, while in many draughts he is placed not far from the middle, or in the prow of the vessel, it is a variation from the text, which distinctly saith "at the poop," which being the highest part, was freest from the billows. Again, in some pieces he is made sleeping with his head hanging down; in others, on his elbow; which amounteth not unto the textual expression, "upon a pillow," or some soft support, or at least (as some conceive that emphatical expression may imply) some part of the ship convenient to lean down the head. Besides, this picture might properly take in the concurrent account of the Scripture, and not describe a single ship, since the same delivereth that there went off other *naviculæ*, or small vessels with it.

11. Whilst the text delivereth that the tempter placed our Saviour (as we read it) upon the *pinnacle* of the temple, some draughts do place him upon the point of the highest turrets; which, notwithstanding, Josephus describeth to have been made so sharp that birds might not light upon them; and the word πτερύγιον signifying a *pinna*,[2] or some projecture of the building, it may probably be conceived to have been some plain place or jetty, from whence he might well cast himself down upon the ground, not falling upon any part of the temple; if there were no wing or prominent part of the building peculiarly called by that name.

12. That piece of the three children in the fiery furnace, in several draughts, doth not conform unto the historical

---

[2] *the word, &c.*] Unquestionably it could not have been any thing like a turret or pinnacle. Some commentators (Le Clerc) consider it a projecting portion of the building outside the parapet. Others (Rosenmüller) call it the flat roof of a portico.

accounts: while in some they are described naked and bareheaded; and in others with improper coverings on their heads. Whereas the contrary is delivered in the text, under all learned languages, and also by our own, with some expositions in the margin: not naked in their bodies, (according to their figure in the *Roma Sotterranea* of Bosio,[3] among the sepulchral figures in the monument of St. Priscilla), but having a loose habit, after the Persian mode, upon them, whereby it might be said that their garments did not so much as smell of the fire; nor bare on their heads, as described in the first chamber of the cemetery of Priscilla, but having on it a tiara, or cap, after the Persian fashion, made somewhat reclining or falling agreeable unto the third table of the fifth cemetery, and the mode of the Persian subjects; not a peaked, acuminated, and erected cap, proper unto their kings, as is set down in the medal of Antoninus, with the reverse, *Armenin*. A standard direction for this piece might probably be that ancient description set down in the calendar used by the Emperor Basilius Porphyrogenitus, and by Pope Paul the Fifth, given unto the Vatican, where it is yet conserved.[4]

[3] *Roma, &c.*] Jacques Bosio, *Roma Sotterranea*; left imperfect by him, but published by his executor, Aldrovandini, fol. 1632; since translated into Latin, and reprinted several times, with additions.—*Gr*.

[4] Numerous additions might yet further be made to our author's collection of pictorial inaccuracies, if such were fairly within our province. It may be allowed to us, at least, to give one or two references to such additions. John Interian de Ayala, a Spanish monk, who died at Madrid, in 1770, published a work on the errors of painters in representing religious subjects; it is entitled *Pictor Christianus Eruditus*, fol. 1720.

In the European Magazine, for 1786, vol. ix. p. 241, is noticed a very curious work (little known), by M. Phil. Rohr, entitled *Pictor Errans*, which was abridged by Mr. W. Bowyer. Mr. Singer, in his *Anecdotes of Spence*, and Mr. D'Israeli, in his *Curiosities of Literature*, have given some very amusing collectanea of the kind. In the Monthly Magazine for 1812, are noticed several singular absurdities in costume; and undoubtedly many other such examples would reward a diligent forage through our numerous periodical publications:—but it is only requisite to compare the *Illustrations* which are constantly issuing from the hands of our artists, with the works they are intended to illustrate, in order to be frequently reminded of the proverbial conclusion of the whole matter;—"*it is even as pleaseth the painter.*"

CHAPTER XXIII.

Compendiously of many popular Customs, Opinions, &c. viz. of an Hare crossing the High-way; of the ominous appearing of Owls and Ravens; of the falling of Salt; of breaking the Egg-shell: of the True Lovers' Knot; of the Cheek Burning or Ear Tingling; of speaking under the Rose; of Smoke following the Fair; of Sitting cross-legged; of hair upon Moles; of the set time of pairing of Nails; of Lions' heads upon Spouts and Cisterns; of the saying, Ungirt, Unblest; of the Sun dancing on Easter-day; of the Silly-how; of being Drunk once a Month; of the appearing of the Devil with a Cloven hoof.

IF an hare cross the high-way,[5] there are few above threescore years that are not perplexed thereat; which notwithstanding is but an augurial terror, according to that received expression, *Inauspicatum dat iter oblatus lepus.* And the ground of the conceit was probably no greater than this, that a fearful animal passing by us, portended unto us something to be feared: as upon the like consideration, the meeting of a fox presaged some future imposture; which was a superstitious observation prohibited unto the Jews, as is expressed in the idolatry of Maimonides, and is referred unto the sin of an observer of fortunes, or one that abuseth events unto good or bad signs; forbidden by the law of Moses; which notwithstanding sometimes succeeding, according to fears or desires, have left impressions and timorous expectations in credulous minds for ever.

2. That owls and ravens[6] are ominous appearers, and pre-

---

[5] *hare.*] When a hare crosseth us, wee thinke itt ill lucke shee should soe neerely escape us, and we had not a dog as neere to catch her.—*Wr.*

[6] *ravens.*] The raven, by his accute sense of smelling, discerns the savour of the dying bodyes at the tops of chimnies, and that makes them flutter about the windows, as they use to doe in the searche of a carcasse. Now bycause whereever they doe this, itt is an evident signe that the sick party seldome escapes deathe: thence ignorant people counte them ominous, as foreboding deathe, and in some kind as causing deathe, whereof they have a sense indeed, but are noe cause at all. Of owles there is not the same opinion, especially in country-men, who thinke as well of them in the barne as of the cat in the house: but in great cityes where they are not frequent, their shriking and horrid note in the night is offensive to women and children, and such as are weake or sicklye.—*Wr.*

On the owl, as an ominous bird, see *The Queen Bee*, ii. 22.—*Jeff.*

signifying unlucky events, as Christians yet conceit, was also an augurial conception. Because many ravens were seen when Alexander entered Babylon, they were thought to preominate his death; and because an owl appeared before the battle,[7] it presaged the ruin of Crassus. Which, though decrepit superstitions, and such as had their nativity in times beyond all history, are fresh in the observation of many heads, and by the credulous and feminine party still in some majesty among us. And therefore the emblem of superstition was well set out by Ripa,* in the picture of an owl, an hare, and an old woman. And it no way confirmeth the augurial consideration that an owl is a forbidden food in the law of Moses; or that Jerusalem was threatened by the raven and the owl, in that expression of Isa. xxxiv.; that it should be "a court for owls, that the cormorant and the bittern should possess it, and the owl and the raven dwell in it;" for thereby was only implied their ensuing desolation, as is expounded in the words succeeding; "He shall draw upon it the line of confusion, and the stones of emptiness."[8]

3. The falling of salt[9] is an authentic presagement of ill-luck, nor can every temper contemn it; from whence not-

* *Iconologia de Cæsare.*

[7] *the battle.*] With the Parthians near Charræ.

[8] *emptiness.*] It is rather singular that the *cuckoo* is not honoured with a place here. "Plinie writeth that if, when you first hear the cuckoo, you mark well where your right foot standeth, and take up of that earth, the *fleas* will by no means breed, either in your house or chamber, where any of the same earth is thrown or scattered!" *Hill's Natural and Artificial Conclusions,* 1650. In the North, and perhaps all over England, it is vulgarly accounted an unlucky omen, if you have no money in your pocket, when you hear the cuckoo for the first time in a season. *Queen Bee,* ii. 20.—*Jeff.*

It would perhaps be rather difficult to say under what circumstances most people would *not* consider such a state of pocket an "unlucky omen."

It is a still more common popular divination, for those who are unmarried to count the number of years yet allotted to them of single blessedness, by the number of the cuckoo's notes which they count when first they hear it in the spring.

[9] *salt.*] Where salt is deare, 'tis as ill caste on the ground as bread. And soe itt is in France, where they pay for every bushel 40s. to the king; and cannot have itt elsewhere: and soe when a glass is spilt 'tis ill lucke to loose a good cup of wine.—*Wr.*

withstanding nothing can be naturally feared; nor was the same a general prognostick of future evil among the ancients, but a particular omination concerning the breach of friendship. For salt,[1] as incorruptible, was the symbol of friendship, and, before the other service, was offered unto their guests; which, if it casually fell, was accounted ominous, and their amity of no duration. But whether salt[2] were not only a symbol of friendship with man, but also a figure of amity and reconciliation with God, and was therefore observed in sacrifices, is an higher speculation.[3]

4. To break the egg-shell after the meat is out, we are taught in our childhood, and practise it all our lives; which nevertheless is but a superstitious relique, according to the judgment of Pliny; *Huc pertinet ovorum, ut exsorbuerit quisque calices protinus frangi, aut eosdem cochlearibus perforari;* and the intent hereof was to prevent witchcraft;[4]

---

[1] *For salt, &c.*] The hospitality most liberally shown by Mr. Ackerman of the Strand, to the Cossack veteran, Alexander Zemlenuten, in 1815, was highly estimated by the stranger, who in describing his generous reception used the exclamation, "He gave me bread and SALT." This is mentioned in the 41st vol. of the *Monthly Magazine*—and illustrated by a sketch of the opinions and feelings of the ancients respecting this "incorruptible symbol of friendship."—Leonardo da Vinci, in his picture of the last supper, has represented Judas Iscariot as having overturned the salt.—*Jeff.*

Captain M'Leod, in his voyage of the Alceste, says that in an island near the straits of Gaspar, "salt was received with the same horror as arsenic."

[2] *But whether salt, &c.*] First added in 2nd edition.

[3] *also a figure, &c.*] In the first vol. of *Blackwood's Magazine* will be found a paper on the *symbolical* uses of salt, p. 579. In the same volume also occur several papers on the use made formerly of the salt-cellar (which was often large, ornamented and valuable, and placed in the centre of the table) as a point of separation between guests of higher and lower degree.—*To drink below the salt* was a condescension; to attain a seat above it, an object of ambition.—See *Bishop Hall's Satires*, No. vi. b. 28.

Among the regalia used at the king's coronation, is the salt of state, to be placed in the centre of the dinner table, in the form of a castle with towers, richly embellished with various coloured stones, elegantly chased, and of silver, richly gilt. This, it is said, was presented to King Charles II. by the City of Exeter.—*Jeff.*

[4] *to prevent witchcraft.*] "To keep the fairies out," as they say in Cumberland.—*Jeff.*

for lest witches[5] should draw or prick their names herein, and veneficiously mischief their persons, they broke the shell, as Dalecampius hath observed.

5. The true lovers' knot[6] is very much magnified, and still retained in presents of love among us; which though in all points it doth not make out, had perhaps its original from the *nodus Herculanus*, or that which was called Hercules his knot, resembling the snaky complication in the *caduceus* or rod of Hermes; and in which form the zone or woollen girdle of the bride was fastened, as Turnebus observeth in his *Adversaria*.

6. When our cheek burneth or ear tingleth,[7] we usually say that somebody is talking of us, which is an ancient conceit, and ranked among superstitious opinions by Pliny; *Absentes tinnitu aurium præsentire sermones de se, receptum est;* according to that distich noted by Dalecampius;

>Garrula quid totis resonas mihi noctibus auris?
>Nescio quem dicis nunc meminisse mei.

Which is a conceit hardly to be made out without the concession of a signifying genius, or universal Mercury, conducting sounds unto their distant subjects, and teaching us to hear by touch.

7. When we desire to confine our words, we commonly say they are spoken under the rose;[8] which expression is

---

[5] *lest witches.*] Least they perchance might use them for boates (as they thought) to sayle in by night.—*Wr.*

[6] *lovers' knot.*] The true lovers' knot is magnified, for the moral signification not esily untyed; and for the naturall,—bycause itt is a knot both wayes, that is, two knots in one.—*Wr.*

[7] *tingleth.*] The singing of the eare is frequent upon the least cold seizing on the braine: but to make construction hereof, as yf itt were the silent humme of some absent friendly soule (especially falling most to bee observed in the night, when few friends are awake) is one of the dotages of the heathen.—*Wr.*

[8] *rose.*] Of those that commonlye use this proverb few, besides the learned, can give a reason why they use itt: itt is sufficient that all men knowe what wee meane by that old forme of speeche, thoughe (as of manye other such like) they know not the originall.—*Wr.*

Warburton (says Brand) commenting on that passage of Shakspeare in Henry VI.:—

" From off this briar pluck a white rose with me,"

supposes the present saying to have originated in the struggle between

commendable, if the rose from any natural property may be the symbol of silence, as Nazianzen seems to imply in these translated verses;

> Utque latet Rosa verna suo putamine clausa,
> Sic os vincla ferat, validisque arctetur habenis,
> Indicatque suis prolixa silentia labris:

And is also tolerable, if by desiring a secrecy to words spoken under the rose, we only mean in society and compotation, from the ancient custom in symposiack meetings, to wear chaplets of roses about their heads: and so we condemn not the German custom, which over the table describeth a rose in the ceiling. But more considerable it is, if the original were such as Lemnius and others have recorded, that the rose was the flower of Venus, which Cupid consecrated unto Harpocrates the God of silence, and was therefore an emblem thereof, to conceal the pranks of venery, as is declared in this tetrastich:

> Est rosa flos Veneris, cujus quò facta laterent,
> Harpocrati matris, dona dicavit amor;
> Inde rosam mensis hospes suspendit amicis,
> Convivæ ut sub eâ dicta tacenda sciant.[9]

8. That smoke doth follow the fairest,[1] is an usual saying with us,[2] and in many parts of Europe; whereof although there seem no natural ground, yet is it the continuation of a very ancient opinion, as Petrus, Victorius, and Casaubon have observed from a passage in Athenæus; wherein a parasite thus describeth himself:

the two houses of York and Lancaster; in which secrecy must very often have been enjoined, on various occasions, and probably was so "under the rose."

In Pegge's *Anonymiana*, the symbol of silence is referred to the rose on a clergyman's hat, and derived from the silence which popish priests kept as to the confessions of their people.—*Jeff*.

[9] *sciant.*] The discourses of the table among true loving friendes require as stricte silence, as those of the bed between the married.—*Wr*.

[1] *fairest.*] The fairest and tenderest complexions are soonest offended with itt: and therefore when they complain, men use this suppling proverb.—*Wr*.

[2] *an usual saying with us.*] An observation of Brand (*Popular Antiquities*) seems to imply that he considered the saying to have become extinct since the days of Browne. This is by no means the case. It is still very common in Norfolk.

> To every table first I come,
> Whence porridge I am call'd by some.
> A Capaneus at stairs I am,
> To enter any room a ram;
> Like whips and thongs to all I ply,
> Like smoke unto the fair I fly.

9. To sit cross-legged,[3] or with our fingers pectinated or shut together, is accounted bad, and friends will persuade us from it. The same conceit religiously possessed the ancients as is observable from Pliny; *poplites alternis genibus imponere nefas olim:* and also from Athenæus, that it was an old veneficious practice, and Juno is made in this posture to hinder the delivery of Alcmæna. And therefore, as Pierius observeth, in the medal of Julia Pia, the right-hand of Venus was made extended with the inscription of Venus Genitrix; for the complication or pectination of the fingers was an hieroglyphick of impediment, as in that place he declareth.

10. The set and statary times of pairing of nails, and cutting of hair,[4] is thought by many a point of consideration; which is perhaps but the continuation of an ancient superstition. For piaculous[5] it was unto the Romans to pare their nails upon the Nundinæ, observed every ninth day; and was also feared by others in certain days of the week; according to that of Ausonius, *Ungues Mercurio, Barbam Jove, Cypride Crines;* and was one part of the wickedness that filled up the measure of Manasses, when 'tis delivered that he observed times.*

11. A common fashion is to nourish hair upon the moles of the face; which is the perpetuation of a very ancient

---

* 1 Chron. xxxv.

[3] *To sit cross-legged.*] There is more incivilitye in this forme of sitting, then malice or superstition; and may sooner move our spleen to a smile then a chafe.—*Wr.*

[4] *hair.*] They that would encrease the haire maye doe well to observe the increasing moone at all times, but especially in Taurus or Cancer: they that would hinder the growthe, in the decrease of the moone, especially in Capricornus or Scorpio: and this is soe far from superstitious folly that it savours of one guided by the rules of the wise in physic. And what is sayd of the haire may bee as fitly applied to the nayles.—*Wr.* Oh! Mr. Dean!

[5] *piaculous.*] Requiring expiation.

custom; and, though innocently practised among us, may have a superstitious original, according to that of Pliny: *Nævos in facie tondere religiosum habent nunc multi.* From the like might proceed the fears of polling elvelocks[6] or complicated hairs off the heads, and also of locks longer than the other hair; they being votary at first, and dedicated upon occasion; preserved with great care, and accordingly esteemed by others, as appears by that of Apuleius, *adjuro per dulcem capilli tui nodulum.*

12. A custom there is in some parts of Europe to adorn aqueducts, spouts and cisterns with lions' heads; which though no illaudable ornament, is of an Egyptian genealogy, who practised the same under a symbolical illation. For because, the sun being in Leo, the flood of Nilus was at the full, and water became conveyed into every part, they made the spouts of their aqueducts through the head of a lion.[7] And upon some celestial respects it is not improbable the great Mogul or Indian king both bear for his arms the lion and the sun.[8]

13. Many conceive there is somewhat amiss, and that as we usually say, they are unblest, until they put on their girdle. Wherein (although most know not what they say) there are involved unknown considerations. For by a girdle or cincture are symbolically implied truth, resolution, and readiness unto action, which are parts and virtues required in the service of God. According whereto we find that the Israelites did eat the paschal lamb with their loins girded;[9]

* Isa. xi.

[6] *elvelocks.*] Such is the danger of cutting a haire in the Hungarian knot that the blood will flow out of itt, as by a quill, and will not bee stanched. And thence perhaps the custome first sprange, though since abused.—*Wr.*

[7] *lion.*] Architects practise this forme still, for noe other reason then the beautye of itt.—*Wr.*

[8] *sun.*] These two are the emblems of majestye: the sonne signifying singularity of incommunicable glory: the lyon sole soveraintye, or monarchall power; and therefore most sutable to their grandour.—*Wr.*

[9] *girded.*] I suppose this innocent custome is most comely and most Christian, partly in observation of the old precept of St. Paule [Ephes. vi. 14], and partly in imitation of him in the first of the revelation, who is described doubly girt, about the paps, and about the loyns. See the Icon of St. Paul before his Epistles, in the Italian Testament, at Lions, 1556.—*Wr.*

and the Almighty challenging Job, bids him gird up his
loins like a man. So runneth the expression of Peter,
" Gird up the loins of your minds, be sober and hope to the
end;" so the high priest was girt with the girdle of fine
linen; so is it part of the holy habit to have our loins girt
about with truth; and so is it also said concerning our
Saviour, " Righteousness shall be the girdle of his loins, and
faithfulness the girdle of his reins."

Moreover by the girdle, the heart and parts which God
requires are divided from the inferior and concupiscential
organs; implying thereby a memento, unto purification and
cleanness of heart, which is commonly defiled from the con-
cupiscence and affection of those parts; and therefore unto
this day the Jews do bless themselves when they put on
their zone or cincture. And thus may we make out the
doctrine of Pythagoras, to offer sacrifice with our feet naked,
that is, that our inferior parts, and farthest removed from
reason, might be free, and of no impediment unto us. Thus
Achilles, though dipped in Styx, yet, having his heel untouched by that water, although he were fortified elsewhere,
he was slain in that part, as only vulnerable in the inferior
and brutal part of man. This is that part of Eve and her
posterity the devil still doth bruise, that is, that part of the
soul which adhereth unto earth, and walks in the path
thereof. And in this secondary and symbolical sense it may
be also understood, when the priests in the law washed their
feet before the sacrifice; when our Saviour washed the feet
of his disciples, and said unto Peter, " If I wash not thy feet,
thou hast no part in me." And thus is it symbolically
explainable, and implieth purification and cleanness, when
in the burnt-offerings the priest is commanded to wash the
inwards and legs thereof in water; and in the peace and sin-
offerings, to burn the two kidneys, the fat which is about
the flanks, and as we translate it, the caul above the liver.
But whether the Jews, when they blessed themselves, had
any eye unto the words of Jeremy, wherein God makes them
his girdle; or had therein any reference unto the girdle,
which the prophet was commanded to hide in the hole of the

The Israelites ate the paschal lamb with their loins girt, as being in
readiness to take their journey (from Egypt).

rock of Euphrates, and which was the type of their captivity, we leave unto higher conjecture.

14. We shall not, I hope, disparage the resurrection of our Redeemer, if we say the sun doth not dance on Easter-day. And though we would willingly assent unto any sympathetical exultation, yet cannot conceive therein any more than a tropical expression. Whether any such motion there were in that day wherein Christ arose, Scripture hath not revealed, which hath been punctual in other records concerning solary miracles; and the Areopagite, that was amazed at the eclipse, took no notice of this. And if metaphorical expressions go so far, we may be bold to affirm, not only that one sun danced, but two arose that day:—that light appeared at his nativity, and darkness at his death, and yet a light at both; for even that darkness was a light unto the Gentiles, illuminated by that obscurity:—that it was the first time the sun set above the horizon:—that although there were darkness above the earth there was light beneath it; nor dare we say that hell was dark if he were in it.

15. Great conceits are raised of the involution or membranous covering, commonly called the silly-how, that sometimes is found about the heads of children upon their birth, and is therefore preserved with great care, not only as medical in diseases, but effectual in success, concerning the infant and others, which is surely no more than a continued superstition. For hereof we read in the *Life of Antoninus*, delivered by Spartianus, that children are born sometimes with this natural cap; which midwives were wont to sell unto credulous lawyers, who had an opinion it advantaged their promotion.[1]

---

[1] *promotion.*] By making them gracious in pleadinge: to whom I thinke itt was sufficient punishment, that they bought not wit, but folly so deare.—*Wr.*

Even till recently the opinion has been held, that a child's caul (silly-how) would preserve a person from drowning! In the *Times* of May 6, 1814, were three advertisements of fine cauls to be sold at considerable prices specified. The following appear at subsequent dates:—" To voyagers. A child's caul to be sold for 15 guineas. Apply, &c." *Times*, Dec. 8th, 1819.

Another for 16 guineas: *Times*, Dec. 16, 1829.

" A child's caul to be disposed of. The efficacy of this wonderful production of nature, in preserving the possessor from all accidents by sea and land, has long been experienced, and is universally acknow-

but to speak strictly, the effect is natural, and thus may be conceived: animal conceptions have (largely taken) three teguments, or membranous films, which cover them in the womb: that is, the *chorion, amnios* and *allantois*. The *chorion* is the outward membrane, wherein are implanted the veins, arteries, and umbilical vessels, whereby its nourishment is conveyed. The *allantois* is a thin coat seated under the *chorion*, wherein are received the watery separations conveyed by the *urachus*, that the acrimony thereof should not offend the skin. The *amnios* is a general investment, containing the sudorous or thin serocity perspirable through the skin. Now about the time when the infant breaketh these coverings, it sometimes carrieth with it, about the head, a part of the *amnois* or nearest coat; which, saith Spigelius,* either proceedeth from the toughness of the membrane, or weakness of the infant that cannot get clear thereof. And therefore, herein significations are natural and concluding upon the infant, but not to be extended unto magical signalities, or any other person.

16. That it is good to be drunk once a month, is a common flattery of sensuality, supporting itself upon physick, and the healthful effects of inebriation.[2] This indeed seems

* *De Formato Fœtu.*

ledged: the present phenomenon was produced on the 4th of March inst. and covered not only the head, but the whole body and limbs of a fine female infant, the daughter of a respectable master tradesman. Apply at No. 49, Gee-street. Goswell-street, where a reference will be given to the eminent physician who officiated at the birth of the child." *Times*, March 9th, 1820. Another advertised, £6, *Times*, Sept. 5th, 1820. Another for 12 guineas, *ditto*, Jan. 23rd, 1824. See *New Monthly Mag.*, May, July, Aug. 1814.

Intellect, surely, was not yet *in full march* at this period.

[2] *inebriation*.] Noe man could more properlye inveighe against this beastly sinn, then a grave and learned physitian, were itt for noe more but the acquitting his noble faculty from the guilt of conntenancinge a medicine soe lothsome and soe odious. Certainlye itt cannot but magnifie his sober spirit, that does make his own facultye (as Hagar to Sarah) vayle to divinity, the handmayd to her lady and mistresse: especially seeinge the naturall man cannot but confesse that itt is base, unworthye the divine offspring of the human soule, which is immortall, to put of itself for a moment, or to assume the shape, or much less the guise of (the uglyest beast) a swine, for any supposable benefit accruing thereby to this outward carcasse, especially when itt may bee far

plainly affirmed by Avicenna, a physician of great authority, and whose religion, prohibiting wine, could less extenuate ebriety. But Averroes, a man of his own faith, was of another belief; restraining his ebriety unto hilarity, and in effect making no more thereof than Seneca commendeth, and was allowable in Cato; that is, a sober incalescence and regulated æstuation from wine; or, what may be conceived between Joseph and his brethren, when the text expresseth they were merry, or drank largely; and whereby indeed the commodities set down by Avicenna, that is, alleviation of spirits, resolution of superfluities, provocation of sweat and urine, may also ensue. But as for dementation, sopition of reason and the diviner particle, from drink; though American religion approve, and Pagan piety of old hath practised it, even at their sacrifices, Christian morality and the doctrine of Christ will not allow. And surely that religion which excuseth the fact of Noah, in the aged surprisal of six hundred years, and unexpected inebriation from the unknown effects of wine, will neither acquit ebriosity[3] nor ebriety, in their known and intended perversions.

And indeed although sometimes effects succeed which may relieve the body, yet if they carry mischief or peril unto the soul, we are therein restrainable by divinity, which circumscribeth physick, and circumstantially determines the use thereof. From natural considerations physick commendeth the use of venery; and haply incest, adultery, or stupration, may prove as physically advantageous as conjugal copulation; which notwithstanding must not be drawn into practice. And truly effects, consequents, or events which we commend, arise ofttimes from ways which we all condemn. Thus from the fact of Lot we derive the generation of Ruth and blessed nativity of our Saviour; which notwithstanding did not extenuate the incestuous ebriety of the generator. And if, as is commonly urged, we think to extenuate ebriety from the benefit of vomit oft succeeding, Egyptian sobriety will con-

better relieved by soe many excellent, easie, warrantable wayes of physick.—*Wr*.

"Drunkenness (methinks) can neither become a wise philosopher to prescribe, nor a virtuous man to practise."—*Bp. Hall, Heaven upon Earth*, § 3.

[3] *ebriosity*.] Habitual drunkenness.

demn us, which purged both ways twice a month without this perturbation; and we foolishly contemn the liberal hand of God, and ample field of medicines which soberly produce that action.

17. A conceit there is, that the devil commonly appeareth with a cloven hoof:[4] wherein, although it seem excessively ridiculous, there may be somewhat of truth; and the ground thereof at first might be his frequent appearing in the shape of a goat, which answers that description. This was the opinion of ancient Christians concerning the apparition of Panites, fauns, and satyrs; and in this form we read of one that appeared unto Antony in the wilderness. The same is also confirmed from expositions of Holy Scriptures; for whereas it is said,* "Thou shalt not offer unto devils," the original word is *seghnirim*, that is, rough and hairy goats, because in that shape the devil most often appeared; as is expounded by the Rabbins, and Tremellius hath also explained; and as the word Ascimah, the god of Emath, is by some conceived. Nor did he only assume this shape in elder times, but commonly in latter times, especially in the place of his worship, if there be any truth in the confession of witches, and as in many stories it stands confirmed by Bodinus.† And therefore a goat is not improperly made the hieroglyphick of the devil, as Pierius hath expressed it. So might it be the emblem of sin, as it was in the sin-offering; and so likewise of wicked and sinful men, according to the expression of Scripture in the method of the last distribution; when our Saviour shall separate the sheep from the goats, that is, the sons of the Lamb from the children of the devil.

* Levit. xvii. † In his *Dæmonomania*.

[4] *hoof.*] 'Tis remarkable that of all creatures the devil chose the cloven-footed, wherein to appeare, as satyrs, and goatishe monsters: the swine whereon to worke his malice: and the calves wherein to bee worshiped as at Dan and Bethel. For which cause the Spirit of God cald those calves (raised by Jeroboam for worship) devils: 2 Chron. xi. 15. And that he chose his priests of the lowest of the people was very suitable. For where their god was a calfe, 'twas not improper that a butcher should be the preiste.—*Wr.*

CHAPTER XXIV.

Of Popular Customs, Opinions, &c.; of the Prediction of the Year ensuing from the Insects in Oak Apples; that Children would naturally speak Hebrew; of refraining to kill Swallows; of Lights burning dim at the Apparition of Spirits; of the wearing of Coral; of Moses' Rod in the Discovery of Mines; of discovering doubtful matters by Book or Staff.

1. THAT temperamental dignotions, and conjecture of prevalent humours, may be collected from spots in our nails, we are not averse to concede; but yet not ready to admit sundry divinations vulgularly raised upon them. Nor do we observe it verified in others, what Cardan * discovered as a property in himself; to have found therein some signs of most events that ever happened unto him. Or that there is much considerable in that doctrine of cheiromancy, that spots in the top of the nails do signify things past; in the middle, things present; and at the bottom, events to come. That white specks presage our felicity; blue ones our misfortunes. That those in the nail of the thumb have significations of honour; those in the forefinger, of riches; and so respectively in other fingers (according to planetical relations, from whence they receive their names), as Tricassus † hath taken up, and Picciolus well rejecteth.⁵

We shall not proceed to query what truth there is in palmistry, or divination from those lines in our hands, of high denomination. Although if any thing be therein, it seems not confinable unto man; but other creatures are also considerable; as is the forefoot of the mole, and especially of the monkey, wherein we have observed the table-line, that of life and of the liver.

2. That children committed unto the school of nature, without institution, would naturally speak the primitive language of the world, was the opinion of ancient heathens, and

* *De Varietate Rerum.* † *De Inspectione Manûs.*

⁵ *spots, &c.*] This saying has remained to the present day. Such superstitions will only cease when the ignorance of the lower orders, through whom they find their way into the nursery, shall have given place to the general diffusion of knowledge—especially of *religious* knowledge.

continued since by Christians; who will have it our Hebrew tongue, as being the language of Adam. That this were true, were much to be desired, not only for the easy attainment of that useful tongue, but to determine the true and primitive Hebrew. For whether the present Hebrew be the unconfounded language of Babel, and that which, remaining in Heber, was continued by Abraham and his posterity;[6] or

[6] *For whether the present Hebrew, &c.*] On the subject of this passage, patient and learned ingenuity has been exercised in successive ages to afford us—only hypothesis and conjectures. And though it must be admitted that nothing more satisfactory can, in the nature of things, be expected, yet is it certain, that in order to constitute a *thorough* competency to propose even these, nothing less would suffice than the most profound acquaintance with history and geography from their remotest traces; and an erudition competent to the analysis and classification, not only of the languages of antiquity, but of those living tongues and dialects which now cover the earth, and to which modern discoveries are daily making additions. On the question, whether the confusion of tongues left one section or family of the existing population in possession of the pure and unadulterated antediluvian language, I cannot perceive the materials for constructing even a conjecture. As to the theory here proposed, on which Abraham might understand those nations among whom he sojourned, by his own means of philological approximation, I cannot help feeling that it is almost like claiming for the patriarch an exemption from the operation of the confusion of tongues. Among the most recent works on this general class of questions, is Mr. Beke's *Origines Biblicæ*, a work in which some novel hypotheses have called down on their author the criticism of those who differ from him; while at the same time the tribute of praise has not been denied to the ability he has displayed, and especially to that spirit of reverence for scriptural authority which pervades his work.

Mr. Beke first states his opinion,—in opposition to the more usual hypothesis which considers the languages of the Jews, Arabians, and other nations of similar character, to be the Semitic or Shemitish family of languages,—that this origin may more probably be assigned to those of Tibet, China, and all those nations of the east and south-east of Asia, which are manifestly distinct from the Japhthitish Hindoos and Tartars; including the islands of the Indian Archipelago and the South Seas. He subsequently gives the following reasons for attributing to the usually-called Semitic languages (namely, Hebrew, Chaldee, Syriac, Arabic, and Ethiopic of Abyssinia), "a Mitzrite, and therefore Hamitish origin." "When the Almighty was pleased to call Abraham from his native country, the land of the Arphaxidites, or Chaldees, first into the country of Aram, and afterwards into that of Canaan, one of two things must necessarily have had place; either that the inhabitants of these latter countries spoke the same language as himself, or else that he acquired the knowledge of the foreign tongues spoken by these people during his residence in the countries in which they were vernacular. That they

rather the language of Phœnicia and Canaan, wherein he lived, some learned men I perceive do yet remain unsatisfied.

all made use of the same language cannot be imagined. Even if it be assumed that the descendants of Arphaxad, Abraham's ancestor, and the Aramites, in whose territories Terah and his family first took up their residence, spoke the same language, or, at the furthest, merely dialects of the same original Shemitish tongue, we cannot suppose that this language would have resembled those which were spoken by the Hamitish Canaanites, and Philistines, in whose countries Abraham afterwards sojourned, unless we at the same time contend that the confusion of tongues at Babel was practically inoperative; a conclusion, I apprehend, in which we should be directly opposed to the express words of Scripture: Gen. xi. 1—9.

"We have no alternative, therefore, as it would seem, but to consider (as, in fact, is the plain and obvious interpretation of the circumstances), that Abraham having travelled from his native place (a distance of above 500 miles) to the 'south country,' the land of the Philistines, where he 'sojourned many days,' he and his family would have acquired the language of the people amongst whom they thus took up their residence. But it may be objected that Abraham and his descendants, although living in a foreign country, and necessarily speaking the language of that country in their communications with its inhabitants, would also have retained the Aramitish tongue spoken in Haran, and that the intercourse between the two countries having been kept up, first by the marriage of Isaac with his cousin Rebekah, and subsequently by that of Jacob also with his cousins Leah and Rachel, and more especially from the circumstance of Jacob's having so long resided in Padan-Aram, and of all his children, with the exception of Benjamin, having been born there, the *family* language of Jacob, at the time of his return into the 'south country,' must indisputably have been the Aramitish. It may be argued farther, that although for the purpose of holding communication with the Canaanities and the Philistines, it was necessary to understand their languages also, yet that the language most familiar to Jacob and his household continued to be the Aramitish, until the period when they all left Canaan to go down into Mitzraim; and hence it might be contended that no good reason exists for opposing the generally received opinion, that the Hebrew is the same Aramitish tongue which was taken by the Israelites into Mitzraim, it being only necessary to suppose that the language was preserved substantially without corruption during the whole time of their sojourning in that country.

"But even admitting this argument, which however I am far from allowing to be conclusive; how are we to explain the origin of the Arabic language? This is clearly not of Aramitish derivation. It is the language which was spoken by the countrymen of Hagar, amongst whom Ishmael was taken by her to reside, and with whom he and his descendants speedily became mixed up and completely identified. Among these people it is not possible that the slightest portion of the

Although I confess probability stands fairest for the former; nor are they without all reason, who think that at the confusion of tongues, there was no constitution of a new speech in every family, but a variation and permutation of the old; out of one common language raising several dialects, the primitive tongue remaining still entire; which they who retained, might make a shift to understand most of the rest. By virtue whereof in those primitive times and greener confu-

Aramitish tongue of Abraham should have existed before the time of Ishmael; nor can it be conceived that the Mitzritish descendants of the latter would have acquired that language through him, even supposing (though I consider it to be far from an established fact) that the Aramitish had continued to be the *only* language which was spoken by Abraham's family during the whole of his residence in the south country among the Canaanites and Philistines; and supposing, also, that Ishmael acquired a perfect knowledge of that language, *and of no other* (which, however, is very improbable, his mother being a Mitzrite), from the circumstance of his childhood having been passed in his father's house.

"I apprehend, indeed, that the Mitzritish origin of the Arabic language is a fact which cannot be disputed; and if this fact be conceded, there remains no alternative but to admit—indeed it is a mere truism to say—that the Hebrew, which is a cognate dialect with the Arabic, must be of common origin with that language, and consequently of Mitzritish derivation also............ The fact of the striking coincidences which may be found in the language of the Berbers, in Northern Africa, with the languages of cognate origin with the Hebrew, is in the highest degree confirmatory of the Hamitish origin which I attribute to the whole of them; and it becomes the more particularly so, on the consideration that I derive the Berbers themselves directly from the country where I conceive the Israelites to have acquired their language."

As to the nature and degree of change which took place in the existing language at its confusion, Mr. Beke contends, "that the idea of an absolute and permanent change of dialect is more strictly in accordance with the literal meaning of the scriptural account of the confusion of tongues, than the supposition that the consequences of that miraculous occurrence were of a temporary nature only, and that the whole of the present diversities in the languages of the world are to be referred to the gradual operation of subsequent causes."

In the foregoing sentence, and still more in the disquisition which precedes it, Mr. Beke's opinion is in opposition to a very high authority both as a natural historian and a philologist,—the Rev. W. D. Conybeare, who supports (in his *Elementary Course of Lectures, on the Criticism, Interpretation, and Leading Doctrines of the Bible*), the more usually received opinion, that Hebrew, and the cognate languages, are of Shemitish origin.

sions, Abraham, of the family of Heber, was able to converse with the Chaldeans, to understand Mesopotamians, Canaanites, Philistines, and Egyptians: whose several dialects he could reduce unto the original and primitive tongue, and so be able to understand them.

3. Though useless unto us, and rather of molestation,[7] we commonly refrain from killing swallows, and esteem it unlucky[8] to destroy them: whether herein there be not a Pagan relick, we have some reason to doubt. For we read in Ælian, that these birds were sacred unto the Penates or household gods of the ancients, and therefore were preserved.* The same they also honoured as the nuncios of the spring; and we find in Athenæus that the Rhodians had a solemn song to welcome in the swallow.

4. That candles and lights burn dim and blue at the apparition of spirits, may be true, if the ambient air be full of sulphureous spirits, as it happeneth ofttimes in mines, where damps and acid exhalations are able to extinguish them. And may be also verified, when spirits do make themselves visible by bodies of such effluviums. But of lower consideration is the common foretelling of strangers, from the fungous parcels about the wicks of candles; which only signifieth a moist and pluvious air about them, hindering the avolation of the light and favillous particles; whereupon they are forced to settle upon the snast.[9]

5. Though coral doth properly preserve and fasten the teeth in men, yet is it used in children to make an easier passage for them: and for that intent is worn about their

* The same is extant in the 8th of Athenæus.

[7] *useless, &c.*] This is a most undeserved censure. The swallows are very useful in destroying myriads of insects, which would be injurious.

[8] *and esteem it unlucky, &c.*] A similar superstition attaches to the robin and the wren;—the tradition is, that if their nests are robbed, the cows will give bloody milk;—schoolboys rarely are found hardy enough to commit such a depredation on these birds, of which the common people in some parts of England have this legend—

    Robinets and Jenny Wrens,
    Are God Almighty's cocks and hens.

[9] *snast.*] The Norfolk (and perhaps other *folk's*) vulgar term, signifying the burnt portion of the wick of the candle; which, when sufficiently lengthened by want of snuffing, becomes crowned with a cap of the purest lamp-black, called here, "the fungous parcels," &c.

necks. But whether this custom were not superstitiously founded, as presumed an amulet or defensative against fascination, is not beyond all doubt. For the same is delivered by Pliny;* *Aruspices religiosum coralli gestamen amoliendis periculis arbitrantur; et surculi infantia alligati, tutelam habere creduntur.*[1]

6. A strange kind of exploration and peculiar way of rhabdomancy is that which is used in mineral discoveries; that is, with a forked hazel, commonly called Moses' rod, which freely held forth, will stir and play if any mine be under it. And though many there are who have attempted to make it good, yet until better information, we are of opinion with Agricola†, that in itself it is a fruitless exploration,[2] strongly scenting of Pagan derivation, and the *virgula divina*, proverbially magnified of old. The ground whereof were the magical rods in poets, that of Pallas in Homer, that of Mercury that charmed Argus, and that of Circe which transformed the followers of Ulysses. Too boldly usurping the name of Moses' rod, from which notwithstanding, and that of Aaron, were probably occasioned the fables of all the rest. For that of Moses must needs be famous unto the Egyptians; and that of Aaron unto many other nations, as being preserved in the ark, until the destruction of the temple built by Solomon.

* Lib. xxxii. † *De Re Metallica*, lib. ii.

[1] *That temperamental, &c.*] The first five sections of this chapter were first added in the 2nd edition.

[2] *exploration.*] This is worthy of note because itt is averred by many authors of whom the world hath a great opinion.— *Wr.*

From a paper by Mr. Wm. Philips, in *Tilloch's Philosophical Magazine*, vol. xiii. p. 309, on the divining rod, it appears that it was ably advocated by De Thouvenel, in France, in the 18th century, and soon after—in our own country—by a philosopher of unimpeachable veracity, and a chemist, Mr. William Cookworthy, of Plymouth. Pryce also informs us, p. 123, of his *Mineralogia Cornubiensis*, that many mines have been discovered by means of the rod, and quotes several; but, after a long account of the mode of cutting, tying, and using it, interspersed with observations on the discriminating faculties of constitutions and persons in its use, altogether rejects it, because "Cornwall is so plentifully stored with tin and copper lodes, that some accident every week discovers to us a fresh vein," and because "a grain of metal attracts the rod as strongly as a pound," for which reason "it has been found to dip equally to a poor as to a rich lode."—See *Trans. Geol. Soc.* ii. 123.

7. A practice there is among us to determine doubtful matters, by the opening[3] of a book, and letting fall a staff, which notwithstanding are ancient fragments of Pagan divinations. The first an imitation of *sortes Homericæ*, or *Virgilianæ*,[4] drawing determinations from verses casually occurring. The same was practised by Severus, who enter-

[3] *opening.*] For the casual opening of a Bible, see *Cardan. de Varietate*, p. 1040.—*Wr.*

[4] *Virgilianæ.*] King Charles I. tried the *sortes Virgilianæ*, as is related by Welwood in the following passage :—

"The king being at Oxford during the civil wars, went one day to see the public library, where he was showed among other books, a Virgil nobly printed, and exquisitely bound. The Lord Falkland, to divert the king, would have his majesty make a trial of his fortune by the *sortes Virgilianæ*, which every body knows was an usual kind of augury some ages past. Whereupon the king opening the book, the period which happened to come up, was that part of Dido's imprecation against Æneas ; which Mr. Dryden translates thus :—

> Yet let a race untamed, and haughty foes,
> His peaceful entrance with dire arms oppose.
> Oppress'd with numbers in th' unequal field,
> His men discouraged and himself expell'd,
> Let him for succour sue from place to place,
> Torn from his subjects, and his son's embrace,
> First let him see his friends in battle slain,
> And their untimely fate lament in vain :
> And when at length the cruel war shall cease,
> On hard conditions may he buy his peace ;
> Nor let him then enjoy supreme command,
> But fall untimely by some hostile hand,
> And lie unburied in the common sand.

It is said King Charles seemed concerned at this accident ; and that the Lord Falkland observing it, would likewise try his own fortune in the same manner ; hoping he might fall upon some passage that could have no relation to his case, and thereby divert the king's thoughts from any impression the other might have upon him. But the place that Falkland stumbled upon was yet more suited to his destiny than the other had been to the king's ; being the following expressions of Evander, upon the untimely death of his son Pallas, as they are translated by the same hand :—

> O Pallas ! thou hast fail'd thy plighted word,
> To fight with reason ; not to tempt the sword.
> I warn'd thee but in vain, for well I knew
> What perils youthful ardour would pursue ;
> That boiling blood would carry thee too far,
> Young as thou wert in dangers, raw to war.
> O curst essay of arms, disastrous doom,
> Prelude of bloody fields and fights to come.

tained ominous hopes of the empire, from that verse in Virgil, *Tu regere imperio populos, Romane, memento;* and Gordianus, who reigned but few days, was discouraged by another; that is, *Ostendunt terris hunc tantùm fata, nec ultra esse sinunt.*[5] Nor was this only performed in heathen authors, but upon the sacred text of Scripture, as Gregorius Turonensis hath left some account; and as the practice of the Emperor Heraclius, before his expedition into Asia Minor, is delivered by Cedrenus.

As for the divination or decision from the staff, it is an augurial relick, and the practice thereof is accused by God himself; "My people ask counsel of their stocks, and their staff declareth unto them."* Of this kind of rhabdomancy was that practised by Nebuchadnezzar in that Chaldean miscellany, delivered by Ezekiel; "The King of Babylon stood at the parting of the way, at the head of two ways to use divination, he made his arrows bright, he consulted with images, he looked in the liver: at the right hand were the divinations of Jerusalem."† That is, as Estius expounded it, the left way leading unto Rabbah, the chief city of the Ammonites, and the right unto Jerusalem, he consulted idols and entrails, he threw up a bundle of arrows to see which way they would light, and falling on the right hand he marched towards Jerusalem. A like way of belomancy or divination by arrows hath been in request with Scythians, Alanes, Germans, with the Africans and Turks of Algier. But of another nature was that which was practised by Elisha,‡ when, by an arrow shot from an eastern window, he presignified the destruction of Syria; or when, according unto the three strokes of Joash, with an arrow upon the ground, he foretold the number of his victories. For thereby the Spirit of God particulared the same, and determined the strokes of the king, unto three, which the hopes of the prophet expected in twice that number.[6]

* Hosea iv.   † Ezek. xxiv.   ‡ 2 Kings xiii. 15.

[5] *sinunt.*] Of all other, I cannot but admire that ominous dreame of Constans, the emperor, the sonne of Heracleonas, and father of Pogonatus, anno imperii 13, who beinge to fight with barbarians the next morne, near Thessalonica, thought hee heard one cryinge Θὲς ἀλλῷ Νικῇν, which the next day proved too true.—*Wr.*

[6] *As for the divination, &c.*] This paragraph, and the three following, were first added in the second edition.

8. We cannot omit to observe the tenacity of ancient customs, in the nominal observation of the several days of the week, according to Gentile and Pagan appellations;* for the original is very high, and as old as the ancient Egyptians, who named the same according to the seven planets, the admired stars of heaven, and reputed deities among them. Unto every one assigning a several day; not according to their celestial order, or as they are disposed in heaven, but after a *diatesseron* or musical fourth. For beginning Saturday with Saturn, the supremest planet, they accounted by Jupiter and Mars unto Sol, making Sunday. From Sol in like manner by Venus and Mercury unto Luna, making Monday: and so through all the rest. And the same order they confirmed by numbering the hours of the day unto twenty-four, according to the natural order of the planets. For beginning to account from Saturn, Jupiter, Mars, and so about unto twenty-four, the next day will fall unto Sol; whence accounting twenty-four, the next will happen unto Luna, making Monday; and so with the rest, according to the account and order observed still among us.

The Jews themselves, in their astrological considerations, concerning nativities and planetary hours, observe the same order upon as witty foundations. Because, by an equal interval, they make seven triangles, the bases whereof are the seven sides of a septilateral figure, described within a circle. That is, if a figure of seven sides be described in a circle, and at the angles thereof the names of the planets be placed in their natural order on it; if we begin with Saturn, and successively draw lines from angle to angle, until seven equicrural triangles be described, whose bases are the seven sides of the septilateral figure; the triangles will be made by this order.† The first being made by Saturn, Sol, and Luna, that is, Saturday, Sunday, and Monday; and so the rest in the order still retained.

But thus much is observable, that however in celestial considerations they embraced the received order of the planets, yet did they not retain either characters or names in common use amongst us; but declining human denomi-

* *Dion. Cassii* lib. xxxvii.
† *Cujus icon apud Doct. Gaffarel*, cap. ii. *et Fabrit. Pad.*

nations, they assigned them names from some remarkable qualities: as is very observable in their red and splendent planets, that is, of Mars and Venus. But the change of their names* disparaged not the consideration of their natures; nor did they thereby reject all memory of these remarkable stars, which God himself admitted in his tabernacle, if conjecture will hold concerning the golden candlestick, whose shaft resembled the sun, and six branches the planets about it.

9. We are unwilling to enlarge concerning many other; only referring unto sober examination, what natural effects can reasonably be expected, when to prevent the *ephialtes* or night-mare, we hang up an hollow stone in our stables; when for amulets against agues we use the chips of gallows and places of execution.[7] When for warts we rub our hands

* *Maadim Nogah.*

[7] *execution.*] See what the Lord St. Alban's sayes for the certaintye of this experimente made upon himself in his natural historye, centurye 10th, and 997 experiment.—*Wr.*

"The sympathy of individuals, that have been entire, or have touched, is of all others the most incredible; yet according unto our faithful manner of examination of nature, we will make some little mention of it. The taking away of warts, by rubbing them with somewhat that afterwards is put to waste and consume, is a common experiment; and I do apprehend it the rather because of my own experience. I had from my childhood a wart upon one of my fingers: afterwards, when I was about sixteen years old, being then at Paris, there grew upon both my hands a number of warts at the least an hundred, in a month's space. The English ambassador's lady, who was a woman far from superstition, told me one day, she would help me away with my warts: whereupon she got a piece of lard with the skin on, and rubbed the warts all over with the fat side; and amongst the rest, that wart which I had had from my childhood: then she nailed the piece of lard, with the fat towards the sun, upon a post of her chamber window, which was to the south. The success was, that within five weeks' space all the warts went quite away: and that wart which I had so long endured, for company. But at the rest I did little marvel, because they came in a short time, and might go away in a short time again: but the going away of that which had stayed so long doth yet stick with me. They say the like is done by the rubbing of warts with a green elder stick and then burying the stick to rot in muck. It would be tried with corns and wens, and such other excrescences. I would have it also tried with some parts of living creatures that are nearest the nature of excrescences; as the combs of cocks, the spurs of cocks, the horns of beasts, &c. And I would have it tried both ways; both by rubbing those parts with lard, or elder, as before; and by cutting off

before the moon,[8] or commit any maculated part unto the touch of the dead. What truth there is in those common female doctrines, that the first rib of roast beef powdered, is a peculiar remedy against fluxes;—that to urine upon earth newly cast up by a mole, bringeth down the menses in women;—that if a child dieth, and the neck becometh not stiff, but for many hours remaineth lithe and flaccid, some other in the same house will die not long after;—that if a woman with child looketh upon a dead body, her child will be of a pale complexion;[9]—our learned and critical philosophers might illustrate, whose exacter performances our adventures do but solicit: meanwhile, I hope they will plausibly receive our attempts, or candidly correct our misconjectures.[1]

> Disce, sed ira cadat naso, rugosaque sanna,
> Dum veteres avias tibi de pulmone revello.

---

some piece of those parts, and laying it to consume: to see whether it will work any effect towards the consumption of that part which was once joined with it."—*Natural History*, Cent. x. No. 997.

[8] *When for warts we rub our hands, &c.*] Hear what Sir Kenelme Digby says of this matter in his *Late Discourse, &c. Touching the Cure of wounds by the Power of Sympathy*, &c. 12mo. 1658.

"I cannot omit to add hereunto another experiment, which is, that we find by the effects, how the rays of the moon are cold and moist. It is without controversy, that the luminous parts of those rays come from the sun, the moon having no light at all within her, as her eclipses bear witness, which happen when the earth is opposite betwixt her and the sun; which interposition suffers her not to have light from his rays. The beams then which come from the moon, are those of the sun, which glancing upon her, reflect upon us, and so bring with them the atoms of that cold and humid star, which participates of the source whence they come: therefore if one should expose a hollow bason, or glass, to assemble them, one shall find, that whereas those of the sun do burn by such a conjuncture, these clean contrary do refresh and moisten in a notable manner, leaving an aquatic and viscous glutining kind of sweat upon the glass. One would think it were a folly that one should offer to wash his hands in a well-polished silver bason, wherein there is not a drop of water, yet this may be done by the reflection of the moonbeams only, which will afford a competent humidity to do it; but they who have tried this, have found their hands, after they are wiped, to be much moister than usually: *but this is an infallible way to take away warts from the hands, if it be often used.*"

[9] *What truth there is, &c.*] This sentence was first added, and the arrangement of the paragraphs in the chapter altered, in the 6th edit.

[1] *misconjectures.*] The perusal of the two preceding chapters calls

powerfully to mind the following lively and eloquent "*character of the superstitious,*" drawn by our author's pious and learned friend, Bishop Hall.

"Superstition is godless religion, devout impiety. The superstitious is fond in observation, servile in fear: he worships God, but as he lists: he gives God what he asks not, more than he asks, and all but what he should give; and makes more sins than the ten commandments. This man dares not stir forth, till his breast be crossed, and his face sprinkled. If but a hare cross him the way, he returns; or, if his journey began, unawares, on the dismal day, or if he stumbled at the threshold. If he see a snake unkilled, he fears a mischief: if the salt fall towards him, he looks pale and red; and is not quiet, till one of the waiters has poured wine on his lap: and when he sneezeth, thinks them not his friends that uncover not. In the morning he listens whether the crow crieth even or odd; and, by that token, presages of the weather. If he hear but a raven croak from the next roof, he makes his will; or if a bittour fly over his head by night: but if his troubled fancy shall second his thoughts with the dream of a fair garden, or green rushes, or the salutation of a dead friend, he takes leave of the world, and says he cannot live. He will never set to sea but on a Sunday; neither ever goes without an *erra pater* in his pocket. St. Paul's day, and St. Swithin's, with the twelve, are his oracles; which he dares believe against the almanack. When he lies sick on his death-bed, no sin troubles him so much, as that he did once eat flesh on a Friday: no repentance can expiate that; the rest need none. There is no dream of his, without an interpretation, without a prediction; and, if the event answer not his exposition, he expounds it according to the event. Every dark grove and pictured wall strikes him with an awful but carnal devotion. Old wives and stars are his counsellors: his night-spell is his guard, and charms, his physicians. He wears Paracelsian characters for the tooth-ache: and a little hallowed wax is his antidote for all evils. This man is strangely credulous; and calls impossible things, miraculous: if he hear that some sacred block speaks, moves, weeps, smiles, his bare feet carry him thither with an offering; and, if a danger miss him in the way, his saint hath the thanks. Some ways he will not go, and some he dares not; either there are bugs, **or** he feigneth them: every lantern is a ghost, and every noise is of chains. He knows not why, but his custom is to go a little about, and to leave the cross still on the right hand. One event is enough to make a rule: out of these rules he concludes fashions proper to himself; and nothing can turn him out of his own course. If he have done his task, he is safe: it matters not with what affection. Finally, if God would let him be the carver of his own obedience, he could not have a better subject: as he is, he cannot have a worse."—*Bishop Hall's Characters of Vices; Works by Pratt*, vol. vii. 102.

THE SIXTH BOOK:

THE PARTICULAR PART CONTINUED.

OF POPULAR AND RECEIVED TENETS, COSMOGRAPHICAL, GEOGRAPHICAL, AND HISTORICAL.

CHAPTER I.

*Concerning the beginning of the World, that the time thereof is **not** precisely known, as commonly it is presumed.*

CONCERNING the world and its temporal circumscriptions, whoever shall strictly examine both extremes, will easily perceive, there is not only obscurity in its end, but its beginning; that as its period is inscrutable, so is its nativity indeterminable; that as it is presumption to enquire after the one, so is there no rest or satisfactory decision in the other. And hereunto we shall more readily assent, if we examine the information, and take a view of the several difficulties in this point; which we shall more easily do, if we consider the different conceits of men, and duly perpend the imperfections of their discoveries.

And first, the histories of the Gentiles afford us slender satisfaction, nor can they relate any story, or affix a probable point to its beginning.[1] For some thereof (and those of the wisest amongst them) are so far from determining its beginning, that they opinion and maintain it never had any at all; as the doctrine of Epicurus implieth, and more positively Aristotle, in his books *De Cœlo*, declareth. Endeavouring to confirm it with arguments of reason, and those appearingly demonstrative; wherein his labours are

[1] *its beginning.*] The beginning of the world.

rational, and uncontrollable upon the grounds assumed, that is, of physical generation, and a primary or first matter, beyond which no other hand was apprehended. But herein we remain sufficiently satisfied from Moses, and the doctrine delivered of the creation; that is, a production of all things out of nothing, a formation not only of matter, but of form, and a materiation even of matter itself.

Others are so far from defining the original of the world or of mankind, that they have held opinions not only repugnant unto chronology, but philosophy; that is, that they had their beginning in the soil where they inhabited; assuming or receiving appellations conformable unto such conceits. So did the Athenians term themselves αὐτόχθονες or Aborigines, and in testimony thereof did wear a golden insect on their heads: the same name is also given unto the Inlanders, or Midland inhabitants of this island, by Cæsar. But this is a conceit answerable unto the generation of the giants; not admittable in philosophy, much less in divinity, which distinctly informeth we are all the seed of Adam, that the whole world perished, unto eight persons before the flood, and was after peopled by the colonies of the sons of Noah. There was therefore never any *autochthon*,[2] or man arising from the earth, but Adam; for the woman being formed out of the rib, was once removed from earth, and framed from that element under incarnation. And so although her production were not by copulation, yet was it in a manner seminal: for if in every part from whence the seed doth flow, there be contained the idea of the whole; there was a seminality and contracted Adam in the rib, which, by the information of a soul, was individuated unto Eve. And therefore this conceit applied unto the original of man, and the beginning of the world, is more justly appropriable unto its end; for then indeed men shall rise out of the earth: the graves shall shoot up their concealed seeds, and in that great autumn, men shall spring up, and awake from their chaos again.

[2] *autochthon*.] Autochthon [rising himselfe from the earthe], which was not to bee granted of the first; who did not spring [as plants now doe] of himselfe. For Adam was created out of the dust by God. The second Adam might bee trulyer called Autochthon, in a mystical sense, not only in respect of his birthe, but of his resurrection alsoe.—*Wr.*

Others have been so blind in deducing the original of things, or delivering their own beginnings, that when it hath fallen into controversy, they have not recurred unto chronology or the records of time; but betaken themselves unto probabilities, and the conjecturalities of philosophy.* Thus when the two ancient nations, Egyptians and Scythians, contended for antiquity, the Egyptians pleaded their antiquity from the fertility of their soil, inferring that men there first inhabited, where they were with most facility sustained; and such a land did they conceive was Egypt.

The Scythians, although a cold and heavier nation, urged more acutely, deducing their arguments from the two active elements and principles of all things, fire and water. For if of all things there was first an union, and that fire over-ruled the rest, surely that part of earth which was coldest would first get free, and afford a place of habitation: but if all the earth were first involved in water, those parts would surely first appear, which were most high, and of most elevated situation, and such was theirs. These reasons carried indeed the antiquity from the Egyptians, but confirmed it not in the Scythians: for, as Herodotus relateth, from Pargitaus their first king unto Darius, they accounted but two thousand years.

As for the Egyptians, they invented another way of trial; for as the same author relateth, Psammitichus their king attempted this decision by a new and unknown experiment; bringing up two infants with goats, and where they never heard the voice of man; concluding that to be the ancientest nation, whose language they should first deliver.[3] But herein he forgot, that speech was by instruction not instinct; by imitation, not by nature; that men do speak in some kind but like parrots, and as they are instructed, that is, in simple terms and words, expressing the open notions of things; which the second act of reason compoundeth into propositions, and the last into syllogisms and forms of ratiocination. And howsoever the account of

* *Diodor. Justin.*

[3] *As for the Egyptians, &c.*] "It is said that after they were two years old, one of the boys cried *becchus*, which in the Phrygian language signifyeth 'bread,' whence it was conjectured that the Phrygians were the first people."—*Jeff.*

Manethon the Egyptian priest run very high, and it be evident that Mizraim peopled that country (whose name with the Hebrews it beareth unto this day), and there be many things of great antiquity related in Holy Scripture, yet was their exact account not very ancient; for Ptolemy their countryman beginneth his astronomical compute no higher than Nabonasser, who is conceived by some the same with Salmanasser. As for the argument deduced from the fertility of the soil, duly enquired it rather overthroweth than promoteth their antiquity; if that country whose fertility they so advance, was in ancient times no firm or open land, but some vast lake or part of the sea, and became a gained ground by the mud and limous matter brought down by the river Nilus, which settled by degrees into a firm land,—according as is expressed by Strabo, and more at large by Herodotus, both from the Egyptian tradition and probable inducements from reason; called therefore *fluvii donum*, an accession of earth, or tract of land acquired by the river.

Lastly, some indeed there are, who have kept records of time, and a considerable duration, yet do the exactest thereof afford no satisfaction concerning the beginning of the world, or any way point out the time of its creation. The most authentick records and best approved antiquity are those of the Chaldeans; yet in the time of Alexander the Great they attained not so high as the flood. For as Simplicius relateth, Aristotle required of Calisthenes, who accompanied that worthy in his expedition, that at his arrival at Babylon, he would enquire of the antiquity of their records; and those upon compute he found to amount unto 1903 years, which account notwithstanding ariseth no higher than ninety-five years after the flood. The Arcadians, I confess, were esteemed of great antiquity, and it was usually said they were before the moon; according unto that of Seneca; *sidus post veteres Arcades editum*, and that of Ovid, *luná gens prior illa fuit*. But this, as Censorinus observeth, must not be taken grossly, as though they were existent before that luminary; but were so esteemed, because they observed a set course of year, before the Greeks conformed their year unto the course and motion of the moon

Thus the heathens affording no satisfaction herein, they are most likely to manifest this truth, who have been acquainted with Holy Scripture, and the sacred chronology delivered by Moses, who distinctly sets down this account, computing by certain intervals, by memorable æras, epochs or terms of time: as, from the creation unto the flood, from hence unto Abraham, from Abraham unto the departure from Egypt, &c. Now in this number have only been Samaritans, Jews, and Christians.

For the Jews; they agree not in their accounts, as Bodine in his method of history hath observed, out of Baal Seder, Rabbi Nassom, Gersom, and others; in whose compute the age of the world is not yet 5400 years. The same is more evidently observable from two most learned Jews, Philo and Josephus; who very much differ in the accounts of time, and variously sum up these intervals assented unto by all. Thus Philo, from the departure out of Egypt unto the building of the temple, accounts but 920 years; but Josephus sets down 1062: Philo, from the building of the temple, to its destruction, 440; Josephus, 470: Philo, from the creation to the destruction of the temple, 3373; but Josephus, 3513: Philo, from the deluge to the destruction of the temple, 1718; but Josephus, 1913. In which computes there are manifest disparities, and such as much divide the concordance and harmony of times.

For the Samaritans; their account is different from these or any others; for they account from the creation to the deluge but 1302 years; which cometh to pass upon the different account of the ages of the patriarchs set down when they begat children. For whereas the Hebrew, Greek, and Latin texts account Jared 162 when he begat Enoch, they account but sixty-two: and so in others. Now the Samaritans were no incompetent judges of times and the chronology thereof; for they embrace the five books of Moses, and as it seemeth, preserve the text with far more integrity than the Jews: who, as Tertullian, Chrysostom, and others observe, did several ways corrupt the same, especially in passages concerning the prophecies of Christ. So that, as Jerome professeth, in his translation he was fain sometime to relieve himself by the Samaritan

Pentateuch; as amongst others in that text, Deuteronomy xxvii. 26; *Maledictus omnis qui non permanserit in omnibus quæ scripta sunt in libro legis.* From hence Saint Paul (Gal. iii. 10) inferreth there is no justification by the law, and urgeth the text according to the Septuagint. Now the Jews, to afford a latitude unto themselves, in their copies expunged the word כל or syncategorematical term *omnis:* wherein lieth the strength of the law, and of the apostle's argument; but the Samaritan Bible retained it right, and answerable unto what the apostle had urged.[4]

As for Christians, from whom we should expect the exactest and most concurring account, there is also in them a manifest disagreement, and such as is not easily reconciled. For first, the Latins accord not in their account; to omit the calculation of the ancients, of Austin, Bede, and others, the chronology of the moderns doth manifestly dissent. Josephus Scaliger, whom Helvicus seems to follow, accounts the creation in 765 of the Julian period; and from thence unto the nativity of our Saviour alloweth 3947 years; but Dionysius Petavius, a learned chronologer, dissenteth from this compute almost forty years; placing the creation in the 730th of the Julian period, and from thence unto the incarnation accounteth 3983 years. For the Greeks; their accounts are more anomalous: for if we recur unto ancient computes, we shall find that Clemens Alexandrinus, an ancient father and preceptor unto Origen, accounted from the creation unto our Saviour, 5664 years; for in the first of his *Stromaticks,* he collecteth the time from Adam unto the death of Commodus to be 5858 years; now the death of Commodus he placeth in the year after Christ 194, which number deducted from the former, there remaineth 5664. Theophilus, bishop of Antioch, accounteth unto the nativity of Christ 5515, deducible from the like way of compute; for in his first book *ad Autolychum,* he accounteth from Adam unto Aurelius Verus 5695 years; now that emperor died in the year of our Lord 180, which deducted from the former sum, there remaineth 5515. Julius Afri-

---

[4] *the Samaritan, &c.*] It is also preserved in six MSS. in the collections of Dr. Kennicott, and De Rossi, in several copies of the Chaldee Targum, and in the LXX.—*Jeff.*

canus, an ancient chronologer, accounteth somewhat less, that is, 5500. Eusebius, Orosius, and others dissent not much from this, but all exceed five thousand.

The latter compute of the Greeks, as Petavius observeth, hath been reduced unto two or three accounts. The first accounts unto our Saviour 5501, and this hath been observed by Nicephorus, Theophanes, and Maximus. The other accounts 5509; and this of all at present is generally received by the church of Constantinople, observed also by the Moscovite, as I have seen in the date of the emperor's letters; wherein this year of ours, 1645, is from the year of the world 7154, which doth exactly agree unto this last account 5509: for if unto that sum be added 1645, the product will be 7154; by this chronology are many Greek authors to be understood: and thus is Martinus Crusius to be made out, when in his Turco-grecian history he delivers, the city of Constantinople was taken by the Turks in the year στθξα that is, 6961. Now according unto these chronologists, the prophecy of Elias the rabbin, so much in request with the Jews, and in some credit also with Christians, that the world should last but six thousand years; unto these I say, it hath been long and out of memory disproved; for the sabbatical and 7000th year wherein the world should end (as did the creation on the seventh day) unto them is long ago expired; they are proceeding in the eighth thousandth year, and numbers exceeding those days which men have made the types and shadows of these. But certainly what Marcus Leo the Jew conceiveth of the end of the heavens, exceedeth the account of all that ever shall be; for though he conceiveth the elemental frame shall end in the seventh or sabbatical millenary, yet cannot he opinion the heavens and more durable part of the creation shall perish before seven times seven or forty-nine, that is, the quadrant of the other seven, and perfect jubilee of thousands.[5]

[5] *Marcus Leo the Jew.*] The text convinceth this dotage of the Jew: St. Paule sayd 1500 years agoe, that the ends of the world were then coming, which was spoken not of hundreds of yeares but of thousands. Yf then Christ were borne in the 4000th yeare of the world, as the late learned Armachanus (Abp. Usher) opines (not without excellent and undeniable reasons easie to bee made good), wee must divide the age of

Thus may we observe the difference and wide dissent of men's opinions, and thereby the great incertainty in this establishment. The Hebrews not only dissenting from the Samaritans, the Latins from the Greeks, but every one from another. Insomuch that all can be in the right it is impossible that any one is so, not with assurance determinable. And therefore, as Petavius confesseth, to effect the same exactly without inspiration, it is impossible, and beyond the arithmetick of any but God himself. And therefore also, what satisfaction may be obtained from those violent disputes, and eager enquiries, in what day of the month the world began, either of March or October; likewise in what face or position of the moon, whether at the prime or full, or soon after, let our second and serious considerations determine.

Now the reason and ground of this dissent is the unhappy difference between the Greek and Hebrew editions of the bible, for unto these two languages have all translations conformed; the Holy Scripture being first delivered in Hebrew, and first translated into Greek. For the Hebrew; it seems the primitive and surest text to rely on, and to preserve the same entire and uncorrupt there hath been used the highest caution humanity could invent. For, as R. Ben Maimon hath declared, if in the copying thereof one letter were written twice, or if one letter but touched another, that copy was not admitted into their synagogues, but only allowable to be read in schools and private families. Neither were they careful only in the exact number of their sections of the law, but had also the curiosity to number every word, and affixed the account unto their several books. Notwithstanding all which, divers corruptions ensued, and several depravations slipt in, arising from many and manifest grounds, as hath been exactly noted by Morinus in his preface unto the Septuagint.

the world into 3 partes. The beginning of the world must bee counted as the first 2000 yeares: the midste 4000: and the end 6000 or perhaps not soe much: for our Saviour sayes evidently there shall be an abbreviation, viz., in the last parte; but when that shall bee Deus novit.— *Wr.*

Our Lord's prediction is usually applied to the destruction of Jerusalem.

As for the Septuagint, it is the first and most ancient translation; and of greater antiquity than the Chaldee version; occasioned by the request of Ptolemeus Philadelphus king of Egypt, for the ornament of his memorable library, unto whom the high priest addressed six Jews out of every tribe, which amounteth unto 72; and by these was effected that translation we usually term the Septuagint, or translation of seventy. Which name, however it obtain from the number of their persons, yet in respect of one common spirit, it was the translation but as it were of one man; if, as the story relateth, although they were set apart and severed from each other, yet were their translations found to agree in every point, according as is related by Philo and Josephus; although we find not the same in Aristæas,* who hath expressly treated thereof. But of the Greek compute there have passed some learned dissertations not many years ago, wherein the learned Isaac Vossius[6] makes the nativity of the world to anticipate the common account one thousand four hundred and forty years.

This translation in ancient times was of great authority. By this many of the heathens received some notions of the creation and the mighty works of God. This in express terms is often followed by the evangelists, by the apostles, and by our Saviour himself in the quotations of the Old Testament. This for many years was used by the Jews themselves, that is, such as did Hellenize and dispersedly dwelt out of Palestine with the Greeks; and this also the succeeding Christians and ancient fathers observed; although there succeeded other Greek versions, that is, of Aquila, Theodosius, and Symmachus. For the Latin translation of Jerome called now the vulgar, was about 800 years after the Septuagint; although there was also a Latin translation before, called the Italic version, which was after lost upon the general reception of the translation of Jerome. Which notwithstanding (as he himself acknowledgeth†) had been needless, if the Septuagint copies had remained pure, and as

* *Aristæas ad Philociatorem de 72 interpretibus.*
† *Præfat. in Paralipom.*

[6] *Isaac Vossius.*] He contended for the inspiration of the Septuagint.—*Jeff.*

they were first translated. But (beside that different copies were used, that Alexandria and Egypt followed the copy of Hesychius, Antioch and Constantinople that of Lucian the martyr, and others that of Origen) the Septuagint was much depraved, not only from the errors of scribes, and the emergent corruptions of time, but malicious contrivance of the Jews; as Justin Martyr hath declared in his learned dialogue with Tryphon, and Morinus* hath learnedly shown from many confirmations.[7]

Whatsoever interpretations there have been since have been especially effected with reference unto these, that is, the Greek and Hebrew text; the translators sometimes following the one, sometimes adhering unto the other, according as they found them consonant unto truth, or most correspondent unto the rules of faith. Now, however it cometh to pass, these two are very different in the enumeration of genealogies, and particular accounts of time: for in the second interval, that is, between the flood and Abraham, there is by the Septuagint introduced one Cainan[8] to be the son of Arphaxad and father of Salah; whereas in the Hebrew there is no mention of such a person, but Arphaxad is set down to be the father of Salah. But in the first interval, that is, from the creation unto the flood, their disagreement is more considerable; for therein the Greek exceedeth the Hebrew and common account almost 600 years. And 'tis indeed a thing not very strange, to be at the difference of a third part, in so large and collective an account, if we consider how differently they are set forth in minor and less mistakable numbers. So in the prophecy of Jonah, both in the Hebrew and Latin text, it is said, "Yet forty days and Nineveh shall be overthrown;" but the Septuagint saith plainly, and that in letters at length, $\tau\rho\epsilon\tilde{\iota}\varsigma\ \dot{\eta}\mu\epsilon\rho\alpha\varsigma$, that is,

* *De Hebraei et Graeci textus sinceritate.*

[7] *which was after lost, &c.*] This concluding sentence was first added in the 2nd edition.

[8] *Cainan.*] How this second Cainan was foisted into the translation of the Septuagint, see that learned tract in *Gregorye's Posthuma*, p. 77, which hee calls Καινὰν δεύτερος. Hee [meaning Sir Thomas] might have called him Ψευδοκαινὰν: which had been most sutable to this learned worke, of discovering comon errors.—*Wr.*

See also *Dr. Hales's New Analysis*, vol. i. pp. 90—94.

"Yet three days and Nineveh shall be destroyed." Which is a difference not newly crept in, but an observation very ancient, discussed by Austin and Theodoret, and was conceived an error committed by the scribe.[9] Men therefore have raised different computes of time, according as they have followed their different texts; and so have left the history of times far more perplexed than chronology hath reduced.

Again, however the texts were plain, and might in their numerations agree, yet were there no small difficulty to set down a determinable chronology or establish from hence any fixed point of time. For the doubts concerning the time of the judges are inexplicable; that of the reigns and succession of kings is as perplexed; it being uncertain whether the years both of their lives and reigns ought to be taken as complete, or in their beginning and but current accounts. Nor is it unreasonable to make some doubt whether in the first ages and long lives of our fathers, Moses doth not sometime account by full and round numbers, whereas strictly taken they might be some few years above or under: as in the age of Noah, it is delivered to be just five hundred when he begat Sem; whereas perhaps he might be somewhat above or below that round and complete number. For the same way of speech is usual in divers other expressions: thus do we say the Septuagint, and using the full and articulate number, do write the translation of seventy; whereas we have shown before the precise number was seventy-two. So is it said that Christ was three days in the grave; according to that of Matthew, "As Jonas was three days and three nights in the whale's belly, so shall the Son of man be three days and three nights in the heart of the earth:" which notwithstanding must be taken synecdochically, or by understanding a part for a whole day; for he remained but two nights in the grave: for he was buried in the afternoon of the first day, and arose very early in the morning on the third; that is, he was interred in the eve of the sabbath, and arose the morning after it.[1]

[9] *scribe.*] Writing γ for μ, which might easily bee, not in the original, but in the second transcript.—*Wr.*

[1] *after it.*] Before day: the whole being scarce 34 houres while he was in the grave, which is not the one halfe of three days and three nights, nor can be salved synechdochicallye.

Moreover, although the number of years be determined and rightly understood, and there be without doubt a certain

'Tis strange to see how all the nation of expositors, since Christe, as yf they were infected with a disease of supinity, thinke they have abundantly satisfied the texte, by telling us, that speech of Christe comparinge himself to Jonas, must be understood synechdochically, which is: 1. not only a weak interpretation; 2. but ridiculous to Jews, Turks, and Infidels; 3. and consequently derogatory to the truth; who expressly puts in the reddition, 3 dayes and 3 nights, by an emphaticall expression. Which as itt was punctually fortold, the express time of 3 dayes and 3 nights; soe itt was as punctually performed (*usque ad apices*) for as Jonas was 3 days and 3 nights in the whale, which admits noe *synechdoche*; soe the sonn of man was in the grave 3 dayes and 3 nights without any abatement of a moment. That which begat this error was, a mistake of the dayes and nights, spoken of Jonas. And from thence not only unwarrantably but untruly applied to Christ's stay in the grave. Wee must therefore distinguish of dayes and nights, and take them either in Moses' sense, for the whole revolution of the ☉ to the eastern pointe after 24 houres: which most men by like contagion of error, call the natural day, wheras itt is rather to bee cald artificiall, as being compounded of a day and a night, wheras the night is properly noe parte univocall of a day, but a contradistinct member thereto. Now in this sense yf the days and nights bee conceived; itt is impossible to make good the one halfe of 3 dayes and 3 nights by any figurative or synechdochical sense: for from the time of his entering, very neer 6 at even on Friday to 6 at even on Saturday are but 24 houres: to which adde from 6 at even to 3 or 4 next morne (for itt was yet darke, when Mary Magd. came and saw the stone removed), viz. 10 houres more, they will make in all but thirty foure houres, that is but $1\frac{1}{2}$ day and night of æquinoctial revolution. Or else in our Saviour's sense, Jo. xi. 9, where by the day Christe understands, the very day-light, or natural day, caused by the presence of the sun; to the which night is always opposed as contradistinct, as is manifest from that very place. For as itts alwayes midday directly under the ☉, soe there is midnight alwayes opposite to midnoone through the world. And these 2 have runn opposite round the world, *simul et semel* every 24 houres since the creation, and soe shall doe, while time shall bee noe more. I say therefore that thoughe in respect of Jesus' grave in the garden he lay but 36 houres in the earthe, yet in respect of the world for which he suffered, there were 3 distincte dayes and nights actually in being, while hee lay in the bowels of the earthe (which is to be distinctly noted to justifie of him, who did not, could not, æquivocate): Friday night in Judæa, and a day opposite therto in the other hemisphere, just 12 houres; Saturday 12 houres in Judæa, and the opposite night 12 hours; Saturday night in Judæa, and the opposite day elsewhere at the same time. And hee that denyes this, hath lost his sense: for I ask were there not actually 3 essentiall dayes and 3 nights (*sub coelo*) during his sepulture. And yf this cannot be denyed truth herein, yet the text speaking obscurely or dubiously, there is ofttimes no slender difficulty at what point to begin or terminate the account. So when it is said, Exod. xii., the sojourning of the children of Israel who dwelt in Egypt was 430 years, it cannot be taken strictly, and from their first arrival into Egypt, for their habitation in that land was far

by any but a madman, I aske againe did Christe suffer for Judæa only, or for the whole world? least of all for Judæa, which for his unjust death was exterminate and continues accursed. Soe that henceforth wee shall need no synechdoche to make good the prophetick speech of him that could not lie: who sayde, *sic erit Filius hominis in corde terræ tribus diebus et tribus noctibus:* and this was truly fulfilled *usque ad momenta,* and therefore I dare believe it, and noe Jew or Turk can contradict itt. (Hee that made the several natures of day and night in this sense; sayd hee would lye in the grave 3 of these dayes and 3 nights.)—*Wr.*

This is ingenious, and to its author it seems abundantly satisfactory, proceeding on the hypothesis that as our Lord suffered for the whole world, the duration of his suffering must be understood with reference to the whole earth. The Dean adds to the two nights and one day which elapsed in Palestine,—the corresponding two days and one night, which elapsed at the antipodes of Judea. But this is liable to objection. It is just as truly *synechdochical* as the interpretation of Sir Thomas:— only that it takes two points on the earth's surface instead of one for the whole. Besides the ingenuity is needless. The Jews were in the habit of speaking *synechdochically* in that very respect that they speak of each part of a day and night (or of 24 hours) as a day and night—$\nu\dot{\nu}\kappa\theta\eta\mu\epsilon\rho\alpha$. So that if Jonah was in the deep during less than 48 hours, provided that period comprised, in addition to one entire 24 hours, a portion of the preceding and of the following 24 hours,—then the Jews would say that he had been in the deep 3 day-nights or 3 days and 3 nights. As if we should say of a person who had left home on Friday afternoon and returned on Sunday morning, that he was from home Friday, Saturday, and Sunday—this might be thought to imply considerable portions of the day of Friday and of Sunday—but certainly it would not be necessary to the accuracy of such a report that he should have started immediately after midnight of Thursday, and returned at the same hour on Sunday. And yet he would otherwise not have been from home on Friday, Saturday, and Sunday—but only during parts of those days. With the Jews common parlance would only require that our Redeemer should have been in the heart of the earth, from the eve of the (Jewish) sabbath, however late, to the morning of the first day, however early, in order to justify the terms in which they would universally have spoken of the duration of his abode there—as comprising three days and three nights. We may observe too, that three days are uniformly spoken of as the time of our Lord's abode in the grave, whether it is spoken of typically or literally. Thus he says of himself, "I do cures to-day and to-morrow, and the third day I am perfected."

less; but the account must begin from the covenant of God with Abraham, and must also comprehend their sojourn in the land of Canaan, according as is expressed Gal. iii., " The covenant that was confirmed before of God in Christ, the law which was 430 years after cannot disannul." Thus hath it also happened in the account of the seventy years of their captivity, according to that of Jeremy, " This whole land shall be a desolation, and these nations shall serve the king of Babylon seventy years."* Now where to begin or end this compute, ariseth no small difficulty; for there were three remarkable captivities and deportations of the Jews. The first was in the third or fourth year of Joachim, and first of Nabuchodonozor, when Daniel was carried away; the second in the reign of Jeconiah, and the eighth year of the same king; the third and most deplorable in the reign of Zedechias, and in the nineteenth year of Nabuchodonozor, whereat both the temple and city were burned. Now such is the different conceit of these times, that men have computed from all; but the probablest account and most concordant unto the intention of Jeremy is from the first of Nabuchodonozor unto the first of King Cyrus over Babylon; although the prophet Zachary accounteth from the last. " O Lord of hosts, how long! wilt thou not have mercy on Jerusalem, against which thou hast had indignation these threescore and ten years?"† for he maketh this expostulation in the second year of Darius Hystaspes, wherein he prophesied, which is about eighteen years in account after the other.

Thus also although there be a certain truth therein, yet is there no easy doubt concerning the seventy weeks, or seventy times seven years of Daniel; whether they have reference unto the nativity or passion[2] of our Saviour, and

* Chap. xx. † Chap. i. 12.

[2] *nativity or passion.*] The learned thinke they have reference [that is of their determination] to neither of them. For most of the learned conceive, that those 70 weeks, or seven times seventy [viz. 490 years] ended with the destruction of the citye; which was 70 yeares after the nativitye, and 38 after the passion of Christe: and then 'twill bee noe hard matter to compute the pointe from whence those 490 yeares must bee supposed to begin: which wee shal find to bee in the 6th yeare of Darius Nothus; at what time the temple being finished by Artaxerxes commaund, formerly given Ao. Regni 20°. the commaund for the build-

especially from whence or what point of time they are to be computed. For thus it is delivered by the angel Gabriel: "Seventy weeks are determined upon thy people;" and again in the following verse: "Know therefore and understand, that from the going forth of the commandment to restore and to build Jerusalem, unto the Messiah the prince, shall be seven weeks, and threescore and two weeks, the street shall be built again, and the wall even in troublesome times; and after threescore and two weeks shall Messiah be cut off."[3] Now the going out of the commandment, to build the city, being the point from whence to compute, there is no slender controversy when to begin. For there are no less than four several edicts to this effect, the one in the first year of Cyrus,[4] the other in the second of Darius, the third and fourth in the seventh and in the twentieth of Artaxerxes Longimanus: although as Petavius accounteth, it best accordeth unto the twentieth year of Artaxerxes, from whence Nehemiah deriveth his commission. Now that computes are made uncertainly with reference unto Christ, it is no wonder, since I perceive the time of his nativity is in controversy, and no less his age at his passion. For Clemens and Tertullian conceive he suffered at thirty; but Irenæus

ing of Jerusalem also was given by this Darius Nothus, Ao. Mundi 3532, which agrees exactlye with Scaliger's irrefragable computation. But to see this difficult question fully decided, and in a few lines, I can give no such direction, as that which Gregorye hath lately given us in his excellent tract *de Æris et Epochis,* cap. xi. which was publisht this last year 1649, and is a work worthye of a diligent reader.—*Wr.*

On referring to Rev. T. H. Horne's analytical view of Daniel, I find the following brief summary of this period. Its commencement "is fixed (Dan. ix. 25) to the time when the order was issued for rebuilding the temple in the seventh year of the reign of Artaxerxes (Ezra vii. 11), seven weeks, or forty-nine years, was the temple in building (Dan. ix. 25); sixty-two weeks, or four hundred and thirty-four years more, bring us to the public manifestation of the Messiah, at the beginning of John the Baptist's preaching; and one prophetic week or seven years, added to this, will bring us to the time of our Saviour's passion, or the thirty-third year of the Christian æra,—in all 490 years."—*Introduction, &c.* vol. iv. p. 1, ch. vi. § 4.

[3] *Know, &c.*] Dan. ix. 25.
[4] *the one in the first year, &c.*] A.M. 3419; 3430; 3492; 3505.—*Wr.*
These dates however differ from those assigned by the most eminent of our more recent chronologists.

a father nearer his time, is further off in his account, that is, between forty and fifty.

Longomontanus, a late astronomer, endeavours to discover this secret from astronomical grounds, that is, the apogeum of the sun; conceiving the eccentricity invariable, and the apogeum yearly to move one scruple, two seconds, fifty thirds, &c. Wherefore if in the time of Hipparchus, that is, in the year of the Julian period 4557, it was in the fifth degree of Gemini, and in the days of Tycho Brahe, that is, in the year of our Lord 1588, or of the world 5554, the same was removed unto the fifth degree of Cancer; by the proportion of its motion, it was at the creation first in the beginning of Aries, and the perigeum or nearest point in Libra. But this conceit how ingenious or subtile soever, is not of satisfaction; it being not determinable, or yet agreed in what time precisely the apogeum absolveth one degree, as Petavius[*] hath also delivered.

Lastly, however these or other difficulties intervene, and that we cannot satisfy ourselves in the exact compute of time, yet may we sit down with the common and usual account; nor are these differences derogatory unto the advent or passion of Christ, unto which indeed they all do seem to point, for the prophecies concerning our Saviour were indefinitely delivered before that of Daniel; so was that pronounced unto Eve in Paradise, that after of Balaam, those of Isaiah and the prophets, and that memorable one of Jacob, " the sceptre shall not depart from Israel until Shilo come ;" which time notwithstanding it did not define at all. In what year therefore soever, either from the destruction of the temple, from the re-edifying thereof, from the flood, or from the creation, he appeared, certain it is, that in the fulness of time he came. When he therefore came, is not so considerable as that he is come: in the one there is consolation, in the other no satisfaction. The greater query is, when he will come again; and yet indeed it is no query at all; for that is never to be known, and therefore vainly enquired: 'tis a professed and authentick obscurity, unknown to all but to the omniscience of the Almighty. Certainly the ends of things are wrapt up in the hands of God, he that undertakes

---

[*] *De Doctrina Temporum,* l. 4.

the knowledge thereof forgets his own beginning, and disclaims his principles of earth. No man knows the end of the world, nor assuredly of any thing in it: God sees it, because unto his eternity it is present; he knoweth the ends of us, but not of himself; and because he knows not this, he knoweth all things, and his knowledge is endless, even in the object of himself.

CHAPTER II.

Of Men's Enquiries in what season or point of the Zodiack it began, that, as they are generally made, they are in vain, and as particularly, uncertain.

CONCERNING the seasons, that is, the quarters of the year some are ready to enquire, others to determine, in what season, whether in the autumn, spring, winter, or summer, the world had its beginning. Wherein we affirm, that, as the question is generally and in respect of the whole earth proposed, it is with manifest injury unto reason in any particular determined; because whenever the world had its beginning it was created in all these four. For, as we have elsewhere delivered, whatsoever sign the sun possesseth (whose recess or vicinity defineth the quarters of the year) those four seasons were actually existent; it being the nature of that luminary to distinguish the several seasons of the year; all which it maketh at one time in the whole earth, and successively in any part thereof.[4] Thus if we suppose the sun created in Libra, in which sign unto some it maketh autumn; at the same time it had been winter unto the northern pole, for unto them at that time the sun beginneth to be invisible, and to show itself again unto the pole of the south. Unto the position of a right sphere, or directly under the equator, it had been summer; for unto that situation the

---

[4] *thereof.*] According as he makes his access too, or recess from the several [parts] of the earthe: now in that his accesse to the one is a recess from the other, it followes, that those from whom he partes have their autumne, those within the tropicks, over whose heads he passes, have their summer, and those on the other side beyond the tropicke towards whome hee goes have their new spring beginning in exchange of their former, causd by his absence.—*Wr.*

sun is at that time vertical. Unto the latitude of Capricorn, or the winter solstice, it had been spring; for unto that position it had been in a middle point, and that of ascent, or approximation; but unto the latitude of Cancer, or the summer solstice, it had been autumn; for then had it been placed in a middle point, and that of descent, or elongation.

And if we shall take literally what Moses describeth popularly, this was also the constitution of the first day. For when it was evening unto one longitude, it was morning unto another; when night unto one, day unto another. And therefore that question, whether our Saviour shall come again in the twilight (as is conceived he arose) or whether he shall come upon us in the night, according to the comparison of a thief, or the Jewish tradition, that he will come about the time of their departure out of Egypt, when they ate the passover, and the angel passed by the doors of their houses; this query, I say, needeth not further dispute. For if the earth be almost every where inhabited, and his coming (as divinity affirmeth) must needs be unto all; then must the time of his appearance be both in the day and night. For if unto Jerusalem, or what part of the world soever he shall appear in the night, at the same time unto the antipodes it must be day; if twilight unto them, broad day unto the Indians; if noon unto them, yet night unto the Americans; and so with variety according unto various habitations, or different positions of the sphere, as will be easily conceived by those who understand the affections of different habitations, and the conditions of Antœci, Periœci, and Antipodes. And so, although he appear in the night, yet may the day of judgment, or doomsday, well retain that name;* for that implieth one revolution of the sun, which maketh the day and night, and that one natural day. And yet, to speak strictly, if (as the apostle affirmeth) we shall be changed in the twinkling of an eye,[5] and (as the schools determine) the

* Νυχθήμρον.

[5] *twinkling, &c.*] Taking this for granted [which noe man, dare denye] yet it is most truly sayde, that doomes day is the last daye, i. e. the last daye of the sons circling this lower world by his daylye course: which as itt hath [in itt selfe] noe rising or settinge, but caryeth the daye and midnoone always directly under him round the world perpetuallye: soe in what parte of the world that course shall

destruction of the world shall not be successive but in an instant, we cannot properly apply thereto the usual distinctions of time; calling that twelve hours, which admits not the parts thereof, or use at all the name of time, when the nature thereof shall perish.

But if the enquiry be made unto a particular place, and the question determined unto some certain meridian; as, namely, unto Mesopotamia,⁶ wherein the seat of Paradise is presumed, the query becomes more reasonable, and is indeed in nature also determinable. Yet positively to define that season, there is no slender difficulty; for some contend that it began in the spring; as (beside Eusebius, Ambrose, Bede, and Theodoret), some few years past, Henrico Philippi in his chronology of the Scripture. Others are altogether for autumn; and from hence do our chronologers commence their compute, as may be observed in Helvicus, Jo. Scaliger, Calvisius, and Petavius.⁷

bee determind [and the day therewith] is noe waye considerable, and much lesse in what parte of the daye of 24 houres, that sodaine instant] of change shall bee; which of necessity must bee to some inhabitants of the world at the time of his risinge, to others at midnoone, to others at his sittinge, and to others at midnight: for all these are all at once, and in the very same instant, every day, in several partes of the worlde: as for example: in April when tis midday at London; 'tis just sonrise at Virginia; and just sonset at the hithermost partes of Nova Guinea, and yet itt is the same daye to all these three parcels of the world at once. But when that greate doome shall come, the course of the son shall instantly cease, and consequently the natural and usual course of day and night with itt: yet there shall bee noe want of lighte in that parte of the aire, or that parte of the earthe under the place, where the sonn of man shall call the world before his judgment-seate; unless any man bee soe simple to thinke that in the presence of God there shall be lesse light then in the presence of the son.—*Wr.*

⁶ *Mesopotamia.*] Most thinke the valley of Jehosaphat.—*Wr.*
The valley of Jehoshaphat was situated eastward of Jerusalem, between that city and the Mo⋅⋅nt of Olives; and through which ran the brook Kedron:—Mesopotamia was a province between the Euphrates and Tigris.

⁷ *Petravius.*] And yet itt must bee confest, that the spring, or sonns entrance into Aries is *rerum caput et naturale Principium Anni*, renewing and reviving all things, as of old in Paradise, æqualling dayes and nights in all places, within the pole circles especially: and as to this all astronomers agree, soe, consonant thereto, all geographers consent, that Paradise was neere under the Æquinoctiall, or on this side of itt, under rise of the spring with the sonn.—*Wr.*

CHAPTER III.

Of the Divisions of the Seasons and Four Quarters of the Year, according unto Astronomers and Physicians; that the common compute of the Ancients, and which is still retained by some, is very questionable.

As for the divisions of the year, and the quartering out this remarkable standard of time, there have passed especially two distinctions. The first in frequent use with astronomers according to the cardinal intersections of the zodiack, that is, the two equinoctials and both the solstitial points, defining that time to be the spring of the year, wherein the sun doth pass from the equinox of Aries unto the solstice of Cancer; the time between the solstice and the equinox of Libra, summer; from thence unto the solstice of Capricornus, autumn; and from thence unto the equinox of Aries again, winter. Now this division, although it be regular and equal, is not universal; for it includeth not those latitudes which have the seasons of the year double; as have the inhabitants under the equator, or else between the tropicks. For unto them the sun is vertical twice a year, making two distinct summers in the different points of verticality. So unto those which live under the equator, when the sun is in the equinox, it is summer, in which points it maketh spring or autumn unto us; and unto them it is also winter when the sun is in either tropick, whereas unto us it maketh always summer in the one. And the like will happen unto those habitations, which are between the tropicks and the equator.

A second and more sensible division there is observed by Hippocrates, and most of the ancient Greeks, according to the rising and setting of divers stars; dividing the year, and establishing the account of seasons from usual alterations, and sensible mutations in the air, discovered upon the rising and setting of those stars: accounting the spring from the equinoctial point of Aries; from the rising of the Pleiades, or the several stars on the back of Taurus, summer; from the rising of Arcturus, a star between the thighs of Boëtes, autumn; and from the setting of the Pleiades, winter. Of these divisions, because they were unequal, they were fain to subdivide the two larger portions, that is, of the summer and winter quarters; the first part of the summer they named θέρος, the second unto the rising of the dog-star, ὥρα, from thence unto the setting of Arcturus, ὀπώρα. The winter they divide also into three parts; the first part, or that of seed-time, they named σπορετὸν, the middle or proper winter, χειμὼν, the last, which was their planting or grafting time, φυταλιάν. This way of division was in former ages received, is very often mentioned in poets, translated from one nation to another; from the Greeks unto the Latins, as is received by good authors; and delivered by physicians, even unto our times.

Now of these two, although the first in some latitude may be retained, yet is not the other in any way to be admitted. For in regard of time (as we elsewhere declare) the stars do vary their longitudes, and consequently the times of their ascension and descension. That star which is the term of numeration, or point from whence we commence the account, altering his site and longitude in process of time, and removing from west to east, almost one degree in the space of seventy-two years, so that the same star, since the age of Hippocrates, who used this account, is removed *in consequentia* about twenty-seven degrees. Which difference of their longitudes doth much diversify the times of their ascents, and rendereth the account unstable which shall proceed thereby.

Again, in regard of different latitudes, this cannot be a settled rule, or reasonably applied unto many nations. For, whereas the setting of the Pleiades, or seven stars, is designed the term of autumn, and the beginning of winter, unto some latitudes these stars do never set, as unto all beyond 67 degrees. And if in several and far distant latitudes we observe the same star as a common term of account unto both, we shall fall upon an unexpected, but an unsufferable absurdity; and by the same account it will be summer unto us in the north, before it be so unto those, which unto us are southward, and many degrees approaching nearer the sun. For if we consult the doctrine of the sphere, and observe the ascension of the Pleiades, which maketh the beginning of summer, we shall discover that in the latitude of 40 these stars arise in the 16th degree of Taurus, but in the latitude of 50, they ascend in the eleventh degree of the same sign, that is, five days sooner; so shall it be summer unto London, before it be unto Toledo, and begin to scorch in England, before it grow hot in Spain.

This is therefore no general way of compute, nor reasonable to be derived from one nation unto another; the defect of which consideration hath caused divers errors in Latin poets, translating these expressions from the Greeks; and many difficulties even in the Greeks themselves, which, living in divers latitudes, yet observed the same compute. So that, to make them out, we are fain to use distinctions; sometimes computing cosmically what they intended heliacally, and sometimes in the same expression accounting the rising heliacally, the setting cosmically. Otherwise it will be hardly made out, what is delivered by approved authors; and is an observation very considerable unto those which meet with such expressions, as they are very frequent in the poets of elder times, especially Hesiod, Aratus, Virgil, Ovid, Manilius, and authors geoponical, or which have treated *de re rustica*, as Constantine, Marcus Cato, Columella, Palladius, and Varro.

Lastly, the absurdity in making common unto many nations those considerations whose verity is but particular unto some, will more evidently appear, if we examine the rules and precepts of some one climate, and fall upon consideration with what incongruity they are transferable unto others.

Thus it is advised by Hesiod:—

> Pleiadibus Atlante natis orientibus
> Incipe Messem, Arationem vero occidentibus,—

implying hereby the heliacal ascent and cosmical descent of those stars. Now herein he setteth down a rule to begin harvest at the arise of the Pleiades; which in his time was in the beginning of May. This indeed was consonant unto the clime wherein he lived, and their harvest began about that season; but is not appliable unto our own, for therein we are so far from expecting an harvest, that our barley-seed is not ended. Again, correspondent unto the rule of Hesiod, Virgil affordeth another:—

> Ante tibi Eoæ Atlantides abscondantur,
> Debita quam sulcis committas semina,—

understanding hereby their cosmical descent, or their setting when the sun ariseth; and not their heliacal obscuration, or their inclusion in the lustre of the sun, as Servius upon this place would have it; for at that time these stars are many signs removed from that luminary. Now herein he strictly adviseth, not to begin to sow before the setting of these stars; which notwithstanding, without injury to agriculture cannot be observed in England; for they set unto us about the 12th of November, when our seed-time is almost ended.

And this diversity of clime and celestial observations, precisely observed unto certain stars and months, hath not only overthrown the deductions of one nation to another, but hath perturbed the observation of festivities and statary solemnities, even with the Jews themselves. For unto them it was commanded, that at their entrance into the land of Canaan, in the fourteenth of the first month (that is Abib or Nisan, which is spring with us), they should observe the celebration of the passover; and on the morrow after, which is the fifteenth day, the feast of unleavened bread; and in the sixteenth of the same month, that they should offer the first sheaf of the harvest. Now all this was feasible and of an easy possibility in the land of Canaan, or latitude of Jerusalem; for so it is observed by several authors in later times; and is also testified by Holy Scripture in times very far before.* For when the children of Israel passed the river Jordan, it is delivered by way of parenthesis, that the river overfloweth its banks in the time of harvest; which is conceived the time wherein they passed; and it is after delivered, that in the fourteenth day they celebrated the passover:† which according to the law of Moses, was to be observed in the first month, or month of Abib.

And therefore it is no wonder, what is related by Luke, that the disciples upon the *deuteroproton*, as they passed by, plucked the ears of corn. For the *deuteroproton* or second first sabbath, was the first sabbath after the *deutera* or second of the passover, which was the sixteenth of Nisan or Abib. And this is also evidenced from the received construction of the first and latter rain: " I will give you the rain of your

---

* Josh. iii. † Josh. v.

land in his due season, the first rain and the latter rain:"*
for the first rain fell upon the seed-time about October, and
was to make the seed to root; the latter was to fill the ear,
and fell in Abib or March, the first month: according as is
expressed, "And he will cause to come down for you the
rain, the former rain and the latter rain in the first month,"†
that is, the month of Abib, wherein the passover was
observed. This was the law of Moses, and this in the land
of Canaan was well observed, according to the first institution: but since their dispersion, and habitation in countries,
whose constitutions admit not such tempestivity of harvests
(and many not before the latter end of summer), notwithstanding the advantage of their lunary account, and intercalary month Veader, affixed unto the beginning of the year,
there will be found a great disparity in their observations,
nor can they strictly, and at the same season with their
forefathers, observe the commands of God.

To add yet further, those geoponical rules and precepts of
agriculture, which are delivered by divers authors, are not to
be generally received, but respectively understood unto climes
whereto they are determined. For whereas one adviseth to
sow this or that grain at one season, a second to set this or
that at another, it must be conceived relatively, and every
nation must have its country farm; for herein we may
observe a manifest and visible difference, not only in the
seasons of harvest, but in the grains themselves. For with
us barley-harvest is made after wheat-harvest, but with the
Israelites and Egyptians it was otherwise. So is it expressed
by way of priority, Ruth ii.; "So Ruth kept fast by the
maidens of Boaz, to glean unto the end of barley-harvest and
of wheat-harvest;" which in the plague of hail in Egypt is
more plainly delivered, Exod. ix.; "And the flax and the
barley were smitten, for the barley was in the ear, and the
flax was bolled; but the wheat and the rye were not smitten,
for they were not grown up."

And thus we see, the account established upon the arise
or descent of the stars can be no reasonable rule unto distant
nations at all; and, by reason of their retrogression, but
temporary unto any one. Nor must these respective expres-

* Deut. xi. † Joel ii.

sions be entertained in absolute consideration; for so distinct is the relation, and so artificial the habitude of this inferior globe unto the superior, and even of one thing in each unto the other, that general rules are dangerous, and applications most safe that run with security of circumstance, which rightly to effect, is beyond the subtilty of sense, and requires the artifice of reason.[8]

CHAPTER IV.

Of some computation of days, and deductions of one part of the year unto another.

FOURTHLY, there are certain vulgar opinions concerning days of the year, and conclusions popularly deduced from certain days of the month; men commonly believing the days increase and decrease equally in the whole year; which notwithstanding is very repugnant unto truth. For they increase in the month of March, almost as much as in the two months of January and February: and decrease as much in September, as they do in July and August. For the days increase or decrease according to the declination of the sun, that is, its deviation northward or southward from the equator. Now this digression is not equal, but near the equinoxial intersections, it is right and greater, near the solstices more oblique and lesser. So from the eleventh of March the vernal equinox, unto the eleventh of April, the sun declineth to the north twelve degrees; from the eleventh of April, unto the eleventh of May, but eight; from thence unto the fifteenth of June, or the summer solstice, but three

[8] *reason.*] Hence itt may appeare that those rules of prognostic and signification, which the Ægyptian, Arabian, Græcian, yea, and Italian astronomers, have given concerning the starrs, and those clymates wherein they lived, cannot bee applied to our remote and colder clymes, nor to these later times (wherein the constellations of all the twelve signes are moved eastward almost 30 degrees; Aries into Taurus and that into Gemini, &c.) without manifest errors and grosse deceptions, and are therefore of late rejected by the most famous astronomers, Tycho, Copernicus, Longomontanus, and Kepler (as diabolical impostures). *De Cometis Anni* 1618.— *Wr.*

and a half: all which make twenty-two degrees and an half, the greatest declination of the sun.

And this inequality in the declination of the sun in the zodiack or line of life, is correspondent unto the growth or declination of man. For setting out from infancy, we increase, not equally, or regularly attain to our state or perfection; nor when we descend from our state, is our declination equal, or carrieth us with even paces unto the grave. For as Hippocrates affirmeth, a man is hottest in the first day of his life, and coldest in the last; his natural heat setteth forth most vigorously at first, and declineth most sensibly at last. And so though the growth of man end not perhaps until twenty-one, yet is his stature more advanced in the first septenary than in the second, and in the second more than in the third, and more indeed in the first seven years, than in the fourteen succeeding; for what stature we attain unto at seven years, we do sometimes but double, most times come short of at one and twenty. And so do we decline again: For in the latter age upon the tropick and first descension from our solstice, we are scarce sensible of declination: but declining further, our decrement accelerates, we set apace, and in our last days precipitate into our graves. And thus are also our progressions in the womb, that is, our formation, motion, our birth, or exclusion. For our formation is quickly effected, our motion appeareth later, and our exclusion very long after: if that be true which Hippocrates and Avicenna have declared, that the time of our motion is double unto that of formation, and that of exclusion treble unto that of motion. As if the infant be formed at thirty-five days, it moveth at seventy, and is born the two hundred and tenth day, that is, the seventh month; or if it receives not formation before forty-five days, it moveth the ninetieth day, and is excluded in the two hundred and seventieth, that is, the ninth month.

There are also certain popular prognosticks drawn from festivals in the calendar, and conceived opinions of certain days in months; so is there a general tradition in most parts of Europe, that inferreth the coldness of succeeding winter from the shining of the sun upon Candlemas day, or the purification of the Virgin Mary, according to the proverbial distich,

> Si Sol splendescat Mariâ purificante,
> Major erit glacies post festum quam fuit ante.

So is it usual among us to qualify and conditionate the twelve months of the year, answerable unto the temper of the twelve days in Christmas; and to ascribe unto March certain borrowed days from April, all which men seem to believe upon annual experience of their own, and the received traditions of their forefathers.

Now it is manifest, and most men likewise know, that the calendars of these computers, and the accounts of these days are very different: the Greeks dissenting from the Latins, and the Latins from each other: the one observing the Julian or ancient account, as Great Britain and part of Germany; the other adhering to the Gregorian or new account, as Italy, France, Spain, and the United Provinces of the Netherlands. Now this latter account, by ten days at least, anticipateth the other; so that before the one beginneth the account, the other is past it; yet in the several calculations, the same events seem true, and men with equal opinion of verity, expect and confess a confirmation from them all. Whereby is evident the oraculous authority of tradition, and the easy seduction of men,[9] neither enquiring into the verity of the substance, nor reforming upon repugnance of circumstance.

And thus may divers easily be mistaken who superstitiously observe certain times, or set down unto themselves an observation of unfortunate months, or days, or hours. As did the Egyptians, two in every month, and the Romans the days after the nones, ides, and calends. And thus the rules of navigators must often fail, setting down, as Rhodiginus observeth, suspected and ominous days in every month, as the first and seventh of March, and fifth and sixth of April, the sixth, the twelfth, and fifteenth of February. For the accounts hereof in these months are very different in our days, and were different with several nations in ages past, and how strictly soever the account be made, and even by the selfsame calendar, yet it is possible that navigators may be out. For so were the Hollanders, who passing west-

[9] *men.*] By the jugling Priests in the old mythologies of the heathen deytyes, trulye taxte by the poet under that "*Quicquid Græcia mendax mandat in historiis.*—*Wr.*

ward through *fretum le Mayre*, and compassing the globe, upon their return into their own country found that they had lost a day. For if two men at the same time travel from the same place, the one eastward, the other westward, round about the earth, and meet in the same place from whence they first set forth, it will so fall out that he which hath moved eastward against the diurnal motion of the sun, by anticipating daily something of its circle with its own motion, will gain one day; but he that travelleth westward,[1] with the motion of the sun, by seconding its revolution, shall lose or come short a day; and therefore also upon these grounds that Delos was seated in the middle of the earth, it was no exact decision, because two eagles let fly east and west by Jupiter, their meeting fell out just in the island Delos.

CHAPTER V.

A digression of the Wisdom of God in the Site and Motion of the Sun.

HAVING thus beheld the ignorance of man in some things, his error and blindness in others, that is, in the measure of duration both of years and seasons, let us awhile admire the wisdom of God in this distinguisher of times, and visible deity (as some have termed it) the sun, which, though some from its glory adore, and all for its benefits admire, we shall advance from other considerations, and such as illustrate the artifice of its Maker. Nor do we think we can excuse the duty of our knowledge, if we only bestow the flourish of poetry hereon, or those commendatory conceits which popularly set forth the eminency of this creature, except we

[1] *westward.*] Captain Bodman, an auncient and discreete gentleman, and learned, for his many services to the State, being admitted a poore Knight at Windsor, was wont to tell mee, that at their returne from surrounding the world with Sir Francis Drake in the yeare 1579, they found that they lost a daye in their accomptes of their daylye saylinge, which agrees with this excellent observation of Dr. Browne; for their voyage was from England to the Streits of Magellan, and soe round by the Moluccas and Cape of Good Hope, back to England, which was totalye with the sonne, and therefore what they observed with admiration, concerning the losse of a day in their accompt, had a manifest reason and cause to justifie the trueth of that observation, and that itt could not possiblye bee otherwise.—*Wr.*

ascend unto subtiler considerations, and such, as rightly understood, convincingly declare the wisdom of the Creator. Which since a Spanish physician* hath begun, we will enlarge with our deductions, and this we shall endeavour from two considerations, its proper situation and wisely ordered motion.

And first, we cannot pass over his providence, in that it moveth at all, for had it stood still, and were it fixed like the earth, there had been then no distinction of times, either of day or year, of spring, of autumn, of summer, or of winter; for these seasons are defined by the motions of the sun: when that approacheth nearest our zenith, or vertical point, we call it summer; when furthest off, winter; when in the middle spaces, spring or autumn; whereas, remaining in one place, these distinctions had ceased, and consequently the generation of all things, depending on their vicissitudes; making in one hemisphere a perpetual summer, in the other a deplorable and comfortless winter.[2] And thus had it also

* *Valerius de Philos. Sacr.*

[2] *winter.*] All this must of necessity evidentlye follow, unlesse (according to the supposition of Copernicus, for I suppose it was but a postulate of art, noe parte of his creed) that the son is fixed in the midst or center of this universal frame of the world, altogether immoovable, and that the earth, with all the rest of the elements, is annually caryed round about the sonne in the sphere between Mars and Venus, parting that lovinge couple of godlings by its boysterous intrusion, but the mischeef is that besides this annual motion of the earth, mounted like Phæthon in the chariot and throne of the sonue, the Copernicans are forced, contrary to their own principles, that *unius corporis cælestis* (for soe you must nowe accompte itt, though a dul and opacous planet, *unius est motus simplex*), to ascribe two other motions to the earth; the one a vertiginous rotation, whirling about his own center, wherby turning toward the son causeth daye, and turning from the son, night; both of them every twenty-four hours; the other a tottering motion of inclination to the son the sommer halfe yeare, and of reclination from the son in the halfe halfe, from whence must of necessity follow two vast and unconcedable postulates. First, that as the son, in his old sphere, is supposed in respect of his distance from the center to moove noe lesse than 18,000 miles every minute of an hour, yf the earth bee in the sons place, they must perforce acknowledge the same pernicitye in the earth, and yet not perceptible to our sense, nor to the wisest of the world, since the creation till our times. But to salve this, as they thinke, they suppose and postulate the second motion of rotation or whirling on his owne center, which others conceive to bee diametrally opposite to Scripture: but then there recoyles upon them this strange

been continual day unto some, and perpetual night unto others, for the day is defined by the abode of the sun above the horizon, and the night by its continuance below; so should we have needed another sun, one to illustrate our hemisphere, a second to enlighten the other, which inconvenience will ensue in what site soever we place it, whether in the poles or the equator, or between them both; no spherical body, of what bigness soever, illuminating the whole sphere of another, although it illuminate something more than half of a lesser, according unto the doctrine of the opticks.

His wisdom is again discernible, not only in that it moveth at all, and in its bare motion, but wonderful in contriving the line of its revolution which is so prudently effected, that by a vicissitude in one body and light it sufficeth the whole earth, affording thereby a possible or pleasurable habitation in every part thereof, and that is the line ecliptick, all which to effect by any other circle it had been impossible. For first, if we imagine the sun to make its course out of the ecliptick, and upon a line without any obliquity, let it be conceived within that circle that is either on the equator, or else on either side; for if we should place it either in the meridian or colures, beside the subversion of its course from east to west, there would ensue the like incommodities. Now if we conceive the sun to move between the obliquity of this ecliptick in a line upon one side of the equator, then would the sun be visible but unto one pole, that is the same which was nearest unto it. So that unto the one it would be perpetual day, unto the other perpetual night; the one would be oppressed with constant heat, the other with insufferable cold, and so the defect of alternation would utterly impugn the generation of all things, which naturally require a vicissitude of heat to their production, and no less to their increase and conservation.

But if we conceive it to move in the equator, first unto a parallel sphere, or such as have the pole for their zenith, it would have made neither perfect day nor night. For being in the equator it would intersect their horizon, and be half above and half beneath it, or rather it would have made

consequence that the earthe being 21,600 miles in compass, and whirling rounde every twenty-four howres, caryes every towne and howse 895 miles every houre, and yet not discernablye.—*Wr.*

perpetual night to both; for though in regard of the rational horizon, which bisecteth the globe into equal parts, the sun in the equator would intersect the horizon; yet in respect of the sensible horizon, which is defined by the eye, the sun would be visible unto neither. For if, as ocular witnesses report, and some also write, by reason of the convexity of the earth, the eye of man under the equator cannot discover both the poles, neither would the eye under the poles discover the sun in the equator. Thus would there nothing fructify either near or under them, the sun being horizontal to the poles, and of no considerable altitude unto parts a reasonable distance from them. Again, unto a right sphere, or such as dwell under the equator, although it made a difference in day and night, yet would it not make any distinction of seasons; for unto them it would be constant summer, it being always vertical, and never deflecting from them. So had there been no fructification at all, and the countries subjected would be as unhabitable, as indeed antiquity conceived them.

Lastly, it moving thus upon the equator, unto what position soever, although it had made a day, yet could it have made no year, for it could not have had those two motions[3] now

[3] *two motions.*] The motion from east to west is cald the motion of the world, bycause by itt all the whole frame of the universe is caryed round every 24 howres, and among the rest of the cælestial lights the sun alsoe, to whom this motion does not belong but passively onlye, and therefore heere was noe feare of crossing that undoubted principle which unavoydably recoyls upon the Copernicans, who to make good their hypothesis, fancye a rotation of dinetical, that is, a whirlinge rapture of the earthe about his owne axe every 24 houres, that is, 900 miles every howre, which is more impossible then for the heaven which wee call the primum mobile to turne about 400,000 miles every houre; unless they thinke that he who made itt soe infinitelye vast in compasse and in distance from us, could not make itt as swift in motion alsoe, as he makes his angels, or has he made his owne bodye in his ascention, or as he makes the lightning or the light itself.

The compass of the earth, which is 21,600 miles, divided by 24 leaves in the quotient $937\frac{12}{24}$ i. e. $\frac{1}{2}$ of miles, and soe many the Copernicans thinke the earth turnes every howre; that is above 15 miles every minute of an houre, and about $\frac{1}{4}$ of a mile every second, i. e. swifter then the natural motion of the heart. Proculdubio loca terræ sub polis sita, nequeunt ab æquatoris subjectis cerni: cum horison terrestris nusquam in ipso oceano tranquillo 60 miliarium visu terminetur: at polos cœli posse ab iisdem terræ incolis simul conspici, manifestum ex rarefactione quæ sydera attollit ultra distantiam horizontis rationalis.—*Wr.*

ascribed unto it, that is, from east to west, whereby it makes the day, and likewise from west to east, whereby the year is computed. For according to received astronomy, the poles of the equator are the same with those of the *primum mobile*. Now it is impossible that on the same circle,[4] having the same poles, both these motions, from opposite terms, should be at the same time performed, all which is salved, if we allow an obliquity in his annual motion, and conceive him to move upon the poles of the zodiack, distant from those of the world twenty-three degrees and an half. Thus may we discern the necessity of its obliquity, and how inconvenient its motion had been upon a circle parallel to the equator, or upon the equator itself.

Now with what providence this obliquity is determined, we shall perceive upon the ensuing inconveniences from any deviation. For first, if its obliquity had been less (as instead of twenty-three degrees, twelve or the half thereof) the vicissitude of seasons appointed for the generation of all things would surely have been too short; for different seasons would have huddled upon each other, and unto some it had not been much better than if it had moved on the equator. But had the obliquity been greater than now it is, as double, or of 40 degrees, several parts of the earth had not been able to endure the disproportionable differences of seasons, occasioned by the great recess, and distance of the sun. For unto some habitations the summer would have been extreme hot, and the winter extreme cold; likewise the summer temperate unto some, but excessive and in extremity unto others, as unto those who should dwell under the tropick of Cancer, as then would do some part of Spain, or ten degrees beyond, as Germany, and some part of England, who would have summers, as now the Moors of Africa. For the sun would sometime be vertical unto them; but they would have winters like those beyond the arctic circle, for in that season the sun would be removed above 80 degrees from them. Again, it would be temperate to some habitations in the summer, but very extreme in the winter; temperate to those in two or three degrees beyond the arctic circle, as now it is unto us, for they would be equidistant from that tropic, even as we

[4] *circle.*] Globe.—*Wr.*

are from this at present. But the winter would be extreme, the sun being removed above an hundred degrees, and so consequently would not be visible in their horizon, no position of sphere discovering any star distant above 90 degrees, which is the distance of every zenith from the horizon. And thus, if the obliquity of this circle had been less, the vicissitude of seasons had been so small as not to be distinguished; if greater, so large and disproportionable as not to be endured.

Now for its situation, although it held this ecliptic line, yet had it been seated in any other orb,[5] inconveniences would ensue of condition unlike the former; for had it been placed in the lowest sphere of the moon, the year would have consisted but of one month, for in that space of time it would have passed through every part of the ecliptic; so would there have been no reasonable distinction of seasons required for the generation and fructifying of all things, contrary seasons which destroy the effects of one another so suddenly succeeding. Besides, by this vicinity unto the earth, its heat had been intolerable; for if, as many affirm,[6] there is a different sense of heat from the different points of its proper orb, and that in the apogeum, or highest point, which happeneth in Cancer, it is not so hot under that tropic, on this side the equator, as unto the other side in the perigeum or lowest part of the eccentric, which happeneth in Capricornus, surely, being placed in an orb far lower, its heat would be unsufferable, nor needed we a fable to set the world on fire.

But had it been placed in the highest orb, or that of the eighth sphere, there had been none but Plato's year, and a far less distinction of seasons; for one year had then been many, and according unto the slow revolution of that orb which absolveth not his course in many thousand years, no man had lived to attain the account thereof. These are the inconveniences ensuing upon its situation in the extreme orbs; and had it been placed in the middle orbs of the planets, there would have ensued absurdities of a middle nature unto them.

[5] *orb.*] Orbit.
[6] *as many affirm.*] Especially Scaliger, in that admirable work of his exercitations upon Cardan de Subtilitate. *Exercit.* 99, § 2, p. 342.—*Wr.*

Now whether we adhere unto the hypothesis of Copernicus,[7] affirming the earth to move and the sun to stand still; or whether we hold, as some of late have concluded, from the spots in the sun, which appear and disappear again, that besides the revolution it maketh with its orbs, it hath also a dinetical[8] motion, and rolls upon its own poles; whether I say we affirm these or no, the illations before mentioned are not thereby infringed. We therefore conclude this contemplation, and are not afraid to believe it may be literally said of the wisdom of God, what men will have but figuratively spoken of the works of Christ, that if the wonders thereof were duly described, the whole world, that is, all within the last circumference, would not contain them. For as his wisdom is infinite, so cannot the due expressions thereof be finite, and if the world comprise him not, neither can it comprehend the story of him.

CHAPTER VI.

Concerning the vulgar opinion, that the Earth was slenderly peopled before the Flood.

BESIDE the slender consideration, men of latter times do hold of the first ages, it is commonly opinioned, and at first thought generally imagined, that the earth was thinly inhabited, at least not remotely planted, before the flood, whereof there being two opinions, which seem to be of some extremity, the one too largely extending, the other too narrowly

---

[7] *Copernicus.*] Copernicus, to make good his hypothesis, is forced to ascribe a triple motion to the earthe: the first annuall, round about the sonne, which hee places in the midst of the universe, and the earthe to bee caryed, as the sonne was ever supposed to be, in a middle orbe between Venus and Mars; the second not a motion of declination from the æquator to bothe the tropicks onlye, causinge the different seasons of the yeare, but more properlye a motion of inclination likewise to the sonne, which supposes also the poles of the earth to bee mooved, and the third motion is that called dineticall, or rotation upon his owne axis, causing day and night.—*Wr.*

[8] *dinetical.*] Signifies whirlinge, from δίνη, which in the Greeke is a whirlpole, soe that the dineticall motion of the son is such, in their opinion, as that of the materiall globes, which wee make to turne upon their axis in a frame.—*Wr.*

contracting the populosity of those times, we shall not pass over this point without some enquiry into it.[9]

Now for the true enquiry thereof, the means are as obscure as the matter, which being naturally to be explored by history, human or divine, receiveth thereby no small addition of obscurity. For as for human relations, they are so fabulous in Deucalion's flood, that they are of little credit about Ogyges' and Noah's. For the heathens, as Varro accounteth, make three distinctions of time. The first from the beginning of the world unto the general deluge of Ogyges, they term *Adelon*,[1] that is, a time not much unlike that which was before time, immanifest and unknown ; because thereof there is almost nothing or very obscurely delivered ; for though divers authors have made some mention of the deluge, as Manethon the Egyptian priest, Xenophon, *De Æquivocis*, Fabius Pictor, *De Aureo seculo*, Mar. Cato, *De Originibus*, and Archilochus the Greek, who introduceth also the testimony of Moses, in his fragment *De Temporibus;* yet have they delivered no account of what preceded or went before. Josephus, I confess, in his discourse against Appion, induceth the antiquity of the Jews unto the flood, and before, from the testimony of human writers, insisting especially upon Maseus of Damascus, Jeronymus Ægyptius, and Berosus ; and confirming the long duration of their lives, not only from these, but the authority of Hesiod, Erathius, Hellanicus, and Age-

---

[9] *whereof, &c.*] Instead of this passage, the first five editions have the following :—" So that some conceiving it needless to be universal, have made the deluge particular, and about those parts where Noah built his ark ; which opinion, because it is not only injurious to the text, human history, and common reason, but also derogatory to the great work of God, the universal inundation, it will be needful to make some further inquisition ; and although predetermined by opinion, whether many might not suffer in the first flood, as they shall in the last flame, that is who knew not Adam nor his offence, and many perish in the deluge, who never heard of Noah or the ark of his preservation."

[1] *Adelon.*] To the heathen who either knew nothing of the creation, or at least beleeved itt not, the first distinction of time must needs bee ἄδηλον, that is utterly unknowne, for the space of 1656 from the creation to the flood, and the second, the *mythicon*, little better, as the very name they give itt (yt is fabulous), importes, whereas in the church of God, the third (which they call historicall, and began not till after the 3000th yeare of the world's creation with them) was continued in a perfect narration and unquestionable historye from the beginning of time through those 3000 yeares.—*Wr.*

silaus. Berosus, the Chaldean priest, writes most plainly, mentioning the city of Enos, the name of Noah and his sons, the building of the ark, and also the place of its landing. And Diodorus Siculus hath in his third book a passage, which examined, advanceth as high as Adam; for the Chaldeans, saith he, derive the original of their astronomy and letters forty-three thousand years before the monarchy of Alexander the Great; now the years whereby they computed the antiquity of their letters, being, as Xenophon interprets, to be accounted lunary, the compute will arise unto the time of Adam. For forty-three thousand lunary years make about three thousand six hundred thirty-four years, which answereth the chronology of time from the beginning of the world unto the reign of Alexander, as Annius of Viterbo computeth, in his comment upon Berosus.

The second space or interval of time is accounted from the flood unto the first Olympiad, that is, the year of the world 3174, which extendeth unto the days of Isaiah the prophet, and some twenty years before the foundation of Rome. This they term *mythicon* or fabulous, because the account thereof, especially of the first part, is fabulously or imperfectly delivered. Hereof some things have been briefly related by the authors above mentioned, more particularly by Dares Phrygius, Dictys Cretensis, Herodotus, Diodorus Siculus, and Trogus Pompeius. The most famous Greek poets lived also in this interval, as Orpheus, Linus, Museus, Homer, Hesiod; and herein are comprehended the grounds and first invention of poetical fables, which were also taken up by historical writers, perturbing the Chaldean and Egyptian records with fabulous additions, and confounding their names and stories with their own inventions.

The third time succeeding until their present ages, they term *historicon*, that is, such wherein matters have been more truly historified, and may therefore be believed. Of these times also have written Herodotus,[2] Thucydides, Xeno-

---

[2] *Herodotus.*] Yet the first parte of his historye begins not till the times of Apries, that is, Hophreas, whose reign began not till the seige of Jerusalem by Nabuchodonosor, 475 yeares after Saul, the first king of Israel, and at least 1224 yeares after the flood, of all which time (which to them was most obscure and fabulous) the sacred storye is soe plaine that thence Eusebius tooke his argument to convince the heathen

phon, Diodorus, and both of these and the other preceding such as have delivered universal histories or chronologies; as (to omit Philo, whose narrations concern the Hebrews) Eusebius, Julius Africanus, Orosius, Ado of Vienna, Marianus Scotus, *Historia tripartita, Urspergensis,* Carion, Pineda, Salian, and with us Sir Walter Raleigh.

Now from the first hereof, that most concerneth us, we have little or no assistance, the fragments and broken records hereof inforcing not at all our purpose. And although some things not usually observed may be from thence collected, yet do they not advantage our discourse, nor any way make evident the point in hand. For the second, though it directly concerns us not, yet in regard of our last medium and some illustrations therein, we shall be constrained to make some use thereof. As for the last, it concerns us not at all; for treating of times far below us, it can no way advantage us. And though divers in this last age have also written of the first, as all that have delivered the general accounts of time, yet are their tractates little auxiliary unto ours, nor afford us any light to detenebrate and clear this truth.

As for Holy Scripture and divine relation, there may also seem therein but slender information, there being only left a brief narration hereof by Moses, and such as affords no positive determination. For the text delivereth but two genealogies, that is, of Cain and Seth; in the line of Seth there are only ten descents, in that of Cain but seven, and those in a right line with mention of father and son, excepting that of Lamech, where is also mention of wives, sons, and a daughter. Notwithstanding, if we seriously consider what is delivered therein, and what is also deducible, it will be probably declared what is by us intended, that is, the populous and ample habitation of the earth before the flood. Which we shall labour to induce not from postulates and entreated maxims, but undeniable principles declared in Holy Scripture, that is, the length of men's lives before the flood, and the large extent of time from creation thereunto.

We shall only first crave notice, that although in the relation of Moses there be very few persons mentioned, yet are there many more to be presumed; nor when the Scripture

of their novel idolatryes, the most whereof sprang upp in the end of these fabulous times.—*Wr.*

in the line of Seth nominates but ten persons, are they to be conceived all that were of this generation. The Scripture singly delivering the holy line, wherein the world was to be preserved, first in Noah, and afterward in our Saviour. For in this line it is manifest there were many more born than are named, for it is said of them all, that they begat sons and daughters. And whereas it is very late before it is said they begat those persons which are named in the Scripture, the soonest at 65, it must not be understood that they had none before, but not any in whom it pleased God the holy line should be continued. And although the expression that they begat sons and daughters, be not determined to be before or after the mention of those, yet must it be before in some; for before it is said that Adam begat Seth at the 130th year, it is plainly affirmed that Cain knew his wife, and had a son, which must be one of the daughters of Adam, one of those whereof it is after said, he begat sons and daughters. And so, for ought can be disproved, there might be more persons upon earth than are commonly supposed when Cain slew Abel, nor the fact so heinously to be aggravated in the circumstance of the fourth person living. And whereas it is said, upon the nativity of Seth, God hath appointed me another seed instead of Abel, it doth not imply he had no other all this while; but not any of that expectation, or appointed (as his name implies) to make a progression in the holy line, in whom the world was to be saved, and from whom he should be born, that was mystically slain in Abel.

Now our first ground to induce the numerosity of people before the flood, is the long duration of their lives, beyond seven, eight, and nine hundred years. Which how it conduceth unto populosity, we shall make but little doubt, if we consider there are two main causes of numerosity in any kind or species, that is, a frequent and multiparous way of breeding, whereby they fill the world with others, though they exist not long themselves; or a long duration and subsistence, whereby they do not only replenish the world with a new annumeration of others, but also maintain the former account in themselves. From the first cause we may observe examples in creatures oviparous, as birds and fishes; in verminiparous, as flies, locusts, and gnats; in animals also viviparous, as swine and conies. Of the first there is a great example in the herd of swine in Galilee, although an unclean beast and forbidden unto the Jews. Of the other a remarkable one in Athenæus, in the Isle Astipalea, one of the Cyclades, now called Stampalia, wherein from two that were imported, the number so increased, that the inhabitants were constrained to have recourse unto the oracle of Delphos, for an invention how to destroy them.

Others there are which make good the paucity of their breed with the length and duration of their days, whereof there want not examples in animals uniparous. First, in bisulcous or cloven-hoofed, as camels and beeves, whereof there is above a million annually slain in England. It is also said of Job, that he had a thousand yoke of oxen, and six thousand camels; and of the children of Israel passing into the land of Canaan, that they took from the Midianites threescore and ten thousand beeves; and of the army of Semiramis, that there were therein one hundred thousand camels. For solipeds or firm-hoofed animals, as horses, asses, mules, &c., they are also in mighty numbers; so it is delivered that Job had a thousand she asses; that the Midianites lost sixty-one thousand asses. For horses, it is affirmed by Diodorus, that Ninus brought against the Bactrians two hundred eighty thousand horses; after him Semiramis five hundred thousand horses, and chariots one hundred thousand. Even in creatures sterile, and such as do not generate, the length of life conduceth much unto the multiplicity of the species; for the number of mules which live far longer than their dams or sires, in countries where they are bred, is very remarkable, and far more common than horses.

For animals multifidous, or such as are digitated or have several divisions in their feet, there are but two that are uniparous, that is, men and elephants, who, though their productions be but single, are notwithstanding very numerous. The elephant, as Aristotle affirmeth, carrieth the young two years, and conceiveth not again, as Edvardus Lopez affirmeth, in many years after, yet doth their age requite this disadvantage, they living commonly one hundred, sometime two hundred years. Now although they be rare with us in Europe, and altogether unknown unto America, yet in the two other parts of the world they are in great abundance, as appears by the relation of Garcias ab Horto, physician to the Viceroy at Goa, who relates that at one venation the king of Siam took four thousand, and is of opinion they are in other parts in greater number than herds of beeves in Europe. And though this, delivered from a Spaniard unacquainted with our northern droves, may seem very far to exceed, yet must we conceive them very numerous, if we consider the number of teeth transported from one country to another, they having only two great teeth, and those not falling or renewing.

As for man, the disadvantage in his single issue is the same with these, and in the lateness of his generation somewhat greater than any; yet in the continual and not interrupted time hereof, and the extent of his days, he becomes at present, if not than any other species, at least more numerous than these before mentioned. Now being thus numerous at present, and in the measure of threescore, fourscore, or an hundred years, if their days extended unto six, seven, or eight hundred, their generations would be proportionably multiplied, their times of generation being not only multiplied, but their subsistence continued. For though the great-grandchild went on, the *petrucius** and first original would subsist and make one of the world, though he outlived all the terms of consanguinity, and became a stranger unto his proper progeny. So, by compute of Scripture, Adam lived unto the ninth generation, unto the days of Lamech, the father of Noah; Methuselah unto the year of the flood, and Noah was contemporary unto all from Enoch unto Abraham. So that although some died, the father beholding so many descents, the number of survivors must still be very great; for if half the men were now alive which lived in the last century, the earth would scarce contain their number. Whereas in our abridged and septuagesimal ages, it is very rare, and deserves a distich† to behold the fourth generation. Xerxes' complaint still remaining, and what he lamented in his army, being almost deplorable in the whole world; men seldom arriving unto those years whereby Methuselah ex-

---

* The term for that person for whom consanguineal relations are accounted, as in the *Arbor civilis*.

† *Mater ait natæ, dic natæ filia, &c.*

ceeded nine hundred, and what Adam came short of a thousand, was defined long ago to be the age of man.

Now, although the length of days conduceth mainly unto the numerosity of mankind, and it be manifest from Scripture they lived very long, yet is not the period of their lives determinable, and some might be longer livers than we account that any were. For, to omit that conceit of some that Adam was the oldest man, in as much as he is conceived to be created in the maturity of mankind, that is, at sixty, for in that age it is set down they begat children, so that adding this number unto his 930, he was 21 years older than any of his posterity; that even Methuselah was the longest liver of all the children of Adam we need not grant, nor is it definitively set down by Moses. Indeed of those ten mentioned in Scripture, with their several ages, it must be true, but whether those seven of the line of Cain and their progeny, or any of the sons' and daughters' posterity after them outlived those, is not expressed in Holy Scripture, and it will seem more probable that of the line of Cain some were longer lived than any of Seth, if we concede that seven generations of the one lived as long as nine of the other. As for what is commonly alleged that God would not permit the life of any unto a thousand, because, alluding unto that of David, no man should live one day in the sight of the Lord, although it be urged by divers, yet is it methinks an inference somewhat rabbinical, and not of power to persuade a serious examiner.

Having thus declared how powerfully the length of lives conduced unto the populosity of those times, it will yet be easier acknowledged if we descend to particularities, and consider how many in seven hundred years might descend from one man; wherein considering the length of their days, we may conceive the greatest number to have been alive together. And this, that no reasonable spirit may contradict, we will declare with manifest disadvantage: for whereas the duration of the world unto the flood was above 1600 years, we will make our compute in less than half that time. Nor will we begin with the first man, but allow the earth to be provided of women fit for marriage the second or third first centuries, and will only take as granted, that they might beget children at sixty, and at an hundred years have twenty, allowing for that number forty years. Nor will we herein single out Methuselah, on account from the longest livers, but make choice of the shortest of any we find recorded in the text, excepting Enoch, who, after he had lived as many years as there be days in the year, was translated at 365. And thus from one stock of seven hundred years, multiplying still by twenty, we shall find the product to be one thousand three hundred forty-seven millions, three hundred sixty-eight thousand, four hundred and twenty.

$$\text{Century} \begin{Bmatrix} 1 \\ 2 \\ 3 \\ 4 \\ 5 \\ 6 \\ 7 \end{Bmatrix} \begin{matrix} 20 \\ 400 \\ 8000 \\ 160{,}000 \\ 3{,}200{,}000 \\ 64{,}000{,}000 \\ 1{,}280{,}000{,}000 \end{matrix}$$

Product   1,347,368,420

Now, if this account of the learned Petavius will be allowed, it will make an unexpected increase, and a larger number than may be found in Asia, Africa, and Europe; especially if in Constantinople, the greatest city thereof, there be no more than Botero accounteth, seven hundred thousand souls. Which duly considered, we shall rather admire how the earth contained its inhabitants, than doubt its inhabitation; and might conceive the deluge not simply penal, but in some way also necessary, as many have conceived of translations,[3] if Adam had not sinned, and the race of man had remained upon earth immortal.

Now, whereas some to make good their longevity, have imagined that the years of their compute were lunary, unto these we must reply; that if by a lunary year they understand twelve revolutions of the moon, that is, 354 days, eleven fewer than in the solary year; there will be no great difference, at least not sufficient to convince or extenuate the question. But if by a lunary year they mean one revolution of the moon, that is, a month; they first introduce a

---

[3] *translations.*] That is, that after some terme of yeares they should not dye, but have been translated as Henoch was, into Heaven.— *Wr.*

year never used by the Hebrews in their civil accounts; and what is delivered before of the Chaldean years (as Xenophon gives a caution) was only received in the chronology of their arts. Secondly, they contradict the Scripture, which makes a plain enumeration of many months in the account of the deluge; for so it is expressed in the text: "In the tenth month, in the first day of the month, were the tops of the mountains seen." Concordant whereunto is the relation of human authors; *Inundationes plures fuere, prima novimestris inundatio terrarum sub prisco Ogyge. Meminisse hoc loco par est post primum diluvium Ogygi temporibus notatum, cum novem, et amplius mensibus diem continua nox inumbrasset, Delon ante omnes terras radiis solis illuminatum sortitumque ex eo nomen.** And lastly, they fall upon an absurdity, for they make Enoch to beget children about six years of age. For, whereas it is said he begat Methuselah at sixty-five, if we shall account every month[4] a year, he was at that time some six years and an half, for so many months are contained in that space of time.

Having thus declared how much the length of men's lives conduced unto the populosity of their kind, our second foundation must be the large extent of time, from the creation unto the deluge (that is, according unto received computes, about 1655 years), almost as long a time as hath passed since the nativity of our Saviour.[5] And this we

* *Xenophon de Æquivocis. Solinus.*

[4] *month.*] The spirit in many places (as of Daniel, and the Apocalyps) by dayes means yeares: but in noe place yeares for dayes or monthes.—*Wr.*

[5] *Saviour.*] And according to this number there are, that take upon them to judge that when the yeares of the church's age comes to as many since Christ's birthe, as those yeares of the world had from the creation to the flood, the consummation or consumption of the world by fire prophesyed by St. Peter, 2nd Epist. 3 chap. v. 10, must needs bee then or thereabouts fulfilled, as itt was before by water at those years. For counting (say they) as the Apostle there does, that with God 1000 yeares are but as one daye, and that (as all agree) in this yeare of Christ, 1650, there are just 5600 yeares of the world past since the creation, that is almost 6 dayes of the weeke, and that the dayes of the world shal bee, as our Saviour foretold, much shortened, i. e. shall not continue to the full end of 6000 yeares, i. e. 6 of God's dayes: they conclude that the seventh day of æternal rest of the world and all the works

cannot but conceive sufficient for a very large increase, if we do but affirm what reasonable enquirers will not deny,—that the earth might be as populous in that number of years before the flood, as we can manifest it was in the same number after. And, whereas there may be conceived some disadvantage, in regard that at the creation the original of mankind was in two persons, but after the flood their propagation issued at least from six; against this we might very well set the length of their lives before the flood, which were abbreviated after, and in half this space contracted into hundreds and threescores. Notwithstanding, to equalize accounts, we will allow three hundred years, and so long a time as we can manifest from the Scripture, there were four men at least that begat children, Adam, Cain, Seth, and Enos; so shall we fairly and favourably proceed, if we affirm the world to have been as populous in sixteen hundred and fifty years before the flood, as it was in thirteen hundred after. Now how populous and largely inhabited it was within this period of time, we shall declare from probabilities, and several testimonies of Scripture and human authors.

And first, to manifest the same near those parts of the earth where the ark is presumed to have rested, we have the relation of Holy Scripture, accounting the genealogy of Japhet, Cham, and Sem, and in this last, four descents unto the division of the earth in the days of Peleg, which time although it were not upon common compute much above an hundred years, yet were men at this time mightily increased. Nor can we well conceive it otherwise, if we consider they began already to wander from their first habitation, and were able to attempt so mighty a work as the building of a city and a tower, whose top should reach unto the heavens. Whereunto there was required no slender number of persons, if we consider the magnitude thereof, expressed by some,

---

therin cannot bee far of. But how far off, or how neere, is not for man to enquire, much less to define otherwise then by way of Christian caution, to bee always readye for the coming of that kingdome, which wee every (day) pray, may come speedilye. For doubtles yf 1600 yeares agoe the Spirit thought itt requisite to rowse them up with that memento, "the Lord is at hand, bee yee therefore sober and watche," itt may well bee an alarum to us, on whom the ends of the world are some.— *Wr.*

and conceived to be *turris Beli* in Herodotus;[6] and the multitudes of people recorded at the erecting of the like or inferior structures; for at the building of Solomon's temple there were threescore and ten thousand that carried burdens, and fourscore thousand hewers in the mountains, beside the chief of his officers three thousand and three hundred; and at the erection of the pyramids in the reign of king Cheops, as Herodotus reports, there were *decem myriades*, that is, an hundred thousand men. And though it be said of the Egyptians,

Porrum et cæpe nefas violare et frangere morsu;*

yet did the sums expended in garlick and onions amount unto no less than one thousand six hundred talents.

The first monarchy or kingdom of Babylon is mentioned in Scripture under the foundation of Nimrod, which is also recorded in human history; as beside Berosus, in Diodorus and Justin; for Nimrod of the Scriptures is Belus of the Gentiles, and Assur the same with Ninus his successor. There is also mention of divers cities, particularly of Nineveh and Resen, expressed emphatically in the text to be a great city.

That other countries round about were also peopled, appears by the wars of the monarchs of Assyria with the Bactrians, Indians, Scythians, Ethiopians, Armenians, Hyrcanians, Parthians, Persians, Susians; they vanquished (as Diodorus relateth) Egypt, Syria, and all Asia Minor, even from Bosphorus unto Tanais. And it is said, that Semiramis in her expedition against the Indians brought along with her the king of Arabia. About the same time of the Assyrian monarchy, do authors place that of the Sycionians in Greece, and soon after that of the Argives, and not very long after, that of the Athenians under Cecrops; and within our period assumed are historified many memorable actions of the Greeks, as the expedition of the Argonauts, with the most famous wars of Thebes and Troy.

* Juvenal.

[6] *conceived to be, &c.*] Mr. Beke, however, is of opinion that "the city and tower of Babel, the Babel of Nimrod and the Babel or Babylon of Nebuchadnezzar, were three totally distinct places."—*Origines Biblicæ*, p. 17.

That Canaan also and Egypt were well peopled far within this period, besides their plantation by Canaan and Misraim, appeareth from the history of Abraham, who in less than 400 years after the flood, journeyed from Mesopotamia unto Canaan and Egypt, both which he found well peopled and policied into kingdoms. Wherein also in 430 years, from threescore and ten persons which came with Jacob into Egypt, he became a mighty nation; for it is said, at their departure, there journeyed from Rhamesis to Succoth about six hundred thousand on foot, that were men, besides children. Now how populous the land from whence they came was, may be collected not only from their ability in commanding such subjections and mighty powers under them, but from the several accounts of that kingdom delivered by Herodotus. And how soon it was peopled, is evidenced from the pillar of their king Osyris, with this inscription in Diodorus: *Mihi pater est Saturnus deorum junior, sum vero Osyris rex, qui totum peragravi orbem usque ad Indorum fines, ad eos quoque sum profectus qui septentrioni subjacent usque ad Istri fontes, et alias partes usque ad Oceanum.* Now, according unto the best determinations, Osyris was Misraim, and Saturnus Egyptius the same with Cham; after whose name Egypt is not only called in Scripture the land of Ham, but thus much is also testified by Plutarch; for in his treatise *de Osyride*, he delivereth that Egypt was called *Chamia, à Chamo Noe filio*, that is, from Cham the son of Noah. And if, according to the consent of ancient fathers, Adam was buried in the same place where Christ was crucified, that is Mount Calvary, the first man ranged far before the flood, and laid his bones many miles from that place, where it's presumed he received them. And this migration was the greater, if, as the text expresseth, he was cast out of the east side of paradise to till the ground; and as the position of the Cherubim implieth, who were placed at the east end of the garden to keep him from the tree of life.

That the remoter parts of the earth were in this time inhabited, is also inducible from the like testimonies, for (omitting the numeration of Josephus and the genealogies of the sons of Noah) that Italy was inhabited appeareth from the records of Livy and Dionysius Halicarnasseus, the story of Æneas, Evander, and Janus, whom Annius of

Viterbo, and the chorographers of Italy, do make to be the same with Noah. That Sicily was also peopled is made out from the frequent mention thereof in Homer, the records of Diodorus and others, but especially from a remarkable passage touched by Aretius and Ranzanus, bishop of Lucerium, but fully explained by Thomas Fazelli, in his accurate history of Sicily, that is, from ancient inscription in a stone at Panormo, expressed by him in its proper characters, and by a Syrian thus translated: *Non est alius Deus præter unum Deum, non est alius potens præter eundem Deum, neque est alius victor præter eundem quem colimus Deum: Hujus turris præfectus est* Sapha *filius* Eliphat, *filii* Esau, *fratris* Jacob, *filii* Isaac, *filii* Abraham; *et turri quidem ipsi nomen est* Baych, *sed turri huic proximæ nomen est* Pharath. The antiquity of the inhabitation of Spain is also confirmable, not only from Berosus in the plantation of Tubal, and a city continuing yet in his name, but the story of Gerion, the travels of Hercules and his pillars, and especially a passage in Strabo, which advanceth unto the time of Ninus, thus delivered in his fourth book: the Spaniards (saith he) affirm that they have had laws and letters above six thousand years. Now the Spaniards or Iberians observing (as Xenophon hath delivered) *annum quadrimestrem*, four months unto a year, this compute will make up 2000 solary years, which is about the space of time from Strabo, who lived in the days of Augustus, unto the reign of Ninus.

That Mauritania and the coast of Africa were peopled very soon, is the conjecture of many wise men, and that by the Phœnicians,[7] who left their country upon the invasion of Canaan by the Israelites. For beside the conformity of the Punick or Carthaginian language with that of Phœnicia, there is a pregnant and very remarkable testimony hereof in Procopius, who in his second *de bello Vandalico*, recordeth that in a town of Mauritania Tingitana, there was to be seen upon two white columns in the Phœnician language these ensuing words; *Nos Maurici sumus qui fugimus*

---

[7] *by the Phœnicians.*] "Tyri et Sidonis in Phœnicis litore civitatum Carthago colonia; unde et *Pœni*, sermone corrupto quasi *Phœni* appellantur."—*Hieron.* See *Selden, De Diis Syriis, Prolegomena,* cap. 2, p. 10-24.—*Jeff.*

à facie Jehoschue filii Nunis prædatoris. The Fortunate Islands or Canaries were not unknown; for so doth Strabo interpret that speech in Homer of Proteus unto Menelaus.

> Sed te qua terræ postremus terminus extat,
> Elysium in Campum cœlestia numina ducunt.

The like might we affirm from credible histories both of France and Germany, and perhaps also of our own country. For omitting the fabulous and Trojan original delivered by Jeffrey of Monmouth, and the express text of Scripture, that the race of Japhet did people the isles of the Gentiles; the British original was so obscure in Cæsar's time, that he affirmeth the inland inhabitants were Aborigines, that is, such as reported that they had their beginning in the island. That Ireland our neighbour island was not long time without inhabitants, may be made probable by sundry accounts, although we abate the tradition of Bartholanus the Scythian, who arrived three hundred years[8] after the flood, or the relation of Giraldus, that Cæsaria, the daughter of Noah, dwelt there before.

Now should we call in the learned account of Bochartus,[*] deducing the ancient names of countries from Phœnicians, who by their plantations, discoveries, and sea negociations, have left unto very many countries, Phœnician denominations, the enquiry would be much shorter; and if Spain, in the Phœnician original, be but the region of conies, Lusitania, or Portugal, the country of almonds, if Britannica were at first Baratanaca, or the land of tin, and Ibernia or Ireland were but Ibernae, or the farthest inhabitation, and these names imposed and dispersed by Phœnician colonies, in their several navigations, the antiquity of habitations might be more clearly advanced.

Thus though we have declared how largely the world was

---

[*] *Bochart. Geog. Sacr. part* 2.

[8] *three hundred years.*] This yeare, 1650, is the 5600 yeare of the worlde since the creation; out of which, yf you take the yeare of the floodd, viz. in the yeare of the world 1656, and also the 300 yeares more here mentioned, the summe will be 1956, which being againe deducted out of the present yeare of the world 5600, there remaine 3644 yeares this yeare, since Bartolanus is said to arrive in Irelande, which neither Scripture nor any story mentions, and therefore is a feigned and foolish tradition.—*Wr.*

inhabited within the space of 1300 years, yet must it be conceived more populous than can be clearly evinced; for a greater part of the earth hath ever been peopled, than hath been known or described by geographers, as will appear by the discoveries of all ages. For neither in Herodotus or Thucydides do we find any mention of Rome, nor in Ptolemy of many parts of Europe, Asia, or Africa; and because many places we have declared of long plantation, of whose populosity notwithstanding or memorable actions we have no ancient story; if we may conjecture of these by what we find related of others, we shall not need many words, nor assume the half of 1300 years. And this we might illustrate from the mighty acts of the Assyrians, performed not long after the flood, recorded by Justin and Diodorus, who makes relation of expeditions by armies more numerous than have been ever since. For Ninus,[9] king of Assyria, brought against the Bactrians 700,000 foot, 200,000 horse, 10,600 chariots. Semiramis, his successor, led against the Indians 1,300,000 foot, 500,000 horse, 100,000 chariots, and as many upon camels. And it is said Staurobates, the Indian king, met her with greater forces than she brought against him; all which was performed within less than four hundred years after the flood.

Now if any imagine the unity of their language did hinder their dispersion before the flood, we confess it some hindrance at first, but not much afterward. For though it might restrain their dispersion, it could not their populosity, which necessarily requireth transmigration and emission of colonies; as we read of Romans, Greeks,

---

[9] *Ninus*] Soe Ninus had in his armye 974,200, reckoning to every chariot six fighting men (on each side three) besides the charioteer; but Semiramis her army was not less then 2,000,000, i. e. above twice soe manye; and yf Staurobates his army were greater, doubtless never any since that time came neere those numbers. Then reckoninge at the least of horses, 4 in each chariot, and of camels, in all 500,000 beasts in her armye, and as many or more on the adverse side, what countryes could hold, much less feed them? For Sennacherib's army did not reach to the twentithe parte of these conjoyned numbers, and yet he boasted to have drunk the rivers drye.—*Wr.*

[1] *upon camels.*] 300,000 ox hides stuffed to represent elephants, and carried upon camels.—*Jeff.*

Phœnicians, in ages past, and have beheld examples thereof in our days. We may also observe that after the flood, before the confusion of tongues, men began to disperse. For it is said they journeyed towards the east, and the Scripture itself expresseth a necessity conceived of their dispersion, for the intent of erecting the tower is so delivered in the text, "lest we be scattered abroad upon the face of the earth."

Again, if any apprehend the plantation of the earth more easy in regard of navigation and shipping discovered since the flood, whereby the islands and divided parts of the earth are now inhabited; he must consider that whether there were islands or no before the flood, is not yet determined, and is with probability denied by very learned authors.

Lastly, if we shall fall into apprehension that it was less inhabited, because it is said in the sixth of Genesis, about 120 years before the flood, "And it came to pass that when men began to multiply upon the face of the earth;" beside that this may be only meant of the race of Cain, it will not import they were not multiplied before, but that they were at that time plentifully increased; for so is the same word used in other parts of Scripture. And so is it afterward in the ninth chapter said, that "Noah began to be an husbandman," that is, he was so, or earnestly performed the acts thereof; so is it said of our Saviour, that he "began to cast them out that bought and sold in the temple," that is, he actually cast them out, or with alacrity effected it.

Thus have I declared some private and probable conceptions in the enquiry of this truth; but the certainty hereof let the arithmetic of the last day determine, and therefore expect no further belief than probability and reason induce. Only desire men would not swallow dubiosities for certainties, and receive as principles points mainly controvertible; for we are to adhere unto things doubtful in a dubious and opinionative way. It being reasonable for every man to vary his opinion according to the variance of his reason, and to affirm one day what he denied another. Wherein although at last we miss of truth, we die notwithstanding in harmless and inoffensive errors, because we adhere unto that, whereunto the examen of our reasons, and honest enquiries induce us.[2]

CHAPTER VII.

Of East and West.

THE next shall be of east and west; that is, the proprieties and conditions ascribed unto regions respectively unto those situations; which hath been the obvious conception of philosophers and geographers, magnifying the condition of India, and the eastern countries, above the setting and occidental climates: some ascribing hereto the generation of gold, precious stones, and spices, others the civility and natural endowments of men; conceiving the bodies of this situation to receive a special impression from the first salutes of the sun, and some appropriate influence from his ascendent and oriental radiations. But these proprieties, affixed unto bodies, upon considerations reduced from east, west, or those observable points of the sphere, how specious and plausible soever, will not upon enquiry be justified from such foundations.

For to speak strictly, there is no east and west in nature, nor are those absolute and invariable, but respective and mutable points, according unto different longitudes, or distant parts of habitation, whereby they suffer many and considerable variations. For first, unto some the same part will be east or west in respect of one another, that is, unto such as inhabit the same parallel, or differently dwell from east to west. Thus, as unto Spain Italy lieth east, unto Italy Greece, unto Greece Persia, and unto Persia China; so again, unto the country of China Persia lieth west, unto Persia Greece, unto Greece Italy, and unto Italy Spain. So that the same country is sometimes east and sometimes west; and Persia though east unto Greece, yet is it west unto China.

Unto other habitations the same point will be both east

---

[2] *induce us.*] And whatsoever is beyond this search must bee imputed to an invincible ignorance.— *Wr.*

and west; as unto those that are Antipodes or seated in points of the globe diametrically opposed. So the Americans are antipodal unto the Indians, and some part of India is both east and west unto America, according as it shall be regarded from one side or the other, to the right or to the left; and setting out from any middle point, either by east or west, the distance unto the place intended is equal, and in the same space of time in nature also performable.

To a third that have the poles for their vertex[3] or dwell in the position of a parallel sphere, there will be neither east nor west, at least the greatest part of the year. For if (as the name oriental implieth) they shall account that part to be east wherever the sun ariseth, or that west where the sun is occidental or setteth; almost half the year they have neither the one nor the other. For half the year it is below the horizon, and the other half it is continually above it, and circling[4] round about them intersecteth not the horizon, nor leaveth any part for this compute. And if (which will seem very reasonable) that part should be termed the eastern point where the sun at equinox, and but once in the year, ariseth, yet will this also disturb the cardinal accounts, nor will it with propriety admit that appellation. For that surely cannot be accounted east which hath the south on both sides; which notwithstanding this position must have. For if, unto such as live under the pole, that be only north which is above them, that must be southerly which is below them, which is all the other portion of the globe, beside that part possessed by them. And thus, these points of east and west being not absolute in any, respective in some, and not at all relating unto others, we cannot hereon establish so general considerations, nor reasonably erect such immutable assertions, upon so unstable foundations.

Now the ground that begat or promoted this conceit

[3] *vertex.*] This is spoken by way of supposition, yf any such there be, that dwell under the pole.— *Wr.*

[4] *and circling.*] And aboutt the tenthe of Marche, before and after, the discus of the son wheles about the verge of the horizon, and rises not totally above itt for the space of almost as many dayes as there are minutes in his diameter: appearing by those degrees in every circulation (of 24 houres time) more and more conspicuous, as hee uses to doe, when he gets out of total eclypse.— *Wr.*

was, first, a mistake in the apprehension of east and west, considering thereof as of the north and south, and computing by these as invariably as by the other. But herein, upon second thoughts, there is a great disparity: for the north and southern pole are the invariable terms of that axis whereon the heavens do move, and are therefore incommunicable and fixed points, whereof the one is not apprehensible in the other. But with east and west it is quite otherwise: for the revolution of the orbs being made upon the poles of north and south, all other points about the axis are mutable; and wheresoever therein the east point be determined, by succession of parts in one revolution every point becometh east. And so, if where the sun ariseth that part be termed east, every habitation, differing in longitude, will have this point also different, in as much as the sun successively ariseth unto every one.[5]

The second ground, although it depend upon the former, approacheth nearer the effect; and that is, the efficacy of the sun, set out and divided according to priority of ascent; whereby his influence is conceived more favourable unto one country than another, and to felicitate India more than any after. But hereby we cannot avoid absurdities, and such as infer effects controlable by our senses. For first, by the same reason that we affirm the Indian richer than the American, the American will also be more plentiful than the Indian, and England or Spain more fruitful than Hispaniola or golden Castile;[6] in as much as the sun ariseth unto the one sooner than the other; and so accountably unto any nation subjected unto the same parallel, or with a considerable diversity of longitude from each other. Secondly, an unsufferable absurdity will ensue; for thereby a country may be more fruitful than itself. For India is more fertile than Spain, because more east, and that the sun ariseth first unto it; Spain likewise by the same reason more fruitful than America, and America than India; so that Spain is less fruitful than that country, which a less fertile country than itself excelleth.

Lastly, if we conceive the sun hath any advantage by

---

[5] *every one.*] Every generall meridian hath a several east pointe and west (in their horizon) that live under itt.—*Wr.*

[6] *Castile.*] Virginia is about 7 houres distant from London, for when 'as noone heere, 'tis 5 in the morne with them.—*Wr.*

priority of ascent, or makes thereby one country more happy than another, we introduce injustifiable determinations, and impose a natural partiality on that luminary, which being equidistant from the earth, and equally removed in the east as in the west, his power and efficacy in both places must be equal, as Boëtius hath taken notice, and Scaliger* hath graphically declared. Some have therefore forsaken this refuge of the sun, and to salve the effect have recurred unto the influence of the stars, making their activities national, and appropriating their powers unto particular regions. So Cardan conceiveth, the tail of Ursa Major peculiarly respecteth Europe: whereas indeed once in twenty-four hours it also absolveth its course over Asia and America. And therefore it will not be easy to apprehend those stars peculiarly glance on us, who must of necessity carry a common eye and regard unto all countries, unto whom their revolution and verticity is also common.

The effects therefore, or[7] different productions in several countries, which we impute unto the action of the sun, must surely have nearer and more immediate causes than that luminary.[8] And these if we place in the propriety of clime, or condition of soil wherein they are produced, we shall more reasonably proceed, than they who ascribe them unto the activity of the sun. Whose revolution being regular, it hath no power nor efficacy peculiar from its orientality, but equally disperseth his beams unto all which equally, and in the same restriction, receive his lustre. And being an universal and indefinite agent, the effects or productions we behold receive not their circle from his causality, but are determined by the principles of the place, or qualities of that region which admits them. And this is evident not only in gems, minerals, and metals, but observable in plants and animals; whereof some are common unto many countries, some peculiar unto one, some not communicable unto another. For the hand of God that first

* *De gemmis exercitat.*

[7] *or.*] Reade *of.*—*Wr.* The Dr.'s is the true reading; see it repeated a few lines further on.
[8] *luminary.*] Cald by God the greate lighte.—*Wr.*

created the earth, hath with variety disposed the principles of all things; wisely contriving them in their proper seminaries, and where they best maintained the intention of their species; whereof if they have not a concurrence, and be not lodged in a convenient matrix, they are not excited by the efficacy of the sun; nor failing in particular causes, receive a relief or sufficient promotion from the universal. For although superior powers co-operate with inferior activities, and many (as some conceive) carry a stroke in the plastick and formative draught of all things, yet do their determinations belong unto particular agents, and are defined from their proper principles. Thus the sun, which with us is fruitful in the generation of frogs, toads, and serpents, to this effect proves impotent in our neighbour island;[9] wherein as in all other, carrying a common aspect, it concurreth but unto predisposed effects, and only susci-

[9] *which with us, &c.*] Itt is a true and remarkable thing that wheras Islip and Bletchinton, in Oxon shire, are not distant above 2 miles, and noe river between, yet noe man living remembers a snake or adder found alive in Bletchinton (which abounds with frogs and toods), and yf they bee brought from Islip, or other partes, unto that towne, they dye, as venemous things doe on Irish earthe, brought thence by ship into our gardens in England: nor is this proper to Irish earthe, but to the timber brought thence, as appeares in that vast roof of King's College Chappel in Cambridge, where noe man ever saw a spider, or their webs, bycause itt is all of Irish timber.—*Wr.*

On reading the preceding passage, I wrote to a friend in Cambridge requesting that some inquiry might be made as to the matter of fact. I subjoin an extract from his reply:—

"Ever since I was a boy, I have heard the traditional account of the roof, and more particularly the organ loft of King's College Chapel, being formed of Irish oak, and that no spiders or their webs are to be found upon it. I yesterday took an opportunity of making a personal enquiry and examination—two curators had, I found, since passed to the silent tomb, a third whom I now met with had not even heard of the circumstance, though an intelligent man, and who seemed to enter at once into the nature of my enquiries. He wished me to go up to the roof and examine for myself, assuring me, that no trouble was taken to sweep it over at any time; I went up and could not succeed in discovering the least appearance of a cobweb, much less of a spider; from the stone roof, which is underneath the wooden roof, he informed me that in some parts the spider's webs were very abundant and troublesome.

"I saw the organist, who seemed to be aware of the tradition, though almost forgotten, and who told me there was plenty of dust for want of proper care of the place, but he believed there were no spiders; he had officiated many years, but had never seen one.

tates those forms, whose determinations are seminal, and proceed from the idea of themselves.

Now, whereas there be many observations concerning east, and divers considerations of art which seem to extol the quality of that point, if rightly understood they do not really promote it. That the astrologer takes account of nativities from the ascendant, that is, the first house of the heavens, whose beginning is toward the east, it doth not advantage the conceit. For he establisheth not his judgment upon the orientality thereof, but considereth therein his first ascent above the horizon; at which time its efficacy becomes observable, and is conceived to have the signification of life, and to respect the condition of all things, which at the same time arise from their causes, and ascend to their horizon with it. Now this ascension indeed falls out respectively in the east; but, as we have delivered before, in some positions there is no eastern point from whence to compute these ascensions. So is it in a parallel sphere; for unto them six houses are continually depressed, and six never elevated; and the planets themselves, whose revolutions are of more speed, and influences of higher consideration, must find in that place a very imperfect regard; for half their period they absolve above, and half beneath the horizon. And so, for six years, no man can have the happiness to be born under Jupiter: and for fifteen together all must escape the ascendant dominion of Saturn.

That Aristotle, in his *Politicks*, commends the situation of a city which is open towards the east, and admitteth the rays of the rising sun, thereby is implied no more particular efficacy than in the west: but that position is commended, in regard the damps and vaporous exhalations, engendered in the absence of the sun, are by his returning rays the sooner dispelled; and men thereby more early enjoy a clear and healthy habitation.[1] Upon the like considerations it is, that

"The curator has promised to bring me a spider or web if he can find one, and seemed much pleased with the, to him, novel information."

The Hon. D. Barrington (in the *Philosophical Transactions*, vol. lix. p. 30) says, that he had examined several ancient timber roofs, without being able to detect any spider's webs. He accounts, however, for this, on the principle that *flies* are not to be found in such situations, and therefore spiders do not frequent them. How would this remark agree with the number of cobwebs found in the stone roof of King's College?

[1] *habitation.*] The waters of those springs are held to bee most medi

Marcus Varro* commendeth the same situation, and exposeth his farm unto the equinoxial ascent of the sun; and that Palladius adviseth the front of his edifice should so respect the south, that in the first angle it receive the rising rays of the winter sun, and decline a little from the winter setting thereof. And concordant hereunto is the instruction of Columella, *De positione villæ;* which he contriveth into summer and winter habitations, ordering that the winter lodgings regard the winter ascent of the sun, that is south-east; and the rooms of repast at supper, the equinoxial setting thereof, that is, the west; that the summer lodgings regard the equinoxial meridian: but the rooms of cenation in the summer, he obverts unto the winter ascent, that is, south-east; and the balnearies, or bathing-places, that they may remain under the sun until evening, he exposeth unto the summer setting, that is, north-west; in all which, although the cardinal points be introduced, yet is the consideration solary, and only determined unto the aspect or visible reception of the sun.

Jews and Mahometans in these and our neighbour parts are observed to use some gestures towards the east, as at their benediction, and the killing of their meat. And though many ignorant spectators, and not a few of the actors, conceive some magick or mystery therein, yet is the ceremony only topical, and in a memorial relation unto a place they honour. So the Jews do carry a respect and cast an eye upon Jerusalem, for which practice they are not without the example of their forefathers, and the encouragement of their wise king; for so it is said that Daniel "went into his house, and his windows being opened towards Jerusalem, he kneeled upon his knees three times a day, and prayed." † So is it expressed in the prayer of Solomon: "What prayer or supplication soever be made by any man, which shall spread forth his hands towards this house; if thy people go out to battle, and shall pray unto the Lord towards the city which thou

---

* *De Re Rustica.* † Dan. vi.

cinal (of all others) which rise into the easte, for this very reason here alleaged: hence in the west parts of England, to difference such from all others, they call them by a significant name, East-up-springs, intimating by that proper name, a proper kind of excellencye, above other springs, especially yf the soile from whence they rise bee chalke, or pure gravell. — *Wr.*

hast chosen, and towards the house which I have chosen to build for thy name, then hear thou in heaven their prayer and their supplication, and maintain their cause." Now the observation hereof, unto the Jews that are dispersed westward, and such as most converse with us, directeth their regard unto the east; but the words of Solomon are appliable unto all quarters of heaven, and by the Jews of the east and south must be regarded in a contrary position. So Daniel in Babylon looking toward Jerusalem had his face toward the west. So the Jews in their own land looked upon it from all quarters: for the tribe of Judah beheld it to the north; Manasses, Zabulon, and Napthali unto the south; Reuben and Gad unto the west; only the tribe of Dan regarded it directly or to the due east. So when it is said: "When you see a cloud rise out of the west, you say there cometh a shower, and so it is;"* the observation was respective unto Judea; nor is this a reasonable illation, in all other nations whatsoever. For the sea lay west unto that country, and the winds brought rain from that quarter; but this consideration cannot be transferred unto India or China, which have a vast sea eastward, and a vaster continent toward the west. So likewise, when it is said in the vulgar translation, "Gold cometh out of the north,"† it is no reasonable inducement unto us and many other countries, from some particular mines septentrional unto his situation, to search after that metal in cold and northern regions, which we most plentifully discover in hot and southern habitations.

For the Mahometans, as they partake with all religions in something, so they imitate the Jews in this. For in their observed gestures, they hold a regard unto Mecca and Medina Talnaby, two cities in Arabia Felix, where their prophet was born and buried, whither they perform their pilgrimages, and from whence they expect he should return again. And therefore they direct their faces unto these parts; which, unto the Mahometans of Barbary and Egypt, lie east, and are in some point thereof unto many other parts of Turkey. Wherein notwithstanding there is no oriental respect; for with the same devotion on the other side, they regard these parts toward the west, and so with variety wheresoever they are seated, conforming unto the ground of their conception.

* Luke xii. † Job xxxvii.

Fourthly, whereas in the ordering of the camp of Israel, the east quarter is appointed unto the noblest tribe, that is, the tribe of Judah, according to the command of God, " In the east side toward the rising of the sun shall the standard of the tribe of Judah pitch ;"* it doth not peculiarly extol that point. For herein the east is not to be taken strictly, but as it signifieth or implieth the foremost place ; for Judah had the van, and many countries through which they passed were seated easterly, unto them. Thus much is implied by the original, and expressed by translations which strictly conform thereto. So Tremellius, *Castra habentium ab anteriore parte Orientem versus, vexillum esto castrorum Judæ* : so hath R. Solomon Jarchi expounded it ; the foremost or before is the east quarter, and the west is called behind. And upon this interpretation may all be salved that is allegeable against it. For if the tribe of Judah were to pitch before the tabernacle at the east, and yet to march first, as is commanded, Numb. x., there must ensue a disorder in the camp, nor could they conveniently observe the execution thereof. For when they set out from Mount Sinai, where the command was delivered, they made northward unto Rithmah ; from Rissah unto Eziongaber about fourteen stations they marched south ; from Almon Diblathaim through the mountains of Abarim and plains of Moab toward Jordan the face of their march was west. So that if Judah were strictly to pitch in the east of the tabernacle, every night he encamped in the rear ; and if (as some conceive) the whole camp could not be less than twelve miles long, it had been preposterous for him to have marched foremost, or set out first, who was most remote from the place to be approached.

Fifthly, that learning, civility, and arts, had their beginning in the east, it is not imputable either to the action of the sun, or its orientality, but the first plantation of man in those parts, which unto Europe do carry the respect of east. For on the mountains of Ararat, this is, part of the hill Taurus, between the East Indies and Scythia, as Sir W. Raleigh accounts it, the ark of Noah rested ; from the east they travelled that built the tower of Babel : from thence they were dispersed and successively enlarged, and learning, good arts, and all civility communicated. The progression whereof was very

* Numb. ii.

sensible, and if we consider the distance of time between the confusion of Babel, and the civility of many parts now eminent therein, it travelled late and slowly into our quarters. For notwithstanding the learning of bards and Druids of elder times, he that shall peruse that work of Tacitus, *De moribus Germanorum*, may easily discern how little civility two thousand years had wrought upon that nation; the like he may observe concerning ourselves from the same author in the life of Agricola, and more directly from Strabo, who, to the dishonour of our predecessors, and the disparagement of those that glory in the antiquity of their ancestors, affirmeth the Britons were so simple, that though they abounded in milk, they had not the artifice of cheese.

Lastly, that the globe itself is by cosmographers divided into east and west, accounting from the first meridian, it doth not establish this conceit. For that division is not naturally founded, but artificially set down, and by agreement, as the aptest terms to define or commensurate the longitude of places. Thus the ancient cosmographers do place the division of the east and western hemisphere, that is, the first term of longitude, in the Canary or Fortunate Islands; conceiving these parts the extremest habitations westward. But the moderns have altered that term, and translated it unto the Azores or islands of St. Michael, and that upon a plausible conceit of the small or insensible variation of the compass in those parts. Wherein nevertheless, and though upon a second invention, they proceed upon a common and no appropriate foundation; for even in that meridian farther north or south the compass observably varieth;[2] and there are also other

---

[2] *varieth*.] Mr. Gunter, about 35 yeares agoe, observd the variation of the compass at Redriff not to bee greate by an excellent needle of 8 inches lengthe; yet now at this day the variation in the very same place is about halfe a pointe different, as some artizans confidently avouch upon experience; and our best mathematicians aver that there is a variation of the former variations dayly; whereof the cause may bee in the several loadstones brought from several places. For the mines of iron, whence they are taken, not running all exactly north and southe, may imprinte a different force, and verticity in the needles toucht by them, according to the difference of their own situation. Soe that the variation is not, or can bee in respect of the pole, but of the needles. It would be therefore exactly inquired by several large stones old and new, whether the verticity of them severally be alwayes the same in the same place or noe.—*Wr.*

places wherein it varieth not, as Alphonso and Rodoriges de Lago will have it about Capo de las Agullas, in Africa; as Maurolycus affirmeth in the shore of Peloponnesus, in Europe; and as Gilbertus averreth, in the midst of great regions, in most parts of the earth.

CHAPTER VIII.
Of the River Nilus.

HEREOF uncontrollably and under general consent many opinions are passant, which notwithstanding, upon due examination, do admit of doubt or restriction. It is generally esteemed, and by most unto our days received, that the river of Nilus hath seven ostiaries, that is, by seven channels disburdened itself into the sea. Wherein, notwithstanding, beside that we find no concurrent determination of ages past, and a positive and undeniable refute of these present, the affirmative is mutable, and must not be received without all limitation.

For some, from whom we receive the greatest illustrations of antiquity, have made no mention hereof. So Homer hath given no number of its channels, nor so much as the name thereof in use with all historians. Eratosthenes in his description of Egypt hath likewise passed them over. Aristotle is so indistinct in their names and numbers, that in the first of *Meteors* he plainly affirmeth, the region of Egypt (which we esteem the ancientest nation of the world) was a mere gained ground, and that by the settling of mud and limous matter brought down by the river Nilus, that which was at first a continued sea,[3] was raised at last into a firm and habitable country. The like opinion he held of Mæotis Palus, that by the floods of Tanais and earth brought down thereby, it grew observably shallower in his days, and would in process of time become a firm land. And though [4] his

[3] *sea.*] Moore.
[4] *And though.*] Yet after Aristotel 740 yeares, about the yeare of Christ 410, itt became soe fordable that the Huns and Vandals (observing a hinde to goe usually through itt to the pastures in Natolia) came in such swarms over the same way, that at last they overrann all Europe also.—*Wr.*

conjecture be not as yet fulfilled, yet is the like observable in the river Gihon,[5] a branch of Euphrates and river of Paradise, which having in former ages discharged itself into the Persian Sea, doth at present fall short, being lost in the lakes of Chaldea, and hath left between them and the sea a large and considerable part of dry land.

Others expressly treating hereof, have diversely delivered themselves. Herodotus in his *Euterpe* makes mention of seven, but carelessly of two hereof, that is, Bolbitinum and Bucolicum;[6] for these, saith he, were not the natural currents, but made by art for some occasional convenience. Strabo, in his geography, naming but two, Peleusiacum and Canopicum, plainly affirmeth there were more than seven; *Inter hæc alia quinque*, &c. There are, saith he, many remarkable towns within the currents of Nile, especially such which have given the names unto the ostiaries thereof, not unto all, for they are eleven,[7] and four besides, but unto seven and most considerable, that is, Canopicum, Bolbitinum, Selenneticum, Sebenneticum,[8] Pharniticum, Mendesium, Taniticum, and Pelusium, wherein to make up the number, one of the artificial channels of Herodotus is accounted. Ptolemy, an Egyptian, and born at the Pelusian mouth of Nile, in his geography maketh nine,[9] and in the third map of Africa, hath unto their mouths prefixed their several names, Heracleoticum, Bolbitinum, Sebenneticum, Pineptum, Diolcos, Pathmeticum, Mendesium, Taniticum, Peleusiacum, wherein notwithstanding there are no less than three different names from those delivered by Pliny. All which considered, we may easily discern that authors accord not either in name or number, and must needs confirm the judgment of Maginus, *de Ostiorum Nili numero et nominibus, valde antiqui scriptores discordant*.

[5] *Gihon.*] The river which rann by Verulam was once navigable up to the wals thereof, as appears by story, and anchors digd up, but is now rich land, 20 miles lower.—*Wr.*

[6] *but carelessly, &c.*] Yet these are now the principal branches remaining.

[7] *eleven.*] Thirteen in all by Strabo, yet Honterus reckons 17.—*Wr.*

[8] *Sebenneticum.*] Is aunciently divided into Saiticum and Mendesium.—*Wr.*

[9] *nine.*] Of note, the rest smaller branches, and soe not considerable, and therefore omitted.—*Wr.*

Modern geographers[1] and travellers do much abate of this number, for as Maginus and others observe, there are now but three or four mouths thereof; as Gulielmus Tyrius long ago, and Bellonius since, both ocular enquirers, with others have attested. For below Cairo, the river divides itself into four branches, whereof two make the chief and navigable streams, the one running to Pelusium of the ancients, and now Damietta;[2] the other unto Canopium, and now Rosetta;[3] the other two, saith Mr. Sandys, do run between these, but poor in water. Of those seven mentioned by Herodotus, and those nine by Ptolemy, these are all I could either see or hear of. Which much confirmeth the testimony of the bishop of Tyre, a diligent and ocular enquirer, who in his Holy War doth thus deliver himself: "We wonder much at the ancients, who assigned seven mouths unto Nilus, which we can no otherwise salve than that by process of time, the face of places is altered, and the river hath lost its channels, or that our forefathers did never obtain a true account thereof."[4]

And therefore, when it is said in Holy Scripture, "The Lord shall utterly destroy the tongue of the Egyptian sea, and with his mighty wind he shall shake his hand over the river, and shall smite it in the seven streams, and make men go over dry-shod,"* if this expression concerneth the river Nilus, it must only respect the seven principal streams. But the place is very obscure, and whether thereby be not meant the river Euphrates, is not without some controversy; as is collectible from the subsequent words; "And there shall be an high way for the remnant of his people, that shall be left from Assyria;" and also from the bare name river, emphatically signifying Euphrates, and thereby the division of the Assyrian empire into many fractions, which might facilitate their return; as Grotius† hath observed, and is more plainly

* Isa. xi. 15. † *Gr. Not. in Isaiam.*

[1] *geographers.*] But Honterus, in his geographical map of Ægypt, sets downe 17, distinct in situation and name, and hee wrote not soe long agoe, that they should since bee varyed.—*Wr.*
[2] *now Damietta.*] This is the Bucolic of Herodotus.
[3] *now Rosetta.*] The Bolbitine branch of Herodotus.
[4] *Which much confirmeth, &c.*] This sentence and the following paragraph were first added in the 2nd edition.

made out, if the* Apocrypha of Esdras, and that of the †
Apocalypse have any relation hereto.⁵

Lastly, whatever was or is their number, the contrivers of
cards and maps afford us no assurance or constant description therein. For whereas Ptolemy hath set forth nine;
Hondius in his map of Africa, makes but eight, and in that
of Europe ten: Ortelius, in the map of the Turkish empire,
setteth down eight, in that of Egypt eleven; and Maginus,
in his map of that country, hath observed the same number.
And if we enquire farther, we shall find the same diversity
and discord in divers others.

Thus may we perceive that this account was differently
related by the ancients, that it is undeniably rejected by the
moderns, and must be warily received by any. For if we
receive them all into account, they were more than seven;
if only the natural sluices they were fewer; and however we
receive them, there is no agreeable and constant description
thereof; and therefore how reasonable it is to draw continual and durable deductions from alterable and uncertain
foundations; let them consider who make the gates of
Thebes, and the mouths of this river a constant and
continued periphrasis for this number,⁶ and in their

* 2 Esdr. xiii. 43, 47.   † Apoc. xvi. 12.

⁵ *And therefore, &c.*] Bishop Lowth considers this passage as conveying an allusion to the passage of the Red Sea. But he cites a story told by "Herodotus (i. 189), of his Cyrus, that may somewhat illustrate this passage; in which it is said that God would inflict a kind of punishment and judgment on the Euphrates, and render it fordable by dividing it into seven streams. Cyrus, being impeded in his march to Babylon by the Gyndes, a deep and rapid river, which falls into the Tygris, and having lost one of his sacred white horses that attempted to pass it, was so enraged against the river, that he threatened to reduce it, and make it so shallow that it should be easily fordable, even by women, who should not be up to their knees in passing it. Accordingly he set his whole army to work, and cutting 360 trenches from both sides of the river, turned the waters into them, and drained them off."

⁶ *number.*] Why should wee call the ancients to accompt for that which, tho' then true, is now altered after 2000 yeares. Let us rather hence collect the mutability of all things under the moone.—*Wr.*

In the first edition the following words are added to this paragraph, but have been omitted in all the subsequent editions:—"conceiving a perpetuity in mutability upon unstable foundations erecting eternal assertions."

poetical expressions do give the river that epithet unto this number.

The same river is also accounted the greatest of the earth, called therefore *Fluviorum pater*, and *totius Orbis maximus*, by Ortelius. If this be true, many maps must be corrected, or the relations of divers good authors renounced.

For first, in the delineations of many maps of Africa, the river Niger exceedeth it about ten degrees in length, that is, no less than six hundred miles. For arising beyond the equator it maketh northward almost 15 degrees, and deflecting after westward, without meanders, continueth a straight course about 40 degrees, and at length with many great currents disburdeneth itself into the occidental ocean. Again, if we credit the descriptions of good authors, other rivers excel it in length, or breadth, or both. Arrianus, in his history of Alexander, assigneth the first place unto the river Ganges; which truly according unto later relations, if not in length, yet in breadth and depth, may be granted to excel it. For the magnitude of Nilus consisteth in the dimension of longitude, and is inconsiderable in the other; what stream it maintaineth beyond Syene or Esna, and so forward unto its original, relations are very imperfect; but below these places, and further removed from the head, the current is but narrow; and we read, in the history of the Turks, the Tartar horsemen of Selimus swam over the Nile from Cairo to meet the forces of Tonumbeus. Baptista Scortia,* expressly treating hereof, preferreth the river of Plate in America, for that, as Maffeus hath delivered, falleth into the ocean in the latitude of forty leagues, and with that force and plenty, that men at sea do taste fresh water before they approach so near as to discover the land. So is it exceeded by that which by Cardan is termed the greatest in the world, that is the river Oregliana in the same continent; which, as Maginus delivereth, hath been navigated 6000 miles, and opens in a channel of ninety leagues broad, so that, as Acosta, an ocular witness, recordeth, they that sail in the middle can make no land on either side.[7]

Now the ground of this assertion was surely the magni-

* *De naturâ et incremento Nili.*

[7] *side.*] Oregliana river is 6000 miles longe, 270 miles broad at the mouth.—*Wr.*

fying esteem of the ancients, arising from the indiscovery of its head.[8] For as things unknown seem greater than they are, and are usually received with amplifications above their nature; so might it also be with this river, whose head being unknown and drawn to a proverbial obscurity, the opinion thereof became without bounds, and men must needs conceit a large extent of that to which the discovery of no man had set a period. And this is an usual way, to give the superlative[9] unto things of eminency in any kind, and when a thing is very great, presently to define it to be the greatest of all. Whereas indeed superlatives are difficult; whereof there being but one in every kind, their determinations are dangerous, and must not be made without great circumspection. So the city of Rome is magnified by the Latins to be the greatest of the earth; but time and geography inform us that Cairo is bigger, and Quinsay, in China, far exceedeth both. So is Olympus extolled by the Greeks, as an hill attaining unto heaven; but the enlarged geography of after times makes slight account hereof, when they discourse of Andes in Peru, or Teneriffe in the Canaries.[1] And we understand, by a person who hath lately had a fair opportunity to behold the magnified Mount Olympus, that it is exceeded by some peaks of the Alps. So have all ages conceived, and most are still ready to swear, the wren is the least of birds;

[8] *head.*] Maximus Tyrius, tutor to Aurel. Antonin. emperor, taxeth the vaine solicitude of Alexander to discover the head of the Nile, and enquired rather *si a Deo bona omnia, unde mala fluunt, &c.*—*Wr.*

[9] *superlative.*] A noble lord was wont to say the best trowts are in as many places of England, as afford any trowtes, for every place magnifies theire owne. Hence Tullye wittily drew an argument from the mouths of all the philosophers against themselves, that the secte of the Academicks (whereof he was one) was the best. For, saythe hee, aske the Stoicke which is the best, and he will say the Stoick. But then aske which is the next best, hee will say the Academick. Soe aske of the Peripatetick, the Cynicke, the Pythagorian, the Platonick, and the Pyrronian or sceptick, which of all is the best, each of these will magnifie and advance his owne as the prime, but next his owne the Academicke. Therefore hee concludes, and that most invinciblye, that which by the confession of all interests in severall is the second, is in every truthe the firste: for what each speakes of his owne is partiall, but whatt all confesse to be the second best after their owne, is by all confession the very prime of all.—*Wr.*

[1] *Canaries.*] Pico, in the Azores, 3 miles highe like a sugar loafe.—*Wr.*

yet the discoveries of America, and even of our own plantations, have showed us one far less, that is, the humbird, not much exceeding a beetle. And truly, for the least and greatest, the highest and the lowest of every kind, as it is very difficult to define them in visible things, so is it to understand in things invisible. Thus is it no easy lesson to comprehend the first matter, and the affections of that which is next neighbour unto nothing, but impossible truly to comprehend God, who indeed is all in all. For things, as they arise into perfection, and approach unto God, or descend to imperfection, and draw nearer unto nothing, fall both imperfectly into our apprehensions, the one being too weak for our conceptions, our conceptions too weak for the other.

Thirdly, divers conceptions there are concerning its increment or inundation. The first unwarily opinions, that this increase or annual overflowing is proper unto Nile, and not agreeable unto any other river, which notwithstanding is common unto many currents of Africa. For about the same time the river Niger and Zaire do overflow, and so do the rivers beyond the Mountains of the Moon, as Suama and Spirito Santo. And not only these in Africa, but some also in Europe and Asia;[2] for so is it reported of Menan in India, and so doth Botero report of Duina in Livonia, and the same is also observable in the river Jordan, in Judea, for

---

[2] *some in Europe and Asia.*] And in America, where the *Rio de la Plata* is flooded at certain periods, and like the Nile inundates and fertilizes the country. The Indians then leave their huts, and betake themselves to their canoes, in which they float about, until the waters have retired. In the month of April, in 1793, it happened that a current of wind, of an extraordinary nature and violence, heaped up the immense mass of water of this river to a distance of ten leagues, so that the whole country was submersed, and the bed of the river remained dry in such a manner, that it might be walked over with dry feet. The vessels which had foundered and sunk, were all exposed again, and there was found, among others, an English vessel, which had perished in 1762. Many people descended into this bed, visited and spoiled the vessels thus laid dry, and returned with their pockets filled with silver and other precious articles, which had been buried more than thirty years in the deep. This phenomenon, which may be regarded as one of the greatest convulsions of nature, lasted three days, at the expiration of which the wind abated, and the waters returned with fury into their natural bed.—*Bulletin Universel.*

so is it delivered that "Jordan overfloweth all his banks in the time of harvest."*³

The effect indeed is wonderful in all, and the causes surely best resolvable from observations made in the countries themselves, the parts through which they pass, or whence they take their original. That of Nilus hath been attempted by many, and by some to that despair of resolution, that they have only referred it unto the providence of God, and his secret manuduction of all things unto their ends. But divers have attained the truth, and the cause alleged by Diodorus, Seneca, Strabo, and others, is allowable; that the inundation of Nilus in Egypt proceeded from the rains in Ethiopia, and the mighty source of waters falling towards the fountains thereof. For this inundation unto the Egyptians happeneth when it is winter unto the Ethiopians, which habitations, although they have no cold winter, the sun being no further removed from them in Cancer than unto us in Taurus, yet is the fervour of the air so well remitted, as it admits a sufficient generation of vapours, and plenty of showers ensuing thereupon.⁴ This theory of the ancients is since confirmed by experience of the moderns: by Franciscus Alvarez, who lived long in those parts, and left a description of Ethiopia, affirming that from the middle of June unto September, there fell in this time continual rains. As also Antonius Ferdinandus, who in an epistle written from thence, and noted by Codignus, affirmeth that during the winter, in those countries, there passed no day without rain.

Now this is also usual, to translate a remarkable quality into a propriety, and where we admire an effect in one, to opinion there is not the like in any other. With these conceits do common apprehensions entertain the antidotal and

* Josh. iii.

³ *harvest.*] Maio ineunte.

⁴ *thereupon.*] This observation is worthye of notinge, yf you understand itt of that Æthiopia, which borders on the springs of Nilus, supposed generally to flow out of the Mountains of the Moon, that is, 15 degrees beyond the æquinoctiall. Whereas Prester John's courte, of residence wherein Alvarez lived, is 12 degrees on this side the line, i. e. 27 degrees, or 1620 miles at least. And this rayne, which fell in his courte from June to September overthrows the former instance of the winter raines at the Mountains of the Moon, although that bee the only and the true cause of the rising of Nilus.—*Wr.*

wondrous condition of Ireland, conceiving only in that land an immunity from venomous creatures; but unto him that shall further enquire, the same will be affirmed of Creta, memorable in ancient stories, even unto fabulous causes, and benediction from the birth of Jupiter. The same is also found in Ebusus or Evisa, an island near Majorca, upon the coast of Spain. With these apprehensions do the eyes of neighbour spectators behold Etna, the flaming mountain in Sicilia; but navigators tell us there is a burning mountain[5] in Iceland, a more remarkable one in Teneriffe of the Canaries, and many volcanoes or fiery hills elsewhere. Thus crocodiles were thought to be peculiar unto Nile, and the opinion so possessed Alexander, that when he had discovered some in Ganges, he fell upon a conceit he had found the head of Nilus; but later discoveries affirm they are not only in Asia and Africa, but very frequent in some rivers of America.

Another opinion[6] confineth its inundation, and positively affirmeth, it constantly increaseth the seventeenth day of June; wherein perhaps a larger form of speech were safer, than that which punctually prefixeth a constant day thereto. For this expression is different from that of the ancients, as Herodotus, Diodorus, Seneca, &c., delivering only that it happeneth about the entrance of the sun into Cancer; wherein they warily deliver themselves, and reserve a reasonable latitude.[7] So, when Hippocrates saith, *Sub Cane et ante Canem difficiles sunt purgationes*, there is a latitude of days comprised therein; for under the dog-star he containeth not only the day of his ascent, but many following, and some ten days preceding. So Aristotle delivers the affections of animals, with the very terms of *circa, et magna ex parte*; and, when Theodorus translateth that part of his " *coeunt thunni et scombri mense Februario post Idus, pariunt Junio ante Nonas*," Scaliger for " *ante Nonas*" renders it " *Junii initio*," because that exposition affordeth the latitude of divers days.

[5] *burning mountain.*] Called Hecla.
[6] *Another, &c.*] Lord Bacon, *Natural History*, Experiment 743.
[7] *latitude.*] This is all one with the former, for in their times the ☉ then entered ♋ or rather soner soe that this *about* hath a large latitude: for at the sumer solstice, or his coming to Cancer, hee does little varye his declination for almost a month's space.—*Wr.*

For affirming it happeneth before the Nones, he alloweth but one day, that is the Calends; for in the Roman account, the second day is the fourth of the Nones of June.[9]

Again, were the day definitive, it had prevented the delusion of the devil, nor could he have gained applause by its prediction; who, notwithstanding (as Athanasius in the life of Anthony relateth), to magnify his knowledge in things to come, when he perceived the rains to fall in Ethiopia, would presage unto the Egyptians the day of its inundation. And this would also make useless that natural experiment observed in earth or sand about the river; by the weight whereof (as good authors report) they have, unto this day, a knowledge of its increase.[1]

Lastly, it is not reasonable from variable and unstable causes to derive a fixed and constant effect, and such are the causes of this inundation, which cannot indeed be regular, and therefore their effects not prognosticable, like eclipses. For, depending upon the clouds and descent of showers in Ethiopia, which have their generation from vaporous exhalations, they must submit their existence unto contingencies, and endure anticipation and recession from the moveable condition of their causes. And therefore some years there hath been no increase at all, as some conceive in the years of famine under Pharaoh; as Seneca and divers relate of the eleventh year of Cleopatra; nor nine years together, as is testified by Calisthenes. Some years it hath also retarded, and come far later than usually it was expected, as according

---

[9] *June.*] Reckoning the nones as they doe the calends *a retro.*—*Wr.*

[1] *increase.*] They have now a more certain way, for all the ancients agree that Nilus begins to flow about the beginning of July (the sonn going out of Cancer into Leo), and about the end of September returnes within his bankes againe. From the first rise to his wonted level are commonly 100 days: the just hight is 16 cubits. In 12 cubits they are sure of a famine, in 13 of scarcitye and dearthe, 14 cubits makes them merye, 15, secure, and 16, triumphe, beyonde this (which is rare) they looke sad agen, not for feare of want, but lest the slow fall of the waters should defer the seed-time to longe; which usually begins in 9ber, and the harvest is in Maye. But of this you may read at large in Plinye's *Natural Historye*, lib. v. cap. 9, and lib. xviii. cap. 18. But most excellently in Seneca's iv. lib. of natural quæstions, which is worthe the reading. Itt seems that in the 7 yeares of famine wherof Joseph (instructed by God) prophesyed, there had noe rain faln in Æthiopia, and that therefore Nilus had not overflowed.—*Wr.*

to Sozomen and Nicephorus it happened in the days of Theodosius; whereat the people were ready to mutiny, because they might not sacrifice unto the river, according to the custom of their predecessors.

Now this is also an usual way of mistake, and many are deceived who too strictly construe the temporal considerations of things. The books will tell us, and we are made to believe, that the fourteenth year males are seminifical and pubescent; but he that shall enquire into the generality, will rather adhere unto the cautelous assertion of Aristotle, that is, *bis septem annis exactis*, and then but *magna ex parte*. That whelps are blind nine days, and then begin to see, is generally believed; but as we have elsewhere declared, it is exceeding rare, nor do their eyelids usually open until the twelfth, and sometimes not before the fourteenth day. And to speak strictly, an hazardable determination it is, unto fluctuating and indifferent effects to affix a positive type or period. For in effects of far more regular causalities, difficulties do often arise, and even in time itself, which measureth all things, we use allowance in its commensuration. Thus while we conceive we have the account of a year in 365 days, exact enquirers and computists will tell us, that we escape six hours,[2] that is, a quarter of a day. And so in a day, which every one accounts twenty-four hours, or one revolution of the sun; in strict account we must allow the addition of such a part as the sun doth make in his proper motion, from west to east, whereby in one day he describeth not a perfect circle.

Fourthly, it is affirmed by many, and received by most, that it never raineth in Egypt, the river supplying that defect, and bountifully requiting it in its inundation: but this must also be received in a qualified sense, that is, that it rains but seldom at any time in the summer, and very rarely in the winter. But that great showers do sometimes fall

---

[2] *escape six hours.*] *Lege* overreckon every common yeare 10′ 44″ according to Alphonsus, and every 4th yeare, 42′ 56″. But Tycho by long and exact observation sayes the retrocession made by this overreckoninge is now but 41′, precisely: so that in 300 yeares to come the retrocession of the æquinoxes in the Julian kalendar (for in heaven they are fixed) cannot bee above one day: soe that the kalendar reformed would remaine to all times.—*Wr.*

upon that region, beside the assertion of many writers, we can confirm from honourable and ocular testimony,* and that not many years past it rained in Grand Cairo divers days together.

The same is also attested concerning other parts of Egypt, by Prosper Alpinus, who lived long in that country, and hath left an accurate treatise of the medical practice thereof. *Cayri rarò decidunt pluviæ; Alexandriæ, Pelusiique et in omnibus locis mari adjacentibus, pluit largissime et sæpe;* that is, it raineth seldom at Cairo, but at Alexandria, Damietta, and places near the sea, it raineth plentifully and often. Whereto we might add the latter testimony of learned Mr. Greaves, in his accurate description of the Pyramids.[4]

Beside, men hereby forget the relation of Holy Scripture. "Behold I will cause it to rain a very great hail,[5] such as hath not been in Egypt since the foundation thereof, even until now."† Wherein God threatening such a rain as had not happened, it must be presumed they had been acquainted with some before, and were not ignorant of the substance, the menace being made in the circumstance. The same concerning hail is inferrible from Prosper Alpinus, *Rarissimè nix, grando,* it seldom snoweth or haileth: whereby we must concede that snow and hail do sometimes fall, because they happen seldom.[6]

Now this mistake ariseth from a misapplication of the bounds or limits of time, and an undue transition from one unto another; which to avoid, we must observe the punctual differences of time, and so distinguish thereof, as not to confound or lose the one in the other. For things may come to pass, *semper, plerumque, sæpe; aut nunquam, aliquando, raro;* that is, always, or never, for the most part, or sometimes, oft-times, or seldom. Now the deception is usual which is made by the mis-application of these; men pre-

---

* Sir William Paston, Baronet. † Exod. ix.

[4] *The same is also, &c.*] First added in 2nd edition.
[5] *rain—hail.*] Haile is raine as itt fals first out of the clowde, but freeses as itt fals, and turnes into haile-stones, yf the lower ayre bee colder then that from whence it fals.—*Wr.*
[6] *The same concerning hail, &c.*] First added in 2nd edition.

sently concluding that to happen often, which happeneth but sometimes: that never, which happeneth but seldom; and that always, which happeneth for the most part. So is it said, the sun shines every day in Rhodes, because for the most part it faileth not. So we say and believe that a chameleon never eateth, but liveth only upon air; whereas indeed it is seen to eat very seldom, but many there are who have beheld it to feed on flies. And so it is said, that children born in the eighth month live not, that is, for the most part, but not to be concluded always: nor it seems in former ages in all places, for it is otherwise recorded by Aristotle concerning the births of Egypt.

Lastly, it is commonly conceived that divers princes have attempted to cut the isthmus or tract of land which parteth the Arabian and Mediterranean seas. But upon enquiry I find some difficulty concerning the place attempted; many with good authority affirming, that the intent was not immediately to unite these seas, but to make a navigable channel between the Red Sea and the Nile, the marks whereof are extant to this day. It was first attempted by Sesostris, after by Darius, and in a fear to drown the country, deserted by them both, but was long after re-attempted and in some manner effected by Philadelphus. And so the Grand Signior, who is lord of the country, conveyeth his galleys into the Red Sea by the Nile; for he bringeth them down to Grand Cairo, where they are taken in pieces, carried upon camels' backs, and rejoined together at Suez, his port and naval station for the sea; whereby in effect he acts the design of Cleopatra, who after the battle of Actium in a different way would have conveyed her galleys into the Red Sea.

And therefore that proverb to cut an isthmus, that is, to take great pains, and effect nothing, alludeth not unto this attempt, but is by Erasmus applied unto several other; as that undertaking of the Cnidians to cut their isthmus, but especially that of Corinth so unsuccessfully attempted by many emperors. The Cnidians were deterred by the peremptory dissuasion of Apollo, plainly commanding them to desist, for if God had thought it fit, he would have made that country an island at first. But this, perhaps, will not be thought a reasonable discouragement unto the activity of those spirits which endeavour to advantage nature by art, and upon good grounds to promote any part of the universe; nor will the ill success of some be made a sufficient determent unto others, who know that many learned men affirm, that islands were not from the beginning, that many have been made since by art, that some isthmuses have been eat through by the sea, and others cut by the spade. And if policy would permit, that of Panama, in America, were most worthy the attempt, it being but few miles over, and would open a shorter cut unto the East Indies and China.[5]

CHAPTER IX.

Of the Red Sea.

CONTRARY apprehensions are made of the Erythræan or Red Sea, most apprehending a material redness therein, from whence they derive its common denomination; and some so lightly conceiving hereof, as if it had no redness at all, are fain to recur unto other originals of its appellation. Wherein to deliver a distinct account, we first observe that without

---

[5] *China.*] Betweene Panama and the Nombre de Dios, which lyes on bothe sides that strip of lande, the Spaniards accompte about 40 miles at most; but the Spaniard enjoying both those havens, and consequentlye having the free trade of both seas without corrivalitye of other nations (which yf that passage were open would not longe bee his alone), will never endure such an attempt, and for that cause hath fortified bothe those havens soe stronglye that hee may enjoye this proprietye without controule. But itt withall supposes that to cutt through the ridge of mountains which lies betweene those 2 havens is impossible, and would prove more unfecible then that of Ægypt, which yf itt might be compassed would be of more advantage to these 3 parts of the world than that of Panama, and nearer by 1000 leagues to us, the remotest kingdome trading to the East Indyes.—*Wr*.

This long projected intercourse with the East Indies seems—under the present enterprising Pacha of Egypt, to be in a fair way of accomplishment. Letters thither having been actually sent off by the Mediterranean mail in the spring of 1835. The Pacha has sent to M. Brunel requesting his assistance in carrying on the great work of improvement in the channel of the Nile; and one of our British engineers, Mr. Galloway, who has the conduct of a railway constructing between Cairo and Suez, has been created a Bey of Egypt.

consideration of colour it is named the Arabian Gulph. The Hebrews, who had best reason to remember it, do call it Zuph, or the weedy sea,[6] because it was full of sedge, or they found it so in their passage. The Mahometans, who are now lords thereof, do know it by no other name than the Gulph of Mecca, a city of Arabia.

The stream of antiquity deriveth its name from King Erythrus, so slightly conceiving of the nominal deduction from redness, that they plainly deny there is any such accident in it. The words of Curtius are plainly beyond evasion: *Ab Erythro rege inditum est nomen, propter quod ignari rubere aquas credunt.* Of no more obscurity are the words of Philostratus, and of later times, Sabellicus; *Stultè persuasum est vulgo rubras alicubi esse maris aquas, quin ab Erythro rege nomen pelago inditum.* Of this opinion was Andreas Corsalius, Pliny, Solinus, Dio Cassius, who although they denied not all redness, yet did they rely upon the original from King Erythrus.

Others have fallen upon the like, or perhaps the same conceit under another appellation, deducing its name not from King Erythrus, but Esau or Edom, whose habitation was upon the coasts thereof.* Now Edom is as much as Erythrus, and the Red Sea no more than the Idumean, from whence the posterity of Edom removing towards the Mediterranean coast, according to their former nomination by the Greeks, were called Phœnicians, or red men, and from a plantation and colony of theirs, an island near Spain was by the Greek describers termed Erythra, as is declared by Strabo and Solinus.

* More exactly hereof Bochartus and Mr. Dickinson.

[6] *the weedy sea.*] Bruce however says that he never saw a weed in it: and attributes this name to the plants of coral with which it abounds.

"Heb. xi. 29, commonly called the Red Sea. But this is a vulgar error, and the appellation rather arose from its proper name *Mare Erythræum*, which (the commentators say) was derived from king Erythrus, undoubtedly the same with Esau and Edom, who was a *red* man—so Grotius and others. It is called by Moses, at Exod. xv. 22, ים סוף, the weedy sea, and such the accounts of modern tourists, as Niebuhr and others (see Huruen), testify it to be. But whether these weeds give a colour to it, so as to originate the name Red Sea, is, I think, very doubtful."—*Bloomfield, Recensio Synoptica, in loc.*

Very many, omitting the nominal derivation, do rest in the gross and literal conception thereof, apprehending a real redness and constant colour of parts. Of which opinion are also they which hold, the sea receiveth a red and minious tincture from springs, wells, and currents that fall into it; and of the same belief are probably many Christians, who conceiving the passage of the Israelites through the sea to have been the type of baptism, according to that of the apostle, " All were baptized unto Moses in the cloud, and in the sea,"* for the better resemblance of the blood of Christ, they willingly received it in the apprehension of redness, and a colour agreeable unto its mystery; according unto that of Austin,† *Significat mare illud rubrum baptismum Christi, unde nobis baptismus Christi, nisi sanguine Christi consecratus?*

But divers moderns not considering these conceptions, and appealing unto the testimony of sense, have at last determined the point, concluding a redness herein, but not in the sense received. Sir Walter Raleigh, from his own and Portugal observations, doth place the redness of the sea in the reflection from red islands, and the redness of the earth at the bottom, wherein coral grows very plentifully, and from whence in great abundance it is transported into Europe. The observations of Albuquerque, and Stephanus de Gama (as, from Johannes de Bairros, Fernandius de Cordova relateth), derive this redness from the colour of the sand and argillous earth at the bottom, for being a shallow sea, while it rolleth to and fro, there appeareth redness upon the water, which is most discernible in sunny and windy weather. But that this is no more than a seeming redness, he confirmeth by an experiment: for in the reddest part taking up a vessel of water, it differed not from the complexion of other seas. Nor is this colour discoverable in every place of that sea, for, as he also observed, in some places it is very green, in others white and yellow, according to the colour of the earth or sand at the bottom. And so may Philostratus be made out, when he saith, this sea is blue; or Bellonius denying this redness, because he beheld not that colour about Suez; or when Corsalius at the mouth thereof could not discover the same.

---

* 1 Cor. x. 2.   † *Aug. in Johannem.*

Now although we have enquired the ground of redness in this sea, yet are we not fully satisfied. For (what is forgot by many, and known by few) there is another Red Sea, whose name we pretend not to make out from these principles, that is, the Persian Gulph or Bay, which divideth the Arabian and Persian shore, as Pliny hath described it, *Mare rubrum in duos dividitur sinus, is qui ab Oriente est, Persicus appellatur;* or, as Solinus expresseth it, *Qui ab Oriente est, Persicus appellatur, ex adverso unde Arabia est, Arabicus;* whereto assenteth Suidas, Ortelius, and many more. And therefore there is no absurdity in Strabo, when he delivereth that Tigris and Euphrates do fall into the Red Sea, and Fernandius de Cordova justly defendeth his countryman Seneca in that expression:—

> Et qui renatum prorsus excipiens diem
> Tepidum Rubenti Tigrin immiscet freto.

Nor hath only the Persian Sea received the same name with the Arabian, but what is strange and much confounds the distinction, the name thereof is also derived from King Erythrus, who was conceived to be buried in an island of this sea, as Dionysius, Afer, Curtius, and Suidas do deliver. Which were of no less probability than the other, if (as with the same authors Strabo affirmeth), he was buried near Caramania, bordering upon the Persian Gulph. And if his tomb was seen by Nearchus, it was not so likely to be in the Arabian Gulph; for we read that from the river Indus he came unto Alexander, at Babylon, some few days before his death. Now Babylon was seated upon the river Euphrates, which runs into the Persian Gulph; and therefore, however the Latin expresseth it in Strabo, that Nearchus suffered much in the Arabian Sinus, yet is the original κόλπος πέρσικος, that is, the Gulph of Persia.

That therefore the Red Sea, or Arabian Gulph, received its name from personal derivation, though probable, is but uncertain; that both the seas of one name should have one common denominator, less probable; that there is a gross and material redness in either, not to be affirmed; that there is an emphatical or appearing redness in one, not well to be denied. And this is sufficient to make good the allegory of the Christians, and in this distinction may we justify the name of the Black Sea, given unto Pontus Euxinus; the name of Xanthus, or the Yellow River of Phrygia; and the name of Mar Vermeio, or the Red Sea in America.

CHAPTER X.

Of the Blackness of Negroes.

It is evident, not only in the general frame of nature, that things most manifest unto sense, have proved obscure unto the understanding; but even in proper and appropriate objects, wherein we affirm the sense cannot err, the faculties of reason most often fail us. Thus of colours in general, under whose gloss and varnish all things are seen, few or none have yet beheld the true nature, or positively set down their incontrollable causes. Which while some ascribe unto the mixture of the elements, others to the graduality of opacity and light, they have left our endeavours to grope them out by twilight, and by darkness almost to discover that whose existence is evidenced by light. The chemists have laudably reduced their causes unto sal, sulphur, and mercury, and had they made it out so well in this as in the objects of smell and taste, their endeavours had been more acceptable: for whereas they refer sapor unto salt, and odor unto sulphur, they vary much concerning colour; some reducing it unto mercury; some to sulphur; others unto salt. Wherein indeed the last conceit doth not oppress the former; and though sulphur seem to carry the master-stroke, yet salt may have a strong co-operation. For beside the fixed and terrestrious salt, there is in natural bodies a sal nitre referring unto sulphur; there is also a volatile or armoniack salt retaining unto mercury; by which salts the colours of bodies are sensibly qualified, and receive degrees of lustre or obscurity, superficiality or profundity, fixation or volatility.

Their general or first natures being thus obscure, there will be greater difficulties in their particular discoveries; for being farther removed from their simplicities, they fall into more complexed considerations; and so require a subtiler act of reason to distinguish and call forth their natures. Thus although a man understood the general nature of colours, yet were it no easy problem to resolve, why grass is green? Why garlic, molyes, and porrets have white roots, deep green leaves, and black seeds? Why several docks and sorts of rhubarb with yellow roots, send forth purple flowers? Why also from lactory or milky plants, which have a white and lacteous juice dispersed through every part, there arise flowers blue and yellow? moreover, beside the special and first digressions ordained from the creation, which might be urged to salve the variety in every species, why shall the marvel of Peru produce its flowers of different colours, and that not once, or constantly, but every day, and variously? Why tulips of one colour produce some of another, and running through almost all, should still escape a blue?[7] And lastly, why some men, yea and they a mighty and considerable part of mankind, should first acquire and still retain the gloss and tincture of blackness? Which whoever strictly enquires, shall find no less of darkness in the cause, than in the effect itself; there arising unto examination no such satisfactory and unquarrellable reasons, as may confirm the causes generally received, which are but two in number;—the heat and scorch of the sun, or the curse of God on Cham and his posterity.

The first was generally received by the ancients, who in obscurities had no higher recourse than unto nature; as may appear by a discourse concerning this point in Strabo: by Aristotle it seems to be implied, in those problems which enquire, why the sun makes men black, and not the fire? why it whitens wax, yet blacks the skin? by the word Ethiops itself, applied to the memorablest nations of negroes, that is, of a burnt and torrid countenance. The fancy of the fable infers also the antiquity of the opinion; which deriveth the complexion from the deviation of the sun: and the conflagration of all things under Phaeton. But this opinion, though generally embraced, was I perceive rejected by Aristobulus, a very ancient geographer, as is discovered by Strabo. It hath been doubted by several modern writers, particularly by Ortelius; but amply and satisfactorily discussed as we know by no man. We shall therefore endeavour a full delivery hereof, declaring the grounds of doubt, and reasons of denial,

---

[7] *should still escape a blue.*] Dr. Shaw remarks, in his *Panorama of Nature*, p. 619, that shells are of almost all colours but blue. The reason seems to be the effects of salt water on that colour.—*Jeff.*

which rightly understood, may, if not overthrow, yet shrewdly shake the security of this assertion.

And first, many which countenance the opinion in this reason, do tacitly and upon consequence overthrow it in another. For whilst they make the river Senega to divide and bound the Moors, so that on the south side they are black, on the other only tawny, they imply a secret causality herein from the air, place, or river; and seem not to derive it from the sun, the effects of whose activity are not precipitously abrupted, but gradually proceed to their cessations.

Secondly, if we affirm that this effect proceeded, or as we will not be backward to concede, it may be advanced and fomented from the fervour of the sun; yet do we not hereby discover a principle sufficient to decide the question concerning other animals; nor doth he that affirmeth that heat makes man black, afford a reason why other animals in the same habitations maintain a constant and agreeable hue unto those in other parts, as lions, elephants, camels, swans, tigers, ostriches, which, though in Ethiopia, in the disadvantage of two summers, and perpendicular rays of the sun, do yet make good the complexion of their species, and hold a colourable correspondence unto those in milder regions. Now did this complexion proceed from heat in man, the same would be communicated unto other animals, which equally participate the influence of the common agent. For thus it is in the effects of cold, in regions far removed from the sun; for therein men are not only of fair complexions, gray-eyed, and of light air; but many creatures exposed to the air, deflect in extremity from their natural colours; from brown, russet, and black, receiving the complexion of winter, and turning perfect white. Thus Olaus Magnus relates, that after the autumnal equinox, foxes begin to grow white; thus Michovius reporteth, and we want not ocular confirmation, that hares and partridges turn white in the winter; and thus a white crow, a proverbial rarity with us, is none unto them; but that inseparable accident of porphyry is separated in many hundreds.

Thirdly, if the fervour of the sun, or intemperate heat of clime did solely occasion this complexion, surely a migration or change thereof might cause a sensible, if not a total mutation; which notwithstanding experience will not admit.

For Negroes transplanted, although into cold and phlegmatick habitations, continue their hue both in themselves, and also their generations, except they mix with different complexions; whereby, notwithstanding there only succeeds a remission of their tinctures, there remaining unto many descents a strong shadow of originals, and if they preserve their copulations entire, they still maintain their complexions. As is very remarkable in the dominions of the Grand Signior, and most observable in the Moors in Brasilia, which, transplanted about an hundred years past, continue the tinctures of their fathers unto this day. And so likewise fair or white people translated into hotter countries receive not impressions amounting to this complexion, as hath been observed in many Europeans who have lived in the land of Negroes: and as Edvardus Lopez testifieth of the Spanish plantations, that they retained their native complexions unto his days.

Fourthly, if the fervour of the sun were the sole cause hereof in Ethiopia or any land of Negroes, it were also reasonable that inhabitants of the same latitude, subjected unto the same vicinity of the sun, the same diurnal arch, and direction of its rays, should also partake of the same hue and complexion; which notwithstanding they do not. For the inhabitants of the same latitude in Asia are of a different complexion, as are the inhabitants of Cambogia and Java; insomuch that some conceive the Negro is properly a native of Africa, and that those places in Asia, inhabited now by Moors, are but the intrusions of Negroes, arriving first from Africa, as we generally conceive of Madagascar, and the adjoining islands, who retain the same complexion unto this day. But this defect is more remarkable in America; which although subjected unto both the tropicks, yet are not the inhabitants black between, or near, or under either: neither to the southward in Brasilia, Chili, or Peru; nor yet to the northward in Hispaniola, Castilia, del Oro, or Nicaragua. And although in many parts thereof there be at present swarms of Negroes serving under the Spaniard, yet were they all transported from Africa, since the discovery of Columbus; and are not indigenous or proper natives of America.

Fifthly, we cannot conclude this complexion in nations

from the vicinity or habitude they hold unto the sun; for even in Africa they be Negroes under the southern tropick, but are not all of this hue either under or near the northern. So the people of Gualata, Agades, Garamantes, and of Goaga, all within the northern tropicks, are not Negroes; but on the other side Capo Negro, Cefala, and Madagascar, they are of a jetty black.

Now if to salve this anomaly we say, the heat of the sun is more powerful in the southern tropick, because in the sign of Capricorn falls out the perigeum or lowest place of the sun in his eccentric, whereby he becomes nearer unto them than unto the other in Cancer, we shall not absolve the doubt. And if any insist upon such niceties, and will presume a different effect of the sun, from such a difference of place or vicinity: we shall balance the same with the concernment of its motion, and time of revolution, and say he is more powerful in the northern hemisphere, and in the apogeum: for therein his motion is slower, and so is his heat respectively unto those habitations, as of more duration, so also of more effect. For though he absolve his revolution in 365 days, odd hours and minutes, yet by reason of eccentricity, his motion is unequal, and his course far longer in the northern semicircle, than in the southern; for the latter he passeth in 178 days, but the other takes him 187, that is, nine days more. So is his presence more continued unto the northern inhabitants; and the longest day in Cancer is longer unto us than that in Capricorn unto the southern habitator. Beside, hereby we only infer an inequality of heat in different tropicks, but not an equality of effects in other parts subjected to the same. For in the same degree, and as near the earth he makes his revolution unto the American, whose inhabitants, notwithstanding, partake not of the same effect. And if herein we seek a relief from the dog-star, we shall introduce an effect proper unto a few, from a cause common unto many: for upon the same grounds that star should have as forcible a power upon America and Asia; and although it be not vertical unto any part of Asia, but only passeth by Beach, in *Terra Incognita;* yet is it so unto America, and vertically passeth over the habitations of Peru and Brasilia.

Sixthly, and which is very considerable, there are Negroes

in Africa beyond the southern tropick, and some so far removed from it, as geographically the clime is not intemperate, that is, near the Cape of Good Hope, in 36 of the southern latitude. Whereas in the same elevation northward, the inhabitants of America are fair; and they of Europe in Candy, Sicily, and some other parts of Spain, deserve not properly so low a name as tawny.

Lastly, whereas the Africans are conceived to be more peculiarly scorched and torrified from the sun, by addition of dryness from the soil, from want and defect of water, it will not excuse the doubt. For the parts which the Negroes possess, are not so void of rivers and moisture, as is presumed; for on the other side the Mountains of the Moon, in that great tract called Zanzibar, there are the mighty rivers of Suama, and Spirito Santo; on this side, the great river Zaire, the mighty Nile and Niger; which do not only moisten and contemperate the air by their exhalations, but refresh and humectate the earth by their annual inundations. Beside in that part of Africa, which with all disadvantage is most dry (that is, in situation between the tropicks, defect of rivers and inundations, as also abundance of sands), the people are not esteemed Negroes; and that is Libya, which with the Greeks carries the name of all Africa. A region so desert, dry, and sandy, that travellers (as Leo reports) are fain to carry water on their camels; whereof they find not a drop sometime in six or seven days. Yet is this country accounted by geographers no part of *Terra Nigritarum*, and Ptolemy placeth therein the *Leuco-Æthiopes*, or pale and tawny Moors.

Now the ground of this opinion might be the visible quality of blackness observably produced by heat, fire, and smoke; but especially with the ancients the violent esteem they held of the heat of the sun, in the hot or torrid zone; conceiving that part unhabitable, and therefore, that people in the vicinities, or frontier thereof, could not escape without this change of their complexions. But how far they were mistaken in this apprehension, modern geography hath discovered: and as we have declared, there are many within this zone whose complexions descend not so low as unto blackness. And if we should strictly insist hereon, the possibility might fall into question; that is, whether the heat of the sun, whose fervour may swart a living part, and even black a dead or dissolving flesh, can yet in animals, whose parts are successive and in continual flux, produce this deep and perfect gloss of blackness.

Thus having evinced, at least made dubious, the sun is not the author of this blackness, how, and when this tincture first began is yet a riddle, and positively to determine it surpasseth my presumption. Seeing therefore we cannot discover what *did* effect it, it may afford some piece of satisfaction to know what *might* procure it. It may be therefore considered whether the inward use of certain waters or fountains of peculiar operations, might not at first produce the effect in question. For of the like we have records in Aristotle, Strabo, and Pliny, who hath made a collection hereof, as of two fountains in Bœotia, the one making sheep white, the other black; of the water of Siberis which made oxen black, and the like effect it had also upon men, dying not only the skin, but making their hairs black and curled. This was the conceit of Aristobulus; who received so little satisfaction from the other (or that it might be caused by heat, or any kind of fire), that he conceived it as reasonable to impute the effect unto water.

Secondly, it may be perpended whether it might not fall out the same way that Jacob's cattle became speckled, spotted, and ring-straked, that is, by the power and efficacy of imagination; which produceth effects in the conception correspondent unto the fancy of the agents in generation, and sometimes assimilates the idea of the generator into a reality in the thing engendered. For, hereof there pass for current many indisputed examples; so in Hippocrates we read of one, that from an intent view of a picture conceived a Negro; and in the history of Heliodore,* of a Moorish queen, who upon aspection of the picture of Andromeda, conceived and brought forth a fair one. And thus perhaps might some say was the beginning of this complexion, induced first by imagination, which having once impregnated the seed, found afterward concurrent co-operations, which were continued by climes, whose constitution advantaged the first impression. Thus Plotinus conceiveth white peacocks first came in. Thus many opi-

* Vide *plura apud Tho. Fienum, de viribus imaginationis.*

nion that from aspection of the snow, which lieth along in northern regions, and high mountains, hawks, kites, bears, and other creatures become white; and by this way Austin conceiveth the devil provided they never wanted a white-spotted ox in Egypt; for such an one they worshipped, and called Apis.

Thirdly, it is not indisputable whether it might not proceed from such a cause and the like foundation of tincture, as doth the black jaundice, which meeting with congenerous causes might settle durable inquinations, and advance their generations unto that hue, which were naturally before but a degree or two below it. And this transmission we shall the easier admit in colour, if we remember the like hath been effected in organical parts and figures; the symmetry whereof being casually or purposely perverted their morbosities have vigorously descended to their posterities, and that in durable deformities. This was the beginning of Macrocephali, or people with long heads, whereof Hippocrates* hath clearly delivered himself: *Cùm primum editus est infans, caput ejus tenellum manibus effingunt, et in longitudine adolescere cogunt; hoc institutum primum hujusmodi, naturæ dedit vitium, successu verò temporis in naturam abiit, ut proinde instituto nihil amplius opus esset; semen enim genitale ex omnibus corporis partibus provenit, ex sanis quidem sanum, ex morbosis morbosum. Si igitur ex calvis calvi, ex cæsiis cæsii, et ex distortis, ut plurimum, distorti gignuntur. eademque in cæteris formis valet ratio; quid prohibet cur non ex macrocephalis macrocephali gignantur?* Thus as Aristotle observeth, the deer of Arginusa had their ears divided; occasioned at first by slitting the ears of deer. Thus have the Chinese little feet, most Negroes great lips and flat noses; and thus many Spaniards, and Mediterranean inhabitants, which are of the race of Barbary Moors (although after frequent commixture), have not worn out the Camoys† nose unto this day.

Artificial Negroes, or Gipsies, acquire their complexion by anointing their bodies with bacon and fat substances, and so exposing them to the sun. In Guinea Moors and others, it hath been observed, that they frequently moisten their skins with fat and oily materials, to temper the irksome

* *De Aere, Aquis, et Locis.* † Flat Nose.

dryness thereof from the parching rays of the sun. Whether this practice at first had not some efficacy toward this complexion, may also be considered.⁸

Lastly, if we still be urged to particularities, and such as declare how, and when the seed of Adam did first receive this tincture; we may say that men became black in the same manner that some foxes, squirrels, lions, first turned of this complexion, whereof there are a constant sort in divers countries; that some choughs came to have red legs and bills; that crows became pied.⁹ All which mutations, however they began, depend on durable foundations; and such as may continue for ever. And if as yet we must farther define the cause and manner of this mutation, we must confess, in matters of antiquity, and such as are decided by history, if their originals and first beginnings escape a due relation, they fall into great obscurities, and such as future ages seldom reduce unto a resolution. Thus if you deduct the administration of angels, and that they dispersed the creatures into all parts after the flood, as they had congregated them into Noah's ark before, it will be no easy question to resolve, how several sorts of animals were first dispersed into islands, and almost how any into America. How the venereal contagion began in that part of the earth, since history is silent, is not easily resolved by philosophy. For whereas it is imputed unto anthropophagy, or the eating man's flesh, that cause hath been common unto many other countries, and there have been cannibals or men-eaters in the three other parts of the world, if we credit the relations of Ptolemy, Strabo, and Pliny. And thus if the favourable pen of Moses had not revealed the confusion of tongues, and positively declared their division at Babel; our disputes concerning their beginning had been without end,¹ and I fear we must have left the hopes of that decision unto Elias.*

* *Elias cum venerit, solvet dubium.*

⁸ *Artificial Negroes, &c.*] First added in the 3rd edition.

⁹ *some choughs, &c.*] This, however, is not a parallel case to the *varieties* existing among different individuals of the same *species*. The chough and the pied crow are distinct species.—The former (*Corvus gracula*) has *always* red legs and bills; the latter *Corvus caryocatactes*) is *always* pied.

had not revealed the confusion, &c.] The question which forms the

And if any will yet insist, and urge the question farther still upon me, I shall be enforced unto divers of the like subject of this and the two following chapters, appears to me to be very much of the same class as those adverted to in the present passage: questions utterly incapable of solution, in the absence of positive information. We know the proximate cause of the different complexions existing among the blacker and tawny varieties of the human race, to be the different hues of the colouring matter contained in the *rete mucosum;* but as to the originating cause, we can scarcely arrive at even a probable conjecture. There have existed various opinions as to the original complexion of mankind. Not only have the Negroes deemed themselves the "fairer," describing the devil and all terrible objects as being white;—but they have contended that our first progenitor was, like themselves, black. Job Ben Solomon, an African prince, when in England, was in company with Dr. Watts. The Dr. enquiring of him why he and his countrymen were black, since Adam was white? Job answered, "How you know Adam white? We think Adam black; and we ask how you came to be white?" A question which it is not probable the Dr. was able to answer.—*Mo. Rev.* vol. xxxviii. p. 541. Mr. Payne Knight, in his work *On Taste*, p. 15, is of the same opinion, that Adam in Paradise was an *African Black!!* Dr. Pritchard has also endeavoured to show that all men were originally Negroes. Blumenbach on the other hand supposes the original to have been Caucasian. The influence of climate has been the most generally assigned cause of the blackness of Negroes,—by some of the greatest naturalists both in ancient and modern times; for example by Pliny, Buffon, Smith, and Blumenbach. But it is a theory which surely a careful investigation of facts will be sufficient to overthrow. In addition to our author's observations to this effect, see those of the English editors of *Cuvier's Animal Kingdom*, vol. i. p. 174.

Nor is the difficulty as to the originating cause of the varieties in the human race confined to the mere question of complexion. It extends to the variations in hair and beard—to the configuration of the head—to the character and expression of countenance—the stature and symmetry of the body—and to the still more important—differences in moral and intellectual character. But of what use is it to exercise ingenuity as to the reasons of these particular variations? We see that the most astonishing variety pervades and adorns the whole range of creation. Let us be content to resolve it into the highest cause to which we can ascend, the will of that Being who has thus surrounded himself with the glory of his own works.

I subjoin some remarks by Mr. Brayley, bearing on a part of the subject.

In an elaborate paper by Dr. Stark, on the influence of colour on heat and odours, published in the *Phil. Trans.* for 1833, are contained some observations and experiments which tend to throw considerable light upon this subject. Dr. Franklin, it is stated by the author of the paper, from the result of his experiments with coloured cloths on the absorption of heat, drew the conclusion, " that black clothes are not so

nature, wherein perhaps I shall receive no greater satisfaction. I shall demand how the camels of Bactria came to have two bunches on their backs, whereas the camels of Arabia in all relations have but one? How oxen in some countries began and continue gibbous or bunch-backed? What way those many different shapes, colours, hairs, and natures of dogs came in?[2] How they of some countries became depilous, and without any hair at all, whereas some sorts in excess abound therewith? How the Indian hare came to have a long tail, whereas that part in others attains

fit to wear in a hot sunny climate or season as white ones, because in such clothes the body is more heated by the sun, when we walk abroad and are at the same time heated by the exercise; which double heat is apt to bring on putrid, dangerous fevers;" that soldiers and seamen in tropical climates should have a white uniform; that white hats should be generally worn in summer; and that garden walls for fruit trees would absorb more heat from being blackened.

"Count Rumford and Sir Evrd. Home, on the contrary," Dr. Stark continued, "come to a conclusion entirely the reverse of this. The count asserts, that if he were called upon to live in a very warm climate, he would blacken his skin or wear a black shirt; and Sir Everard, from direct experiments on himself and on a Negro's skin, lays it down as evident, 'that the power of the sun's rays to scorch the skins of animals is destroyed when applied to a dark surface, although the absolute heat, in consequence of the absorption of the rays, is greater.' Sir Humphry Davy explains this fact by saying, 'that the radiant heat in the sun's rays is converted into sensible heat.' With all deference to the opinion of this great man, it by no means explains why the surface of the skin was kept comparatively cool. From the result of the experiments detailed (in Dr. Stark's paper), it is evident, that if a black surface absorbs caloric in greatest quantity, it also gives it out in the same proportions, and thus a circulation of heat is as it were established, calculated to promote the insensible perspiration, and to keep the body cool. This view is confirmed by the observed fact of the stronger odour exhaled by the bodies of black people."—*Br.*

[2] *What way those many, &c.*] Rev. Mr. White, in his delightful *Natural History of Selborne,* describes a very curious breed of edible dogs from China—" such as are fattened in that country for the purpose of being eaten: they are about the size of a moderate spaniel; of a pale yellow colour, with coarse bristling hair on their backs, sharp upright ears, and peaked heads, which give them a very fox-like appearance. They bark much in a short, thick manner, like foxes; and have a surly savage demeanour, like their ancestors, which are not domesticated; but bred up in sties, where they are fed for the table with rice-meal and other farinaceous food." On the subject of canine varieties Sir W. Jardine in a note refers to "some very interesting observations, in the fifth number of the *Journal of Agriculture,* by Mr. J. Wilson."

no higher than a scut? How the hogs of Illyria, which Aristotle speaks of, became solipedes or whole-hoofed, whereas in other parts[3] they are bisulcous, and described cloven-hoofed, by God himself? All which, with many others, must needs seem strange unto those that hold there were but two of the unclean sort in the ark; and are forced to reduce these varieties to unknown originals.

However therefore this complexion was first acquired, it is evidently maintained by generation, and by the tincture of the skin as a spermatical part traduced from father unto son; so that they which are strangers contract it not, and the natives which transmigrate, amit it not without commixture, and that after divers generations. And this affection (if the story were true) might wonderfully be confirmed, by what Maginus and others relate of the emperor of Ethiopia, or Prester John, who, derived from Solomon, is not yet descended into the hue of his country, but remains a Mulatto, that is, of a mongrel complexion unto this day. Now although we conceive this blackness to be seminal, yet are we not of Herodotus' conceit, that their seed is black. An opinion long ago rejected by Aristotle, and since by sense and enquiry. His assertion against the historian was probable, that all seed was white; that is, without great controversy in viviparous animals, and such as have testicles, or preparing vessels, wherein it receives a manifest dealbation. And not only in them, but (for ought I know) in fishes, not abating the seed of plants; whereof at least in most, though the skin and covering be black, yet is the seed and fructifying part not so: as may be observed in the seeds of onions, piony, and basil. Most controvertible it seems in the spawn of frogs and lobsters, whereof notwithstanding at the very first the spawn is white, contracting by degrees a blackness, answerable in the one unto the colour of the shell, in the other unto the porwigle or tadpole; that is, that animal which

---

[3] *in other parts.*] Not in all, for about Aug. 1625, at a farm 4 miles from Winchester, I beheld with wonder a great heard of swine, whole footed, and taller then any other that ever I sawe.— *Wr.*

In several of the examples in this paragraph, the same error has been committed, as in that of the "chough" and "pied crow," just before; viz. the confounding of species with varieties.

first proceedeth from it. And thus may it also be in the generation and sperm of Negroes; that being first and in its naturals white, but upon separation of parts, accidents before invisible become apparent; there arising a shadow or dark efflorescence in the outside, whereby not only their legitimate and timely births, but their abortions are also dusky, before they have felt the scorch and fervor of the sun.

CHAPTER XI.

Of the same.

A SECOND opinion[4] there is, that this complexion was first a curse of God derived unto them from Cham, upon whom it was inflicted for discovering the nakedness of Noah. Which notwithstanding is sooner affirmed than proved, and carried with it sundry improbabilities. For first, if we derive the curse on Cham, or in general upon his posterity, we shall denigrate a greater part of the earth than was ever so conceived, and not only paint the Ethiopians and reputed sons of Cush, but the people also of Egypt, Arabia, Assyria, and Chaldea, for by this race were these countries also peopled. And if concordantly unto Berosus, the fragment of Cato *de Originibus*, some things of Halicarnasseus, Macrobius, and out of them Leandro and Annius, we shall conceive of the travels of Camese or Cham, we may introduce a generation of Negroes as high as Italy, which part was never

---

[4] *a second opinion.*] Possevine, in his 2 tom. and 252 page, does much applaud himself as the first inventor of this conceite. But Scaliger, in his 244 exercitation, sifting that quere of Cardan, why those that inhabite the hither side of the river Senega, in Affrick, are dwarfish and ash colour; those on the other side are tall and Negroes; rejects all arguments drawn from naturall reasons of the soile, &c. and concludes that the Asanegi on this side the river formerly inhabited on both sides of it, but were driven out of their countrye into this side of the river by the black Moores, drawne thither by the richnes of the soile on the further side. And doubtles considering that the maritime Moors of Barbarye, who lye 900 miles on this side the tropicke, are blacker then those of the posteritye of Chus, in Arabia, which lyes under the tropick; wee must needs conclude that this is but a poore conceyte, not unlike many other roving phancyes wherein the Jesuit is wont to vaunt himselfe.—*Wr.*

culpable of deformity, but hath produced the magnified examples of beauty.

Secondly, the curse mentioned in Scripture was not denounced upon Cham, but Canaan, his youngest son; and the reasons thereof are divers. The first from the Jewish tradition, whereby it is conceived that Canaan made the discovery of the nakedness of Noah, and notified it unto Cham. Secondly, to have cursed Cham, had been to curse all his posterity, whereof but one was guilty of the fact. And lastly, he spared Cham because he had blessed him before. Now if we confine this curse unto Canaan, and think the same fulfilled in his posterity, then do we induce this complexion on the Sidonians, then was the promised land a tract of Negroes, for from Canaan were descended the Canaanites, Jebusites, Amorites, Girgashites, and Hivites, which were possessed of that land.

Thirdly, although we should place the original of this curse upon one of the sons of Cham, yet were it not known from which of them to derive it. For the particularity of their descents is imperfectly set down by accountants, nor is it distinctly determinable from whom thereof the Ethiopians are proceeded. For whereas these of Africa are generally esteemed to be the issue of Chus, the elder son of Cham, it is not so easily made out. For the land of Chus, which the Septuagint translates Ethiopia, makes no part of Africa, nor is it the habitation of blackamoors, but the country of Arabia, especially the *Happy* and *Stony* possessions and colonies of all the sons of Chus, excepting Nimrod and Havilah, possessed and planted wholly by the children of Chus, that is, by Sabtah and Ramah, Sabtacha, and the sons of Raamah, Dedan, and Sheba; according unto whose names the nations of those parts have received their denominations, as may be collected from Pliny and Ptolemy, and as we are informed by credible authors, they hold a fair analogy in their names even unto our days. So the wife of Moses translated in Scripture an Ethiopian, and so confirmed by the fabulous relation of Josephus, was none of the daughters of Africa, nor any Negro of Ethiopia, but the daughter of Jethro, prince and priest of Midian, which was a part of Arabia the *Stony*, bordering upon the Red Sea. So the queen of Sheba came not unto Solomon out of Ethiopia, but from Arabia, and that part thereof which bore the name of the first planter, the son of Chus. So whether the eunuch, which Philip the deacon baptized, were servant unto Candace, queen of the African Ethiopia (although Damianus à Goes, Codignus, and the Ethiopic relations aver it), is yet by many, and with strong suspicions, doubted. So that the army of a million, which Zerah, king of Ethiopia, is said to bring against Asa, was drawn out of Arabia, and the plantations of Chus; not out of Ethiopia, and the remote habitations of the Moors. For it is said that Asa pursuing his victory took from him the city Gerar; now Gerar was no city in or near Ethiopia, but a place between Cadesh and Zur, where Abraham formerly sojourned. Since therefore these African Ethiopians are not convinced by the common acception to be the sons of Chus, whether they be not the posterity of Phut or Mizraim, or both, it is not assuredly determined. For Mizraim, he possessed Egypt, and the east parts of Africa. From Lubym, his son, came the Libyans, and perhaps from them the Ethiopians. Phut possessed Mauritania, and the western parts of Africa, and from these perhaps descended the Moors of the west, of Mandinga, Meleguette, and Guinea. But from Canaan, upon whom the curse was pronounced, none of these had their original; for he was restrained unto Canaan and Syria, although in after ages many colonies dispersed, and some thereof upon the coasts of Africa, and prepossessions of his elder brothers.

Fourthly, to take away all doubt or any probable divarication, the curse is plainly specified in the text, nor need we dispute it, like the mark of Cain; *Servus servorum erit fratribus suis,*—" Cursed be Canaan, a servant of servants shall he be unto his brethren;" which was after fulfilled in the conquest of Canaan, subdued by the Israelites, the posterity of Sem. Which prophecy Abraham well understanding, took an oath of his servant not to take a wife for his son Isaac out of the daughters of the Canaanites, and the like was performed by Isaac in the behalf of his son Jacob. As for Cham and his other sons, this curse attained them not; for Nimrod, the son of Chus, set up his kingdom in Babylon, and erected the first great empire; Mizraim and his posterity grew mighty monarchs in Egypt; and the empire of the Ethiopians hath been as large as either. Nor did the curse descend in general upon the posterity of Canaan, for the Sidonians, Arkites, Hamathites, Sinites, Arvadites, and Zemerites seem exempted. But why there being eleven sons, five only were condemned, and six escaped the malediction, is a secret beyond discovery.[5]

Lastly, whereas men affirm this colour was a curse, I cannot make out the propriety of that name, it neither seeming so to them, nor reasonably unto us, for they take so much content therein, that they esteem deformity by other colours, describing the devil and terrible objects white; and if we seriously consult the definitions of beauty, and exactly perpend what wise men determine thereof, we shall not apprehend a curse, or any deformity therein. For first, some place the essence thereof in the proportion of parts, conceiving it to consist in a comely commensurability of the whole unto the parts, and the parts between themselves, which is the determination of the best and learned writers. Now hereby the Moors are not excluded from beauty, there being in this description no consideration of colours, but an apt connection and frame of parts and the whole. Others there be, and those most in number, which place it not only in proportion of parts, but also in grace of colour. But to make colour essential unto beauty, there will arise no slender difficulty. For Aristotle, in two definitions of pulchritude, and Galen in one, have made no mention of colour. Neither will it agree unto the beauty of animals, wherein notwithstanding here is an approved pulchritude. Thus horses are handsome under any colour, and the symmetry of parts obscures the consideration of complexions. Thus in concolour animals and such as are confined unto one colour, we measure not their beauty thereby; for if a crow or blackbird grow white, we generally account it more pretty; and in almost a monstrosity descend not to opinion of deformity. By this way likewise the Moors escape the curse of deformity, there concurring no stationary colour, and sometimes not any unto beauty.

The Platonick contemplators reject both these descriptions founded upon parts and colours, or either, as M. Leo, the Jew, hath excellently discoursed in his *Genealogy of Love*, defining beauty a formal grace, which delights and moves

[5] *Nor did the curse, &c.*] First added in 2nd edition.

them to love which comprehend it. This grace, say they, discoverable outwardly, is the resplendour and ray of some interior and invisible beauty, and proceedeth from the forms of compositions amiable. Whose faculties if they can aptly contrive their matter, they beget in the subject an agreeable and pleasing beauty; if overruled thereby, they evidence not their perfections, but run into deformity. For seeing that out of the same materials, Thersites and Paris, monstrosity and beauty may be contrived, the forms and operative faculties introduce and determine their perfections. Which in natural bodies receive exactness in every kind, according to the first idea of the Creator, and in contrived bodies the fancy of the artificer, and by this consideration of beauty, the Moors also are not excluded, but hold a common share therein with all mankind.

Lastly, in whatsoever its theory consisteth, or if in the general we allow the common conceit of symmetry and of colour, yet to descend unto singularities, or determine in what symmetry or colour it consisted, were a slippery designation. For beauty is determined by opinion, and seems to have no essence that holds one notion with all; that seeming beauteous unto one, which hath no favour with another; and that unto every one, according as custom hath made it natural, or sympathy and conformity of minds shall make it seem agreeable. Thus flat noses seem comely unto the Moor, an aqueline or hawked one unto the Persian, a large and prominent nose unto the Roman; but none of all these are acceptable in our opinion. Thus some think it most ornamental to wear their bracelets on their wrists, others say it is better to have them about their ankles; some think it most comely to wear their rings and jewels in the ear, others will have them about their privities; a third will not think they are complete except they hang them in their lips, cheeks, or noses. Thus Homer to set off Minerva, calleth her γλαυκῶπις, that is, gray, or light-blue eyed; now this unto us seems far less amiable than the black. Thus we that are of contrary complexions accuse the blackness of the Moors as ugly; but the spouse in the Canticles excuseth this conceit, in that description of hers, I am black but comely. And howsoever Cerberus, and the furies of hell be described by the poets under this complexion, yet in the beauty of our Saviour, blackness is commended, when it is said, his locks are bushy and black as a raven. So that to infer this as a curse, or to reason it as a deformity, is no way reasonable; the two foundations of beauty, symmetry and complexion, receiving such various apprehensions, that no deviation will be expounded so high as a curse or undeniable deformity, without a manifest and confessed degree of monstrosity.

Lastly, it is a very injurious method unto philosophy, and a perpetual promotion of ignorance, in points of obscurity, nor open unto easy considerations, to fall upon a present refuge unto miracles; or recur unto immediate contrivance from the unsearchable hands of God. Thus, in the conceit of the evil odour of the Jews, Christians, without a further research into the verity of the thing, or enquiry into the cause, draw up a judgment upon them from the passion of their Saviour. Thus in the wondrous effects of the clime of Ireland, and the freedom from all venomous creatures, the credulity of common conceit imputes this immunity unto the benediction of St. Patrick, as Beda and Gyraldus have left recorded. Thus the ass having a peculiar mark of a cross made by a black list down his back, and another athwart, or at right angles down his shoulders: common opinion ascribes this figure unto a peculiar signation, since that beast had the honour to bear our Saviour on his back. Certainly this is a course more desperate than antipathies, sympathies, or occult qualities; wherein by a final and satisfactive discernment of faith, we lay the last and particular effects upon the first and general cause of all things; whereas in the other, we do but palliate our determinations, until our advanced endeavours do totally reject, or partially salve their evasions.

CHAPTER XII.

A Digression concerning Blackness.

THERE being therefore two opinions repugnant unto each other, it may not be presumptive or sceptical to doubt of both. And because we remain imperfect in the general theory of colours, we shall deliver at present a short discovery of blackness; wherein although perhaps we afford no greater satisfaction than others, yet shall we empirically and sensibly discourse hereof; deducing the causes of blackness from such originals in nature, as we do generally observe things are denigrated by art. And herein I hope our progression will not be thought unreasonable; for, art being the imitation of nature, or nature at the second hand, it is but a sensible expression of effects dependent on the same, though more removed causes: and therefore the works of the one may serve to discover the other. And though colours of bodies may arise according to the receptions, refraction, or modification of light; yet are there certain materials which may dispose them unto such qualities.[7]

And first, things become, by a sooty or fuliginous matter proceeding from the sulphur of bodies, torrified; not taking *fuligo* strictly, but in opposition unto ἀτμίς, that is, any kind of vaporous or madefying excretion, and comprehending ἀναθυμίασις, that is, as Aristotle defines it, a separation of moist and dry parts made by the action of heat or fire, and colouring bodies objected. Hereof in his *Meteors*, from the qualities of the subject, he raiseth three kinds; the exhalations from ligneous and lean bodies, as bones, hair, and the like, he called κάπνος, *fumus;* from fat bodies, and such as have not their fatness conspicuous or separated, he termeth λίγνις, *fuligo,* as wax, resin, pitch, or turpentine; that from unctuous bodies, and such whose oiliness is evident, he named κνίσσα or *nidor.* Now every one of these do blacken bodies objected unto them, and are to be conceived in the sooty and fuliginous matter expressed.

I say, proceeding from the sulphur of bodies torrified, that is, the oil, fat, and unctuous parts, wherein consist the principles of flammability. Not pure and refined sulphur, as in the spirits of wine often rectified; but containing terrestrious parts, and carrying with it the volatile salt of the body, and such as is distinguishable by taste in soot: nor vulgar and usual sulphur, for that leaves none or very little blackness, except a metalline body receive the exhalation.

I say, torrified, singed, or suffering some impression from fire; thus are bodies casually or artificially denigrated, which

---

[7] *And though colours, &c.*] First added in the 6th edit.

in their naturals are of another complexion; thus are charcoals made black by an infection of their own *suffitus;* so is it true what is affirmed of combustible bodies, *adusta nigra, perusta alba:* black at first from the fuliginous tincture, which being exhaled they become white, as is perceptible in ashes. And so doth fire cleanse and purify bodies, because it consumes the sulphurous parts, which before did make them foul, and therefore refines those bodies which will never be mundified by water. Thus camphire, of a white substance, by its *fuligo* affordeth a deep black. So is pitch black, although it proceed from the same tree with resin, the one distilling forth, the other forced by fire. So of the *suffitus* of a torch, do painters make a velvet black; so is lamp-black made; so of burnt hart-horns a sable; so is bacon denigrated in chimneys; so in fevers and hot distempers from choler adust is caused a blackness in our tongues, teeth, and excretions; so are *ustilago,* brant-corn and trees black by blasting; so parts cauterized, gangrenated, siderated, and mortified, become black, the radical moisture, or vital sulphur suffering an extinction, and smothered in the part affected. So not only actual but potential fire—not burning fire, but also corroding water—will induce a blackness. So are chimneys and furnaces generally black, except they receive a clear and manifest sulphur; for the smoke of sulphur will not black a paper, and is commonly used by women to whiten tiffanies, which it performeth by an acid, vitriolous, and penetrating spirit ascending from it, by reason whereof it is not apt to kindle anything: nor will it easily light a candle, until that spirit be spent, and the flame approacheth the match. This is that acid and piercing spirit which, with such activity and compunction invadeth the brains and nostrils of those that receive it. And thus when Bellonius affirmeth the charcoals made out of the wood of oxycedar are white, Dr. Jordan, in his judicious discourse of mineral waters, yieldeth the reason, because their vapours are rather sulphureous than of any other combustible substance. So we see that Tinby coals will not black linen hanged in the smoke thereof, but rather whiten it by reason of the drying and penetrating quality of sulphur, which will make red roses white. And therefore to conceive a general **blackness** in hell, and yet therein the pure and refined flames of sulphur, is no philosophical conception, nor will it well consist with the real effects of its nature.

These are the advenient and artificial ways of denigration, answerably whereto may be the natural progress. These are the ways whereby culinary and common fires do operate, and correspondent hereunto may be the effects of fire elemental. So may bitumen, coals, jet, black-lead, and divers mineral earths become black; being either fuliginous concretions in the earth, or suffering a scorch from denigrating principles in their formation. So men and other animals receive different tinctures from constitution and complexional efflorescences, and descend still lower, as they partake of the fuliginous and denigrating humour. And so may the Ethiopians or Negroes become coal-black, from fuliginous efflorescences and complexional tinctures arising from such probabilities, as we have declared before.

The second way whereby bodies become black, is an atramentous condition or mixture, that is, a vitriolate or copperas[8] quality conjoining with a terrestrious and astringent humidity; for so is *atramentum scriptorium*, or writing ink commonly made by copperas cast upon a decoction or infusion of galls. I say a vitriolous or copperas quality; for vitriol is the active or chief ingredient in ink, and no other salt that I know will strike the colour with galls: neither alum, sal-gem, nitre, nor ammoniack. Now, artificial copperas, and such as we commonly use, is a rough and acrimonious kind of salt drawn out of ferreous and eruginous earths, partaking chiefly of iron and copper; the blue of copper, the green most of iron. Nor is it unusual to dissolve fragments of iron in the liquor thereof, for advantage in the concretion. I say, a terrestrious or astringent humidity; for without this there will ensue no tincture; for copperas in a decoction of lettuce or mallows affords no black, which with an astringent mixture it will do, though it be made up with oil, as in printing and painting ink.[9] But whereas in this composition we use only nut-galls, that is, an excrescence from the oak, therein we follow and beat upon the old receipt; for any plant of austere and stiptick

[8] *copperas.*] Reade *copper-rust*.
[9] *as in printing, &c.*] There is noe copper-rust in printinge ink, which is made of lamp black and oyle.— *Wr.*

parts will suffice, as I have experimented in *bistort*, *myrobalans*, *myrtus brabantica*, *balaustium*, and red roses. And indeed, most decoctions of astringent plants, of what colour soever, do leave in the liquor a deep and muscadine red; which by additon of vitriol descends into a black: and so Dioscorides in his receipt of ink, leaves out gall, and with copperas makes use of soot.[1]

Now, if we enquire in what part of vitriol this atramental and denigrating condition lodgeth, it will seem especially to lie in the more fixed salt thereof. For the phlegm or aqueous evaporation will not denigrate; nor yet spirits of vitriol, which carry with them volatile and nimbler salt. For if upon a decoction of copperas and gall, be poured the spirits or oil of vitriol, the liquor will relinquish his blackness; the gall and parts of the copperas precipitate unto the bottom, and the ink grow clear again, which it will not so easily do in common ink, because that gum is dissolved therein, which hindereth the separation. But colcothar, or vitriol burnt, though unto a redness, containing the fixed salt, will make good ink; and so will the lixivium, or lye made thereof with warm water; but the terra or insipid earth remaining, affords no black at all, but serves in many things for a gross and useful red. And though spirits of vitriol, projected upon a decoction of galls, will not raise a black, yet if these spirits be any way fixed, or return into vitriol again, the same will act their former parts, and denigrate as before. And if we yet make a more exact enquiry, by what this salt of vitriol more peculiarly gives this colour, we shall find it to be from a metalline condition, and especially an iron property or ferreous participation. For blue copperas[2] which deeply partakes of the copper, will do it but weakly, verdigris which is made of copper will not do it at all. But the filings of iron infused in vinegar, will with a decoction of galls make good ink, without any copperas at all; and so will infusion of load-stone, which is of affinity with iron. And though more conspicuously in iron, yet such a calcanthous or atramentous quality we will not wholly reject in other metals; whereby we often observe black tinctures in their solutions. Thus a lemon, quince, or sharp apple cut with a

---

[1] *soot.*] But he meant torche or lamp soote.—*Wr.*
[2] *copperas.* Reade *copper-rust*, and soe itt is.—*Wr.*

knife becomes immediately black. And from the like cause, artichokes. So sublimate beat up with whites of eggs, if touched with a knife, becomes incontinently black. So *aqua fortis*, whose ingredient is vitriol, will make white bodies black. So leather, dressed with the bark of oak, is easily made black by a bare solution of copperas. So divers mineral waters and such as participate of iron, upon an infusion of galls, become of a dark colour, and entering upon black. So steel infused, makes not only the liquor dusky, but, in bodies wherein it concurs with proportionable tinctures, makes also the excretions black. And so also from this vitriolous quality, *mercurius dulcis*, and vitriol vomitive, occasions black ejectious. But whether this denigrating quality in copperas proceedeth from an iron participation, or rather in iron from a vitriolous communication; or whether black tinctures from metallical bodies be not from vitriolous parts contained in the sulphur, since common sulphur containeth also much vitriol, may admit consideration. However in this way of tincture, it seemeth plain, that iron and vitriol are the powerful denigrators.[3]

Such a condition there is naturally in some living creatures. Thus that black humour by Aristotle named ϑολός, and commonly translated *atramentum*, may be occasioned in the cuttle-fish. Such condition there is naturally in some plants, as blackberries, walnut-rinds, black cherries; whereby they extinguish inflammations, corroborate the stomach, and are esteemed specifical in the epilepsy. Such an atramentous condition there is to be found sometime in the blood, when that which some call *acetum*, *vitriolum*, concurs with parts prepared for this tincture. And so from these conditions the Moors might possibly become Negroes, receiving atramentous impressions in some of those ways, whose possibility is by us declared.

Nor is it strange that we affirm there are vitriolous parts, qualities, and even at some distance vitriol itself in living bodies; for there is a sour stiptick salt diffused through the earth, which passing a concoction in plants, becometh milder and more agreeable unto the sense; and this is that vegetable vitriol, whereby divers plants contain a grateful sharpness, as lemons, pomegranates, cherries; or an

[3] *But whether, &c.*] First added in 3rd edition.

austere and inconcocted roughness, as sloes, medlars, and quinces. And that not only vitriol is a cause of blackness, but the salts of natural bodies do carry a powerful stroke in the tincture and varnish of all things, we shall not deny, if we contradict not experience, and the visible art of dyers, who advance and graduate their colours with salts.[4] For the decoctions of simples which bear the visible colours of bodies decocted, are dead and evanid, without the commixtion of alum, argol, and the like. And this is also apparent in chemical preparations. So cinnabar[5] becomes red by the acid exhalation of sulphur, which otherwise presents a pure and niveous white. So spirits of salt upon a blue paper make an orient red. So tartar,[6] or vitriol upon an infusion of violets affords a delightful crimson. Thus it is wonderful what variety of colours the spirits of saltpetre, and especially, if they be kept in a glass while they pierce the sides thereof; I say, what orient greens they will project. From the like spirits in the earth the plants thereof perhaps acquire their verdure. And from such solary* irradiations may those wondrous varieties arise, which are observable in animals, as mallard's heads, and peacock's feathers, receiving intention or alteration according as they are presented unto the light.

Thus saltpetre, ammoniack, and mineral spirits emit delectable and various colours; and common *aqua fortis* will in some green and narrow-mouthed glasses, about the verges thereof, send forth a deep and *gentianella* blue.

Thus have we at last drawn our conjectures unto a period; wherein if our contemplations afford no satisfaction unto others, I hope our attempts will bring no condemnation on ourselves: for (besides that adventures in knowledge are laudable, and the essays of weaker heads afford oftentimes improveable hints unto better), although in this long journey we miss the intended end, yet are there many things of truth disclosed by the way; and the collateral verity may unto reasonable speculations somewhat requite the capital indiscovery.

* Whence the colours of plants, &c. may arise.

[4] *salts.*] And allums, which are a kind of salte.—*Wr.*
[5] *cinnabar.*] See the oyle of tartar poured on the filing of Brasil wood make an excellent red inke.—*Wr.*
[6] *tartar.*] A drop of the oyle of sulphur turns conserve of red roses into a scarlat.—*Wr.*

CHAPTER XIII.[7]

Of Gypsies.

GREAT wonder it is not, we are to seek, in the original of Ethiopians, and natural Negroes, being also at a loss concerning the original of Gypsies[8] and counterfeit Moors, observable in many parts of Europe, Asia, and Africa.

---

[7] Chap. xiii. & xiv. first appeared in 2nd edition.

[8] *concerning the original of Gypsies.*] This question, unlike the greater number of those which have occupied the attention of Sir Thomas, would seem less and less likely to be answered, as years roll on. While the progress of science and the discoveries which reward the patience and acuteness of modern investigation, are daily affording us satisfactory explanations of various phenomena in nature, the origin of Gypsies is a question which the lapse of time is daily removing further from our reach. Little has therefore been done towards its solution, but to collect and compare former opinions and speculations. The criterion, which seems the most to be relied upon, is that of language. Sir Thomas gives us no authority for his assertion that the dialect of the Gypsies is Sclavonian: an assertion which inclines him to the opinion that they came originally from the north of Europe. A very different theory was suggested by Büttner, and advocated after great labour and research with every appearance of probability, by Grellman. He has given a comparative vocabulary showing a striking affinity between the Gypsy and Hindoostanee languages. Captain Richardson, in the *Asiatic Researches* (vol. vii. p. 451), has carried the point still further, and established an affinity between them and a tribe in India, called the Bazeegurs. Professor Pallas and other writers have remarked this similarity of language. Dr. Pritchard is decidedly of opinion that their origin was Indian. Mr. Hoyland, of Sheffield, with the benevolent object of bettering their condition, took great pains some years ago to investigate their history, and especially their present state; and published a volume on this subject, entitled, "*A Historical Survey of the Customs, Habits, and Present State of the Gypsies,*" 8vo. York, 1816.

Brand (in his *Observations on Popular Antiquities,* vol. ii. 432) speaks of the Gypsies as of Hindoo origin, probably of the lowest caste, called Pariars, or Suders; and says, they probably emigrated about 1408, in consequence of the conquests of Timur Beg. Park mentions a wandering tribe named *Libey,* whom he had seen in his travels in Africa, very similar in their habits and customs to the Gypsies. A different solution has been proposed by an anonymous writer in the *Gentleman's Magazine* (vol. lxxii. 291), who thinks it very probable that they are the fulfilment of the prophecy in Gen. xvi. respecting the descendants

Common opinion deriveth them from Egypt, and from thence they derive themselves, according to their own account hereof, as Munster discovered in the letters and pass which they obtained from Sigismund the emperor. That they first came out of lesser Egypt, that having defected from the Christian rule, and relapsed unto pagan rites, some of every family were enjoined this penance to wander about the world. Or, as Aventinus delivereth, they pretend for this vagabond course a judgment of God upon their forefathers, who refused to entertain the Virgin Mary and Jesus, when she fled into their country.

Which account notwithstanding is of little probability:

of Ishmael. He observes that they inhabited in the first place the wilderness of Paran; that they increased prodigiously, and, under the appellation of *Al Arab al mostá-reba*, or *institious Arabs*, hived off from Arabia Deserta and Petræa, then too narrow to contain them, into the neighbouring country of Egypt. So that both the African and Asiatic shores of the Red Sea became inhabited by these nomadic Arabs. He therefore rather inclines to suppose the Gypsies, who made their appearance in Europe in the early part of the 15th century, to have been a migration of these Arabs, whose country had been the theatre of the ferocious contests between Tamerlane and Bajazet—than to have been Suders driven from India by Timur Beg. In corroboration of his theory he remarks, the greater propinquity of Arabia and Egypt to Europe. He concludes by noticing a subsequent migration led from Egypt, a century later, by Zinganeus—when that country was invaded by Solyman the Great.

The appellations *Egyptians* and *Zinganees* are readily accounted for on the supposition of this writer. We are not, after all, perhaps, precluded from availing ourselves, to a certain extent, of both theories.

An amusing account is given, in the *Gentleman's Magazine*, for Dec. 1801, of a Gypsy supper in the New Forest. Dr. Knox relates, in his last *Winter Evening*, the following incident, in proof of the piety of the Gypsies: "A large party had requested leave to rest their weary limbs, during the night, in the shelter of a barn; and the owner took the opportunity of listening to their conversation. He found their last employment at night, and their first in the morning, was prayer. And though they could teach their children nothing else, they taught them to supplicate, in an uncouth but pious language, the assistance of a friend, in a world where the distinctions of rank are little regarded. I have been credibly informed, that these poor neglected brethren are very devout, and remarkably disposed to attribute all events to the interposition of a particular Providence."

It may be doubted, perhaps, with too much probability, whether his benevolent inference in their favour would be borne out by more intimate acquaintance with their general character.

for the general stream of writers, who enquire into their original, insist not upon this; and are so little satisfied in their descent from Egypt, that they deduce them from several other nations. Polydore Virgil accounting them originally Syrians; Philippus Bergomas fetcheth them from Chaldea; Eneas Sylvius from some part of Tartary; Bellonius no further than Wallachia and Bulgaria; nor Aventinus than the confines of Hungaria.*

That they are no Egyptians, Bellonius maketh evident:† who met great droves of Gypsies in Egypt, about Grand Cairo, Mætærea, and the villages on the banks of Nilus, who notwithstanding were accounted strangers unto that nation, and wanderers from foreign parts, even as they are esteemed with us.

That they came not out of Egypt is also probable, because their first appearance was in Germany, since the year 1400; nor were they observed before in other parts of Europe, as is deducible from Munster, Genebrard, Crantsius, and Ortilius.

But that they first set out not far from Germany, is also probable from their language, which was the Sclavonian tongue; and when they wandered afterward into France, they were commonly called Bohemians, which name is still retained for Gypsies. And therefore when Crantsius delivereth, they first appeared about the Baltick Sea; when Bellonius deriveth them from Bulgaria and Wallachia, and others from about Hungaria, they speak not repugnantly hereto: for the language of those nations was Sclavonian, at least some dialect thereof.

But of what nation soever they were at first, they are now almost of all: associating unto them some of every country where they wander. When they will be lost, or whether at all again, is not without some doubt; for unsettled nations have out-lasted others of fixed habitations. And though Gypsies have been banished by most Christian princes, yet have they found some countenance from the great Turk, who suffereth them to live and maintain publick stews near the imperial city in Pera, of whom he often maketh a politick advantage, employing them as spies into other nations, under which title they were banished by Charles the Fifth.

* *Feynand. de Cordua didascal. multipl.*   † *Observat. l. 2.*

CHAPTER XIV.

Of some others.

WE commonly accuse the fancies of elder times in the improper figures of heaven assigned unto constellations, which do not seem to answer them, either in Greek or Barbarick spheres. Yet equal incongruities have been commonly committed by geographers and historians, in the figural resemblances of several regions on earth. While by Livy and Julius Rusticus the island of Britain is made to resemble a long dish or two-edged axe: Italy by Numatianus to be like an oak-leaf, and Spain an ox-hide; while the fancy of Strabo makes the habitated earth like a cloak: and Dionysius Afer will have it like a sling; with many others observable in good writers,[*] yet not made out from the letter or signification:— acquitting astronomy in the figures of the zodiack; wherein they are not justified unto strict resemblances, but rather made out from the effects of sun or moon in these several portions of heaven, or from peculiar influences of those constellations, which some way make good their names.

Which notwithstanding being now authentic by prescription, may be retained in their naked acceptions, and names translated from substances known on earth. And therefore the learned Hevelius, in his accurate *Selenography*, or description of the moon, hath well translated the known appellations of regions, seas, and mountains, unto the parts of that luminary; and rather than use invented names or human denominations, with witty congruity hath placed Mount Sinai, Taurus, Mæotis Palus, the Mediterranean Sea, Mauritania, Sicily, and Asia Minor in the moon.

More hardly can we find the Hebrew letters in the heavens made out of the greater and lesser stars, which put together do make up words, wherein cabalistical speculators conceive they read events of future things.[†] And how, from the stars in the head of Medusa, to make out the word Charab,

---

[*] *Tacit. de vita Jul. Agric. Junctin. in Sph. l. de Sacro bosco,* cap. 2.
[†] The cabala of the stars.

and thereby desolation presignified unto Greece or Javan numerally characterized in that word, requireth no rigid reader.*

It is not easy to reconcile the different accounts of longitude, while in modern tables the hundred and eightieth degree is more than thirty degrees beyond that part where Ptolemy placeth an 180. Nor will the wider and more western term of longitude, from whence the moderns begin their commensuration, sufficiently salve the difference.† The ancients began the measure of longitude from the Fortunate Islands or Canaries, the moderns from the Azores or islands of St. Michael; but since the Azores are but fifteen degrees more west, why the moderns should reckon 180, where Ptolemy accounteth above 220, or though they take in fifteen degrees at the west, why they should reckon thirty at the east, beyond the same measure, is yet to be determined, nor would it be much advantaged, if we should conceive that the compute of Ptolemy were not so agreeable unto the Canaries, as the Hesperides or islands of Capo Verde.‡

Whether the compute of months from the first appearance of the moon, which divers nations have followed, be not a more perturbed way than that which accounts from the conjunction may seem of reasonable doubt;§ not only from the uncertainty of its appearance in foul and cloudy weather, but unequal time in any, that is, sooner or later, according as the moon shall be in the signs of long descension, as Pisces, Aries, Taurus, in the perigeum or swiftest motion, and in the northern latitude; whereby sometimes it may be seen the very day of the change, as did observably happen, 1654, in the months of April and May. Or whether also the compute of the day be exactly made from the visible arising or setting of the sun, because the sun is sometimes naturally set, and under the horizon, when visibly it is above it; from the causes of refraction, and such as make us behold a piece of silver in a bason, when water is put upon it, which we could not discover before, as under the verge thereof.

---

* *Greffarel* out of *R. Chomer.* † *Athan. Kircher. in proœmio.*
‡ *Robertus Hues de globis.* § *Hevel. Selenog.* cap. 9.

Whether the globe of the earth be but a point in respect of the stars and firmament, or how if the rays thereof do fall upon a point, they are received in such variety of angles, appearing greater or lesser from differences of refraction?

Whether if the motion of the heavens should cease awhile, all things would instantly perish; and whether this assertion doth not make the frame of sublunary things to hold too loose a dependency upon the first and conserving cause, at least impute too much unto the motion of the heavens, whose eminent activities are by heat, light, and influence, the motion itself being barren, or chiefly serving for the due application of celestial virtues unto sublunary bodies, as Cabeus hath learnedly observed.

Whether comets or blazing stars be generally of such terrible effects, as elder times have conceived them;[9] for since it is found that many, from whence these predictions are drawn, have been above the moon, why they may not be qualified from their positions, and aspects which they hold with stars of favourable natures, or why, since they may be conceived to arise from the effluviums of other stars, they may not retain the benignity of their originals; or since the natures of the fixed stars are astrologically differenced by the planets, and are esteemed martial or jovial, according to the colours whereby they answer these planets, why, although the red comets do carry the portentions of Mars, the brightly white should not be of the influence of Jupiter or Venus, answerably unto Cor Scorpii and Arcturus, is not absurd to doubt.

[9] *Whether comets, &c.*] Aristotle considered them to be accidental fires or meteors, kindled in the atmosphere. Kepler supposed them to be monsters, generated in celestial space!

Dr. Thomas Burnet says, that the comets seem to him to be nothing else but (as one may say) the dead bodies of the fixed stars unburied, and not as yet composed to rest; they, like shadows, wander up and down through the various regions of the heavens, till they have found out fit places for their residence, which having pitched upon, they stop their irregular course, and being turned into planets, move circularly about some star.—*Charles Blount's Miscellaneous Works*, p. 63.

Tycho Brahe first ascertained, by observations on the comet of 1577, that comets are permanent bodies, like the planets.

THE SEVENTH BOOK:

THE PARTICULAR PART CONCLUDED.

OF POPULAR AND RECEIVED TENETS, CHIEFLY HISTORICAL, AND
SOME DEDUCED FROM THE HOLY SCRIPTURES.

CHAPTER I.

That the Forbidden Fruit was an Apple.

THAT the forbidden fruit of Paradise was an apple, is commonly believed, confirmed by tradition, perpetuated by writings, verses, pictures; and some have been so bad prosodians, as from thence to derive the Latin word *malum*, because that fruit was the first occasion of evil: wherein notwithstanding determinations are presumptuous, and many I perceive are of another belief. For some have conceived it a vine;[1] in the mystery of whose fruit lay the expiation of the transgression. Goropius Becanus, reviving the conceit of Barcephas, peremptorily concludeth it to be the Indian fig-tree, and by a witty allegory labours to confirm the same. Again, some fruits pass under the name of Adam's apples, which in common acception admit not that appellation: the one described by Matthiolus under the name of Pomum Adami, a very fair fruit, and not unlike a citron, but somewhat rougher, chopped and crannied, vulgarly conceived the marks of Adam's teeth: another, the fruit of that plant which Serapion termeth Musa, but the eastern Christians commonly the apples of Paradise; not resembling an apple in figure, and in taste a melon or cucumber.[2] Which fruits

---

[1] *a vine.*] By the fatal influence of whose fruit the nakedness both of Adam and of Noah were exposed. See the *Targum of Jonathan.*—*Jeff.*

[2] *again, &c.*] The fruit-shops of London exhibit a large kind of citron labelled, *Forbidden Fruit*, respecting which, and the *Pomum adami* of Matthiolus, I have the following obliging and satisfactory

although they have received appellations suitable unto the tradition, yet we cannot from thence infer they were this fruit in question. No more than *Arbor vitæ*, so commonly called, to obtain its name from the tree of life in Paradise, or *Arbor Judæ*, to be the same which supplied the gibbet unto Judas.

Again, there is no determination in the text; wherein is only particularised, that it was the fruit of a tree good for food, and pleasant unto the eye, in which regards many excel the apple: and therefore learned men do wisely conceive it inexplicable; and Philo puts determination unto despair, when he affirmeth the same kind of fruit was never produced since. Surely were it not requisite to have been concealed, it had not passed unspecified; nor the tree revealed which concealed their nakedness, and that concealed which revealed it; for in the same chapter mention is made of fig-leaves. And the like particulars, although they seem uncircumstantial, are oft set down in Holy Scripture; so is it specified that Elias sat under a juniper-tree, Absalom hanged by an oak, and Zaccheus got up into a sycamore.

And although, to condemn such indeterminables, unto him that demanded on what hand Venus was wounded, the philosopher thought it a sufficient resolution, to re-inquire upon what leg King Philip halted; and the Jews not undoubtedly resolved of the *sciatica* side of Jacob, do cautiously in their diet abstain from the sinews of both;[3] yet are there many nice particulars which may be authentically determined. That Peter cut off the right ear of Malchus, is beyond all doubt. That our Saviour eat the Passover in an upper room, we may determine from the text. And some we may concede which the Scripture plainly defines not. That the dial of Ahaz[4] was placed upon the west side of the temple,

---

notice from my friend Professor Lindley:—"The forbidden fruit of the London markets is a variety of the *Citrus decumana*, and is in fact a small sort of shaddock. But as to the *Pomum Adami*, no one can make out exactly what it was. The common Italian *Pomo d'Adamo* is a variety of *Citrus limetta*: that of Paris is a thick-skinned orange; and at least three other things have been so called. I do not think it possible to ascertain what Matthiolus meant beyond the fact that it was a *Citrus* of some kind."

[3] *of both.*] And this superstition befooles them alike in both.—*Wr.*

[4] *dial of Ahaz.*] Suggestions have been made respecting this, as

we will not deny, or contradict the description of Adricomius; that Abraham's servant put his hand under his right thigh, we shall not question; and that the thief on the right hand was saved, and the other on the left reprobated, to make good the method of the last judicial dismission, we are ready to admit. But surely in vain we inquire of what wood was Moses' rod, or the tree that sweetened the waters. Or, though tradition or human history might afford some light, whether the crown of thorns was made of *paliurus;* whether the cross of Christ were made of those four woods in the distich of Durantes,* or only of oak, according unto Lipsius and Goropius, we labour not to determine. For though hereof prudent symbols and pious allegories be made by wiser conceivers; yet common heads will fly unto superstitious applications, and hardly avoid miraculous or magical expectations.

Now the ground or reason that occasioned this expression by an apple, might be the community of this fruit, and which is often taken for any other. So the goddess of gardens is termed Pomona; so the proverb expresseth it, to give apples unto Alcinous; so the fruit which Paris decided was called an apple; so in the garden of Hesperides (which many conceive a fiction drawn from Paradise) we read of golden apples guarded by the dragon. And to speak strictly in this appellation, they placed it more safely than any other; for, beside the great variety of apples, the word in Greek comprehendeth oranges,[5] lemons, citrons, quinces; and as Ruellius defineth,† such fruits as have no stone within, and a soft covering without; excepting the pomegranate; and

* *Pes Cedrus est, truncus Cupressus, Oliva supremum, Palmaque transversum Christi sunt in cruce lignum.*

† *Ruel. De Stirpium Natura.*

---

well as some other miracles, which seem to me to proceed too much on the principle of endeavouring to lessen them, so as to bring them within the compass of belief. Thus the *dial* only, not the sun, is supposed to have gone backwards; and that not *really,* but only *apparently,*—by a "miraculous refraction." Is it not better to take the *literal* meaning, content to believe that to omnipotence one miracle is no greater than another?

[5] *word in Greek.*] Not only in Grecke but in Latin also, all these are cald by the very name of apple trees, as *Malus aurantia, citria, cydonia, granata.—Wr.*

will extend much further in the acception of Spigelius,* who comprehendeth all round fruits under the name of apples, not excluding nuts and plums.⁶

It hath been promoted in some constructions from a passage in the Canticles, as it runs in the Vulgar translation, *Sub arbore malo suscitavi te, ibi corrupta est mater tua, ibi violata est genitrix tua.*† Which words, notwithstanding parabolically intended, admit no literal inference, and are of little force in our translation: "I raised thee under an apple-tree, there thy mother brought thee forth, there she brought thee forth that bare thee." So when, from a basket of summer fruits or apples, as the Vulgar rendereth them, God by Amos foretold the destruction of his people, we cannot say they had any reference unto the fruit of Paradise, which was the destruction of man; but thereby was declared the propinquity of their desolation, and that their tranquillity was of no longer duration than those horary ‡ or soon-decaying fruits of summer. Nor, when it is said in the same translation, *Poma desiderii animæ tuæ discesserunt à te*,—"the apples that thy soul lusted after are departed from thee," is there any allusion therein unto the fruit of Paradise; but thereby is threatened unto Babylon, that the pleasures and delights of their palate should forsake them. And we read in Pierius, that an apple was the hieroglyphick of love, and that the statue of Venus was made with one in her hand. So the little cupids in the figures of Philostratus § do play with apples in a garden; and there want not some who have symbolized the apple of Paradise unto such constructions.⁷

Since therefore after this fruit, curiosity fruitlessly inquireth, and confidence blindly determineth, we shall surcease our inquisition; rather troubled that it was tasted, than troubling ourselves in its decision; this only we observe, when things are left uncertain, men will assure them by determination. Which is not only verified concerning the fruit, but the serpent that persuaded; many defining the kind or species thereof. So Bonaventure and Comestor

---

* *Isagoge in rem Herbariam.* † Cant. viii.
‡ *Fructus horæi.* § *Philostrat.* figure vi. *De amoribus.*

⁶ *and will extend, &c.*] First added in 2nd edition.
⁷ *So the little cupids, &c.*] First added in 2nd edition.

affirm it was a dragon, Engubinus a basilisk, Delrio a viper, and others a common snake.[8] Wherein men still continue the delusion of the serpent, who having deceived Eve in the main, sets her posterity on work to mistake in the circumstance, and endeavours to propagate errors at any hand. And those he surely most desireth which concern either God or himself; for they dishonour God, who is absolute truth and goodness; but for himself, who is extremely evil, and the worst we can conceive, by aberration of conceit they may extenuate his depravity, and ascribe some goodness unto him.

CHAPTER II.

That a Man hath one Rib less than a Woman.

THAT a man hath one rib less than a woman, is a common conceit, derived from the history of Genesis, wherein it stands delivered, that Eve was framed out of a rib of Adam; whence it is concluded the sex of men still wants that rib our father lost in Eve. And this is not only passant with the many, but was urged against Columbus in an anatomy of his at Pisa, where having prepared the skeleton of a woman that chanced to have thirteen ribs on one side, there arose a party that cried him down, and even unto oaths affirmed, this was the rib wherein a woman exceeded. Were this true, it would ocularly silence that dispute out of which side Eve was framed; it would determine the opinion of Oleaster, that she was made out of the ribs of both sides, or such as from the expression of the text* maintain there was a plurality of ribs required; and might indeed decry the parabolical exposition of Origen, Cajetan, and such as fearing to concede a monstrosity, or mutilate the integrity of Adam, preventively conceive the creation of thirteen ribs.

But this will not consist with reason or inspection. For if we survey the skeleton of both sexes, and therein the compage of bones, we shall readily discover that men and women have

* *Os ex ossibus meis.*

[8] *snake.*] Itt seemes to bee none of these but rather that species which Scaliger, the great secretary of nature, with noe reference to this storye, wittily cals (Exercitat. 226, §) ἐγχελανθρώπους.—*Wr.*

four and twenty ribs; that is, twelve on each side, seven greater, annexed unto the *sternon*, and five lesser which come short thereof. Wherein if it sometimes happen that either sex exceed, the conformation is irregular, deflecting from the common rate or number, and no more inferrible upon mankind than the monstrosity of the son of Rapha, or the vitious excess in the number of fingers and toes. And although some difference there be in figure, and the female *os innominatum* be somewhat more protuberant, to make a fairer cavity for the infant; the *coccyx* sometime more reflected, to give the easier delivery; and the ribs themselves seem a little flatter; yet are they equal in number. And therefore, while Aristotle doubteth the relations made of nations, which had but seven ribs on a side, and yet delivereth, that men have generally no more than eight; as he rejecteth their history, so can we not accept of his anatomy.

Again, although we concede there wanted one rib in the skeleton of Adam, yet were it repugnant unto reason and common observation that his posterity should want the same. For we observe that mutilations are not transmitted from father unto son; the blind begetting such as can see, men with one eye children with two, and cripples mutilate in their own persons do come out perfect in their generations. For the seed conveyeth with it not only the extract and single idea of every part, whereby it transmits their perfections or infirmities; but double and over again; whereby sometimes it multipliciously delineates the same, as in twins, in mixed and numerous generations. Parts of the seed do seem to contain the idea and power of the whole; so parents deprived of hands beget manual issues, and the defect of those parts is supplied by the idea of others. So in one grain of corn appearing similarly and insufficient for a plural germination, there lieth dormant the virtuality of many other; and from thence sometimes proceed above an hundred ears. And thus may be made out the cause of multiparous productions; for though the seminal materials disperse and separate in the matrix, the formative operator will not delineate a part, but endeavour the formation of the whole; effecting the same as far as the matter will permit, and from dividing materials attempt entire formations. And therefore, though wondrous strange, it may not be impossible what is confirmed at Lausdun concerning the countess of Holland; nor what Albertus reports of the birth of an hundred and fifty. And if we consider the magnalities of generation in some things,[9] we shall not controvert its possibilities in others: nor easily question that great work, whose wonders are only second unto those of the creation, and a close apprehension of the one, might perhaps afford a glimmering light, and crepusculous glance of the other.

CHAPTER III.

Of Methuselah.

WHAT hath been every where opinioned by all men, and in all times, is more than paradoxical to dispute; and so, that Methuselah was the longest liver of all the posterity of Adam, we quietly believe: but that he must needs be so, is perhaps below paralogy to deny.[1] For hereof there is no determination from the text; wherein it is only particularised he was the longest liver of all the patriarchs whose age is there expressed; but that he out-lived all others, we cannot well conclude.[2] For of those nine whose death is mentioned

---

[9] *And if we consider, &c.*] "Many things are useful and convenient, which are not necessary: and if God had seen man might not want it, how easy had it been for him which made the woman of that bone, to turn the flesh into another bone? But he saw man could not complain of the want of that bone, which he had so multiplied, so animated. O God, we can never be losers by thy changes, we have nothing but what is thine, take from us thine own when thou wilt; we are sure thou canst not but give us better!"—*Bp. Hall's Contemp.* book i. chap. 2.

[1] *is perhaps below paralogy to deny.*] "To deny it is not hastily to be condemned as *false reasoning.*"

[2] *we cannot, &c.*] If the learned author had looked into the text, Gen. v. hee woulde have dasht this unnecessary and frivolous discourse, for in that the Holy Ghost does particularly mention all the 9 patriarchs' ages, as of men to whom God gave such long life for the peopling of the world: and tooke away all the rest of the world, not only in Caine's race, but in all the other patriarchal familyes, men, women, and children, that they might not live to propagate that wickedness which had overspread the world by the marriage of Seth's posterityes with Caine's female issue. Itt is fit to beleeve that God would never grant to any of Caine's posterity longer live then to the longest liver among the patriarchs, when he intended to cutt off even that life of theirs which

before the flood, the text expresseth that Enoch was the shortest liver; who saw but three hundred sixty-five years. But to affirm from hence, none of the rest, whose age is not expressed, did die before that time, is surely an illation whereto we cannot assent.

Again many persons there were in those days of longevity, of whose age notwithstanding there is no account in Scripture; as of the race of Cain, the wives of the nine patriarchs, with all the sons and daughters that every one begat: whereof perhaps some persons might out-live Methuselah; the text intending only the masculine line of Seth, conducible unto the genealogy of our Saviour, and the antediluvian chronology. And therefore we must not contract the lives of those which are left in silence by Moses; for neither is the age of Abel expressed in the Scripture, yet is he conceived far elder than commonly opinioned; and if we allow the conclusion of his epitaph as made by Adam, and so set down by Salian, *Posuit morens pater, cui à filio justius positum foret, anno ab ortu rerum* 130; *ab Abele nato* 129, we shall not need to doubt. Which notwithstanding Cajetan and others confirm; nor is it improbable, if we conceive that Abel was born in the second year of Adam,[3] and Seth a year after the death of Abel; for so it being said, that Adam was an hundred and thirty years old when he begat Seth, Abel must perish the year before, which was one hundred and twenty-nine.

And if the account of Cain[4] extend unto the deluge, it may not be improbable that some thereof exceeded any of Seth. Nor is it unlikely in life, riches, power, and temporal blessings, they might surpass them in this world, whose

hee permitted them to prolong till their sinns were fulfild: and therefore tooke away Mathuselah also the yeare that hee sent the flood to take away all (universally) then living, save Noah and his immediate family.—*Wr.*

[3] *second year, &c.*] Abel's birth is not deducible necessarily from Scripture: his death is more probable.—*Wr.*

[4] *Cain.*] Betweene the creation and the flood were 1656 yeares, to which, though Cain's owne accompt did not reach, yet his posterity did. For upon them was the flood sent, yet not on them onlye, for all the posterityes of the patriarchal familyes, which doubtless were innumerable, did all perish in the flood, excepting only eight persons. —*Wr.*

lives related unto the next. For so when the seed of Jacob was under affliction and captivity, that of Ishmael and Esau flourished and grew mighty, there proceeding from the one twelve princes, from the other no less than fourteen dukes and eight kings. And whereas the age of Cain and his posterity is not delivered in the text, some do salve it from the secret method of Scripture, which sometimes wholly omits, but seldom or never delivers the entire duration of wicked and faithless persons, as is observable in the history of Esau, and the kings of Israel and Judah. And therefore when mention is made that Ishmael lived 127 years, some conceive he adhered unto the faith of Abraham, for so did others who were not descended from Jacob, for Job is thought to be an Idumean, and of the seed of Esau.

Lastly, although we rely not thereon, we will not omit that conceit urged by learned men, that Adam was elder[5] than Methuselah; inasmuch as he was created in the perfect age of man, which was in those days 50 or 60 years, for about that time we read that they begat children; so that if unto 930 we add 60 years, he will exceed Methuselah; and therefore if not in length of days, at least in old age he surpassed others; he was older than all, who was never so young as any. For though he knew old age, he was never acquainted with puberty, youth, or infancy, and so in a strict account he begat children at one year old. And if the usual compute will hold, that men are of the same age which are born within compass of the same year, Eve was as old as her husband and parent Adam, and Cain, their son, coetaneous unto both.

Now that conception, that no man[6] did ever attain unto

---

[5] *Adam was elder.*] This phrase, as itt is commonly used, signifies elder in time, and then itt sayes nothing, for who denyes itt? But in lengthe of dayes from the birthe Adam was not soe old as Mathuselah by 20 yeares.—*Wr.*

[6] *that no man, &c.*] This is most true *de facto*, though the reason bee but symbolical, and concludes nothing necessarilye. For granting that Adam was created in the perfect age of man, as then itt was, which was rather 100 then 60, yet he lived noe more then 930 in all, viz. solar, sydereal, tropick years. To which if you add those hypothecall 60 yeares (for they are not reall but imaginary only), yet soe Adam would not reach to 1000 by 10 yeares, and therefore the saying is most true.—*Wr.*

a thousand years, because none should ever be one day old in the sight of the Lord, unto whom, according to that of David, "A thousand years are but one day," doth not advantage Methuselah. And being deduced from a popular expression, which will not stand a metaphysical and strict examination, is not of force to divert a serious inquirer. For unto God a thousand years are no more than one moment, and in his sight Methuselah lived no nearer one day than Abel, for all parts of time are alike unto him, unto whom none are referrible, and all things present unto whom nothing is past or to come; and therefore, although we be measured by the zone of time, and the flowing and continued instants thereof do weave at last a line and circle about the eldest, yet can we not thus commensurate the sphere of Trismegistus,[7] or sum up the unsuccessive and stable duration of God.

CHAPTER IV.

That there was no Rainbow before the Flood.

THAT there shall no rainbow appear forty years before the end of the world, and that the preceding drought unto that great shame shall exhaust the materials of this meteor, was an assertion grounded upon no solid reason; but that there was not any in sixteen hundred years, that is, before the flood, seems deducible from Holy Scripture, Gen. ix., "I do set my bow in the cloud, and it shall be for a token of a covenant between me and the earth." From whence notwithstanding we cannot conclude the non-existence of the rainbow, nor is that chronology naturally established, which computeth the antiquity of effects arising from physical and settled causes, by additional impositions from voluntary determinators. Now by the decree of reason and philosophy, the rainbow hath its ground in nature, as caused by the rays of the sun, falling upon a rorid and opposite cloud, whereof some reflected, others refracted, beget that semicircular

---

[7] *sphere of Trismegistus.*] Trismegistus sayd God was a circle, whose center, that is, his presentiall and immutable essence, from whence all things have their beinge, is every where, but his circumference, that is, his incomprehensible infinity, is noe where.—*Wr.*

variety we generally call the rainbow, which must succeed upon concurrence of causes and subjects aptly predisposed. And therefore to conceive there was no rainbow before, because God chose this out as a token of the covenant, is to conclude the existence of things from their signalities, or of what is objected unto the sense, a coexistence with that which is internally presented unto the understanding. With equal reason we may infer there was no water before the institution of baptism, nor bread and wine before the Holy Eucharist.

Again, while men deny the antiquity of one rainbow, they anciently concede another. For beside the solary iris which God showed unto Noah, there is a lunary, whose efficient is the moon, visible only in the night, most commonly called at full moon, and some degrees above the horizon. Now the existence hereof men do not controvert, although effected by a different luminary in the same way with the other. And probably it appeared later, as being of rare appearance and rarer observation, and many there are which think there is no such thing in nature; and therefore by casual spectators they are looked upon like prodigies, and significations made, not signified by their natures.

Lastly, we shall not need to conceive God made the rainbow at this time, if we consider that in its created and predisposed nature, it was more proper for this signification, than any other meteor or celestial appearancy whatsoever. Thunder and lightning had too much terror to have been tokens of mercy. Comets or blazing stars appear too seldom to put us in mind of a covenant to be remembered often, and might rather signify the world should be once destroyed by fire, than never again by water. The *galaxia* or milky circle had been more probable; for beside that unto the latitude of thirty, it becomes their horizon twice in four and twenty hours, and unto such as live under the equator, in that space the whole circle appeareth, part thereof is visible unto any situation; but being only discoverable in the night, and when the air is clear, it becomes of unfrequent and comfortless signification. A fixed star had not been visible unto all the globe, and so of too narrow a signality in a covenant concerning all. But rainbows are seen unto all the world, and every position of sphere. Unto our own elevation they may appear in the morning, while the sun hath attained about forty-five degrees above the horizon, which is conceived the largest semidiameter of any iris, and so in the afternoon when it hath declined unto that altitude again, which height the sun not attaining in winter, rainbows may happen with us at noon or any time. Unto a right position of sphere they may appear three hours after the rising of the sun, and three before its setting; for the sun ascending fifteen degrees an hour, in three attaineth forty-five of altitude. Even unto a parallel sphere, and such as live under the pole, for half a year some segments may appear at any time and under any quarter, the sun not setting but walking round about them.

But the propriety of its election most properly appeareth in the natural signification and prognostic of itself; as containing a mixed signality of rain and fair weather. For, being in a rorid cloud and ready to drop, it declareth a pluvious disposure in the air; but because, when it appears, the sun must also shine, there can be no universal showers, and consequently no deluge. Thus, when the windows of the great deep were open, in vain men looked for the rainbow; for at that time it could not be seen, which after appeared unto Noah. It might be therefore existent before the flood, and had in nature some ground of its addition. Unto that of nature God superadded an assurance of its promise, that is, never to hinder its appearance or so to replenish the heavens again, as that we should behold it no more. And thus, without disparaging the promise, it might rain at the same time when God showed it unto Noah; thus was there more therein than the heathens understood when they called it the *nuncia* of the gods, and the laugh of weeping heaven;* and thus may be elegantly said, I put my bow, not my arrow in the clouds, that is, in the menace of rain, the mercy of fair weather.

Cabalistical heads, who from that expression in Isaiah,† do make a book of heaven, and read therein the great concernments of earth, do literally play on this, and from its semicircular figure (resembling the Hebrew letter caph, whereby is signified the uncomfortable number of twenty, at which years Joseph was sold, which Jacob lived under Laban, and

---

* *Risus plorantis Olympi.* † Isa. xxxiv. 4

at which men were to go to war), do note a propriety in its signification; as thereby declaring the dismal time of the deluge. And Christian conceits do seem to strain as high, while, from the irradiation of the sun upon a cloud, they apprehend the mystery of the sun of righteousness in the obscurity of flesh, by the colours green and red, the two destructions of the world by fire and water, or by the colours of blood and water, the mysteries of baptism, and the Holy Eucharist.[8]

Laudable therefore is the custom of the Jews, who upon the appearance of the rainbow, do magnify the fidelity of God in the memory of his covenant, according to that of Syracides, "Look upon the rainbow, and praise him that made it." And though some pious and Christian pens have only symbolized the same from the mystery of its colours, yet are there other affections which might admit of theological allusions. Nor would he find a more improper subject, that should consider that the colours are made by refraction of light, and the shadows that limit that light; that the centre of the sun, the rainbow, and the eye of the beholder must be in one right line, that the spectator must be between the sun and the rainbow, that sometime three appear, sometime one reversed. With many others, considerable in meteorological divinity, which would more sensibly make out the epithet of the heathens,* and the expression of the son of Syrach, "Very beautiful is the rainbow, it compasseth the heaven about with a glorious circle, and the hands of the Most High have bended it."

CHAPTER V.

Of Shem, Ham, and Japheth.

CONCERNING the three sons of Noah, Shem, Ham, and Japheth, that the order of their nativity was according to that of enumeration,[9] and Japheth, the youngest son (as

* *Thaumancias.*

[8] *Cabalistical heads, &c.*] The present paragraph was first added in the 2nd edition, in which also the same subject was first noticed in the last chapter of book vi.

[9] *that the order of their nativity, &c.*] Mr. C. T. Beke, in the 5th chapter

most believe, as Austin and others account), the sons of Japheth, and Europeans need not grant, nor will it so well concord unto the letter of the text, and its readiest interpretations. For so is it said in our translation, Shem the father of all the sons of Heber, the brother of Japheth the elder, so by the Septuagint, and so by that of Tremellius. And therefore when the Vulgar reads it, *Fratre Japhet majore*, the mistake, as Junius observeth, might be committed by the neglect of the Hebrew accent, which occasioned Jerome so to render it, and many after to believe it. Nor is that argument contemptible which is deduced from their chronology, for probable it is that Noah had none of them before, and begat them from that year when it is said he was five hundred years old, and begat Shem, Ham, and Japheth. Again it is said he was six hundred years old at the flood, and that two years after Shem was but an hundred; therefore Shem must have been born when Noah was five hundred and two, and some other before in the year of five hundred and one.

of his *Origines Biblicæ*, takes some pains to prove not only that Shem and not Japheth was Noah's eldest son (a point admitting some controversy), but that "the order in which the names of these three great progenitors of the human species are invariably placed when mentioned together in the sacred volume, may therefore be regarded as the order of their birth." Whereas "it is plainly delivered," as Sir Thomas remarks, that Ham, whose name stands invariably second, was the youngest son—a fact which absolutely overthrows this argument in favour of Shem's primogeniture, leaving the way open to consideration on other grounds. Mr. Beke contends that its probability is "strengthened by the situation of the country, which, in his opinion, was occupied by Shem and his descendants, namely, that in which Noah himself resided, while the possessions of Ham and Japheth, Shem's younger brothers, were situated, as they would naturally be imagined to have been, on either side of the paternal seat." He further endeavours to invalidate the argument against Shem's seniority, drawn from the 10th Gen. ver. 21,—"unto Shem also the father of all the children of Eber, the brother of Japheth the elder,"—by an examination of similar passages which would admit, if not favour the interpretation which Sir Thomas notices, as given to this passage by the Vulgate and others, viz., "the elder brother of Japheth." Neither does he admit the chronology to be conclusive against Shem, but concludes, after a lengthened consideration of the point, that "there could not have been a sufficient interval between the 500th year of Noah's life, and the birth of the father of Arphaxad (Shem), to allow of the intervention of an elder son."

Now whereas the Scripture affordeth the priority of order unto Shem, we cannot from thence infer his primogeniture. For in Shem the holy line was continued, and therefore, however born, his genealogy was most remarkable. So is it not unusual in Holy Scripture to nominate the younger before the elder. So it is said, that Terah begat Abraham,* Nachor, and Haram; whereas Haram was the eldest. So Rebecca† is termed the mother of Jacob and Esau. Nor is it strange the younger should be first in nomination, who have commonly had the priority in the blessings of God, and been first in his benediction. So Abel was accepted before Cain, Isaac the younger preferred before Ishmael the elder, Jacob before Esau, Joseph was the youngest of twelve, and David the eleventh son and minor cadet of Jesse.

Lastly, though Japheth were not elder than Shem, yet must we not affirm that he was younger than Cham; for it is plainly delivered, that, after Shem and Japheth had covered Noah, he awaked and knew what his youngest son had done unto him; υἱὸς ὁ νεώτερος is the expression of the Septuagint, *Filius minor* of Jerome, and *minimus* of Tremellius. And upon these grounds perhaps Josephus doth vary from the Scripture enumeration, and nameth them Shem, Japheth, and Cham: which is also observed by the Annian Berosus, Noah *cum tribus filiis, Semo, Jepeto, Chem*. And therefore, although in the priority of Shem and Japheth, there may be some difficulty, though Cyril, Epiphanius, and Austin have accounted Shem the elder, and Salian the annalist, and Petavius the chronologist, contend for the same; yet Cham is more plainly and confessedly named the youngest in the text.

And this is more conformable unto the Pagan history and Gentile account hereof, unto whom Noah was Satan, whose symbol was a ship, as related unto the ark, and who is said to have divided the world between his three sons. Ham is conceived to be Jupiter, who was the youngest son, worshipped by the name of Hamon, which was the Egyptian and African name for Jupiter, who is said to have cut off the genitals of his father, derived from the history of Ham,

---

* Gen. xi. † Gen. xxviii.

who beheld the nakedness of his, and by no hard mistake might be confirmed from the text,* as Bochartus† hath well observed.⁹

CHAPTER VI.

That the Tower of Babel was erected against a second Deluge.

An opinion there is of some generality, that our fathers after the flood attempted the tower of Babel, to secure themselves against a second deluge. Which, however affirmed by Josephus and others, hath seemed improbable unto many who have discoursed hereon. For (beside that they could not be ignorant of the promise of God never to drown the world again,¹ and had the rainbow before their eyes to put them in mind thereof), it is improbable from the nature of the deluge; which, being not possibly causable from natural showers above, or watery eruptions below, but requiring a supernatural hand,² and such as all

* Gen. ix. 22.
† Reading *Veiaggod, et abscidit*, for *Veiegged, et nunciavit.*—*Bochartus de Geographiâ sacrâ.*

⁹ *And this is more conformable, &c.*] This paragraph added in 2nd edition.

¹ *the promise of God, &c.*] This was an argument of beleef in the family of Sem in the Old Testament, and to the familyes of Japhet now in the new, that could not break his promise. But to the familyes of Ham, whereof Nimrod was the cheefe, it was of noe force: with them itt was more easie to slight first and then to forget that promise: when as they had now forgot God himselfe, as appeares by this bold attempt, which therfore most deservedly ended in confusion.—*Wr.*

² *requiring a supernatural hand.*] A late writer, speaking of the Mosaic account of the deluge, says, "What a scene of terrific and awful desolation does this narrative convey! How puerile those comments which exhibit animals and men *escaping* to the highest grounds and hills as the flood advanced. The impossibility of such escape may be immediately seen. Neither man nor beast under such circumstances could either advance or flee to any distance. Any animal, found in the plain when the flood began, would thus be merged in water seven or eight feet deep in a quarter of an hour! And were he to attempt advancing up the rising ground, a cataract of sheet water several feet deep would be gushing all the way in his face, besdes impending water-spouts from the 'flood-gates' of heaven, momentarily bursting over him; he would instantly become a prey to those 'mighty waters.'"

acknowledge irresistible, must needs disparage their knowledge and judgment in so successless attempts.

Again, they must probably hear, and some might know, that the waters of the flood ascended fifteen cubits above the highest mountains. Now, if (as some define) the perpendicular altitude of the highest mountains be four miles, or (as others) but fifteen furlongs, it is not easily conceived how such a structure could be effected, except we allowed the description of Herodotus concerning the tower of Belus; whose lowest story was in height and breadth one furlong, and seven more built upon it; abating that of the Annian Berosus, the traditional relation of Jerome, and fabulous account of the Jews. Probable it is, that what they attempted was feasible, otherwise they had been amply fooled in the fruitless success of their labours, nor needed God to have hindered them, saying, "Nothing will be restrained from them, which they begin to do."[3]

It was improbable from the place, that is, a plain in the land of Shinar. And if the situation of Babylon were such at first as it was in the days of Herodotus, it was rather a seat of amenity and pleasure, than conducing unto this intention: it being in a very great plain, and so improper a place to provide against a general deluge by towers and eminent structures, that they were fain to make provisions against particular and annual inundations by ditches and trenches, after the manner of Egypt. And therefore Sir Walter Raleigh* accordingly objecteth: if the nations which followed Nimrod still doubted the surprise of a second flood, according to the opinions of the ancient Hebrews, it soundeth ill to the ear of reason, that they would have spent many years in that low and overflown valley of Mesopotamia. And therefore in this situation, they chose a place more likely to have secured them from the world's destruction by fire, than another deluge of water: and, as Pierius observeth, some have conceived that this was their intention.

Lastly, the reason is delivered in the text. "Let us

* *History of the World.*

[3] *whose lowest story, &c.*] This passage was altered and enlarged in the 2nd edition.

build us a city and a tower, whose top may reach unto heaven, and let us make us a name, lest we be scattered abroad upon the whole earth;" as we have already begun to wander over a part. These were the open ends proposed unto the people; but the secret design of Nimrod, was to settle unto himself a place of dominion, and rule over his brethren, as it after succeeded, according to the delivery of the text, "The beginning of his kingdom was Babel."

CHAPTER VII.

Of the Mandrakes of Leah.

WE shall not omit the mandrakes[4] of Leah, according to the history of Genesis. "And Reuben went out in the days of wheat-harvest, and found mandrakes in the field, and brought them unto his mother Leah. Then Rachel said unto Leah, Give me, I pray thee, of thy son's mandrakes: and she saith unto her, Is it a small matter that thou hast taken my husband, and wouldst thou take my son's mandrakes also? And Rachel said, Therefore he shall lie with thee this night for thy son's mandrakes." From whence hath arisen a common conceit, that Rachel requested these plants as a medicine of fecundation, or whereby she might become fruitful. Which notwithstanding is very questionable, and of incertain truth.

For, first, from the comparison of one text with another, whether the mandrakes here mentioned be the same plant which holds that name with us, there is some cause to doubt. The word is used in another place of Scripture,* when the church inviting her beloved into the fields, among the delightful fruits of grapes and pomegranates, it is said,

* Cant. vii.

[4] *mandrakes.*] For a brief description of a plant bearing this name, see vol. i.

Ross concludes a page of criticism on our author's reasons for rejecting the popular opinion of Rachel's motives for requesting the mandrakes—by the following pithy expostulation:—"To be brief, I would know, whether it be a greater error in me to affirm that which is denied by some, or in him to deny that which is affirmed by all?"

"The mandrakes give a smell, and at our gates are all manner of pleasant fruits." Now instead of a smell of delight, our mandrakes afford a papaverous and unpleasant odour, whether in the leaf or apple, as is discoverable in their simplicity or mixture. The same is also dubious from the different interpretations: for though the Septuagint and Josephus do render it the apples of mandrakes in this text, yet in the other of the Canticles, the Chaldee paraphrase termeth it balsam. R. Solomon, as Drusius observeth, conceives it to be that plant the Arabians named Jesemin. Oleaster, and Georgius Nenetus, the lily; and that the word *dudaim* may comprehend any plant that hath a good smell, resembleth a woman's breast, and flourisheth in wheat-harvest. Tremellius interprets the same for any amiable flowers of a pleasant and delightful odour. But the Geneva translators have been more wary than any; for although they retain the word mandrake in the text, they in effect retract it in the margin; wherein is set down the word in the original is *dudaim*, which is a kind of fruit or flower unknown.

Nor shall we wonder at the dissent of exposition, and difficulty of definition concerning this text, if we perpend how variously the vegetables of Scripture are expounded, and how hard it is in many places to make out the species determined. Thus are we at variance concerning the plant that covered Jonas: which though the Septuagint doth render *colocynthis*, the Spanish *calabaca*, and ours accordingly a gourd, yet the Vulgar translates it *hedera* or ivy; and as Grotius observeth, Jerome thus translated it, not as the same plant, but best apprehended thereby. The Italian of Diodati, and that of Tremellius have named it *ricinus*, and so hath ours in the margin; for *palma Christi* is the same with *ricinus*. The Geneva translators have herein been also circumspect, for they have retained the original word *kikaion*, and ours hath also affixed the same unto the margin.

Nor are they indeed always the same plants which are delivered under the same name, and appellations commonly received amongst us. So when it is said of Solomon, that he writ of plants, "from the cedar of Lebanus, unto the hyssop that groweth upon the wall," that is **from the** greatest unto the smallest, it cannot be well conceived our common hyssop: for neither is that the least of vegetables, nor observed to grow upon walls; but rather as Lemnius well conceiveth, some kind of the capillaries, which are very small plants, and only grow upon walls and stony places. Nor are the four species in the holy ointment, cinnamon, myrrh, calamus, and cassia, nor the other in the holy perfume, frankincense, *stacte*, *onycha*, and *galbanum*, so agreeably expounded unto those in use with us, as not to leave considerable doubts behind them. Nor must that perhaps be taken for a simple unguent, which Matthew only termeth a precious ointment; but rather a composition, as Mark and John imply by *pistick* nard, that is faithfully dispensed, and may be that famous composition described by Dioscorides, made of oil of ben, *malabathrum, juncus odoratus, costus, amomum,* myrrh, balsam, and nard,* which Galen affirmeth to have been in use with the delicate dames of Rome, and that the best thereof was made at Laodicea, from whence by merchants it was conveyed unto other parts. But how to make out that translation concerning the tithe of mint, anise and cummin, we are still to seek; for we find not a word in the text that can properly be rendered anise, the Greek being ἄνηθον, which the Latins call *anethum*, and is properly Englished dill. Lastly, what meteor that was, that fed the Israelites so many years, they must rise again to inform us. Nor do they make it out,† who will have it the same with our manna; nor will any one kind thereof, or hardly all kinds we read of, be able to answer the qualities thereof, delivered in the Scripture; that is, to fall upon the ground, to breed worms, to melt with the sun, to taste like fresh oil, to be ground in mills, to be like coriander seed, and of the colour of bdellium.†[5]

Again, it is not deducible from the text or concurrent sentence of comments, that Rachel had any such intention, and most do rest in the determination of Austin, that she desired them for rarity, pulchritude, or suavity. Nor is it

---

* V. *Matthioli Epist.*
† V. *Doctissimum Chrysostom. Magnenum de Manna.*

Lastly, &c.] This passage was added in the 2nd edition.

probable she would have resigned her bed unto Leah, when at the same time she had obtained a medicine to fructify herself. And therefore Drucius, who hath expressly and favourably treated hereof, is so far from conceding this intention, that he plainly concludeth, *Hoc quo modo illis in mentem venerit, conjicere nequeo;*—"how this conceit fell into men's minds, it cannot fall into mine;" for the Scripture delivereth it not, nor can it be clearly deduced from the text.

Thirdly, if Rachel had any such intention, yet had they no such effect, for she conceived not many years after, of Joseph; whereas in the mean time Leah had three children, Issachar, Zebulon, and Dinah.

Lastly, although at that time they failed of this effect, yet is it mainly questionable whether they had any such virtue, either in the opinions of those times, or in their proper nature. That the opinion was popular in the land of Canaan, it is improbable; and had Leah understood thus much, she would not surely have parted with fruits of such a faculty; especially unto Rachel, who was no friend unto her. As for its proper nature, the ancients have generally esteemed it narcotick or stupefactive, and it is to be found in the list of poisons, set down by Dioscorides, Galen, Ætius, Ægineta, and several antidotes delivered by them against it. It was, I confess, from good antiquity, and in the days of Theophrastus, accounted a philter or plant that conciliates affection; and so delivered by Dioscorides. And this intent might seem most probable, had they not been the wives of holy Jacob; had Rachel presented them unto him, and not requested them for herself.

Now what Dioscorides affirmeth in favour of this effect, that the grains of the apples of mandrakes mundify the matrix, and applied with sulphur stop the fluxes of women, he overthrows again by qualities destructive unto conception; affirming also that the juice thereof purgeth upward like hellebore; and applied in pessaries[6] provokes the menstruous flows, and procures abortion. Petrus Hispanus, or Pope John the Twentieth, speaks more directly in his *Thesaurus Pauperum:* wherein among the receipts of fecundation, he experimentally commendeth the wine of

[6] *pessaries.*] Medicines made into an oblong shape.

mandrakes given with *triphera magna*. But the soul of the medicine may lie in *triphera magna*, an excellent composition, and for this effect commended by Nicolaus. And whereas Levinus Lemnius, that eminent physician, doth also concede this effect, it is from manifest causes and qualities elemental occasionally producing the same. For he imputeth the same unto the coldness of that simple, and is of opinion that in hot climates, and where the uterine parts exceed in heat, by the coldness hereof they may be reduced into a conceptive constitution, and crasis accommodable unto generation; whereby indeed we will not deny the due and frequent use may proceed unto some effect; from whence, notwithstanding, we cannot infer a fertilitating condition or property of fecundation. For in this way all vegetables do make fruitful according unto the complexion of the matrix; if that excel in heat, plants exceeding in cold do rectify it; if it be cold, simples that are hot reduce it; if dry, moist; if moist, dry correct it; in which division all plants are comprehended. But to distinguish thus much is a point of art, and beyond the method of Rachel's or feminine physic. Again, whereas it may be thought that mandrakes may fecundate, since poppy hath obtained the epithet of fruitful, and that fertility was hieroglyphically described by Venus with an head of poppy in her hand; the reason hereof was the multitude of seed within itself, and no such multiplying in human generation. And lastly, whereas they may seem to have this quality (since opium itself is conceived to extimulate unto venery, and for that intent is sometimes used by Turks, Persians, and most oriental nations), although Winclerus doth seem to favour the conceit, yet Amatus Lusitanus, and Rodericus à Castro, are against it; Garcias ab Horto refutes it from experiment; and they speak probably who affirm the intent and effect of eating opium is not so much to invigorate themselves in coition, as to prolong the act, and spin out the motions of carnality.

CHAPTER VIII.

Of the Three Kings of Collein.[7]

A COMMON conceit there is of the three kings of Collein, conceived to be the wise men that travelled unto our Saviour by the direction of the star. Wherein (omitting the large discourses of Baronius, Pineda, and Montacutius), that they might be kings, beside the ancient tradition and authority of many fathers, the Scripture implieth; "The Gentiles shall come to thy light, and kings to the brightness of thy rising. The kings of Tharsis and the Isles, the kings of Arabia and Saba shall offer gifts." Which places most Christians and many rabbins interpret of the Messiah. Not that they are to be conceived potent monarchs, or mighty kings, but toparchs, kings of cities or narrow territories; such as were the kings of Sodom and Gomorrha, the kings of Jericho and Ai, the one and thirty which Joshua subdued, and such as some conceive the friends of Job to have been.

But although we grant they were kings, yet can we not be assured they were three. For the Scripture maketh no mention of any number; and the number of their presents, gold, myrrh, and frankincense, concludeth not the number of their persons; for these were the commodities of their country, and such as probably the queen of Sheba in one person had brought before unto Solomon. So did not the sons of Jacob divide the present unto Joseph, but are conceived to carry one for them all, according to the expression of their father; "Take of the best fruits of the land in your vessels, and carry down the man a present." And therefore their number being uncertain, what credit is to be given unto their names, Gasper, Melchior, Balthazar,[8] what to the

---

[7] *Three kings of Collein.*] Cologne on the Rhine.

[8] *Gasper, &c.*] According to the following distich in *Festa Anglo-Romana*, p. 7:

>Tres reges regi regum tria dona ferebant;
>Myrrham homini, uncto aurum, thura dedere Deo.

Selden says, that "our chusing kings and queens, on twelfth night, has reference to the three kings."—*Table Talk*, p. 20. See also *Universal Magazine*, 1774; Sir H. Piers's *Westmeath*, 1682, in **Vallancey's Col-**

charm thereof against the falling sickness, or what unto their habits, complexions, and corporal accidents, we must rely on their uncertain story, and received portraits of Collein.

Lastly, although we grant them kings, and three in number, yet could we not conceive that they were kings of Collein. For although Collein were the chief city of the Ubii, then called Ubiopolis, and afterwards Agrippina, yet will no history inform us there were three kings thereof. Beside, these being rulers in their countries, and returning home, would have probably converted their subjects; but according unto Munster, their conversion was not wrought until seventy years after, by Maternus, a disciple of Peter. And lastly, it is said that the wise men came from the east; but Collein is seated westward from Jerusalem; for Collein hath of longitude thirty-four degrees, but Jerusalem seventy-two.

The ground of all was this. These wise men or kings were probably of Arabia, and descended from Abraham by Keturah, who apprehending the mystery of this star, either by the Spirit of God, the prophecy of Balaam, the prophecy which Suetonius mentions, received and constantly believed through all the east, that out of Jewry one should come that should rule the whole world, or the divulged expectation of the Jews from the expiring prediction of Daniel, were by the same conducted unto Judea, returned into their country, and were after baptized by Thomas. From whence about three hundred years after, by Helena, the empress, their bodies were translated to Constantinople. From thence by Eustatius unto Milan, and at last by Renatus, the bishop, unto Collein, where they are believed at present to remain, their monuments shown unto strangers, and having lost their Arabian titles, are crowned kings of Collein.

lectan. i. No. 1. p. 124.—A writer in the *Gentleman's Magazine*, however, vol. xxxiv. p. 599, refers the twelfth night cake to the Roman custom of casting dice to decide who should be *rex convivii*.

It appears from *Gentleman's Magazine*, that on twelfth day, 1736, the king and the prince, at the chapel-royal, St. James's, made their offerings of gold, frankincense, and myrrh. These continue to be annually made—*by proxy.*—*Hone's Every-day Book*, vol. i. p. 59.

CHAPTER IX.

Of the food of John Baptist, Locusts and Wild Honey.

CONCERNING the food of John Baptist in the wilderness, locusts and wild honey, less popular opiniatrity should arise, we will deliver the chief opinions. The first conceived the locusts here mentioned to be that fruit which the Greeks name κεράτιον, mentioned by Luke in the diet of the prodigal son, the Latins *siliqua*, and some *panis sancti Johannis,* included in a broad pod, and indeed a taste almost as pleasant as honey. But this opinion doth not so truly impugn that of the locusts, and might rather call unto controversy the meaning of wild honey.

The second affirmeth that they were the tops or tender crops of trees; for so *locusta* also signifieth. Which conceit is plausible in Latin, but will not hold in Greek, wherein the word is ἀκρίσι; except for ἀκρίδες, we read ἀκρόδρυα, or ἀκρέμονες, which signify the extremities of trees, of which belief have divers been; more confidently Isidore Pelusiota, who in his epistles plainly affirmeth they think unlearnedly who are of another belief. And this so wrought upon Baronius, that he concludeth in neutrality; *Hæc cum scribat Isidorus, definiendum nobis non est, et totum relinquimus lectoris arbitrio; nam constat Græcam dictionem* ἀκρίδες, *et locustam, insecti genus, et arborum summitates significare. Sed fallitur,* saith Montacutius, *nam constat contrarium,* ἀκρίδα *apud nullum authorem classicum* ἀκρόδρυα *significare*. But above all Paracelsus with most animosity promoteth this opinion, and in his book *De Melle* spareth not his friend Erasmus. *Hoc à nonnullis ita explicatur ut dicant locustas aut cicadas Johanni pro cibo fuisse; sed hi stultitiam dissimulare non possunt, veluti Jeronymus, Erasmus, et alii prophetæ neoterici in Latinitate immortui.*

A third affirmeth that they were properly locusts, that is, a sheath-winged and six-footed insect, such as is our grass-hopper. And this opinion seems more probable than the other.[9] For beside the authority of Origen, Jerome, Chry-

---

[9] *and this opinion, &c.*] Ross contends against the Dr. for the greater probability that John's diet was vegetable—on the ground that, as he

sostom, Hilary, and Ambrose to confirm it, this is the proper signification of the word, thus used in Scripture by the Septuagint; Greek vocabularies thus expound it; Suidas on the word ἀκρίς observes it to be that animal whereupon the Baptist fed in the desert: in this sense the word is used by Aristotle, Dioscorides, Galen, and several human authors. And lastly, there is no absurdity in this interpretation, nor any solid reason why we should decline it, it being a food permitted unto the Jews, whereof four kinds are reckoned up among clean meats. Besides, not only the Jews, but many other nations, long before and since, have made an usual food thereof. That the Ethiopians, Mauritanians, and Arabians did commonly eat them, is testified by Diodorus, Strabo, Solinus, Ælian, and Pliny; that they still feed on them is confirmed by Leo, Cadamustus, and others John therefore, as our Saviour saith, "came neither eating nor drinking," that is, far from the diet of Jerusalem and other riotous places, but fared coarsely and poorly, according unto the apparel he wore, that is, of camel's hair; the place of his abode—the wilderness; and the doctrine he preached—humiliation and repentance.

CHAPTER X.

That John the Evangelist should not die.

THE conceit of the long living, or rather not dying, of John the Evangelist, although it seem inconsiderable, and not much weightier than that of Joseph, the wandering Jew, yet being deduced from Scripture, and abetted by authors of all times, it shall not escape our enquiry. It is drawn from the speech of our Saviour unto Peter after the prediction of his martyrdom: "Peter saith unto Jesus, Lord, what shall this man do? Jesus saith unto him, If I will that he tarry

---

Ethiopians, who were accustomed to use *locusts* for food, almost all fell a prey to *phthiriasis*, it is scarcely to be believed that John would have adopted a diet likely to entail so loathsome a disease.—*Arcana*, p. 95.

There is one species of the acacia tribe called the *honey locust*, bearing a large and very sweet pod, which is very commonly boiled and eaten in America; and this is supposed to have been the food of the Baptist.

until I come, what is that to thee? Follow thou me. Then went this saying abroad among the brethren, that this disciple should not die."*

Now the belief hereof hath been received either grossly and in the general, that is, not distinguishing the manner or particular way of this continuation, in which sense probably the grosser and undiscerning party received it; or more distinctly, apprehending the manner of his immortality, that is, that John should never properly die, but be translated into Paradise, there to remain with Enoch and Elias until about the coming of Christ, and should be slain with them under Antichrist, according to that of the Apocalypse; "I will give power unto my two witnesses, and they shall prophesy a thousand two hundred and threescore days clothed in sackcloth; and when they shall have finished their testimony, the beast that ascendeth out of the bottomless pit shall make war against them, and overcome them and kill them." Hereof, as Baronius observeth, within three hundred years after Christ, Hippolytus the martyr was the first assertor, but hath been maintained by Metaphrastes, by Freculphus, but especially by Georgius Trapezuntius, who hath expressly treated upon this text, and although he lived but in the last century, did still affirm that John was not yet dead.

The same is also hinted by the learned Italian poet Dante, who in his poetical survey of Paradise, meeting with the soul of St. John, and desiring to see his body, received answer from him, that his body was in earth, and there should remain with other bodies until the number of the blessed were accomplished.[1]

> In terra è terra il mio corpo, et saragli
> Tanto con gli altri, che l' numero nostro
> Con l' eterno proposito s' agguagli.

As for the gross opinion that he should not die, it is sufficiently refuted by that which first occasioned it, that is, the Scripture itself, and no further off than the very subsequent verse: "Yet Jesus said not unto him, he should not die, but

* John xxi.

[1] *The same is also hinted, &c.*] This paragraph, together with the Italian quotation which follows it, was first added in the 6th edition.

if I will that he tarry till I come, what is that to thee?" And this was written by John himself, whom the opinion concerned, and (as is conceived) many years after, when Peter had suffered and fulfilled the prophecy of Christ.

For the particular conceit, the foundation is weak, nor can it be made out from the text alleged in the Apocalypse; for beside that therein two persons only are named, no mention is made of John, a third actor in this tragedy. The same is also overthrown by history, which recordeth not only the death of John, but assigneth the place of his burial, that is, Ephesus, a city in Asia Minor; whither, after he had been banished into Patmos by Domitian, he returned in the reign of Nerva, there deceased, and was buried in the days of Trajan. And this is testified by Jerome, by Tertullian, by Chrysostom, and Eusebius* (in whose days his sepulchre was to be seen), and by a more ancient testimony alleged also by him, that is, of Polycrates, bishop of Ephesus, not many successions after John; whose words are these, in an epistle unto Victor, bishop of Rome: *Johannes ille qui supra pectus Domini recumbebat, doctor optimus, apud Ephesum dormivit.* Many of the like nature are noted by Baronius, Jansenius, Estius, Lipellous, and others.

Now the main and primitive ground of this error was a gross mistake in the words of Christ, and a false apprehension of his meaning; understanding that positively which was but conditionally expressed, or receiving that affirmatively which was but concessively delivered. For the words of our Saviour run in a doubtful strain, rather reprehending than satisfying the curiosity of Peter: as though he should have said, " thou hast thy own doom, why enquirest thou after thy brother's?—what relief unto thy affliction will be the society of another's?—why pryest thou into the secrets of God's will?—if he stay until I come, what concerneth it thee, who shalt be sure to suffer before that time?" And such an answer probably he returned, because he foreknew John should not suffer a violent death, but go unto his grave in peace. Which had Peter assuredly known, it might have cast some water on his flames, and smothered those fires which kindled after unto the honour of his Master.

* *De Scriptor. Ecclesiast. De anima.*

Now why among all the rest John only escaped the death of a martyr, the reason is given: because all others fled away or withdrew themselves at his death, and he alone of the twelve beheld his passion on the cross. Wherein notwithstanding, the affliction that he suffered could not amount unto less than martyrdom: for if the naked relation, at least the intentive consideration of that passion, be able still, and at this disadvantage of time, to rend the hearts of pious contemplators, surely the near and sensible vision thereof must needs occasion agonies beyond the comprehension of flesh; and the trajections of such an object more sharply pierce the martyred soul of John, than afterwards did the nails the crucified body of Peter.

Again, they were mistaken in the emphatical apprehension, placing the consideration upon the words, "If I will," whereas it properly lay in these, "until I come." Which had they apprehended, as some have since, that is, not for his ultimate and last return, but his coming in judgment and destruction upon the Jews; or such a coming, as it might be said, that generation should not pass before it was fulfilled; they needed not, much less need we, suppose such diuturnity. For after the death of Peter, John lived to behold the same fulfilled by Vespasian: nor had he then his *nunc dimittis*, or went out like unto Simeon; but old in accomplished obscurities, and having seen the expire of Daniel's prediction, as some conceive, he accomplished his revelation.

But besides this original and primary foundation, divers others have made impressions according unto different ages and persons by whom they were received. For some established the conceit in the disciples and brethren which were contemporary unto him, or lived about the same time with him. And this was, first, the extraordinary affection our Saviour bare unto this disciple, who hath the honour to be called the disciple whom Jesus loved: now from hence they might be apt to belive their Master would dispense with his death, or suffer him to live to see him return in glory, who was the only apostle that beheld him to die in dishonour. Another was the belief and opinion of those times, that Christ would suddenly come; for they held not generally the same opinion with their successors, or as descending ages after so many centuries, but conceived his coming would not be long after his passion, according unto several expressions of our Saviour grossly understood, and as we find the same opinion not long after reprehended by St. Paul:* and thus, conceiving his coming would not be long, they might be induced to believe his favourite should live unto it. Lastly, the long life of John might much advantage this opinion; for he survived the other twelve—he was aged twenty-two years when he was called by Christ, and twenty-five (that is the age of priesthood) at his death, and lived ninety-three years, that is sixty-eight after his Saviour, and died not before the second year of Trajan: now, having outlived all his fellows, the world was confirmed he might still live, and even unto the coming of his Master.

The grounds which promoted it in succeeding ages, were especially two. The first his escape of martyrdom; for whereas all the rest suffered some kind of forcible death, we have no history that he suffered any; and men might think he was not capable thereof; for as history informeth, by the command of Domitian he was cast into a caldron of burning oil, and came out again unsinged. Now future ages apprehending he suffered no violent death, and finding also the means that tended thereto could take no place, they might be confirmed in their opinion, that death had no power over him; that he might live always, who could not be destroyed by fire, and was able to resist the fury of that element which nothing shall resist. The second was a corruption, crept into the Latin text, for *si* reading *sic eum manere volo;* whereby the answer of our Saviour becometh positive, or that he will have it so; which way of reading was much received in former ages, and is still retained in the Vulgar translation: but in the Greek and original the word is $\dot{\epsilon}\dot{\alpha}\nu$, signifying *si* or if, which is very different from $o\ddot{\upsilon}\tau\omega$, and cannot be translated for it: and answerable hereunto is the translation of Junius, and that also annexed unto the Greek by the authority of Sixtus Quintus.

The third confirmed it in ages farther descending, and proved a powerful argument unto all others following—because in his tomb at Ephesus there was no corpse or relick

---

* 2 Thess. ii.

thereof to be found; whereupon arose divers doubts, and many suspicious conceptions; some believing he was not buried, some, that he was buried but risen again, others, that he descended alive into his tomb, and from thence departed after. But all these proceeded upon unveritable grounds, as Baronius hath observed; who allegeth a letter of Celestine, bishop of Rome, unto the council of Ephesus, wherein he declareth the relicks of John were highly honoured by that city; and a passage also of Chrysostom in the homilies of the apostles, "That John being dead, did cures in Ephesus, as though he were still alive." And so I observe that Estius discussing this point, concludeth hereupon, *quòd corpus ejus nunquam reperiatur, hoc non dicerent si veterum scripta diligenter perlustrassent.*

Now that the first ages after Christ, those succeeding, or any other, should proceed into opinions so far divided from reason, as to think of immortality after the fall of Adam, or conceit a man in these later times should outlive our fathers in the first,—although it seem very strange, yet is it not incredible. For the credulity of men hath been deluded into the like conceits; and, as Irenæus and Tertullian mention, one Menander, a Samaritan, obtained belief in this very point, whose doctrine it was, that death should have no power on his disciples, and such as received his baptism should receive immortality therewith. 'Twas surely an apprehension very strange; nor usually falling either from the absurdities of melancholy or vanities of ambition. Some indeed have been so affectedly vain as to counterfeit immortality, and have stolen their death, in a hope to be esteemed immortal; and others have conceived themselves dead: but surely few or none have fallen upon so bold an error, as not to think that they could die at all. The reason of those mighty ones, whose ambition could suffer them to be called gods, would never be flattered into immortality; but the proudest thereof have by the daily dictates of corruption convinced the impropriety of that appellation. And surely, although delusion may run high, and possible it is that for a while a man may forget his nature, yet cannot this be durable. For the inconcealable imperfections of ourselves, or their daily examples in others, will hourly prompt us our corruption, and loudly tell us we are the sons of earth.

CHAPTER XI.

Of some others more briefly.

MANY others there are which we resign unto divinity, and perhaps deserve not controversy. Whether David were punished only for pride of heart for numbering the people, as most do hold, or whether, as Josephus and many maintain, he suffered also for not performing the commandment of God concerning capitation, that when the people were numbered, for every head they should pay unto God a shekel,*—we shall not here contend. Surely if it were not the occasion of this plague, we must acknowledge the omission thereof was threatened with that punishment, according to the words of the law: "When thou takest the sum of the children of Israel, then shall they give every man a ransom for his soul unto the Lord, that there be no plague amongst them."† Now how deeply hereby God was defrauded in the time of David, and opulent state of Israel, will easily appear by the sums of former lustrations. For in the first, the silver of them that were numbered was an hundred talents, and a thousand seven hundred and threescore and fifteen shekels; a bekah for every man, that is, half a shekel, after the shekel of the sanctuary; for every one from twenty years old and upwards, for six hundred thousand, and three thousand and five hundred and fifty men. Answerable whereto we read in Josephus, Vespasian ordered that every man of the Jews should bring into the Capitol two drachms; which amounts unto fifteen pence, or a quarter of an ounce of silver with us; and is equivalent unto a bekah, or half a shekel of the sanctuary. For an Attick drachm is sevenpence halfpenny, or a quarter of a shekel, and a *didrachmum*, or double drachm, is the word used for tribute money, or half a shekel; and a *stater*, the money found in the fish's mouth, was two *didrachmums*, or a whole shekel, and tribute sufficient for our Saviour and for Peter.

We will not question the metamorphosis of Lot's wife, or whether she were transformed into a real statue of salt;

---

* Exod. xxx.   † Exod. xxxviii.

though some conceive that expression metaphorical,[2] and no more thereby than a lasting and durable column, according to the nature of salt, which admitteth no corruption;[3] in which sense the covenant of God is termed a covenant of salt; and it is also said, God gave the kingdom unto David for ever, or by a covenant of salt.

That Absalom was hanged by the hair of the head, and not caught up by the neck, as Josephus conceiveth, and the common argument against long hair affirmeth, we are not ready to deny. Although I confess a great and learned party there are of another opinion; although if he had his morion or helmet on, I could not well conceive it; although the translation of Jerome or Tremellius do not prove it, and our own seems rather to overthrow it.

That Judas hanged himself—much more that he perished thereby—we shall not raise a doubt. Although Jansenius, discoursing the point, produceth the testimony of Theo-

---

[2] *We will not question, &c.*] Dr. Adam Clarke has given a long note on this question, to which the reader is referred. He enumerates in addition to Browne's two hypotheses, a third:—viz. that, by continuing in the plain, she might have been struck dead with lightning, and enveloped and invested in the bituminous and sulphurous matter which descended. But Dr. C. evidently inclines to accept the *metaphorical* interpretation. A number of absurd and contradictory stories (he remarks) have been told, of the discovery of Lot's wife still remaining unchanged—and indeed *unchangeable*,—her form having still resident in it a continual miraculous energy, reproductive of any part which is broken off: so that though multitudes of visitors have brought away each a morsel, yet does the next find the figure—complete! The author of the poem *De Sodoma*, at the end of Tertullian's works, and with him, Irenæus, asserts the figure to possess certain indications of a remaining portion of animal life, and the latter father in the height of his absurdity, makes her an emblem of the true church, which, though she suffers much, and often loses whole members, yet preserves *the pillar of salt*, that is, *the foundation of the true faith!!* Josephus asserts that he himself saw the pillar. S. Clement also says that Lot's wife was remaining, even at that time, as a pillar of salt. Recent and more respectable travellers however have sought for her in vain, and it is now very generally admitted, either that the statue does not exist—or that some of the blocks of rock salt met with in the vicinity of the Dead Sea—are the only remains of it.

[3] *which, &c.*] Itt admitteth noe corruption in other things, but itselfe suffers liquation, and corruption too, that is, looses its savour, as appears by that remarkable speech of our Saviour, Marc. ix. 50.—*Wr.*

phylact and Euthymius, that he died not by the gallows but under a cart-wheel; and Baronius also delivereth, this was the opinion of the Greeks, and derived as high as Papias, one of the disciples of John. Although, also, how hardly the expression of Matthew is reconcileable unto that of Peter—and that he plainly hanged himself, with that, that falling headlong he burst asunder in the midst — with many other the learned Grotius plainly doth acknowledge. And lastly, although, as he also urgeth, the word ἀπήγξατο in Matthew doth not only signify suspension or pendulous illaqueation, as the common picture describeth it, but also suffocation, strangulation or interception of breath, which may arise from grief, despair, and deep dejection of spirit, in which sense it is used in the history of Tobit concerning Sara, ἐλυπήθη σφόδρα ὥστε ἀπάγξασθαι,—*Ita tristata est ut strangulatione premeretur*, saith Junius; and so might it happen from the horror of mind unto Judas.* So do many of the Hebrews affirm, that Achitophel was also strangled, that is, not from the rope, but passion. For the Hebrew and Arabic word in the text not only signifies suspension, but indignation, as Grotius hath also observed.

Many more there are of indifferent truths, whose dubious expositions worthy divines and preachers do often draw into wholesome and sober uses, whereof we shall not speak. With industry we decline such paradoxes, and peaceably submit unto their received acceptions.

CHAPTER XII.

Of the Cessation of Oracles.

THAT oracles ceased or grew mute at the coming of Christ,[5] is best understood in a qualified sense, and not without all latitude, as though precisely there were none after, nor any decay before. For (what we must confess

* *Strangulat inclusus dolor.*

[5] *That oracles ceased, &c.*] Browne betrays, throughout, his full belief in the supernatural and Satanic character of oracles.

unto relations of antiquity), some pre-decay is observable from that of Cicero, urged by Baronius; *Cur isto modo jam oracula Delphis non eduntur, non modo ætate, sed jam diu, ut nihil possit esse contemptius.* That during his life they were not altogether dumb, is deducible from Suetonius in the life of Tiberius, who attempting to subvert the oracles adjoining unto Rome, was deterred by the lots or chances which were delivered at Præneste. After his death we meet with many; Suetonius reports, that the oracle of Antium forewarned Caligula to beware of Cassius, who was one that conspired his death. Plutarch enquiring why the oracles of Greece ceased, excepteth that of Lebadia; and in the same place Demetrius affirmeth the oracles of Mopsus and Amphilochus were much frequented in his days. In brief, histories are frequent in examples, and there want not some even to the reign of Julian.

What therefore may consist with history;—by cessation of oracles, with Montacutius, we may understand their intercision, not abscission or consummate desolation; their rare delivery, not total dereliction: and yet in regard of divers oracles, we may speak strictly, and say there was a proper cessation. Thus may we reconcile the accounts of times, and allow those few and broken divinations, whereof we read in story and undeniable authors. For that they received this blow from Christ, and no other causes alleged by the heathens, from oraculous confession they cannot deny; whereof upon record there are some very remarkable. The first that oracle of Delphos delivered unto Augustus.

> Me puer Hebræus Divos Deus ipse gubernans,
> Cedere sede jubet, tristemque redire sub orcum;
> Aris ergo dehinc tacitus discedito nostris.
>
> An Hebrew child, a God all gods excelling,
> To Hell again commands me from this dwelling;
> Our altars leave in silence, and no more
> A resolution e'er from hence implore.

A second recorded by Plutarch, of a voice that was heard to cry unto mariners at the sea, *Great Pan is dead;* which is a relation very remarkable, and may be read in his defect of oracles. A third reported by Eusebius in the life of his magnified Constantine, that about that time Apollo mourned, declaring his oracles were false, and that the righteous upon earth did hinder him from speaking truth. And a fourth related by Theodoret, and delivered by Apollo Daphneus unto Julian, upon his Persian expedition, that he should remove the bodies about him before he could return an answer, and not long after his temple was burnt with lightning.

All which were evident and convincing acknowledgments of that power which shut his lips, and restrained that delusion which had reigned so many centuries. But as his malice is vigilant, and the sins of men do still continue a toleration of his mischiefs, he resteth not, nor will he ever cease to circumvent the sons of the first deceived. And therefore, expelled from oracles and solemn temples of delusion, he runs into corners, exercising minor trumperies, and acting his deceits in witches, magicians, diviners, and such inferior seducers. And yet (what is deplorable) while we apply ourselves thereto, and, affirming that God hath left off to speak by his prophets, expect in doubtful matters a resolution from such spirits; while we say the devil is mute, yet confess that these can speak; while we deny the substance, yet practise the effect, and in the denied solemnity maintain the equivalent efficacy;—in vain we cry that oracles are down; Apollo's altar still doth smoke; nor is the fire of Delphos out unto this day.

Impertinent it is unto our intention to speak in general of oracles, and many have well performed it. The plainest of others was that of Apollo Delphicus, recorded by Herodotus, and delivered unto Crœsus; who as a trial of their omniscience sent unto distant oracles: and so contrived with the messengers, that though in several places, yet at the same time they should demand what Crœsus was then a doing. Among all others the oracle of Delphos only hit it, returning answer, he was boiling a lamb with a tortoise, in a brazen vessel, with a cover of the same metal. The style is haughty in Greek, though somewhat lower in Latin.

>Æquoris est spatium et numerus mihi notus arenæ,
>Mutum percipio, fantis nihil audio vocem.
>Venit ad hos sensus nidor testudinis acris,
>Quæ semel agninâ coquitur cum carne lebete,
>Aere infra strato, et stratum cui desuper æs est.

> I know the space of sea, the number of the sand,
> I hear the silent, mute I understand.
> A tender lamb joined with tortoise flesh,
> Thy master, king of Lydia, now doth dress.
> The scent thereof doth in my nostrils hover,
> From brazen pot closed with brazen cover.

Hereby indeed he acquired much wealth and more honour, and was reputed by Crœsus as a deity: and yet not long after, by a vulgar fallacy he deceived his favourite and greatest friend of oracles, into an irreparable overthrow by Cyrus. And surely the same success are likely all to have, that rely or depend upon him. 'Twas the first play he practised on mortality; and as time hath rendered him more perfect in the art, so hath the inveterateness of his malice more ready in the execution. 'Tis therefore the sovereign degree of folly, and a crime not only against God, but also our own reasons, to expect a favour from the devil, whose mercies are more cruel than those of Polyphemus; for he devours his favourites first, and the nearer a man approacheth, the sooner he is scorched by Moloch. In brief, his favours are deceitful and double-headed, he doth apparent good, for real and convincing evil after it; and exalteth us up to the top of the temple, but to tumble us down from it.

CHAPTER XIII.

Of the Death of Aristotle.

THAT Aristotle drowned himself in Euripus, as despairing to resolve the cause of its reciprocation, or ebb and flow seven times a day, with this determination, *Si quidem ego non capio te, tu capies me*, was the assertion of Procopius, Nazianzen, Justin Martyr, and is generally believed among us. Wherein because we perceive men have but an imperfect knowledge, some conceiving Euripus to be a river, others not knowing where or in what part to place it, we first advertise, it generally signifieth any strait, fret, or channel of the sea, running between two shores, as Julius Pollux hath defined it; as we read of Euripus Hellespontiacus, Pyrrhæus, and this whereof we treat, *Euripus Euboicus*, or *Chalcidicus*, that is, a narrow passage of sea dividing Attica and the island of Eubœa, now called *Golfo di Negroponte*, from the name of the island and chief city thereof, famous in the wars of Antiochus, and taken from the Venetians by Mahomet the Great.

Now that in this Euripe or fret of Negroponte, and upon the occasion mentioned, Aristotle drowned himself, as many affirm, and almost all believe, we have some room to doubt. For without any mention of this, we find two ways delivered of his death by Diogenes Laertius, who expressly treateth thereof; the one from Eumolus and Phavorinus, that, being accused of impiety for composing an hymn unto Hermias (upon whose concubine he begat his son Nicomachus), he withdrew into Chalcis, where drinking poison he died; the hymn is extant in Laertius, and the fifteenth book of Athenæus. Another by Apollodorus,[6] that he died at Chalcis of a natural death and languishment of stomach, in his sixty-third, or great climacterical year; and answerable hereto is the account of Suidas and Censorinus. And if that were clearly made out, which Rabbi Ben Joseph affirmeth he found in an Egyptian book of Abraham Sapiens Perizol, that Aristotle acknowledged all that was written in the law of Moses, and became at last a proselyte, it would also make improbable this received way of his death.*[7]

Again, beside the negative of authority, it is also deniable by reason; nor will it be easy to obtrude such desperate attempts upon Aristotle, from unsatisfaction of reason, who so often acknowledged the imbecility thereof. Who in matters of difficulty, and such which were not without abstrusities, conceived it sufficient to deliver conjecturalities. And surely he that could sometimes sit down with high improbabilities, that could content himself, and think to satisfy others, that the variegation of birds was from their living in the sun, or erection made by delibration of the testicles; would not have been dejected unto death with this. He that was so well acquainted with ἢ ὅτι and πότερον, *utrum* and *an quia*, as we observe in the queries of his problems, with ἴσως and ἐπὶ τὸ πολὺ, *fortasse* and *plerumque*, as is

---

* *Licetus de Quæsitis. Epist.*

[6] *Another, &c.*] The most probable account.
[7] *And if that, &c.*] First added in the 2nd edition.

observable through all his works, had certainly rested with probabilities, and glancing conjectures in this. Nor would his resolutions have ever run into that mortal *antanaclasis*, and desperate piece of rhetorick, to be comprised in that he could not comprehend. Nor is it indeed to be made out, that he ever endeavoured the particular of Euripus, or so much as to resolve the ebb and flow of the sea. For, as Vicomercatus and others observe, he hath made no mention hereof in his works, although the occasion present itself in his *Meteors*, wherein he disputeth the affections of the sea; nor yet in his *Problems*, although in the twenty-third section there be no less than one and forty queries of the sea. Some mention there is indeed in a work of the propriety of elements, ascribed unto Aristotle:* which notwithstanding is not reputed genuine, and was perhaps the same whence this was urged by Plutarch.

Lastly, the thing itself whereon the opinion dependeth, that is, the variety of the flux and the reflux of Euripus, or whether the same do ebb and flow seven times a day, is not incontrovertible. For though Pomponius Mela, and after him Solinus and Pliny have affirmed it, yet I observe Thucydides, who speaketh often of Euboea, hath omitted it. Pausanias, an ancient writer, who hath left an exact description of Greece, and in as particular a way as Leandro of Italy, or Camden of Great Britain, describing not only the country towns and rivers, but hills, springs, and houses, hath left no mention hereof. Æschines in Ctesiphon only alludeth unto it; and Strabo, that accurate geographer, speaks warily of it, that is, ὡς φασὶ, and as men commonly reported. And so doth also Maginus, *Velocis ac varii fluctûs est mare, ubi quater in die, aut septies, ut alii dicunt, reciprocantur æstus*. Botero more plainly, *Il mar cresce e cala con un impeto mirabile quatra volte il di, ben che communimente si dica sette volte, &c.*—" this sea with wondrous impetuosity ebbeth and floweth four times a day, although it be commonly said seven times; and generally opinioned, that Aristotle despairing of the reason, drowned himself therein." In which description by four times a day, it exceeds not in number the motion of other seas, taking the words properly, that is,

* *De placitis Philosophorum.*

twice ebbing and twice flowing in four and twenty hours. And is no more than what Thomaso Porrchachi affirmeth in his description of famous islands, that twice a day it hath such an impetuous flood, as is not without wonder. Livy speaks more particularly, *Haud facile infestior classi statio est et fretum ipsum Euripi, non septies die (sicut fama fert) temporibus certis reciprocat, sed temerè in modum venti, nunc hunc nunc illuc verso mari, velut monte præcipiti devolutus torrens rapitur :*—" there is hardly a worse harbour, the fret or channel of Euripus not certainly ebbing or flowing seven times a day, according to common report: but being uncertainly, and in the manner of a wind, carried hither and thither, is whirled away as a torrent down a hill." But the experimental testimony of Gillius is most considerable of any; who having beheld the course thereof, and made enquiry of millers that dwelt upon its shore, received answer, that it ebbed and flowed four times a day, that is, every six hours, according to the law of the ocean; but that indeed sometimes it observed not that certain course. And this irregularity, though seldom happening, together with its unruly and tumultuous motion, might afford a beginning unto the common opinion. Thus may the expression in Ctesiphon be made out. And by this may Aristotle be interpreted, when in his *Problems* he seems to borrow a metaphor from Euripus; while in the five and twentieth section he enquireth, why in the upper parts of houses the air doth Euripize, that is, is whirled hither and thither.

A later and experimental testimony is to be found in the travels of Monsieur Duloir; who about twenty years ago, remained sometime at Negroponte, or old Chalcis, and also passed and repassed this Euripus; who thus expresseth himself: " I wonder much at the error concerning the flux and reflux of Euripus; and I assure you that opinion is false. I gave a boatman a crown, to set me in a convenient place, where for a whole day I might observe the same. It ebbeth and floweth by six hours, even as it doth at Venice, but the course thereof is vehement."[8]

Now that which gave life unto the assertion, might be his death at Chalcis, the chief city of Euboea, and seated upon

---

[k] *A later and experimental, &c.*] First added in 6th edition.

Euripus, where 'tis confessed by all he ended his days. That he emaciated and pined away in the too anxious enquiry of its reciprocations, although not drowned therein, as Rhodiginus relateth some conceived, was a half confession thereof not justifiable from antiquity. Surely the philosophy of flux and reflux was very imperfect of old among the Greeks and Latins; nor could they hold a sufficient theory thereof, who only observed the Mediterranean, which in some places hath no ebb, and not much in any part. Nor can we affirm our knowledge is at the height, who have now the theory of the ocean and narrow seas beside. While we refer it unto the moon, we give some satisfaction for the ocean, but no general salve for creeks and seas which know no flood; nor resolve why it flows three or four feet at Venice in the bottom of the gulph, yet scarce at all at Ancona, Durazzo, or Corcyra, which lie but by the way. And therefore old abstrusities have caused new inventions; and some from the hypotheses of Copernicus, or the diurnal and annual motion of the earth, endeavour to salve the flows and motions of these seas, illustrating the same by water in a bowl, that rising or falling to either side, according to the motion of the vessel; the conceit is ingenious, salves some doubts, and is discovered at large by Galileo.*⁹

But whether the received principle and undeniable action of the moon may not be still retained, although in some difference of application, is yet to be perpended; that is not by a simple operation upon the surface or superior parts, but excitation of the nitro-sulphureous spirits, and parts disposed to intumescency at the bottom; not by attenuation of the upper part of the sea, (whereby ships would draw more water at the flow than at the ebb,) but intergescencies caused first at the bottom, and carrying the upper part before them; subsiding and falling again, according to the motion of the moon from the meridian, and languor of the exciting cause: and therefore rivers and lakes who want these fermenting parts at the bottom, are not excited unto æstuations; and therefore some seas flow higher than others,

* *Rog. Bac. Doct. Cabeus Met.* 2.

⁹ *and is discovered at large by Galileo.*] And by the **Lord Bacon** rejected in his booke, *De Fluxu et Refluxu Maris.*—*Wr.*

according to the plenty of these spirits, in their submarine constitutions. And therefore also the periods of flux and reflux are various, nor their increase or decrease equal: according to the temper of the terreous parts at the bottom; which as they are more hardly or easily moved, do variously begin, continue, or end their intumescencies.

From the peculiar disposition of the earth at the bottom, wherein quick excitations are made, may arise those agars[9] and impetuous flows in some estuaries and rivers, as is observed about Trent and Humber in England; which may also have some effect in the boisterous tides of Euripus, not only from ebullitions at the bottom, but also from the sides and lateral parts, driving the streams from either side, which arise or fall according to the motion in those parts, and the intent or remiss operation of the first exciting causes, which maintain their activities above and below the horizon; even as they do in the bodies of plants and animals, and in the commotion of catarrhs.[1]

How therefore Aristotle died, what was his end, or upon what occasion, although it be not altogether assured, yet that his memory and worthy name shall live, no man will deny, nor grateful scholar doubt. And if according to the elogy of Solon, a man may be only said to be happy after he is dead, and ceaseth to be in the visible capacity of beatitude; or if according unto his own ethicks, sense is not essential unto felicity, but a man may be happy without the apprehension thereof; surely in that sense he is pyramidally happy; nor can he ever perish but in the Euripe of ignorance, nor till the torrent of barbarism overwhelmeth all.

A like conceit there passeth of Melisigenes, *alias* Homer, the father poet, that he pined away upon the riddle of the fishermen. But Herodotus, who wrote his life, hath cleared this point; delivering, that passing from Samos unto Athens, he went sick ashore upon the island Ios, where he died, and was solemnly interred upon the sea-side; and so decidingly concludeth, *Ex hac ægritudine extremum diem clausit Homerus in Io, non, ut arbitrantur aliqui, ænigmatis perplexitate enectus, sed morbo.*

[9] *agar.*] The tumultuous influx of the tide.
[1] *But whether the received principle, &c. From the peculiar, &c.*] These two paragraphs were first added in the 2nd edition.

CHAPTER XIV.

Of the Wish of Philoxenus to have the Neck of a Crane.

That relation of Aristotle, and conceit generally received, concerning Philoxenus, who wished the neck of a crane, that thereby he might take more pleasure in his meat, although it pass without exception, upon enquiry I find not only doubtful in the story, but absurd in the desire or reason alleged for it.[2] For though his wish were such as is delivered, yet had it not perhaps that end to delight his gust in eating, but rather to obtain advantage thereby in singing, as is declared by Mirandula. Aristotle, saith he, in his *Ethicks* and *Problems*, accuseth Philoxenus of sensuality, for the greater pleasure of gust desiring the neck of a crane, which desire of his (assenting unto Aristotle), I have formerly condemned. But since I perceive that Aristotle for his accusation hath been accused by divers writers;—for Philoxenus was an excellent musician, and desired the neck of a crane, not for any pleasure at meat, but fancying thereby an advantage in singing or warbling, and dividing the notes in music:—and many writers there are which mention a musician of that name; as Plutarch in his book against *Usury*, and Aristotle himself, in the eighth of his *Politicks*, speaks of one Philoxenus, a musician, that went off from the Dorick dithyrambics unto the Phrygian harmony.

Again, be the story true or false, rightly applied or not, the intention is not reasonable, and that perhaps neither one way nor the other. For if we rightly consider the organ of

---

[2] *That relation, &c.*] Our author's observations on this absurd story are quoted by Dr. John Bulwer, in his *Anthropometamorphosis*, &c. p. 276.

Ross goes into the history of Philoxenus at great length, and adheres, as usual, most tenaciously to the legend. He contends, and with some reason, that the *absurdity* of the wish, if granted, were no argument against its having been expressed, seeing that many have entertained wishes far more so. But he even asserts its reasonableness, "that there is much pleasure in deglutition of sweet meats and drinks, is plain by the practice of those who, to supply the want of long necks, used to suck their drink out of long small cranes, or quills, or glasses with long narrow snouts, &c. &c.!!"

taste, we shall find the length of the neck to conduce but little unto it; for the tongue being the instrument of taste, and the tip thereof the most exact distinguisher, it will not advantage the gust to have the neck extended; wherein the gullet and conveying parts are only seated, which partake not of the nerves of gustation, or appertaining unto sapor, but receive them only from the sixth pair; whereas the nerves of taste descend from the third and fourth propagations, and so diffuse themselves into the tongue; and therefore cranes, herons, and swans, have no advantage in taste beyond hawks, kites, and others of shorter necks.

Nor, if we consider it, had nature respect unto the taste in the different contrivance of necks, but rather unto the parts contained, the composure of the rest of the body, and the manner whereby they feed. Thus animals of long legs have generally long necks, that is, for the conveniency of feeding, as having a necessity to apply their mouths unto the earth. So have horses, camels, dromedaries, long necks, and all tall animals, except the elephant, who in defect thereof is furnished with a trunk, without which he could not attain the ground. So have cranes, herons, storks, and shovelards long necks; and so even in man, whose figure is erect, the length of the neck followeth the proportion of other parts; and such as have round faces or broad chests and shoulders, have very seldom long necks. For the length of the face twice exceedeth that of the neck, and the space between the throat-pit and the navel, is equal unto the circumference thereof. Again, animals are framed with long necks, according unto the course of their life or feeding; so many with short legs have long necks, because they feed in the water, as swans, geese, pelicans, and other fin-footed animals.[3] But hawks and birds of prey have short necks and trussed legs; for that which is long is weak and flexible, and a shorter figure is best accommodated unto that intention. Lastly, the necks of animals do vary, according to the parts that are contained in them, which are the weazand and the gullet. Such as have no weazand and breathe not, have

---

[3] *fin-footed animals.*] Wee usually call them lether-footed,* but this terme suites with the use more significantlye.— *Wr.*

* Web-footed rather.

scarce any neck, as most sorts of fishes; and some none at all, as all sorts of pectinals, soles, thornback, flounders, and all crustaceous animals, as crevises,[4] crabs, and lobsters.

All which considered, the wish of Philoxenus will hardly consist with reason. More excusable had it been to have wished himself an ape,[5] which if common conceit speak true, is exacter in taste than any. Rather some kind of granivorous bird than a crane, for in this sense they are so exquisite, that upon the first peck of their bill, they can distinguish the qualities of hard bodies, which the sense of man discerns not without mastication. Rather some ruminating animal, that he might have eat his meat twice over; or rather, as Theophilus observed in Athenæus, his desire had been more reasonable, had he wished himself an elephant or a horse; for in these animals the appetite is more vehement, and they receive their viands in large and plenteous manner. And this indeed had been more suitable, if this were the same Philoxenus whereof Plutarch speaketh, who was so uncivilly greedy, that, to engross the mess,[6] he would preventively deliver his nostrils in the dish.[7]

---

[4] *crevises.*] Now called *cray-fish.*

[5] *an ape.*] I thinke an ape is more exacte in the smel then in the taste: for he never tastes that which hee first smels not too. And how pleasant soever any food seeme to us, yf itt displease his smel, he throws it away with a kind of indignation.—*Wr.*

[6] *to engross the mess.*] I was assured by a friend that the following somewhat similar exploit was performed in a commercial traveller's room at ——. A dish of green peas was served very early in the season. One of the party, who preferred high-seasoned peas to most other vegetables, and himself to everybody besides, took an early opportunity of offering his services to help the peas, but he began by peppering them so unmercifully, that it was not very probable they would suit any other palate than his own. His neighbour, perceiving his own chance thus demolished, expostulated; and was told in reply of the virtues of *pepper*, as the only thing to make green peas wholesome. He instantly drew forth his snuff-box, and dextrously scattered its contents over the dish, as the most summary means which occurred to him of defeating such palpable selfishness and gluttony, observing drily that he thought snuff an excellent addition to the pepper.

[7] *dish.*] There have been some whose slovenleyeness and greedines have æqualed his, by throwing a candles end into a messe of creame. But, more ingenious, frame a peece of aple like a candle, and therein stick a clove to deceave others of their deyntyes, in fine eating the counterfet candle.—*Wr.*

As for the musical advantage, although it seem more reasonable, yet do we not observe that cranes and birds of long necks have any musical, but harsh and clangous throats. But birds that are canorous, and whose notes we most commend, are of little throats and short necks, as nightingales, finches, linnets, Canary birds, and larks. And truly, although the weazand, throttle, and tongue be the instruments of voice, and by their agitations do chiefly concur unto these delightful modulations, yet cannot we distinctly and peculiarly assign the cause unto any particular formation: and I perceive the best thereof, the nightingale, hath some disadvantage in the tongue, which is not acuminate[8] and pointed as the rest, but seemeth as it were cut off, which perhaps might give the hint unto the fable of Philomela, and the cutting off her tongue by Tereus.

CHAPTER XV.

Of the Lake Asphaltites.

Concerning the Lake Asphaltites, the Lake of Sodom, or the Dead Sea, that heavy bodies cast therein sink not, but by reason of a salt and bituminous thickness in the water float and swim above, narrations already made are of that variety, we can hardly from thence deduce a satisfactory determination, and that not only in the story itself, but in the cause alleged. As for the story, men deliver it variously.[9]

Counterfeit candles' ends are now made of peppermint, which are admirable imitations of the attractive originals, and would have perfectly supplied the occasion related by the Dean.

[8] *acuminate.*] Yf the acuminate did any thinge to the songe or speech of birds, how comes itt that the blunt toung in the parat and the gaye [jay?] speake best, and in the bulfinch expresses the most excellent whistle.—*Wr.*

[9] *As for the story itself, &c.*] It is to be reckoned among the many strange and incredible stories, which both ancients and moderns have told respecting this lake. Dr. Pococke swam in it for nearly a quarter of an hour, and felt no inconvenience. He found the water very clear, and to contain no substances besides salt and alum. The fact is, that its waters are very salt, and therefore bodies float readily in it; and probably on that account few fish can live in it. Yet the monks of St. Saba assured Dr. Shaw that they had seen fish caught in the lake. —See *Dr. Adam Clarke's note in lo*.

Some I fear too largely, as Pliny, who affirmeth that bricks will swim therein. Mandevil goeth further, that iron swimmeth, and feathers sink. Munster in his *Cosmography* hath another relation, although perhaps derived from the poem of Tertullian, that a candle burning swimmeth, but if extinguished sinketh.[1] Some more moderately, as Josephus, and many others, affirming that only living bodies float, nor peremptorily averring they cannot sink, but that indeed they do not easily descend. Most traditionally, as Galen, Pliny, Solinus, and Strabo, who seems to mistake the Lake Serbonis for it. Few experimentally, most contenting themselves in the experiment of Vespasian, by whose command some captives bound were cast therein, and found to float as though they could have swimmed. Divers contradictorily, or contrarily, quite overthrowing the point.[2] Aristotle, in the second of his *Meteors*, speaks lightly thereof, ὥσπερ μυθολογοῦσι, which word is variously rendered, by some as a fabulous account, by some as a common talk. Biddulphus* divideth the common accounts of Judea into three parts; the one, saith he, are apparent truths, the second apparent falsehoods, the third are dubious or between both, in which form he ranketh the relation of this lake. But Andrew Thevet, in his *Cosmography*, doth ocularly overthrow it, for he affirmeth he saw an ass with his saddle cast therein and drowned. Now of these relations so different or contrary unto each other, the second is most moderate and safest to be embraced, which saith that living bodies swim therein, that is, they do not easily sink, and this, until exact experiment further determine, may be allowed as best consistent with this quality, and the reasons alleged for it.

As for the cause of this effect, common opinion conceives it to be the salt and bituminous thickness of the water. This indeed is probable, and may be admitted as far as the second opinion concedeth. For certain it is that salt water

---

* *Biddulphi Itinerarium, Anglicè.*

[1] *sinketh.*] Soe it will doe in anye water, if kept upright.—*Wr.*

[2] *divers contradictorily.*] This diversity may proceed from the diverse experiments that have been made on severall sides of the lake, which have not all the like effecte: in some partes it beares that which in another part will sinke, as hath been experimented by some late travelers.—*Wr.*

will support a greater burden than fresh; and we see an egg will descend in fresh water, which will swim in brine. But that iron should float therein, from this cause, is hardly granted; for heavy bodies will only swim in that liquor, wherein the weight of their bulk exceedeth not the weight of so much water as it occupieth or taketh up. But surely no water is heavy enough to answer the ponderosity of iron, and therefore that metal will sink in any kind thereof, and it was a perfect miracle which was wrought this way by Elisha. Thus we perceive that bodies do swim or sink in different liquors, according unto the tenuity or gravity of those liquors which are to support them. So salt water beareth that weight which will sink in vinegar; vinegar that which will fall in fresh water; fresh water that which will sink in spirits of wine; and that will swim in spirits of wine which will sink in clear oil; as we made experiment in globes of wax pierced with light sticks to support them. So that although it be conceived a hard matter to sink in oil, I believe a man should find it very difficult, and next to flying to swim therein. And thus will gold sink in quicksilver, wherein iron and other metals swim; for the bulk of gold is only heavier than that space of quicksilver which it containeth; and thus also in a solution of one ounce of quicksilver in two of *aqua fortis*, the liquor will bear amber, horn, and the softer kinds of stones, as we have made trial in each.

But a private opinion there is which crosseth the common conceit, maintained by some of late, and alleged of old by Strabo, that the floating of bodies in this lake proceeds not from the thickness of water, but a bituminous ebullition from the bottom, whereby it wafts up bodies injected, and suffereth them not easily to sink. The verity thereof would be enquired by ocular exploration, for this way is also probable. So we observe, it is hard to wade deep in baths where springs arise; and thus sometime are balls made to play upon a spouting stream.[3]

And therefore, until judicious and ocular experiment confirm or distinguish the assertion, that bodies do not sink

---

[3] *spouting stream.*] This confirmeth what I noted before, for, as in the hot bathe, so here, the bituminous ebullition is but in some places stronge, and in some places of the lake not at all.— *Wr.*

herein at all, we do not yet believe; that they do, not easily, or with more difficulty, descend in this than other water, we shall readily assent.[4] But to conclude an impossibility from a difficulty, or affirm whereas things not easily sink, they do not drown at all; beside the fallacy, is a frequent addition in human expression, and an amplification not unusual as well in opinions as relations; which oftentimes give indistinct accounts of proximities, and without restraint transcend from one another. Thus, forasmuch as the torrid zone was conceived exceeding hot, and of difficult habitation, the opinions of men so advanced its constitution, as to conceive the same unhabitable, and beyond possibility for man to live therein. Thus, because there are no wolves in England, nor have been observed for divers generations, common people have proceeded into opinions, and some wise men into affirmations, they will not live therein, although brought from other countries. Thus most men affirm, and few here will believe the contrary, that there be no spiders in Ireland; but we have beheld some in that country; and though but few, some cobwebs we behold in Irish wood in England. Thus the crocodile from an egg growing up to an exceeding magnitude, common conceit, and divers writers deliver, it hath no period of increase, but groweth as long as it liveth.[5] And thus in brief, in most apprehensions the conceits of men extend the

---

[4] *readily assent.*] And hee should adde, in some places itt beares, in others not.—*Wr*.

[5] *groweth, &c.*] This may bee true inoughe in regard of the vast bignes which is reported of some of them; and what should hinder? For in men and creatures also kept for food, their bulke growes still greater, though not their stature.—*Wr*.

It is probably true, of the whole order to which the crocodile belongs (*the saurians*), that they have "no period of increase"—they have no *metamorphosis*, like many other animals (and some in the same class), to place a limit, by its completion, to the further growth of the individual. Nor do they, like the vertebrate animals, arrive early at a maximum of growth, which is not afterwards increased, except in corpulency. Congeniality of climate makes a striking difference in magnitude, at the same age, between saurians of different countries (for example, the crocodile of the Nile is larger than any other of its species), but in all, growth, though *very* slow, is probably continued through life; unless, indeed, extreme old age may begin the end, by ending the vital power of growth, which seems probable, but would not impugn our author's position.

considerations of things, and dilate their notions beyond the propriety of their natures.

In the maps of the Dead Sea or Lake of Sodom, we meet with the destroyed cities, and in divers the city of Sodom placed about the middle, or far from the shore of it; but that it could not be far from Segor, which was seated under the mountains, near the side of the lake, seems inferrible from the sudden arrival of Lot, who coming from Sodom at daybreak, attained Segor at sun-rising; and therefore Sodom ought to be placed not many miles from it, and not in the middle of the lake, which is accounted about eighteen miles over; and so will leave about nine miles to be passed in too small a space of time.

CHAPTER XVI.

Of Divers other Relations, viz. :—Of the Woman that Conceived in a Bath ;—Of Crassus that never Laughed but once ;—That our Saviour never Laughed ;—Of Sergius the Second, or Bocca di Porco ;—That Tamerlane was a Scythian Shepherd.

THE relation of Averroes, and now common in every mouth, of the woman that conceived in a bath, by attracting the sperm or seminal effluxion of a man admitted to bathe in some vicinity unto her,[6] I have scarce faith to believe; and had I been of the jury, should have hardly thought I had found the father in the person that stood by her. 'Tis a new and unseconded way in history to fornicate at a distance, and much offendeth the rules of physick, which say, there is no generation without a joint emission, nor only a virtual, but corporal and carnal contaction. And although Aristotle and his adherents do cut off the one, who conceive no effectual ejaculation in women; yet in defence of the other they cannot be introduced. For if, as he believeth, the inordinate longitude of the organ, though in its proper recipient, may

[6] *by attracting, &c.*] No absurdity, which Browne undertakes to refute—though so gross as not to merit notice, appears too monstrous to find acceptance with Ross. He finds it "quite possible, even as the stomach attracteth meat and drink, though in some distance from it." The conceit respecting Lot is not suggested by the scriptural account, which only asserts that he did not recognise his daughters.

be a mean to inprolificate the seed; surely the distance of place, with the commixture of an aqueous body must prove an effectual impediment, and utterly prevent the success of a conception. And therefore that conceit concerning the daughters of Lot, that they were impregnated by their sleeping father, or conceived by seminal pollution received at distance from him, will hardly be admitted. And therefore what is related of devils, and the contrived delusions of spirits, that they steal the seminal emissions of men, and transmit them into their votaries in coition, is much to be suspected; and altogether to be denied, that there ensue conceptions thereupon; however husbanded by art, and the wisest menagery of that most subtile impostor. And therefore also that our magnified Merlin was thus begotten by the devil, is a groundless conception; and as vain to think from thence to give the reason of his prophetical spirit. For if a generation could succeed, yet should not the issue inherit the faculties of the devil, who is but an auxiliary, and no univocal actor; nor will his nature substantially concur to such productions.

And although it seems not impossible, that impregnation may succeed from seminal spirits, and vaporous irradiations, containing the active principle, without material and gross immissions; as it happeneth sometimes in imperforated persons, and rare conceptions of some much under puberty or fourteen. As may be also conjectured in the coition of some insects, wherein the female makes intrusion into the male; and from the continued ovation in hens, from one single tread of a cock, and little stock laid up near the vent, sufficient for durable prolification. And although also in human generation the gross and corpulent seminal body may return again, and the great business be acted by what it carrieth with it; yet will not the same suffice to support the story in question, wherein no corpulent immission is acknowledged; answerable unto the fable of Talmudists, in the story of Benzira, begotten in the same manner on the daughter of the prophet Jeremiah.[7]

2. The relation of Lucillius, and now become common concerning Crassus, the grandfather of Marcus the wealthy

---

[7] *And although, &c.*] This paragraph first added in 3rd edition.

Roman, that he never laughed but once in all his life, and that was at an ass eating thistles, is something strange. For, if an indifferent and unridiculous object could draw his habitual austereness unto a smile, it will be hard to believe he could with perpetuity resist the proper motives thereof. For the act of laughter, which is evidenced by a sweet contraction of the muscles of the face, and a pleasant agitation of the vocal organs, is not merely voluntary, or totally within the jurisdiction of ourselves, but, as it may be constrained by corporal contaction in any, and hath been enforced in some even in their death, so the new, unusual, or unexpected, jucundities which present themselves to any man in his life, at some time or other, will have activity enough to excitate the earthiest soul, and raise a smile from most composed tempers. Certainly the times were dull when these things happened, and the wits of those ages short of these of ours; when men could maintain such immutable faces, as to remain like statues under the flatteries of wit, and persist unalterable at all efforts of jocularity. The spirits in hell, and Pluto himself, whom Lucian makes to laugh at passages upon earth, will plainly condemn these Saturnines, and make ridiculous the magnified Heraclitus, who wept preposterously, and made a hell on earth; for rejecting the consolations of life, he passed his days in tears, and the uncomfortable attendments of hell.[8]

3. The same conceit[9] there passeth concerning our blessed Saviour, and is sometime urged as a high example of gravity. And this is opinioned, because in Holy Scripture it is recorded he sometimes wept, but never that he laughed. Which, howsoever granted, it will be hard to conceive how he passed his younger years and childhood without a smile, if as divinity affirmeth, for the assurance of his humanity

---

[8] *the uncomfortable, &c.*] Ross remarks with much reason on this observation, that "oftentimes there is hell in laughing, and a heaven in weeping:" and that "good men find not the uncomfortable attendments of hell in weeping, but rather the comfortable enjoyments of heaven."—*Arcana*, p. 176.

[9] *The same conceit, &c.*] Tis noe argument to say tis never read in Scripture that Christ laughed, therefore he did never laughe, but on the other side to affirme, that hee did laughe is therefore dangerous bycause unwarrantable and groundles.—*Wr.*

unto men, and the concealment of his divinity from the devil, he passed this age like other children, and so proceeded until he evidenced the same. And surely herein no danger there is to affirm the act or performance of that, whereof we acknowledge the power and essential property; and whereby indeed he most nearly convinced the doubt of his humanity.[1] Nor need we be afraid to ascribe that unto the incarnate Son, which sometimes is attributed unto the uncarnate Father; of whom it is said, "He that dwelleth in the heavens shall laugh the wicked to scorn." For a laugh there is of contempt or indignation, as well as of mirth and jocosity: and that our Saviour was not exempted from the ground hereof, that is, the passion of anger, regulated and rightly ordered by reason, the schools do not deny; and, besides the experience of the money-changers and dove-sellers in the temple, is testified by St. John, when he saith the speech of David was fulfilled in our Saviour.*

Now the alogy of this opinion consisteth in the illation; it being not reasonable to conclude from Scripture negatively in points which are not matters of faith, and pertaining unto salvation. And therefore, although in the description of the

* *Zelus domûs tuæ comedit me.*

[1] *humanity.*] The doubt of his humanity was convinced soe many other wayes (before his passion) as by his birth, his circumcision, his hunger at the fig-tree, his compassion and teares over his friend Lazarus, and those other instances here alleaged, that the propertye of risibilitye (which is indeed the usuall instance of the schooles) though it bee inseparable from the nature of man, and incommunicable to any other nature, yet itt does not infer the necessitye of the acte in every individuall subject or person of man; noe more then the power and propertye of numeration (whereof no other creature in the world is capable) can make every man an arithmetician. Itt is likewise recorded of Julius Saturninus, sonne to Philippus (Arabs) the emperor, that from his birth *nullo prorsus cujusquam commento ad ridendum moveri potuerit.*—*Wr.*

It is the characteristic description of our Redeemer that "he was a man of sorrows and acquainted with grief." Will it not be felt by every Christian, that *laughter* is utterly out of keeping with the dignity, the character, and office of him, who himself took our infirmities, and bare our sins: who spent a life in the endurance of the contradiction of sinners against himself,—and in the full and constant contemplation of that awful moment when he was to lay down that life for their sakes? The difficulty would have been to credit the contrary tradition, had it existed.

creation there be no mention of fire,[2] Christian philosophy did not think it reasonable presently to annihilate that element, or positively to decree there was no such thing at all.[3] Thus, whereas in the brief narration of Moses there is no record of wine before the flood, we cannot satisfactorily conclude that Noah[4] was the first that ever tasted thereof.* And thus, because the word brain is scarce mentioned once, but heart above a hundred times in Holy Scripture, physicians that dispute the principality of parts are not from hence induced to bereave the animal organ of its priority. Wherefore the Scriptures being serious, and commonly omitting such parergies, it will be unreasonable from hence to condemn all laughter, and from considerations inconsiderable to discipline a man out of his nature. For this is by rustical severity to banish all urbanity: whose harmless and confined condition, as it stands commended by morality, so is it consistent with religion, and doth not offend divinity.

4. The custom it is of Popes to change their name at their creation; and the author thereof is commonly said to be *Bocca di Porco*, or Swines-face; who therefore assumed the style of Sergius the 2nd, as being ashamed so foul a name should dishonour the chair of Peter; wherein notwithstanding, from Montacutius and others, I find there may be

* Only in the vulgar Latin, Judg. ix. 53.

[2] *fire.*] There is no mention of metals or fossiles; and yet wee know they were created then, or else they could not now bee.—*Wr.*

[3] *at all.*] Many things may perchance be past over in silence in Holy Scripture, which notwithstandinge are knowne to bee partes of the creation, and many things spoken to the vulgar capacity, which must be understood in a modified sense. But never any thinge soe spoken as might be convinced of falshood; soe that either God or Copernicus, speaking contradictions, cannot both speak truthe. And therefore, *sit Deus verus et omnis homo mendax*, that speakes contradictions to him.—*Wr.*

[4] *Noah.*] Noah was not the first that tasted of the grape: but itt is expresly sayd, Genes. ix. 21, that Noah was the first husbandman that planted a vineyard, and that first made wine, and therfore was the first that dranke of the wine; which does not only satisfactorily but necessarily oblige us to a beleefe that wine made by expression into a species of drinke was not knowne, and therfore not used in that new (dryed) world till Noah invented itt. Itt was then, as itt is now in the new westerne plantations, where they have the vine, and eate the grapes but do not drinke wine, bycause they never began to plant vineyardes till now of late.—*Wr.*

some mistake. For Massonius, who writ the lives of Popes, acknowledgeth he was not the first that changed his name in that see; nor as Platina affirmeth, have all his successors precisely continued that custom; for Adrian the sixth, and Marcellus the second, did still retain their baptismal denomination. Nor is it proved, or probable, that Sergius changed the name of Bocca di Porco, for this was his surname,[5] or gentilitious appellation; nor was it the custom to alter that with the other: but he commuted his Christian name Peter for Sergius, because he would seem to decline the name of Peter the second. A scruple I confess not thought considerable in other sees, whose originals and first patriarchs have been less disputed; nor yet perhaps of that reality as to prevail in points of the same nature. For the names of the apostles, patriarchs, and prophets have been assumed even to affectation. The name of Jesus[6] hath not been appropriated; but some in precedent ages have borne that name, and many since have not refused the Christian name of Emmanuel. Thus are there few names more frequent than Moses and Abraham among the Jews. The Turks without scruple affect the name of Mahomet, and with gladness receive so honourable cognomination.

And truly in human occurrences there ever have been many well directed intentions, whose rationalities will never bear a rigid examination, and though in some way they do commend their authors, and such as first began them, yet have they proved insufficient to perpetuate imitation in such as have succeeded them. Thus was it a worthy resolution of Godfrey, and most Christians have applauded it, that he refused to wear a crown of gold where his Saviour had worn one of thorns. Yet did not his successors durably inherit

[5] *surname.*] Itt might bee his sirename: but doubtles it was first a nicuame fastened on some of his progenitors.— *Wr.*

[6] *The name, &c.*] The name of Jesus was not the same, *per omnia*, in Joshua; and Jesu was never given to any before the angel brought itt from heaven. The names of patriarches and prophets have been imposed (not assumed) as memorials (to children) of imitation; and that of Emmanuel in a qualified sense onlye. But that never any Pope would bee stiled Peter the second, proceeds from a mysterye of policye; that they may rather seeme successors to his power, then to his name, which they therefore decline of purpose; that Christ's vicariate authoritye may seeme to descend not from personal succession, but immediately from [him] who first derived it on Peter.— *Wr.*

that scruple, but some were anointed, and solemnly accepted the diadem of regality. Thus Julius, Augustus, and Tiberius with great humility or popularity refused the name of Imperator, but their successors have challenged that title, and retained the same even in its titularity. And thus, to come nearer our subject, the humility of Gregory the Great would by no means admit the stile of universal bishop; but the ambition of Boniface made no scruple thereof, nor of more queasy resolutions have been their successors ever since.

5. That Tamerlane[7] was a Scythian shepherd, from Mr. Knollis and others, from Alhazen a learned Arabian who wrote his life, and was spectator of many of his exploits, we have reasons to deny. Not only from his birth,—for he was of the blood of the Tartarian emperors, whose father Og had for his possession the country of Sagathy, which was no slender territory, but comprehended all that tract wherein were contained Bactriana, Sogdiana, Margiana, and the nation of the Massagetes, whose capital city was Samarcand, a place, though now decayed, of great esteem and trade in former ages)—but from his regal inauguration, for it is said, that being about the age of fifteen, his old father resigned the kingdom and men of war unto him. And also from his education, for as the story speaks it, he was instructed in the Arabian learning, and afterwards exercised himself therein. Now Arabian learning was in a manner all the liberal sciences, especially the mathematicks, and natural philosophy; wherein, not many ages before him there flourished Avicenna, Averroes, Avenzoar, Geber, Almanzor, and Alhazen, cognominal unto him that wrote his history, whose chronology indeed, although it be obscure, yet in the opinion of his commentator, he was contemporary unto Avicenna, and hath left sixteen books of opticks, of great esteem with ages past, and textuary unto our days.

[7] *Tamerlane.*] His true Scythian name was Temur-Can, which all storyes corruptly and absurdlye call Tamberlane.—*Wr.*

From the best authorities it appears that the parentage here assigned to Timur Beg (Tamerlane) is erroneous. His father was Targuï, a chief of the tribe of Berlas, tributary to Jagatai, one of the sons of Jenghis- (or Chingis-) Khan. He was born at Sebz, a suburb of the city of Kesch. See *Biographie Universelle; Universal History; Lardner's Outlines of History.*

Now the ground of this mistake was surely that which the Turkish historian declareth. Some, saith he, of our historians will needs have Tamerlane to be the son of a shepherd. But this they have said, not knowing at all the custom of their country; wherein the principal revenues of the king and nobles consisteth in cattle : who, despising gold and silver, abound in all sorts thereof. And this was the occasion that some men call them shepherds, and also affirm this prince descended from them. Now, if it be reasonable, that great men whose possessions are chiefly in cattle should bear the name of shepherds, and fall upon so low denominations, then may we say that Abraham was a shepherd, although too powerful for four kings ; that Job was of that condition, who beside camels and oxen had seven thousand sheep,[8] and yet is said to be the greatest man in the east. Thus was Mesha, king of Moab, a shepherd, who annually paid unto the crown of Israel, an hundred thousand lambs, and as many rams. Surely it is no dishonourable course of life which Moses and Jacob have made exemplary : 'tis a profession supported upon the natural way of acquisition, and though contemned by the Egyptians, much countenanced by the Hebrews, whose sacrifices required plenty of sheep and lambs. And certainly they were very numerous ; for, at the consecration of the temple, beside two-and-twenty thousand oxen, king Solomon sacrificed an hundred and twenty thousand sheep: and the same is observable from the daily provision of his house ; which was ten fat oxen,[9] twenty oxen out of the pastures, and a hundred sheep, beside roebuck, fallow deer, and fatted fowls. Wherein notwithstanding (if a punctual relation thereof do rightly inform us), the Grand Seignior doth exceed ; the daily provision of whose seraglio in the reign of Achmet, beside beeves, consumed[1] two hundred sheep, lambs and kids when they were in season

[8] *sheep.*] Sir Wm. Jorden, of Wiltes, in the plaines, aspired to come to the number of 20,000 : but with all his endeavour could never bring them beyond 18,000. He lived since 1630.— *Wr.*

[9] *oxen, &c.*] That is, in the yeare, of beeves, 10,950, of sheep, 36,500. — *Wr.*

[1] *consumed, &c.*] Of sheep, lambs, kids, 109,500. And yet this cann raise noe greate wonder considering how manye mouthes were dayly fed at Solomon's tables, his concubines, his officers, his guards, and all sorts of inferior attendants on him and them: of which kinles

one hundred, calves ten, geese fifty, hens two hundred, chickens one hundred, pigeons a hundred pair.

And therefore this mistake, concerning the noble Tamerlane, was like that concerning Demosthenes, who is said to be the son of a blacksmith, according to common conceit, and that handsome expression of Juvenal;

> Quem pater ardentis massa fuligine lippus,
> A carbone et forcipibus, gladiosque parente
> Incude, et luteo Vulcano, et Rhetora misit.

Thus Englished by Sir Robert Stapleton:

> Whom's Father with the smoky forge half blind,
> From blows on sooty Vulcan's anvil spent
> In ham'ring swords, to study Rhet'rick sent.

But Plutarch, who writ his life, hath cleared this conceit, plainly affirming he was most nobly descended, and that this report was raised, because his father had many slaves that wrought smith's work, and brought the profit unto him.[2]

CHAPTER XVII.

Of some others, viz.,—of the poverty of Belisarius; of Fluetus Decumanus, or the tenth wave; of Parisatis that poisoned Statira by one side of a knife; of the Woman fed with poison that should have poisoned Alexander; of the Wandering Jew; of Pope Joan; of Friar Bacon's brazen head that spoke; of Epicurus.

WE are sad when we read the story of Belisarius, that worthy chieftain of Justinian; who, after his victories over Vandals, Goths, Persians, and his trophies in three parts of the world, had at last his eyes put out by the emperor, and was reduced to that distress, that he begged relief on the highway, in that uncomfortable petition, *date obolum Belisario*.[3] And this we do not only hear in discourses, orations,

the Grand Signeur mainteyns greater multitudes daylye in the Seraglio.—*Wr.*

[2] *And this mistake, &c.*] This paragraph was first added in the 2nd edition, except the translation, which was added in the 6th edition.

[3] *We are sad, &c.*] Lord Mahon, in his life of Belisarius, adopts this traditional account of him, as the most likely to be true: and gives at the close of the work his reasons at large.

and themes, but find it also in the leaves of Petrus Crinitus, Volaterranus, and other worthy writers.

But, what may somewhat consolate all men that honour virtue, we do not discover the latter scene of his misery in authors of antiquity, or such as have expressly delivered the stories of those times. For, Suidas is silent herein, Cedrenus and Zonaras, two grave and punctual authors, delivering only the confiscation of his goods, omit the history of his mendication. Paulus Diaconus goeth farther, not only passing over this act, but affirming his goods and dignities were restored. Agathius, who lived at the same time, declared he suffered much from the envy of the court; but that he descended thus deep into affliction, is not to be gathered from his pen. The same is also omitted by Procopius,* a contemporary and professed enemy unto Justinian and Belisarius, who hath left an opprobrious book against them both.

And in this opinion and hopes we are not single, but Andreas Aniatus the civilian in his *Parerga*, and Franciscus de Corduba in his *Didascalia*, have both declaratorily confirmed the same, which is also agreable unto the judgment of Nicolaus Alemannus, in his notes upon that bitter history of Procopius. Certainly sad tragical stories are seldom drawn within the circle of their verities; but as their relators do either intend the hatred or pity of the persons, so are they set forth with additional amplifications. Thus have some suspected it hath happened unto the story of Œdipus: and thus do we conceive it hath fared with that of Judas, who, having sinned above aggravation, and committed one villany which cannot be exasperated by all other, is also charged with the murder of his reputed brother, parricide of his father, and incest with his own mother,[4] as

---

* Ἀνέκδοτα, or *Arcana Historia*.

---

[4] *is also charged, &c.*] Surely yf these had been true, St. John, who cals him a theefe in plaine termes, would never have concealed such unparalleled villanyes. They could not bee don after his treason, the halter followed that soe closelye; and had they been don before, neither could he have escaped the laws of Judæa, most severe against such hideous crimes; nor would the Sonne of God have endured the scandal of such a knowne miscreant, much lesse have chosen him among the twelve apostles. Judas deserved as much detestation as his **unparaleld**

Florilegus or Matthew of Westminster hath at large related. And thus hath it perhaps befallen the noble Belisarius; who, upon instigation of the Empress, having contrived the exile, and very hardly treated Pope Serverius, Latin pens, as a judgment of God upon this fact, have set forth his future sufferings; and, omitting nothing of amplification, they have also delivered this; which, notwithstanding Johannes the Greek makes doubtful, as may appear from his *Iambicks* in Baronius, and might be a mistake or misapplication, translating the affliction of one man upon another, for the same befell unto Johannes Cappadox,* contemporary unto Belisarius, and in great favour with Justinian; who being afterwards banished into Egypt, was fain to beg relief on the highway.[5]

2. That *fluctus decumanus*,[6] or the tenth wave is greater and more dangerous than any other, some no doubt will be

* *Procop. Bell, Persic,* 1. Ἄρτον ἢ ὀβολὸν αἰτεῖσθαι.

and matchless crimes could any way deserve. But noe cause of such detestation could be soe just, as to produce such prodigious fictions in the writings of Christians: whome the recorded example of the Archangel Michael hath taught, not to rayle against, much less to belye the Divel himselfe.—*Wr.*

[5] *and might be a mistake, &c.*] First added in 2nd edition.

[6] *Fluctus decumanus, &c.*] Ross says that our author "troubles himself to no purpose in refuting the greatness of the tenth wave and tenth egg: for the tenth of anything was not counted the greatest, but the greatest of anything was called the tenth, because that is the first perfect number; therefore anything that was greater than another was called *decumanus.* So *porta decumana, limes decumanus, decumana pyra,* and *pomum decumanum* as well as *ovum decumanum.*"—*Arc.* p. 178.

Mr. Forbes, in his *Oriental Memoirs,* describing the effect of the monsoon upon the ocean, says, "every *ninth* wave is observed to be more tremendous than the rest, and threatens to overwhelm the settlement of Anjengo."

The following passage occurs in *Dr. Henderson's Iceland,* vol. ii. p. 109: "Owing to a heavy swell from the ocean, we found great difficulty in landing, and were obliged to await the alternation of the waves in the following order:—first, three heavy surges broke with a tremendous dash upon the rocks; these were followed by six smaller ones, which just afforded us time to land; after which the three large ones broke again, and so on in regular succession."

"The typhon is a strong swift wind, that blows from all points, and is frequent in the Indian seas; raising them, with its strong whirling about, to a great height, every *tenth* wave rising above the rest."—*Loss of the ship Fanny.*

offended if we deny; and hereby we shall seem to contradict antiquity; for, answerable unto the literal and common acception, the same is averred by many writers, and plainly described by Ovid.

> Qui venit hic fluctus, fluctus supereminet omnes,
> Posterior nono est, undecimoque prior.

Which notwithstanding is evidently false; nor can it be made out by observation either upon the shore or the ocean, as we have with diligence explored both. And surely in vain we expect a regularity in the waves of the sea, or in the particular motions thereof, as we may in its general reciprocations, whose causes are constant, and effects therefore correspondent. Whereas its fluctuations are but motions subservient; which winds, storms, shores, shelves, and every interjacency irregulates. With semblable reason we might expect a regularity in the winds; whereof though some be statary, some anniversary, and the rest do tend to determine points of heaven, yet do the blasts and undulary breaths thereof maintain no certainty in their course, nor are they numerally feared by navigators.

Of affinity hereto is that conceit of *ovum decumanum*; so called, because the tenth egg is bigger than any other, according unto the reason alleged by Festus, *decumana ova dicuntur, quia ovum decimum majus nascitur*. For the honour we bear unto the clergy, we cannot but wish this true: but herein will be found no more of verity than in the other; and surely few will assent hereto without an implicit credulity, or Pythagorical submission unto every conception of number.

For surely the conceit is numeral, and, though in the sense apprehended, relateth unto the number of ten, as Franciscus Sylvius hath most probably declared. For, whereas amongst simple numbers or digits, the number of ten is the greatest: therefore whatsoever was the greatest in every kind, might in some sense be named from this number. Now, because also that which was the greatest, was metaphorically by some at first called *decumanus*, therefore whatsoever passed under this name, was literally conceived by others to respect and make good this number.

The conceit is also Latin; for the Greeks, to express the

greatest wave, do use the number of three, that is, the word τρικυμία, which is a concurrence of three waves in one, whence arose the proverb, τρικυμία κακῶν, or a trifluctuation of evils, which Erasmus doth render, *malorum fluctus decumanus*. And thus although the terms be very different, yet are they made to signify the self-same thing: the number of ten to explain the number of three, and the single number of one wave the collective concurrence of more.

3. The poison of Parysatis,[7] reported from Ctesias by Plutarch in the life of Artaxerxes (whereby, anointing a knife on the one side, and therewith dividing a bird, with the one half she poisoned Statira, and safely fed herself on the other), was certainly a very subtle one, and such as our ignorance is well content it knows not. But surely we had discovered a poison that would not endure Pandora's box, could we be satisfied in that which for its coldness nothing could contain but an ass's hoof, and wherewith some report that Alexander the Great was poisoned. Had men derived so strange an effect from some occult or hidden qualities, they might have silenced contradiction; but ascribing it unto the manifest and open qualities of cold, they must pardon our belief; who perceive the coldest and most Stygian waters may be included in glasses; and by Aristotle, who saith that glass is the perfectest work of art, we understand they were not then to be invented.

And though it be said that poison will break a Venice glass,[8] yet have we not met with any of that nature. Were there a truth herein, it were the best preservative for princes and persons exalted unto such fears; and surely far better than divers now in use. And though the best of China dishes, and such as the emperor doth use, be thought by some of infallible virtue unto this effect, yet will they not, I fear, be able to elude the mischief of such intentions. And though also it be true, that God made all things double, and that if we look upon the works of the Most

---

[7] *The poison of Parysatis.*] This is treated as fabulous by Paris and Fonblanque, in the 20th vol. of whose *Medical Jurisprudence*, p. 131, &c. will be found a long article on poisons.

[8] *poison will break a Venice glass.*] Such is the venom of some spiders that they will crack a Venice glass, *as I have seen;* and Scaliger doth witness the same—however the doctor denies it.—*Ross, Arc.* 146

High, there are two and two, one against another; that one contrary hath another, and poison is not without a poison unto itself; yet hath the curse so far prevailed, or else our industry defected, that poisons are better known than their antidotes, and some thereof do scarce admit of any. And lastly, although unto every poison men have delivered many antidotes, and in every one is promised an equality unto its adversary, yet do we often find they fail in their effects: *moly* will not resist a weaker cup than that of Circe; a man may be poisoned in a Lemnian dish; without the miracle of John, there is no confidence in the earth of Paul;* and if it be meant that no poison could work upon him, we doubt the story, and expect no such success from the diet of Mithridates.

A story there passeth of an Indian king, that sent unto Alexander a fair woman, fed with aconites and other poisons, with this intent, either by converse or copulation complexionally to destroy him. For my part, although the design were true, I should have doubted the success.[9] For, though it be possible that poisons may meet with tempers whereto they may become aliments, and we observe from fowls that feed on fishes, and others fed with garlick and onions, that simple aliments are not always concocted beyond their vegetable qualities; and therefore that even after carnal conversion, poisons may yet retain some portion of their natures; yet are they so refracted, cicurated,[1] and subdued, as not to make good their first and destructive malignities. And therefore [to] the stork that eateth snakes, and the stare that feedeth upon hemlock, [these] though no commendable aliments, are not destructive

* *Terra Melitca.*

[9] *success.*] Hee that remembers how the Portuguez mixing with the women in the eastern islands founde such a hot overmatching complexion in them, that as the son puts out a candle, soe itt quentcht their hot luste with the cold gripes of deathe; may easilye conceive, without an instance, what a quick effect such venemous spirits make by a contagious transfusion. Nor is there the same danger in eatinge of a duck that feeds on a toade, as in the loathsome copulation with those bodyes, whose touch is formidable as the fome of a mad dog, the touch whereof has been found as deadly to some, as the wound of his teeth to others.—*Wr.*

[1] *cicurated.*] Tamed:—a *Brownism.*

poisons.* For, animals that can innoxiously digest these poisons, become antidotal unto the poison digested. And therefore, whether their breath be attracted, or their flesh ingested, the poisonous relicks go still along with their antidote; whose society will not permit their malice to be destructive. And therefore also, animals that are not mischieved by poisons which destroy us, may be drawn into antidote against them; the blood or flesh of storks against the venom of serpents, the quail against hellebore, and the diet of starlings against the draught of Socrates.[2] Upon like grounds are some parts of animals alexipharmical unto others; and some veins of the earth, and also whole regions,[3] not only destroy the life of venomous creatures, but also prevent their productions. For though perhaps they contain the seminals of spiders and scorpions, and such as in other earths by suscitation[4] of the sun may arise unto animation; yet lying under command of their antidote, without hope of emergency they are poisoned in their matrix by powers easily hindering the advance of their originals, whose confirmed forms they are able to destroy.

5. The story of the wandering Jew is very strange, and will hardly obtain belief; yet is there a formal account thereof set down by Matthew Paris, from the report of an Armenian bishop,[5] who came into this kingdom about four

* [to] [these] these words seem indispensable to complete the sense evidently intended.

[2] *Socrates.*] That is, henbane.—*Wr.*
[3] *whole regions.*] As Ireland and Crete neither breede nor brooke any venemous creature, which was a providence of God, considering that noe creature can be worse than the natives themselves.—*Wr.*
Is this remark perfectly in keeping with the character of a Christian minister?
[4] *suscitation.*] Excitement.
[5] *Armenian bishop.*] And that reporte of a wandering bishop is the ground of this absurd figment: for what's become of him ever since that time? But 'tis noe wonder to finde a wandring Jew in all partes of the world; for what are all the nation but wanderers? Inmates to the world, and strangers noe where soe much as in their owne countrye.—*Wr.*

"This fable of the wandering Jew, once almost generally believed, probably suggested the fabrication of the tale of the wandering Gentile in later times: they are both included in a work, entitled *News from*

hundred years ago, and had often entertained this wanderer at his table. That he was then alive, was first called Cartaphilus, was keeper of the judgment hall, whence thrusting out our Saviour with expostulation for his stay, was condemned to stay until his return;* was after baptized by Ananias, and by the name of Joseph; was thirty years old in the days of our Saviour, remembered the saints that arose with him, the making of the apostles' creed, and their several peregrinations. Surely were this true, he might be an happy arbitrator in many Christian controversies; but must unpardonably condemn the obstinacy of the Jews, who can contemn the rhetorick of such miracles, and blindly behold so living and lasting conversions.

6.[6] Clearer confirmations must be drawn for the history of Pope Joan, who succeeded Leo the Fourth, and preceded Benedict the Third, than many we yet discover. And since it is delivered with *aiunt* and *ferunt* by many; since the learned Leo Allatius hath discovered† that ancient copies of Martinus Polonus, who is chiefly urged for it, had not this story in it; since not only the stream of Latin historians have omitted it, but Photius the Patriarch, Metrophanes Smyrnæus, and the exasperated Greeks have made no mention of it, but conceded Benedict the Third to be successor unto Leo the Fourth; he wants not grounds that doubts it.[7]

* *Vade, quid moraris? ego vado, tu autem morare donec venio.*
† *Confutatio fabulæ de Joanna Papissa cum Nibusio.*

Holland; or a short relation of two witnesses, now living, of the suffering and passion of our Saviour Jesus Christ: the one being a Gentile, the other a Jew," &c. in High Dutch. Amsterdam, 1647, London, 1648, 4to. See *Huttman's Life of Christ,* p. 67. The *Spaniard,* who wrote one of the most amusing of critiques on *John Bull,* under the title of *Don Manuel Alvarez Espriella's Letters from England,* has enlivened his narrative of the wandering Jew with the following incident: "The Jew had awarded his preference to Spain above all the countries he had seen; as perhaps"—ingeniously remarks the soi-disant *Spanish* narrator—"a man would who had really seen all the world." But on being reminded that it was rather extraordinary that a Jew should prefer the country of the Inquisition, the ready rogue answered, with a smile and a shake of the head, "that it was long before Christianity when he last visited Spain, and that he should not return till long after it was all over."

[6].] The remainder of the chapter was first added in 2nd edition.
[7] *the history of Pope Joan.*] Not only the final catastrophe of this lady's career, as recorded in the well-known Latin line, "*Papa, pater*

Many things historical, which seem of clear concession, want not affirmations and negations, according to divided pens: as is notoriously observable in the story of Hildebrand or Gregory the Seventh, repugnantly delivered by the imperial and papal party. In such divided records, partiality hath much depraved history, wherein if the equity of the reader do not correct the iniquity of the writer, he will be much confounded with repugnancies, and often find, in the same person, Numa and Nero. In things of this nature moderation must intercede; and so charity may hope that Roman readers will construe many passages in Bolsec, Fayus, Schlusselberg, and Cochlæus.

7. Every ear is filled with the story of Friar Bacon, that made a brazen head to speak these words, *time is*.[b] Which though there want not the like relations, is surely too literally received, and was but a mystical fable concerning the philosopher's great work, wherein he eminently laboured: implying no more by the copper head, than the vessel wherein it was wrought, and by the words it spake, than the opportunity to be watched, about the *tempus ortus*, or birth of the mystical child, or philosophical king of Lullius; the rising of the *terra foliata* of *Arnoldus*, when the earth, sufficiently impregnated with the water, ascendeth white and splendent. Which not observed, the work is irrecoverably lost, according to that of Petrus Bonus: *Ibi est operis perfectio aut annihilatio; quoniam ipsâ die, immo horâ, oriuntur elementa simplicia depurata, quæ egent statim compositione, antequam volent ab igne.**

Now letting slip this critical opportunity, he missed the intended treasure, which had he obtained, he might have made out the tradition of making a brazen wall about England: that is, the most powerful defence, and strongest fortification which gold could have effected.

8. Who can but pity the virtuous Epicurus, who is commonly conceived to have placed his chief felicity in pleasure

* *Margarita pretiosa*.

patrum, peperit Papissa papillum,"—but even her very existence itself seems now to be universally rejected by the best authorities, Protestant as well as Catholic, as a fabrication from beginning to end.

[b] *a brazen head.*] This ridiculous story was originally imputed, not to Roger Bacon, but to Robert Grosseteste, bishop of Lincoln.

and sensual delights, and hath therefore left an infamous name behind him? How true, let them determine who read that he lived seventy years, and wrote more books than a philosopher but Chrysippus, and no less than three hundred without borrowing from any author: that he was contented with bread and water; and when he would dine with Jove, and pretend unto epulation, he desired no other addition than a piece of Cytheridian cheese: that shall consider the words of Seneca,⁹ *Non dico, quod plerique nostrorum, sectam Epicuri flagitiorum magistrum esse: sed illud dico, male audit, infamis est, et immerito:* or shall read his life, his epistles, his testament in *Laërtius*, who plainly names them calumnies, which are commonly said against them.

The ground hereof seems a misapprehension of his opinion, who placed his felicity not in the pleasures of the body, but the mind, and tranquillity thereof, obtained by wisdom and virtue, as is clearly determined in his epistle unto Menæceus. Now how this opinion was first traduced by the Stoicks, how it afterwards became a common belief, and so taken up by authors of all ages, by Cicero, Plutarch, Clemens, Ambrose, and others, the learned pen of Gassendus hath discovered.*¹

CHAPTER XVIII.

More briefly of some others, viz.: that the Army of Xerxes drank whole Rivers dry; that Hannibal eat through the Alps with Vinegar; of Archimedes, his burning the Ships of Marcellus; of the Fabii that were all slain; of the Death of Æschylus; of the Cities of Tarsus and Anchiale built in one day; of the great Ship Syracusia or Alexandria; of the Spartan Boys.

1. OTHER relations there are, and those in very good authors, which though we do not positively deny, yet have

* *De vita et moribus Epicuri.*

⁹ *That shall consider the words of Seneca.*] That is, "let them determine the words of Seneca," &c.

¹ *Who can but pity, &c.*] Ross is unmerciful in his reprobation of our author's defence of Epicurus. Yet some of those who were among the opponents of that philosopher's doctrines,—for example, Cicero, Plutarch, and Seneca, have awarded him, in reference to the particular charges here spoken of, the same acquittal which Browne has pronounced.

they not been unquestioned by some, and at least as improbable truths have been received by others. Unto some it hath seemed incredible what Herodotus reporteth of the great army of Xerxes, that drank whole rivers dry. And unto the author himself it appeared wondrous strange, that they exhausted not the provision of the country, rather than the waters thereof. For as he maketh the account, and Buddeus *de Asse* correcting their miscompute of Valla delivereth it, if every man of the army had had a *chenix* of corn a day, that is, a sextary and a half, or about two pints and a quarter, the army had daily expended ten hundred thousand and forty medimnas, or measures containing six bushels.[2] Which rightly considered, the Abderites had reason to bless the heavens, that Xerxes eat but one meal a day, and Pythius, his noble host, might with less charge and possible provision entertain both him and his army; and yet may all be salved, if we take it hyperbolically, as wise men receive that expression in Job, concerning behemoth or the elephant, " Behold, he drinketh up a river and hasteth not; he trusteth that he can draw up Jordan into his mouth."

2. That Hannibal ate or brake through the Alps with vinegar may be too grossly taken, and the author of his life annexed unto Plutarch, affirmeth only he used this artifice upon the tops of some of the highest mountains. For as it is vulgarly understood, that he cut a passage for his army through those mighty mountains, it may seem incredible, not only in the greatness of the effect, but the quantity of the efficient, and such as behold them may think an ocean of vinegar too little for that effect.[3] 'Twas a work indeed

[2] *bushels.*] But the wonder is not soe much how they could consume soe much corne, as where they could have it soe sodenly. But it seemes the learned author heere mistooke his accompte. For 1,000,000 quarts (allowing for every one in his army a quarte, and 16 quartes to a bushell), amount to noe more then 62,499 bushels, or 10,416 medimnas, which would not loade 1000 wagons, a small baggage for so great an army not to be wondered at.— *Wr.*

[3] *an ocean, &c.*] There needed not more than some few hogsheads of vinegar, for having hewed downe the woods of firr growing there, and with the huge piles thereof calcined the tops of some cliffes which stood in his waye; a small quantity of vinegar poured on the fired glowing rocks would make them cleave in sunder, as is manifest in calcined flints, which being often burned and as often quentcht in

rather to be expected from earthquakes and inundations, than any corrosive waters, and much condemneth the judgment of Xerxes, that wrought through Mount Athos with mattocks.

3. That Archimedes burnt the ships of Marcellus, with speculums of parabolical figures, at three furlongs, or as some will have it, at the distance of three miles, sounds hard unto reason and artificial experience, and therefore justly questioned by Kircherus, who after long enquiry could find but one made by Manfredus Septalius* that fired at fifteen paces. And therefore more probable it is that that the ships were nearer the shore or about some thirty paces, at which distance notwithstanding the effect was very great. But whereas men conceive the ships were more easily set on flame by reason of the pitch about them, it seemeth no advantage; since burning glasses will melt pitch or make it boil, not easily set it on fire.

4. The story of the Fabii, whereof three hundred and six marching against the Veientes were all slain, and one child alone to support the family remained, is surely not to be

* *De luce et umbra.*

vinegar, will in fine turne into an impalpable powder, as is truly experimented, and is dayly manifest in the lime kilnes.— *Wr.*

Dr. McKeever, in a paper in the 5th vol. of the *Annals of Philosophy, N. S.* discusses this question, and arrives at the conclusion that, in all probability, the expansive operation of the fire on the water which had been percolating through the pores and fissures of the rocks, occasioned the detachment of large portions of it by explosion, just as masses of rock are frequently detached from cliffs, and precipitated into adjoining valleys, by a similar physical cause. Dr. M. notices the annual disruption of icebergs in the Polar seas, on the return of summer, as a phenomenon bearing considerable analogy to the preceding. Mr. Brayley supposes that Hannibal might have used vinegar to dissolve partially a particular mass of limestone, which might impede his passage through some narrow pass. Dr. M. suggests that he might attribute to the vinegar and fire what the latter actually effected by its action on the water, and would have effected just as well without the vinegar. But perhaps after all the only vinegar employed might be pyroligneous acid, produced from the wood by its combination, without any intention on the part of Hannibal, though its presence would very naturally have been attributed to design by the ignorant spectators of his operations, which, on this theory, may be supposed to have been conducted on a full knowledge of the effects they would produce, in the explosive removal of the obstacles which obstructed his advance.

paralleled, nor easy to be conceived, except we can imagine that of three hundred and six, but one had children below the service of war, that the rest were all unmarried, or the wife but of one impregnated.[4]

5. The received story of Milo, who by daily lifting a calf, attained an ability to carry it being a bull, is a witty conceit, and handsomely sets forth the efficacy of assuefaction. But surely the account had been more reasonably placed upon some person not much exceeding in strength, and such a one as without the assistance of custom could never have performed that act, which some may presume that Milo, without precedent, artifice, or any other preparative, had strength enough to perform. For as relations declare, he was the most pancratical man of Greece, and as Galen reporteth, and Mercurialis in his *Gymnastics* representeth, he was able to persist erect upon an oiled plank, and not to be removed by the force or protrusion of three men. And if that be true which Athenæus reporteth, he was little beholding to custom for his ability; for in the Olympic games, for the space of a furlong, he carried an ox of four years[5] upon his shoulders, and the same day he carried it in his belly; for as it is there delivered, he eat it up himself. Surely he had been a proper guest at Grandgousier's feast, and might have matched his throat that eat six pilgrims for a salad.*

6. It much disadvantageth the panegyrick of Synesius,† and is no small disparagement unto baldness, if it be true what is related by Ælian concerning Æschylus, whose bald pate was mistaken for a rock, and so was brained by a tortoise

---

* *In Rabelais.*
† Who writ in the praise of baldness. An argument or instance against the motion of the earth.

[4 3.] This and the following paragraph, as well as § 12, were first added in 2nd edition.
[5 *an ox, &c.*] An ox of 4 years in Greece did not æqual one with us of 2; whereof having taken out the bowels and the heade and the hide, and the feete and all that which they call the offall, we may well thinke the four quarters, especially yf the greate bones were all taken out, could not weigh much above a 100lb. weight. Now the greater wonder is how he could eate soe much, then to carry itt. Itt is noe newes for men in our dayes to carry above 400 weight; but few men can eate 100 weight, excepting they had such a gyant-like bulke as hee had.—*Wr.*

which an eagle let fall upon it. Certainly it was a very great mistake in the perspicacy of that animal. Some men critically disposed, would from hence confute the opinion of Copernicus, never conceiving how the motion of the earth below, should not wave him from a knock perpendicularly directed from a body in the air above.

7. It crosseth the proverb, and Rome might well be built in a day, if that were true which is traditionally related by Strabo; that the great cities, Anchiale and Tarsus,[6] were built by Sardanapalus, both in one day, according to the inscription of his monument, *Sardanapalus Anacyndaraxis filius, Anchialem et Tarsum unâ die ædificavi, tu autem hospes, ede, lude, bibe, &c.* Which if strictly taken, that is, for the finishing thereof, and not only for the beginning; for an artificial or natural day, and not one of Daniel's weeks, that is, seven whole years; surely their hands were very heavy that wasted thirteen years in the private house of Solomon. It may be wondered how forty years were spent in the erection of the temple of Jerusalem, and no less than an hundred in that famous one of Ephesus. Certainly it was the greatest architecture of one day, since that great one of six; an art quite lost with our mechanics, a work not to be made out, but like the walls of Thebes, and such an artificer as Amphion.

8. It had been a sight only second unto the ark to have beheld the great Syracusia, or mighty ship of Hiero, described in Athenæus; and some have thought it a very large one, wherein were to be found ten stables for horses, eight towers, besides fish-ponds, gardens, tricliniums, and many fair rooms paved with agath and precious stones. But nothing was

---

[6] *Anchiale and Tarsus.*] A single fortress, as that of Babell, is called a city. Genes. xi. 4. In imitation whereof, built by Nimrod, the first Assyrian Monarch, itt is possible that Sardanapalus, the last Monarch, but withall the greatest in power, and purse, and people, might easily raise such a fortresse in a daye, having first brought all the materials in place, and if one, he might as well have built ten in several places. Now these cityes were about 4 hundred miles distant, Tarsus on the banke of Sinus, Issicus in Cilicia, and Anchiala on the banke of the Euxine Sea in Pontus, both border townes, dividing Natolia on the lesser Asia from the greater Asia, and were the 2 frontire townes of the Assyrian Monarchie, and were built for the ostentation of his vast spreading dominions, and both in a day raised, for ostentation of his power.—*Wr.*

impossible unto Archimedes, the learned contriver thereof; nor shall we question his removing the earth, when he finds an immoveable base to place his engine unto it.

9.[7] That the Pamphilian sea gave way unto Alexander, in his intended march toward Persia, many have been apt to credit, and Josephus is willing to believe, to countenance the passage of the Israelites through the Red Sea. But Strabo, who writ before him, delivereth another account; that the mountain climax, adjoining to the Pamphilian sea, leaves a narrow passage between the sea and it; which passage at an ebb and quiet sea all men take; but Alexander coming in the winter, and eagerly pursuing his affairs, would not wait for the reflux or return of the sea; and so was fain to pass with his army in the water, and march up to the navel in it.

10. The relation of Plutarch, of a youth of Sparta that suffered a fox, concealed under his robe, to tear out his bowels before he would, either by voice or countenance, betray his theft; and the other, of the Spartan lad, that with the same resolution suffered a coal from the altar to burn his arm; although defended by the author that writes his life, is I perceive mistrusted by men of judgment, and the author, with an *aiunt*, is made to salve himself. Assuredly it was a noble nation that could afford an hint to such inventions of patience, and upon whom, if not such verities, at least such verisimilities of fortitude were placed. Were the story true, they would have made the only disciples for Zeno and the Stoicks, and might perhaps have been persuaded to laugh in Phalaris his bull.

11. If any man shall content his belief with the speech of Balaam's ass, without a belief of that of Mahomet's camel, or Livy's ox; if any man makes a doubt of Giges' ring in Justinus, or conceives he must be a Jew that believes the sabbatical river[8] in Josephus; if any man will say he doth

---

[7] 9.] First added in the 6th edition.

[8] *the sabbatical river.*] A singular discrepancy exists on this point between the statement of Josephus and that of Pliny. The former (*De Bell. Jud.* lib. vii. c. 24) saying that the river flows on sabbath, but rests on every other day:—while Pliny (*Hist. Nat.* xxxi. § 18) relates that it flows most impetuously all the week, but is dry on the sabbath. All the Jewish rabbinical authorities adopt the latter as the fact, in opposition to Josephus, whose account is so singular, that several of his commentators have not hesitated to suppose a transposition to have

not apprehend how the tail of an African wether out-weigheth the body of a good calf, that is, an hundred pounds, according unto Leo Africanus,[9] or desires, before belief, to behold such a creature as is the ruck[1] in Paulus Venetus,—for my part I shall not be angry with his incredulity.

12. If any one shall receive, as stretched or fabulous accounts, what is delivered of Cocles, Scævola, and Curtius, the sphere of Archimedes, the story of the Amazons, the taking of the city of Babylon, not known to some therein in three days after, that the nation was deaf which dwelt at the fall of Nilus, the laughing and weeping humour of Heraclitus and Democritus, with many more, he shall not want some reason and the authority of Lancelotti.*

13. If any man doubt of the strange antiquities delivered by historians, as of the wonderful corpse of Antæus untombed

* *Farfalloni Historici.*

occurred in his text, producing the error in question. Our poetical Walton alludes to this marvellous river, but he has adopted the proposed correction, citing Josephus as his authority, but giving the Plinian version of the story, doubtless thinking it most fit that the river should allow the angler to repose on Sunday, and afford him, during the six other days, "choice recreation." The classical authorities declare that the river has long since vanished. But recently, a learned Jew, Rabbi Edrehi, has announced a work, asserting the discovery of the lost river, but affirming it to be a *river of sand!* This is apt to recal to mind an old proverb about "twisting a *rope* of sand!"

As for the "marvellous" of the story, it strikes me, that—only grant the existence of *water-corn-mills* in the time of the Emperor Titus (which it is not for me to deny),—and the whole is perfectly intelligible. The mills had been at work during the week, keeping up a head of water which had rushed along with a velocity (as Josephus describes it) sufficient to carry with it stones and fragments of rocks. On sabbath-day the miller "shut down," and let all the water run through, by which means the river was laid almost dry. What should hinder, in these days of hypothesis, our adopting so ready and *satisfactory* a solution?

[9] *Leo Africanus.*] What weights Leo Africanus meanes is doubtfull. Some have been brought hither, that being fatted, coulde scarcely carye their tayles: though I know not, why nature, that hung such a weight behinde, shoulde not enable the creature to drag itt after him by the strength of his backe, as the stag to carye as great weight on his heade only.—*Wr.*

[1] *ruck.*] Surely the ruc was but one, like the phœnix, but revives not like the phœnix.—*Wr.*

The roc of the Arabian Nights, conjectured to have originated in the American condor.

a thousand years after his death by Sertorius; whether there were no deceit in those fragments of the ark, so common to be seen in the days of Berosus; whether the pillar which Josephus beheld long ago, Tertullian long after, and Bartholomeus de Saligniaco and Bochardus long since, be the same with that of Lot's wife; whether this were the hand of Paul, or that which is commonly shown the head of Peter; if any doubt, I shall not much dispute with their suspicions. If any man shall not believe the turpentine-tree betwixt Jerusalem and Bethlehem, under which the Virgin suckled our Saviour as she passed between those cities; or the fig-tree of Bethany, showed to this day, whereon Zaccheus ascended to behold our Saviour; I cannot tell how to enforce his belief, nor do I think it requisite to attempt it. For, as it is no reasonable proceeding to compel a religion, or think to enforce our own belief upon another, who cannot without the concurrence of God's Spirit have any undubitable evidence of things that are obtruded, so is it also in matters of common belief; whereunto neither can we indubitably assent, without the co-operation of our sense or reason, wherein consist the principles of persuasion. For, as the habit of faith in divinity is an argument of things unseen, and a stable assent unto things inevident, upon authority of the Divine Revealer, — so the belief of man, which depends upon human testimony, is but a staggering assent unto the affirmative, not without some fear of the negative. And as there is required the Word of God, or infused inclination unto the one, so must the actual sensation of our senses,[2] at least the non-opposition of our reasons, procure our assent and acquiescence in the other. So when Eusebius, an holy writer, affirmeth, there grew a strange and unknown plant near the statue of Christ, erected by his hæmorrhoidal patient in the gospel, which attaining unto the hem of his vesture, acquired a sudden faculty to cure all diseases; although,[3] he saith, he saw the statue in his days,

[2] *senses.*] And that this was not wanting to make good the storye in parte, is evident in the very next section.— *Wr.*

[3] *although, &c.*] Why may wee not beleave that there was such a plant at the foote of that statue upon the report of the ecclesiastick story, publisht in the third ecumenical council at Ephesus, as wel as the statue itselfe upon the report of Eusebius at the first ecumenical coun-

yet hath it not found in many men so much as human belief. Some believing, others opinioning, a third suspecting it might be otherwise. For indeed, in matters of belief, the understanding assenting unto the relation, either for the authority of the person, or the probability of the object, although there may be a confidence of the one, yet if there be not a satisfaction in the other, there will arise suspensions; nor can we properly believe until some argument of reason, or of our proper sense, convince or determine our dubitations.

And thus it is also in matters of certain and experimented truth. For if unto one that never heard thereof, a man should undertake to persuade the affections of the loadstone, or that jet and amber attract straws and light bodies, there would be little rhetorick in the authority of Aristotle, Pliny, or any other. Thus although it be true that the string of a lute or viol will stir upon the stroke of an unison or diapason in another of the same kind; that alcanna being green, will suddenly infect the nails and other parts with a durable red; that a candle out of a musket will pierce through an inch board, or an urinal force a nail through a plank; yet can few or none believe thus much without a visible experiment. Which notwithstanding falls out more happily for knowledge; for these relations leaving unsatisfaction in the hearers, do stir up ingenuous dubiosities unto experiment, and by an exploration of all, prevent delusion in any.

CHAPTER XIX.

Of some Relations whose truth we fear.

LASTLY, as there are many relations whereto we cannot assent, and make some doubt thereof, so there are divers

cil at Nice; who sayes he saw the statue, but repeates the storye of the plant out of Africanus, who lived within the 200th yeare of Christ: and out of Tertullian, who lived within 120 yeares after this miracle was wrought upon the hæmorrhoidall that erected the statue. For though the plant lived not till his time, yet itt was as fresh in memorye in the church as when it first grewe.—*Wr.*

others whose verities we fear, and heartily wish there were no truth therein.

1. It is an insufferable affront unto filial piety, and a deep discouragement unto the expectation of all aged parents, who shall but read the story of that barbarous queen, who, after she had beheld her royal parent's ruin, lay yet in the arms of his assassin, and caroused with him in the skull of her father. For my part, I should have doubted the operation of antimony, where such a potion would not work; 'twas an act, methinks, beyond anthropophagy, and a cup fit to be served up only at the table of Atreus.[4]

---

[4] *barbarous queen, &c.*] If this relates to the story of Alboin, it is not correctly noticed. I give it from *Lardner's Cyclopædia.—Europe during the Middle Ages.*

"Few dynasties have been so unfortunate as that of the Lombards. Alboin, its founder, had not wielded the sceptre four years, when he became the victim of domestic treason: the manner is worth relating, as characteristic of the people. During his residence in Pannonia, this valiant chief had overcome and slain Cunimond, king of the Gepidæ, whose skull, in conformity with a barbarous custom of his nation, he had fashioned into a drinking cup. Though he had married Rosamond, daughter of Cunimond, in his festive entertainments he was by no means disposed to forego the triumph of displaying the trophy. In one held at Verona, he had the inhumanity to invite his consort to drink to her father, while he displayed the cup, and, for the first time, revealed its history in her presence. His vanity cost him dear: if she concealed her abhorrence, it settled into a deadly feeling. By the counsel of Helmich, a confidential officer of the court, she opened her heart to Peredeo, one of the bravest captains of the Lombards; and when she could not persuade him to assassinate his prince, she had recourse to an expedient, which proves, that in hatred as in love, woman knows no measure. Personating a mistress of Peredeo, she silently and in darkness stole to his bed; and when her purpose was gained, she threatened him with the vengeance of an injured husband, unless he consented to become a regicide. The option was soon made: accompanied by Helmich, Peredeo was led to the couch of the sleeping king, whose arms had been previously removed; and, after a short struggle, the deed of blood was consummated. The justice of heaven never slumbers: if Alboin was thus severely punished for his inhumanity, fate avenged him of his murderers. To escape the suspicious enmity of the Lombards, the queen and Helmich fled to Ravenna, which at this period depended on the Greek empire. There the exarch, coveting the treasures which she had brought from Verona, offered her his hand, on condition she removed her companion. Such a woman was not likely to hesitate. To gratify one passion she had planned a deed of blood—to gratify another, her ambition, she presented a poisoned cup to her lover,

2. While we laugh at the story of Pygmalion, and receive as a fable that he fell in love with a statue; we cannot but fear it may be true, what is delivered by Herodotus concerning the Egyptian pollinctors, or such as anointed the dead; that some thereof were found in the act of carnality with them. From wits that say 'tis more than incontinency for Hylas to sport with Hecuba, and youth to flame in the frozen embraces of age, we require a name for this: wherein Petronius or Martial cannot relieve us. The tyranny of Mezentius* did never equal the vitiosity of this incubus, that could embrace corruption, and make a mistress of the grave; that could not resist the dead provocations of beauty,[5] whose quick invitements scarce excuse submission. Surely, if such depravities there be yet alive, deformity need not despair; nor will the eldest hopes be ever superannuated, since death hath spurs, and carcasses have been courted.

3. I am heartily sorry, and wish it were not true, what to the dishonour of Christianity is affirmed of the Italian; who after he had inveigled his enemy to disclaim his faith for the redemption of his life, did presently poiniard him, to prevent repentance, and assure his eternal death. The villany of this Christian exceeded the persecution of heathens, whose malice was never so longimanous† as to reach the soul of their enemies, or to extend unto an exile of their elysiums. And though the blindness of some ferities have savaged on the bodies of the dead, and been so injurious unto worms, as to disinter the bodies of the deceased, yet had they therein no design upon the soul; and have been so far from the destruction of that, or desires of a perpetual death, that for the satisfaction of their revenge they wish them many souls, and were it in their power would have reduced them unto life again. It is a great depravity in our natures, and surely an affection that somewhat savoureth of hell, to desire the society, or comfort

---

* Who tied dead and living bodies together. † Long-handed.

in the bath. After drinking a portion, his suspicions were kindled, and he forced her, under the raised sword, to drink the rest. The same hour ended their guilt and lives. Peredeo, the third culprit, fled to Constantinople, where a fate no less tragical awaited him."

[5] *dead provocations of beauty.*] Provocations of dead beauty.—*Wr.*

ourselves in the fellowship of others that suffer with us; but to procure the miseries of others in those extremities, wherein we hold an hope to have no society ourselves, is methinks a strain above Lucifer, and a project beyond the primary seduction of hell.

4. I hope it is not true, and some indeed have probably denied, what is recorded of the monk that poisoned Henry the emperor, in a draught of the holy Eucharist. 'Twas a scandalous wound unto the Christian religion, and I hope all Pagans will forgive it, when they shall read that a Christian was poisoned in a cup of Christ, and received his bane in a draught of his salvation.[6] Had he believed transubstantiation, he would have doubted the effect; and surely the sin itself received an aggravation in that opinion. It much commendeth the innocency of our forefathers, and the simplicity of those times, whose laws could never dream so high a crime as parricide: whereas this at the least may seem to out-reach that fact, and to exceed the regular distinctions of murder. I will not say what sin it was to act it; yet may it seem a kind of martyrdom to suffer by it. For, although unknowingly, he died for Christ his sake, and lost his life in the ordained testimony of his death. Certainly had they known it, some noble zeals would scarcely have refused it; rather adventuring their own death, than refusing the memorial of his.[7]

Many other accounts like these we meet sometimes in history, scandalous unto Christianity, and even unto humanity; whose verities not only, but whose relations, honest minds do deprecate. For of sins heteroclital, and such as want either name or precedent, there is oft-times a sin even in their histories. We desire no records of such enor-

---

[6] *'Twas a scandalous wound, &c.*] It is said that Ganganelli, Pope Clement XIV. was thus despatched by the Jesuits. In the *Universal Magazine* for 1776, vol. v. p. 215, occurs an account of that poisoning of the sacramental wine at Zurich, by a grave-digger, by which a number of communicants lost their lives.

[7] *Than refusing, &c.*] Itt had been a very foolishe zeale, and little less than selfe murder to have taken that sacramentall, wherin they had knowne poyson to have been put. The rejection of that particular cup had not been any refusal of remembring his death. This therefore needs an index expurgatorius, and a deleatur, and soe wee have according canceld itt.— *Ur.*

mities; sins should be accounted new, that so they may be esteemed monstrous. They amit of monstrosity as they fall from their rarity; for men count it venial to err with their forefathers, and foolishly conceive they divide a sin in its society. The pens of men may sufficiently expatiate without these singularities of villany; for, as they increase the hatred of vice in some, so do they enlarge the theory of wickedness in all. And this is one thing that may make latter ages worse than were the former; for, the vicious examples of ages past poison the curiosity of these present, affording a hint[8] of sin unto seducible spirits, and soliciting those unto the imitation of them, whose heads were never so perversely principled as to invent them. In this kind we commend the wisdom and goodness of Galen, who would not leave unto the world too subtle a theory of poisons; unarming thereby the malice of venomous spirits, whose ignorance must be contented with sublimate and arsenic. For, surely there are subtler venerations, such as will invisibly destroy, and like the basilisks of heaven. In things of this nature silence commendeth history: 'tis the veniable part of things lost; wherein there must never rise a Pancirollus,* nor remain any register, but that of hell.

And yet, if, as some Stoicks opinion, and Seneca himself disputeth, these unruly affections that make us sin such prodigies, and even sins themselves be animals, there is a history of Africa and story of snakes in these. And if the transanimation of Pythagoras, or method thereof were true, that the souls of men transmigrated into species answering their former natures; some men must surely live over many serpents, and cannot escape that very brood, whose sire Satan entered. And though the objection of Plato should take place, that bodies subjected unto corruption must fail at last before the period of all things, and growing fewer in number must leave some souls apart unto

* Who writ *De antiquis deperditis,* or of inventions lost.

[8] *Affording, &c.*] Itt is noe doubte but that some casuists have much to answere for that sinn of curiosity, who by proposing some quæstions to the confitents teach them to knowe some sinns wherof they would never have thought.—*Wr.*

themselves, the spirits of many long before that time will find but naked habitations; and, meeting no assimilables wherein to re-act their natures, must certainly anticipate such natural desolations.

Primus sapientiæ gradus est, falsa intelligere.—LACTANT.

Also from Benediction Books ...

Wandering Between Two Worlds: Essays on Faith and Art
Anita Mathias
Benediction Books, 2007
152 pages
ISBN: 0955373700

Available from www.amazon.com, www.amazon.co.uk
www.wanderingbetweentwoworlds.com

In these wide-ranging lyrical essays, Anita Mathias writes, in lush, lovely prose, of her naughty Catholic childhood in Jamshedpur, India; her large, eccentric family in Mangalore, a sea-coast town converted by the Portuguese in the sixteenth century; her rebellion and atheism as a teenager in her Himalayan boarding school, run by German missionary nuns, St. Mary's Convent, Nainital; and her abrupt religious conversion after which she entered Mother Teresa's convent in Calcutta as a novice. Later rich, elegant essays explore the dualities of her life as a writer, mother, and Christian in the United States-- Domesticity and Art, Writing and Prayer, and the experience of being "an alien and stranger" as an immigrant in America, sensing the need for roots.

About the Author

Anita Mathias was born in India, has a B.A. and M.A. in English from Somerville College, Oxford University and an M.A. in Creative Writing from the Ohio State University. Her essays have been published in The Washington Post, The London Magazine, The Virginia Quarterly Review, Commonweal, Notre Dame Magazine, America, The Christian Century, Religion Online, The Southwest Review, Contemporary Literary Criticism, New Letters, The Journal, and two of HarperSanFrancisco's The Best Spiritual Writing anthologies. Her non-fiction has won fellowships from The National Endowment for the Arts; The Minnesota State Arts Board; The Jerome Foundation, The Vermont Studio Center; The Virginia Centre for the Creative Arts, and the First Prize for the Best General Interest Article from the Catholic Press Association of the United States and Canada. Anita has taught Creative Writing at the College of William and Mary, and now lives and writes in Oxford, England.

"Yesterday's Treasures for Today's Readers"
Titles by Benediction Classics available from Amazon.co.uk

Religio Medici, Hydriotaphia, Letter to a Friend, Thomas Browne

Pseudodoxia Epidemica: Or, Enquiries into Commonly Presumed Truths, Thomas Browne

Urne Buriall and The Garden of Cyrus, Thomas Browne

The Maid's Tragedy, Beaumont and Fletcher

The Custom of the Country, Beaumont and Fletcher

Philaster Or Love Lies a Bleeding, Beaumont and Fletcher

A Treatise of Fishing with an Angle, Dame Juliana Berners.

Pamphilia to Amphilanthus, Lady Mary Wroth

The Compleat Angler, Izaak Walton

The Magnetic Lady, Ben Jonson

Every Man Out of His Humour, Ben Jonson

The Masque of Blacknesse. The Masque of Beauty,. Ben Jonson

The Life of St. Thomas More, William Roper

Pendennis, William Makepeace Thackeray

Salmacis and Hermaphroditus attributed to Francis Beaumont

Friar Bacon and Friar Bungay Robert Greene

Holy Wisdom, Augustine Baker

The Jew of Malta and the Massacre at Paris, Christopher Marlowe

Tamburlaine the Great, Parts 1 & 2 AND Massacre at Paris, Christopher Marlowe

All Ovids Elegies, Lucans First Booke, Dido Queene of Carthage, Hero and Leander, Christopher Marlowe

The Titan, Theodore Dreiser

Scapegoats of the Empire: The true story of the Bushveldt Carbineers, George Witton

All Hallows' Eve, Charles Williams

The Place of The Lion, Charles Williams

The Greater Trumps, Charles Williams

My Apprenticeship: Volumes I and II, Beatrice Webb

Last and First Men / Star Maker, Olaf Stapledon

Last and First Men, Olaf Stapledon

Darkness and the Light, Olaf Stapledon

The Worst Journey in the World, Apsley Cherry-Garrard

The Schoole of Abuse, Containing a Pleasaunt Invective Against Poets, Pipers, Plaiers, Iesters and Such Like Catepillers of the Commonwelth, Stephen Gosson

Russia in the Shadows, H. G. Wells

Wild Swans at Coole, W. B. Yeats

A hundreth good pointes of husbandrie, Thomas Tusser

The Collected Works of Nathanael West: "The Day of the Locust", "The Dream Life of Balso Snell", "Miss Lonelyhearts", "A Cool Million", Nathanael West

Miss Lonelyhearts & The Day of the Locust, Nathaniel West

The Worst Journey in the World, Apsley Cherry-Garrard

Scott's Last Expedition, V1, R. F. Scott

The Dream of Gerontius, John Henry Newman

The Brother of Daphne, Dornford Yates

The Downfall of Robert Earl of Huntington, Anthony Munday

Clayhanger, Arnold Bennett

The Regent, A Five Towns Story Of Adventure In London , Arnold Bennett

The Card, A Story Of Adventure In The Five Towns , Arnold Bennett

South: The Story of Shackleton's Last Expedition 1914-1917, Sir Ernest Shackketon

Greene's Groatsworth of Wit: Bought With a Million of Repentance, Robert Greene

Beau Sabreur, Percival Christopher Wren

The Hekatompathia, or Passionate Centurie of Love, Thomas Watson

The Art of Rhetoric, Thomas Wilson

Stepping Heavenward, Elizabeth Prentiss

Barker's Delight, or The Art of Angling, Thomas Barker

The Napoleon of Notting Hill, G.K. Chesterton

The Douay-Rheims Bible (The Challoner Revision)

Endimion - The Man in the Moone, John Lyly

Gallathea and Midas, John Lyly,

Mother Bombie, John Lyly

Manners, Custom and Dress During the Middle Ages and During the Renaissance Period, Paul Lacroix

Obedience of a Christian Man, William Tyndale

St. Patrick for Ireland, James Shirley

The Wrongs of Woman; Or Maria/Memoirs of the Author of a Vindication of the Rights of Woman, Mary Wollstonecraft and William Godwin

De Adhaerendo Deo. Of Cleaving to God, Albertus Magnus

Obedience of a Christian Man, William Tyndale

A Trick to Catch the Old One, Thomas Middleton

The Phoenix, Thomas Middleton

A Yorkshire Tragedy, Thomas Middleton (attrib.)

The Princely Pleasures at Kenelworth Castle, George Gascoigne

The Fair Maid of the West. Part I and Part II. Thomas Heywood

Proserpina, Volume I and Volume II. Studies of Wayside Flowers, John Ruskin

Our Fathers Have Told Us. Part I. The Bible of Amiens. John Ruskin

The Poetry of Architecture: Or the Architecture of the Nations of Europe Considered in Its Association with Natural Scenery and National Character, John Ruskin

The Endeavour Journal of Sir Joseph Banks. Sir Joseph Banks

Christ Legends: And Other Stories, Selma Lagerlof; (trans. Velma Swanston Howard)

Chamber Music, James Joyce

Blurt, Master Constable, Thomas Middleton, Thomas Dekker

Since Yesterday, Frederick Lewis Allen

The Scholemaster: Or, Plaine and Perfite Way of Teachyng Children the Latin Tong , Roger Ascham

The Wonderful Year, 1603, Thomas Dekker

Waverley, Sir Walter Scott

Guy Mannering, Sir Walter Scott

Old Mortality, Sir Walter Scott

The Knight of Malta, John Fletcher

The Double Marriage, John Fletcher and Philip Massinger

Space Prison, Tom Godwin

The Home of the Blizzard Being the Story of the Australasian Antarctic Expedition, 1911-1914, Douglas Mawson

Wild-goose Chase , John Fletcher

If You Know Not Me, You Know Nobody. Part I and Part II, Thomas Heywood

The Ragged Trousered Philanthropists, Robert Tressell

The Island of Sheep, John Buchan

Eyes of the Woods, Joseph Altsheler

The Club of Queer Trades, G. K. Chesterton

The Financier, Theodore Dreiser

Something of Myself, Rudyard Kipling

Law of Freedom in a Platform, or True Magistracy Restored, Gerrard Winstanley

Damon and Pithias, Richard Edwards

Dido Queen of Carthage: And, The Massacre at Paris, Christopher Marlowe

Cocoa and Chocolate: Their History from Plantation to Consumer, Arthur Knapp

Lady of Pleasure, James Shirley

The South Pole: An account of the Norwegian Antarctic expedition in the "Fram," 1910-12. Volume 1 and Volume 2, Roald Amundsen

A Yorkshire Tragedy, Thomas Middleton (attrib.)

The Tragedy of Soliman and Perseda, Thomas Kyd

The Rape of Lucrece. Thomas Heywood

Myths and Legends of Ancient Greece and Rome, E. M. Berens

In the Forbidden Land, Henry Savage Arnold Landor

Across Unknown South America, by Arnold Henry Savage Landor

Illustrated History of Furniture: From the Earliest to the Present Time, Frederick Litchfield

A Narrative of Some of the Lord's Dealings with George Müller Written by Himself (Parts I-IV, 1805-1856), George Müller

The Towneley Cycle Of The Mystery Plays (Or The Wakefield Cycle): Thirty-Two Pageants, Anonymous

The Insatiate Countesse, John Marston.

Spontaneous Activity in Education, Maria Montessori.

On the Art of Writing, Sir Arthur Quiller-Couch

The Well of the Saints, J. M. Synge

Bacon's Advancement Of Learning And The New Atlantis, Francis Bacon.

Catholic Tales And Christian Songs, Dorothy Sayers.

Two Little Savages: Being the Adventures of Two Boys who Lived as Indians and What they Learned, Ernest Thompson Seton

The Sadness of Christ, Thomas More

The Family of Love, Thomas Middleton

The Passing of the Aborigines: A Lifetime Spent Among the Natives of Australia, Daisy Bates

The Children, Edith Wharton

A Record of European Armour and Arms through Seven Centuries., (Volumes I, II, III, IV and V) Francis Laking

The Book of the Farm: - Detailing The Labours Of The Farmer, Steward, Plowman, Hedger, Cattle-Man, Shepherd, Field-Worker, and Dairymaid. (Volume I), Henry Stephens

The Book of the Farm: - Detailing The Labours Of The Farmer, Steward, Plowman, Hedger, Cattle-Man, Shepherd, Field-Worker, and Dairymaid. (Volume II), Henry Stephens

The Book of the Farm: - Detailing The Labours Of The Farmer, Steward, Plowman, Hedger, Cattle-Man, Shepherd, Field-Worker, and Dairymaid. (Volume III). by Henry Stephens

The Naturalist On The River Amazons, by Henry Walter Bates.

Antarctic Penguins: A Study of their Social Habits, Dr. George Murray Levick

and many others…

Tell us what you would love to see in print again, at affordable prices!
Email: **benedictionbooks@btinternet.com**